D1552868

A HISTORY OF THE BOOK IN AMERICA

The Colonial Book in the Atlantic World is the first of a five-volume series extending through the twentieth century; it carries the interrelated stories of publishing, writing, and reading from the beginning of the colonial period of American history up to 1790. Three major themes run through the volume: the persisting connection between the book trades in the Old World and the New, as evidenced in modes of intellectual and cultural exchange and the dominance of imported, chiefly English texts; the gradual emergence of a competitive book trade, in which newspapers were the largest form of production; and the institution of a "culture of the Word," organized around an essentially theological understanding of print, authorship and reading, complemented by other frameworks of meaning that included the culture of republicanism. The volume also traces the histories of literary and learned culture, censorship and "freedom of the press," and literacy and orality.

Hugh Amory retired as Senior Rare Book Cataloger at the Houghton Library, Harvard University.

David D. Hall is Professor of American Religious History at the Harvard Divinity School.

A HISTORY OF THE BOOK IN AMERICA

David D. Hall, General Editor

Volume One, *The Colonial Book in the Atlantic World,* edited by Hugh Amory & David D. Hall

Volume Two, *An Extensive Republic: Print, Culture, and Society in the New Nation,* edited by Robert A. Gross & Mary Kelley

Volume Three, *The Industrial Book, 1840–1880,* edited by Stephen W. Nissenbaum & Michael Winship

Volume Four, *Print in Motion: Books and Reading in the United States, 1880–1945,* edited by Carl F. Kaestle & Janice Radway

Volume Five, *The Enduring Book, 1945–1995,* edited by David Paul Nord, Joan Shelley Rubin, & Michael Schudson

This work has been made possible in part by a series of grants from the National Endowment for the Humanities, an independent federal agency, and The Elisabeth Woodburn Fund of the Antiquarian Booksellers' Association of America, American Booksellers Association Inc., James J. Colt Foundation, Richard A. Heald Fund, John Ben Snow Memorial Trust, and the Center for the Book in the Library of Congress

A HISTORY OF THE BOOK IN AMERICA

Volume One

The Colonial Book in the Atlantic World

Edited by

HUGH AMORY & DAVID D. HALL

AMERICAN ANTIQUARIAN SOCIETY

CAMBRIDGE UNIVERSITY PRESS
Cambridge, New York, Melbourne, Madrid, Cape Town, Singapore, São Paulo, Delhi

Cambridge University Press
32 Avenue of the Americas, New York, NY 10013-2473, USA

www.cambridge.org
Information on this title:www.cambridge.org/9780521482561

First published 2000
Reprinted 2001, 2005, 2007

Printed in the United States of America

A catalogue record for this book is available from the British Library

Library of Congress Cataloguing in Publication Data
The colonial book in the Atlantic world / edited by Hugh Amory, David D. Hall.
p. cm.– (A history of the book in America; v. 1)
Includes bibliographical references and index.
ISBN 0-521-48256-9
1. Book industries and trade – United States – History – 17th
century. 2. Book industries and trade – United States – History – 18th
century. I. Amory, Hugh. II. Hall, David D. III. Series.
Z473.C686 1999
381'.45002'0973–dc21 99-12595
CIP

ISBN 978-0-521-48256-1 hardback

Contents

Illustrations

Figures

Tables

Graphs

Contributors

Hugh Amory retired as senior rare book cataloger at the Houghton Library, Harvard University.

Ross W. Beales is professor of history, The College of the Holy Cross.

John Bidwell is curator of graphic arts, Princeton University Library.

Richard D. Brown is professor of history, University of Connecticut.

Charles E. Clark is professor of history emeritus, University of New Hampshire.

James N. Green is associate librarian, Library Company of Philadelphia.

David D. Hall is professor of American religious history, Harvard Divinity School.

Russell L. Martin is curator of newspapers and periodicals at the American Antiquarian Society

E. Jennifer Monaghan is professor of English, Brooklyn College of The City University of New York.

Elizabeth Carroll Reilly is an independent scholar.

A. Gregg Roeber is professor of early modern history and religious studies and co-director, Max Kade German-American Research Institute, The Pennsylvania State University.

James Raven is university lecturer in modern history and tutorial fellow, Mansfield College, Oxford.

David S. Shields is professor of English, The Citadel.

Calhoun Winton is professor of English emeritus, University of Maryland.

Authors' and Editors' Acknowledgments

The Colonial Book in the Atlantic World is a collaborative work of scholarship, fashioned out of an abundance of consultations, exchanges, and critiques among the contributors. On the part of the volume's editors, therefore, the most appropriate acknowledgment is of the generosity, seriousness, and spirit of cooperation that our authors have shown each other: a generosity in sharing expertise with fellow contributors, a seriousness about breaking new ground, doing fresh research, and attempting new kinds of connections, and a spirit of cooperation in responding to requests for revisions. Two of our authors, E. Jennifer Monaghan and Elizabeth Carroll Reilly, lent a helping hand at close to the last moment; we thank them for responding so promptly. The editors owe much to the Editorial Board that supervises the broader project of which *The Colonial Book in the Atlantic World* is the first volume; the tradition of vigorous questioning that prevails within this group has served us well. We are grateful for the good will that so many others have expressed for this project, a good will that, like our very subject, spans the Atlantic ocean.

It is no less appropriate to acknowledge the generosity and good will of the American Antiquarian Society (AAS), which undertook to sponsor "A History of the Book in American Culture" during the presidency of Marcus A. McCorison and with the warm encouragement of the then Director of Research and Publication and Editor of Publications, John B. Hench, who, as vice president of the society with responsibility for the overall project, has remained closely involved with this volume. Caroline F. Sloat, administrative assistant for *A History of the Book in America* and the society's editor of publications, played a major role in preparing the final version of the manuscript. Georgia B. Barnhill, the Andrew W. Mellon curator of graphic arts at the AAS, gave generously of her time, suggesting illustrations, drafting captions, and providing a selection of basic references for the bibliography.

We also thank Ellen Dunlap, the current president of AAS, for her support. Generous funding from the National Endowment for the Humanities made it possible for the contributors to meet twice for crucial face-to-face discussions; at the first of these, we also benefited from the presence of Jerome Anderson, Susan Berg, Kevin J. Hayes, David McKitterick, Thomas Siegel, Michael Turner, and Michael Warner. The same funding has enabled Russell L. Martin, cataloguer on the North American Imprints Program (NAIP) and research assistant for *A History of the Book in America*, to master the NAIP database and to carry out the often quite complicated calculations that lie behind the charts and tables; his participation has been indispensable in other ways as well. Without the services, invariably selfless, of archivists, bibliographers, librarians, and curators of rare book and manuscript collections, much of the information brought together in this volume would not have been available. We thank all those (and they are many) who have contributed in this fashion to *The Colonial Book in the Atlantic World*.

Financial support for this volume, and for the project as a whole, has also been provided by The Elisabeth Woodburn Fund of the Antiquarian Booksellers' Association of America, Inc., American Booksellers Association, Inc., the Richard A. Heald Fund, the James J. Colt Foundation, the John Ben Snow Memorial Trust, and the Center for the Book in the Library of Congress. We are very grateful for these contributions.

The several authors wish to make the following particular acknowledgments:

Hugh Amory: the late William J. Gilmore-Lehne kindly read and commented on drafts of Chapters 3 and 9; Jerome Anderson allowed me to illustrate his exceptionally interesting copy of Edward Phillips's *New World of English Words* and patiently advised me on matters historical; Alan N. Degutis, head of cataloguing services, AAS, printed out records of early Massachusetts imprints from NAIP, an indispensable resource; and my former Houghton colleague Roger E. Stoddard's friendly encouragement and inspiring example sustained me.

John Bidwell: I would like to acknowledge support received from the American Society for Eighteenth-Century Studies, for a fellowship to work at the American Antiquarian Society in the summer of 1994.

Charles E. Clark: Eliga Gould, who read an early draft of the essay and offered helpful comments. Work on this essay has been facilitated enormously by the endowment of, and my appointment to, the James H. Hayes and Claire Short Hayes Chair in the Humanities at the University of New Hampshire, for which I am particularly grateful. Much of what appears here has been informed in some way by the research that resulted in *The Public*

Prints (1994). It is appropriate that I reinforce here the acknowledgments that appear in that volume, since most of the persons named there have contributed, at least indirectly, to this chapter.

James N. Green: Keith Arbour, Donald Farren, David Haugaard, Joseph Felcone II, J. A. Leo Lemay, Warren McDougall, Karen Nipps, Rosalind Remer, Richard Sher, Willman Spawn, William A. Speck, Daniel Traister, and, above all, the late Edwin Wolf 2nd.

David D. Hall: Jessica Marshall, Timothy Milford, John O'Keefe, and Jennifer Wardowski for assisting with research; Richard Cogley and Jill Lepore for advice on the Introduction, Part 2; Warren M. Billings, Lois Green Carr, J. William Frost, Kevin Kelly, Ann Smart Martin, David Moltke-Hansen, the late Darrett and Anita Rutman, Brent Tarter, and Thad W. Tate for material and advice relating to Chapter 2; Michael McGiffert, Roger Thompson, and Joy Young for assistance with Chapter 4; Mary S. Bilder, Ann Blair, Kenneth Carpenter, Joyce Chaplin, James McLachlan, and Daniel Walker Howe for materials and suggestions concerning Chapter 12.

Russell L. Martin: Alan N. Degutis, head of cataloging services, AAS, for setting up a pre-1801 segment of the NAIP database specifically for statistical research and suggesting some of the better ways of extracting information from it.

E. Jennifer Monaghan: Konstantin Dierks for sharing his unpublished research.

James Raven: The Bibliographical Society of America (Fredson Bowers Award); Giles Barber, Alan Clark, Elizabeth G. Durkee, Jinny Crum-Jones and Ian Jones, Catherine Sadler and the staff of the Charleston Library Society, and Warren McDougall.

Elizabeth Carroll Reilly: Kevin Hayes and the late Victor E. Neuburg.

A. Gregg Roeber: Fred Kopp and Joseph Lucas for research assistance; I am indebted to Eric Nooter and Ruth Piwonka for assistance on Dutch-language books; to Ursula Hans, and to David Skaggs for alerting me to her work; to Charles Mann, Special Collections, The Pattee Library, The Pennsylvania State University, for searching the relevant literature on Weisse, Berquin, and other popular children's authors, and to David William Voorhees for alerting me to this source as well as for information on Dutch probate inventories; Renate Wilson.

Calhoun Winton: The General Research Board of the University of Maryland for a Summer Research Grant and the John Carter Brown Library (Norman Fiering, director) for a fellowship.

Abbreviations

Bond and Amory, *Harvard Catalogues*	W. H. Bond and Hugh Amory, eds., *The Printed Catalogues of the Harvard College Library, 1723–1790*, *Pubs. CSM* 68 (1996)
Brigham	Clarence S. Brigham, *History and Bibliography of American Newspapers, 1690–1820*, 2 vols. (Worcester, Mass.: American Antiquarian Society, 1947).
Coll. MHS	*Collections of the Massachusetts Historical Society*
Conn. Records	*The Public Records of the Colony of Connecticut*, ed., J. Hammond Trumbull and Charles J. Hoadly, 15 vols. (Hartford, 1850–1890).
Duniway, *Freedom of the Press*	Clyde Augustus Duniway, *The Development of Freedom of the Press in Massachusetts* (New York and London: Longmans Green, and Co., 1906).
EAL	*Early American Literature*
EIHC	*Essex Institute Historical Collections*
Evans	Charles Evans, *American Bibliography*, 14 vols. (Chicago: Privately printed, 1903–1934; Worcester, Mass.: American Antiquarian Society, 1955–59).
Ford, *Boston Book Market*	Worthington C. Ford, *The Boston Book Market, 1679–1700* (Boston: Club of Odd Volumes, 1917).
Ford, *Mass. Broadsides*	Worthington C. Ford, *Broadsides, Ballads, &c. Printed in Massachusetts, 1639–1800* (Boston: Massachusetts Historical Society, 1922).
Franklin, *Autobiography*	Benjamin Franklin, *Writings*, ed. J. A. Leo Lemay (New York: Library of America, 1987).
Franklin Papers	*The Papers of Benjamin Franklin*, ed. Leonard W. Labaree et al., 33 vols. (New Haven, Conn: Yale University Press, 1959–).

Hall, *Narratives Md.*	Clayton Colman Hall, ed. *Narratives of Early Maryland, 1633–1684* (New York, 1910).
Hall, *Worlds*	David D. Hall, *Worlds of Wonder, Days of Judgment: Popular Religious Belief in Early New England* (New York: Knopf, 1989).
HLB	*Harvard Library Bulletin*
Hening, *Statutes*	William Waller Hening, ed., *The Statutes at Large; Being a Collection of all the Laws of Virginia,* 13 vols., 2nd ed. (New York, 1819–1823).
Holmes, *Cotton Mather*	Thomas J. Holmes, *Cotton Mather: A Bibliography of His Works,* 3 vols. (Cambridge: Harvard University Press, 1940).
HLQ	*Huntington Library Quarterly*
Lemay	J. A. Leo Lemay, *A Calendar of American Poetry in the Colonial Newspapers and in the Major English Magazines through 1765* (Worcester, Mass.: AAS, 1972).
Littlefield, *Boston Booksellers*	George E. Littlefield, *Early Boston Booksellers, 1642–1711,* 2 vols. (Boston: Club of Odd Volumes, 1900).
Littlefield, *Boston Printers*	George E. Littlefield, *The Early Massachusetts Press, 1638–1711,* 2 vols. (Boston: Club of Odd Volumes, 1907).
Md. Arch.	*Archives of Maryland,* ed. William Hand Brown et al., 73 vols. to date (Baltimore: Maryland Historical Society, 1883–).
Mass. Records	*Records of the Governor and Company of the Massachusetts Bay in New England,* ed. Nathaniel B. Shurtleff, 5 vols. (Boston, 1853–1854).
MdHM	*Maryland Historical Magazine*
Mather, *Diary*	*The Diary of Cotton Mather,* ed. Worthington C. Ford, 2 vols. (New York: Frederick Ungar, [1957]).
Mather, *Magnalia*	Cotton Mather, *Magnalia Christi Americana,* 2 vols. (1702; Hartford, Conn., 1853–1854).
Miller, *Franklin's Philadelphia Printing*	C. William Miller, *Benjamin Franklin's Philadelphia Printing 1728–1766: A Descriptive Bibliography* (Philadelphia, Pa.: American Philosophical Society, 1974).
Morison, *Harv. Coll.*	Samuel Eliot Morison, *Harvard College in the Seventeenth Century,* 2 vols. (Cambridge, Mass.: Harvard University Press, 1936).

NEHGR	*New England Historic Genealogical Register*
NEQ	*New England Quarterly*
PBSA	*Papers of the Bibliographical Society of America*
PMLA	*Publications of the Modern Language Association*
PMHB	*Pennsylvania Magazine of History and Biography*
Press & Am. Rev.	*The Press and the American Revolution,* ed. Bernard Bailyn and John B. Hench (Worcester, Mass.: American Antiquarian Society, 1980; repr. Boston: Northeastern University Press, 1981).
Printing and Society	*Printing and Society in Early America,x* ed. William L. Joyce et al. (Worcester, Mass.: American Antiquarian Society, 1987).
Procs. AAS	*Proceedings of the American Antiquarian Society*
Procs. Am. Phil. Soc.	*Proceedings of the American Philosophical Society*
Procs. MHS	*Proceedings of the Massachusetts Historical Society*
Pubs. CSM	*Publications of the Colonial Society of Massachusetts*
Recs. Va. Co.	*The Records of the Virginia Company of London,* ed. Susan M. Kingsbury, 4 vols. (Washington, D.C.: Library of Congress, 1906–1935).
Sewall, *Diary.*	*The Diary of Samuel Sewall, 1674–1729,* ed. M. Halsey Thomas, 2 vols. (New York: Farrar, Straus, and Giroux, 1973).
Sibley	John L. Sibley et al., *Biographical Sketches of the Graduates of Harvard College,* 17 vols. (Cambridge, Mass.: Harvard University Press, 1873–1975).
SB	*Studies in Bibliography*
Thomas, *Hist. Printing*	*The History of Printing in America,* ed. Marcus McCorison, 2 vols. (1874; repr., New York: Weathervane Books, [1975]).
VMHB	*Virginia Magazine of History and Biography*
WMQ	*William and Mary Quarterly*
Winans, *Book Catalogues*	Robert B. Winans, *A Descriptive Checklist of Book Catalogues Separately Printed in America, 1693–1800* (Worcester, Mass.: American Antiquarian Society, 1981).
Winship, *Cambridge Press*	George Parker Winship, *The Cambridge Press, 1638–1692* (Philadelphia: University of Pennsylvania Press, 1946).
Winthrop Papers	*Winthrop Papers* (Boston: Massachusetts Historical Society, 1929–).

Wroth, *Printing in Col. Md.*	Lawrence C. Wroth, *A History of Printing in Colonial Maryland, 1686–1776* (Baltimore, Md.: Typothetae of Baltimore, 1922).
Wroth, *Col. Printer*	Lawrence C. Wroth, *The Colonial Printer*, 2nd ed. (Portland, Me: Southworth-Anthoesen Press, 1938).

Introduction

DAVID D. HALL

PART ONE. SOME CONTEXTS AND QUESTIONS

The Colonial Book in the Atlantic World is a collaborative history of the uses of print and books in the thirteen mainland British colonies that in 1776 formed the United States. Ours is a history of beginnings – of booksellers and the stores they opened, of printers using imported presses, of writers who sought in some manner to "publish," and of readers who, in the strange setting of the New World, welcomed such familiar texts as the almanac, the catechism, and the Bible. Ours is also a story of change – of a book trade that, initially dependent on the patronage of the civil government or church and on importations from abroad, slowly became competitive and commercial, of shifting strategies for regulating printers and booksellers as licensing and censorship gave way to suits for libel and an ethos of "free inquiry," and of new choices emerging for readers and writers. In this, the first volume of *A History of the Book in America,* we carry these threads of change and continuity down to the close of the Revolutionary period, when national independence had been declared and the new federal government had come into being.

Our purpose in this introduction is to specify what we mean by "the book" and to suggest in advance the main arguments or interpretations that unify our narrative. A story arranged chronologically and by regions has seemed the most adequate means of dealing with two centuries of time and the sharpness of regional differences in early America. But in keeping with the growing cosmopolitanism and consolidation that happened in the course of the eighteenth century, three chapters (11, 12, and 13), which are best understood as an interrelated whole, deal thematically and topically with that period. Here in this introduction, we want also to reflect on certain key terms or categories. In a separate, concluding section – placed where it is because the subject matter cuts across the chronological and regional structure of this volume – we describe the encounter between Europeans and Native Americans from the vantage of book history.

As we use the term "book" in these pages, it encompasses the familiar format of the codex, whether in manuscript or print, as well as its intellectual content. When the seventeenth-century colonists used the word "book," they had in mind both writing and printing, sometimes differentiating the latter as "printed."[1] For us, the term also encompasses items that had some of the uses of books: for example, single-sheet broadsides and issues of newspapers. Even though we understand the term this broadly, the totality of written and printed matter was even greater, for we exclude such matters as store signs and blank forms and, more for want of space than for any other reason, do not deal with printed images or music.[2]

The book history of early America must be generously defined in other respects, for it was framed by the great social, economic, religious, and political movements of the sixteenth century, movements that prompted the migration of thousands of Europeans to these shores. The title of this volume is meant to evoke the multiple connections with European history that are so consequential for the story that we tell. Three events or movements are especially pertinent: the two Reformations of the sixteenth century, but chiefly the Protestant; the strengthening of the civil state in several European countries, together with the rivalry between these states that was played out in the colonization of the New World; and mercantile capitalism. Let us consider each in turn.

The history of the book in early America was profoundly shaped by ideas and practices that emerged within the Protestant Reformation. Ever since the early centuries of the Christian era, Christianity had been a text-based religion.[3] Protestantism was even more so, for the sixteenth-century Reformers rejected the "idolatry" of images as well as most forms of sacramentalism. Asserting the authority of the Word as revealed in Scripture and declaring that the door to salvation lay through knowledge of the Bible, the early Reformers labored to make it available in the vernacular by providing new translations. To abet the religious instruction of the common people, Protestants published an abundance of catechisms and other devotional or liturgical texts such as the *Book of Common Prayer* (1549) in England. All together, these practices and expectations had a considerable impact: Book production in Germany exploded in the 1520s, reaching a level four times higher than in 1517.[4]

Another legacy of the Reformation was a particular understanding of printing, reading, and writing. Famously, the Reformers came to view the invention of printing as a divinely ordained means of emancipating the

Church from the "tyranny" of the Roman popes. "The Gospel freely preached" also meant the Gospel openly printed and dispersed in the vernacular: this axiom of the Reformation was represented on the illustrated title page of the English martyrologist and church historian John Foxe's *Actes and Monuments* (1563), which showed women and men who "sit listening to the Word with Bibles in their laps," as contrasted with Catholics who merely finger their beads. Considering "to what end and purpose the Lord hath given this gift of printing to the earth," Foxe argued that the new technology was part of God's providential design: "the blessed wisdom and omnipotent power of the Lord began to work for his church; not with sword and target to subdue his exalted adversaries, but with printing, writing and reading: to convince darkness by light, error by truth, ignorance by learning." Foxe also celebrated the expansive, multiplying consequences of the technology: "by this printing, as by the gift of tongues . . . the doctrine of the gospel soundeth to all nations and countries under heaven; and what God revealeth to one man, is dispersed to many, and what is made known in one nation, is opened to all."[5]

This understanding of printing prevailed among the Protestants who colonized the mainland British colonies on which we focus. As a social and political event, the Reformation was no less consequential for these colonists. The divisions that arose between Catholics and Protestants in Europe, together with schisms and differences among Protestants themselves as they debated the nature of the true church, led to waves of persecution and exclusion. Among those so treated, some sought refuge or asylum in the New World. So it happened that the "Pilgrims" set out on the *Mayflower,* that thousands of English Puritans would follow soon thereafter, that English Catholics would simultaneously undertake the founding of Maryland, and that in the late seventeenth century Quakers, Mennonites, German sectarians, and Huguenots would begin to people the middle colonies. These groups would be joined by others who brought with them the traditions of a national or state church: the Dutch Reformed, Anglicans, and Scotch Presbyterians. Because these communities relied on books to sustain their religious practice, they were quick to import them from overseas and to patronize printers on this side of the Atlantic. Thanks to the uses of books within such groups, they were able to maintain a degree of coherence even though they were often decentralized or lacked strong regulating structures.

Each of the European civil states resisted the divisive consequences of the Reformation. On their own, moreover, these states were undertaking a major phase of consolidation, adding to the powers of the central government at the very moment when the exploration and colonization of the New World were getting underway, which in England happened by means of chartered, joint-stock companies. Peace among the settlements that arose up and down the Atlantic coast and the Gulf of Mexico was always fragile and wars were recurrent, the most important of them being the series of conflicts between France, Spain, and Britain that broke out in 1689 and continued down to 1763. These conflicts spurred the English government to strengthen and extend its presence among the colonists, a process that also encompassed certain forms of recordkeeping the Crown imposed on the colonies and the regulating of trade via a series of laws collectively known as the Navigation Acts, the earliest of which was enacted in 1651.[6]

In England, this process of regulation extended to the book trades. No sooner had the new technology of printing taken hold in Europe than church and state interested themselves in what was being printed and distributed. Unable to regard opposition as legitimate, the early modern civil state treated the criticism and dissent that appeared in print as "sedition." The civil state was no less anxious about the flow of news, which it wished to regulate for its own benefit. Hence it was that gossip, rumor, letters, and speech were deemed potentially subversive.[7] Religious leaders were no less certain that any wavering from the official system was heresy. The outbreak of the Reformation brought a new intensity to the task of regulation, for the authorities, both civil and religious, had to contend with Protestants who believed in making the vernacular Bible available to everyone. Even before Henry VIII of England broke with Rome in 1536, control of the press remained a priority. In 1530 Henry denounced as "blasphemous and pestiferous" certain Protestant books on the grounds that their intent was "to stir and incense [the people] to sedition, and disobedience against their princes, sovereigns, and heads"; as for the vernacular Bible, the king ruled that its distribution "dependeth onely upon the discretion of the superiors [in the Church hierarchy], as they shall think it convenient." Not only monarchs but also the most zealous of reformers rejected a free market in books lest the wrong kinds of texts reach the common people.[8]

From the start, the regulating mechanisms of the civil state were entwined with the self-interest of the book trade. For England, the key instrument of state policy became a system of licensing mediated through the Stationers' Company, chartered by the Crown in 1557. According to the charter, every member of the Company was required to "register" the titles of books he wished to publish, to secure a license from ecclesiastical or governmental officials before proceeding any further, and to specify the name of the printer on the title page. Imported books were to pass through London, where inspectors examined them for any that were seditious or heretical. The Company willingly accepted these rules because the system of permissions or licensing was simultaneously a system for ensuring each bookseller the exclusive rights to publish certain texts. These rights to "copy" – that is, to multiply copies of a given text – served in principle to prevent any other printer or bookseller from issuing a competing edition, a practice that booksellers on both the Continent and in England condemned as "piracy."[9]

In this respect, the Licensing Act of 1662, which renewed or restated the provisions of the charter of 1557, was typical. As Michael Treadwell has pointed out, it contained clauses specifically "designed for the commercial advantage of the Company and its copyright-owning members" and which reveal that "the Company feared sedition much less than it feared uncontrollable printing of other men's copies." When Parliament in 1695 did not renew the Licensing Act, as it had more or less routinely for thirty years, the reasons for this inaction were again commercial or economic – in this instance, a rising tide of complaints against the monopolistic practices of the Company.[10] But these were eventually settled by the Copyright Act of Anne (1710), which for the first time recognized the limited right of persons outside the Company to their "copy."

In actuality, this system of licensing was never fully effective. It lapsed from time to time, notably so during the 1640s and in 1679–1685, when King and Parliament were at odds. As happened during the early years of the German Reformation, this unintentional legitimizing of religious and political dissent during the Civil War period and the Popish Plot led to an explosion of imprints. Radicals like John Milton, moreover, urged the benefits to the progress of truth from free expression and criticized the monopolistic aspects of permissions and licensing. During those periods when the civil government was acting more effectively, an important alternative to state regulation was to operate a clandestine press or to print and import seditious and heretical texts from the other side of the Channel. Famously, the early English Protestant William Tyndale used the Netherlands as his base for producing Bibles in the vernacular. Almost a century later, the Separatist and exile William Brewster would do the same in order to publish manifestoes of the radical wing of the Puritan movement. Despite its dangers, the trade in underground books on the Continent and in England flourished, for, early on, printers and booksellers realized that suppression could stimulate demand. Another means of circumventing the system of regulation – the motive usually being to gain commercial advantage by subverting another bookseller's rights to copy – was to disguise the piracy or clandestine text under a deceitful title or a false designation of place, date, or printer.[11] As for writers, they too adapted to the system of state regulation, some by circulating their work only in manuscript and others by a self-censorship that masked their real opinions.[12] Predictably, the attentiveness of the licensers waxed and waned, in keeping with the political winds of the moment.

When and under what circumstances these practices were employed in the colonies is a principal thread of the following narrative. In advance of these chapters, it is important to reiterate that regulation occurred within the trade and, for that matter, within the act of writing as well as being imposed from without.

The third of the great movements affecting the book history of early America was mercantile capitalism, which financed the colonization of North America. The settlements that arose up and down the coast, whether initiated by the English, Dutch, French, or Spanish, would all participate in a vast network of trade, an Atlantic economy that bound together fisheries in the Gulf of Maine, sugar plantations in the West Indies, those in the Chesapeake and lower South that raised tobacco, rice, and indigo, and family farms in New England and the middle colonies that produced surpluses of lumber, grain, and cattle. European merchants provided the credit that enabled this system of exchange to function. The colonial economy was similarly dependent on the Atlantic world for its labor force. Labor was a commodity in the specific sense that ordinary people sold themselves into service for a fixed term of years in return for certain benefits. Thus it happened that tens of thousands of persons arrived in the mainland colonies as indentured servants. From Africa came many more thousands who, deprived of choice, had their labor bound in perpetuity and could not use writing to communicate with their home societies.[13]

The exchange structures of the Atlantic world included books, for they were also a commodity financed and distributed in keeping with the credit mechanisms and geographies of mercantile capitalism. This was not true of all books, for printers and booksellers were also subsidized by civil governments, churches, and learned or philanthropic societies; works of learning and belles lettres frequently attracted the support of private patrons, and some religious or social movements – notably the Society of Friends, or Quakers, in England, and the Pietists based at Halle, in Germany – developed their own systems of nonprofit production and distribution. But in general, the book trade relied on commercial credit to finance the acquisition of paper (the largest single cost in bookmaking) and to survive while waiting for returns from sales, which were always unpredictable and often slow in coming. The methods of advertising and distributing books included many kinds of catalogues, as well as fairs, like the international one held twice a year at Frankfurt, where booksellers exchanged each other's imprints or bought stock outright.[14] The reach of the book trade was extended through merchants, who routinely carried stocks of books, and peddlers, who traveled the highways and byways of England.[15]

Beginning in the sixteenth century, the European economy entered a long phase of expansion that eventually prompted a "consumer revolution," or a heightening of demand for many kinds of goods, including books.[16] Enterprising printers and booksellers abetted this heightening of demand by experimenting with format, as the Venetian printer Aldus Manutius had done, in "a series of [classical texts] which would at the same time be scholarly, compact, handy, and cheap," a feat he accomplished by "cram[ming] as much text as possible on to the octavo format which he allowed for his 'pocket editions.'" Price was always a constraint, as was the extent of literacy, but certain forms of print such as chapbooks and broadsides, a format used for almanacs, "histories" (i.e., fiction), and ballads, were being printed in late seventeenth-century England in quantities that ranged well into the thousands.[17]

Not only must the early American book trade be located within the contexts of mercantile capitalism, an imperial state system, and religious reformation, it should also be understood as "colonial" in the sense of being structurally interrelated with the book trades of western Europe, and especially England. Isaiah Thomas, who wrote the first history of the American book trades, *The History of Printing in America* (1810), was aware of this dependence and filled his pages with accounts of the origin and progress of printing in Europe and the English colonies in the New World from Canada to the Caribbean. Thomas revealed something else in the structure of the *History,* a certain "cultural cringe," as an Australian might call it, before the mother country. Without a qualified technical ancestry, the production of print in America seemed inexplicable to him, and he all too readily argued the descent of early colonial printers from the mere coincidence of names: of Stephen Day from the Elizabethan printer John Daye; of John Allen from Benjamin and Hannah Allen[18] – fallacious arguments but, setting aside their cultural implications, based on sound instincts, for American imprints often relied on European authors for their texts and on European presses, paper, and type for their production.

Though we in *The Colonial Book in the Atlantic World* resist imposing autonomy on the practices we describe, others before us have worked from different premises in attempting to describe how a book or broadside printed in the colonies differed from an import. The mistakes that have been made in this enterprise of favoring American originality and difference – an enterprise paralleled among historians of art, literature, religion, and politics in early America – have been repeated in the practice of imprint bibliography: The fact that hundreds of entries in Charles Evans's *American Bibliography* (1903–1955) are based solely on advertisements of British imports underlines the possibility of confusion. Important as it has been to identify these "ghosts" and to exclude them from Evans's descendants, the purified text has become less representative thereby of a confused historical reality. Imprint bibliography, as exemplified in the work of three great scholars – Evans, Douglas McMurtrie, and Roger P. Bristol – defines an American imprint as a book printed in the area that would one day become the continental United States. A very different picture (and a different form of bibliography) would emerge if we considered with Edwin Wolf 2nd the predominance of English books in the catalogues of colonial libraries, in the advertisements and sale catalogues of booksellers, and in the rather more loosely described contents of probate inventories. As another bibliographer has sadly observed, Evans and Bristol "[do] not tell one very much about what was being read in America, or even what was available in bookshops." Their continuations by Clifford K. Shipton and James E. Mooney tell us even less. Indeed, the *Short-Title Evans*, unlike its equivalents for England, theoretically excludes even titles that were printed abroad for sale in the national area.[19]

Eschewing, we trust, a perspective that values any book printed in America more highly than those imported from overseas, we use the term "colonial" deliberately in order to emphasize the continuing dependence of the book trade in the mainland colonies on its European (chiefly British) sources of supply for paper, type and presses, as well as for books, texts, and wider cultural practices. Within cultural and social history, the colonial situation meant that the colonists were minor figures in a commercial and intellectual traffic that originated within cosmopolitan centers on the other side of the Atlantic. Although this traffic ran in both directions, the realities of dependence, coupled with the frustrations that came in the train of trying to keep up with and not seem inferior to the metropolis, account for a certain restlessness, a confusion of identity, among the colonists that found notable expression in writers at the turn of the century such as William Byrd II and Cotton Mather. For our volume, therefore, the term "colonial" designates not only certain structures of the British empire and the Atlantic economy but also long-lasting aspects of intellectual life and cultural identity.[20]

The book history of early America intersects with several other arguments about print and culture, each of which we shall briefly describe.

1. Orality, Writing, and Print. It is common within some versions of cultural and social history to evoke a great transition from orality to literacy or writing or from the age of the manuscript book to the age of printing. Each of these transitions has been represented as deeply consequential, even "revolutionary," in its consequences for western culture. The case for printing as "an agent of change" has been forcefully argued by the historian Elizabeth Eisenstein. Limiting herself to the literate, learned community that was already accustomed to owning and using manuscript books, she proposes that the technology of printing, by making it possible to duplicate a text in large quantities, opened the way to standardization, order, and much wider dissemination; hence she contrasts the emergence of alphabet-

ical indexes, the purification of corrupted texts, and the operations of science and natural history in the early modern period with the "disorder" and limited reach of texts in the age of scribal production. Her larger goal is to link the Renaissance, the Reformation, and the beginnings of the scientific revolution with a "communications revolution" caused by the shift from script to print.[21]

The transition from orality to literacy as sketched by Walter J. Ong is less chronologically precise, for Ong's purpose is twofold: To sketch a decline in the "presence of the word" as it was displaced by the visual (i.e., printed) word, and yet to emphasize the residual presence of orality in the West. For him, a major difference between orality and writing is that the latter lends itself to "elaborate analytical categories to structure knowledge." Writing separates and isolates; it leads to "abstractions."[22] A third possibility, argued half a century ago by the anthropologist Claude Lévi-Strauss, is that writing should be understood as a form of power that overcame and suppressed the authority of speech.[23]

What is the pertinence of these assertions to our history? Eisenstein is right to argue that printing as a technology made a difference, for it greatly enlarged the scale by which texts could be reproduced and lowered the cost of these copies. This was a problem as well as a solution, however, since it also raised the cost of entry into the market, and the sheer numbers of copies outran their initial markets. Both factors figured in the making of the Reformation.[24] By the mid-seventeenth century in England, moreover, printing was clearly overtaking and, in certain situations, displacing oral and scribal publication; proclamations and the structure of legal "memory" are cases in point. Yet we fall into difficulties, at once conceptual and practical, in attempting to specify a "logic of print," as though the technology were itself an actor, and in pinpointing when this logic may have become dominant.[25] Indeed Ong's grand narrative has seduced some historians of early America into proposing this or that moment as marking the definitive rupture with orality.[26]

But let us rethink the terms of the problem. One way of understanding Ong's narrative of decline is to regard it as an episode in the "anxiety about language" that, within western culture, may be traced back to Aristotle and the New Testament. The literary historian Sandra Gustafson, to whom we owe this suggestion, goes on to remark that the cultural historian of the post-Gutenberg period inevitably encounters a series of oppositions that have shown a remarkable persistence: "stable text/dead letter; living speech/demonic speech." The same could be said of assertions about writing as power; here, the anxiety about the possibilities for freedom, resistance, and subversion within a routinized, bureaucratic (and, for others, patriarchal and racist) culture is palpable. But as Gustafson aptly observes, the task of the historian, as distinct from that of the prophet or cultural critic, is not to reiterate these oppositions but to uncover "the cultural and historical imperatives that bring one opposition to the fore, and thus privilege speech or writing in a given community at a given period."[27] For us, therefore, orality is a flexible category or practice, persisting in America well into the nineteenth century. We have also attended to the practice of scribal publication and some of the ways in which it competed with or was eventually displaced by printing.

2. Literacy and Illiteracy. Like printing, literacy (usually signifying the ability both to read *and* write, a misleading conjunction as we will see) can be considered an autonomous skill, a technology that carries with it certain automatic consequences. But for us, literacy is akin to orality in being not a fixed term or condition but a practice that was mediated by different frames of meaning and social circumstances. The polarity of literacy and illiteracy or of literacy and orality must give way, therefore, to a contextualized description of the uses – discursive or ideological as well as practical or social – to which literacy was put. Otherwise, we run the risk in early American history of representing literacy as hierarchical and excluding, labels that overlook the important distinction between reading and writing literacy and that ignore the possibilities for knowledge and participation among the so-called illiterate.[28]

3. Print and the Public Sphere. According to Jürgen Habermas, printing abetted the construction of a "bourgeois public sphere" in eighteenth-century Europe, a space that enabled the work of social criticism and the forming of public opinion to proceed to the point of becoming an alternative to the mystifications and personal rule of the monarchy.[29] Yet on this side of the Atlantic, social and political criticism were never fully differentiated from the language and practices of radical Protestantism, which during the English Civil War had already fashioned a certain kind of public sphere. In the American colonies, moreover, political, religious, and social authority was remarkably local and decentralized in comparison with France, Britain, or Prussia. Here, too, the term "bourgeois" is less applicable, and the consequences of printing and bookselling for the making of a public sphere are less easily differentiated from the world of commerce. Nor can we equate "public" with any broad distribution of printed matter, for the simple reason that, with very few exceptions, no such distribution occurred in eighteenth-century America. For these reasons, we have preferred to describe the emergence of a "republic of letters" and an ethos of "free inquiry" that flourished within learned culture and that made it more legitimate to expose the private and sacred qualities of personal rule.[30] Our narrative also takes account of literary and cultural coteries, some of which

preferred the medium of scribal publication to the "public" medium of print.

4. Authorship and Intellectual Property. For France and Britain in particular, some historians have argued that the seventeenth and eighteenth centuries witnessed the "birth" of the author, as evidenced by the construction of an "autonomous" literary sphere and changes in the understanding of rights to intellectual property in relation to capitalism and state control.[31] Such a transition occurred for *some* writers in Europe (Alexander Pope comes immediately to mind). We may also understand this transition as the creation of distinctive social sites for the practice of belles lettres. The literary history of early America was affected by this transition. Yet our literary history also encompasses a quite different understanding of writing, authorship, and literature, one that denied the very possibility of literature being separated from moral and social life. Moreover, the earliest legal privileging of authors only occurred at the very end of our period.[32]

5. The "Reading-Revolution." It has been argued by Rolf Engelsing and others that a "reading-revolution" (*Leserevolution*) unfolded in the eighteenth century as fiction began to displace the traditional stock of devotional texts and as more books became available. Here, too, while we take note in a subsequent chapter of changes under way by the time of the Revolution, the situation in America seems less advanced than in contemporary Europe, in part because of the slower advent of the consumer revolution on this side of the Atlantic and the continuing strength of Protestantism. Reading is perhaps the least understood – or the most difficult to conceptualize – of our topics. Is it the rules within a text or its typographic form that govern the act of reading? If every reader remakes the text, can we make any generalizations about the practice?[33] The familiar antithesis between intensive and extensive reading, which, it is argued, coincided with a decline in the importance of religious texts and a surge in the production of fiction, does not seem pertinent to eighteenth-century Americans except, perhaps, for certain urban reading circles.[34]

The history of reading also intersects with two other important questions or issues, one being gender, the other the categories of "high" and "low." Did women act in a different manner than men as consumers of print, and did they become significantly more visible as consumers in the course of the eighteenth century? These questions we address in Chapter 11, where we also reflect on the argument that genres and readers can be arranged along a spectrum of "high" to "low," elite to popular. To signal in advance our point of view, we prefer a history of reading that acknowledges a middling social and cultural space in which many texts seem to have circulated widely. The principal exception to this rule (and for the seventeenth century, a gendered exception) is learned culture, which was fashioned around a distinctive set of reading practices and a competency in foreign languages. Recognizing, as we do, the social dimensions of reading, literacy, and book ownership, we have also sought to describe reading as a cultural practice mediated by differing rules or representations of readers and texts.

Having indicated our thinking on these broad questions, what should readers expect from *The Colonial Book in the Atlantic World*? We remind our readers that this book is not an encyclopedia but a narrative history. Accordingly, anyone seeking information about a particular printer or bookseller, library or writer will often be disappointed. For the most part we have also forgone explicit comparisons with British and Continental practices, though Chapters 1 and 3, especially, are informed by a comparative perspective. We have chosen, of necessity, to work within certain larger restraints. Ours is not a history of "communication" in early America, which would require a much larger canvas. Nor is it a *histoire totale* of society and culture. Yet we have constantly endeavored to locate our story of writers, readers, and book-trade practices within a wider history of social structures and social movements. These include the workings of the imperial system and the factionalism that drove colonial politics, the religious insurgencies that attempted to extend the Reformation, the evangelical campaigns of the eighteenth century that conventionally are entitled "the Great Awakening," demographic and social tendencies as the population of the mainland colonies began a remarkable phase of expansion after 1700, and in relation to literary and learned culture, the emergence of new forms of sociability and new sites of cultural production that competed with older, long-persisting structures.

The central purpose of *The Colonial Book in the Atlantic World* is to provide a sustained description of book-trade practices, including journalism. Our account of book-trade practices foregrounds the doings of booksellers and establishes the very limited scope of printing and bookselling in the colonies for the seventeenth and the first half of the eighteenth centuries. In appendices that conclude the volume we provide further information on book production in the colonies and new republic, books imported from overseas, book prices, and popular authors and titles. We urge every reader to pay close attention to the first of these appendices and, in light of what is said therein about the limitations of our knowledge, to exercise due caution in citing any of our charts and tables that specify book production. However, we find suggestive the relationships that these charts and tables expose.

No less central is the history we provide of reading and writing, and of efforts to regulate writers, readers, printers, and booksellers. The story that we tell of readers and writers has many dimensions to it. First and foremost is our effort to narrate the changing understandings of writing and, more narrowly, of "literature" or "literary culture." Another important dimension of this story concerns the social contexts or "communities" within which writing and reading occurred, and the differing rhetorics that writers employed in addressing these communities. Here, too, we concern ourselves with self-censorship by authors and whether they controlled the transmission of their texts. No less important is our description of what we term the "modalities of reading," or the differing frameworks of meaning that mediated the practice. We attempt as well to describe the circumstances of literacy, book distribution, and book ownership, together with the history of libraries. The arguments we have advanced earlier in this introduction about orality and literacy, performance and scribal publication, reading and authorship are, we hope, sustained by the details that follow. Much remains to be learned about all of these matters; ours is "a" history of the book in early America, not "the" definitive account. We emphasize that, in experimenting with a fuller synthesis than heretofore attempted, we have often been reminded of what we did not know. That this book will serve to suggest many opportunities for further study and research is, for us, a prospect we welcome and encourage.

PART TWO. THE EUROPEANS' ENCOUNTER WITH NATIVE AMERICANS

THE COLONIAL BOOK IN THE ATLANTIC WORLD is a story of ongoing exchanges between the Old World and the New – of books and paper for tobacco, of intellectual recognition in return for a local naturalist's shipment of native flora and fauna. The Europeans who explored the coast and the colonists who followed in their wake entered into a similar relationship with the Indians, trading clothes, weapons, utensils, and alcohol for information, sustenance, furs, and land. Colonists and Indians were alike – if unequally successful – in using each other to gain political and economic power. Treaties and alliances were the visible signs of these negotiations, which involved an ever-shifting coalition of tribes, colonial governments, and European civil states.[35]

These modalities of exchange coexisted with contradictory attitudes and policies. Notwithstanding the colonists' dependence on the Indians, the English engaged in displays of force and episodes of wholesale slaughter. These actions flowed from the assumption that the colonists were dealing with "bestial dogs" enslaved by Satan. These same actions were regarded as necessary to intimidate the Indians, who it was feared, would rise up and overwhelm the colonists, as nearly happened in Virginia in 1622 and in New England during King Philip's War (1675–1676).[36] Racism, intimidation, war, and the relentless expansion of settlements onto Indian lands were conditions that eventually destroyed the system of exchange.

Nor did exchange prevail in the project of converting the Indians to Christianity, a project premised on the Europeans' assumption that they had much to give and little to receive, other than the satisfaction of saving souls from hell. The instrumentalities of this program were preaching, books, schools for introducing the Indians to literacy in their own languages and in those of the Europeans, and communities or settlements where Indians were brought together to live in a new, more "civilized" manner.

The missionary project originated with the Spanish who, under Cortez, invaded Mexico in 1519. Four years later, in 1523, a small group of Franciscans arrived in Mexico City to begin the task of teaching Christianity to the Indians. Because books were deemed critical to the tasks of conversion and education, the Bishop of Mexico established in 1539 the first printing office in the New World, using it to issue books of religious instruction. By the close of the seventeenth century, Franciscan missionaries in Sante Fe and other nearby outposts were using books produced in New and Old Spain and in Antwerp to instruct the local Indians.[37] To the east, in Florida, and to the north, in French Canada, missionaries were also at work. The earliest reports from Florida and the southwest told of an extraordinary number of baptisms – tens of thousands in the Southwest, some eight thousand in Florida.[38]

The insincerity of such mass conversions offended Jesuits and Protestants alike, who both insisted on rigorous proof of their converts' faith – a task in which the Jesuits were more successful, in part because they were better organized and more tolerant of Indian culture, in part because Catholic ritual and devotion were more appealing, in part, it must be said, because European emigration to Canada was sparser.[39] The religious medals the French Jesuits distributed are found in grave sites as far south as Rhode Island, and the English colonists savagely resisted their incursions in "the Eastern parts" (Maine) and Iroquoia. In Maryland, the Jesuits had to overcome opposition from the Proprietor before undertaking to live among the Indians, as four of them did in 1638; in their annual letter to the head of the English province, one wrote how his companions had dispersed themselves "in places far distant – doubtless because they expect thus to obtain an earlier acquaintance with the barbarian language, and propagate more widely the sacred faith of the Gospel." Three years later, one of the priests succeeded in composing "a short catechism, by the aid of an interpreter."[40] The task of mastering a native language that seemed to have no rules of grammar was daunting; of those who tried, relatively few succeeded, even with the help of native intermediaries.[41]

English Protestants responded as confusedly as French Catholics to the Indians, reporting in almost the same breath that "a more kinde and loving people there can not be found in the worlde," and yet calling them idolators who worshiped Satan.[42] In principle, the English were zealous in the cause of evangelism, the main motive specified in royal charters for the enterprise of colonization. The letters patent of the Virginia Company of London (1606) described the venture as "a work which may . . . tend to the glory of his divine Majesty, in propagating of Christian religion to such people, as yet live in darkness and miserable ignorance of the true knowledge and worship of God."[43] The seal of the Massachusetts Bay Company depicted an Indian uttering the "Macedonian plea" to St. Paul of Acts 16:9: "Come over and help us." Notwithstanding these icons and pronouncements, the Protestant colonists were slow to act and never had the same success as their Catholic counterparts, a success these Protestants refused to acknowledge.[44] Protestant and Catholic missionaries were also handicapped by the inroads that disease and war made on the Indians who lived in the areas of first contact and settlement. The sharp decline of this population, and the threat of pro-French sentiment among Catholic converts in Iroquoia, dictated that the scene of endeavor move inland during the eighteenth century to the New York and Pennsylvania frontier.

Anglicans, Presbyterians, and Moravians each played a role in these eighteenth-century missions. The Society for the Propagation of the Gospel in Foreign Parts, chartered in England in 1701, supported Anglican clergy in the colonies, a few of them specifically as missionaries to the Mohawks of New York; after 1715, these clergy used a translation into Mohawk of parts of the *Book of Common Prayer* (Fig. I.1). The Society in Scotland for the Propagation of Christian Knowledge, founded in 1701 as the Society for the Reformation of Manners, supported a variety of American missions from 1730 on. Another international network was responsible for the effort of the Moravians, who applied their ethic of peace, love, and Biblical simplicity to the mission field in Pennsylvania. Here at midcentury they established a series of communities, most notably, Gnadenhutten, where whites and Indians were to live together.[45]

Among the seventeenth-century English colonists, only the Puritans in New England were able to initiate missions of any scale. Like their contemporaries in Canada and New Spain, the Puritans had to decide whether literacy was requisite to becoming a Christian and, if so, whether to translate religious texts from English into native languages or to teach the Indians to

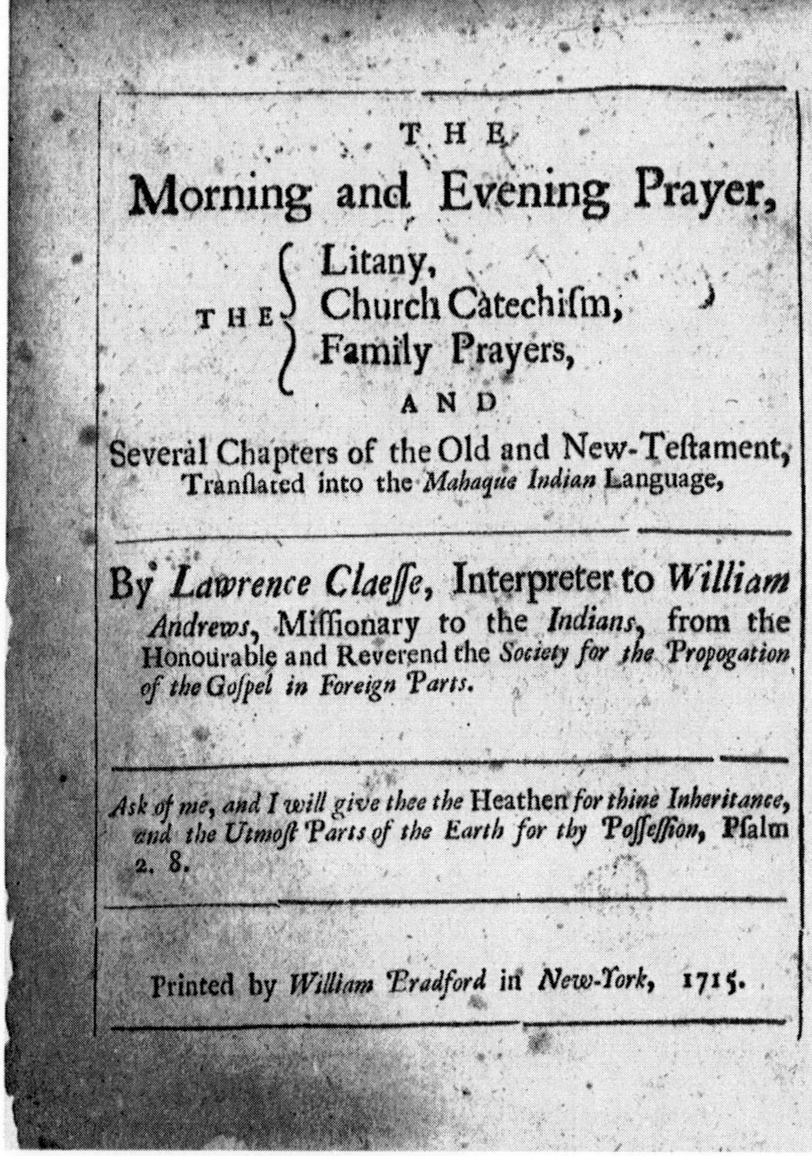

THE

Morning and Evening Prayer,

THE { Litany,
Church Catechiſm,
Family Prayers,

AND

Several Chapters of the Old and New-Teſtament,
Tranſlated into the *Mahaque Indian* Language,

By *Lawrence Claeſſe*, Interpreter to *William Andrews*, Miſſionary to the *Indians*, from the Honourable and Reverend the *Society for the Propogation of the Goſpel in Foreign Parts.*

Ask of me, and I will give thee the Heathen *for thine Inheritance, and the Utmoſt Parts of the Earth for thy Poſſeſſion,* Pſalm 2. 8.

Printed by *William Bradford* in *New-York*, 1715.

Figure I.1. Church of England, *The Morning and Evening Prayer = Ne Orhoengene neon Yogaraskhagh Yondereanayendaghkwa* . . . translated into the Mahaque Indian language, by Lawrence Claesse (New York: William Bradford, 1715). Courtesy of the Library Company of Philadelphia.

NE

Orhoengene neoni Yogaraskhagh

Yondereanayendaghkwa,

NE { Ene Niyoh Raodeweyena,
Onoghſadogeaghtige Yondadderighwanondoentha,
Siyagonnoghſode Enyondereanayendaghkwagge, }

Yotkade Kapitelhogough ne Karighwadaghkweagh Agayea neoni Aſe Teſtament, neoni Niyadegariwagge, ne *Kanninggahaga Siniyewenoteagh*.

Tehoenwenadenyough *Lawrance Claeſſe*, Rowenagaradatsk *William Andrews*, Ronwanha-ugh *Ongwehoenwighne* Rodirighhoeni Raddiyadanorough neoni Ahoenwadigonuyoſthagge Thoderighwawaakhogk ne Wahooni Agarighhowanha Niyoh Raodeweyena Niyadegoghwhenjage.

Eghtſeraggwas Eghtjeeagh ne ongwehoonwe, neoni ne ſiyodoghwhenjooktannighhoegh etho ahadyeandough.

Figure I.1. (*Continued*)

read the Bible and other books in the colonists' own tongue. The decision in favor of translation was largely the doing of John Eliot, the minister of Roxbury, Massachusetts, who spent the last forty years of his life both as pastor and as missionary. To this latter task, he brought the same assumptions that guided his pastorate in Roxbury: converts to Christianity and candidates for admission to church membership should know the Bible, be familiar with Christian doctrine as outlined in a catechism, manifest their faith in a "relation" of spiritual experience, and lead a moral life. Behind this framework of assumptions lay long-established expectations about literacy and reading as crucial to religion. Ritual, sacraments, and images would not do; the true Christian was someone who knew how to read.[46]

In September 1646, Eliot traveled to a nearby Indian settlement, where he conducted a prayer service (in English), with a sermon (in Massachusett), followed by questions and answers. Encouraged to continue by the colony government, which authorized certain grants of land, and aided by funds raised in England by a philanthropic organization, the Society for Propagation of the Gospel in New England (chartered for this purpose in 1649, rechartered in 1662, and known informally as the New England Company), Eliot and co-workers such as Daniel Gookin devised a three-part missions program. Unlike the Franciscans and the Jesuits, Eliot did not propose to live among the Indians himself. Instead, he wanted to introduce the Indians to "civilization," which meant detaching them from their customary ways of living and resettling them in "praying towns" where European patterns of work, dress, and household structure would prevail. Schools where native children learned to read Christian texts translated into Massachusett were a feature of these towns, some fourteen of which had been organized in Massachusetts by 1674. So were churches. The earliest effort at organizing a gathered congregation occurred at Natick in 1652, with a small number of Indians offering spiritual testimony before an audience of visiting clergy. This effort was unsuccessful, but after further testimonies had been received in 1659, the missionary succeeded.

The second part of Eliot's program was to alphabetize the Massachusett language for a translation of the Bible and related texts, in order to print and distribute copies in sufficient quantity to sustain religious instruction and devotion among the Indians. "I having yet but little skill in their language," Eliot wrote to Edward Winslow in 1649, "I must have some Indians, and it may be other help continually about me to try and examine Translations." Aided by three teachers and interpreters, a Montauk Indian from Long Island named Cockenoe and two Massachusett Indians, John Sassamon and Job Nesutan, he was able to see a complete Bible through the press by 1663 (Fig. I.2a). He began, however, with a simpler text, a catechism that was issued in 1654. Along the way, three parts of the Bible – Genesis, the Gospel of Matthew, and a metrical translation of the Psalms – were printed in order to test the adequacy of the translation and to encourage English donors to support so grand a project. Meanwhile, Abraham Pierson, the minister in Branford, Connecticut, prepared another catechism, published in Cambridge in 1659, "to sute these southwest partes where the languige differs from theires whoe live about the Masacheusetts."[47]

With the Bible completed, Eliot decided that the next step was to provide "Books for [the Indians'] private use, of ministerial composing. For their help," as he explained in 1663 to the English minister Richard Baxter, "though the Word of God be the best of Books, yet Humane Infirmity is, you know, not a little helped, by reading the holy Labours of the Ministers of Jesus Christ." A year later, his translation, an abridgment of Baxter's *Call to the Unconverted,* was published, followed in 1665 by a shortened version of Lewis Bayly's *The Practice of Piety* and in 1689 of Thomas Shepard's *The Sincere Convert.* Eliot's most important contribution to the teaching of Massachusett was the *Indian Primer* of 1669. Including the reprintings that were done before and after Eliot died in 1690, some of them occasioned by the destruction of books during King Philip's War, and texts written or translated by others like Josiah Cotton and Experience Mayhew, the number of Indian imprints had reached approximately twenty-eight by 1730.[48] Thereafter, the program came to an end, save for very occasional reprints.

The reasons for giving up on the program of translations were several. From the outset, not everyone shared Eliot's passion for getting books in their own language into the hands of the Indians. Some doubted that the vocabulary of Christian doctrine could be rendered into so different a language. Roger Williams, for one (Fig. I.2b), had remarked on the "mighty paines and hardships undergone by my selfe, or any that would proceed to such a further degree of the Language, as to be able in propriety of speech to open matters of salvation to them."[49] It had been Eliot's hope that Massachusett was derived from Hebrew, which he and others regarded as the original language of all the children of Adam. This expectation, which was linked to his assumption that the Indians were descended from Shem,[50] was not borne out by his struggles with Massachusett. Meanwhile his English sponsors were being told that some New England tribes could not understand the dialect into which he was translating the Bible. The New England Company also pressed on him the importance of using teachers and intermediaries who were fluent in the native language. The press also employed a Nipmuck Indian, named by the English James Printer after his trade, to set type and correct the sheets.[51]

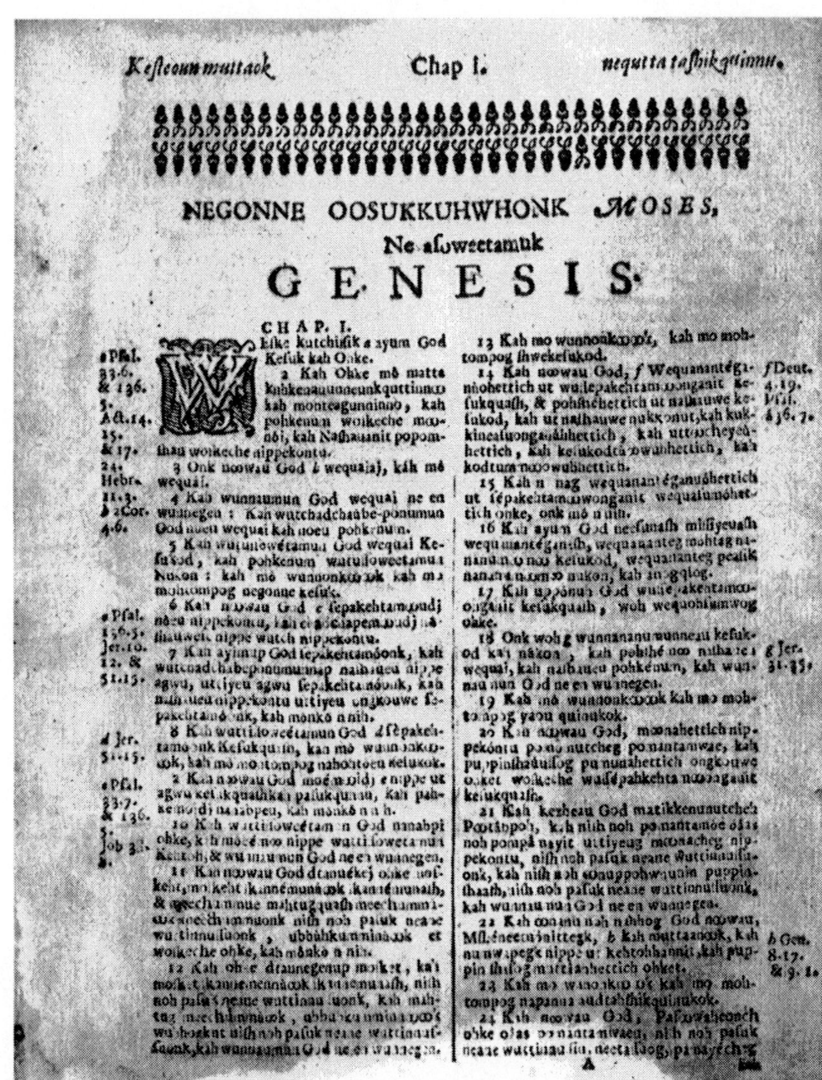

Kesteoun muttaok Chap I. *nequtta tashikquinnu.*

NEGONNE OOSUKKUHWHONK *MOSES,*

Ne asoweetamuk

GENESIS.

CHAP. I.

Figure I.2a. The creation myth (Genesis 1:1–13) in Natick and Narragansett: the Eliot Indian Bible (Cambridge, 1661–1663) (American Antiquarian Society); and (I.2b) Roger Williams, *A Key into the Language of America* (London, 1643). Note the "learned" diacritics of Williams's version, helpful for nonnative speakers. Courtesy of the John Carter Brown Library, Brown University.

124 Of *their Religion.*

Maunaûog Miſhaúnawock.	*Many, great many.*
Netop machàge.	*Friend, not ſo.*
Paûſuck naûnt manìt.	*There is onely one God.*
Cuppíſsittone.	*You are miſtaken.*
Cowauwaúnemun.	*You are out of the way.*

A phraſe which much pleaſeth them, bein proper for their wandring in the woods, an ſimilitudes greatly pleaſe them.

Kukkakótemous, wáchit-quáſhouwe.	*I will tell you, preſentl*
Kuttaunchemókous:	*I will tell you newes.*
Paûſuck naûnt manìt kéeſittin keeſuck, &c	*One onely God made th Heavens, &c.*
Napannetaſhèmittan naugecautúmmonab nſhque.	*Five thouſand yeers ag and upwards.*
Naûgom naûnt wukkeſittinnes wâme teâgun.	*He alone made all thin*
Wuche mateâg.	*Out of nothing.*
Quttataſhuchuckqúnnacauſ-keeſitìnnes wâme.	*In ſix dayes he made things.*
Nquittaqúnne.	*The firſt day Hee ma*
Wuckéeſitin wequâi.	*the Light.*
Néeſqunne.	*The ſecond day Hee*
Wuckéeſitin Keéſuck.	*made the Firmament*

Shúc

Figure I.2b.

The need to convince the New England Company of the feasibility of the project explains why the "Indian library" included a handful of bilingual texts, in which English was interlined with Massachusett: Pierson's catechism (for which Thomas Stanton, Sr., a trader, provided assistance), a preliminary edition of the translation of Genesis (1655), and the *Christian Covenanting Confession* used in admitting persons to church membership. Until 1700, however, the other texts were almost entirely in the native language. But by 1710, the Boston minister Cotton Mather voiced a general opinion when he wrote the New England Company that "The best thing we can do for our Indians is to Anglicise them in all agreeable Instances; and in that of Language, as well as others."[52] Increasingly thereafter, the texts included in the Indian library were bilingual.

A third part of the program was to provide additional training – even, it was hoped, at Harvard College – for a handful of young men who, having learned English and accepted Christianity, would become teachers and ministers among their own people. As Eliot and Thomas Mayhew, Jr., a lay missionary on Martha's Vineyard, realized, only thus would a sufficient number of spiritual leaders be available for native churches and communities. "I find it hopeless," Eliot wrote in 1671, "to expect English Officers in our Indian Churches; the work is full of hardship, hard labour, and chargeable also." It followed, therefore, that natives "must be trained up to be able to live of themselves in the ways of the Gospel of Christ." Though the Harvard end of things was unsuccessful because of the early deaths of some of the most promising Indian students, dozens of persons on Martha's Vineyard and the mainland took on these roles in the seventeenth and eighteenth centuries, several becoming ordained ministers. They were complemented in their public ministry by women converts who were literate.[53]

Of all the intermediaries who participated in the missionary project, the most famous in his own day was the Mohegan Samson Occom, born near New London in 1723 in a "heathen" family. The religious revivals of the late 1730s and early 1740s having led to a renewed concern among the colonists for evangelism, a wave of conversions among the yet unchristianized Indians in New England followed, Occom's being one of them. Setting himself the task of becoming literate in English, he learned within a year "to Read in the New Testament without Spelling." His mother, now herself a Christian, asked a nearby minister, Eleazer Wheelock, if he would instruct her son "in Reading," which Wheelock agreed to do. Training in English was followed by lessons in Latin and, with a different minister, in Hebrew. Because troubles with his eyes prevented him from attending college (which his teachers thought he could do successfully), Occom served briefly as a schoolteacher among Indians on Long Island before being ordained as a

Presbyterian minister in 1759, having delivered a "trial sermon" and been examined "in the learned languages." The organizers of this event had in mind the missions then being instituted among the Oneida in New York, where Occom took up his ministry in 1761, preaching through an interpreter while he started to learn the language.

But by the mid-sixties, Occom was more interested in a school for teaching English to native youth (both boys and girls) that Wheelock was struggling to sustain in eastern Connecticut, Occom's home ground. On behalf of this program and with the support of George Whitefield, the great itinerant revivalist, Occom and a clerical companion toured England and Scotland in 1765–1768, soliciting donations that eventually totalled £12,000. A living witness to the transformations wrought by civilization and Christianity, Occom was something of a celebrity in English society, and admirers had his portrait painted. It shows him in clerical dress pointing to a folio Bible open to the New Testament; a bow and arrow hang on the wall in the background (Fig. I.3). Not much went right thereafter in Occom's life; with some justice, he felt that his singular identity had been exploited by Wheelock, whose decision to move the Indian school to New Hampshire, where it evolved into Dartmouth College, was another blow. In the aftermath of the Revolution, Occom helped organize a movement among the Indians who remained in eastern Connecticut to resettle in the west.[54]

Occom was the first Native American to publish in English.[55] Before him, the persons whose spiritual histories were collected in John Eliot and Thomas Mayhew's *Tears of Repentance* (London, 1653) and in Experience Mayhew's *Indian Converts* (London, 1727) had told their stories through an intermediary. Occom's opportunity to publish arose in 1772, when he was asked to preach a sermon on the day that a Native American convicted of murder was executed in New Haven. A contemporary newspaper remarked on Occom's "honest simplicity and Gospel sincerity"; in his preface, he made a point of having spoken so that ordinary people, both whites and Indians, would understand him. The sensational aspects of the event, however, were probably why his sermon, a plea for temperance, was reprinted three times in the space of three months and another eight times within the next year and a half, as well as being issued as a broadside. In 1774, Occom published a longer work, *A Choice Collection of Hymns and Spiritual Songs,* some of which were of his own composing and others the work of Isaac Watts and Charles Wesley. Any reference to race was conspicuously absent from the title page, for Occom was identified as "Minister of the Gospel" and the subtitle read, "Intended for the Edification of sincere Christians, of all Denominations." That the collection was used by the Indian communities he was organizing in the west seems certain, but the dozen or so editions that ap-

Figure I.3. "The Reverend Mr. Samson Occom," mezzotint (London, 1768) by Jonathan Spilsbury after a lost contemporary portrait by Mason Chamberlain. Courtesy of the Hood Museum of Art, Dartmouth College, Hanover, N.H.; gift of Mrs. Robert W. Birch.

peared by the first decade of the nineteenth century suggest a wider audience and, for Occom, an identity as a Christian that, as in his London portrait, drew much of its force from his past as a "heathen."[56]

The uses of books and literacy among the Native Americans can only be touched on briefly.[57] Early reports from Europeans who showed them books and writing describe a response of wonder. One such story, which, like others of its kind, may be a European fantasy, told of the "unlettered stupiditie" of Indians who "could not conceive the force of writing of Letters; . . . the poore Indian would marvaile how it should be possible that he to whom [a letter] came should be able to know all things . . . : And thereupon divers of them did thinke, that there was some kinde of Spirit in the paper, and marveilously stood in feare of such a thing as a Letter was."[58] If they existed, these feelings of awe and inferiority gave way, in time, to a realism and expertise in the making of records, dealing with civil courts, and handling treaties, a considerable number of which were printed in the eighteenth century for the benefit of each party to the exchange thus formalized in writing.[59] As for how the Indians responded to the thousands of catechisms, psalters, primers, and Bibles printed for their benefit, the narratives collected by Experience Mayhew in *Indian Converts,* together with the material evidence in surviving copies – marginal annotations, signatures of owners, much evidence of being handled – are signs that some Indians became active users of these books.[60] Yet an archeologist's discovery of a native grave site in Connecticut that contained, among other artifacts, a leaf torn from a Bible, suggests that books, or pages from books, may have played a variety of functions far beyond what Eliot and the missionaries intended – possibly as grave goods, perhaps as signs or instruments of healing, or as elements in some system of exchange quite apart from the program set up by the colonists. That the "Indian library" was put to diverse ends seems clear.[61] And that Eliot (in contrast with the missionary work of Thomas Mayhew, Jr. of Martha's Vineyard) did everything possible to override native culture, imposing Eurocentric assumptions about language, speech, author, book, and literacy on the Indians, is all too evident as well.[62] On the other hand, there is abundant evidence that Christian Indians adapted writing to their own purposes. Writings in Massachusett ranging from town records and land transactions to a list of marriages reveal the uses of vernacular literacy as late as the 1770s in support of an oral culture.[63]

CHAPTER ONE

Reinventing the Colonial Book

HUGH AMORY

FROM THE BEGINNING, printers have rejoiced in two ideologies: one vindicates the majesty of their art; the other exculpates its abuses. In the more familiar of these pleas, echoed in many an early colophon, theirs is a divine art and mystery, Laurens Coster's "art that preserves all arts" (ARS ARTIVM OMNIVM CONSERVATRIX), Johann Gutenberg's "artful venture" (*künste vnd afentur*); and it is in this guise that Isaiah Thomas introduces it in his pioneering study *The History of Printing in America* (1810) as an inherently potent, mysterious force, like the philosopher's stone. Nor was Thomas merely a naive, early historian who swallowed the mythical identification of Gutenberg's successor Fust with Doctor Faustus. No less than Lawrence C. Wroth, in his standard account of colonial American printing, claims a visible "spiritual force" for the printing press that is, apparently, denied to "a spinning wheel of the same period"; once more, the man's "spiritual" machine seems to triumph over the woman's merely "material" one.[1]

The alternative ideology, though rarely noticed by historians of the colonial book before Stephen Botein, insists that printing is only a trade, exercised by "mere mechanics" who must print whatever comes to their hand.[2] William Bradford, the first printer in Pennsylvania, claimed that his divine art deserved the special patronage of the colony, yet, only six years after his arrival in 1685, he argued that the Philadelphia magistrates could not blame *him* for printing George Keith's attack on the Quakers, since he had to take what work he could get. If, long afterwards, patriot mobs struck this prop from the printer's trembling hands, they also created new sources of patronage, from which the Boston printer Benjamin Edes, among other "Trumpeters of Sedition," temporarily profited. And after the Revolution, of course, the "mechanics" easily returned to celebrating the mystery of their art, which (so they claimed) had brought the Revolution all about.[3] Whether American printers relied on loyalist or revolutionary factions, on colonial governors or colonial assemblies, on a church, a sect, or their critics, they were rarely ruled by their "art," leaving it an open question whether the printing press in the colonies was an agent of cultural change or cultural change an agent of printing.

Our standard retrospective national bibliographies hunt this question, but the nature of "American literature" proves elusive. It is defined as books "relating to North and South America" in Joseph Sabin's *Bibliotheca Americana* (1868–1936), as books printed in the continental United States in Charles Evans's *American Bibliography* (1903–1955), and as works by North American authors writing in English in Jacob Blanck's *Bibliography of American Literature* (1955–1991), "specifically . . . that many-faceted product called belles-lettres." Finally, Oscar Wegelin, in his *Early American Poetry* (2nd ed., 1930), includes poetry in any language by anyone "born or residing" in America north of the Mexican border. In one way or another, these projects artificially divide production from consumption, the "art" from its distribution, the culture from its origins, and yet arbitrarily yoke culture and nationality to language, geography, or authorship.

The source for these various definitions can readily be identified as either current national bibliographies, like the *National Union Catalogue* and *Publisher's Weekly*, or United States copyright law (for Wegelin, in particular). Since national boundaries change and national identity is far from stable, however, it should be clear that current bibliographical practice is a poor rule for retrospective applications. For most of the period under consideration here, the only copyright law was the Act of Anne (1710), which drew no distinction between British subjects residing in Great Britain, and elsewhere; indeed, the colonists occasionally availed themselves of this act or the protection of the Stationers' Register, beginning as early as 1653. Out of respect for the parallel British and Canadian Histories of the Book, we have scanted our treatment of the Caribbean or Canada, but the distinction would have been foreign to an inhabitant of the British North American colonies before 1776 or even for some time afterwards, as Thomas's *History of Printing in America* shows. An identity that could cover the spectrum from loyalist to revolutionary was obviously somewhat fragile, but it was not wholly "imaginary," as Benedict Anderson would have us believe.[4] Since the "colonial book" has been invented so often and so variously, one may be pardoned for attempting once again to explain how and when its nationality, religion, language, and script were connected.

The "colonial" book has a character that distinguishes it at once from the product of the English provinces (with which it is often compared) and from that of England's nearer colonies, Scotland and Ireland. Like the latter and from a very early date, the American colonies printed their own psalm-books, psalters, primers, and almanacs, otherwise the jealously guarded properties of the London Stationers' Company. Somewhat later, in the eighteenth century, its reprints competed with both London and Edinburgh production. Culturally, however, Boston, Philadelphia, and New York were English provincial capitals and certainly regarded as such by London wholesalers, who by and large controlled the titles most sought-after by the colonists. Nevertheless, American national feeling – or the nostalgic love for a *Heimat* that was its usual eighteenth-century equivalent – had many parallels in John Bull's other kingdoms. We will consider this cultural mixture from two different angles: as an expression of nationality and as a commercial nexus. The technological dimension may be left to the classic introductions of Lawrence C. Wroth and Rollo G. Silver. Throughout our period, print was the servant, not the master, of the relationship between books and culture. The "colonial book" was what the colonists bought and read, as well as what they printed or reprinted, and no special importance was attached to its place of manufacture – in marked contrast to the protectionism that prospered from the Revolution to the Second World War.

Nationality and Print

Maps of the spread of Western printing are among the most familiar demonstrations of the mysterious power of moveable type, a vivid progress summarized in the subtitle of volume 1 of the *Histoire de l'édition française* as "le livre conquérant." The book that conquered in this early phase of its history was Latin and European, however, not vernacular or national, because printers needed the widest possible market to sell their extraordinarily elevated production. Latin was the larger, international market, whereas vernaculars, particularly on the peripheries of Europe, had only a local sale, a distinction that never affected the production of writing but was crucial for print. Printing "spread" along preexisting linguistic, intellectual, and commercial channels, in short, driven but not directed by technology. In the central region where printing originated, along the Rhine, about 77 percent of incunabula were in Latin – not just classics, but new editions of long neglected medieval theology as well; as a result, the proportion of vernacular to Latin texts in this area, particularly the popular German romances, actually declined with the introduction of printing.[5] On the European periphery, in Spain and England, this proportion was reversed and the vernacular triumphed: the periphery now met the demand for Latin by importation, and local production specialized in the vernacular, which was unmarketable in the center.

In general, since manuscript books were written and bound to order, there was no risk of overproduction. The printed book, however, was an "*afentur*," a business venture, and the early printer's options for hedging the risk were limited. He could not readily repackage the text in a smaller format, for example, because he had only a limited range of type sizes, and in any case, as their names still indicate, particular sizes of type were appropriated to specific kinds of book: missals (canon), pies (pica), primers, and breviaries. Aldus was the first printer to break with this tradition, printing "pocket editions" of works that normally appeared in larger formats. Though its cheapness made a printed copy more readily marketable than a manuscript, moreover, and the edition sizes of incunabula were small (250 copies on an average), the local market for a particular title was likely to be saturated well before the edition was exhausted. Already by 1480, the German trade was expressing anxiety about the "*librorum multiplicatio*," and by 1504, trade along the Rhine was at a standstill; it only revived with the Reformation, which, for the first time, provided a substantial market for the vernacular.[6]

The early European book trade eventually solved the problem of distribution by instituting the so-called *Tauschhandel,* the exchange of books on a sheet-for-sheet basis at the spring and autumn Frankfurt book fairs. This practice allowed printers to spread the risk of their investment in any single title by exchanging it for an assortment. It was a good solution for production that was heavily invested in the Latin language and the subject of religion, both of the widest interest, and as nearly fungible as the nature of the book permitted. After the Thirty Years' War, when confessional boundaries hardened, the trade too split: Imperial, Catholic books remained in the Frankfurt fair, and the Protestant trade recentered on Leipzig.[7]

The nexus of language, nationality, religion, and script allows a wide choice of elements in the constitution of a national retrospective bibliography. In his *American Bibliography,* Charles Evans took the "birth of a national literature" as his subject, colonial printing being "American" in embryo. Less teleologically, biologically, and nationalistically, one might define the colonial book as what was written, printed, or published by or for colonials; not a literature, but a scripture. A "scripture" keeps the balance between nationality and religion nicely neutral and directs our study toward the function and culture of the text, matters that are controlled by authors, languages, and printers in a "literature" but by writers, scripts, and publishers in a "scripture."

The "colonial book" may be divided into two scriptures, British and German: British for the national nexus (insofar as there was a single colonial nation); German for the religious and linguistic nexus that provided other emigrants their central identity. The two were distinguished by their scripts, both in print and in writing: roman and italic for British, *Fraktur* and

Schwabacher for German. English was generally the language of colonial government, the medium through which European culture was transmitted, and the usual language of the colonial printer. In this respect, colonial production differed little from that of the metropolis. After the final annexation of New Netherland in 1674, only German regularly served as a supplementary language of colonial government, though Eliot's Indian Bible had important governmental applications, and a selection of the Massachusetts Laws was briefly translated into Massachusett in 1707. The alphabetization of the Indians had proceeded in English at least as early as 1720,[8] and Pennsylvania Germans employed or adapted many English words and expressions. "Germantaun," as their section of Philadelphia was known, defined it in an alien tongue.

Only English scripture functioned continuously and generally as an instrument of culture: the occasional imprints in Swedish, Dutch, French, Spanish, or Welsh followed or exceeded German in their focus on religion. Dutch or German grammars were designed to teach English as a second language, and the standard mathematics text in German was a translation of Daniel Fenning's popular *Ready Reckoner.* The market for European belles lettres, either in the original or in translation, was English: the Pennsylvania Germans might occasionally buy Pope, Milton, and Shakespeare in translation, but rarely Goethe, Gessner, or Kotzebue. "The demand for foreign literature is inconsiderable," noted a contemporary observer of the American market in 1789; "It is very little for French books, and still less for Italian, Spanish, and Portuguese. German books are in some degree, an exception, for they sell in parts inhabited by the Dutch; but principally books of devotion and school books." Though the German press kept the "German subjects of King George III" abreast of political developments, "almost no public discussion of the issue of independence took place among the Germans themselves."[9] Apart from religion, the German press published translations of English (or American) culture: German scripture, but English (or American) literature.

From around 1740, the Scotch began to invade both the provincial and the colonial markets, to the distress of the London trade, which launched a series of lawsuits claiming perpetual copyright, a claim the Donaldsons of Edinburgh and London finally defeated in 1774; and by 1780, Irish trade with the colonies began to assume some importance.[10] No less a bibliophile than Thomas Jefferson appreciated the cheapness of Irish reprints of English legal authorities. The greatest contribution of these two kingdoms to the colonial trade, however, was their enterprising printers and booksellers, who mostly came over after 1750: Hugh Gaine in New York; Mein & Fleeming in Boston; David Hall, Robert Bell, and Mathew Carey in Philadelphia; and Robert Wells in Charleston – independent spirits who operated on their own and were often astonishingly defiant of public opinion (Gaine's timidity was exceptional).

Culturally, though the two kingdoms were perceived as separate nationalities both in England and the colonies, they printed and sold London properties. Scotch loyalism, particularly strong in the book trade, was resented by American patriots. Timothy Green, third in a succession of New London printers of that name and proud scion of a New England clan, was incensed when Robertson and Trumbull of Albany set up a store in "his" market of Norwich, Connecticut: "It appears something strange," he wrote, "that Scotsmen and Irishmen should in this Country have the Preference to Englishmen."[11] These prejudices did not attach to their books, however, whose contents were as English as London's and whose appearance was as provincial as America's.

At all periods, Americans bought books by special order from Europe: John Winthrop, Jr. received Frankfurt book fair catalogues; Increase Mather ordered Hebrew grammars from Utrecht; Thomas Jefferson, French literature from Paris. Commercial relations are harder to document, however: The bookstores established by Guérard de Nancrède in Boston and by Moreau de Saint-Méry in Philadelphia lie outside our period. Joseph Brunning, in seventeenth-century Boston, was the son of Mercy Brunning, in Amsterdam, who published Increase Mather's *Diatriba de signo hominis* (1684); we may assume that he dealt in Continental books, but the market cannot have been very large. Latin literature was surely its most important sector, and by the eighteenth century European sales were mediated through London. Both British and French mercantilism underwrote the "special relationship" of the colonies to Great Britain, even after the Revolution.

This chapter, then, explores how the English language and loyalties and the curve of the colonists' economic and imperial dependence on London defined colonial books, whether native imprints or imports. The German book trade and the economics of trade with Great Britain will be treated elsewhere, in Chapters 8 and 5, respectively. Evans seems a less suitable archive for our purposes than the imprint bibliographies of Pollard and Redgrave, Wing, and the ESTC, which cover printing in British dominions as well as English language titles wherever printed. Some works by colonial Americans that were first printed outside the continental United States will illustrate the difference. They range from London editions of the laws of Bermuda (1621), Barbados (1654, etc.), New Haven (1656), and Virginia (1662, etc.), to Samuel Newman's standard concordance to the Bible (1643), Franklin's *Experiments and Observations on Electricity* (1751), Anne Bradstreet's *Fifth Muse Lately Sprung up in America* (1650), and Phillis Wheatley's

Poems on Various Subjects (1773). Around 1625, Lewis Hughes, a minister from Bermuda, published A *Copy-book containing Plain and Easie Directions to Fair Writing* "for the benefit of the new planted Vineyards of the Lord Jesus in Virginia, Sommer Islands, and New England"; later London editions followed in 1653.[12] Copies of Cotton Mather's *Magnalia Christi Americana* (London, 1702), with two leaves of errata printed in Boston, or of Samuel Willard's *Compleat Body of Divinity* (Boston, 1726), with a frontispiece portrait engraved in London, are hybrids. One may also note hybrid authors like Susanna Rowson or George Whitefield, whose writings enjoyed a denser vogue in America than in their native country; indeed, copies of the first (and for a long time, the only) London edition of *Charlotte Temple* were only recently identified.

The context of English imperial authority also qualified the special significance that Evans assigns to colonial printing. An authorized London edition of the Cambridge *Platform of Church Discipline,* entered for the Massachusetts Bay Colony in the Stationers' Register (19 October 1652), certainly reached a wider audience than the original; there was also a London "piracy" (1652). As Perry Miller remarks, the early colonists did not write "for home consumption, but for an audience that stretched across half Europe,"[13] and they reached this audience by European, not domestic production. The most interesting instance of such a book is probably the *Declaration of Independence.* Is its audience European – as the invocation of "a decent respect for the opinions of mankind" might imply – or rather American – "the good people" whose grievances it details? In a sense it depends on whether we incarnate the text in script or print, script being its most familiar textual image today.

Indeed it is notoriously scriptural, providing such proverbial expressions for a signature as "a John Hancock." One naturally attributes the authorship of the *Declaration* to the signers, one of whom claimed it on his tombstone, though it speaks in the name of "the good people" they represented. In a logical paradox explored by Jacques Derrida and Michael Warner, however, its authority is circular, derived from "the people" whom it incorporates and purports to give a voice: "The signature invents the signatory." And Warner proceeds, superbly, to contrast the "personal" writtenness of the *Declaration* with the "anonymous" printedness of the Federal Constitution, "which deprived signing of personal meaning." Orality, script, and print mark off the stages in which the authorial voice of "the people" is silenced by the sovereignty that they themselves created.[14]

As Warner is aware, however, his analysis rests on a "fable" that was retroactively imposed on the *Declaration,* perhaps beginning in 1817 when facsimiles of the engrossed copy began to proliferate.[15] Nevertheless, "as it actually was," the text was first published in thirty newspaper editions (one in German translation) and some fourteen broadside editions (three in two impressions) before it was ever engrossed on parchment and signed.[16] These printed texts were also proclaimed orally to various assemblies of "the good people," who signalled their assent in festivities that included melting down a statue of George III into bullets for the Continental Army. *Then* it was signed, though it would not be clear before the Civil War that the new nation was established in July 1776, not in August by the signers, and not in a "more perfect union" by the thirteen states in 1789. By the suppression of its earliest, printed form, the *Declaration* has become permanently "unpublished," as it were, a merely personal prequel to the anonymous consensus embodied in the Constitution. The letters of the republic have been obliterated or, more precisely, placed under a spell.

The "unpublished," "prepublished," or, as Evans expresses it, "embryonic" status of the *Declaration* typifies most colonial American imprints. The only editions of the Bay Psalm Book since 1773, for example, have been facsimiles of the first edition (1640), though it received authoritative textual revisions in 1651, and the entire canon of colonial printing is now facsimiled in Readex microprint. Cotton Mather's multitudinous pamphlets, though most of them were were written for a wider audience than his own congregation, were distributed privately, for the most part, not commercially. Much colonial literature looked to a coterie and remained in manuscript or was first printed in unauthorized editions, like Anne Bradstreet's poetry. The colonial laws were perhaps the closest American printers ever came to a "public" property, and yet many American colonies chose to "publish" their laws by subscription – the ultimate form of privatization – or in manuscript. One third of the subscribers to the 1733 Laws of Virginia were located outside of the colony, as far away as London, York, Glasgow, and Bristol.[17]

The "spiritual force" of the printing press in colonial America is thus not as easily discovered as one might suppose. On closer examination, many forceful expressions of the American spirit were first printed in England, the press itself was ordinarily manufactured in England, and its first editions were *préoriginale* to a London reprint or reissue, which registered as the "original edition" in the current national bibliographies of the *Term Catalogues* or the *London Catalogue*. We can only perceive the provinciality of the colonial book, and the "presence" of English, Scotch, and Irish imports, by insisting on these alien originations. This was also a native perception: the "London Bookstore" flourished in eighteenth-century Boston, and one of its proprietors, John Mein, promoted his wares by equipping them with false London or Dublin imprints (a familiar tactic in the provinces, and in Scottish "piracies" as well). Had it not been for American independence,

London might ultimately have dominated the American trade as thoroughly as it would Australia's where, even as late as 1953, 80 percent of the books sold were imports.[18]

London's Commerce with the Colonies

As seen from London, the colonies were only another, more distant province of England, and the mechanisms by which the London trade supplied books to Norwich, York, or Exeter also operated to supply Boston, New York, and Philadelphia. The privileges that the Stationers' Company originally enjoyed by royal charter were gradually qualified by statute and by private combinations in restraint of trade, and the wholesalers and distributors who took over the country trade at the end of the seventeenth century also promoted trade with the colonies. Colonial, provincial, and metropolitan booksellers alike operated within a system of privileges and agreements designed to keep the risk of doing business as predictable as possible and to ward off not just competition, but the displeasure of church and state. Naturally, colonial printers and publishers were less dependent on London than their provincial brethren – their commerce rather resembled the Irish or Scottish trades; but the booksellers and printer–booksellers did a growing business in imports from London, on London's terms, to be considered now.

The Reformation had turned printing into a potentially dangerous, political activity, as John Foxe never wearied of pointing out in the *Book of Martyrs.* English authorities responded by an attempt to incorporate the printers, limit their numbers, and confine their production to a few, easily supervised centers. The London Stationers were originally a guild of retail booksellers ("stationers"), lymners (i.e. illuminators), rubricators, and bookbinders; printers were first incorporated in the company by the charter of 1557, which forbade the exercise of the art outside of London except at the two universities of Oxford and Cambridge. The charter also established a register, by which members of the company might enter a "copy" or title and claim exclusive rights to print it, whether or not they ever actually exercised the rights. This is the so-called booksellers' copyright, which was limited to guild members: no author or "foreign" (i.e., non-Londoner) bookseller might enter a work, and entries were only assigned, divided, or inherited within the London Stationers. The system nominally endured down to 1911, though the House of Lords in *Donaldson* v. *Becket* (1774) reduced the extent of the privilege to a statutory term of years.[19]

The Stationers' monopoly did not extend to wholesale bookselling, which they shared with other London guilds and with aliens for most of the sixteenth century: with Mercers, or Drapers like Andrew Maunsell, who drew up the first English trade catalogue (1595) and Christopher Barker, who monopolized the printing of the English Bible (1575, etc.); with aliens like the Birckmanns of Cologne, who maintained a branch in London. These wholesalers were essential to the early English book trade, providing the necessary capital and credit in an otherwise one-sided commerce with the Continent. The Stationers suppressed the encroachments of the Drapers in 1600 and formed a "Latin Stock" for the importation of books in 1616, but it fizzled out only eleven years later. Individual Stationers like Samuel Smith, and later John Nourse, finally took over the trade with the Continent, but little Latin and small Greek came from English presses before the eighteenth century, apart from schoolbooks. So strong was the flood of imported classics that most English editions were "pirated" from Continental properties.[20]

The charter's exclusion of "foreigners" from membership was less damaging than one might suppose: the Catholic or Puritan whom London shut out might still turn to a coreligionist in St. Omer or Amsterdam, the "foreign" bookseller might still buy London or Continental printing, and many more books in English or for sale in England were printed on the Continent than in the English provinces. In consequence, printing never "spread" in England as it did in Europe: even without government regulation, the strength of printing across the Channel, as well as the economic dominance of London, would have sufficed to keep the number of provincial printers down. In all of sixteenth-century England and Wales, the revised STC records presses at only four locations outside of London, Southwark, and Westminster before the charter, and even afterwards, Oxford and Cambridge forbore any exercise of their privileges for twenty-five years. Of the thirteen "secret" recusant and Puritan presses that can be located, eight set up shop in London, presumably because they considered it safer and more convenient than the country. A total of twenty-five locations outside London supported booksellers,[21] and one may doubt that there would have been more if they had printed for themselves.

Apart from entries in the Stationers' Register, literary property might be secured by a royal privilege or patent, the preferred method where one needed to protect a subject or a genre, and the sole recourse for authors before the Copyright Act of 1710. The Stationers soon patented the more lucrative properties – Bibles, lawbooks, liturgies, schoolbooks, and almanacs – in this manner. In 1602 they consolidated the patents on psalters, almanacs, and schoolbooks in an "English Stock" and shared it out among the leading booksellers. Except in Oxford and Cambridge, no provincial bookseller could participate in the printing and wholesaling of these texts, and even Oxford and Cambridge were eventually brought to heel. In 1631, the company reduced the Cambridge press to printing schoolbooks for the English Stock, and in 1637, for £200 a year, Oxford agreed to refrain from overprinting the company's patents.[22] With occasional renegotiations, these arrangements lasted into the eighteenth century: The use of English-language textbooks for teaching Latin and grammar, like the popular series of Charles Hoole or John Clarke, owes much to the relative profitability of the English Stock over imports. The Bible patent eventually came into the hands of John Baskett, and from his editions, printed in Oxford or Edinburgh, stems the present empire of Oxford University Press.

Control of the company gradually shifted from the printers to the booksellers who had amassed rights in the most profitable "copies" in the Register, and to owners of patents like the King's Printer, the Law Printer, or that "company within a company," the holders of shares in the English Stock. Printers sank into an underclass that multiplied steadily in the seventeenth century, despite edicts from the Star Chamber and Parliament limiting their numbers. The Stationers battled throughout the seventeenth century against the encroachments of other guilds on retail bookselling – Haberdashers, Ironmongers, and Chandlers being the worst offenders – but with little success. The same exploitation of the printer that ensured the profits of the "topping" Stationers also multiplied opportunities for lesser breeds; even within patented properties, there was no way in which editions of fifty or sixty thousand almanacs, "small books," and "pleasant histories" could be confined to what the company considered authorized outlets.[23]

As the institution of *Tauschhandel* suggests, relatively few properties were worth monopolizing under the *ancien régime,* and the risk of overproduction encouraged exchanges. The value of an entry in the Stationers' Register only accrued by hindsight, since 90 percent of the entries were never reprinted, and some of them were never printed at all. Even steady sellers like the English Stock were more safely shared, if only to discourage wasteful competition and piracy. The straightforward exchange of sheet for sheet became impractical, however, as publications became more various and specialized, and seventeenth-century booksellers replaced it with an exchange of titles by value. William Darrell's popular *Gentleman Instructed,* part 2 (1707) may illustrate how the new system operated: it was advertised at 6*s*., bound; offered by exchange, unbound, to the trade at 4*s*. 9*d*.; sold by the publisher and distributor to the trade at 3*s*. 4*d*.; and sold by the publisher to distributors at 2*s*. 10*d*.[24] The bookseller John Dunton, when he set up business in 1681, printed off a single title and exchanged it around the London trade for the necessary assortment. Three years later, his catalogue of *Books Printed for, and are to be Sold by John Dunton* listed 168 titles, besides "all sorts of Bibles and Bible-Cases, and all sorts of School-Books, &c."; only fourteen of these titles were actually Dunton's properties (Fig. 1.1).[25]

Dunton's expedient was necessarily confined to members of the London trade; the provinces had no titles to exchange and acquired their stock by

(1)

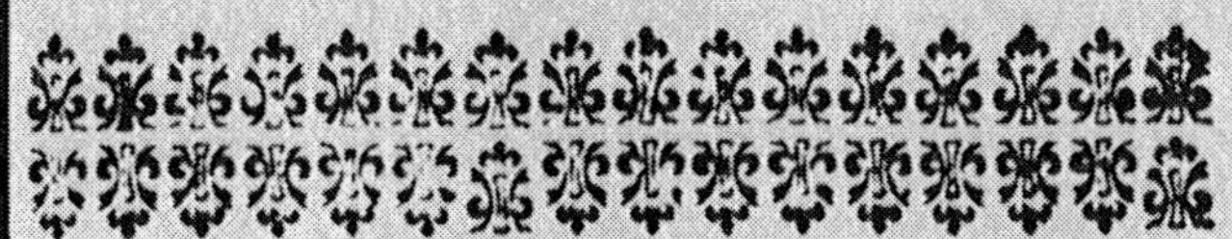

BOOKS

Printed for, and are to be Sold by *John Dunton* at the *Black Raven* in the *Poultrey*, over againſt the *Stocks-Market*, London.

Note, Thoſe Books that are mark'd with a Hand are lately Printed.

Folio.

A *General Martyrology*, containing a Collection of all the greateſt Perſecutions which have befaln the Church of Chriſt from the Creation to our preſent Times; wherein is given an exact Account of the Proteſtants Sufferings in Queen *Maries* Reign; whereunto is added the Lives of 32 *Engliſh* Divines, famous in their Generations for Learning and Piety, and moſt of them Sufferers in the Cauſe of Chriſt, &c. By *Samuel Clarke*, late Paſtor of St. *Bennet Fink*, London.

Figure 1.1. *Books Printed for, and are to be Sold by John Dunton* [London, 1684]; a list of the books that he sold in London and probably exported to America.

cash or services (e.g., on sale or return). When the country bookseller had any prospect of a considerable sale, as with items of local interest, he might buy into a London edition, however, acquiring copies at the cost of paper and print (e.g., for *A Gentleman Instructed,* at about 1*s.* 3*d.* a copy), a temporary partnership that benefited the London bookseller as well, by reducing the risk of his investment. Niccolò Balbani's *Italian Convert,* for example, printed by Anne Griffin for Michael Sparke and Anne Moore (London, 1635), was also issued with cancel title-pages by country booksellers in Salisbury, Dorchester, Coventry, Exeter, and Northampton: one edition, divided into eight issues, distributed in six cities. Wing's standard seventeenth-century imprint bibliography lists some hundred such provincial "editions": London sheets that the country bookseller had issued over his own imprint, either altering the London imprint during production or cancelling the London title-page.

In the fifteenth and sixteenth centuries, retailing had been essentially equivalent to binding up sheets that the binder acquired wholesale. By the era of the Restoration, however, most new titles were offered bound and advertised in the quarterly London trade periodical called the *Term Catalogues* (1668–1709); the exceptions were "Acts of Parliament, Proclamations, Speeches, Declarations, Letters, Orders, Commissions, Articles of War or Peace, Books of Church Government, Sermons, Histories [i.e., fiction], Plays, etc.," in short, fugitive tracts and ephemera. These were printed in uniform formats and sold stitched, allowing purchasers to arrange and bind up their collections by genre or subject if they wished.[26] The popular fiction, jestbooks, and godly admonitions collectively known as "small books," which were distributed by hawkers and traveling chapmen, were wholesaled bound from an early period, though the binding probably responded to orders for a specific quantity of copies.

The *Term Catalogues* clearly addressed a clientele of tradesmen and gentry outside of London, and the wholesaler Richard Chiswell enclosed free copies with the invoices of books that he shipped to the merchant John Usher in colonial Boston. In the early seventeenth century, the London bookseller "would bill the provincial bookseller at a price very little below the retail selling price in London," and the provincial bookseller advanced his price accordingly; a country customer could order new books directly from London about as cheaply as from his local bookseller. The fixed prices of the *Term Catalogues,* however, imply that the country trade received a discount, and in general, as John Feather argues, these booksellers probably acted as agents for their country customers when they ordered books from London, just as Usher himself did.[27] Wholesale, London offered recent titles at seven copies for the price of six and staples like the English Stock and "small books" at thirteen for the price of twelve or twenty-five for the price of twenty-four; discounts for quantity that applied equally to the prices in sheets, stitched, in wrappers, boards, or variously bound.

The retail price of London books rose from three times to five times the cost of paper and print during the seventeenth century,[28] and this in turn allowed a middleman profit for authors (the earliest surviving publisher's agreement is for *Paradise Lost* [1664]), binders, and distributors. Groups of booksellers known as "congers" who shared a group of copyrights on the model of the English Stock formed in the late seventeenth and early eighteenth century, and around 1718, the trade initiated sales at which particular titles (usually popular steady sellers) were divided into shares, offered for sale exclusively to members of the London trade, and regularly kept in print for the shareholders. By these combinations, the "topping booksellers" not only acquired their assortment at the cheapest possible rate but settled the prices at which they were to be exchanged or sold. After the Copyright Act of Anne (1710) granted literary property to persons outside the Stationers, the advantages of membership in the company declined: entry in the Stationers' Register continued to secure older properties like Shakespeare, Milton, and Dryden, but recent publications diluted the commercial value of this form of copyright, and *Donaldson* v. *Becket* (1774) ended it. Booksellers were then free to specialize as publishers, who offered only their own properties instead of sharing them with the trade, and by 1800 the Stationers had become a guild of paper stationers (i.e., retailers of stationery), binders, and printers.[29]

The explosion of country printing in the eighteenth century is usually ascribed to the lapse of the Licensing Act in 1695, an event that is supposed to have secured the freedom of the press and commerce that would have prevailed but for the monopolies of the Stationers' Company.[30] Commercial dominance was as least as effective as government regulation, however, and London now maintained its grip by combinations of the "topping booksellers," not by royal patents and privileges. Eighteenth-century country booksellers functioned mostly as retailers for London production and did little printing for themselves; even the copublication of London properties died out. One may also question how vital binding continued to be for the country trade, when they might order their books ready-bound – and probably better bound than anything the country bookseller could offer. Only 4 of more than 500 country printers, booksellers, and other craftsmen listed in the earliest book-trade directory (1785) describe themselves as binders.[31]

Richard Chiswell (formerly a Haberdasher), in the seventeenth century, and the firms of Thomas Longman and Edward and Charles Dilly, in the eighteenth, were prominent distributors who also dealt with the colonies. "A Catalogue of Mr. Richard Royston's Copies" (1703) that Chiswell (Royston's son-in-law) probably managed for the Royston heirs describes 254 entries in the Stationers' Register, extending from 1628 to 1686 (Fig. 1.2). The potentialities for exchange within the trade were manifold: Dunton, after all, had parlayed only 14 titles into 168. According to a well-known but rather schematic account by Dr. Johnson in 1776, the distributor allowed the country bookseller a unit discount of about 17½ percent off the London retail price, for "with less profit than this," Johnson, the son of a Lichfield bookseller, alleged, "the Country Bookseller cannot live."[32] This roughly corresponds to the 21 percent discount allowed by publishers at the beginning of the century for exchange of the *Gentleman Instructed*, but it is less than half the 44½ percent then allowed by distributors to the trade; the later distributors must have assumed the binding and transportation costs. Stock moved out of London by a regular series of discounts, instead of by added value in stages of manufacture, and this system accompanies the beginnings of edition binding in the 1730s.[33]

The colonial bookseller's greater distance from his supplier meant that he required longer terms of credit than his provincial brother, and payment was complicated and dilatory, as James Raven shows in Chapter 5. Trade with the colonies took many forms to deal with this difficulty. Thomas Cox, a London stationer and stockbroker, established an agency under his former apprentice George Vaux in Boston, but in general the London trade avoided branch offices. Booksellers and auctioneers might offer shipments of books at fixed prices for stated periods, after which the prices advanced or the books were returned; or the shippers themselves accompanied their offerings across the Atlantic, as John Dunton did as early as 1686; and there were always auctions. All of these devices ensured a quick return.[34] The London supplier could also compensate for longer credit by sending older, slower-selling stock: the fate of a "dull" author, sang Pope, was to be "shipp'd with Ward to ape and monkey lands" – to wit, the American colonies, where Pope's imaginary fauna matched the dullness of their reading. Gerrish's sale catalogue in 1720, Cox's in 1734, and Franklin's in 1744 list antiquated stock, broken sets, and, as Pope predicted, the *Miscellaneous Works* of Ward.[35] The personal friendship between David Hall and William Strahan, and Jeremy Condy's religious affiliations underwrote the quality of their shipments, whereas without such support the offerings of the New York bookseller James Rivington remained dubious and ill-sorted.

The colonial bookseller could have eased some of his problems of credit by buying into a London edition, like his provincial confreres, but he only rarely did so. *The Mystery of God Incarnate* (1650) by Samuel Eaton, formerly a minister at New Haven but by 1650 residing at Dukinfield near Manchester, appeared under four separate imprints: For H. Cripps and for L. Lloyd (both in London); to be sold by William Fugill (in Hull); and "to be sold by Hezekiah Vsher at Boston in New-England" and in fact, the third known book with his imprint. William Fugill was probably a kinsman of Thomas

A CATALOGUE *of Mr.* Richard Royſton's COPIES *as they ſtand Entred in the Regiſter of the Company of* Stationers. *Now belonging to the Children of Mr.* Luke Meredith; *deceaſed.*

January 26. 1628. ONE Copy call'd, An Elegy upon the Death of the moſt hopeful young Prince, *Henry*, eldeſt Son to his Majeſty of *Bohemia*.

October 1. 1629. *Francis Coles* and the ſaid *Richard Royſton* enter a Copy call'd, The Sacrifice of a Contrite Heart. Penned by *John Evans*, M. A.

May 10. 1630. *Richard Royſton* enters a Copy call'd, A Banquet of Jeſts; or, change of Cheer; being a Collection of Modern Jeſts, witty Jeers, pleaſant Taunts, merry Tales, *&c.*

April 26. 1631. Mr. *Young* and *Richard Royſton* enter a Book call'd, The Compleat Gentlewoman.

June 16. *Ditto*. *Richard Royſton* enters a Copy call'd, The Fair Maid of the *Weſt*, 1ſt. and 2d. Part.

July 28. *Ditto*. True Religion explained and defended againſt the Arch enemies thereof in theſe Times. Written By *Hugh Creſhaw*, and Tranſlated into Engliſh by *Fra. Coventry*, Eſquire.

Febr. 6. *Ditto*. Aſſigned over to him by *Martha Swaler*, a Copy call'd, The Promiſes, or, Saints Legacy.

March 22. 1632. *Richard Royſton* entred a Copy call'd, The Lover beguiled.

March 10. 1633. Mr. *Allot*, Mr. *Griſmond*, Mr. *Milburn*, *Richard Royſton*, and *Hen. Taunton*, entred a Copy call'd, Emblems Ancient and Modern, with Metrical Illuſtrations, *&c.* By *Geo. Wither*, Gent.

June 6. 1635. Aſſigned to *Richard Royſton* by *John Crouch*, a Copy call'd, The Chriſtian Directory; or, Rules of Chriſtian Piety and Wiſdom, *&c.*

Sept. 19. 1639. *Richard Royſton* entred a Copy call'd, The Exemplary Lives and Memorable Acts of Nine moſt worthy Women; three Jews, three Gentiles, and three Chriſtians. By Mr. *Thomas Heywood*.

Feb. 19. *Ditto*. A full third part in the Book call'd, Fourſcore Sermons, penn'd and preach'd by the Reverend *John Donne*, D. D. late Dean of St. *Paul's*; aſſigned to him by Mr. *Fleſher* and Mr. *Marriott*.

Ditto. Mr. *Fleſher*, Mr. *Marriot*, and *Richard Royſton* entred a Book call'd, Fifty Sermons, penn'd and preach'd by the ſaid *John Donne*; with his Picture and the Tables to all the Sixſcore and Ten Sermons.

Sept. 5. 1640. *Richard Royſton* entred two Copies aſſigned to him by *John Colby*, call'd, *Hermina*, &c. By Mr. *Geo. Rivers*. And, The Loſt Lady.

Octob. 5. *Ditto*. A Copy aſſign'd to him by *Richard Clutterbuck*, called, Meditations for Prayer upon the Seven Days of the Week. By Sir *Rich. Baker*.

April 5. 1642. A Sermon preached in St. *Paul's* Church on the King's Coronation-day, by Dr. *Gardner*.

Decemb. 17. 1644. Mr. *Bourne* and *Richard Royſton* entred a Book call'd, *Anabaptiſtarum Catacriſis*; or, the Anabaptiſt dipt and plunged. By *Dan. Featly*, D. D.

Ditto. *Richard Royſton* entred a Book called, *Boanerges Sinai*; or, Judgment and Mercy for afflicted Souls. By *Francis Quarles*, with his Picture engraven in Copper.

April 18. 1645. *Solomon's* Recantation, entituled *Eccleſiaſtes* paraphras'd, with twelve Soliloquies. And alſo Mr. *Quarles's* Life written by his Wife.

April 23. 1645. *Enchiridion* of Fortifications; or, a handful of Knowledge in Martial Affairs, with 20 Braſs Cuts and a Copper Title belonging to the ſaid Book.

May 5. *Ditto*. A Sermon preached at the Funeral of Dr. *Featly* by Dr. *Low*, with a Relation of his Life and Death, and a Braſs-plate of his Monument, with Verſes underneath it.

June 2. *Ditto*. The Shepherd's Oracle delivered in an Eclogue.

3. *Ditto*. A Comedy call'd, The Jealous Lover; by *Thomas Randall*, which ſaid Copy was formerly printed at *Cambridge*, as by a Note under their Hands appears, which is put upon the File.

July 26. 1645. A Practical Catechiſm in *Octavo*, containing two and twenty Sheets and a half.

Octob. 15. *Ditto*. Of Conſcience, *&c.*

Novemb. 20. *Ditto*. Five learned Treatiſes, *viz.* 1. Of Scandal. 2. Of Worſhip. 3. Of Superſtition. 4. Of Sins of Weakneſs and Wilfulneſs. 5. Of a late or Death-bed Repentance. By Dr. *Hammond*.

Ditto. Several Speeches made by Dr. *Featly* before the Aſſembly of Divines, with King *James's* Advice.

Ditto. The Cure of the Kingdom's great Curſe; or, an Antidote for the Tongue that is accuſtomed to Swearing. By *Robert Boerman*.

April 17. 1645. Certain Prayers grounded on the *Pſalms* of *David*, with certain Devotions thereunto annexed, *&c.* by Sir *Chriſt. Hatton*.

May 23. 1646. A Treatiſe of Self-denial, *&c.*

Sept. 4. 1646. The Additions and Appendix to the *Practical Catechiſm*, by Dr. *Hammond*.

Nov. 30. 1646. Directions for the Reading of the Scriptures with profit, with the Deſcription of a Spiritual Man, both in his Nature and Operations, and the clearing and aſſerting of the Morality of the Fourth Commandment in all things. By Mr. *John White* of *Dorcheſter*.

Dec. 1. *Ditto*. A Warning for *England*, eſpecially for *London*, in the famous Hiſtory of the Frantick Anabaptiſts, their wild Preaching and Practices in *Germany*.

Dec. 21. *Ditto*. A new and eaſie Inſtitution of Grammar, in which the Labour of many Years uſually ſpent in learning the Latin Tongue is ſhortened and made eaſie.

March 8. *Ditto*. A Diſcourſe of the Liberty of Propheſying; ſhewing the unreaſonableneſs of preſcribing to other Men's Faith, and the Iniquity of perſecuting differing Opinions, *&c.*

March 12. *Ditto*. Several Letters written between Dr. *Hammond* and Mr. *Francis Cheynell*.

April 23. 1647. Notes and Obſervations upon ſome Paſſages of Scripture, *&c.* By Mr. *Gregory*.

April 29. *Ditto*. The Diſcovery of Witches, by *Mat. Hopkins*.

July 24. *Ditto*. Of Fraternal Admonition or Correption.

Sept. 3. *Ditto*. Of the Power of the Keys, or, of Binding and Looſing, by Dr. *Hammond*.

Octob. 2. *Ditto*. The Privileges of the Univerſity of *Oxford* in point of Viſitation.

Nov. 10. 1648. The Soul's Soliloquy, and a Conference with Conſcience, *&c.* By Dr. *Duppa* Biſhop of *Salisbury*.

May 23. 1649. The Papers which paſſed at *Newcaſtle*, between his Sacred Majeſty and Mr. *Alexander Henderſon*, concerning the change of Church Government.

Dec. 31. *Ditto*. A Sovereign Salve to cure wounded Spirits, *&c.* By *Rich. Gove*.

Ditto. The Returns of Spiritual Comfort and Grief in a Devout Soul, *&c.* By *John Durton*.

Ditto. *Mercurius Pædaneus*; or, a ſhort way to the Latin Tongue. By *Jo. Phillips*.

Dec. 31. 1649. *Tropoſchematologia*, &c. By Mr. *Streter*.

March 11. The Reaſonableneſs of Chriſtian Religion for the ſatisfying of ſome Diſputes of theſe Evil Times.

Octob. 21. 1650. Some Animadverſions and Obſervations upon Sir *Walter Rawleigh's* Hiſtory of the World, *&c.* By *Alexander Roſſe*.

Ditto. Additionals, or certain Caſes of Doubt.

Nov. 7. The true Citizen; or, the Elements of Philoſophy, *&c.* reſerving every Man's Right.

Nov. 30. *La Stratonica di Luca Aſſarino Libri Tres*, tranſlated into Engliſh.

Dec. 16. *Barnabas*; or, Wine and Oyl for afflicted Souls. By *Francis Quarles*.

Jan. 7. *Diſſertationes quinque quibus Epiſcopatus jura ex S. Scriptura*, &c. *contra Sententiam D. Blondelli & aliorum.* Authore H. H.

14. *Grotii opera*, *viz.* *Annotationes in Libros Evangelii & in Acta Apoſtolorum, & Epiſtolas Apoſtolicas, & in Novum Teſtamentum, & in Apocalypſin.*

Ditto. *Hugonis Grotii de jure belli ac pacis.*

April 8. 1651. Sermons; the 1ſt. intituled, The Spirit of Grace, *&c.* By *Jeremy Taylor*, D. D.

Ditto. A Paraphraſe and Annotations upon all the Books of the *New Teſtament*, briefly explaining all the difficult places thereof. By *H. Hammond*, D. D.

Ditto. *Certamen Religioſum*; or, a Conference between the late King of *England* and the late Lord Marqueſs of *Worceſter*; together with a Vindication of the Proteſtant Cauſe from the Pretences of the Marqueſs's laſt Papers, which the neceſſity of the King's Affairs denied him opportunity to anſwer.

June 23. The Rule and Exerciſe of Holy Dying, *&c.* together with Prayers and Acts of Vertue to be uſed by the Sick, *&c.* Alſo Rules for the Viſitation of the Sick, *&c.* By *Jeremy Taylor*, D. D.

Sept. 16. The Gallantry of Heroick Women, written in French by *F. Peter le Moyne* of the S. of J. and tranſlated into Engliſh by *M.* of *W.*

Nov. 24. Two Copies, *viz.* The great Exemplar; or, the Life of Chriſt; and, The Rule and Exerciſe of Holy Living.

Feb. 9. *Tabulæ Feneratoriæ*; or, a moſt eaſie and compendious way to find out the Simple Intereſt of any Number to a Shilling for 365 Days, *&c.* Calculated by *Roger Clavell*.

March 18. 1651. A ſhort Catechiſm for the Inſtitution of young Perſons in the Chriſtian Religion. To which is added, an Explication of the Apoſtolical Creed. By *Jer. Taylor*, D. D.

April 21. 1652. A Diſcourſe of holy Love, by which the Soul is united unto God; containing, *&c.* Written in Spaniſh by *Chriſt. de Fonſeca*, and tranſlated into Engliſh by Sir *George Strode*, Knight.

May 27. Obſervations upon *Ariſtotle's* Politicks, touching Forms of Government: Together with Directions for Obedience to Governours in dangerous and doubtful Times.

July 1. Devotion digeſted, in ſeveral Diſcourſes upon the Lord's Prayer. Together with Nine Additional Exerciſes,

A (*&c.*)

Figure 1.2. *A Catalogue of Mr. Richard Royston's Copies* in Jeremy Taylor, *Antiquitates Christianæ* (London, 1703); a list of eight folio columns, beginning with entries made in 1629, of "conger" properties, probably managed by Richard Chiswell. Courtesy of Andover-Harvard Theological Library, Harvard Divinity School.

Fugill, the first secretary of New Haven, who had returned to Yorkshire excommunicated and disgraced in 1646, which may explain the special appeal of Eaton in Hull. Cotton Mather's *Eleutheria* (1698) appeared under three imprints: for A. Baldwin (London), John Mackie (Edinburgh) and Samuel Phillips (Boston).[36] Other examples of such arrangements, possibly printed in Holland for sale in the colonies, may be "Hezekiah Usher's" editions of the Bay Psalm Book, discussed in Chapter 3; but issues with a Dutch imprint have never been identified. Experience Mayhew's *Indian Converts* has the portmanteau imprint "London: Printed for Samuel Gerrish, bookseller in Boston in New England; and sold by J. Osborn and T. Longman in Pater-Noster-Row, 1727," where Gerrish was acting as an agent for the American subscribers as well as on his own account.[37]

The exchange of American for English sheets (or vice versa) was another possible device for facilitating transatlantic credit. It was used as early as 1675, when John Usher offered Richard Chiswell a stock of the 1672 Massachusetts Laws "as nouelties," an explanation that betrays some ignorance of how frequently the Londoners had printed editions of colonial laws. Chiswell reissued these sheets over his own imprint.[38] Sporadic exchanges of this kind continued into the eighteenth century: the London reissue of Priestley's *Discourses Relating to the Evidences of Revealed Religion* (Philadelphia, 1796), for example.[39] The firm of Berry and Rogers (later Berry, Rogers, and Berry) in New York at the end of the century made something of a specialty of reissuing London or Dublin sheets with cancel title-pages bearing their own imprint. Franklin's edition of Lewis Evans's *Geographical Essays* (1755) is an early instance of a colonial title with an alternate metropolitan imprint, for the Dodsleys in London. All such alterations of the imprint imply the shipment of copies in sheets.

Beginning in the 1740s, there was an ever-rising tide of intercolonial commerce in books, though their imprints fail to acknowledge it in such formulas as "Printed for X in Philadelphia, and are to be sold by Y in New York and Z in Boston." Booksellers were reluctant to commit capital to "foreign" editions in advance of publication and postponed their purchases to the latest possible moment. Thus the Boston bookseller Benjamin Eliot and the Boston binder Charles Harrison bound and sold Philadelphia editions in the 1740s, but because they bought their copies after publication, they do not appear in the imprints. Newspaper proprietors advertised "foreign" editions free of charge, and therefore they probably had a few copies on hand for sale or return.[40]

Serial or quasi-serial publications were the most widely distributed properties: newspapers, magazines, and almanacs. Publishers exchanged newspapers in order to acquire the news that made up their text, since what was old hat in Boston might still be "news" in Philadelphia, and vice versa. As Ian Steele observes, the first Boston newspaper circulated so widely that an advertisement of some runaway slaves in New England alerted their captors in South Carolina.[41] The first publication with an intercolonial imprint was *The American Magazine and Historical Chronicle* (1743–1746), sold in Boston, Philadelphia, New York, New Haven, and Newport. The serial format extended the market wider and lower, for the relatively small size of each issue limited the risk of failure, and its sale in turn financed and advertised the next issue. Editors hedged the risk of publication by subscription and the labor of composition by compilation. An essay reprinted from a Philadelphia newspaper that had borrowed it from the *Gentleman's Magazine,* which took it in turn from a London newspaper like *The Craftsman,* had proven value, far better attested than any book's could be. The full extension of this rationale to books, by the serialized publication of titles "in numbers," only came in the Federal period, though Samuel Keimer experimented with it as early as 1724; before 1790, Bell's British Poets, Cooke's British Classics and their many imitations probably preempted American competition.

At least after 1740, then, the location of the colonial printer only roughly corresponds to the readership and distribution of his product, and at all times colonial imprints imperfectly index consumption; one might indeed invert Wroth's famous tribute and conclude that history is a "matrix of Evans," for no "spiritual force" attaches to the location of a press, and the normal lag between production and consumption greatly weakens the testimony of imprint dates, all of which must be controlled by what bibliographers casually dismiss as "external evidence."[42] Where is the Oxford University Press today? Conventionally, despite its name, in London; but in fact, and more significantly, in Glasgow, New York, Toronto, Melbourne, Wellington, Cape Town, Ibadan, Nairobi, Dar-es-Salaam, Lusaka, Addis Ababa, Delhi, Bombay, Calcutta, Madras, Karachi, Lahore, Dacca, Kuala Lumpur, Singapore, Hong Kong, and Tokyo.

Mutatis mutandis, one might similarly "distribute" the Stationers' Company among the major cities of colonial America, and yet "devolve" colonial printing from that of the English provinces. No English county or municipal corporation issued regular laws; no provincial printer would have reprinted Richardson's *Pamela,* as Benjamin Franklin did, and the Stationers clung to their monopoly of that most characteristic and widely printed of colonial productions, the almanac. Warfare with the French and Indians was a continuing feature of colonial life, and apparently required manuals to be done properly; American politics, once it developed a printed dimension in the eighteenth century, had no resemblance to a county or borough election, and its products were often reprinted in London. "The ubiquity of chapbooks and ballads is apparent everywhere in the country trade," John Feather observes,[43] yet they were rarely printed in the colonies outside of New England. Even as early as the Eliot Indian Bible (1663), colonial printing began to attract the services of binders, moreover, so that the trade eventually developed a wholesaling dimension and possibilities of exchange that the provinces never enjoyed. Even so, the "ghettoization" of colonial book markets was partly a function of their connection to Great Britain, since cheap Scottish reprints of London properties discouraged similar colonial ventures and limited opportunities for intercolonial commerce.

Colonial production most distinctively differs from that of the provinces in the printing of books. English copyright, either statutory or by entry in the Stationers' Register, did not extend outside the realms of England, Wales, and Scotland, and royal patents operated unevenly. Before the Glorious Revolution of 1688, colonial laws were evidently considered municipal ordinances, which the patents of the King's (or Queen's) Printer and the Law Printer did not cover. The advent of royal charters and the superintendence of the Privy Council changed their status, and later London editions, at least – Bermuda (1719), Barbados (1721), Massachusetts (1724), the Leeward Islands (1734), and St. Kitt's (1739, etc.) – fell to the King's Printer.[44] Conversely, royal governors and occasionally assemblies ordered colonial editions of English laws, like the Stamp Act, despite the patent of the Law Printer. In 1688, William Bradford openly proposed to violate the Bible patent, but later printers generally respected it, at least to the extent of concealing their responsibility for their own piracies under false imprints. Nevertheless, the colonists regularly infringed the patents of the English stock by printing almanacs, psalmbooks, and psalters. "Ancient custom" going back to the Bay Psalm Book no doubt sanctioned these little piracies, whereas the mere size of the Bible prompted caution.

Despite considerable differences of scale, the Irish and Scottish book trades provide better models for colonial production and marketing than the provinces. Colonial editions, like Dublin's, compulsively echoed London's, reprints outnumbered first editions, and native authors and printers could not protect their literary property except by printing or copublishing in London. Scotch booksellers challenged London's monopolies in the colonies, just as they did in the English provinces. Like the two kingdoms, the colonies were united to England by language yet separated by differences of religion: Ireland, in particular, with its separate Parliament was a constant example for colonial meditations on loyalty and independence. John Clive and Bernard Bailyn call our attention to cultural parallels between the colonies and Scotland: two middle-class societies, led by lawyers and officials; a sense of isolation and rootlessness; distinctive dialects; a prickly pride, nurtured in a secret sense of inferiority.[45] Print maintained the ascendancy of English over native languages in all these places and proclaimed the distinctiveness of their laws, and Scotland, Ireland, and the colonies alike freely reprinted English laws. Seen from London, colonial customers may not have seemed very different from provincial booksellers, and Londoners allowed them much the same discounts, if sometimes longer credit. Internally, however, the colonial trade operated by different rules.

The Colonial Trade

The colonial printing office, as the establishment is often called in America (the *OED* gives Benjamin Franklin as its earliest citation, in 1733), is a multifarious affair (Fig. 1.3). In London, printing was a separate trade, but in the colonies, it was generally combined with a "bookstore" (Fig. 1.4) – a distinctively American term for the English "bookshop," denoting that the printer also stored sheets ready for binding and wholesaling to other booksellers in what the London trade distinguished as a "warehouse."[46] The colonial trade thus differed from London's in its lack of specialization. Only in Boston were printing and bookselling carried on as separate trades; elsewhere, "printer–booksellers" combined them.[47]

New and Old England also resemble each other in the centralization of their trades. Printers moved out of Boston tardily and reluctantly, but printer–booksellers elsewhere – Benjamin Franklin, James Parker, James Rivington, John Conrad – formed widespread networks. Isaiah Thomas was the first printer to introduce such networks into New England, after the Revolution. The separation of printing and bookselling was a powerful argument for centralization, if only because booksellers and binders were the printers' main market; their combination was surely a condition of the wider "spread of printing" in the South and Mid-Atlantic than in New England, but it also implies that the local markets of New York and Philadelphia were relatively small and had to be eked out by networking.

Seen through the medium of imprints, as in our standard reference works, colonial printers of course remain devoted to their trade, but in real life, they often plied it as a more or less profitable sideline: as booksellers, postmasters, binders, and auctioneers; stocking not only stationery, but musical and mathematical instruments, patent medicines, and lottery tickets – even "whalebone, live goosefeathers, pickled sturgeon, chocolate, Spanish snuff, &c."[48] Since they might be paid in "commodity currency" like corn, salt pork, or salt beef, the successful bookseller or printer might easily develop into a general merchant, like Thomas Hancock. Merchants, another class that dealt in books, rarely appear in colonial imprints. Outside the larger cities, they regularly stock Bibles, Testaments, psalters (the psalms in prose), psalmbooks (in verse), primers, almanacs, and other staples; even in Boston, merchants often advertise Bibles, Testaments, and psalters at the end of recent shipments of various cloth fabrics, reminding us of the early role played by the Drapers in London.[49]

Figure 1.3. The first illustration of an American printing office, from Samuel Saur's *Neue hoch deutsche americanische Calender für 1791* [1790]. One pressman is "beating" the type with inkballs, while the other is about to open the frisket to insert a fresh sheet from the dampened pile on his right; the compositor stands in front of the cases. Copy for this year's almanac is on his left, and with his right hand he hails Mercury, bearing copy for 1792, inscribed *Was ich jetzt nicht offenbar, bring ich dir das nächste Jahr* ("what I don't publish here, I will bring you next year"). Octavo, quarto, and folio books are stored in a bookcase. The press appears to be English, without the ingenious *Himham* that German printers used to close the frisket, and the type-cases have an English (upper/lower case) lay. Courtesy of The Historical Society of Pennsylvania.

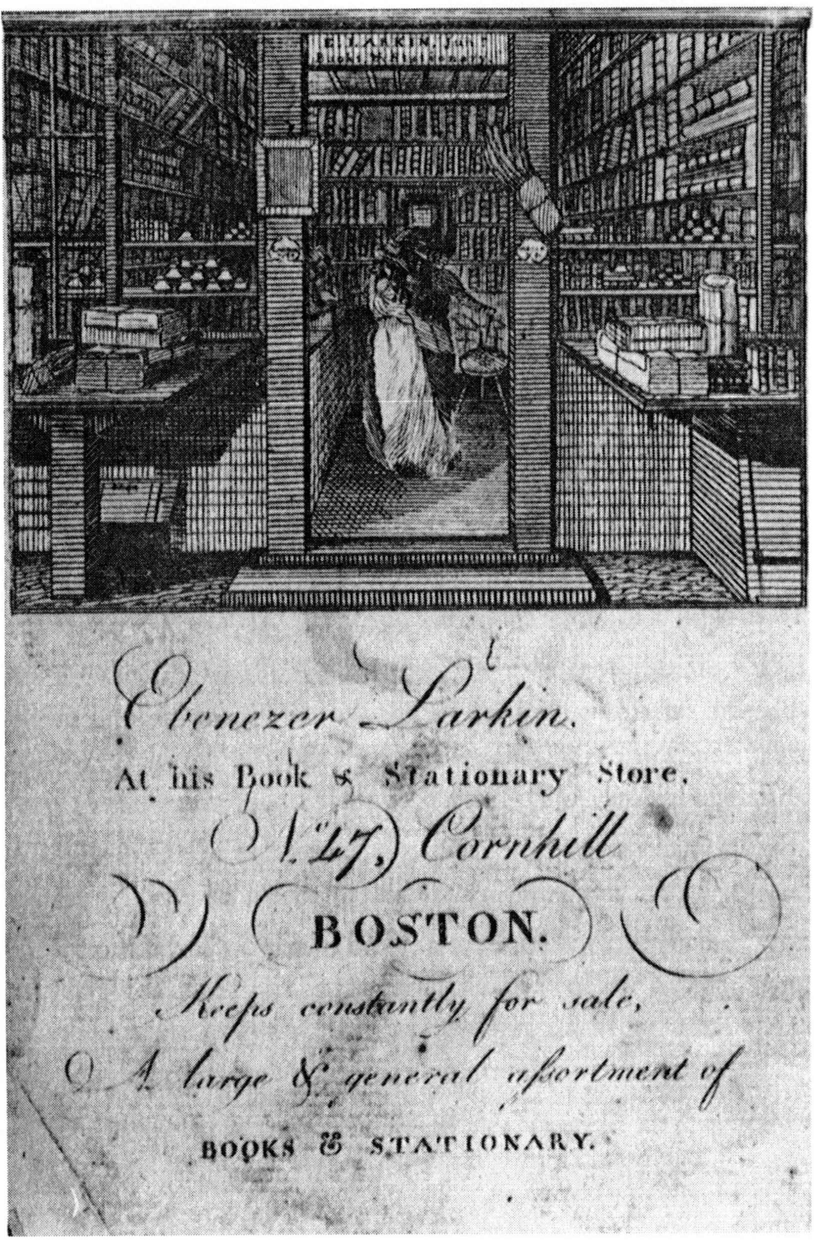

Figure 1.4. The trade card of the "Book & Stationary Store" of Ebenezer Larkin, Jun., 47 Cornhill, Boston (ca. 1796; J. T. Winterich illustrates an earlier state, at 50 Cornhill [ca. 1790), as a frontispiece to his *Early American Books & Printing* [1935]). The shopman holds a chair for an elegant woman inside; outside, two shutters are folded down as counters to display his wares. On the right doorpost is a parcel of quill pens, on the left, a slate; reams of writing paper and rolls of cartridge paper or possibly wallpaper are on the counters; the little triangular objects on shelves above them may be packets of ink powder or bottles of ink. The size of the bookstore may have been artistically exaggerated by the engraver. American Antiquarian Society.

Colonial imprints commonly locate printing offices and bookstores near state houses, churches, markets, prisons, taverns, coffeehouses, and other places of frequent resort. The all-out favorite colonial sign is a Bible and/or Crown (the Crown, of course, fell into disfavor with the Revolution). Signs do not parade the connection of bookselling to literature before the late eighteenth century: "Shakespeare's Head" in Providence, 1763, and Boston, 1786; "Dean Swift's Head" in Philadelphia, 1769, "Franklin's Head" in Boston, 1787 (Fig. 1.5) and Charleston, 1788; "Yorick's [i.e., Sterne's] Head" in Philadelphia, 1786. The Bible and the intensive reading associated with it must have been the rule before that time.

As in England, the wealthier members of the trade tended to be booksellers like Daniel Henchman, and the poorer members binders like Andrew Barclay (Fig. 1.6), with printers like Bartholomew Green falling somewhere between. Before 1750, bookbinders tended to settle in Boston simply because its religious establishment generated the largest number of unbound sheets. In Philadelphia, Franklin issued his edition of *Pamela* [1743] stitched in paper wrappers, whereas Charles Harrison in Boston sold his copies bound in unlettered calf. Neither issue sold well, it seems, but predictably, a single copy of Harrison's stouter production is all that survives. Quakers had no use for liturgical books, and though Presbyterians and Anglicans used as many psalmbooks in New York and the South as Congregational Boston, they printed them only infrequently, and imported them bound.[50]

Apart from Franklin's early initiatives, most colonial partnerships were cosily local, whether they served to finance a single publication, like Willard's *Compleat Body of Divinity*, to keep a steady-selling title in print, as a group of Bostonians did the psalter and the almanac in the 1760s, or to form a regular business, like Mein and Fleeming or Franklin and Hall. The commonest colonial organization is rather the family or clan – the prolific Greens, the Bradfords, the Franklins, and the Fleets (whose celibate tendencies threatened their succession). These relationships also underwrote their partnerships, as with the Fleets and the Drapers, but no formal professional organizations of booksellers or printers emerge before the Federal period, though partnerships of unrelated printers certainly became commoner. In 1724, James Franklin reported that the Boston booksellers had "lately had several Meetings in order to establish themselves into a Company, and raise the Price of their Goods. Accordingly many of them begin to sell Bib[les, Testa]ments, Psalters, Psalm-Books, Primers, &c. [considera]bly dearer than they were sold a f[ew Years ago . . . (?)]."[51] Nothing is ever heard of this "Company" again, however, and Franklin may have manufactured the news item (along with a report of a hike in the price of wigs) as "proof" of a currency crisis.

Our knowledge of colonial personnel mostly concerns master printers and booksellers; we know practically nothing about the apprentices, jour-

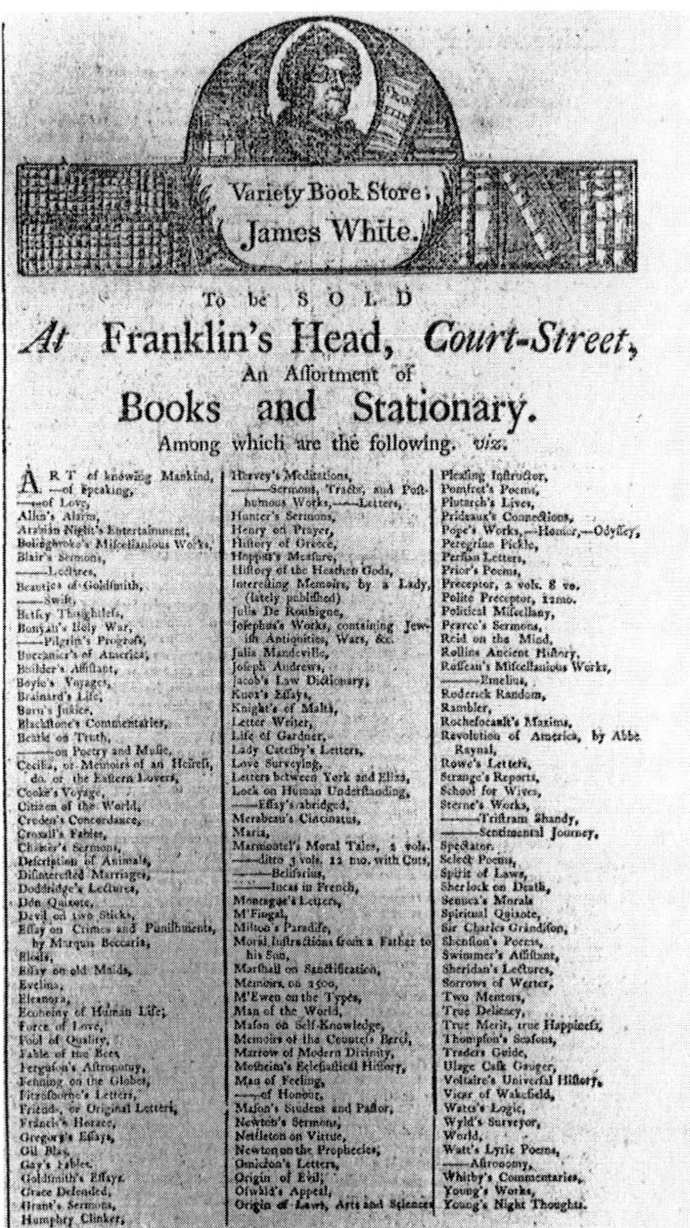

Variety Book Store;
James White.

To be SOLD
At Franklin's Head, *Court-Street*,
An Assortment of
Books and Stationary.
Among which are the following. *viz.*

ART of knowing Mankind,
—of Speaking,
—of Love,
Allen's Alarm,
Arabian Night's Entertainment,
Bolingbroke's Miscellanious Works,
Blair's Sermons,
——Lectures,
Beauties of Goldsmith,
——Swift,
Betsy Thoughtless,
Bunyan's Holy War,
——Pilgrim's Progress,
Buccanier's of America,
Builder's Assistant,
Boyle's Voyages,
Brainard's Life,
Burn's Justice,
Blackstone's Commentaries,
Beattie on Truth,
———on Poetry and Music,
Cecilia, or Memoirs of an Heiress,
do. of the Eastern Lovers,
Cooke's Voyage,
Citizen of the World,
Cruden's Concordance,
Crosall's Fables,
Chaucer's Sermons,
Description of Animals,
Disinterested Marriages,
Doddridge's Lectures,
Don Quixote,
Devil on two Sticks,
Essay on Crimes and Punishments, by Marquis Beccaria,
Eloisa,
Essay on old Maids,
Evelina,
Eleanora,
Economy of Human Life;
Force of Love,
Fool of Quality,
Fable of the Bees,
Ferguson's Astronomy,
Fenning on the Globes,
Fitzosborne's Letters,
Friends, or Original Letters,
Francis's Horace,
Gregory's Essays,
Gil Blas,
Gay's Fables,
Goldsmith's Essays,
Grace Defended,
Grant's Sermons,
Humphry Clinker,
Hervey's Meditations,
———Sermons, Tracts, and Posthumous Works,——Letters,
Hunter's Sermons,
Henry on Prayer,
History of Greece,
Hoppus's Measure,
History of the Heathen Gods,
Interesting Memoirs, by a Lady, (lately published)
Julia De Roubigne,
Josephus's Works, containing Jewish Antiquities, Wars, &c.
Julia Mandeville,
Joseph Andrews,
Jacob's Law Dictionary,
Knox's Essays,
Knight's of Malta,
Letter Writer,
Life of Gardner,
Lady Catesby's Letters,
Love Surveying,
Letters between York and Eliza,
Lock on Human Understanding,
——Essay's abridged,
Merabeau's Cincinatus,
Maria,
Marmontel's Moral Tales, 2 vols.
——ditto 3 vols. 12 mo. with Cuts,
———Belisarius,
———Incas in French,
Montague's Letters,
M'Fingal,
Milton's Paradise,
Moral Instructions from a Father to his Son,
Marshall on Sanctification,
Memoirs, on 2500,
M'Ewen on the Types,
Man of the World,
Mason on Self-Knowledge,
Memoirs of the Countess Berci,
Marrow of Modern Divinity,
Mosheim's Eclesiastical History,
Man of Feeling,
——of Honour,
Mason's Student and Pastor,
Newton's Sermons,
Nettleton on Virtue,
Newton on the Prophecies,
Omicron's Letters,
Origin of Evil,
Oswald's Appeal,
Origin of Laws, Arts and Sciences
Pleasing Instructor,
Pomfret's Poems,
Plutarch's Lives,
Prideaux's Connections,
Pope's Works,—Homer,—Odyssey,
Peregrine Pickle,
Persian Letters,
Prior's Poems,
Preceptor, 2 vols. 8 vo.
Polite Preceptor, 12mo.
Political Miscellany,
Pearce's Sermons,
Reid on the Mind,
Rollins Ancient History,
Rosseau's Miscellanious Works,
———Emelius,
Roderick Random,
Rambler,
Rochefocault's Maxims,
Revolution of America, by Abbe Raynal,
Rowe's Letters,
Strange's Reports,
School for Wives,
Sterne's Works,
———Tristram Shandy,
———Sentimental Journey,
Spectator,
Select Poems,
Spirit of Laws,
Sherlock on Death,
Seneca's Morals
Spiritual Quixote,
Sir Charles Grandison,
Shenston's Poems,
Swimmer's Assistant,
Sheridan's Lectures,
Sorrows of Werter,
Two Mentors,
True Delicacy,
True Merit, true Happiness,
Thompson's Seasons,
Traders Guide,
Ulage Cask Gauger,
Voltaire's Universal History,
Vicar of Wakefield,
Watts's Logic,
Wyld's Surveyor,
World,
Watt's Lyric Poems,
——Astronomy,
Whitby's Commentaries,
Young's Works,
Young's Night Thoughts.

Figure 1.5. Advertisement of stock by James White at Franklin's Head, *Independent Chronicle*, January 18, 1787 (detail). American Antiquarian Society.

Figure 1.6. Binder's label of Andrew Barclay, near the "Three Kings" in Cornhill, Boston (a coffeehouse), inserted in volume 1 of a set of the Massachusetts Laws (1759–1765), bound in full blindtooled calf, spines gilt, with red morocco labels. He is plowing the edges of a book in the press, with gilding tools heating on a brazier nearby. Plain books, with numbered spines, stand about him, ready for gilding and labelling to the customer's order. By permission of the Houghton Library, Harvard University.

neymen, and foremen who did most of the work. The exceptions tend, as usual, to be exceptional: Franklin and Thomas themselves, of course, and others who eventually rose to be masters; but also children, women, blacks, and Indians, whom the historian considered normally illiterate or otherwise unqualified for printing. Ann Franklin in Newport and Thomas Fleet in Boston employed black pressmen, and one of Fleet's was a wood-engraver, but we know little about them but their names: the wood-engraver's sons "Pompey" and "Cesar," who were free; "Primus," who worked for the Fowles in Boston and Portsmouth; Andrew Cain, in Philadelphia.[52]

American apprenticeships seem to have been diverse and informal; their terms range from the fifty years that the Greens extracted from that unfortunate Nipmuck James Wowaus, to three years or less.[53] During the seventeenth century, only Marmaduke Johnson, William Bradford, and John Allen could claim a regular English apprenticeship in their craft, but neither Johnson nor Bradford came of their own initiative. Franklin's colonial skills, acquired as an apprentice to his brother James from 1718 to 1723, won him employment in Philadelphia and London as a compositor, and perhaps we may assume that by this date colonial technology had matured. It is symptomatic that when an anonymous Irish "Book Printer" arrived in Boston in 1716, the advertisement muddled him together with other servants; possibly he moved on to another occupation, like the prototypographer of Cambridge, Stephen Day.[54]

Colonial workmen were as versatile as their masters. Franklin was surprised that compositors and pressmen formed separate callings in London. His reluctance to observe the usual rules of a London printer's chapel, requiring him to treat his fellows to beer on his promotion to compositor, may suggest that such customs were unusual in the colonies. Journeymen and even apprentices occasionally supervised the operations of an office, as shop foremen. The distinction between masters and journeymen, too, was not strictly observed. Thomas reports that the master might allow his journeyman the use of a press in return for a share of the profits, an arrangement that may have lain behind the confusing imprints of Samuel Green and Marmaduke Johnson. It might also explain the baffling similarity of the type stocks used by John Allen, Timothy Green, and Thomas Fleet, which even a bibliographer as skillful as Thomas J. Holmes was unable to disentangle.[55] The life of an apprentice or journeyman was no doubt stormier than that of a master printer. "Tramping" up and down the Atlantic coast looking for work typified the lives of colonial journeymen.[56]

Authorities agree that "a wife was a necessity if the printer wanted to succeed in business." The widowed Joanna Perry continued her husband's business by bookbinding, Deborah Franklin folded and quired her husband's printing, and in Federal Philadelphia, women specialized in this service.[57] Colonial women also worked as compositors and even as pressmen and, like Ann Franklin, Sarah Goddard, Mary Katharine Goddard and Jane Aitken, stepped into the shoes of their male relations as masters – but they never "tramped."[58] In gender, too, the colonial trade was relatively unspecialized.

"Before the Revolution and for some years after," notes Isaiah Thomas, "500 Copies of a Book were thought a handsome Edition, as to number[,] excepting Almanacks, Psalters, Psalm and Spelling Books, and Primers. – Of these 5,000, 10,000, 15,000 & 20,000 were not uncommon."[59] Cotton Mather occasionally boasts of editions of 1,000 to 2,000 copies, but he was the most eminent clergyman in Boston and in any case had no reason to mention the usual, less flattering figures. The Salem clergyman William Bentley, at the end of the eighteenth century, says that American sermons were usually printed in editions of 400 copies. Thomas is silent on the edition size of government documents and of paper currency (an important source of income to Franklin). In New England, church "platforms" and cumulated editions of colonial laws might run from 600 to 800, or even 1,500, and election sermons from 100 to 700 copies; editions of sessions acts and of blank forms, however, were often tiny. In Philadelphia and Charleston, editions even of the cumulated laws often amount to no more than 100 to 200 copies; Delaware was content to take twenty-one unbound copies of its 1741 Laws, and twenty-one bound copies with the supplement of temporary and obsolete acts [1743], leaving the rest (if any) for the printer.[60]

The larger editions of almanacs and primers were produced by returning standing type to the press for impressions of a few thousand each, as the earlier impressions sold off. Editions of more than 10,000 (the size of *Poor Richard's Almanack*) were often cooperative ventures. In 1759, Benjamin Mecom undertook to print 30,000 copies of the *New England Psalter* (300,000 octavo sheets): it was "two years worrying through the press" (an average of only 500 sheets a day! presumably sandwiched between other jobs), and it was finally issued with three imprints, for Mecom alone, for Green and Russell, and for a partnership of D. Henchman and six others.[61] Thomas reports that Nathaniel Ames's little twenty-four page almanac sold 50 or 60,000 copies a year in the 1760s and 1770s, a figure that is independently confirmed by Margaret Draper. To speed this enormous production, the proprietors divided the almanac in thirds, taking a half-sheet octavo signature apiece (25,000 or 30,000 sheets).[62]

Large paper, large format, and large type all enjoyed a high social status, generated not only by the "louder," attention-grabbing volume of the text but also by the conspicuous waste of paper. Roughly speaking, paper and binding account for two-thirds of the colonial book's cost, and the need to conserve paper pressed harder on colonial printers than on their metropolitan colleagues. At all periods, a few copies of a sermon or of a poem might be printed on writing paper for presentation. The general production of special issues on fine (usually wove) paper, however, attends the 1790s, when it became a perfect craze: even the Massachusetts Laws were published on two grades of paper. Willard's *Compleat Body of Divinity* (1726) was issued on two grades of paper, and the Harvard *Pietas et Gratulatio* on George III's accession (1761) was issued on three grades of paper, but these examples are exceptionally early.[63]

In general, colonial books were a dingy lot, confined to a smaller, narrower range of types, papers, and formats than that of the metropolis. In 1772, the firm of Green and Russell alleged that they had imported an imperial press for the (detested) Board of Custom Commissioners, claiming that "such another is not in America, and they have been informed there is [sic] but four such presses in all England." This monstrous press and its paper had lain idle and unused since their appointment as printers to the Board in 1767.[64] William McCulloch wondered at *Dunlap's American Daily Advertiser* (1791–1795), printed in five columns on super-royal paper, "the first perhaps of that size on the continent"; Isaiah Thomas's royal-paper *Massachusetts Spy* was

Figure 1.7. Isaac Newton, *Opticks* (London, 1704); shelved in the Harvard College Library, case 19, the third shelf up, no. "20" on that shelf, as marked on the foredge (showing that it was shelved spine inwards), and so recorded in the 1723 Harvard *Catalogus.* Together with Increase Mather, *The Duty of Parents to Pray for their Children* (Boston, 1703), a foolscap duodecimo, beside Robert Boyle, *Love and Religion Demonstrated* (London, 1703), a demy duodecimo, showing the difference in size. The Mather work is bound in the original unlettered sprinkled sheep, with endpapers from the 1685 Eliot Indian Bible; stamped on covers EC and signed on the front flyleaf "Ebenezer [&] Elizabeth Clap ther Book"; with the later, childish inscription "Benjamin french his book god give him grace there to lok [sic]." By permission of the Houghton Library, Harvard University.

the largest newspaper in Boston, 1771.[65] Demy paper (52 × 40 cm) was the commonest size used for printing books in England, yet generally the largest used in the colonies. "Demy Printing large sort" at 18*s*. a ream was the largest produced by Massachusetts mills in 1785; John Carter, in Providence, used nothing larger than crown paper (46 × 35 cm) from 1768 to 1774; Franklin, from 1728 to 1766, printed nothing larger than demy.[66] Seventeenth-century presses (and papers) were even smaller.

By order of the Stationers' Company, English books of any size and consequence were to be bound in calf; only the "small books and pleasant histories" that Dunton dismissed as "*Sheeps-Leather Books*" were regularly bound in sheep, a cheaper, less durable leather. In the colonies, however, sheep was the most common covering, probably because the production of salt beef for the Caribbean discouraged the early slaughter of cattle. Colonial sermons were thus nearly indistinguishable, in size and texture, from metropolitan children's books, and English imprints, which were largely imported bound, were elegantly recommended by their covers (Fig. 1.7).[67] Pamphlets needed for immediate distribution received temporary bindings: election sermons in marbled wrappers; funeral sermons and elegies in mourning wrappers, with black edges.[68]

At the option of the purchaser, the colonial binder might add spine labels, supra libris, gilt decoration, and clasps (for Bibles, psalmbooks, and other books that were too frequently used to be shelved); but before 1750 or 1760, colonial bindings usually have unlabeled spines, and even imports may be lettered on the foredge, indicating that the book was shelved with the edges outward (Fig. 1.7); Charles Harrison, in 1739, advertised his services to refurbish them: "Any Gentlemen desirous of having their Libraries Gilt or Letter'd may have them done by the said Harrison as cheap as in London."[69] Pamphlets were issued "stabbed," in blue-gray cartridge-paper wrappers, sewn through three holes in the sides, for immediate hawking through the streets. From around 1743, about the same period as in England, the wrappers might also bear a printed title or advertisement,[70] and owners at all times bound books for themselves in limp parchment or wallpaper.

Since the technology of printing changed little for three centuries, and since so many colonial books in any case were printed in Europe, the advent and spread of the craft in the colonies is of relatively little historical and cultural importance. More significant were the ways in which books were distributed and bound, the supply of paper and type, and the organization and recruitment of personnel. In these respects, the colonial trade is amphibious, at once part of and distinct from the metropolitan trade. We can neither isolate it in a culture all its own nor entirely subsume it in British provincial culture; even in the colonies themselves, there were important regional differences, to be addressed in the following chapters.

CHAPTER TWO

The Chesapeake in the Seventeenth Century

DAVID D. HALL

THE ENGLISH CAME LATE as colonists to the New World. A century after the Spanish embarked on the conquest and colonization of the Americas, the Virginia Company of London, chartered in 1606, dispatched a group of colonists in 1607 to the coast of Virginia. Early on, the chances of success at Jamestown seemed little greater than they had proved to be for the "lost colony" of Roanoke, attempted in the 1580s in Albemarle Sound. An adverse disease environment, the hostility of local Indians, and shortages of food caused near-catastrophic rates of sickness and death, and failures of leadership made matters worse. Even so, the stockholders in the Virginia Company continued to finance shipments of people and supplies in the hope of carrying out an expansive economic program directed at producing silk, glass, wine, and iron. Individual entrepreneurs, using dividends of land grants from the company, turned instead to raising tobacco. The high price it brought in Europe and the absence of any alternative ensured that the economy became oriented around an export, "staple" crop. To the north, a separate political jurisdiction was created in 1632 when Charles I awarded George Calvert, Lord Baltimore, the territory Calvert named Maryland. Here, too, tobacco became the basis of the economy.

At first glance, the history of the book trades in the seventeenth-century Chesapeake is a history of absences and censorship. Not until the 1680s was a printing office opened in Maryland, after being transferred from Virginia, where the authorities closed it down before William Nuthead, the printer, had issued a single book. Books were an insignificant element in the trade that brought scores of ships to the Chesapeake each year to exchange European goods for tobacco. No merchant in the two colonies specialized in bookselling, and few stores carried more than a miniscule supply of printed books. The institutions that in England served as patrons of learnedness, and therefore as patrons of printing and bookselling, did not exist or, as in the case of the colonial version of the Church of England, were repeatedly short of clergy and funds. Not until the very end of the century did this situation begin to change in Virginia with the relocation of the capital to Williamsburg and the founding of the first college in the south, William and Mary.[1]

Was the absence of a printing press intentional, the doing of a civil state bent on domination and well aware of how, in England, printers always seemed to elude regulation? This possibility is suggested by William Berkeley's critique of printers and schools. Answering queries from the English government in 1670, the governor of Virginia linked the stability of church and state to the absence of printers and free (Latin) schools: "But I thank God, there are no free schools nor printing, and I hope we shall not have these [for a] hundred years; for learning has brought disobedience, and heresy, and sects into the world, and printing has divulged them, and libels against the best government. God keep us from both!"[2] The reference in this passage to "sects" suggests that Berkeley was thinking of the Civil War period in England when the Church of England had splintered into a variety of groups, some of which veered off into heterodoxy. He may also have been thinking of the Licensing Act of 1662, which reestablished a system of state control over printers and booksellers. When, with a different governor in office, the Virginia government thwarted the attempt in 1683 to found a printing office, its action flowed from the assumption, not unique to Berkeley but a commonplace in the seventeenth century, that the civil state was empowered to limit the uses of printing to those which served the purposes of constituted authority, both civil and ecclesiastical.

Yet Berkeley and his political allies were not hostile to printing, per se. At one moment in his governorship he arranged for a London printer to issue an edition of the Virginia statutes, a practice he intended to continue. Depending on the circumstances, therefore, the assumption that a civil government was entitled to supervise the press could in practice result in more, not less or no, production. Indeed it was the patronage of the civil government in Maryland that enabled William Nuthead's press to survive as long as it did, and William Bladen counted on the same patronage when he set up another press in Maryland in 1700. A better explanation for the absence of a printing office in the Chesapeake is economic. Even under the best of circumstances there was little work for printers in any of the seventeenth-century colonies to do, a situation exacerbated in the Chesapeake by the dispersal of settlement, the effectiveness of scribal publication, and the paucity of literary patrons.

For reasons unrelated to the presence or absence of a press, the vision of political and cultural order that Berkeley voiced in 1671 is not what came to pass in the Chesapeake. A near-endemic restlessness with political authority is apparent in the abundance of oppositional texts, some of them scribally published in the two colonies and others ushered into print in London. This restlessness had much to do with the tug-of-war between periphery and center, colonies and empire. Another source of opposition was the very sectarianism that Berkeley feared. No group in the colonies controlled the interpretation of the vernacular Bible, which many of the colonists owned. Nor was any government able to monopolize ink and paper and thereby silence groups such as the Quakers, who made their presence felt in the Chesapeake as early as the 1650s. Within sectarian communities, people who might ordinarily have remained silent became writers and readers despite efforts by the civil state to silence them. Hence it happened that the history of the book in the Chesapeake involved different and sometimes openly contested versions of authority in religion and civil government.

The story of scarcity is, like Berkeley's vision of perfect order, also but a half-truth, for much was made available in the Chesapeake by the means of scribal production, as when the civil state issued handwritten "books" containing the sessions laws enacted by the assemblies in each of the colonies. Texts were also "published" by the age-old method of being read aloud. When the colonists used the word "publish," it usually signified this mode of communication. Taking into account these modes of production, scarcity becomes relative, for handwritten books and legal documents circulated in abundance. But in emphasizing the effectiveness of scribal and oral publication, we must not ignore the colonists' own perception that for certain kinds of texts, printing was more advantageous than other technologies of preservation and communication.

Record-Keeping and Law Making

Governments in the seventeenth century depended on information being written down. So did people with property. Living on the nearer side of the transition "from memory to written record" that was under way in England by the twelfth century,[3] and recognizing, as the Virginia government declared in 1664, that "in all Countryes the well or ill keeping of the Records, is of the highest Consequence, as being the only means to preserve the Rights and Properties of all the Inhabitants of the same," the colonists began at once to create an archive of documents.[4] The setting in which many of these documents accumulated was the civil court system, and especially the county courts. To these courts came hundreds of men and women seeking to secure their claim to property – to land, to pigs and cattle, to indentured servants, to a share of someone's estate. To these same courts came creditors wanting to enforce a contract or bargain. All of this business generated a stream of deeds, inventories, warrants, indentures, accounts, bonds, writs, receipts, patents, surveys, bills of sale, subpoenas, depositions, actions, executions, attachments, and petitions, each and every one of them scribally produced.[5] Other documents emerged from governors and assemblies – in particular, orders, commissions, statute laws and proclamations. Agencies in England imposed various forms of recordkeeping or reportage on local officials who themselves required lesser bodies – county sheriffs, parish ministers, church vestries – to enumerate "tithables" and preserve vital statistics.[6]

This archive was complemented by oral knowledge. In the early years, much was not put on paper – a dying man's instructions on how to dispose of his property, an exchange of services or goods, an agreement between master and servant over a term of indenture, the ages of children who became orphans. Illiteracy, and especially the inability to write, ensured the continuing presence of oral knowledge even after the civil courts indicated their preference that things be written down. This preference became a matter of statute law – for example, in 1663 when the Maryland legislature ordered that indentures and land transfers must be in writing.[7] Ordinary people also liked having their rights and intentions preserved on paper. On his deathbed Benjamin Gill of Maryland craved a written instrument to convey his property. But he had to settle for second best; "there being nobody then there lyung that could write, he requested this deponent to bear [oral] witness."[8] Early on, many must have felt the same disappointment.

That so much was written down reflects the expectation that these texts made economic transactions more secure and civil government more legitimate. Yet the materiality of scribal production could undercut this expectation. It was common knowledge that handwritten texts could easily be altered by the simple insertion or deletion of words. Moreover, errors inevitably occurred as a consequence of the process of making copies. Thus it was that civil courts had to inquire into whether a document was "authentic" or why so many signatures "are all of one hand," and to seek corroborating testimony for the attribution of a text to someone on the basis of handwriting. To signify the finality of certain documents, governments stamped them with a seal and had them "engrossed" (written in a distinctive clerical hand) on the more permanent medium of parchment. The very quality of the handwriting, as when a document was "fairely" or "legibly" written, could also abet the authenticating of a text.[9]

Notwithstanding the uncertain authority of scribal texts, everyone in the Chesapeake accepted the premise that written or printed documents embodied political legitimacy. Assertions of sovereignty sometimes involved the displaying or performance of such texts in a public setting. So, too, insurgents produced and displayed alternative texts and challenged others as inauthentic. At the outset of colonization, the single most important category of document was the royal charter and its equivalent, a commission from a proprietor or chartered company declaring the sovereignty of the king's representatives and affirming their right to the land. The performance of these texts in open-air ceremonies was a distinctive feature of colonization. Thus the proprietor of Maryland, knowing in advance that his patent had been encroached upon and that the Virginia government was opposed to the new colony, gave careful instructions to the first group of colonists on how they should deploy the documents on which his authority rested, to the point of outlining the scenario for the moment when the colonists first reached Maryland: "That [his agents] . . . do assemble all the people together in a fitt and decent manner and then cause his majesties letters pattents to be publikely read by his Lordships Secretary John Bolles, and afterwards his Lordships Commission to them."[10] The uncertainties surrounding political authority in early Virginia led to similiar scenes, as when John Smith, temporarily in the office of "President," had "the letters patent" read aloud "each week" in order to bolster his office.[11]

Essential as these texts and ceremonies were to the process of establishing political order, they could not keep at bay the discontents that led to armed insurrection in both Maryland and Virginia. During the period of the English civil war and commonwealth, a "puritan" faction in each colony agitated against representatives of the king, and vice versa. Protestants in Maryland exploited this situation to depose the Calverts from control in the mid-1650s, revolted unsuccessfully in 1676 and 1681, and deposed the proprietor anew in 1689. In Virginia the royalist–parliamentarian schism caused a change of government in the 1650s. And in 1676 the colony fell into near-anarchy during the insurgency known as Bacon's Rebellion.

A class of document that loomed large in these situations was the proclamation. In the context of English political culture the proclamation embodied the oral, the written, and the printed (this last in those versions where it reached this stage). An instrument of royal sovereignty, any English proclamation issued before 1640 had the status of statute law. Conceptually, it embodied the monarch's speech, or spoken will. Transposed into written text, the proclamation was an elaborate artifact bearing not only the royal seal and appropriate signatures but also decorative lettering. Some of this decorative lettering was carried over into the printed form, usually a single-sheet broadside. Written or printed, these sheets were commonly posted in public for everyone to read and see. The text was turned back into speech when it was read aloud, or published, in markets or other open-air settings.[12]

As in England, so in the Chesapeake proclamations were central to the process of governing, put to use by governors in lieu of statute law or as the means of communicating orders.[13] Shortly after Governor Thomas Dale arrived in Virginia in 1611, he "made divers proclamations which I caused to be set up for the publique view."[14] In Maryland, the Parliamentary commissioners repeatedly "published" what they termed "declarations" asserting their authority; in riposte, William Stone, who represented the proprietor, issued counterproclamations, one of which was "published . . . in the Church meeting." These performances accelerated in the early months of 1655, with Stone (as seen by his enemies) "publish[ing] a proclamation to deceive the amazed and distract[ed] people." Hoping by force of arms to overcome the commissioners, Stone "sent two men [before him] to publish a proclamation" of Lord Baltimore's authority. The commissioners replied in kind. Boarding a ship at anchor in the Severn, they "fix[ed] a proclamation in the main mast, directed to [the] . . . commander of the said ship, wherein he was required" to aid and assist the parliamentarians, who ended up victorious in the "Battle of the Severn."[15]

The history of Bacon's Rebellion parallels the turmoil in Maryland, for the antagonists in that uprising, Nathaniel Bacon and the reigning governor, William Berkeley, improvised the appropriate documents to suit rapidly changing conditions. When Berkeley learned in May 1676 that the young planter had allied himself with colonists discontented with the government's response to the incursion of a few Indians, the governor issued two proclamations, reproduced in enough manuscript copies to reach each county, the first of them denouncing Bacon as a rebel and the second calling for new elections to the House of Burgesses. Yet Bacon forced Berkeley to grant the one document he most wanted, a commission authorizing him to pursue military action against the Indians. Thus empowered, he sought to expand his new-found authority via scribal production. Immediately after receiving the commission in June 1676, Bacon, then in Jamestown, where a session of the assembly was coming to an end, prevailed on a member of the burgesses to "Sit the Whole Night by him filling up" a parcel of "unfolded Papers" which this temporary clerk "then Saw were blank Commissions Sign'd by the Governour, incerting such Names and Writing other matters as he [Bacon] Dictated." With Bacon away from Jamestown, Berkeley once again proclaimed him a rebel and repudiated the commission. After the rebellion collapsed, the governor was challenged from another quarter when newly arrived royal commissioners, acting in the name of Charles II, sought to distribute a proclamation of general pardon they brought with them. Berkeley refused to cooperate, issuing, instead, a counterproclamation of his own sanctioning the execution of more rebels.[16]

These proclamations were supplemented in the workings of government by another category of document, the statute laws enacted by each session of the general assemblies in Virginia and Maryland. Here too, the colonists inherited a well-established form, for English printers had issued statutes or sessions laws since the end of the fifteenth century. In English practice individual laws were commonly printed as broadsides in order to facilitate the process of distribution, which, as in the case of proclamations, included the reading aloud of statutes.[17] The very nature of the process ensured that statute books, which brought together a series of laws, fell out of date almost as rapidly as they were printed. Keeping up with laws that were current, and differentiating these from older laws that were "temporary" (as certain English statutes, like those authorizing grants of money, usually were), repealed, revised, or superseded was no easy business. These difficulties were compounded in the Chesapeake for two reasons. On this side of the Atlantic it was never easy to keep up with the flow of English statutes. But the greater difficulty lay in the division of authority between local governments and proprietors or agencies of the Crown, for every law enacted by the governments in Virginia and Maryland was reviewed in London by one or another of these bodies. This process of review, which frequently resulted in laws being suspended or revoked, made for a persistent confusion that was exacerbated by the recurrent struggle for power between royal or proprietary governors and local assemblies.[18]

The one technology the colonists had at hand for producing copies of statute laws was scribal publication. The task of making these handwritten copies became the responsibility of the clerk of the assembly in Virginia and the secretary of the colony in Maryland. It was important that these men and their assistants produce copies for the authorities back in England. It was even more important that copies reach each county court, for until this happened these courts could not function properly. Recognizing this fact, the commissioners of newly designated Somerset County on the eastern shore of Maryland asked the proprietary governor, Charles Calvert, to "Cause acts of the last Session of [the] grand assembly to be sent over to us That wee may knowe the better to keepe ourselves in due observance of the Lawes."[19] In this instance, the county was requesting a copy of all current statutes, for the Maryland government had recently undertaken a complete revision of the statutes in force.[20]

All did not go well with this system of production. As the nineteenth-century Virginia legal historian William Hening discovered in preparing the early volumes of *The Statutes at Large; Being a Collection of all the Laws of Virginia,* few versions of the laws sent out to the counties were alike. From some, entire statutes were missing, and the textual variations were many. The great struggle between royalists and parliamentarians in the 1650s added yet another layer of complications, for it left the colonists suspended between two sources of sovereignty. A revision of the Virginia statutes in

1652 resolved this conflict in favor of Parliament. But in the aftermath of the Restoration, the colonists had to change everything around again to indicate the authority of the Crown.[21]

In 1660–1661, the Virginia government tried a different approach to the problems arising from scribal production of what, in essence, was a periodical. The moment was propitious, for the restoration of Charles II in 1660 ended the uncertainty about what language to use in writs. Realizing, too, that the new government in London wanted assurances that things were in good order in the colonies, the General Assembly went through the entire body of accumulated statutes, eliminating some and reaffirming others while adding new laws to the whole. In the final stages the task of fashioning this body of laws fell to the deputy governor, Francis Moryson, and the clerk of the assembly, Henry Randolph. By prearrangement, it seems, they dispatched a copy to the governor, William Berkeley, who was then in London.[22] Berkeley turned the manuscript over to a London printer, who in the late summer of 1662 issued in folio *The Lawes of Virginia Now in Force.* Berkeley gave copies to members of the newly formed Council for Foreign Plantations, reporting as he did so that the colonists intended to continue having each year's laws printed in London.[23] Presumably he also carried home with him enough copies for each county court and probably for each member of the assembly and council. Almost immediately, the assembly and council had to pass new laws correcting errors of omission in the book.[24]

By the early 1680s the situation was becoming critical once again in Virginia. For reasons unknown, in the years since 1662 the assembly contented itself with scribal publication. That system yielded an interesting set of artifacts in the wake of Bacon's Rebellion, for the reformist legislation enacted by the assembly that met in June 1676 was subsequently repealed, obliging county clerks to eliminate the offending pages from their cache of manuscripts.[25] The initiative to resume the technology of printing came from a first-generation planter–merchant and sometime member of the House of Burgesses, John Buckner, who imported a press to Virginia along with an experienced printer, William Nuthead, to run it.[26] Nuthead set to work in late 1682 printing the sessions laws from the assembly that met in 1680, only to encounter the wrath of Governor Culpeper and the council, who in February 1683, having reviewed the first "two sheets" to pass the press, halted the process on the grounds that Buckner and his printer had not been duly licensed. When further advice was sought from the Lords of Trade and Plantation, the response was an order, inserted in December 1683 into the instructions for Culpeper's successor, Lord Howard of Effingham, that he not allow any further printing.[27]

In the event it was an unauthorized edition that gave Virginians their second statute book in the customary format of folio: *A Complete Collection of all the Laws of Virginia now in Force . . . Copied from the Assembly Records* (1684?). The intermediary was John Purvis, a London-based ship captain and merchant who came often to Virginia; laying hands on a manuscript compilation, Purvis took it back to London to be printed and returned with copies, some of which contained additional blank pages. In April 1684 the Virginia government repudiated the book on the grounds that it was published "without Licence" and directed county courts not to use it.[28] Even so, and in spite of the imperfections of the text, from which entire laws were missing, the book seems to have passed into general use, for several of the surviving copies bear handwritten notations indicating the repeal or altering of laws. Of more importance, some owners used these books to record new sessions laws on blank pages bound in with the printed text for this purpose.[29]

Not until 1696 did the General Assembly in Maryland move toward having its laws printed; the actual work, done on William Bladen's newly established local press, occurred in 1700. Throughout the century the colony made do with scribal publication, ordering in 1664, in the aftermath of a thoroughgoing revision of the laws, that the secretary of the colony prepare a copy on parchment for each county "to the End that all the good people of this Province may have sufficient notice of" the laws.[30] As in Virginia, the Maryland Assembly responded to the ever-growing pile of statutes by periodically repealing all existing laws, only to reenact in the same session a nearly identical set. This tactic helped the government clarify the troublesome distinction between laws current and laws repealed or revised, a distinction that in Maryland was overlaid with the difference, arising in part from the right of the proprietor in England to approve legislation, between "perpetuall" and "temporary" statutes.[31] Reflecting in 1676 on the situation in their colony, the members of the assembly were acutely aware of the problem of "knowing what Lawes are in force & unrepealed"; similarly, they were frank in acknowledging that confusion arose from "the multiplicity of Lawes to one and the same thing which many tymes interfer one with another."[32]

A decade later, in 1685, the first printing office was set up in Maryland when William Nuthead, thwarted by the authorities in Virginia, moved his press to St. Mary's City and began to issue printed legal forms. Other business was scant until the insurgents of 1689, needing to justify the overthrow of the proprietor, hired Nuthead to print copies of documents they were sending to the new government of William III. In 1693 the government ordered Nuthead to print nothing but blank bonds without permission. After he died, his widow, Dinah, moved the press to Annapolis, where the capital had been relocated, and received permission to resume issuing legal forms.[33]

It was not this printing office, however, but a new venture welcomed by the royal governor and sponsored by the clerk of the assembly, William

Bladen, that gained the necessary approval from the government to issue the colony's laws. In 1696 Bladen proposed the establishment of a printing press in Annapolis to the end of "printing the Laws made every Sessions." He urged this step anew in May 1700, at a moment when the assembly was struggling to affirm its selection of laws against the King's veto, on the grounds of the evident benefit of having enough copies on hand so that "every person might easily have them in their houses without being troubled to goe to the County Court house to have recourse thereto." Guaranteed the patronage of the government, Bladen went ahead with the production of *All the Laws of Maryland Now in Force* – the actual work was done by a printer who was brought from England, using type left over from the Nuthead press – though he had to suffer the embarrassment of being officially informed that, when compared with the manuscript "originalls," the printed text proved to contain "many Erata's." The new press also undertook to issue a variety of printed writs, encouraged to do so by an order of the Maryland Assembly in 1700 that "noe other writts be made use of but such as shalbe printed." By 1704 the craftsman who ran the press, Thomas Reading, was issuing sessions laws, as Bladen had envisaged from the outset.[34]

Looking back on the interplay between scribal production and letterpress printing, our sympathies may lie with the author of the preamble to the Maryland printed laws of 1700, who felt that the first of these technologies made it impossible for judges to obtain a "perfect knowledge of the Laws," the reason being the shortage and expense of copies, so that "Very few gentlemen of this Province, nay not all the Justices of the Provincial and County Courts have yet had the Body of Laws by them so as to read, meditate and digest them, without which it is impossible rightly to know them, for indeed they were not to be had but at a great charge and difficult to get at any cost, and then but in a [written] hand."[35] A parallel critique was voiced in the preface to the Maryland printed laws of 1718, with its backward glance at the "Ill-Written Manuscripts, Lodged in the Hands of particular Officers, and not more than Twelve or Fourteen of them in the whole Province," and again in 1730 by a Virginian in *Typographia,* a poem written to celebrate the opening of William Parks' Williamsburg office. Anticipating the first locally printed edition of Virginia laws, John Markland evoked the "blotted Manuscripts" in which, hitherto, "Virginia's Laws . . . lay . . . obscur'd. By vulgar Eyes unread."[36] Yet as Hening pointed out and as the Maryland Assembly learned to its dismay in 1701, printed editions of the laws were also plagued with errors. The advantages of printing lay, it seems, in the multiplication of uniform copies and the lower cost per copy.

There is no evidence, in any case, that the everyday workings of justice were seriously impaired under the scribal system; whatever the confusion, local magistrates, very few of whom had been formally trained in the law, continued to issue judgments on the basis of the common law and English statutes as adapted to the needs of the colonists. The advantages and disadvantages of the various technologies may have mattered less, therefore, than the workaday pragmatism of these magistrates, who rarely owned law books other than those of the "how-to-do-it" kind.[37] Yet the material production of colonial statutes was politically consequential in the context of the endemic tension between local rights and imperial or proprietary sovereignty. That the colonists were bothered by the supervisory privileges of the Crown, that the printing of statutes was in some situations construed as a means of protest against these privileges, and that scribal publication made for more confusion both at home and in London, seems certain. The situation in Maryland between the mid-1670s and the overthrow of the Proprietor in 1689, as the antiproprietary forces were increasingly angered by the uncertainties of the scribal system, is a case in point.[38]

Books and their Owners

Printed books figured in the culture of the Chesapeake from the very outset of colonization, be these informational tracts on silkworm culture shipped there by the Virginia Company, Bibles brought by individual adventurers and servants, or personal libraries carefully transferred by men of learning.[39] Thereafter, the colonists had to make do without the network of entrepreneurial printers and booksellers who, in England, stocked the commercial marketplace with a large and ever-changing supply of books. In the absence of a retail trade, books arrived in the colonies because someone chose to bring them over, as a schoolmaster was doing shortly after the turn of the century,[40] or because a local institution deemed them necessary. The only other means was for persons to order books via the overseas merchants and ship captains who thronged the Chesapeake each fall exchanging goods of many kinds for tobacco. On this basis a handful of the colonists continued to add to their libraries.

Books were significant to the colonists for several reasons. Early on, while the Virginia Company was in charge, a remarkable number of educated men made their way to Jamestown. In that unfamiliar and disruptive setting they attempted to resume the cultural practices familiar to them back in England, practices that, originating in Renaissance humanism, symbolized the condition of being "cultivated" or civilized. Thus it was that a minister wrote in 1621 that he was "no statesman nor love[d] to meddle with any thing but [his] Bookes"; that George Percy, having received writing materials and books from his brother, the Earl of Northumberland, kept a daily journal and wrote "the earliest known account" of the colonizing venture; that John Pory, in a letter of September 1619 to an English friend, voiced a longing "to have some good book always in store, being in solitude the best and choicest company"; and that George Sandys, educated at Oxford and the Middle Temple and son of an archbishop, continued to work on a translation of Ovid's *Metamorphoses* published after he returned from the colony (Fig. 2.1). Long after these dreams of a rural arcadia had faded away, books in Latin and Greek remained central to the identity of planters like William Byrd II.[41]

For others, the rationale for having books was rooted in Protestantism – or among the Catholics of Maryland, in Catholicism. Accustomed to owning and reading the vernacular English Bible, many of the Protestant colonists carried copies with them to the New World; a colonist of Puritan sympathies brought over the notes he had taken on sermons preached in London by John Davenport, a minister who ended up in New England.[42] During the period of the Virginia Company, donors in London anxious about the supply of Bibles and other religious books helped out by providing extra copies; "By this Shipp the Hopewell," the company wrote in August 1623, "you shall receaue three great Bibles, two Common prayer booke and Ursinaes Catechisme; being the guift of an unknowne person for the use of those Churches that most need them." The perception that the colonists were short of Bibles lasted throughout the century, for in 1683 the Bishop of London arranged for a shipment of 39 copies (undoubtedly the folios known as "Church" Bibles), to be distributed to parishes in need.[43] In order to get the Church of England up and running the Jamestown colony also needed clergymen. That men of this profession depended on books was acknowledged by the company when it agreed to pay an allowance for this purpose to emigrating ministers.[44]

For still others, books were utilitarian. The men who practiced medicine in the Chesapeake commonly owned manuals of surgery and pharmacology, and books of "physick" also turn up in other inventories.[45] Officers of the courts relied on collections of English statutes and handbooks containing legal forms and procedures, both of which county courts ordered and paid for directly.[46] A few men took a broader view of the law. Wanting to align the legal system in the colonies with the English common law, yet also preferring a measure of local autonomy, these men turned to works of history, English statutes, and treatises of jurisprudence in their search for such a middle way. This sense of need was expressed early on, in 1621, by a Virginia colonist who asked the Virginia Company to send "the newe booke of thabridgment of Statutes and Stamfordes pleases of the Crowne and mr westes presidents and what other Lawe bookes you shall thinke fitt," the reason being that "in the matter of our Government here wee are many times perplexed . . . for . . . wante of bookes." Near the end of the century, William Fitzhugh, a wealthy planter who was active in affairs of state, told the Virginia Assembly at a moment when it was frustrated by not knowing

Figure 2.1. Levinus Lemnius, *De Miraculis Occultis Naturæ* (Francofurti: Joannis Saurii, impensis Jacobi Fischeri, 1611); from the library of the Virginia colonist and translator of Ovid George Sandys, with his arms stamped in gilt on the covers, and his signature and motto (*Habere eripitur, habuisse nunquam*) on the title page; later owned by Isaac Norris of Philadelphia, the son-in-law of James Logan. Courtesy of The Library Company of Philadelphia.

whether Charles II had assented to certain laws that the colony should be able to enact statutes of its own when and where local "expedient" justified such action. Fitzhugh's position made him all the more concerned to keep abreast of English legislation. To this end he assembled a library of legal materials that included (as did similar libraries in Virginia) John Rushworth's *Historical Collections*. Ordering books directly from England in 1698, he specified "All the Statues [*sic*] made since the twenty second of King Charles the second to this year," further volumes in Rushworth's *Collections*, an English translation of a Latin treatise on government in Scotland, and three works dealing with recent or contemporary English politics.[47]

Viewed in the ensemble, the quantity of books carried to the Chesapeake in the seventeenth century was considerable. Referring only to Virginia, one historian has estimated that the total reached 20,000, dispersed among a thousand or more households.[48] But let us look at three specific bodies of data, the evidence of book holdings in the probate inventories that survive from three counties: Surry and York in Virginia and St. Mary's in Maryland. Taken as a whole, 35 percent of these inventories indicate the ownership of books. As in England, so in the Chesapeake this figure varied with what people did for a living and how much wealth they had. Clergy and doctors invariably owned books. But among the lowest wealth cohort in St. Mary's County for the period 1658–1705 (347 inventories out of a total of 638 indicating an estate of less than £50), 19 percent owned books. This figure more than doubles for the next two wealth cohorts, doubling again to 80 percent for those whose probated wealth was in the range of £400–£999. The numbers that James Horn has worked out for four Virginia counties are roughly comparable.[49]

When the inventories are analyzed more closely, they reveal that most household libraries were rather small. In Surry, of forty-one inventories containing books, twenty-four had five or fewer; in only three instances is it certain that the number exceeded ten. In St. Mary's County, only about one in eight inventories indicate a personal library that exceeded ten books. In York County, close to 50 percent of the households with books had no more than five, the few libraries of any size belonging to clergy and, in one instance, a learned physician. The story of readers and their books in the Chesapeake is properly a tale not of the few great libraries but of households more than half of which did without books and of book owners satisfied with having only the Bible and a few others, most probably religious in their subject matter.[50] Comparatively speaking, these patterns represent an improvement on the situation in some parts of England, though they fall behind the percentages for New England.[51]

As well as indicating patterns of ownership, the inventories inform us of books that were commonly owned. The title cited most widely in the Surry County, Virginia inventories was the Bible (fifteen out of forty-one); for St.

Mary's the figure is twenty-nine of seventy-eight, and for York, thirty-three of seventy-one. People owned the Bible in a variety of formats and sometimes in multiple copies.[52] Few other books are mentioned by title, the prevailing reference being to "old books," a "parcel" of books, "small books," and the like, with valuations that rarely exceed one or two hundred pounds of tobacco or the equivalent in shillings and pence. Other than the Bible, the book most often named was a Protestant work of devotion, a steady seller of the first two-thirds of the century, Lewis Bayly's *The Practice of Piety*, the only "small book" identified by title in a York County merchant's inventory of 1657 (two copies, out of a total stock of twelve or thirteen). Some seven of the York County inventories included Bayly's much-reprinted book, an amount that equals the total references to psalters, psalmbooks, and the *Book of Common Prayer* (but a single copy).[53] Whenever the appraisers of an estate provide a list of specific titles, the subject matter is invariably religious. It seems reasonable to assume, therefore, that religion predominated as the subject matter of the "old" or "small books" left nameless in so many inventories.[54] Books we may lump together as "secular" are a very distant second to religious books; some of these were manuals or handbooks that taught specific skills.[55] In keeping with the importance of the commerce in tobacco, land, and servants, a sixth of the York County inventories note the presence of "writings" (commonly preserved in a chest or trunk), account books and paper. Some of the colonists assembled a substantial archive of these writings or ledgers and, in the course of time, used up a great deal of loose paper.[56]

Two circumstances worked to limit the ownership of books. One of these was the near-complete absence of booksellers handling new or used books, and a second was the rate of literacy. No one in the seventeenth-century Chesapeake seems to have specialized in bookselling, as was happening by the 1690s in Boston. Nor does anyone seem to have practiced the trade of bookbinding, though there must have been someone with the necessary tools and knowledge who worked alongside the Bladen/Reading printing office.[57] Local merchants in the Chesapeake – that is, permanent residents, in contrast to the transient Dutch or English merchants who exchanged merchandise from their ships for tobacco – carried supplies of paper in their stores as well as "paper books" (i.e., blank books). Most of them also had a small supply of primers and hornbooks of the kind used by children learning how to read. The inventory of the store that Richard Willis kept in Middlesex County at the end of the seventeenth century included thirty quires of paper, twenty primers, and five hornbooks; the latter must have been barely visible amid the extensive quantities of fabrics, clothes, tools, nails, pipes, and buttons.[58] An inventory made in 1675 of the store of Robert Farrar, in St. Mary's County, Maryland, listed five primers and three hornbooks. Another of 1675 from York County included eight "gilt" hornbooks and six "plain," the former valued at two pence each, the latter at one, among a great mass of linens, tools, pots and pans, tapes, shoes, and the like.[59] In 1668 Jonathan Hubbard of the same county had twelve hornbooks (valued, in total, at *2s.*), one testament, and one psalter in his inventory; three years later, the York County store kept by Jonathan Newell included eight hornbooks valued at one pound of tobacco apiece. So insignificant were printed books as a commodity that some merchants stocked none at all, though paper was almost ubiquitous.[60] Only in a single instance, the store maintained by John Sampson of Rappahannock County, Virginia, were books a significant feature of the inventory, and this because in 1685, the year he died, the store goods included a chest containing ninety-one copies of the 1684 edition of the Virginia statutes.[61]

Was this absence of demand linked to the rate of literacy in the Chesapeake? In assessing that rate, we learn little from remarks that were made by contemporaries, as when the Virginia Council denounced Nathaniel Bacon's followers as "the Rascallity and meanest of the people . . . there being . . . very few who can either write or read," or when three observers at the end of the century observed that some of the magistrates could not read or write.[62] We learn more from the wills and legal documents to which people had to add their signature, for a good many of the colonists signed with a mark. According to one careful study of Virginia wills, the rate of signature literacy for men dying before 1650 was 45 percent and rose to about 60 percent by 1680. These and other surveys indicate that men were able to sign their names at twice the rate of women, and that relative wealth influenced the rate of male literacy.[63] Court records provide further evidence of persons who lacked the ability to write and who turned to someone else to prepare a document. Thus in a case of fornication in York County, Virginia, a woman servant testified that her lover used the excuse of needing to have a letter written to come to the house where she lived.[64]

The people who signed with a mark may have been able to read. Since there is no quantitative basis for ascertaining this skill, the evidence for reading literacy must be indirect. That evidence includes court records that capture in one way or another the presence of thousands of men and women, young and old, servants, leaseholders, merchants, and planters. Rarely do these records suggest that someone could not read, and though it may be the case that women were less literate, their participation in the world of reading is evident from the references to them as givers and receivers of books.[65] The sheer mass of written documents that both women and men handled in making property transactions points toward the same presumption, that most of them had some capacity as readers. This presumption is strengthened by the fact that children were taught to read before they learned to write; many who started down the path to literacy halted midway, never advancing to the more specialized skill of writing.[66]

To the premise of widespread reading-literacy we must add another, that people who were unable to write could nonetheless participate in the workings of politics and the economy. At certain moments of high political tension, crowds gathered to sign their names to oaths or protests.[67] Administrators in the civil government were not always literate; it happened, for example, that certain burgesses and justices of county courts signed their names with a mark, and it was very common for the men who compiled probate inventories and appraised estates to use marks, as did many of the persons who witnessed legal documents and served on juries.[68] These episodes of the supposedly "illiterate" acting side-by-side with the "literate" force on us the recognition that the practical significance of literacy in the Chesapeake was relative to specific situations. Moreover, the traditional method of "publishing" many documents by reading them aloud served to enlarge the possibilities for participation. Literacy was thus a two-sided situation, involving a hierarchy of skills but also open-ended and performative in ways that sharply reduced the significance of gender and property.

As to how and when children learned to read and write in the Chesapeake, the evidence is again mostly indirect. Where they learned to read can be answered in the negative: not in schools organized or financed by the civil state. The continual flow of new immigrants to the Chesapeake, most of them indentured servants in their teens, included a certain number of young men and women who had become literate back in England. Children born and raised in the Chesapeake learned to read, and a smaller proportion, heavily male, learned to write, either in a household or by attending local schools so informally organized that it is hard to document their presence. One clue to these local possibilities is the preference expressed in wills that children be taught to read and write. By the end of the century the indentures of orphans and servants, both male and female, sometimes included a provision that the master teach reading and, in some instances, writing. These indentures reflect the common assumption that children learned how to read in a household.[69] Alternatively, or afterwards, children studied under a schoolmaster. Responding individually to inquiries from the Bishop of London in 1724, twelve Anglican clergy in Virginia informed him that the possibilities for schooling in their parishes included "small" or "little" schools where reading, writing, and, less commonly, arithmetic were taught.[70] Another form of school, the "free" or "grammar" school, where boys learned the classical languages, existed intermittently in Virginia and Maryland; such a school was established alongside (and for two decades in lieu of) the newly founded College of William and Mary.

Learned culture nonetheless survived in the Chesapeake, reconstituting itself in the aftermath of the dissolution of the Virginia Company, though never again, perhaps, as closely attached to cosmopolitan practices as in those early years. Little evidence remains of the libraries that the earliest of the learned to arrive brought with them to Virginia. It seems probable that, under the chaotic conditions of the first decades, such collections were dispersed or abandoned once their owners died. But a clergyman who lived for half a century on the eastern shore of Virginia, Thomas Teackle, enjoyed a library that had grown to 333 books when he died in 1697. In Maryland the chancellor of the colony, Philip Calvert, a graduate of the College of Saints Peter and Paul in Lisbon, Portugal, lived amid a hundred or so books; the more utilitarian of them – Coke's *Institutes,* the ubiquitous Dalton on the office of justice of the peace, a "Lattin booke of writts" and a "Treatise of Wills" – were stored in the office where he did his legal business. The library of Henry Randolph, sometime clerk of the Virginia Assembly and one of the persons responsible for the printed laws of 1662, contained 29 titles in folio out of a total of some 160. Books relating to the law constituted half of the collection of 114 titles belonging to Arthur Spicer of Richmond County, who was active as an attorney. Ralph Wormeley of Middlesex County, Virginia, owned 410 titles according to an inventory made in 1701; broken down by subject, 86 of these were works of history and biography and 123 pertained to religion and morality. In 1686 Henry Willoughby, a doctor, had seventy-four books described by the appraisers of his estate as "divinity," another thirty-eight characterized as dealing with the law, and forty-four on "physic." By the turn of the century, the largest personal libraries in the Chesapeake were probably those of Presbyterian clergymen from Scotland; when Francis Makemie, the most prominent of these ministers, died in 1708 he owned 992 titles.[71]

More common were collections in the range of twenty to one hundred titles. Robert Slye of St. Mary's County had "forty printed Bookes great and Small" when he died in 1671. The first of the Virginia Carters, John, owned some sixty titles at his death in 1659; many of these passed into the collection of his son John II, who had about the same number in his estate when it was inventoried in 1690.[72] The library of a physician and native German, George Hack, inventoried in 1665, contained some ninety books in a number of languages ("High German," "Dutch," Latin, and English) and formats, from folio to duodecimo; Hack must have brought the greater part of these with him to Virginia. A collection of forty-nine books belonging to Sarah Willoughby of Lower Norfolk County was inventoried by title in 1673; aside from two Testaments and four Bibles, one of them in Latin, the collection included another ten or so books in Latin as well as a potpourri of history, religion, travel, and how-to-do-it manuals.[73] Where such books were stored – in a "closet," a chest, a hall or the infrequent "study" – varied from one house to the next.[74]

How it was the colonists added to or acquired their stock of books once they reached the Chesapeake is largely unknown. Early on, the Virginia Company advised a clergyman that he could assemble a decent library in Virginia out of the collections of his predecessors.[75] This grim truth was pertinent to much of the seventeenth century and may help explain why so many of Teackle's books had been printed before 1620. Some books passed as gifts within families or to a circle of friends, or in acknowledgment of another's professional needs – a surgeon bequeathing his Latin and English books and instruments to another would-be doctor or, in a separate instance, designating a folio Greek Testament as a gift to a much-admired minister; a man bequeathing a Bible and sermon books to a godson and goddaughter; a county clerk willing each of his executors "a booke as they Shall Choose for their reading."[76] Arriving in Virginia relatively late in the seventeenth century, a clergyman naturalist, John Banister, was given a copy of Descartes's *Meditations* (an Elzevir) by one of the Blands. There is some evidence that the learned borrowed from each other, as William Fitzhugh did from Ralph Wormeley in 1682 when he wanted to use Rushworth's *Historical Collections* and the latest statutes.[77] English correspondents sent books; George Calvert was grateful in 1664 to receive the latest printed "news books, which are a great divertisement to us," from his father; one of the naturalist John Banister's patrons sent him books; and William Fitzhugh asked overseas friends and in another instance, a brother, to send him "printed News" and other "newest" items of their own selection.[78] It was also possible to order specific titles, as Teackle must have done in building up his library. In the early 1630s William Claiborne of Kent Island was buying "bibles and bookes of prayers" to use in church services. Later in the century, George Hack had copies of the *London Gazette* that he probably acquired from a transient tobacco merchant. William Byrd I relied on the Reverend John Clayton, who spent two years in Virginia, to act as his intermediary in securing items of natural science, and Fitzhugh ordered schoolbooks for his sons, along with political and legal books, from a London bookseller.[79] Aside from individuals, orders for books from England came from vestries in Virginia needing copies of the Bible and the *Book of Common Prayer*.[80] Quakers had their own system for acquiring and distributing books.[81]

Learned culture in the Chesapeake was like popular culture in being linked to Protestantism. Invariably the larger collections included the Bible and examples of the literature of devotion. More telling than the proportion of devotional books is the importance they had for their owners, an importance revealed in four specific legacies that involved women readers. In 1659 John Carter willed his wife three works of devotion, one of them a steady seller of Anglican devotion, Richard Allestree's *The Whole Duty of Man* (he also specified that his wife should retain "her own books"). In 1673 the widow of Colonel John Catlett divided up her late husband's library, giving each of her two daughters "a small Bible" and leaving the rest to be shared equally between her sons. At the end of the century William Sherwood willed his "Divinity bookes to my Loving wife Rachell," empowering her to pass "such of them as shee shall see fit" to another person. In 1701 William Fitzhugh's widow Sarah made a selection of books from his library that she wished to keep for herself: the Bible, the *Book of Common Prayer, The Whole Duty of Man, The Practice of Piety,* "Smith's Sermon Book," and *The Queen's Closett Opened.*[82] These were the same books that so many middling-status English readers preferred, books deemed of "practical" significance (as they advertised themselves) in teaching the reader how to set things right with God. No less utilitarian were other sections of these learned libraries – notably, books on navigation, horticulture, surgery and medicine, the law, and scriptural exegesis, this last category constituting a third of Teackle's books. Books of a different kind altogether, the romances, miscellanies, plays, satires, and collections of epigrams that constituted the light reading of English gentlemen and gentlewomen, were thinly represented.[83] Even for the wealthy and the learned, reading was no leisurely pastime but something undertaken to meet specific needs.[84]

At the end of the century the founding of William and Mary became the first real counterweight to the dispersal of learned culture. Thirty years before this event, in the aftermath of the Restoration, the Virginia government, noting "the want of able & faithfull ministers," envisioned a college, as had the Virginia Company in its heyday. Not until the appointment in 1689 of James Blair, a Scotsman, as commissary of the clergy in Virginia did these long-nurtured hopes began to ripen, with a charter in hand by 1693 and the first students enrolled in a grammar school by 1694. Like the founders of Harvard before them, the founders wanted their new college to function as "a seminary of ministers of the gospel" capable of providing a sufficient supply of native-born clergy.[85]

The new college needed books, which came to it mainly through private donations. Back in 1619, when the Virginia Company entertained the project of a college, an anonymous donor responded with a gift of a three-volume folio set of William Perkins's works and Augustine's *City of God.* In the mid-1690s, the key figure in the making of the college library was Francis Nicholson, a soldier turned administrator who served a term as lieutenant governor of Virginia and a second as governor. Initially he gave seven books, and shortly thereafter, probably upon becoming governor, donated the remainder of a personal collection of more than two hundred volumes, the majority of them relating to religion. Other donations arrived from

England in response to solicitations made in person by James Blair. Certain bishops of the Church gave generously, for in May 1699 a student thanked two bishops for "makeing a noble present of well chosen bookes to our Library, intending hereby to take care that our Youth be well seasoned with the best principles of religion and Learning that can be taught by the most sound & Orthodox Divines." Only two examples of expenditures for "books Mapps & papers" are noted in the surviving records, and in only one of these is a title specified, a history of the Bible.[86]

Since William and Mary remained a grammar school for its first two decades, the library, which was stored in a second-floor room in the main college building, may not have seen much use, especially if Blair, the first president, refused to let the books circulate. For sure, only the faculty, and not the students, had access to the collection. When the college building burned in 1705, the library went up in smoke. The story of its prolonged rebuilding would carry us far into the eighteenth century. But it is appropriate to suggest that in size and breadth the college library never rivaled the great personal collections formed early in that century by William Byrd II and Landon Carter.

Modes of Authorship

From the outset of colonization people who came to the Chesapeake colonies as transient observers or to stay were eager to share their impressions of the New World. Most of these reports ended up in family papers or the cache of administrative records maintained by the Church of England and the Crown,[87] though some, like John Rolfe's "A true Relation of the state of Virginia," circulated in the colonies and England in handwritten copies.[88] Others appeared in print, frequently abridged or recast by someone else's hand, as parts of a compilation, a tradition exemplified by Samuel Purchas's four-volume folio *Purchas his Pilgrimes* (1625). The political crises that erupted in Maryland and Virginia drove certain colonists to write and publish, notably in the mid-1650s and a second time in response to Bacon's Rebellion. Much of the more casual work has not survived, like the almanac contradicting "judicial astrology" that John Catlett wrote in 1664 and a play entitled "the Bare and the Cubb" acted by three men in 1665.[89] An enterprising merchant born in Prague and reared in the Netherlands only to become a naturalized resident of Maryland, Augustine Herrman, prepared a map of the Chesapeake that was engraved and published in London in 1674; Herrman earned the reward of a large land grant for his cartography, which served the political purposes of Lord Baltimore.[90]

Our literary historians have commonly approached these seventeenth-century writers wanting to know which of them to credit for composing the "first American book" or asking which texts fit within the category of "American literature."[91] From the standpoint of book history, the more appropriate task is to examine the social practice of authorship. As a series of individual examples will make clear, no single system of rules prevailed in the Chesapeake or in the metropolis of London. In general, authors had little control over what they wrote once their material was passed on to intermediaries. To be a writer was to enter into a relationship of dependence. For some, this relationship was with a patron, for others with a bookseller, for still others with a coterie or (as in the case of the Quakers) with a religious community. Certain forms of writing – most specifically letters but also texts that were deliberately withheld from the marketplace – were deemed "private," though it often happened that such texts were published. Anonymity, as in the use of initials on a title page, was a means of combining privacy and publication. To enter the public realm was to encounter the possibility of censorship by the civil state or ecclesiastical authorities. The sensible response to this situation was to engage in self-censorship. An alternative was to write a "libel," a genre that, because it lacked the attributions of author, printer, and bookseller, usually spurred the civil state into searching for and punishing the libellers.[92] The most crucial fact that bore upon authorship in the Chesapeake was the paucity of local patrons, including much by way of a reading public. Almost without exception, to become an author in these two colonies could only be accomplished by looking to readers and patrons overseas, in England.

The literary career of Captain John Smith is revealing of how someone who was neither learned nor a "gentleman" exploited the possibilities for patronage. Before Smith signed on with the Virginia Company of London to take part in the founding expedition of 1607, he had not thought of himself as a writer. He became one accidentally (though he surely knew of the market for travel narratives) when a long letter-narrative "to a friend of his" sent back by ship in June 1608 passed through the hands of the Virginia Company to a member of the Stationers' Company, who registered *A True Relation of Such Occurrences and Accidents of Noate as Hath Hapned in Virginia since the First Planting of That Collony* for publication as a quarto in August. The text, an account of dissension and disease in Jamestown and of Smith's negotiations with the Indians, was less frank than it might have been because someone in the employ of the company edited out certain information; justifying the abridgment, the editor invoked the distinction between private and public, noting that "somewhat more was by him written, which being as I thought (fit to be private) I would not adventure to make it publicke." Initially the printer attributed the text to "a Gentleman," then to a "Th. Watson Gent," and only in the third version of the title page to Smith himself, identified as "Coronell of the said Collony."[93]

This casualness about the author's name and text, with the printer playing a large role in deciding the spelling of place names and an editor – someone unknown to Smith – intervening as censor, gave way to a different set of circumstances once he began to publish regularly after he returned from Virginia. The longest of his books was *The General History of Virginia, Summer Isles, and New England,* published as a folio in 1624 and reprinted four times by 1632. The origins of the *General History* lay in the embattled circumstances of the Virginia Company. Even though its self-interest was crucially involved in shaping the flow of news from Jamestown, the company was unable to prevent negative reports from being published. Almost immediately, therefore, the company had to improvise a program of literary patronage, sponsoring sermons and travel narratives that offered a more encouraging view of Virginia's prospects. In 1621, with the success of the venture much in doubt and its finances tied to raising money through public lotteries, a leading member of the company proposed that it undertake "a faire and perspicuous history, compiled of that Country, from her first discouery to this day." The company agreed, and, after joining forces with John Smith, probably financed the printing of a four-page prospectus advertising the contents.[94]

For the final page of this prospectus, Smith wrote a statement about authorship that situated the practice within three different contexts. The first of these concerned the sources of the *General History,* which Smith identified as data "discovered, observed, or collected" by himself, though he also acknowledged his dependence on "an infinite nomber of variable Relations" written by others. Like other travel writers of the period, Smith the author–observer was also Smith the compiler–editor. A second context concerned truth: who was telling it and who was not. The third had to do with money: who would pay the cost of having the copperplate maps engraved and, of more importance, who would pay *him,* the author, for by this point in his career as a writer Smith understood authorship not as something that happened inadvertently and without yielding any financial return but as providing "satisfaction[s]" that merited due reward.

Money is the subject of the very first sentence of the prospectus, money Smith himself had invested, together with the "eighteene yeeres of time" he had given "gratis" to the enterprise of discovery. Now he needed money from some other source, for the book would be a long one (by far the longest he would ever write or compile) of "eighty sheets, besides the three Maps," the whole requiring a subsidy of "neere in an hundred pounds, which summe I cannot disbursse." Who would patronize the work and provide this sum? Smith addressed himself to members of the nobility and the gentry, "humbly entreat[ing]" them "either to adventure [i.e., invest in the hope of getting some return] or give me what you please towards the impression."

In the event, the Duchess of Richmond responded with a subsidy; nothing, it seems, was contributed by the hard-pressed company. And who would recompense him as author? Here Smith shifted his voice, no longer representing himself as someone "accountable and thankful" to a great patron but speaking to the members of the Stationers' Company as an experienced writer sensible of the value of literary property: "nor shall the Stationers have the copy for nothing."[95]

In a single paragraph Smith thus tried out two alternative possibilities for financing a book and earning money as an author: relying on disinterested great patrons or on booksellers intent on making money themselves. By implication, booksellers drove hard bargains and were unpleasant to deal with. Yet to seek out great patrons involved another kind of unpleasantness, of admitting the difference in rank between sponsor and writer and of embodying that difference in flattery. Addressing "the illustrious and most noble Princess, the Lady Francis, Duchesse of Richmond" in the dedication, Smith contrasted the inadequacy of his prose – "poore ragged lines" written by a "rude military hand" wielding a "rough Pen" – with the "Judicious" discernment seemingly intrinsic to persons blessed with a "glorious Name": "If therefore your *Grace* shall daigne to cast your eye on this poore Booke, view I pray you rather your owne *Bountie* (without which it had dyed in the wombe) then my *imperfections,* which have no helpe but the shrine of your *glorious Name* to be sheltered from censorious condemnation." According to this scheme, noble patrons were a writer's ideal readers – that is, if they chose to read at all.[96]

The reference to "censorious condemnation" points us toward another complication, the contested situation in which Smith as author found himself. This situation was generic to authorship in the period, as the Maryland writer George Alsop indicated some decades later in imagining the fate of his manuscript once it entered the public realm: "Farewell, poor brat! thou in a monstrous world, / In swaddling clothes, thus up and down art hurled; / There to receive what destiny doth contrive, / Either to perish or be saved alive / Good fate protect thee from a critic's power."[97] But the situation was also specific to the genre of travel narrative or history, and especially to any retrospective account of the Virginia Company, which, long since, had found itself immersed in a sea of "calumnies and slanders" that "run (like wilde fire) from man to man,"[98] in part because of the large discrepancies between company-sponsored travel narratives representing Virginia as a veritable paradise and the reports reaching England of disease, starvation, and death. Moreover, Smith's own reputation as an explorer and adventurer was open to challenge. Was he telling the truth? This insistent question lay behind Smith's oft-repeated assertion that he had "observed" much of what he wrote about, as it also did behind the apparatus of testimonials professing admiration for him as "Author." Could he appropriate the authority of the patron to whom he dedicated the *General History*? If the position of such patrons (who for an earlier work included the Prince of Wales) in the hierarchies of culture allowed them to stand above the fray, could he repair his own reputation by associating his work with their names?

But we must set these circumstances and Smith's quest for authority in a still broader context. Here, the tension involved in going public as an author arose out of the assumption, common to the times, that anyone who published merely for the sake of earning money was certain to lie. John Hammond, a Maryland colonist who wrote in defense of the proprietor in 1656, voiced this assumption in representing himself as "not [having] written for profit, for it is known I have given away the copy, and therefore am the less to be mistrusted for a deluder, for popular applause I did it not."[99] A parallel assumption was that persons of "gentle" status, surely not in need of money, preferred to remain anonymous, or even not to publish, rather than to allow their handiwork – and their persons – to become soiled in the commercial marketplace. In the very years in which Smith was fashioning his career as writer, the clergyman-poet John Donne, reacting to the "stigma of print," limited himself to the medium of scribal publication. Colonial writers and editors also had to wonder, as George Alsop did, if going public was worth the cost to personal reputation; although the editor of the English-language version of the New World explorer John Lederer's *Discoveries* reasoned that "the printing of these Papers . . . might prove a service to the Publick," he had to reassure himself that their publication "was no injury to the Author."[100]

John Smith wanted to be recognized as a man of civic virtue selflessly using his "best abilities to the good of my Prince and Countrey." But he also wanted to make money, which meant being of service to the booksellers. That he was no gentleman but a bargainer tainted by the market is evident from the final page of the prospectus for the *General History*, with its appeal for fair treatment from booksellers.[101]

Here, at the beginning of the seventeenth century, we see authors involved in long-lasting issues of truth, disinterestedness, anonymity, and commerce. A further case in point was William Fitzhugh's effort to secure the publication of a "short description of Virginia & a methodicall Digestion of the Laws thereof." In 1694 he sent a copy of the manuscript, based on a revision of the Virginia statutes he had recently supervised, to a London merchant with whom he had business dealings, accompanying it with a letter advising that he "would not have the Impression neither in my name nor at my charge" and offering the encouragement that, since his friends expected "every one that can read both here & in Maryland would have one," the bookseller who published it could anticipate selling "some thousands," and that "suddenly." This being the case, was it not appropriate that Fitzhugh be paid "liberally for the Copy of it," more even "than is given for the Copy of the ordinaryest Play book, which is twenty shillings a sheet"? As it happened, no one bit. Three years later, Fitzhugh was providing detailed instructions to the London bookseller Hugh Newman on how additional laws should be incorporated and certain information highlighted, in part to compensate for the loss of "the fairest & best Copy" to French privateers. Reluctantly admitting that "some small Erratas will happen," yet hoping that "if this Impression sells well [these] will be easily corrected in the next," he left to Newman the decision as to format (the bookseller had suggested octavo). What concerned him more was his own presence as author – or rather, the suppression of his presence, for he wanted Newman to "write a . . . new preface . . . as from your self, the Printer giving an account of the Casuall meeeting with the Copy," to the end of suggesting that "it were an accidentall Copy & no Author known thereto." Fitzhugh may have wished to remain anonymous in keeping with the conventions of the amateur or gentleman writer or because, as an office-holder in Virginia, he wished to shield himself from criticism of the kind that Purvis and Buckner had encountered. Yet like Smith before him, he framed his relationship with the world of London booksellers as a business transaction, willing by 1697 to accept an offer of £20 (contingent on Newman's finding "a chapman that . . . would take off five hundred of them"), to be rendered not in cash but in books. In the event, the manuscript never passed into print, possibly because the bookseller thought the risk of earning back his investment was too great.[102]

Authorship had a somewhat different meaning for two men, both of them college educated and ordained clergy, who came to Virginia to undertake scientific studies. After spending two years in the colony (1684–86), John Clayton returned to England, where he wrote a series of letters that were published in the *Philosophical Transactions* of the Royal Society of London. John Banister came in 1678 and stayed, living long enough to begin a "Naturall History of Virginia," parts of which were incorporated into publications by other English naturalists. Each of these men depended on a newly emerging community of scientists for the funding that brought them to Virginia. It was this community, based both in the Royal Society (1660) and in coffeehouse culture, that defined the program of research these naturalists should follow. It was also this community that provided a means of making public new discoveries – means that included an elaborate network of correspondents, the *Philosophical Transactions,* and the publishing of books by subscription.

These modes of publication offered two advantages to men like Banister and Clayton. The first was a certain distance from the religious and dynastic politics of the period, for, early on, the Royal Society refused to be drawn into the great conflict between Nonconformists and Anglicans. The second was a certain distance from the marketplace. In proposing to publish by subscription his "Naturall History" – had the project come to fruition, he would have been among the earliest writers in America to use this method – Banister acted in the awareness that (as his fellow English naturalist John Ray complained in 1686) "the greatest part of Natural historie has been starved and abused by the Avarice of Stationers who have beat down the Artist." To be sure, Banister worried about the consequences of publishing the "History" in parts as a serial in order to reduce the expense to those who subscribed. But at least he could count on a patronage that was sympathetic to his ends.[103]

The leaders of the Royal Society wanted to free themselves from practices within the book trade that undercut an author's control of his text. In doing so they were also seeking to remove the natural philosopher's criterion of "truth," meaning true to nature, from the rough-and-tumble of the marketplace, where, as John Smith and so many other writers realized, all and any claims to truth were easily compromised.[104]

For another writer, the planter John Cotton, we must guess at the circumstances of production and distribution since little is known beyond the fact that, in the immediate aftermath of Bacon's Rebellion, he wrote a sardonic history of the event that remained in manuscript in his own day. It seems likely that Cotton prepared "The History of Bacon's and Ingram's Rebellion" for a coterie of readers, possibly members of a coffeehouse set in London, among whom it circulated in a small number of handwritten copies. The members of this circle may have shared other, related texts, for Cotton included in the "History" two examples of the "many copp[i]es of verses made after [Bacon's death]." Like Alsop's *Character of Maryland*, the style of the "History" was based on the satirical and jestbook culture that was wholly opposite to the literature of religious devotion.[105]

Colonial writers contributed to the last of these genres as well. Here, the meaning of authorship shifted yet again. The title page of *A Song of Sion*, written in Virginia by a transient Quaker, John Grave, and printed in London in 1662, immediately suggests one major difference: The author is described as a "Citizen" of "Sion" and we do not learn his name until the end of the tract/poem, where he signed himself "your fellow-friend." Grave preferred this quasianonymity because he believed that a worldly identity would get in the way of conveying divine truth. And although we know nothing of his dealings with the bookseller who issued *Song of Sion*, it is certain that Grave regarded the spiritual truths he rhymed in ballad metre as no one's private property for sale to booksellers but as the voice of God: "O mind you all, these words most true, / proceeding from above. . . ." Grave as author was a self-effacing intermediary.[106]

These case histories are revealing of the ambiguities that encompassed the meaning and nature of intellectual property: To whom or to what did a text belong? They underscore the paradoxical relationship between authenticity and the marketplace, for a literary work that rejected the taint of the market may have made itself more attractive to patrons and readers. These examples also underscore the mutual dependence between writers in the Old World and writers in the New: Colonial authors depended on patrons in the metropolis, but cosmopolitan writers and patrons were needy in their turn for information from the colonies.

CHAPTER THREE

Printing and Bookselling in New England, 1638–1713

HUGH AMORY

THE COLONIZING OF NEW ENGLAND happened in a rush. The "separatist" Pilgrims found a haven at New Plymouth in 1620. The Massachusetts Bay Company, a joint-stock venture chartered in 1628, initiated the "Great Migration" of 1630, founding Boston and several neighboring towns in that year. As more people arrived during the 1630s, they dispersed up and down the coast and as far inland as the settlements that became Hartford, Windsor, and Springfield along the Connecticut River. In 1640, when the first book was printed in British North America, New England contained five separate jurisdictions: New Plymouth; Massachusetts Bay, which claimed the future territories of Maine, New Hampshire, and Vermont (the last also claimed by New York); Connecticut; New Haven; and an aggregation of towns and land grants that were later incorporated under a royal charter as Rhode Island and Providence Plantations.

Freedoms and Licenses

Despite this chaotic scatter of jurisdictions, from which yet others later split off, the localized origins of the Great Migration in East Anglia, Hampshire, and Dorset, and the motives that impelled emigration, together with the covenanted character of New England churches, enforced a highly homogeneous culture, at least outside of the Quaker and Baptist settlements of Rhode Island. In the United Colonies of Massachusetts, Connecticut, and New Plymouth, communication (and indeed communion) was essentially equivalent to agreement.[1] From the arrival of a press in December 1638 down to 1689, the Massachusetts General Court and later, the Governor and Council of the Dominion of New England not only limited the number of presses and confined them to either Cambridge or Boston, but also directly controlled their management. Dissident opinion had no alternative but to go overseas: John Eliot might exhibit his views by writing to England, but Thomas Lechmere, Roger Williams, and other critics had to remove themselves bodily from New England in order to break into print.

In these respects, New England's censorship differed little from Old England's, though it was more visible, more effective, and culturally more accepted. Some marginal titles, moreover, were imported that would not have been licensed for printing: the *Book of Common Prayer*, for example, was regularly bound up with the Authorized Version of the Bible, which New Englanders owned at least as frequently as the Geneva version.[2] The Bay Colony suppressed a Cambridge edition of the *Imitatio Christi* in 1669, though a 1658 Leiden edition would find its way into Harvard College Library by 1723. The merchant John Usher imported a salacious novel, *The London Jilt,* a pornographic classic, *Venus in the Cloister* and the Earl of Rochester's libertine *Poems.*[3] Massachusetts and Connecticut ports were officially closed to Catholic, Quaker, and Baptist books, but Benjamin Lynde, a future Massachusetts chief justice, had acquired copies of Dryden's agnostic poem, *Religio Laici* (1682) and his allegorical apology for Catholicism, *The Hind and the Panther* (1687) shortly after their publication.[4] Such importations imply that the ultimate constraint on the books that the colonists read was not their local, Puritan preference, but rather the conditions governing the English trade. This was regulated by the Licensing Act of 1662, in force to 1679, when it lapsed for six years, and again from 1685 to 1695, when it lapsed altogether.[5]

The Licensing Act certainly complicated existence for English Catholics and Nonconformists, but it also enforced trade privileges that went back to the beginnings of the Stationers' Company; the only new element was the enactment of these privileges by Parliament, instead of by royal decree. In the colonies, too, the licenser's propriety and the printer's property went hand in hand; if anything, the licensed printer preferred more, not less, prior restraint on his trade. Serjeant Samuel Green in Cambridge treated his license to print English as a privilege from which the printer of Indian, Marmaduke Johnson, should rightly have been excluded. Timothy Green would not settle for a mere monopoly over Connecticut printing; he demanded and got a contract guaranteeing him £50 a year – more than the salary of the deputy governor – and a free supply of paper. The Boston merchant John Usher secured a seven-year privilege on his edition of the 1672 Massachusetts Laws, apparently to protect it from overprinting by Samuel Green, the colony printer.[6]

The colonial press, especially in Cambridge, thus took on some of the features of a mint, setting an official seal of authenticity on a text. The market for books was a separate matter, of secondary concern to the authorities, and managed by merchants and booksellers. New England's characteristic separation of printing from bookselling owed something to its institution of censorship, which divided the world of the covenanted from the world of the commercial, "a plantation of religion," as the minister John Higginson insisted, from "a plantation of trade." The colonies' abandonment of this ideal, pilloried as a shameful "declension" in many an election sermon, is a tale of two cities, a gradual triumph of Boston merchants, royal governors, and the English Board of Trade over the Cambridge press, the General Court, and the "New England Way" of its Congregational churches.[7]

Technologically, Boston and Cambridge were roughly on a par: from 1639 to 1692, there were one or two presses operating in Cambridge; from 1675 to 1713, one to three presses in Boston; and in New England as a whole down to 1713, there were usually two, and occasionally three or four presses. During this period, Boston presses printed 81 percent of the New England editions still surviving, and in only half the time it took Cambridge to print nearly all the rest: with 361 editions in Cambridge, of which 116 are now lost, we may compare 48 editions in New London, of which 23 no longer survive, and some 1,239 editions (including separate issues of the *Boston News-Letter*) in Boston, of which 96 have perished.[8] Despite uncertainties in the assignment of lost editions, the measure of Boston's commercial importance seems assured.

Intellectually, no Boston imprints have the stature of the Bay Psalm Book (1640), the *Platform of Church Discipline* (1649), or the Eliot Indian Bible (1661–1663), all of them first printed in Cambridge, and yet these early monuments were oddly specialized.[9] The Cambridge press contributed nothing to medicine, science, or technology, and little to belles lettres, politics, or news; its production centered on ecclesiastical and municipal laws, Indian texts, and practical divinity. It printed no schoolbooks but catechisms, and most of its poems were funeral elegies that the mourners cast in the grave; even regular sequences of blank forms, the ubiquitous staple of later printers, date only from the 1680s. The exceptions that are sometimes urged are unconvincing: Is *God's Terrible Voice in the City of London* (1667) – an account of the Great Fire and plague of 1665 by the London minister Thomas Vincent – really "the first American medical work"? Is the Earl of Winchilsea's *True and Exact Relation of the Late Prodigious Earthquake & Eruption of Mount Aetna* (1669) the "prototype" of "Eye Witness News"?[10] The Eye that witnessed and the Voice that spoke in these events was divine.

Boston's strength was in history and biography and in its sheer uncovenanted diversity: Thomas Thacher's *Brief Rule* for dealing with "the small pocks or measels" (1678); Benjamin Harris's almanacs, his *Publick Occurrences* (1690), and *Protestant Tutor Enlarged* (1685); *The New England Primer Enlarged* (1691) and *The New England Psalter* (1682), long-time staples of the trade; to say nothing of *Pilgrim's Progress* (1681). How did Bostonians ever live without *The Names of the Streets . . . within the Town of Boston* (1708)? How did they wage war – and they fought continually – without *An*

Abridgment of the English Military Discipline (1690)? A number of these titles, including the *Abridgment,* were reprints of London properties, but the colonial editions were often "enlarged" or, in the case of the *Abridgment,* improved for the colonial market. The editor (Benjamin Harris?), who engagingly ascribed it to that Protestant martyr the Duke of Monmouth, decorated the title page with a cut of the royal arms and the pious motto, "God Save KING William & QVEEN Mary"; the recency of their ascent to the throne had caught the printer short, but he made do with the (barely recognizable) arms of Charles I.[11] These Boston imprints are, quite simply, the first of any practical importance for the lives of "the Common People of New England" to whom Thacher addressed his broadsheet.

The ascendancy of the Green family provides a technological link between the two cities. This "dynasty of printers," as it is often called, owed their genes to a government monopoly. "Sergeant" Samuel, the founder of the family fortunes, had five sons, three of whom had no innate inclination for printing: Joseph became a tailor, Jonas a mariner, and Samuel Jr. carried on "a convenient way of trading" and cattle ranching in Hartford and later, New London, Connecticut, for about six years before his father forced him to return to Boston to take over its printing in 1681.[12] The Greens eventually secured the contracts for Massachusetts, Connecticut, New Plymouth, and New Hampshire, and they gratefully internalized the values of these masters. Bartholomew, the most productive and least prolific of his clan, operated from 1685 to 1732, ever loyal to this past. He "always spoke of the wonderful spirit of piety that prevailed in the land of his youth with a singular pleasure," his obituarist reported, and was "cautious of publishing anything offensive, light or hurtful" even after the licensing regime had loosened. A certain lack of enterprise accompanied these beliefs, which Isaiah Thomas, that Revolutionary patriot and empire-builder, found puzzling: "He [Bartholomew] was the most distinguished printer of that period in this country, and did more business than any other of the profession; *yet he worked chiefly for the booksellers* [emphasis added]."[13] That was no way to get ahead in 1776, but Bartholomew appears as the printer of some 1,073 entries in the on-line North American Imprints Program (NAIP), about a quarter of all the titles printed in the continental United States down to his death in 1732, nearly all of them printed for the colonial government, booksellers, or private customers. Here is a concrete explanation of his "singular pleasure" in the "wonderful spirit of piety" of early New England.

Cambridge and Boston Presses

Our records are exceptionally complete for the Cambridge press because it was a tool of government and of John Eliot's mission to the Indians, on which the authorities reported progress to the sponsoring English agency, the New England Company. The first press and £60 worth of paper belonging to it were also the subject of a lawsuit by the rightful owners in 1654 against Henry Dunster, president of Harvard College, who managed it for the authorities.[14] This documentation, and the majesty of its product for the early church and state, have naturally won the Cambridge press the affection of later bibliographers, despite the much more varied and commercially valuable production of Boston.

Jose Glover, a wealthy Surrey clergyman, brought over the first press and secured the services of Stephen and Matthew Day, a locksmith and his son from Cambridge, England, possibly to operate it. He died on the passage over, however, his plans died with him, and the management of the press fell to Henry Dunster, the new president of Harvard, who married his widow in 1641. The General Court treated the press as Harvard property from the start, and the college later claimed title to it and "all its impressions" since its arrival.[15] Nevertheless, Glover's heirs sued Dunster in 1654 for an accounting of the profits and recovered £20 for the press and £30 worth of paper, amounting to 120 reams. This seems to be a judgment that Dunster had managed the press as their stepfather and guardian during their minority, and not as president of Harvard, an office in any case he had resigned in 1654 when he sold the press to the college.[16]

This record, unfortunately, leaves many questions unanswered. The college steward Samuel Green had leased the press for 10*s.* a sheet, on the decease of Matthew Day in 1649; yet if the college owned "all the impressions," why would Green pay for printing them? All that seems clear is that the college, Green, and the colony were entangled in a common public enterprise, though Green moonlighted from time to time, just as employees today abuse the office xerox and the company letterhead. Well into the eighteenth century, the college printer will not be held to his bargains, if they pinch him, and the government was surprisingly lenient on violations of the law by the printer of the New England Company if he promised to reform.[17] Government, college, and Indian printing were never carried on at arm's length, but collusively. Downy private enterprise only just peeps forth from beneath these sheltering wings.

Glover's plans for his two indentured servants are not recorded. Stephen had only contracted to serve for two years and immediately afterwards left to explore for black lead in the valley of the Blackstone River. He strongly resented his brief stint as prototypographer of British North America and demanded and got extra compensation for it from the colony. The literature of emigration, moreover, might lead us to believe that the colony wanted locksmiths far more urgently than printers; perhaps Jose Glover planned to operate the press himself. A late tradition reports that the Days were "assisted" by Gregory Dexter, a London printer who had moved to Rhode Island in 1643.[18] This transient initiation may have sufficed to teach them the "mystery" of printing, but the authorities made little demand on their time, and all the early printers combined more important occupations with occasional stints at the press. The elder Green, indeed, was generally known as "Serjeant Green" from his joy in the maneuvres of the Ancient and Honorable Artillery Company, a Boston militia; Samuel Jr., his better-equipped Bostonian son, was "Printer Green."

The peculiar type, faulty spelling, and frequent misprints of the Bay Psalm Book (1640) prompted its historian George Parker Winship to joke that it "looks the part that the fates assigned it to play"; yet the type was english (14 pt.), "a very good letter," in Isaiah Thomas's opinion, and the composition was not much worse than London's rather low standard.[19] The signatures follow an English register of twenty-four letters, including *W*, whereas London books followed a Latin alphabet of twenty-three. The Days also set the running-heads afresh for every sheet as though they were the first words on the page, occasionally making the catchwords "catch" with them. These are hardly faults, but they fairly illustrate the Days' innocence of London practice.

A press was symbolic of larger, more plaintive needs, one suspects, than the need for printing. The image of New England that enticed the settlers over changed from a welcoming paradise to a "howling wilderness" as the reality struck home;[20] the press was a visible sign that they had never left – perhaps even a promise of return. In 1669, when a Royal Commission was challenging the validity of the Bay Colony charter, President Charles Chauncy anxiously addressed the New England Company, begging them to transfer the Indian press and its types to the college. He wrote in Latin, to make sure they saw the point:

> we fear (alas!) that if the printing press fall to wreck, or in any wise fail us, and the Characters be taken from us, not only, to begin with, will America be without printers, & the Academy with its Scholars suffer damage in the progress of its Studies, & our very meetings with opportunity for taking Degrees be hindered, but also the Common weal & the Civil laws passed for the general good will, to the unspeakable, almost irreparable, loss of the Christian Religion and the Churches of the whole Community of New England, utterly perish & come to destruction.[21]

His concern for the commonweal was genuine enough, at a time when England had unleashed the Clarendon Code against his coreligionists and dispatched a commission to review the charter and administration of Massachusetts. The presidential rhetoric, however, surely exaggerated the needs of Harvard College, which had subsisted on a meager annual diet of two broadside *Theses* and *Quæstiones* and a sixteen-page almanac since 1639 – a total of from two to two-and-a-half printed sheets a year. All the printed texts assigned to the students were imported from Europe; others they copied out. They commonplaced their reading, and they wrote out the college laws and school-texts in manuscript, multiple copies of which still survive (Fig. 4.3).[22]

Besides these anxieties, justified or unjustified, the proliferation of printers in the aftermath of the Indian Bible would have worried the president. The project grew out of John Eliot's mission to the Massachusett Indians. In 1659 the New England Company had unleashed a second press and Marmaduke Johnson, a competent printer, on a colony long accustomed to the unskillful and subservient Samuel Green. Eliot carried out the translation with the assistance of two converts, Job Nesutan and John Sassamon, and printed it with the help of a third, James Wowaus, known as James the Printer. In 1661 1,500 copies of the New Testament were printed, of which 200 were provisionally bound up in limp vellum; and 1,000 copies of the Old Testament in 1663, of which 40 copies were sent in sheets to England for presentation to the officers of the company, and other dignitaries, bound in full morocco, or to be lodged with learned institutions. As of August 1664, only forty-two complete Bibles had been bound in America, and the binder was complaining that he could not afford to bind any more.

The size and speed of the project were unprecedented. The first edition alone (including the metrical psalms) required 353 reams, more paper than the entire output of the press down to 1660, and it was completed in only three years. Its effect on its intended audience is not much contested: Samuel Eliot Morison called it "the most notable – and least useful – production of the press at this period"; other historians have often seen it as an instrument of domination over an ambivalent and demoralized group of Indians – even James the Printer later joined King Philip, the leader of a native insurrection in 1675.[23] The binding of 200 New Testaments suggests that Eliot had converted no more than 200 families by 1661, and few of the surviving Bibles have an Indian provenance. It seems that production was calculated to ensure an ample future supply after Johnson had returned to England, and certainly the only occasion for a second edition was the wanton destruction of most of the first edition in King Philip's War.

Johnson declined to return to England, however, and launched into initiatives of his own. The first trained printer in the colonies, he had been apprenticed to the printer John Field of Cambridge, England in 1645 and freed in 1652. Johnson was a constant thorn in the side of the commissioners who supervised the progress of the Bible: he sought "to draw away the affections" of Green's daughter, though he had a wife still living in England, and he "absented himselfe" from the press;[24] when he returned to England in 1664 with instructions to buy a new supply of type for the "improvement" of the Indian press, he bought more type and a third press on his own account, which remained idle and unlicensed long after its arrival. There was simply not enough work for two printers without the Bible, and both Johnson and Green, for sheer want of copy, began to reprint London pamphlets, completing some fourteen exceptionally vendible titles in 1667–1668 before the magistrates investigated. The magistrates may have objected to the use of the college and Indian presses for private profit, they may have felt that colonial reprints were a kind of piracy, or they may simply have rejected commerce as such. No official order suppressing this promising line of new titles is recorded, but it ended abruptly in 1668, and surviving copies are suspiciously rare.

Green and Johnson were thus cast onto other shifts, one to earn and the other to protect his living. Their first instinct was to lighten the competition: Johnson petitioned the General Court for permission to operate his own press in Boston, and Green counterpetitioned to suppress his rival's operations in Cambridge. Despite the perfect symmetry of their requests, neither obtained his wish. For a while John Eliot, who felt an uneasy responsibility for Johnson's predicament as the Indian printer who had no Indian to print, tried to supply or translate enough for his support. Eventually, Johnson gave up the unequal effort and entered into partnership with Green in late 1668. In 1671, the partnership broke up, and Johnson began to work for Edmund Ranger, Joseph Farnum, or John Usher, and Green for John Tappan, John Ratcliffe, or William Avery, all of them in Boston.

"In 1672," says Winship, summarizing this development, "all at once, smaller shops specializing in books and stationery hung out their signs."[25] It is a pretty thought, but based solely on the deceptive evidence of imprints. Ratcliffe had been working as a binder since 1662, and as we shall see, neither Avery, Tappan, nor Farnum specialized in books and stationery, though they commissioned books. Hezekiah Usher was a merchant who had occasionally paid for both colonial and London printing since 1647 (Fig. 3.1). His son John took over the business in 1663.[26] When the English bookseller John Dunton visited Boston in 1686, John was his main competitor.

The printers, however, had broken out of the cage where the magistrates had confined their craft. In 1673, Harvard leased the Indian press for 30*s*. a year to Johnson (a bitter blow to Green); and in 1674, the magistrates finally accepted the *fait accompli* and permitted Johnson to set up a press in Boston. His triumph was brief: he died a few months later, and his latest imprint was still dated from Cambridge, but there was no turning back. Despite a final petition by Samuel Green to lock up printing again in Cambridge, the magistrates allowed John Foster, a Harvard graduate, to purchase and operate Johnson's press. In Green's opinion, he was "a young man, that had no

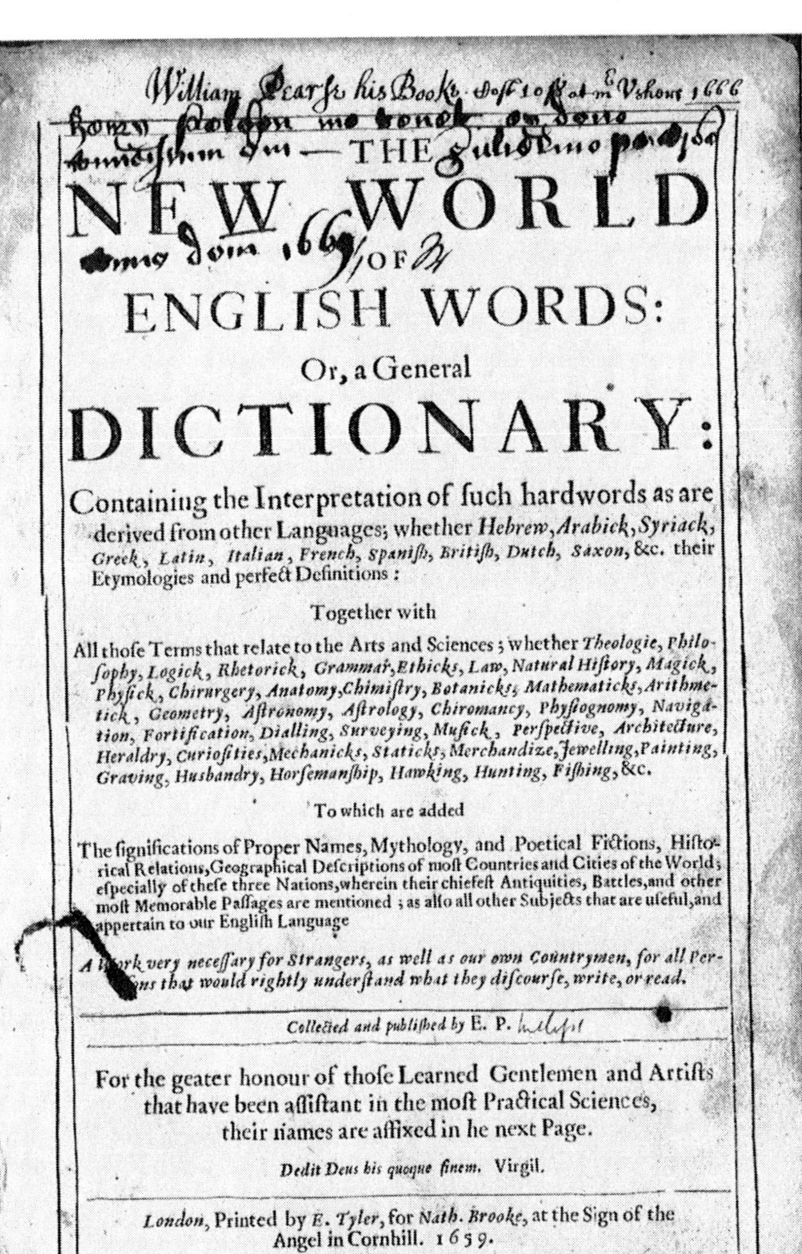

THE

NEW WORLD

OF

ENGLISH WORDS:

Or, a General

DICTIONARY:

Containing the Interpretation of ſuch hardwords as are derived from other Languages; whether *Hebrew*, *Arabick*, *Syriack*, *Greek*, *Latin*, *Italian*, *French*, *Spaniſh*, *Britiſh*, *Dutch*, *Saxon*, &c. their Etymologies and perfect Definitions:

Together with

All thoſe Terms that relate to the Arts and Sciences; whether *Theologie*, *Philoſophy*, *Logick*, *Rhetorick*, *Grammar*, *Ethicks*, *Law*, *Natural Hiſtory*, *Magick*, *Phyſick*, *Chirurgery*, *Anatomy*, *Chimiſtry*, *Botanicks*, *Mathematicks*, *Arithmetick*, *Geometry*, *Aſtronomy*, *Aſtrology*, *Chiromancy*, *Phyſiognomy*, *Navigation*, *Fortification*, *Dialling*, *Surveying*, *Muſick*, *Perſpective*, *Architecture*, *Heraldry*, *Curioſities*, *Mechanicks*, *Staticks*, *Merchandize*, *Jewelling*, *Painting*, *Graving*, *Husbandry*, *Horſemanſhip*, *Hawking*, *Hunting*, *Fiſhing*, &c.

To which are added

The ſignifications of Proper Names, Mythology, and Poetical Fictions, Hiſtorical Relations, Geographical Deſcriptions of moſt Countries and Cities of the World; eſpecially of theſe three Nations, wherein their chiefeſt Antiquities, Battles, and other moſt Memorable Paſſages are mentioned; as alſo all other Subjects that are uſeful, and appertain to our Engliſh Language

A Work very neceſſary for Strangers, as well as our own Countrymen, for all Perſons that would rightly underſtand what they diſcourſe, write, or read.

Collected and publiſhed by E. P.

For the geater honour of thoſe Learned Gentlemen and Artiſts that have been aſſiſtant in the moſt Practical Sciences, their names are affixed in he next Page.

Dedit Deus his quoque finem. Virgil.

London, Printed by *E. Tyler*, for *Nath. Brooke*, at the Sign of the Angel in Cornhill. 1659.

Figure 3.1. [Edward Phillips], *The New World of English Words* (London, 1659 [i.e., 1658]); inscribed "William Pearse his Booke. Cost 10*s.* at m[ist]er Vshers 1666." The earliest known evidence of Boston bookselling, apart from imprints. At the end is a booklist of eighty-nine titles in print and twenty-six "ready for Printing"; 10*s.* was also the price bound in London. Wing (2nd ed.) P2068 (variant state, with imprint correctly dated 1658). Courtesy of Jerome Anderson, Boston, Mass.

skill of printing but what he had taken notice by the by," but it was skill enough for him as it had been for Green, and before his untimely death in 1681 he had produced the first printed portrait, of Richard Mather (Fig. 3.2), and the first printed map of New England.

His widow sold the press and its equipment to Samuel Sewall, then at the beginning of his career as merchant; the General Court granted him the "management" of the press and prohibited others from setting up a second press without their permission. Though Sewall actually printed a catechism and a sermon on his own – and proudly dispatched some hundreds of copies of the catechism to his native town of Bishop's Stoke in England – he ordinarily "assigned" the operation of the press to others: John Ratcliffe, James Glen, Samuel Green, Jr., and Richard Pierce. Green moved to Boston from New London in 1681 and took over the government printing from his father, who had previously shared it with Foster.[27]

In 1684, when Sewall became a magistrate of the General Court, the court released him from the "management" of the press, which he sold to Green. Benjamin Harris later described it as "the best furnished PRINTING PRESS, of those few we know of in America," and its fonts included the long primer Greek and pointed Hebrew that Johnson had cadged from his employers, as well as a pica black letter that was first used in 1686.[28] Green petitioned the General Court for permission to succeed Sewall as "manager" in 1685,[29] but their decision is not recorded and the evidence of imprints is confused. In 1685, Green printed the New Plymouth Laws and began an abortive edition of the Massachusetts Laws, but Pierce printed William Adams's election sermon. The revocation of the colony charter and the advent of the Dominion of New England threw the colony into turmoil, and when the air cleared in 1686, Pierce was appointed the government printer for the Dominion of New England.[30]

Little is known about Pierce beyond his bare name in imprints, which begin in 1684, when he was presumably working under Sewall's "assignment," though the imprints do not say so. In his history of early Massachusetts printing, George E. Littlefield supposed, logically enough, that Pierce got the government press along with the government contract, but if so, he certainly did not acquire Johnson's types and ornaments.[31] An entrenched bibliographical dogma holds that presses may be distinguished by their stocks of type and ornaments; by this criterion, we may assume that the Dominion allowed Pierce to set up a press of his own in 1685, an assumption that, as we shall see, helps explain the continuity of printing in 1690, when Johnson's press was destroyed.

In 1686 Pierce cut a seal for the Dominion, and in 1688, a rather crude royal arms, for use at the head of proclamations – a public identification with Governor Edmund Andros's regime that would soon cost him his con-

Figure 3.2. John Foster, "Richardus Matherus," ca. 1670. The earliest state of this woodcut portrait, signed by the engraver. By permission of the Houghton Library, Harvard University.

tract.[32] The printing of the Massachusetts Laws was suspended while the General Court haggled over the drafting of an article on "Courts" and collapsed with the arrival of Andros, who preferred to engross them on parchment; in the end, the colonists (who had no intention of obeying them) cunningly complained that they did not know what the law was.[33] The Dominion fell in 1689, and a provisional Council of Safety took up the reins of government, leaving the future of the colony hanging before order was finally reimposed by the new charter in 1692. In the interim, the Council of Safety restored the government printing to Samuel Green, Jr., and after Green's death in July 1690 transferred it to Benjamin Harris and John Allen. Pierce continued printing down to 1691, when he either worked as a journeyman for Harris and Allen, as he had previously done for Sewall, or left Boston, or died.

At the Cambridge press, Serjeant Green had apprenticed his younger son Bartholomew in the early 1680s, when he needed help with a large (2,000 copies) edition of the Indian Bible; Bartholomew appears as a partner with his father in Cambridge imprints from 1691, about the time when his indentures should have expired. He seems to have split his time between his father's office in Cambridge and his brother Sam's in Boston, where he completed some government orders in August 1690, after his brother's death. The business of the Cambridge press shrank to printing Harvard commencement exercises, an annual almanac, and an occasional Indian title, and Serjeant Green finally closed it down in 1692. Cambridge had never been able to support two printers for long.[34]

Samuel Green Jr.'s press was destroyed by fire in September 1690 and, though Bartholomew saved some of the type, Harris and Allen kept possession of the only remaining press in Boston. Bartholomew Green did not finally receive permission to settle in Boston until June 6, 1693,[35] and he presumably used their press in 1692 to print Samuel Lee's *Great Day of Judgement* and, with Allen, Cotton Mather's *Blessed Unions*. The latter imprint foreshadows Harris's return to England in 1694, when Green and Allen took over the press and the government contract. Green himself had only one press, as appears from the inventory of his estate (1733), where it was valued at £15; and Allen had no other press before 1707, when he set up printing on his own. Harvard's two presses remained idle after 1692, the "Indian College" that housed them was torn down in 1698, and printing would not be permanently reestablished in Cambridge for more than a century.

Despite the plethora of printers in imprints, then, Isaiah Thomas is probably correct to say "there had never been more than two printing houses open at the same time in Boston" before 1700.[36] Green and Allen protected their monopoly by voluntarily declining to print any "Books of Controversy" without the approval of the lieutenant governor or their "particular Friends and Imployers," Increase and Cotton Mather. This became clear from a public scuffle over the printing of a reply to the Mathers. The *casus belli* was a *Manifesto* (1699) by the newly founded Fourth (Brattle Street) Church, a liberal congregation that admitted members without a public relation of their conversion – deviance from "the New England Way" that Increase Mather attacked in *The Order of the Gospel* (1700). When Green refused to print the church's anonymous riposte, its principals resorted to the press of William Bradford in New York, adding some venomous remarks on the Mathers' control of the press in a preface.

Prior restraint of free speech had certainly loosened, since critics of the New England Way no longer had to emigrate in order to put their attacks in print, but the colony had always followed a more liberal standard for imports than for native printing. Solomon Stoddard's *Doctrine of Instituted Churches* (1699), defending the indiscriminate admission of parishioners to Holy Communion, and Robert Calef's *More Wonders of the Invisible World* (1700), attacking the Mathers' hushed handling of the Salem witchcraft trials, were printed in London. William Bradford, in Philadelphia, printed *The People's Right to Election* (1689), an attack on the Connecticut Charter government by the eccentric ex-minister of Wethersfield, Gershom Bulkeley, though Bulkeley's sequel, *Will and Doom,* remained in manuscript down to the nineteenth century.[37] Later, in New York, Bradford printed George Keith's Anglican responses to the venerable Samuel Willard (1702) and Increase Mather (1703). All of these pieces circulated in Boston, prompting Increase Mather to lament that the glory of New England had departed, but the pattern of foreign attack and native reply was at least as old as John Norton's *Heart of N-England Rent* (1659).

Legally, the control of the press had been transferred from the General Court to the governor, which at least ensured that New England did not observe a peculiar standard of public decorum: the *Boston News-Letter* (1704–1775) and almanacs were long "Published by Authority," and Samuel Shute affixed his imprimatur to books as late as 1719 during his unhappy tenure as governor. The importation of controversial literature was one thing, however, and the admission of a hostile press into the colony was another. A "wicked company of Manifesto-men," Cotton Mather learned in 1703, "a year or two ago, procured a Press and Letters, to be sent for, unto London," but Governor Dudley apparently denied permission to operate it, and they were obliged to sell the plant to Bartholomew Green and John Allen.[38] There was no officially appointed "manager" of the Boston press after 1692, but with the help of Green and Allen, the Mathers held all the cards; from 1695 down to 1713, the only printers in all of New England were the Greens or their associates.

Timothy Green, the youngest and laziest of Sergeant Samuel's sons, began to print books in 1700 and sold them at a shop in Middle (now Hanover) Street in the North End, near Second Church, where the Mathers presided. Perhaps at first he used Green and Allen's office, where he was certainly at work in 1700, but later he may have taken over the "Manifesto-men's" press. He continued printing, specializing in the Mathers' writings, down to 1707, when Allen, who had disappeared from Boston imprints for three years, opened a third office in Pudding Lane near the State House.

This competition from their former associate seems to have disconcerted the Greens. Bartholomew proposed to assign the Connecticut government printing to Timothy, if he would move to New London, but Timothy declined, declaring that he did not wish to exchange "a certainty for an uncertainty," and Bartholomew was obliged to equip the colony with his brother-in-law, Thomas Short.[39]

To judge by his imprints, Timothy avoided competition with Allen by concentrating on bookselling after 1708, a year in which he printed only one piece, Cotton Mather's *Winthropi Justa.* "It has been said of him," Thomas remarked, "that whenever he heard a sermon which he highly approved, he would solicit a copy from the author, and print it for his own sales" – adding, severely, that he thus ended up with bushels of unsaleable sermons.[40] Timothy's record of printing in Boston can make this gossip more precise: of eighty-two editions that he printed between 1700 and 1714, sixty-three (76 percent) were written by the Mathers, and almost all of these were heavily subvened by Cotton and his friends.[41] Timothy printed nine of the eleven pieces that Cotton published in 1704, when he ran what was virtually an in-house press for Second Church. The Great Fire of 1711 destroyed Allen's shop, Short died in 1712, Timothy moved to New London two years later, and the Mathers switched their custom to Thomas Fleet. The destruction of the stock of most Boston booksellers in the Great Fire must have been some comfort to Bartholomew, but two new printers sprang up in Allen's place.

Boston Booksellers

The Greens and the Mathers are good examples of what the historian Edmund S. Morgan called Puritan "tribalism," associations that fitted smoothly into their intellectual and contractual commitments; they may even have been related by marriage.[42] The younger Greens' businesses were infinitely more diverse than that of their father, whose "spirit of piety" they looked back to. Like his father, Bartholomew was set in motion by his customers' interests and ambitions, but the number and interests of these customers had proliferated, and his "spirit of piety" was sometimes at odds with theirs. Just as New England town meetings, unable to reach total agreement on the location of a meeting-house, divided into different towns and separate meeting-houses, so printers, if they were unable to work under a single roof, set up shop as distant as practicable from one another:[43] in Cambridge and Boston (1675–1691); in the north, south, and middle of Boston (1700–1713); in Massachusetts and Connecticut (1708–1714). The printers form a striking contrast with the booksellers, a group of much more varied religious and social beliefs, who clustered together, companionably, beneath the Boston Exchange.

The Exchange was a wooden structure in the marketplace, also known as the "Town House," erected under a bequest of the merchant Robert Keayne in 1657. On the ground floor, where most of the booksellers had their tiny stalls, was an open concourse where the merchants gathered to exchange news and transact business. Above it were rooms for the legislature and the town library. The route connecting Boston to the country led into the square by Cornhill (now Washington) Street, where it met King (now State) Street ascending from the harbor and the merchants' warehouses. The booksellers' imprints refer to the London Coffee House, the Blue Anchor Inn, and the "Old Meeting House" (First Church), ranged about the outside of the square. Every Thursday, a market day, the preachers of Boston and the adjacent communities preached a lecture in rotation at First Church, providing a prime source of texts for the booksellers. The justices met in quarter sessions in the "Court Room" of the Blue Anchor Inn, and merchants exchanged news and read the latest gazettes at the London Coffee House.

These addresses advertise the booksellers' valuable association with the center of church, state, and commerce, but there were a few outliers. Duncan Campbell, down at Dock Square at the northern end of Cornhill, was the postmaster, but his son John, the publisher of the *Boston News-Letter*, moved closer. Nicholas Buttolph set up shop a little farther out on Marlborough Street (another section of Washington Street) next to his brother-in-law Robert Gutteridge's coffeehouse. There, at the corner of School Street, the pupils of the famous Boston schoolmaster Ezekiel Cheever, merchants interested in foreign news, and the congregation of Third Church came together.

The books that were printed in Cambridge and Boston were published over a wide area, from New Hampshire to the Barbados, privately, officially, and commercially. Increase Mather's *Essay for the Recording of Illustrious Providences* (1684) and his *Two Plain and Practical Discourses* (1699) were simultaneously issued in Boston and London. The largest editions of books distributed outside their place of production were the early laws and election sermons of Connecticut, New Plymouth, and New Hampshire, all of them printed in Boston or Cambridge for official distribution in these jurisdictions. John Eliot's *Communion of Churches* (1665) was "not published, only committed privately to some godly and able hands to be viewed, corrected, amended, rejected, as it shall be found to hold weight in the sanctuary balance, or not," according to his preface; his collection of *The Dying Speeches of Several Indians* [ca. 1683–1685?] was "printed, not so much for publishment, as to save charge of writing out of copyes for those that did desire them." The imprint of neither piece announced that it was to be had in Roxbury. None of Cotton Mather's sermons acknowledged (as they might have, in England) that they were "printed for the author"; many of them were, however, as some naughty people pointed out, to his irritation.[44]

When such private interests found their way into imprints, they show that Boston printers served sundry other communities. The imprint of the church covenant of the First Church in Salem stated that it was printed "for themselves and their children" in 1680. Nathaniel Porter of Windsor, Connecticut, sponsored a sermon of his pastor's, in 1707; and "Capt. Benjamin Marston, Merchant in Salem," commissioned an almanac for the latitude of the Barbados in 1712. *A Thankfull Remembrance of Gods Mercy . . . at Quabaug or Brookfield* (1676) was "published by Capt. Thomas Wheeler" of that town, a little west of Worcester. Nehemiah Walter, a Roxbury minister, delivered a sermon on *Unfruitful Hearers Detected,* "published by some of the hearers" under that title in 1696. Clearly, these are cases of private printing; even if Capt. Marston hoped to get something for his almanacs, he was obviously not in a regular way of bookselling.

The largest genre of such sponsored texts was the catechism, printed both in New and Old England. The earliest such New England printing was Edward Norris's, "published for the use of the Church of Christ at Salem" in 1649. Other catechisms were printed in Boston or Cambridge for the churches at Chelmsford (1657), Hampton, New Hampshire (1663), Norwich, Connecticut (1679), Newbury (1661) – by James Noyes, and popular enough to be reprinted in 1684 and 1714 – Farmington, Connecticut (1684), and even Bermuda (1699). Before the Boston press allowed an alternative venue to Cambridge in 1675, New England ministers also resorted to London, where the catechisms of Ezekiel Rogers of Rowley, John Norton of Ipswich, Thomas Shepard of Cambridge, Richard Mather of Dorchester, and John Davenport of New Haven were printed.[45]

When the person who sponsored the book did not identify his occupation, he may easily be mistaken for a bookseller, though in fact this might not have been his chief calling. John Tappin (or Tappan), a feltmaker, died worth £5,000, of which only £16 were in "Bibles and other books" (possibly a private library); he had married Mary, widow of William Avery, and William, Mary, and John each appear in one or two imprints (1672, 1679, and 1682). William was a physician who set up the first apothecary's shop in Boston. William Gibbons, who reprinted Samuel Stone's catechism in 1699, was a Boston feltmaker. Obadiah Gill was a shipwright who, according to Cotton Mather, clubbed together with other godly persons to sponsor worthy books, including, of course, Cotton's;[46] he appears in two imprints. Elkanah Pembroke, by profession a weaver but repeatedly described as a "shopkeeper" in his numerous lawsuits, also appears in two imprints (1699, 1712), the second printed by William Bradford in New York, when Pembroke had moved to Newport, Rhode Island. Joseph Farnum (otherwise Farnham), a shopkeeper, and Thomas Baker, otherwise unknown, "printed" only one title apiece; another shopkeeper or stationer, Joseph Wheeler, is master of only two imprints, one no longer extant.[47]

Private persons, like Gill and his associates, not only "printed" (i.e., sponsored) books but also distributed them. In 1704, Sewall, after three years of steady benefaction, dispensed a remainder of five dozen copies of Samuel Willard's *Fear of an Oath* (1701), one dozen of them to Nicholas Boone, "for whom" they were originally printed, and yet Sewall appears in only one imprint after 1684.[48] Cotton Mather saw print as a means of preaching to a wider audience than Second Church, though this "audience" did not always find the message congenial. "I will now have my Agents in several parts of the Countrey, to lodge the Book where it is intended," Mather wrote in 1711; his agents ranged from good Mr. Penhallow in Portsmouth down to Connecticut, and by 1706 they were distributing some fifty dozen sermons a year.[49] Such pious work was not necessarily limited to distributing New England editions. The best customers for Dunton's imports in 1686 were ministers, and John Usher imported London books for the Reverend Thomas Shepard II in Charlestown, and John Wise in Chebacco (Essex) in quantities that suggest that they were also acting as distributors and possibly trading for profit. Governor Thomas Prence of New Plymouth left a parcel of a hundred psalmbooks and fifty "smale paper bookes" (exercise books), to be bound and distributed to the four Old Colony schools that he had recently established.[50]

The wealth of the trade varied enormously, from Hezekiah Usher's estate of £15,538 down to Michael Perry, who died some hundreds of pounds worse than nothing. In a Boston tax list of 1687, we find six booksellers assessed from 1*s.* 10*d.* (Samuel Phillips) to 3*s.* (Benjamin Harris and Joseph Brunning); Samuel Sewall, a merchant and magistrate, paid 14*s.* 10*d.* or roughly five times as much. John Usher, merchant, treasurer of the Dominion of New England, and later lieutenant governor of New Hampshire, was even wealthier, though he, too, kept his shop under the Exchange. Books may have formed a relatively small part of Usher's or Sewall's business, which stretched across the Atlantic to London, the Azores, and down to the Caribbean. Because they had credit in London, however, they could provide English books to the humbler members of the trade. Other Boston booksellers who appear in only one or two imprints may well have been persons who dealt principally in English books: James Cowse, a stationer, or Job How, who came over with Dunton, perhaps qualify here. Samuel Sewall Jr. was certainly apprenticed to a bookseller, though he appears in only two imprints; Richard Wilkins, a major customer of Dunton's, appears in only four, and Hezekiah Henchman (d. 1692), father of the leading printer and bookseller of the next generation, in none. John Hayward, a scrivener whom Sewall reproved for wearing a wig, seems to have dealt in schoolbooks in a small way, to judge from his account with Usher, but he appears in no imprint.[51]

If we define a bookseller as someone who traded sheets with other booksellers, the core of the trade was small. Their stock may be represented by the inventory of Michael Perry's estate in 1700, containing a wide selection of both English and American imprints. Ignoring single titles in the inventory, some of which may form Perry's personal library, his stock may be divided into schoolbooks; Bibles, psalters and New Testaments; local lawbooks; practical divinity; and miscellaneous titles. The schoolbooks for instruction in English, including catechisms, were all American reprints of English properties; those for grammar schools were imported from London. There were no English lawbooks, which were little cited in colonial courts before the Dominion of New England, though Perry had supplied some to John Usher and the Dominion in 1689. Anything resembling English literature – *Pilgrim's Progress,* chapbook histories like *Fortunatus* and the *Seven Champions of Christendom* – was all printed in England, though *Pilgrim's Progress* had already received an American edition in 1681. Otherwise, literature is represented only by Latin schooltexts of Ovid, Virgil, or Cicero. There is an interesting group of practical handbooks on navigation, accounting, and husbandry. Newsbooks (in which remarkable providences, books of wonders, and execution sermons may be included) divided fairly equally between London and Boston printing. Perry had a stock well worth browsing, even in a shop of less than thirty-six feet square.[52]

On Michael Perry's level, as of 1695, we might include Duncan Campbell, Nicholas Buttolph, and Perry's cousin Benjamin Eliot. Somewhat earlier, there was Joseph Brunning or Browning, Benjamin Harris, Samuel Phillips, and John Griffin; and somewhat later, Nicholas Boone, who eventually also undertook printing, Eleazar Phillips, and Timothy Green. Samuel Phillips, who had advertised a very similar stock to Perry's at the end of Solomon Stoddard's *Safety of Appearing at the Day of Judgment* (1687), moved into a much larger "Brick Shop" (240 square feet) next to the Meeting House in 1694; probably he was switching his business to imports, which required more space to display. Brunning was the son of Mercy Brunning, an English refugee bookseller in Amsterdam, Harris was a Baptist, Campbell was from Scotland, John Griffin was the third person to be buried by *The Book of Common Prayer* in Boston, and Dunton himself was Presbyterian. This is a remarkably "mixed" group of people for seventeenth-century New England, a settlement of tribalist landsmen who found even French Huguenots a little strange, but the trade pitched its tents on the wide-open Atlantic, where King Street led down to the harbor and out to the great world.

Benjamin Harris may be singled out from his fellows as a bookseller who was also an author and publicist. A London bookseller and radical Protestant with a hatred of the Catholics, especially James, Duke of York, he had already been in trouble with the English authorities during the Popish Plot and Exclusion crisis for printing the *Protestant Intelligence* (1679–1681) and Henry Care's *English Liberties* (1682). After James succeeded to the throne in 1685, Harris prudently moved to Boston, opening a bookstore and the London Coffee House near the Exchange. Coffeehouses had been one of the main venues for political discussion and the distribution of unlicensed news. His *Publick Occurrences* (1690) may or may not be the first Boston newspaper (only a single number issued before it was suppressed by the Boston authorities); his *Protestant Tutor* (2 eds., 1682; reprinted in Boston, 1689), a violently anti-Catholic tract for children, is supposed to be one of the ancestors of the *New England Primer*; and he was the publisher of some overtly political pieces (then a new genre in Boston) attacking the Andros regime and praising the Prince of Orange. In 1687, he launched a series of Boston almanacs by John Tulley of Saybrook, Connecticut, that shocked and entertained Bostonians by prognostications of the imminent death of Louis XIV, instead of the sophomoric verse and disquisitions on comets that filled their Cambridge counterparts. It would be nearly thirty years before another printer, James Franklin, ventured into public political controversy.[53]

Richard Wilkins, too, is less typical of the Boston trade. He came over from Limerick with his son-in-law John Baily, a Nonconformist who had been ejected from his ministry there and settled in Boston around 1683. It seems unlikely that Wilkins was ever actually a bookseller in Limerick, as Thomas supposed, since John Baily stated that new books were unobtainable there. Dunton, with whom he had been in correspondence, does not describe him as a bookseller, and his business, which he carried on until his death in 1704, may have been fairly indiscriminate, in cloth, haberdashery, books, and other dry goods.[54] Only four Boston imprints bear his name: his son-in-law's farewell sermon to the congregation in Limerick (1690), with a preface by Increase Mather; two pieces by Increase Mather (1693, 1696); and Samuel Sewall's *Phænomena Quædam Apocalyptica* (1697). The intensely focused authorship of these pieces indicates that Wilkins published them more out of conviction than for commercial profit, and their dates cover only a small part of his bookselling career.

A little eighth-sheet broadside "Advertisement" mounted at the back of a Harvard copy of Cotton Mather's life of John Eliot (1691), printed for Joseph Brunning, describes Wilkins's stock of books. The Harvard cataloguer assumed that the "Advertisement" was published together with the book, but it is mounted on a flyleaf autographed by that melancholy poet "Michael Wigglesworth Ejus Liber 1700," the probable date of the original sprinkled sheep binding. According to Dunton, Brunning was "a Compleat Bookseller . . . [who]'d promote a good Book whoever printed it,"[55] yet it seems unlikely that he would ever have advertised another bookseller. Wilkins probably inserted the flyer when he bound and sold the book to Wigglesworth. It describes a business chiefly devoted to providing books for the learned and gentry, who "may be Supplyed with Various Treatises both of Polemical and Practical Divinity; & Commentaries upon the Scriptures; together with useful Treatises in Grammer, School-Books, Chyrurgery, Merchandize, Husbandry, Astronomy, Geometry, Law, Military Affayrs, and other Subjects; all at such Reasonable Rates, as have not heretofore been afforded in these parts of the World [italic reversed]." Wilkins stocked a range of subjects normally confined to English printing; it finds no counterpart in Perry's inventory and is considerably broader than the collection of divinity that John Dunton advertised in his catalogue of 1684 and probably imported to Boston.

At the other end of the economic spectrum from Wilkins, James Gray of Charlestown was a peddler who, according to his obituary (1705) "used to go up and down the Country selling of Books." The inventory of his estate consisted in eight bags of silver money (£591 1*s.* 2*d.*), a gold ring (£1), and "old clothes, books, & some small haberdashers ware" (£5). In addition, his executors sued to recover "£200 current silver money" from Edward Thomas, merchant, and Mary, widow and administratrix of David Jesse, goldsmith, in 1707.[56] Gray may have operated as a banker as well as a peddler. He is the only named representative of that occupation in our period, but it did not die with him, for Cotton Mather attacked it in 1711: "the Minds and Manners of many People about the Countrey are much corrupted, by foolish Songs and Ballads, which the Hawkers and Pedlars carry into all parts of the Countrey."[57] These foolish objects were probably imported, which Gray could well have afforded to do. His astonishing hoard of silver came from a cash business, whereas Perry and other booksellers on his level dealt for credit, and might be paid in "marchantable [i.e., salt] beefe," or pork, Indian corn, wampum and other "commodity currency."[58]

At the bottom of the trade were bookbinders: Richard Wilkins, whose stock was dominated by English books, probably did less bookbinding than Michael Perry. The first person to be called a bookbinder is one John

Sanders, a name, no more, recorded 1636–1651; John Ratcliffe, possibly a Plymouth (England) bookseller who appears in a single English imprint (1662), and Edmund Ranger are the first binders whose work is identifiable today. Both, as we would expect, appear in imprints, which they commissioned in order to provide the raw material for their occupation, Ratcliffe's dated 1664–1682, and Ranger's, 1673–1679. Ratcliffe, in a petition of 1664, complained that he had removed to New England in hopes to bind Indian Bibles, and yet he had lost money by it since "in things belonging to my trade, I here pay 18*s*. for that which in England I could buy for four shillings, they being things not formerly much used in this country."[59] Ranger was more successful, opening a tavern in 1697, which he kept to his death in 1705. The occupation of bookbinding is otherwise only sporadically attested: William Nowell and Thomas Rand, bookbinders, petition to settle in Boston in 1672; Bartholomew Sprint in 1685; but there is no evidence that their petitions were granted.[60]

In seventeenth-century New England, there were few genuine booksellers outside of Boston. Primers, hornbooks, almanacs, catechisms and "other Small books" were generally available – from Eliza Cutler, for instance, the widow of a Charlestown merchant, in 1694; or from the merchants William Pynchon of Springfield and Joseph Hawley of Northampton, who supplied the grammar school of Hadley, Massachusetts in the seventeenth century.[61] The merchants and ministers of Salem, Norwich, Brookfield, Farmington, and Windsor announced themselves in imprints of sermons and catechisms because there was no one else to distribute these books for them. Salem merchants like George Corwin (d. 1685) and Timothy Lindall (d. 1698) sold such staples as paper, inkhorns, psalmbooks, Bibles, primers, and almanacs; we rarely find less generic books, such as those in the estate of the Salem merchant William Bowditch (d. 1681), which Harriet S. Tapley mistook for a private library. The estate of Colonel Bartholomew Gedney (d. 1698) in Salem had "tools for a bookbinder," but his library consisted of a small stock of divinity, law, physic, history, and military matters, which were typically imported bound.[62]

The sale of anything more diverse than Bibles, primers, psalmbooks, and almanacs (the Waldenbooks of the seventeenth century) followed wealth and population density, the same factors associated with literacy. The Massachusetts General Court actually used these criteria to distribute the Laws of 1660.[63] The townsfolk of the neighboring communities came to market in Boston "more or less every day," when they crossed Roxbury Neck or took the Winnisimmet (Charlestown) ferry to exchange their produce for books and other urban goods. Salem, the other port of entry in Massachusetts, provided a smaller center for such commerce to the north.[64] Boston lay on the periphery of London, which in turn operated on the periphery of Frankfurt and Amsterdam in the heart of the European book trade.

Imports and Native Production

Bookselling was a risky business. Big winners like Daniel Henchman were few, and colonial trade in general thought exceedingly small, putting most of their capital into steady sellers. They financed their newspapers by subscription, and their hottest-selling items – execution sermons and captivity narratives – were short and issued in small editions. John Usher's edition of *Pilgrim's Progress* (1681) was a relatively sizeable book, but already by that date a sure steady seller. Daniel Henchman's secret editions of the Bible and New Testament, traditionally dated in 1752, though probably printed in 1731,[65] were certainly the earliest New England projects with a substantial element of risk. When colonial booksellers gambled, in short, they tended to gamble on London titles, and preferably on an imported parcel of 20 to 50 copies than on a colonial reprint of 500.

The lapse of the Licensing Act in 1679 depressed the London book market, according to both John Dunton and Richard Chiswell: Dunton and three other booksellers – Andrew Thorncomb, Job How, and Benjamin Harris – and the printer John Allen all came over in the 1680s to try their luck in Boston, the first such exodus of the London trade; Robert Boulter and Richard Chiswell, who stayed behind, were offering books to the colonists at cut-rate discounts of from 25 to 33 percent off. The number of London imprints soared, spurred on by the Popish Plot, and Nonconformist voices were once more heard in print, but profits dropped, as they would do again in 1695 after the final lapse of the Licensing Act, when there was a second exodus to the English provinces. Whatever its other virtues, freedom of the press does not pay: the margin of profit shrinks as the market grows more competitive.

The invoices of shipments sent between 1678 or 1679 and April 1685 by Boulter and Chiswell to a single Boston merchant, John Usher, are the only direct evidence we have of this transatlantic commerce in the seventeenth century.[66] Some of these were wholesale orders for ministers and other persons who do not appear in imprints; others he or his clerk Michael Perry retailed to the colony and the citizens of Boston. Booksellers like Samuel Phillips or Richard Wilkins were probably more important customers than the likes of Joseph Brunning, Nicholas Buttolph or Benjamin Eliot, whose trade lay more in colonial imprints, which they commissioned, exchanged, and bound. Boulter sent books and stationery worth £445 11*s.* 6*d.* from 1679 to 1683. John Dunton's Bostonian customers owed him some £500 by 1686, when he took a "ramble" to America to collect; he began business in 1681 and, assuming they had paid something on account, his sales must have at least equalled Chiswell's, who sent over £567 worth of books in roughly the same period.[67] In the years when these three booksellers' shipments overlapped (1681–1682), they shipped an annual average of over £300 worth of books and stationery to Boston. Itemized invoices for this period do not survive, but Chiswell's invoices for 1683–1685 record a total of 3,544 volumes worth about £295 and stationery worth about £35. One may conclude that between 3,500 and 4,000 volumes were annually exported to Boston in the 1680s, and that they sold out, since orders would not otherwise have continued.

For a comparable segment of colonial production, one may exclude the almanacs, session acts, and broadsides recorded in NAIP, which leaves only eighty-two titles printed in Boston and Cambridge from 1681 to 1689. Their edition sizes ranged from the revised Indian Bible (1680–1685) of 2,000 copies, to catechisms and primers of perhaps 1,000 copies, down to 500 copies or less (all the rest), amounting to some 45,500 volumes in all. These almost certainly took longer to sell than imports, however. Samuel Sewall's purchases in the eighteenth century are one indication of their rate of sale: in 1728–1729, the last year of his life, he distributed some 400 sermons, and there still survives a bill from Benjamin Eliot for purchases of nearly 190 copies of seven sermons, bound and/or gilt, worth £31 19*s.* 6*d.* One of these books had been printed twenty-eight years earlier, and clearly the edition was not yet exhausted; the median imprint date of his purchases fell around 1716.[68] To take another indicative example, at the end of Daniel Travis's *Almanac for 1711* [1710], there is a list of fifteen titles "Printed for, and are to be Sold by Nicholas Boone," the earliest of which was printed in 1700; a substantial number must still have remained "in print" to be worth advertising. Assuming an average edition-life of twelve years, and that sales over this period were steady, we can estimate that only 19,585 copies of the titles printed between 1681 and 1689 had actually sold by the end of that period, an average of 2,177 volumes a year. Sales of local production would thus have amounted to no more than 60 percent of imports.

The 3,500 to 4,000 volumes imported annually at Boston in the 1680s was only part of the total for New England, moreover. From 1700 to 1713, British customs records show that an average of 68.81 cwt. (or 7,607 lbs.) of books were exported annually to New England: the figures range from 19.5 cwt. (2,184 lbs.) in 1705 to 116.5 cwt. (13,048 lbs.) in 1710. The conversion of these weights into books is necessarily conjectural, but we are probably safe in assuming that most of them were bound and that the proportions of folios, quartos, and small formats was roughly the same as in Usher's invoices of 1683–1685. A trial "shopping basket" of forty late seventeenth-century books made up in these proportions (1:3:36) weighed 41.5 lbs., averaging about a pound a volume.[69]

The sixfold variation between the smallest and the largest annual eighteenth-century figures should caution us not to rely too confidently on a few, probably favorable years in the 1680s. Indeed, the figure for all of New England in 1705 was only half as large as the number of books annually imported for Boston alone in the 1680s. When demand was strong, Boston booksellers relied more heavily on English than on local editions, even for colonial titles. The history of two such texts, the Bay Psalm Book, a steady seller, and Michael Wigglesworth's spectacular success, *The Day of Doom,* is instructive in this regard. In both cases, their editions divide between Boston and London, but for very different reasons.

The Cambridge press printed 1,700 copies of the Bay Psalm Book in quarto, 1640, followed by an unauthorized London reprint in 1647; Matthew Day printed 2,000 copies of a revised edition in octavo for Hezekiah Usher in 1651. The next colonial printings were an "eighth" edition for Samuel Phillips in Boston, 1695, and a "ninth" for Michael Perry in 1698. In between fall three London editions of the revised text printed for Richard Chiswell in London. John Usher imported a hundred copies of Chiswell's 1680 edition for Thomas Shepard II fifty of them unbound, in quires, and seventy bound copies on his own account. Besides these London editions, there were three surreptitious printings, ostensibly "for Hezekiah Usher of Boston," without date. These deceptive psalmbooks are often found bound with eighteenmo Bibles having an engraved imprint "Cambridge, 1648," but actually printed by Joachim Nosche in Amsterdam, ca. 1675 to ca. 1680.[70] The psalmbooks were certainly not printed in Boston, however, and if, as most authorities suppose, they were printed around the date of their Bibles, they were probably not printed for Hezekiah Usher, who had left business in 1663 and died in 1676. The Bibles may well have been a shipment "bound . . . in holland" that Usher's agent John Ive dispatched in 1675, half of which were spoiled "by sending them to Barbados first."[71]

The imprint of these psalmbooks was modeled on the 1651 Cambridge edition's, which the "eighth" and "ninth" Boston editions implicitly assume to be the first: Michael Perry, as John Usher's former clerk, should have been intimately familiar with the contraband trade of his master. Richard Chiswell told John Usher that the smallest number of the *New England Primer* worth printing in London was "Ten Gross"; the known editions of the Bay Psalm Book were only a third larger, and we may fairly take their size as a norm.[72] Eight editions of 2,000 copies each between 1651 and 1698 means that 16,000 copies sold over forty-seven years at roughly 340 copies a year. Better yet, the Bibles with which they were bound did not come with a complementary *Book of Common Prayer,* unlike most of those printed in England.

The psalmbook was a steady seller, an exceptionally profitable one if, like Chiswell or the Ushers, you have the capital for 2,000 copies, but it sold in a very different way from *The Day of Doom*. Psalmbooks were quotidian and ubiquitous, carried by most merchants in New England; *The Day of Doom* had far fewer outlets, and even its author thought its sale miraculous: "It pleased the Lord . . . to give vent for my books & greater accepta[n]ce then I could have expected: so yt of 1800 there were scarce any unsold (or but few) at ye yeers end."[73] It was the more miraculous since the first edition, of which only a fragment survives, was printed at the author's expense in Cambridge, 1662; the second (Cambridge, 1666?), surviving in three fragmentary copies, appeared at the expense of the printer or bookseller. The numbering of the "fifth edition" (Boston, 1701) reflects the appearance of three London editions in 1666, 1673, and 1687, and the private character of the first edition. All of the English editions reprint the unrevised text and, to judge from the provenance of their copies, sold mostly in England. The "first edition" for the London trade, in short, was 1662, but for Boston, 1666.[74]

Did nearly 1,800 purchasers, then, as is generally believed, each end up with a copy of *The Day of Doom* in only a year? It seems unlikely, even supposing that the copies were stitched, in paper wrappers – and there were certainly not enough binders to issue them bound. Wigglesworth no doubt had consigned his stock in varying quantities among his friends and the Boston book trade, but he could hardly have known how many of these were still on their hands at the end of the year. The trade, after all, declined to enter this lucrative market for some four years, presumably because they still had copies to sell. With the full apparatus of the state, Connecticut was unable to dispose of a much smaller edition of its 1673 Laws in a like period, and Cotton Mather and his associates were unable to give away more than 600 books a year in 1706. Either by pious benefactions or by bargain and sale, the distribution of *The Day of Doom* must have continued over at least four years, before the edition was exhausted.

Nevertheless, an average sale of 450 copies a year is an astonishing record, which even the Bay Psalm Book cannot match; it is nearly twice the number of copies of the 1660 Laws that the General Court hoped to sell in the Greater Boston area in a similar period. The aftermarket for the "trade" edition must have been correspondingly smaller (500 copies?), and no more were required for thirty-five years. In 1688, Judge Sewall presented his cousin Stephen Greenleaf with "the Catechise, Day of Doom, &c. bound together in a good Cover"; his language strongly suggests that Sewall had this tract volume bound locally from sheets of the 1666 Cambridge edition, which was therefore still "in print."[75] At that rate, the Bay Psalm Book's Tortoise would have caught up with our Hare in only six years, if they had started selling together. The numbering of the "fifth edition," moreover, acknowledges the continuing popularity of the work in London, which a changed, more "English" Boston recognized and rewarded. The society that would later pour out editions of *The Day of Doom* had outgrown the society that produced it; indeed, the work would become a children's book, but it was written in a very different spirit. Like *Gulliver's Travels* or *Robinson Crusoe, The Day of Doom* ultimately moved into a new market niche, without which it might have remained a day's wonder.

The success of these exceptional titles sets an upper limit on the size of the Boston market, which could absorb 450 copies of a single title in a year, or some 3,500 volumes of an imported assortment, including parcels of from twenty to fifty copies of the more popular titles. Most seventeenth- and early eighteenth-century colonial editions were printed in small runs and sold off slowly – perhaps at the rate of only forty copies or so a year; only a few English titles achieved this rate, but the titles that were printed in the colonies were not very numerous either. The 600 sermons that Cotton Mather and his cronies handed out each year was about a ninth of his printers' annual production. The booksellers almost certainly realized a higher profit on colonial sheets than on English books, and at lower risk, since their printing was frequently subsidized. Colonial printing also reached a broader segment of the population than most English books, but the wonderful variety attested by library catalogues, inventories, and advertisements was nearly all printed in Europe, as, indeed, was the Bible itself, before 1731.

The Ubiquity and Poverty of Print

If one had to characterize print culture in New England in brief, one might call it ubiquitous, but poor, and shallow: "poor" because monotonous – only a few titles were widespread; "shallow" because few colonial titles were ever reprinted, and most of its European editions were of recent date. The Harvard College Library catalogue of 1723 records the cumulated gifts and bequests of seventeenth-century ministers and magistrates. Despite some large English benefactions from Theophilus Gale and Sir John Maynard, no more than a fifth of the 3,516 volumes date from before 1600. Only 5.6 percent date from before 1560, and before 1501, we find only eight incunables in ten volumes. All of these incunables perished in a fire of 1764, and St. Augustine's *Opuscula plurima* (1491), which the Rev. Thomas Prince purchased in 1742, may be the first surviving incunable with an authentic American provenance (see Fig. 4.2).[76]

Colonial libraries soon descended from these dizzy heights. The average minister's "study" might have a few hundred titles, some in the three learned languages of Latin, Greek, and Hebrew. The commonest description of a library in seventeenth-century Essex inventories, however, is just "a Bible and other books," the others being between five and ten volumes, when they are enumerated. When the editions can be identified, they are usually English, written by the authors venerated by an older generation, and a number reappear in later estates, as they are handed down in ever-shrinking parcels.[77] There were probably colonial imprints as well, too little valued to be worth listing (and no inventory was required of estates of less than £5).

"Other books" were rather more prevalent and varied in urban Middlesex than in rural Essex,[78] yet we need not conclude that our Essex Man felt especially poor or deprived. The Bible was print enough: indeed, Puritans honored the Reformation doctrine of *sola scriptura* to the point of arguing that Protestants should read little else. Together with the Bible, translations of Lewis Bayly's *Practice of Piety* (abridged), Richard Baxter's *Call to the Unconverted,* Thomas Shepard's *Sincere Convert,* and a few primers and catechisms sufficed for the Indians. What was sauce for the native goose was sauce for the European gander. Ann Hopkins, daughter of a Connecticut governor, "was fallne into a sadd infirmytye . . . by occasion of her givinge her selfe wholly to readinge & writinge," Winthrop noted (she showed Anabaptist symptoms); John Higginson recommended the "remarkable providence" of "godly Mr. Sharp" (as he later became) who, misled by "a strong inclination & eager affection to books" and a "stranger's" gift of an attractively unfamiliar title, found himself overcome by "a strange kind [of] Horror both of Body & minde" as he read. Thereafter he confined himself "to reading the Bible & other known good books of Divinity." Judge Sewall's bookplate cautioned (in Latin) that Life without Literature is an Image of Death, But Life without Christ is Worse than Death.[79] The Puritans honored learning and encouraged widespread literacy, but they feared unlicensed "bookishnes," even at the level of a deacon like Mr. Sharp.

Since the Bible served as a manual of law, literature, history, and warfare, as well as a primer for reading and, of course, religion, the sphere of "the book" remained wide, but its content was remarkably uniform, and print was used as sparingly as iron in colonial hoes, ploughs, and shovels. Blank forms are among the commonest productions of the colonial press, as ubiquitous in their way as Bibles (Fig. 3.3). "In examining the records of the colonial communities," remarks L. C. Wroth, "one is appalled by the amount of legal and official business that was transacted in this new country, but whoever else may have been the sufferer by this frequent lawing, it is certain that it was not the printer."[80] And he goes on to instance the first production of the Cambridge press, the Freeman's Oath. As with all such "firsts," there is a powerful implication that the press continued to pour out more editions of the same, but peculiarly, the Massachusetts presses never printed another edition. Later oaths (1676, 1678, 1692, etc.), which Winship

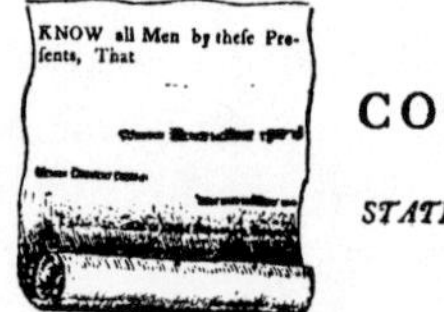

SAMUEL COOPER,

At his OFFICE, *STATE-STREET,*

Opposite the North-east corner of the State-House,—
Has for SALE, *the following*

B L A N K S,

Which are executed in the best manner, on good Paper, and sold by the *sheet, quire* or *ream,* as CHEAP as at any place in the Commonwealth *viz*—

J U S T I C E S.

WRITS and Summonses on the Confession Act,
Executions on the same act,
Writs and Summonses not exceeding £. 4,
Executions not exceeding that sum,
Subpaenas or Summonses for witnesses,
Agreements for Reference,
Acknowledgment of Debt,
Recognizances civil,
——— criminal,
Certificates to the Common Pleas upon the Parties not agreeing to a Reference,
Complaints on suspicion of stolen Goods, being secreted, and Search Warrants thereon,
Records for Judgments in Civil Actions, above £. 4,
Records for Judgments in Civil Actions not exceeding £. 4,
Records for Judgments on Default in Actions above £. 4,
Records for Judgments on Default in Actions not exceeding £. 4,
Records for Judgment on Trials for Theft,
Records for Judgment on Trials for Assaults,
Judgment on Trials for Assaults,
Appeals from Judgment of Justices, in Civil Actions,
Complaints against and Warrants for apprehending Riotous Persons,
Commitments for being concerned in a Riot,
Complaints against and Warrants for apprehending Persons guilty of profane Cursing and Swearing,
Complaints for fear of Mischief, and Warrants for apprehending,
Commitments of Persons threatning Mischief, who refuse to find sureties for their appearance at Court,
Complaints against and Warrants for apprehending absconding Seamen,
Commitments for such *as have absconded,*
Complaints against Paupers and Warrants for conveying them before a Justice,
Warrants for removing Paupers,
Complaints and Warrants for apprehending in cases of Assaults,
Commitments on conviction of an Assault and a refusal to comply with the sentence of the Justices,
Examination and Warrants for apprehending in cases of Bastardy,
Commitments on refusal to give security for appearance at Court, in cases of Bastardy,
Complaints and Warrants for Defamation,
Complaints against Thieves, and Warrants for apprehending them,
Commitments on charge of Theft for refusing to recognize,
Commitments on conviction of Theft, for refusing to comply with the sentence of the Justice,

P R O B A T E.

Administration Bonds,
——— Letters,
Warrants for Appraisement,
Guardian Bonds for Minors,
——— Letters under fourteen years of age,
——— Letters above fourteen years of age,
Letters Testamentary,
Bonds for paying Debts and Legacies,
Bonds to exhibit Inventory, and settle Accounts,
Guardian Bonds, for persons non compos mentis,
[illegible] ditto,
Orders for distribution of Personal Estate,
Orders for distribution of Insolvent Estate,
Certificates to the Judicial Courts when Real Estate is necessary to be sold for payment of Debts,
Bonds and settlements of Real Estate,
Bonds for Sale of Real Estate,
Warrants appointing Commissioners on Insolvent Estates
Citations,
Warrants for setting off Widow's Dower,
Warrants for division of Estates,

N A V A L.

Shipping Papers,
Policies of Insurance,
Bills of sale of Vessels,
Bills of Health,
Long Clearances, Short Clearances,
Coaster's Bonds,
Bills of Lading,
Charter Parties,
Permits to take on board,
Manifests, outwards and inwards,
Cockets,
Permits to unload
Coaster's Certificates,

A L S O,

Bills of Exchange,
Excise Certificates,
Blank, Bank Lists,
Deeds, both of the long and short forms
Quit-Claim ditto,
Mortgage ditto,
Bonds, Counter Bonds,
Complaints to Supreme Judicial Court for not entering Appeals,
Apprentices Indentures,
County and Town Treasurer's Warrants, against delinquent Collectors,
Articles of Excise and Impost,
Prices Current,
Bills of Sale,
Long Powers of Attorney,
Short ditto,
Lawyer's ditto,
Sheriffs Bail Bonds, Constables ditto,
Long Leases, Short ditto,
Coroner's Inquisitions,
Assessors Orders to Surveyor of Highways,
Assessors Warrants to Collectors of Town, County and State Tax, Excise Blanks &c. &c. &c.

Figure 3.3. Advertisement of blank forms, "sold by the sheet, quire or ream," by Samuel Cooper, *Independent Chronicle,* October 23, 1788. American Antiquarian Society.

describes as revised editions of the Freeman's Oath, and which Shipton and Mooney enter under Massachusetts (Colony), are in fact editions of the Oaths of Supremacy and Abjuration required by English law.[81] Instead of reprinting the Freeman's Oath separately, the magistrates appended it with other legal forms at the end of the colonial Laws, whence town clerks presumably promulgated it in manuscript. Even the oaths of Supremacy and Abjuration, moreover, were signed by groups, beginning at the foot of the document, and continuing on the back, as necessary. It is not clear whether each of the signers read the document individually, or whether it was read to them in a group before signing, but the latter seems more likely, if only to save time, paper, and print.[82]

As legalities comparable to these oaths, one might cite orders to the town constable to bring in a rate, which the town meeting would then subdivide among the constabulary, recording their individual responsibilities in manuscript. The earliest such printed warrant dates from 1679, and the treasurer of the colony would have required no more than thirty or forty copies a year, one for every township.[83] Printed orders to the constable to "warn" the inhabitants of the date for electing deputies to the General Assembly, or to pick jurors for the quarter sessions appear somewhat later in the Massachusetts archives. All of these orders differ from blanks that record transactions, such as recognizances, subpoenas, deeds, or letters of attorney, whose virtue lies in what Benjamin Franklin called their "correctness." The parties to the transaction want to be sure that they are following proper legal form, and print is their guarantee. Apart from bills of lading, whose earliest New England examples were probably printed in London, in my opinion (Fig. 3.4), transactional forms date from the Dominion of New England, 1686–1689. They reflect the heightened taxation, challenges to land titles, and insistence on "correct" English procedure introduced by Sir Edmund Andros. When the Andros regime fell, the parties resumed the use of manuscript subpoenas, only to return to printed forms when the 1692 Massachusetts Charter restored order.

The colonies experimented with various commercial or official schemes for distributing their laws, with uneven success. The 600 copies of the 1648 Massachusetts Laws were "to be solde at the shop of Hezekiah Usher in Boston," but over a quarter of the impression was still on the hands of the colony treasurer, Richard Russell, in 1651, "unvendible" because of later revisions and additions.[84] The General Court sent out the 1660 Laws to the four county recorders, with instructions to apportion them to their towns pro rata, by tax rate. Since Watertown paid £41 5*s*. of a total rate of £616 4*s*. 6*d*., and received 35 copies, we may estimate that 525 copies were so distributed: about 203 copies to Suffolk County, 154 to Middlesex, 151 to Essex, and 17 to

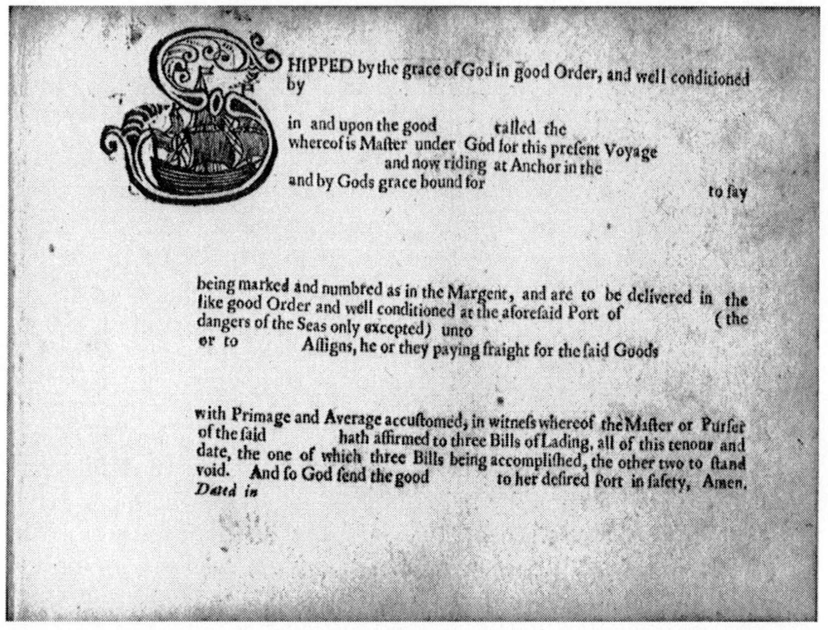
SHIPPED by the grace of God in good Order, and well conditioned by

in and upon the good called the
whereof is Maſter under God for this preſent Voyage
and now riding at Anchor in the
and by Gods grace bound for to ſay

being marked and numbred as in the Margent, and are to be delivered in the like good Order and well conditioned at the aforeſaid Port of (the dangers of the Seas only excepted) unto
or to Aſſigns, he or they paying fraight for the ſaid Goods

with Primage and Average accuſtomed, in witneſs whereof the Maſter or Purſer of the ſaid hath affirmed to three Bills of Lading, all of this tenour and date, the one of which three Bills being accompliſhed, the other two to ſtand void. And ſo God ſend the good to her deſired Port in ſafety, Amen.
Dated in

Figure 3.4. A bill of lading, printed in England (?); from a bound volume of bills belonging to Samuel Sewall and used by his successors down to the mid-eighteenth century. Courtesy of the Massachusetts Historical Society.

Norfolk. Hampshire County, in western Massachusetts, was only formed in 1662, but its three townships and their court may have taken a handful more. With twenty copies apiece for Portsmouth and Dover, New Hampshire, fifty for the "eastern parts" (Maine), and sixty-six official copies designated for magistrates, deputies, and county recorders, an edition of 700 copies is accounted for.[85] This scheme also proved unsatisfactory, however, for in 1670, the Court declared that "there is a great want of law books . . . and very few of them that are extant are complete," and in 1672 they returned to the private sector, granting John Usher a seven-year privilege on the edition, to keep the value up; nevertheless, Usher still had 190 copies unsold in 1675. Connecticut resolved that every family should buy a copy of the 1673 Laws, but even with this mandate, the constables were unable to collect and 400 copies still remained unsold in 1677.[86]

Even when towns could afford to lodge a copy in the hands of each constable and selectman, the constables might not pass along their copies to their successors; Watertown bought a fresh supply for this reason in 1697, but it is also clear that the constables were able to carry out their duties without them. In 1642, Massachusetts appointed a broadside *Capital Laws*, extracted from Ward's *Body of Liberties*, for the instruction of children: it was still "in print" in 1674, when Watertown duly ordered that "Each man heaue in his house a coppy," to be paid for out of the rates, as the law required.[87] Even this minimal, compendious summary, it seems, failed of its intended audience; the readers of the *Capital Laws* petered out with succeeding generations, and its provisions became obsolete.

None of this should be surprising. Knowledge of the law at a personal or local level is still generally imperfect today, and New England had its proper share of Dogberries and Shallows. Most laymen encounter the law through blank forms, not by reading statutes and decisions, and since the colonial judges themselves cited the Bible as a legal authority,[88] John Cotton's "Moses his Judicialls," unauthorized editions of which escaped into print at London in 1641 and 1655, was perhaps a more realistic "code" than the colony's *Laws and Liberties*. Otherwise, plaintiff and defendant crossed swords over a little quarter-sheet scrap of a subpoena, the only bit of printed law (when it was printed) that either of them would ever see.

Before the Glorious Revolution of 1688, the function of cumulated editions of the Laws was to establish the agreement of the magistrates and the deputies and to transmit it to the towns. The sessions acts, by which the cumulations were updated, were printed in editions too small for even this distribution, and probably served, like legislative bills, for internal use. The contents and arrangement of the lawbook strikingly resemble that of Michael Dalton's *Countrey Justice* (1618, etc.), a standard English handbook for justices of the peace: alphabetical by topic, with blank forms at the end, and for the most part concerned with criminal law. This format complicated revision of the law, since it obscured the historical context of the articles, but it better communicated their substance to a largely untrained magistracy and constabulary.[89]

After the Revolution of 1688, metropolitan authority brought about an "adjustment to empire," as Richard R. Johnson has called it, in the uses of print as in other matters. The colonial legislature now followed parliamentary procedure, where bills were read three times before being passed on to the governor and council for consent; and the validity of the law was subject to disallowance by the Board of Trade in London.[90] The laws themselves were now arranged chronologically, by session and regnal year, just like the English sessions acts and *Statutes at Large*. Benjamin Harris and John Allen adorned the 1692 Massachusetts Laws with a cut of the royal arms which, unlike Richard Pierce's pitiful effort, was engraved in England. Print now served the imperial function of communicating between the colony and the mother country, whose delegation of authority to the colonies was explicitly proclaimed by the inclusion of the royal charter in the lawbook. Other New England colonies followed suit: the first printing of the New Hampshire Laws responded to an order from the Board of Trade in 1698, not to a purely colonial initiative, and Massachusetts submitted a revised edition for the same purpose. Only Rhode Island resisted, sending an illegible manuscript "abstract" to gloss over its insubordination.

The "adjustment to empire" transformed even the meaning of colonial type faces. In England, the black-letter (or "english") face lingered on in a few books long after it had been generally superseded by roman: in laws, folio Bibles, and popular literature, like ballads and chapbook romances. In particular, an exceptionally large size (great primer, or 18 pt.), characterized the metropolitan printing of laws, whereas colonial laws had usually been printed in roman, english (14 pt.) or pica (12 pt.). The first New England printer to use black letter was Samuel Green, Jr., and he had little of it, since he was unable to set more than the initial words of paragraphs in blacks for his edition of the 1628 Massachusetts Bay Charter (1689), in pica. *A Vindication of Nevv-England* [1690?], ascribed to Increase Mather and Charles Morton, attacked the "Church of England" faction for their support of Andros, but the printer (Richard Pierce?) had no type of the proper size to express this invidious, "English" distinction. He therefore engraved "Church of England" in the characters proper to it on a woodblock. It seems an improbably laborious way of expressing his feelings for a mere pamphlet, especially since he was unlikely ever to use these words in the same way again.

The black-letter face had thus acquired a "foreign" connotation for the colonists. Time passed, however, the colonists took up wigs, drinking healths, celebrating Christmas, naming weekdays by their traditional, "pagan" names, and even acknowledging bishops and the *Book of Common Prayer*. English traditions and black letter became familiar. The publication of the law also took a new turn in 1704 with the *Boston News-Letter*, founded by the colony postmaster John Campbell. It was "published by authority," an explicit recognition of state property in "foreign intelligence,"[91] which Campbell had previously distributed to a select group in manuscript; and it regularly reprinted proclamations by the governor and council. It was printed down to 1707 by Bartholomew Green, and from 1707 to 1711, by John Allen.

In 1710, Francis Nicholson led an expedition against Port Royal in Nova Scotia, which capitulated without much of a fight. To celebrate the victory, John Campbell drew up an exceptionally expansive, twelve-page *Boston News-Letter* (October 30/November 6, 1710), containing Nicholson's journal of events and two of Dudley's proclamations, for a fast, and a day of thanksgiving. John Allen, the printer, had recently advertised his importation of "all sorts of good new Letter" from London, and the generous format of this victory issue gave him a brief chance to display his wares. The first proclamation was in the traditional great primer "blacks" (Fig. 3.5), which, however took up so much space that the next proclamation, after opening with a

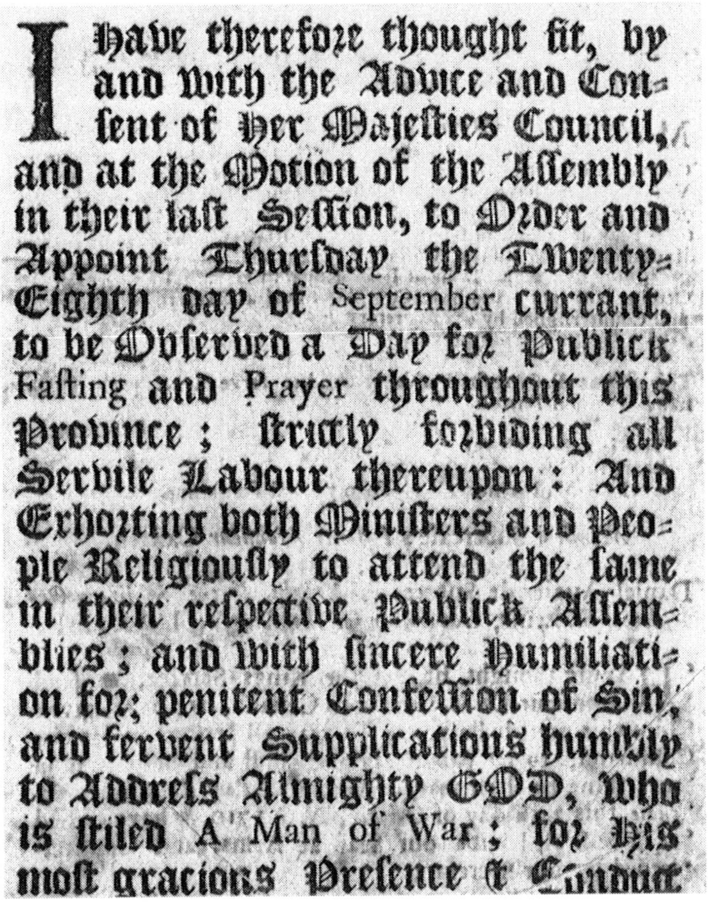

I Have therefore thought fit, by and with the Advice and Consent of Her Majesties Council, and at the Motion of the Assembly in their last Session, to Order and Appoint Thursday the Twenty-Eighth day of September currant, to be Observed a Day for Publick Fasting and Prayer throughout this Province; strictly forbiding all Servile Labour thereupon: And Exhorting both Ministers and People Religiously to attend the same in their respective Publick Assemblies; and with sincere Humiliation for; penitent Confession of Sin, and fervent Supplications humbly to Address Almighty GOD, who is stiled A Man of War; for His most gracious Presence & Conduct

Figure 3.5. "A Proclamation for a General Fast," preliminary to the reduction of Port-Royal, N.S., printed in the *Boston News-Letter,* October 30/November 6, 1710. The first legal text in the colonies printed in great primer blackletter, the size and face proper to it. Courtesy of the Massachusetts Historical Society.

paragraph of great primer roman, gradually dwindled in ever less vocal paragraphs to long primer (9 pt., or half the size). One can imagine Allen gloating "Just like in England!" before cringing back to his true provincial status.

Puritan New England, Richard D. Brown observes, controlled information hierarchically.[92] Print shared this structure, and not simply as a consequence of government licensing. From the populated shelves of Harvard College Library, down to the still numerous, but scantier collections of the Winthrops and the Mathers, English printing dwindled to the "Bible and other books" of rural Essex; colonial imprints descended from folio lawbooks and church platforms to local catechisms, almanacs, and sermons in small formats; literacy cadenced from writing to reading, from manuscript to print, from Latin to English to Indian. All of these hierarchical distinctions in the sources, uses, scripts, languages, quantities, and distribution of print mark out center and periphery, rulers and ruled, commercial and religious spheres. Because print was licensed and sanctioned, it was intimately associated with power, as it could not be under a "free press," serving "the diffusion of useful knowledge." The first step toward that distant nineteenth-century goal was often the advent of a second press and printers of enterprise like Marmaduke Johnson, Benjamin Harris, or John Allen. Prototypographers have held center stage far too long in our histories of printing. The Days, Greens, and Bradfords were neither Gutenbergs nor Caxtons, nor were meant to be, and we can only distort their achievement by isolating it from its English sources.

CHAPTER FOUR

Readers and Writers in Early New England

DAVID D. HALL

LITERARY CULTURE IN SEVENTEENTH-CENTURY New England was a child of long-lasting tensions that arose out of the hesitancies of the English Reformation. In the aftermath of Henry VIII's decision to break with the authority of Rome, the clergy and the English government were divided on how thoroughly Protestant the Church of England should become. Those who insisted on a purging of all Catholic "remnants" were moved to do so by the example of the Reformed (Calvinist) tradition, which some English clergy had encountered first-hand when they fled England during the reign of Mary Tudor (1552–1558). Regarding the English people as ignorant and undisciplined in matters of religion and most of the parish clergy as little better,[1] the reformers set themselves the task of bringing into being a cadre of university-educated ministers committed to fervent, systematic preaching as an instrument of change. Institutions like Emmanuel College, founded for this purpose in 1584, were the seedbed of a "spiritual brotherhood" that became increasingly numerous and effective in the early seventeenth century.[2]

The larger task of transforming the "mixt multitude" of the English parish into a zealous, godly people was less easily accomplished. In this campaign books were as crucial as sermons; as a latter-day activist observed, printed sermons were a public means of carrying the gospel to places where preaching did not reach. In spite of competition from many "profane" kinds of books, certain genres enjoyed a remarkable success, in one or two instances because specific books became widely used within the Church. This was the case with a new translation of the psalms in ballad meter, initiated by Thomas Sternhold during the reign of Edward VI and designed explicitly to displace "ungodly songs and ballades," which passed through some 500 editions by 1660, and with the vernacular Bible in whole or in parts, published in a variety of translations and some in smaller formats cheap enough to bring the cost within the reach of middling readers, who bought up 300 English-language editions of a psalter, or psalmbook, by 1640. Early in the reign of Elizabeth, other reformers introduced a repertory of pious ballads that, for a decade or two, enjoyed considerable success. Readers were also receptive to books of surprising length and substance that were advertised as guides to how to be a Christian. A notable example was Arthur Dent's *The Plain Mans Pathway to Heaven* (1601) – written, Dent declared, "to all of all sorts: I speak not to some few of one sort" – which went through twenty-five editions by 1640. "Cheap" forms of print, especially the many broadsides and tracts interpreting certain "wonders" as providential signs of God's impending wrath against an erring people, were much relished. Godliness and the appetite for sensation converged in chapbook "penny godlies" that dramatized the fate awaiting sinners.[3] Only a few years into the seventeenth century, the success of the reformers in the marketplace was properly cause for celebration: "yea . . . never such plentie of good and plaine bookes printed, never so good cheape."[4]

The modes of writing and reading that arose within English Puritanism (to name the reforming impulse)[5] and that the colonists who founded the New England colonies in the 1620s and 1630s brought with them were premised on a particular understanding of "literature" and the written word. Prefacing the term "literature" with the adjectives "usefull" and "good," Puritans insisted that the purpose of speech and writing was to communicate divine truth, a truth that was inherently transformative in how it affected sinful humankind. Utilitarian or "practical" in attempting change, good writing was also modeled on the archetypal patterns of pilgrimage, exile, suffering, and providential deliverance that were "the touchstone" for all of human experience. The Bible was the great source of these archetypes. In the "humble" speech of Jesus, the Bible also modeled a "plain style" of speech and writing that was best suited to the work of reform.[6]

This understanding of literature was deeply political, for it existed in conscious opposition to other possibilities.[7] The most important of these was the academic or humanist argument, dating from Aristotle and of great importance in the English Renaissance, that literature was artifice, a formal employment of rhetorical devices manipulated to achieve certain effects. A second, overlapping possibility was the frank appeal to pleasure that Elizabethan poets such as Philip Sidney voiced. A third was the stuff of traditional popular culture, the revels and rituals that were celebrated in countless ballads and stories. Puritans denounced these forms of writing and performance as ungodly and called on readers to forswear all such "idle" books – idle in the sense of diverting attention from the great end of life. In so doing the reformers were challenging both the workings of the market and a system of literary production that depended on the patronage of the court and aristocracy. The dedications in godly books were not to these patrons but to the figure of the "Christian reader." Implicit in this form of dedication was the assumption that literary authority flowed less from learnedness or worldly status than from service to the godly. In keeping with the latent populism of this politics, the reformers welcomed vernacular translations of the Bible and argued that the meaning of Scripture was so readily apparent "that not only the learned, but the unlearned . . . may attain unto a sufficient understanding of them." Meanwhile, some of their opponents fretted that ordinary people should not be trusted with the Bible; contrary to the strategies of the "spiritual brotherhood," who wanted to persuade large numbers of persons to change how they lived, writers who worked within the system of court patronage assumed that their audience was essentially personal (centrally, the person of the monarch) and private.[8] Despite much middle ground where moderates on both sides met, the opposition between these two systems of literary production was visibly manifested in ecclesiastical and civil censorship of the more "forward" or radical of the reformers and, in turn, their resort to underground or illicit publication.[9]

This politics of opposition and critique was but half the story, for it was always joined with a politics of regulation or control: godly writers understood the practices of writing, reading, and speaking as means by which ordinary people would be persuaded to act in certain ways. Always, therefore, writing, speaking, and reading were political in being vehicles for conveying a particular vision of collective life; always, too, the reformers were challenged from one side by radical Protestants who wanted to pursue a more "thorough" transformation of church and state "without tarying for anie," and, from another, by those who were contentedly conservative and cosmopolitan.

Literacy and Reading

The continuities of culture between the godly in England and New England included an important intersection of cultural and social history. In the course of making the Bible the rule of everyday life, the early English reformers had moved to secure its translation into the vernacular. Simultaneously they had urged that everyone learn to read. "If (as hath been showed) all ought to read the scriptures," the Elizabethan Thomas Cartwright declared, "then all ages, all sexes, all degrees and callings, all high and low, rich and poor, wise and foolish have a necessary duty therein."[10] Transplanted to New England, this argument for a broad-based *reading* literacy became embodied in a series of laws in the colonies of Massachusetts, Connecticut, Plymouth, and New Haven. The first of these laws, passed in Massachusetts in 1642, voiced the expectation that children, servants and apprentices should acquire the "ability to read & understand the principles of religion & the capitall lawes of this country" and empowered the selectmen of each town to "take account" of whether this was happening. A 1650 Connecticut statute specified that children should know "perfectly to read the english tongue" and that parents should "catachise their children and servants" weekly or otherwise ensure that they "learn some short orthodox catachism without book" (i.e., orally, by memorization). New Haven Colony required children and apprentices to "attain at least so much, as to be able duly to read the Scriptures, and other good and profitable printed Books in the English tongue." A beginning on the necessary fabric of institutions was made in 1647 when the Massachusetts government ordered that towns of fifty households appoint someone to teach reading and writing and that those of one hundred households or more add a "grammar" school, where Latin was taught, to the mix.[11]

The effects of these laws must not be exaggerated. Though indentures commonly specified that a master must teach his servant how to read, no law in any of the colonies but New Haven mandated that children learn to write or that they attend school for any period of time. Many did not, relying instead on instruction at home. Others went to unregulated (i.e., unlicensed) "reading" schools, some of which were run by women. The ability to write, a skill acquired far more commonly by men than by women, usually was gained in "general" schools with writing teachers, who often doubled as instructors in Latin and in certain situations also taught reading. Some of these schools did not admit women.[12]

This patchwork system worked relatively well, for the colonists were able to sustain a distinctively high rate of reading and writing literacy, far higher than in the seventeenth-century Chesapeake and in most parts of England. Using the signature-count method, Kenneth Lockridge has suggested that, as of 1660, 60 percent of adult males in the eastern counties of Massachusetts and 40 percent of the adult women were able to write; according to his calculations, by 1710 the figure for men had risen to 70 percent and for women, to 42 percent. Because reading was taught prior to writing, we may safely conclude that the ability to read exceeded the ability to write by a considerable margin. As in the Chesapeake, court records reveal the presence of persons who could read but not write (or, in some instances, not read handwriting); only a small number of the colonists seem wholly illiterate.[13] Even so, the leadership of the colonies became concerned in the late 1660s about the state of literacy. In 1668 thc Massachusetts General Court asked the selectmen in each town to report on enforcement of the laws that required children to be "taught to read perfectly the English tongue" and to learn an "orthodoxe chattechisme." According to a Massachusetts statute of

1679, towns were to appoint tithingmen charged with uncovering any deficiencies of "family government," including the duty of instruction. The returns from individual towns seem to have been reassuring; in Watertown, Massachusetts, periodic surveys during the 1670s turned up only two or three families in which children had failed to become literate. About the same time, the Connecticut General Court tightened the enforcement of its school laws, though systematic pressure on local communities did not really take hold in Massachusetts until the 1690s.[14]

Linked as the actions of the 1660s and 1670s were to the emergence of Anglicans, Quakers, and Baptists (who by 1665 had established an independent congregation in Charlestown, Massachusetts) and to a perceived restlessness among "youth," they may have had more to do with an ideology of social order the colonists shared with their Catholic and Protestant contemporaries than with any actual decline in literacy. In the context of the Protestant revolt against Catholicism, the mythic significance of becoming a literate, catechized, and Bible-reading people was freedom from "popish tyranny." Reading signified liberation – from sin, falsehoods, and unjust claims to authority. But in the context of a state-supported orthodoxy of the kind that prevailed in all of the New England colonies save Rhode Island, literacy, catechizing, and print were means of buttressing a moral order premised on the authority of parents, magistrates, and ministers. Hence the iconic function of certain forms of print, notably a Massachusetts broadside of 1642 listing a newly enacted set of capital laws. Among the steps taken by the selectmen of Watertown in the 1670s, when order and literacy were much on their minds, was to purchase enough copies of this broadside so that every household could own one. Hence, too, the endlessly reiterated association between households and literacy, for children who learned to read in a well-governed household were also learning the lesson, at once political and moral, of obedience to their superiors. *The New England Primer*, which came into general use after 1700, drove this lesson home in a series of aphorisms for children to memorize: "I will honour my Father & Mother. I will Obey my Superiours. I will Submit to my Elders."[15]

The rationale for teaching children to read was to start them on the path to knowledge of God, a knowledge contained, above all, in the Scriptures. It was also possible to gain this knowledge by listening to sermons and hearing the Bible read aloud. In one of his epistles St. Paul had declared that "faith cometh by hearing, and hearing by the Word of God," a verse reformers within the Church of England had interpreted as requiring ministers to preach frequently and to ground their sermons in an explication of the Bible. Any lay man or woman who absorbed a steady diet of sermons, as, year in and year out, most of the colonists did, was bound to acquire a fluency in Scripture and a similar fluency in the language of devotion or religious experience. Though we cannot establish the exact proportions between these two ways of learning, orality or speech was surely more important than reading or writing in the colonists' repertory of communicative practices. The spiritual relations that lay men and women gave in churches suggest as much, for the references to sermons far outweigh those to books and reading.[16] As in the Chesapeake, moreover, speech remained an important aspect of the political and legal system. Thus in early 1649 "the whole Towne" of Springfield gathered to hear "all the printed lawes" read aloud to them, as required by a Massachusetts statute.[17]

The written and the oral converged in practices that intermingled the two. As the literary historian Larzer Ziff has noted, the much-published Cotton Mather worked within an oral tradition in the specific sense of performing orally his printed sermons and, in some instances, of performing them extemporaneously.[18] Speech turned into writing, and writing into speech, when people in a congregation took notes on sermons that afterwards were read aloud in households. The spoken and the written also converged in the method of learning how to read, which consisted of chanting aloud and memorizing the contents of a primer or a catechism, genres that were based on the oral tradition of the liturgy.[19] At a deeper level, the significance of speech and hearing flowed from a theological understanding of Scripture as living speech, the spoken Word of God. Starting from the assumption that the revelation of God occurred through speech before being turned into writing, the colonists regarded the printed Bible as a "speaking" book and argued that extempore sermons were preferable to those delivered from a written text, or even notes. Accordingly, ministers were advised to preach their sermons from memory "in the demonstration of the Spirit."[20] Hearing, reading, and memorizing were thus intertwined with each other in ways that made them covalent as means of knowing God.

None of these practices worked in the absence of a spiritual capacity for receiving the Word. Appropriating a traditional distinction between first- and second-hand knowledge, Puritans theorized that hearing and reading Scripture were empty actions unless the "heart" or soul were engaged, which happened only when the inner self was open to the transforming power of the Holy Spirit. "Printed books will do little good," a minister wrote in 1666, "except Gods Spirit print them in our hearts. Gods words written with Ink will not profit, except they be also written with the Spirit of the Living God." Properly performed, the practices of reading and hearing became spiritual exercises that abetted the ever-necessary, ever-continuing process of self-examination. Reading was also a "duty" God had prescribed as a means of learning truth, or sound doctrine. Like all such duties, godly reading was a disciplined practice, a matter of routine, presumably daily, resort to the Bible and other worthy books. This very repetitiousness was predicated on the permanence of the printed book, which, unlike speech, always remained the same.[21]

In scores of prefaces addressed "To the Reader," writers within the Protestant vernacular tradition reiterated the distinction between "idle" and "spiritual" reading and specified the "studious" manner in which godly texts should be approached. John Foxe advised readers of the *Book of Martyrs* to this effect:

> The grace of the Lord Jesus work with thee, gentle reader, in all thy studious readings. And while thou hast space, so employ thyself to read, that by reading thou mayest learn daily to know that which may profit thy soul, may teach thee experience, may arm thee with patience, and instruct thee in all spiritual knowledge more and more to thy perpetual comfort and salvation in Christ Jesus our Lord, in whom be glory.

The same inward intensity was prescribed as the right way of listening to sermons: "Remember . . . to intreat God with tears before you come to hear any sermon, that thereby God would powerfully speak to your heart, and make his truth precious to you." The substance of these admonitions was succinctly captured in a letter from the New England minister Thomas Shepard II to a son who was newly enrolled at Harvard College: "Reading without meditation will be useless; meditation without reading will be barren."[22]

These instructions shaped the manner of reading for many colonists. Returning to a devotional text again and again, and repeating passages from memory, seem to have been common practices; the Boston merchant Robert Keayne reported, for example, that he had "read over I think 100 and 100 times" his own treatise "on the sacrament of the Lord's Supper." Few may have gone to this extreme. Yet thousands of persons in New England read certain books, and especially the Bible, repeatedly. So, too, they found that certain books stirred them to self-examination and repentance.[23] Wondering if they were "worthy" of participation, some people turned to books like Cotton Mather's *A Companion for Communicants,* in which young Joseph Green, who became a minister, found the reassuring rule that "if a person could not conclude themselves to be unconverted they ought to" receive the sacrament.

This modality of reading was resumed when people opened their Bibles. No book was read more often or in so many different ways: privately in silence, aloud in households where the reading may sometimes have proceeded "in course" through the Old and New Testaments,[24] and in church services as the text for Sunday sermons. In keeping with the practice of meditation, the Bible enabled people to "see" themselves truly. Making her relation before the Cambridge church, Ann Errington recalled how a text for a sermon she heard preached in England on Lamentations 3:40, "Let us search and turn unto the Lord," "came as a light into me and the more the text was opened [the] more I saw my heart."[25] For Mary Rowlandson, a minister's wife who in February 1676 was taken captive by the Indians, the Bible she was handed by one of her captors became an extraordinary resource in the midst of tribulations. She knew the Bible well enough to seek out particular chapters, though she may also have opened it at random, trusting to divine guidance to direct her reading. Thus it happened that "the Lord helped" her "still to go on reading till" she came to a passage in Deuteronomy in which God promised his protection to the repentant. Long after she had been released from captivity the "comfort" of this verse remained in her mind. She remembered as well another moment when a "quieting scripture came to my hand . . . which stilled my spirit for the present." An unexpected reunion in the wilderness with one of her sons led them both to the Bible. She asked him to read, "and he lighted upon that comfortable scripture, Psalms 118:17, 18, 'I shall not die but live. . . .' 'Look here, Mother,' says he, 'did you read this?' "[26]

Mother and son thus acted out the meaning of the Bible as the gift of life. For them it was also a book that bound its readers together in a holy circle or community, differentiating this circle from communities that worshiped falsely or were deprived of the Word. The importance of the Bible in this culture is suggested by the fact that no other book appears in probate inventories in multiple copies or was willed, as Bibles so often were, explicitly to other members of the family. Probate inventories reveal that Bibles in a variety of formats – folio, quarto, and the smaller sizes – were the most widely owned and, in a number of households, the only book that people had at hand. In Essex County, Massachusetts, a third of all probate inventories made after death indicate ownership of a Bible, and the proportion rises to two-thirds of those inventories that indicate the presence of books in the household; in Middlesex, these percentages were 20 and 30 percent, respectively. Though Bibles were commonly owned, a Massachusetts minister complained in 1673 that "in multitudes of Families there is (it may be) . . . no Bible, or onely a torn Bible to be found[.] I mean, but a part of the Bible." Not until the early eighteenth century did a coalition of clergy and the civil government in Massachusetts and Connecticut seek some means of determining which families lacked Bibles and of providing copies for "People unable through Poverty to furnish themselves."[27]

The discrepancies between expectation and reality underline the limited workings of the book market in seventeenth-century New England. To be sure, more households in New England contained books than in the Chesapeake: 60 percent in Middlesex County, Massachusetts, in the middle of the seventeenth century, 52 percent in Essex County, and, as correlated with wealth according to the calculations of Gloria L. Main, 60 percent in several southern New England counties for those who ranked in the *lowest* wealth cohort. Probate inventories, the basis for these figures, reveal approximately the same scale of ownership as in the Chesapeake: Most book-owning households (68 percent in Middlesex) contained five or fewer books, and collections of any real size (more than twenty) invariably belonged to ministers or magistrates. Wealth and occupation were decidedly important in allowing (or obliging) a handful of persons to assemble these larger collections. But the prevalence of book ownership among persons of very modest means demonstrates that these factors were far less significant in New England than they were in the Chesapeake.[28] Not surprisingly, the subject matter identified by the inventories was overwhelmingly religious: Bibles, psalmbooks, works of spiritual devotion, and the like. As a general rule, the inventories do not record the flow of unbound, inexpensive books and pamphlets, some of them locally printed – almanacs, schoolbooks, catechisms – that were deemed expendable.

Many of the books in these inventories were redistributed over time, some by gift or legacy, others by being made available for purchase. When learned men with extensive libraries made out their wills, they preferred that their books pass to someone who, for professional reasons, had need of them. A more common concern was to specify who received the Bible. Often the recipients were women; excluded for the most part from the world of learned books, wives and daughters were quite likely to inherit Bibles or "godly books," a phrase used by the schoolmaster and Harvard graduate Ezekiel Cheever in 1708 in designating which books his wife could select from his library.[29] People without books sometimes borrowed from a neighbor, as his Plymouth Colony neighbors frequently did from William Brewster. An Essex County farmer also turned to neighbors in the 1650s when a family member who was learning to read needed a Bible. Some personal libraries were built up out of second-hand books. One careful study of this process, based on early Plymouth Colony inventories, shows that books owned by Samuel Fuller entered Brewster's library, which in turn was dispersed after his death to others, including Miles Standish and William Bradford.[30]

Notwithstanding the barriers of cost and the limited scope of the book trade, certain categories of books passed into general circulation. The largest selling items were undoubtedly hornbooks and primers. These schoolbooks constituted a fifth of the total stock (in all, some 1,200 copies) of the Boston bookseller Michael Perry when he died in 1700. Another measure of their importance in the local trade is a bill submitted by a printer to the bookseller Daniel Henchman in 1727 for the printing of 4,000 primers. Psalmbooks ran a close second; by 1710, booksellers had issued nearly a dozen editions of the Bay Psalm Book, and the same printer's bill of 1727 covered

3,000 copies of a collection of psalms and hymns by Isaac Watts and another, unspecified psalmbook.[31] Catechisms were a third genre that became widely owned thanks to orders by the civil government that children and servants be taught a "short orthodox catechis," and to towns like Chelmsford, Massachusetts, where the church took the initiative in ordering copies – one hundred of the Shorter Westminster Catechism in 1665 – for families to purchase.[32] In the course of the century, nineteen different ministers wrote catechisms, some of which circulated in manuscript copies before being printed in Cambridge, Boston, or London.[33] The only other book that rivaled primers, psalmbooks, and catechisms was the annual almanac, the earliest of which were issued in very limited quantities by the Cambridge Press in the 1640s. By the late 1670s the popularity of the genre encouraged printers to issue competing versions.

A few other books were widely owned thanks to occasions of sponsorship, as when the town of Dorchester, Massachusetts, paid for the printing of *A Farewel Exhortation* by its minister, Richard Mather, thereby enabling him to provide copies for every household in his congregation. Every town was also on the receiving end of publications sponsored and paid for by the civil government: collections of laws, broadside proclamations, *A Platform of Church Discipline* (1649), John Norton's attack on Quakerism, *The Heart of N-England Rent* (1659). Individuals also acted as patrons and distributors; in 1677 the minister in Plymouth requested twenty copies of a defense of a controversial decision by a synod of ministers, and Cotton Mather, who was constantly handing out copies of his books to anyone who would accept them, estimated in 1706 that he gave away upwards of 600 books a year.[34] Books were also available at "public" libraries in Boston (located on the second floor of the town market), Concord, and New Haven. The stock of these libraries, which consisted in the main of legacies from the estates of ministers and magistrates, saw little use.[35]

Small or large, household libraries, the stocks of booksellers, and personal records (relations of spiritual experience; the occasional diary) are informative about the writers and genres that the colonists preferred and those which they ignored. Not surprisingly, these sources indicate that first-generation colonists relied on Bayly's *Practice of Piety*, Dent's *The Plain Mans Pathway to Heaven*, and Scudder's *Daily Walk*. After 1660 the favorites became such Nonconformist writers as Richard Baxter, Joseph Alleine, James Janeway, Thomas Vincent, John Flavel, William Dyer, Thomas Wilcox, and, in the eighteenth century, Isaac Watts. Books by these men gradually became staples of the New England book trade, steady sellers that, decade after decade, were imported or reprinted, as Watts's *Spiritual Songs* was some thirty-three times by New England booksellers before 1790.[36] That so many readers in New England and elsewhere in the colonies preferred these older books is an apt reminder of the difference between the rhythms of literary fashion and the rhythms of popular consumption.

But the colonists also had access to books that represented alternative ways of thinking. One of these alternatives was the radical Puritanism that flowered into numerous sects: "Antinomians," Baptists, Quakers, Gortonists, and Rogerenes, to name those most active in New England. In keeping with the general pattern of their outreach, the Quaker missionaries who came to Massachusetts in the 1650s brought books and pamphlets with them and carried back to London reports of how they had been persecuted. Quaker books, some of them dispatched by George Fox, continued to arrive in the colonies. Baptists such as Obadiah Holmes prepared reports of their treatment that were published in London. Rogerenes, a sect founded in the late seventeenth century in southeastern Connecticut by John Rogers, issued their tracts through William Bradford in Philadelphia and New York. By the 1720s Rhode Island printers, though not wanting to identify themselves by name, were willing to publish the Rogerenes.[37]

Orthodox culture was also disturbed by books that were distinctively *not* religious: jestbooks and "merriments," ballads, almanacs, courtly poetry, pornography, and chivalric romances. English booksellers shipped modest quantities of some of these books, usually in response to individual orders, to the Boston merchant John Usher, though in Michael Perry's stock of 1700 they were all but absent. It is unlikely that the secular and, according to its critics, profane ballad culture of seventeenth-century England was transferred to the colonies. But by the early 1670s some of the ministers were upset by Anglican primers that a merchant had imported, and they also worried about books that peddlers were distributing. About 1700 Cotton Mather warned female readers of "Books . . . seen and sold at Noon-day, among us; . . . There are Plays, and Songs, and Novels, and Romances, and foolish and filthy Jests, and Poetry prostituted unto Execrable Ribaldry."[38] Details of the peddlers' stock are hard to come by. Other evidence reveals that the traditional prohibition of "idle" reading did not prevent some people – even some who were godly – from enjoying such books. The commonplace book Elnathan Chauncy compiled as a student at Harvard College in the late 1650s shows that he was reading widely in contemporary "secular literature," including "a collection of Elizabethan and Jacobean epigrams, love lyrics, and the like." About 1670, a group of young men in Dedham "sat up many a time a great part of the night at Dedham sawmill to heare a book read" which, according to one of those present, taught him "to give maids such things as would make them follow him about so that he could do with them what he would."[39]

But for much of the seventeenth century the market aligned itself with godliness and orthodoxy because to do otherwise was to risk the intervention of the civil government. Back in England, aggressively "forward" Puritans had benefitted from illicit or underground printing when they were a much-beleaguered minority. On these shores, however, the civil rulers in each of the colonies (with the sole exception of Rhode Island) undertook to defend religious truth and their own authority, and to regulate the press accordingly. Like speech, all writing was political in potentially being able to encourage sedition or heresy. Yet there were limits on what the state could do, limits growing out of the distinction, articulated in 1648 in the Cambridge Platform, between "erronious opinions not vented" (i.e., held in private and not communicated to others) and those "acted by the outward man," and also out of divisions of opinion among the orthodox on the proper response to dissent. (For the moment, colonial practice and thinking were not affected by the English radicals who in the 1640s proposed, on the grounds of "Christian liberty" and "conscience," that the civil state should allow most opinions to circulate freely.) Hence the story is one of negotiation and compromise as well as of repression and, on the part of dissidents, recourse to the London trade.[40]

From the very outset of settlement, the colonial governments in Massachusetts and elsewhere acted to suppress manuscripts and seize printed books. Not until 1649 did the Massachusetts government entertain a proposal, which in the event was not endorsed by the magistrates, authorizing certain licensers to approve or disallow books and pamphlets before they were printed. Books printed overseas posed another set of problems. When, as in the case of William Pynchon's *The Meritorious Price of Our Redemption*, the writer was someone local, the General Court acted both to suppress the book, on the grounds that it was "erronyous and hereticale," and to punish the author if he would not recant.[41] The government also seized and destroyed Quaker imprints, at the same time imposing fines on anyone who imported them. The condemnation of John Eliot's antimonarchical speculations about *The Christian Commonwealth* (London, 1660) was based on reasons of state at a time of high tension between the newly restored monarchy and the Puritan colonies.

This tension, together with the active resumption of state censorship in England with the Licensing Act of 1662, may have moved the Massachusetts General Court to order in the same year that "henceforth no copie shall be printed" by the two Cambridge printers unless, beforehand, they had received the "allowance" of Captain Daniel Gookin and the Cambridge minister, Jonathan Mitchell. This order was repealed the following spring, possibly because of divisions of opinion over the Synod of 1662, but in October 1664, the government began the practice of appointing ministers and high-ranking laymen to review and license the Cambridge and, after 1674, the Boston printers.[42] After the licensing system disappeared with the revocation of the Massachusetts charter in 1685, the officers of the short-lived Dominion of New England asserted the right to approve all "Papers, Bookes, Pamphlets." As a matter of standard imperial policy, the royal governors who held office after 1692 were authorized to supervise the press. One other kind of publication that infuriated the government was the anonymous, handwritten "libel" surreptitiously posted or otherwise distributed in public places.[43]

These interventions and, more spectacularly, the scenes of public book-burnings (as happened with Pynchon's *Meritorious Price*) were infrequent.[44] Other writers chose the path of self-censorship. The major examples of self-censorship occurred among magistrates and clergy who were comfortably orthodox. For them, the practice was a means of concealing differences of opinion which, if made public, would jeopardize their authority and the carefully crafted compromises that the clergy had fashioned on matters of church order and doctrine. John Cotton tried to suppress an early treatise on the "Congregational Way" after he became more conservative, but a London bookseller obtained a copy of the manuscript and issued it in 1644. The precarious situation of the colonies in the 1630s provided another reason for engaging in self-censorship. Writing to John Winthrop in 1639, at a moment when the colonists were unsure whether the English government would take action against them, Thomas Shepard commended him for attempting a history of New England but warned that, unless Winthrop were careful in selecting what he recorded, the book "may prejudice vs in regard of the state of England if" some "secret hid things" were "divulged." The concealing and rearranging that mark Winthrop's journal-history were strategies that became almost second nature among the magistrates and clergy. Accordingly, most of the published sermons of the period are couched in a code that historians are still learning to penetrate.[45]

To be sure, the experience of John Cotton suggests that self-censorship could provoke others into exposing what an author wished to conceal; texts infused with the aura of repression were, for that very reason, more powerful and potentially more in demand. But to defy the pressures of self-censorship, as Increase Mather did in his outspoken election-day sermon of 1676, was to run the risk of going unpublished, which happened to Mather when the magistrates refused to play their customary role as patrons. During the Salem witch hunt, Cotton Mather's *Wonders of the Invisible World* (1693 [i.e., 1692]) was the only authorized account; other, more critical narratives appeared in manuscript, or under false imprints. Thomas Brattle, who did not want to be seen as a man "of . . . factious spirit," chose the least explicit way of voicing his criticism of the judges by writing a private letter, which he assumed others would read. Samuel Willard published his *Some Miscellany Observations on Our Present Debates* (1692) anonymously, as from

"Philadelphia: Printed by William Bradford for Hezekiah Vsher." The imprint was transparently false, since Hezekiah Senior had been dead for twenty years, while Hezekiah Jr., a merchant who appears in no other imprint, had fallen under suspicion of witchcraft and fled for his life to New York. Willard was hardly an outsider to church and state, so the publication was probably not clandestine; rather, the imprint functioned to provide the authorities with deniability and to ensure that Mather's version was not officially contested. In Paris it would have been called a *permission tacite*.[46]

A major exception to this history of suppression and concealment was the controversy over church membership that erupted in 1662 when a majority of the ministers attending a special synod voted that the children of a parent who had been baptized were by definition members of the church covenant and entitled to the sacrament of baptism themselves. The handful of ministers who opposed this policy were irritated by the "unseasonable printing" (which the Massachusetts General Court had ordered) of the synod's "propositions" and used the event to justify appealing to church members who were also affected. Even so, they were not sure that the General Court would allow them to publish their responses. "All the answer we could get [from the government]," one of them wrote to a fellow critic, "was that we might do as we would. We count it a favour we were not commanded to be silent." Some of these responses circulated in manuscript, one was issued in London in 1662, and a second made it through the Cambridge Press in 1663. Spokesmen for the majority, though critical of the dissenters for breaking "silence" and for acting to "amuse and trouble the People by Printing a Dissent," implied that this openness was possible because the controversy was not about "damnable Heresies" but concerned "lesser differences." A more likely reason for allowing the minority to publish was its political weight, including strong support within the Massachusetts General Court.[47]

Do controversies, censorship, and self-censorship suggest that seventeenth-century New England (which is to say, the orthodox colonies) was a divided, contentious society or that it was tightly ordered, with Puritanism providing the cohesion? Social and intellectual historians cannot agree on the answer. From the perspective of book history the answer is both yes and no. Infused as it was with the language of hierarchy and obedience, the Puritan project of a literate, Bible-reading people was an instrument of order. But because these same people were entitled to challenge "unlawful" authority, the much-encouraged practice of reading the Bible was inherently unstable, for its message was always open to interpretation. Moreover, the story of control is complicated by the disagreements that arose among the clergy and magistrates, disagreements that limited the capacity of the civil government to impose uniformity. Book history brings the imperfect workings of the system into view – the shortages of Bibles, the conflicts of opinion among the elite, the presence of insurgents like the Baptists, the continuing appeal of a popular culture of "merry jests," and the inconsistencies of censorship. But the story is also one of the prevalence of godly books, the remarkable extent of book ownership and literacy, a book trade closely allied with the civil state, and the mobilization of speech and writing in behalf of a core set of values. These circumstances bespeak the coherence of culture in New England, a coherence manifested in the continuities, stretching far beyond the seventeenth century, of a Protestant literary tradition.

Learned Culture

Writing and reading in early New England were shaped not only by the Reformation but also by scholastic and humanist ways of thinking that converged in learned culture.[48] The transfer of learned culture occurred because a hundred or so of the founding generation had attended one of the English universities, especially Emmanuel College, Cambridge. Most of this group had been ordained as ministers in the Church of England. Advocates of an alternative church order, the "Congregational Way," the immigrants quickly realized that both the preservation of "Learning" and the success of their new system of church government depended on producing more clergy. Plans were therefore laid in 1636 for a college, soon to be named Harvard in honor of a wealthy young minister who, dying in 1638, left half of his estate and the entirety of his books for the benefit of the institution. The first class graduated in 1642, an event that was celebrated in *New Englands First Fruits* (1643), which also described the requirements for being admitted and the course of study.

One central purpose of a Harvard education was to acquire a mastery of Latin, Greek, and Hebrew; to be learned meant being "literate" in the root sense of knowing Latin. A working knowledge of Latin and a preliminary knowledge of Greek were necessary to gain admission to the college, and the requirements for the A.B. degree specified that "Every Scholer" be "able to read extempore the Pentateuch, and the New Testament in Latin out of the Original Tongues." As this rule indicates, gaining a mastery of Scripture was a second major purpose. The allied "arts" of logic and rhetoric were also part of the curriculum, which was filled out with instruction in ethics, divinity, mathematics, physics, and, depending on who was president or available to teach, other ancient languages (Hebrew, Aramaic, Syriac) pertinent to mastering the Old Testament. When a second college, eventually named Yale, was founded in Connecticut in 1701, its organizers, all of them Harvard graduates, re-created this curriculum.[49]

Anyone who passed through these colleges learned how to speak, read, and write in a special manner. What was special was not simply the ability to decipher or quote from the classical languages. The real difference between everyday writing and speaking and the "school" techniques taught and learned at Harvard lay in the "arts" of disputation, which in turn involved syllogistic reasoning, the arcane vocabulary of Protestant scholasticism, and stylized forms of rhetoric. These arts came into play during the Antinomian controversy of the mid-1630s when the ministers debated each other in private and in public over matters of doctrine. Describing the climactic synod of August 1637, which proscribed eighty-two "errors," Thomas Weld recalled that the clergy spent a "fortnight . . . in a plaine Syllogisticall dispute . . . gathering up nine of the chiefest points . . . and disputed of them all in order, pro and con. In the forenoones we framed our arguments, and in the afternoones produced them in publick, and next day the Adversary gave in their answers, and produced also their arguments on the same questions; then we answered them, and replyed also upon them the next day."[50] At every college commencement the graduates displayed their mastery of these techniques – a mastery honed on "disputing" with each other during the school year – by defending *theses* and *quaestiones* on a variety of subjects. For each commencement the graduates paid the Cambridge press to issue a broadside listing the program of these disputes.[51]

Reading was another skill that the learned put to use in a special manner. The uses of literacy within this group included, first and foremost, an ability to go behind the English text of the Bible to its predecessors in Hebrew, Greek, and Latin. Accordingly, pride of place in a clergyman's library went to a non-English version of the Bible, with commentaries close behind. So it was that Henry Dunster, the first president of Harvard, owned the Old Testament in Hebrew and Aramaic and the New Testament in Greek, with a Syriac version bound in.[52] A further aspect of learned reading was "commonplacing," or the practice of excerpting a text in a special notebook, where these extracts were arranged under appropriate topics and with "proper indices." This system of information storage and retrieval was used by students when their turn came to participate in the exercise of disputation. Most of the notebooks that survive from the seventeenth century are not true commonplace books but contain notes on sermons the students had heard preached and were required to discuss. For seasoned ministers, commonplace books were a place to work out arguments in defense of orthodox divinity. Another means of organizing information was to insert in books "a brief idea of the whole . . . with memorandums of more notable passages occuring in it."[53]

Above all, reading was (as a New England minister instructed a son who had just enrolled at Harvard) a matter of "order and method." When

Thomas Shepard II employed this phrase, he implied that the immensity of the world of learning could only be tamed by hard work. But he was also voicing the assumption, which the learned took for granted, that knowledge was a whole or "summe" that could be laid out in clearly articulated principles. The true measure of learnedness was being able to perceive this coherence and knowing how to analyze it logically. The means of doing so that another minister urged on a Harvard student was that of "the incomparable P[eter] Ramus," a French Huguenot academic of the mid-sixteenth century. "Get his definitions and distributions into your mind and memory," Leonard Hoar advised his nephew in 1661. "Let these be the titles of your severall pages and repositoryes in the [commonplace] books aforesaid." Generation after generation, Harvard students arranged their arguments according to the procedures of Ramean logic. Candidates for a master's degree were assigned a related task of preparing "a written Synopsis, or Compendium" of theology, ethics, and philosophy.[54]

The distinctiveness of the world of the learned extended to the kinds of books they owned and the size of their libraries. Textbooks used at Harvard or Yale were the initial basis for these collections; some of these books, or others useful to them, passed through the hands of several student owners (Fig. 4.1).[55] During their careers clergy commonly accumulated two or three hundred volumes, a total achieved by piecing together legacies, gifts, and purchases or, as in the case of Edward Taylor, by making handwritten copies. Some of the wealthier immigrants had much larger libraries; John Harvard, though but thirty years old when he died in 1638, owned 400 volumes and John Winthrop the Younger's collection was "above a thousand" by 1642.[56] A substantial percentage of books in these libraries were in Latin – more than three-fourths in some, though a third seems to have been typical (Fig. 4.2). The intellectual range was wide, encompassing, as John Harvard's library did, classical antiquity (sometimes in schoolbook editions), Catholic and Protestant scholasticism (much of the latter written by German and Dutch scholars), encyclopedias, Luther and Calvin, church history, commentaries on the Bible, the practical divinity of the English Puritan tradition, and belles lettres. Relative to sixteenth-century academic collections, Aristotle and the church fathers were much less widely owned. By the early eighteenth century, some of these libraries included a significant number of local publications.[57] Apart from the clergy, magistrates needed legal and historical books and surgeons owned medical treatises, though books in these fields were also owned more generally.[58]

No seventeenth-century New England printer or bookseller issued a single learned book or schoolbooks of the kind that were used in grammar (Latin) schools or at Harvard. Learned men, and schoolboys on their way to becoming learned, often had to rely on handwritten copies of textbooks,[59]

HOMERI
QVÆ EXTANT
OMNIA
Ilias, Odyssea, Batrachomyomachia, Hymni,
Poematia aliquot
Perpetuis item iustisque in Iliada simul & Odysseam Io. SPONDANI Mauleonensis
COMMENTARIIS.
PINDARI quinetiam Thebani Epitome Iliados Latinis versib. & DARETIS Phrygii de bello Troiano libri à Corn. Nepote eleganter latino versi carmine.
INDICES Homeri textus & Commentariorum locupletissimi.
FAMA
AVRELIÆ ALLOBROGVM
Sumptibus Caldorianæ Societatis.
M. DCVI.

Figure 4.1. Homer, *Opera Quæ Extant* (Aureliæ Allobrogum [Geneva], 1606). A copy first owned by Henry Dunster, President of Harvard, 1640–1654; and by Elnathan Chauncy, 1657, with his printed label; passing to Samuel Mather and James Winthrop, with their signatures on the front flyleaf; then to Harvard College Library, with its eighteenth-century bookplate but rejected as a duplicate, and presented by William Bentley to Allegheny College, 1818. Courtesy of the Bentley Collection, Special Collections Department, Allegheny College.

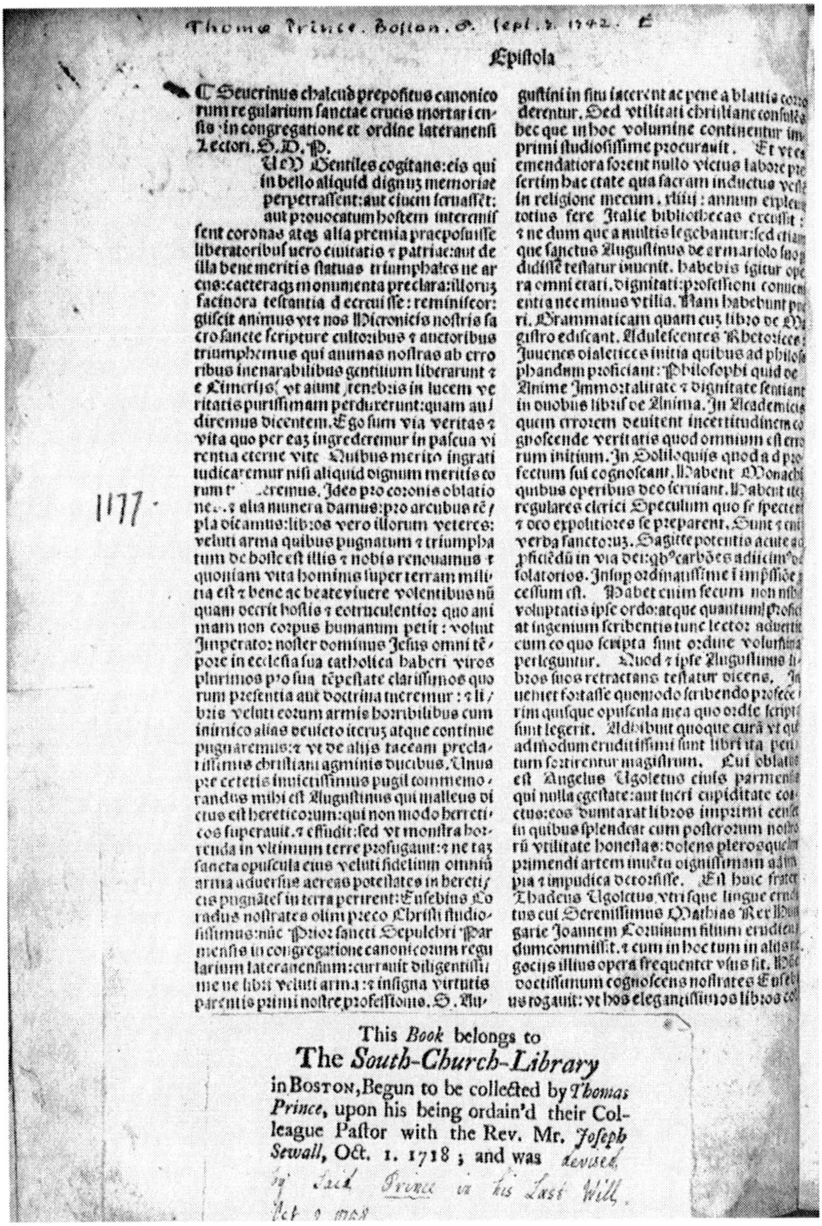
Thomas Prince. Boston. 7. Sept. 1742.

Epistola

This *Book* belongs to
The *South-Church-Library*
in BOSTON, Begun to be collected by *Thomas Prince*, upon his being ordain'd their Colleague Pastor with the Rev. Mr. *Joseph Sewall*, Oct. 1. 1718; and was devised by said Prince in his Last Will.

Figure 4.2. St. Augustine of Hippo, *Opuscula Plurima* (Venice, 1491), with the signature (?) of John Norton (1606–1663), who settled in Plymouth in 1635; acquired by Thomas Prince, September 7, 1742; perhaps the earliest attested American provenance of a still surviving incunabulum. Courtesy of the Boston Public Library.

on borrowed or redistributed books, or on those received from overseas, some of which arrived as gifts and others through booksellers. In the early 1630s a friend in England was sending the Frankfurt book fair catalogues to John Winthrop the Younger, whose correspondents both in England and the colonies often forwarded books and manuscripts to him. So did others in England for friends in the New World.[60] Subsidies were occasionally available; the town of Hartford, seeking to recruit Jonathan Mitchell as its minister, offered to help pay for books he wanted. Increase Mather had the benefit of legacies and gifts from kinfolk, other ministers, and friends; the widow of Leonard Hoar let him choose ninety-seven books from her late husband's library.[61] Newly arriving immigrants helped to freshen the stock of second-hand books. This was notably so in the case of the Reverend Samuel Lee, a Nonconformist minister who died in 1691, five years after immigrating. The thousand volumes he brought with him became the first private collection in New England to be advertised for sale in a printed catalogue.[62]

By this decade, booksellers such as Duncan Campbell were stocking items for their learned customers.[63] Meanwhile Increase and Cotton Mather, but especially Cotton, were building up libraries remarkable for their size and breadth and for being so current. "Seldom any *new Book* of Consequence finds the way from beyond-Sea, to these parts of *America*, but I bestow the Perusal upon it," Cotton Mather noted in a diary entry in 1706. The sheer size of his library bears him out; by 1700, when he was thirty-five years old, he had between two and three thousand books, and by 1728, the year he died, the collection was much larger. As happened often with learned books, some of those in Cotton's library descended to him from his father and grandfather. The same lines of descent enabled Cotton to assemble a manuscript archive of the first importance.[64]

The library of Harvard College mirrored these private collections. Donations, most of them solicited from English benefactors, were the only means of adding to the collection that John Harvard left to the college. The largest of these gifts, totalling perhaps a thousand volumes, arrived in 1680 from England as a bequest from Theophilus Gale, a former fellow of Magdalen College, Oxford, author of an important history of the European languages, and a Nonconformist after 1662. With an eye to encouraging more donations, in 1723 the college issued the *Catalogus Librorum Bibliothecae Collegij Harvardini Quod est Cantabrigiae in Nova Anglia*. Starting with the folios, which constituted more than a third of the collection, the arrangement of the catalogue was alphabetical according to three different sizes. The shelf arrangement was similar. As calculated by Samuel Eliot Morison, the largest of the subject classifications was "theology, bibles, patristic works, scholastic philosophy," numbering 2183 volumes out of a total of 3516. The category of "history, politics, geography, description, travel" was second, with a mere 367. Another 300 volumes concerned Hebrew, Greek, and Latin grammar and literature, or were works of academic reference. According to a list of rules drawn up in 1667, clergy and governing officers had borrowing privileges, but seniors were the only students who could do so. Because the library was akin to a rare-book collection, this rule was not as restrictive as, at first glance, it may seem to be.[65]

To what uses were these books put? Few direct references to the apparatus of learned culture appear in the more pastoral or practical printed sermons. Nonetheless, this apparatus was regarded as essential to the ongoing work of the ministry. When Thomas Mayhew, Jr. began to preach to the Indians on Martha's Vineyard, his fellow missionary John Eliot described him as in "extreme want of books" and in need, especially, of "*Commentaries* and *Common Places* for the body of Divinity." Writing in 1649 to Edward Winslow in London, Eliot asked that Winslow arrange for someone to "send over such books as may be necessary for a young Scholer; I will name no books, he needs all."[66] Apart from the ever-present task of preparing sermons, a scholar's books were of critical importance when the task at hand was apologetic or controversial. John Norton's *The Orthodox Evangelist*, a thickly scholastic text that relied on concepts like the "order of nature" in explaining the role of faith in salvation, abounded with citations to English and continental works of Protestant divinity. Like so many others in the seventeenth century, Norton also relied on compendia or encyclopedias.[67]

The apparatus of learnedness was crucial to another area of knowledge, natural science. During the first two decades, instruction in physics and mathematics at Harvard was rudimentary and traditional. In this area as in that of theology, learnedness did not mean critical thinking or the advancement of knowledge but reiterating the accumulated wisdom of the past and defending truth against error. Nonetheless the colonists responded to the winds of change that began to blow by mid-century. In 1659, the graduates of Harvard who prepared the annual almanac shifted to Copernican astronomy. John Winthrop the Younger, who had been visiting in London in 1661 when the Royal Society was just getting under way, became the first English colonist to be elected a Fellow. After he returned to Connecticut in 1663, Winthrop continued to participate via letters, forwarding, among other information, observations of comets he made with a telescope. By the late 1660s he was sharing the newly begun *Philosophical Transactions* of the Royal Society with Thomas Shepard II of Charlestown.[68] Winthrop also shared an interest in alchemy with some of his correspondents, and his library included an extensive collection of books dealing with the occult. When the Nonconformist educator Charles Morton arrived in Boston in 1686, he brought with him a manuscript "compendium" of the physical sciences that, because it was more up-to-date, quickly passed into use at Harvard; never printed, it was copied and recopied by successive undergraduates for another generation (Fig. 4.3).[69]

For many of the learned the Bible remained the most important text to study. Cotton Mather aspired to make a contribution to biblical scholarship, but the annotations and commentary he assembled in a near-lifetime of laboring on his "Biblia Americana" never interested any London bookseller.[70] In the everyday work of interpreting the Bible, learnedness played a number of roles. Though the meaning of the Scriptures was, in principle, immediately apparent to readers enlightened by the "inward work of the holy Spirit," the annotators of the Geneva Bible and the authors of the Westminster Confession had reported that the Word contained "hard places" in the sense that "all things in Scripture are not alike plain in themselves, nor alike clear to all." Consequently, learnedness was indispensable as a means of unravelling the "mysteries" of the Bible.[71] Despite a veritable mountain of commentaries and annotations, much remained unclear. Hence Hugh Peter's plea in 1636 that John Cotton be given the time to "go through the Bible, and raise marginal notes upon all the knotty places of the scriptures." Had Cotton done so, he would have relied on philology, or a knowledge of the ancient languages, in order to work out the meaning of words like "church" and "bishop." The tools of logic and rhetoric would have helped him resolve aspects of Scripture that were contradictory or incomplete. Still another task would have been to analyze the interlocking "types" and "figures," a mode of analysis that Samuel Mather, brother of Increase and a Harvard College graduate who became a minister in Dublin, Ireland, attempted to codify in *Figures and Types of the Old Testament* (1683).[72]

Throughout the seventeenth century the esoteric chapters of the Bible attracted lay or unlearned readers – famously, the Fifth Monarchists – who turned prophecy into an instrument of social and religious criticism. Some of these radicals regarded the spiritually transmitted Word as prior to and more authentic than anything written down. On this ground, they rejected the authority of learnedness, which they regarded as contrary to the practice of depending on the guidance of the Holy Spirit. Others insisted that revelation, by which they meant the direct witness of the Holy Spirit, was ongoing.

These ideas circulated in New England as early as the Antinomian controversy. When Anne Hutchinson, the central figure in the controversy, wanted to "expound [the] dark places of Scripture" she did so by claiming the authority of inspiration: "The Lord knows that I could not open scripture; he must by his prophetical office open it unto me." A hostile contemporary, Edward Johnson, recalled a supporter of hers in Boston saying,

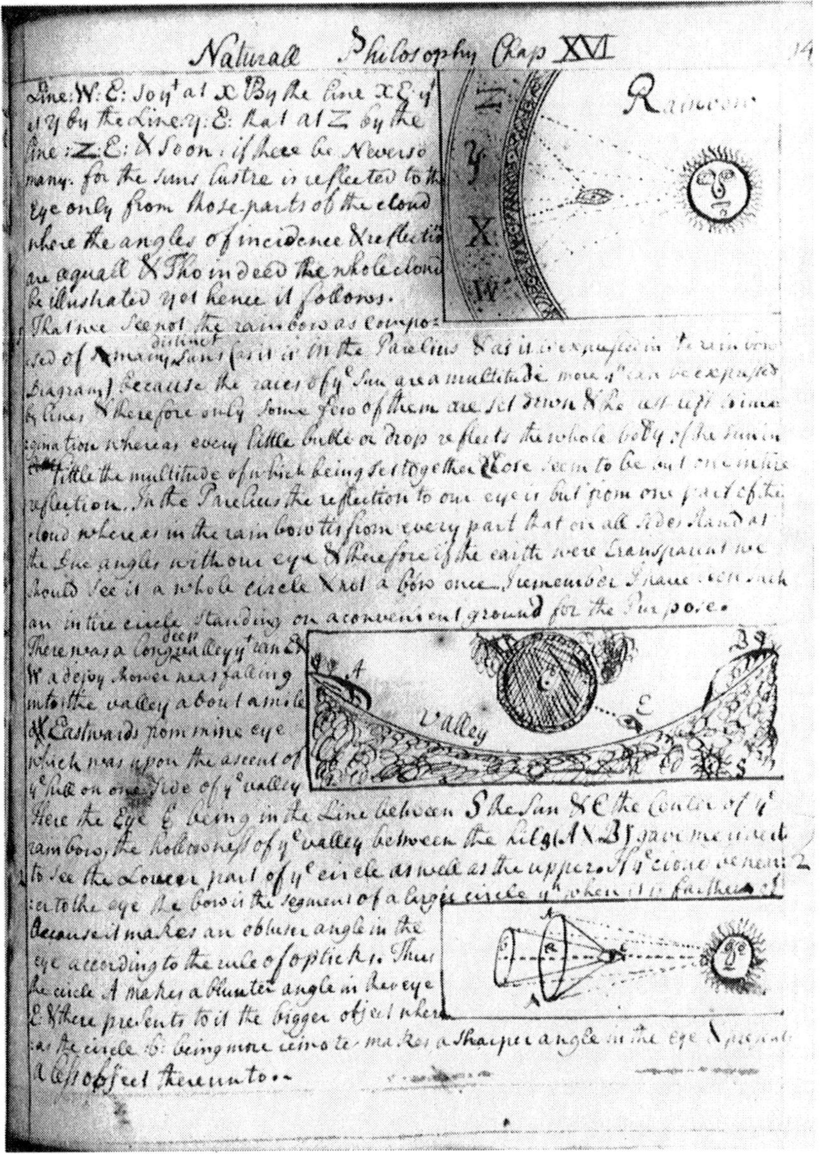

Naturall Philosophy Chap XVI

Line: W: E: Joyn at X By the Line X E y
& Y by the Line: Y: E: that at Z by the
Line: Z: E: & Soon: if there be Never so
many. for the suns Lustre is reflected to the
Eye only from those parts of the cloud
where the angles of incidence & reflectio[n]
are equall & Tho indeed the whole cloud
be illustrated yet hence it follows.
That wee See not the rainbow as compo-
sed of many distinct Suns (as it is in the Parelius & as it is expressed in the rainbow
Diagram) because the raies of ye Sun are a multitude more yn can be expressed
by lines & therefore only some few of them are set down & the rest left to imagination whereas every little bubble or drop reflects the whole body of the sun in
little the multitude of which being set together those seem to be but one intire
reflection. In the Parelius the reflection to our eye is but from one part of the
cloud whereas in the rainbow tis from every part that on all sides stand at
the due angles with our eye & therefore if the earth were transparent we
should see it a whole circle & not a bow once I remember I have seen such
an intire circle standing on a convenient ground for the purpose.
There was a long deep valley yt ran E & W a dewy shower was falling
into the valley about a mile Eastwards from mine eye
which was upon the ascent of ye hill on one side of ye valley
Here the Eye E being in the Line between S the Sun & C the Center of ye
rainbow, the hollowness of ye valley between the hills A & B gave me liberty
to see the Lower part of ye circle as well as the upper. If ye cloud be nearer to the eye the bow is the segment of a bigger circle yn when it is farther of
because it makes an obtuse angle in the
eye according to the rule of opticks. Thus
the circle A makes a blunter angle in the eye
E & there presents to it the bigger object where-
as the circle B being more remote makes a sharper angle in the eye & presents
a less object thereunto.

Figure 4.3. Charles Morton, *Compendium Physicæ;* one of the many manuscript copies of this seventeenth-century textbook by Harvard College students. American Antiquarian Society.

"Come along with me . . . i'le bring you to a Woman that Preaches better Gospell then any of your black-coates that have been at the Ninneversity . . . for my part, saith hee, I had rather hear such a one that speakes from the meere motion of the spirit, without any study at all, then any of your learned Scollers."[73] Long after Mrs. Hutchinson was silenced, some lay men and women, veterans of the conventicle and accustomed in that setting to arguing that lay people were entitled to "try the Doctrine of preachers whether they be consonant to the Scriptures or not," continued to insist on the privilege of speaking out in private meetings or even in church; others, like the early Baptists, resented the fact that "none but such as had *humane learning*" were allowed to be ministers.[74] Another challenge to the authority of learnedness came from readers of the Bible who felt that the Holy Spirit was speaking to them directly as they turned its pages.[75]

All of these challenges were authentically Puritan in affirming the power of the Holy Spirit and the priority of Scripture over "high learning." So the martyrs chronicled by John Foxe had constantly affirmed.[76] It was equally in keeping with mainstream Puritanism that the ministers and their allies in New England vigorously defended learnedness, insisted that "Extraordinarie Revelations are now ceased," categorized the prophecies voiced by lay people as delusions created by the Devil, and accused their critics, especially the women among them, of being "ignorant and unlettered." Baptists, Quakers, and other insurgents were the targets of the same accusations, Winthrop, for example, writing of the Gortonists that "they were all illiterate men, the ablest of them could not write true English, no not common words, yet they would take upon them the interpretation of the most difficult places of scripture, and wrest them any way to serve their own turns."[77]

The authority of men over the "weaker sex" was as much at stake as the authority of learnedness over unlearnedness or truth over error; one of Mrs. Hutchinson's faults had been that she dared to "interpret . . . Mens Sayings and sermons after" her own mind. *Any* woman who stepped out of line made herself vulnerable to the argument that the female mind was intrinsically weak and, because of this weakness, unsuited to the honor and work of being learned. A characteristic example of this reasoning, all the more revealing because of being applied to someone who was not an insurgent, was John Winthrop's explanation for the mental illness of Ann Hopkins, wife of the governor of Connecticut, which he blamed on "her giving herself wholly to reading and writing. . . . For if she had attended her household affairs, and such things as belong to women, and not gone out of her way and calling to meddle in such things as are proper for men, whose minds are stronger, etc., she had kept her wits."[78] But the orthodox clergy had other reasons for defending learnedness than wanting to protect a gendered authority. They worried about living so "farre removed from the more cultivated parts of the world," a situation that required them "to use utmost care & diligence to keep up Learning . . . lest degeneracy, Barbarism, Ignorance and irreligion . . . breake in upon us."[79]

This assertiveness had three consequences: barring from orthodox pulpits anyone who lacked a college education, keeping Harvard College going even when funds and students were scarce, and protecting the authority of the ministers. Yet within the very house of learnedness there were doubts about the use of "pagan" authors and, in the longer term, a growing uneasiness about the relationship between faith and natural reason. Winthrop, who was bothered by favorable references to the "heathen commonwealths" of Greece and Rome in the election sermon of 1641 and responded by observing that "the word of God makes men wiser," had to be reassured by Thomas Shepard that his "apprehensions agaynst reading and learning heathen authors . . . will be easily answered." Even in defending learnedness, however, the orthodox clergy always assumed that it was not an end in itself but a means of advancing true religion. This way of thinking, which they inherited from the humanists, was embodied in the original statutes of the college, which laid out a program of regular Bible reading, and addressed again in a college statute of 1655 ordering that "in the teaching of all Arts such Authors bee read as doe best agree with the Scripture truths."[80]

These efforts at balance were vulnerable to the charge that the scale had been tipped too far in one direction. The radicals who lamented the privileging of learnedness may have had a point, for in certain situations it served to set the clergy apart from the laity. The brute fact of difference emerged from Thomas Weld's account of how the ministers at the Synod of 1637, debating before a general audience, had spoken "syllogistically, *ad vulgus* as much as might be." The same distance was remarked upon by a minister on the losing side of the Synod of 1662 who characterized the lay delegates as "over-born" because they were "no Logitians, and so unable to answer Syllogisms, and discern Ambiguities," and remarked upon anew by a former president of Harvard, Henry Dunster, when he asked in his will that "Judicious and learned Men" be appointed to appraise the value of his library, since "some of my bookes [are] in such languages wherein common Englishmen know not one letter."[81] Another means of imposing distance was the sarcasm learned writers turned against the stock figure of the bumbling and credulous "Countryman." As early as 1670 this tried-and-true trope was appearing in the Cambridge almanacs, on its way to becoming a staple of coffeehouse culture in the eighteenth century. No humor was involved in the bluntness with which other writers spoke of the "ruder and more ignorant sort" or, reiterating a misogynist trope, of "Credulous" women.[82]

These literary and cultural strategies, which seem so different in their tone and consequences from the plain style, underscore the paradoxical situation of the learned. They were members of a great tradition of learnedness that by its very nature was cosmopolitan and hierarchical. Overcoming the space between colony and metropolis was a critical task for the New England clergy, one they most easily accomplished by corresponding with Nonconformist clergy in England and, more rarely, with Protestant scholars and clergy on the Continent, which John Norton did in Latin.[83] Yet a sense of being out of touch, of falling behind, also weighed upon the colonists. Writing to John Winthrop the Younger in 1669 to thank him for sending the *Philosophical Transactions*, Thomas Shepard II spoke candidly about the difficulties and, by implication, the importance, of keeping in touch: "it is no small part of our great unhappinesse who dwell in these out-skirts of the earth that we are so little acquainted with those Excellent things that are done, and found out in the world and discoursed of by those learned and worthy personages."[84] The deeper paradox was this, that an oppositional culture remained dependent on the center. Negotiating this paradox was a persistent issue for learned writers in New England.

Authors and Writing

Many people in seventeenth-century New England expressed themselves in writing. For most of the century those who wrote could not publish through the book trades in New England for the simple reason that no printer or bookseller cared to risk his capital on sales to the local market. This situation had little effect on first-generation ministers like Thomas Hooker, John Cotton, and Thomas Shepard, who were able to publish their sermons in London thanks to their literary reputations and to the presence of a well-established market for godly books. Second-generation ministers like Increase Mather and Samuel Willard began to publish locally in the 1670s after John Foster opened his printing office in Boston. All along, however, some of what was written circulated through the means of scribal publication, as happened with John Winthrop's "Modell of Christian Charity" and the elegies that printers also issued as broadsides (Fig. 4.4).[85] Other texts that remained unpublished, like William Bradford's history of Plymouth, could be consulted in an archive; still others, like Samuel Sewall's diary, were cherished within a family, sometimes in multiple copies.[86]

The diverse modes of literary production in early New England all had in common the framework of the Protestant vernacular tradition. Within this tradition, the great watchword for writers was "plain," which signified truth and utility as well as certain qualities of literary style. Plainness must not be

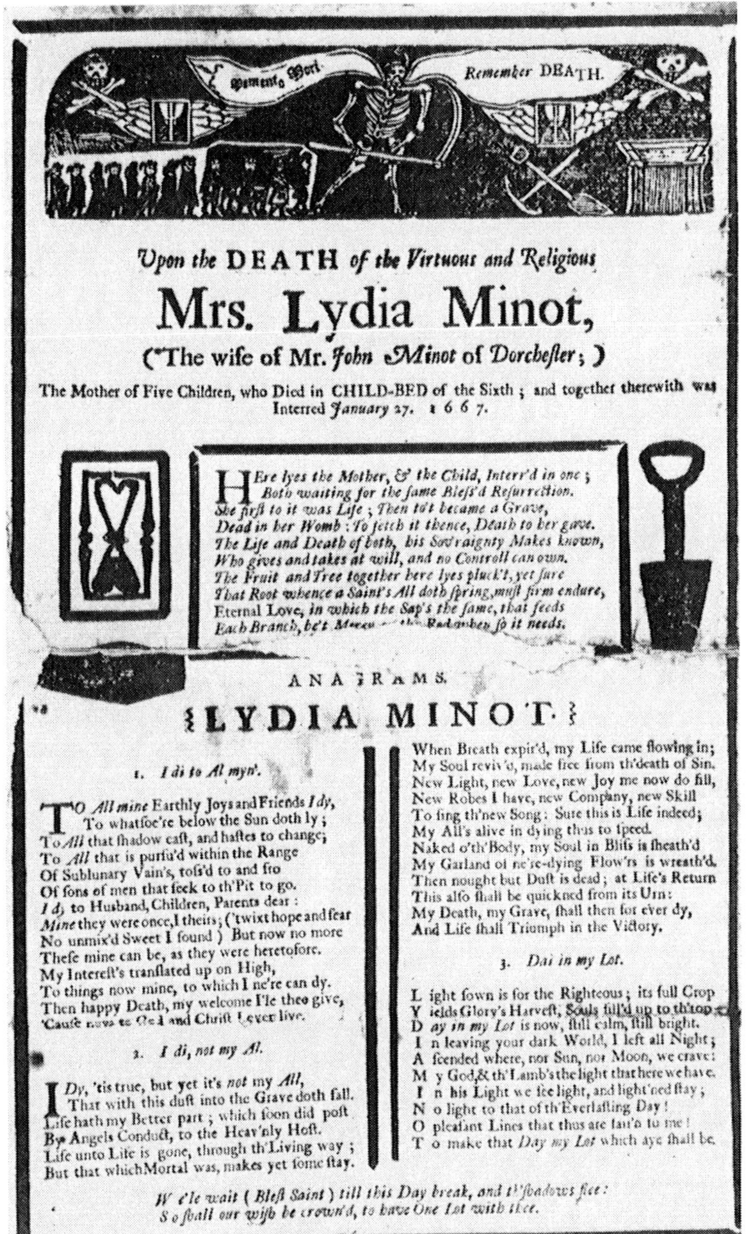

Upon the DEATH of the Virtuous and Religious

Mrs. Lydia Minot,

(The wiſe of Mr. *John Minot* of *Dorcheſter*;)

The Mother of Five Children, who Died in CHILD-BED of the Sixth; and together therewith was Interred *January* 27. 1 6 6 7.

HEre lyes the Mother, & the Child, Interr'd in one;
Both waiting for the ſame Bleſs'd Reſurrection.
She firſt to it was Life; Then to't became a Grave,
Dead in her Womb: To fetch it thence, Death to her gave.
The Life and Death of both, his Sov'raignty Makes known,
Who gives and takes at will, and no Controll can own.
The Fruit and Tree together here lyes pluck't, yet ſure
That Root whence a Saint's All doth ſpring, muſt firm endure,
Eternal Love, *in which the Sap's the ſame, that feeds*
Each Branch, be't [illegible] *Rod when ſo it needs.*

ANAGRAMS.

LYDIA MINOT.

1. *I di to Al myn'.*

TO *All mine* Earthly Joys and Friends *I dy*,
To whatſoe're below the Sun doth ly;
To *All* that ſhadow caſt, and haſtes to change;
To *All* that is purſu'd within the Range
Of Sublunary Vain's, toſs'd to and fro
Of ſons of men that ſeek to th'Pit to go.
I dy to Husband, Children, Parents dear:
Mine they were once, I theirs; ('twixt hope and fear
No unmix'd Sweet I found) But now no more
Theſe mine can be, as they were heretofore.
My Intereſt's tranſlated up on High,
To things now mine, to which I ne're can dy.
Then happy Death, my welcome I'le thee give,
'Cauſe [illegible] and Chriſt I ever live.

2. *I di, not my Al.*

I *Dy*, 'tis true, but yet it's *not* my *All*,
That with this duſt into the Grave doth fall.
Life hath my Better part; which ſoon did poſt
By Angels Conduct, to the Heav'nly Hoſt.
Life unto Life is gone, through th'Living way;
But that which Mortal was, makes yet ſome ſtay.
When Breath expir'd, my Life came flowing in;
My Soul reviv'd, made free from th'death of Sin.
New Light, new Love, new Joy me now do fill,
New Robes I have, new Company, new Skill
To ſing th'new Song: Sure this is Life indeed;
My All's alive in dying thus to ſpeed.
Naked o'th'Body, my Soul in Bliſs is ſheath'd
My Garland of ne're-dying Flow'rs is wreath'd.
Then nought but Duſt is dead; at Life's Return
This alſo ſhall be quickned from its Urn:
My Death, my Grave, ſhall then for ever dy,
And Life ſhall Triumph in the Victory.

3. *Dai in my Lot.*

L ight ſown is for the Righteous; its full Crop
Y ields Glory's Harveſt, Souls fill'd up to th'top.
D *ay in my Lot* is now, ſtill calm, ſtill bright.
I n leaving your dark World, I left all Night;
A ſcended where, nor Sun, nor Moon, we crave:
M y God, & th'Lamb's the light that here we have.
I n his Light we ſee light, and light'ned ſtay;
N o light to that of th'Everlaſting Day!
O pleaſant Lines that thus are fall'n to me!
T o make that *Day my Lot* which aye ſhall be.

We'le wait (Bleſt Saint) till this Day break, and th'ſhadows flee:
So ſhall our wiſh be crown'd, to have One Lot with thee.

Figure 4.4. *Upon the Death of the Virtuous and Religious Lydia Minot* [Boston, Mass., ca. 1710?]. Probably copied from a lost manuscript or printed original, 1667. Courtesy of the Massachusetts Historical Society.

construed to mean that the Puritan literary aesthetic was truncated or inadequate. This judgment has given way to an understanding of the role of figural or typological interpretation in the "Puritan imagination." The idea of "figure," that persons and events in the Old Testament foreshadowed those in the New, with ever-extending replications of these types in the history of Christianity, opened up vast possibilities for the play of symbolic language. The idea of providence held similar possibilities, as did motifs such as pilgrimage and wilderness. So, too, literary Puritanism embodied a thaumaturgy of Christ contending against Satan that for some writers pointed toward sensationalism and, for others, toward allegory.

Godly writing attempted to replicate the transformative power of the Word. In asserting the close dependence of writing on the Word, Puritans emphasized the role of the Holy Spirit: Without the presence of the Spirit, preaching and writing were empty acts. Contrary to the humanist and classical traditions, godly writing thus involved a stance of self-effacement, a renunciation of any "worldly" aspirations for monetary gain or literary reputation. Another aspect of this ethic was a representation of authors as "God's workmen," mere pens in his hands. The layman Nathaniel Morton, who was commissioned by the Plymouth Colony government to prepare a history (which he based on Bradford's manuscript) of that colony, spoke of himself in this way: "So then, gentle Reader, thou mayest take notice, that the main Ends of publishing this small History, is, That God may have his due Praise, His Servants the Instruments have their Names embalmed, and the present and future Ages may have the fruit and benefit of Gods great work." In the midst of writing *The Day of Doom,* Michael Wigglesworth wrote in his commonplace book, "I desire with all my heart and might to serve my Lord Christ (who is my best and onely friend and supporter) . . . if he shall please to accept such a poor piece of service at my hands. . . . I delight in his service and glory, and the good of poor souls, though my endeavors this way should rather occasion loss then outward advantage to my self." The same self-understanding was voiced by Anne Bradstreet. Dedicating a collection of prose meditations to her children, she explained that she wrote them in order "that you may gain some spiritual Advantage by my experience. I have not studyed in this you read to show my skill, but to declare the Truth – not to sett forth myself, but the Glory of God."[87]

This understanding of authorship established a distinctive relationship between the writer/speaker and his or her audience. This audience was the selective community of the godly, a community that, in John Winthrop's famous phrase from the "Modell of Christian Charity" of 1630, regarded itself as "knit together in the bonds of love." Not the world of commerce but the spiritual interdependence he evoked constituted the ground on which writers and readers met. The meetinghouse was the place where, each Sunday, this interdependence was visibly enacted as the clergy preached in the vernacular to the farmers and housewives who had elected them to office and provided them their "maintenance." Aside from these congregations, other godly audiences – which is to say, other sites of patronage or literary production – were the household, the conventicle (or, after 1690, the private society), the town, the commonwealth, and like-minded people in other parts of the western world. Thus it was that the town of Dorchester sponsored the publication of Richard Mather's sermons, that the colony of Plymouth paid for Morton's *New-Englands Memoriall*, and that parents like Anne Bradstreet passed on to their children the "legacy" of moral counsel in the form of handwritten texts. None of these writers presumed to be original or independent. The goal was representativeness, to convey in an exemplary manner the pattern of godly living.

Because the spiritual experience of ordinary people was no less exemplary than the histories of people higher up in the social scale, the possibility of being representative was available to everyone in the godly community regardless of age, gender, or learning. A long-lasting trope, antedating the rise of the vernacular tradition but revivified within it, was that "ploughmen" were closer to God and better vehicles of truth than the learned. In New England the feeling of self-worth among the laity was palpable in the setting of the church. Here, in the course of becoming members, ordinary men and women spoke of how they had experienced the "work of grace." In these relations, as in most of what they wrote, unlearned writers relied on the Bible, quoting it directly and evoking its great motifs of wilderness and pilgrimage. The most common narrative pattern may have been to represent the similitudes between their lives and God's providential design. The long autobiographical "Narrative" (in prose and poetry) of John Dane, the 456-line poem "Captan Perse and his coragios Company" by Philip Walker, the "Last Will & Testament" of the Baptist Obadiah Holmes, the "Valedictory and Monitory Writing" of Sarah Goodhue, the "Book of Remembrance of Gods Provydences towards mee" kept by Abraham Browne and willed to his son, the occasional poems and meditations of Benjamin Franklin the Elder, the deathbed reflections of pious children that Cotton Mather preserved in *A Token, for the Children of New England* (1700) – these and many other texts, most of them circulating only in manuscript (if circulating at all), are a forceful reminder of how the practice of writing encompassed all ages and ranks.[88]

To be sure, some of these people were conscious of the limitations of their prose style or found themselves introduced, as the mason John Goodwin was, by a minister who characterized him as writing with a "Hand used only to the Trowel." In this instance as in many others, the openness of the vernacular tradition clashed with the regulating hierarchies imbedded in the practices of speaking, reading, and writing.[89] We may also discern the power of the clergy and the printers and booksellers allied with them in the voice of these lay writers. Theirs was not a wholly independent voice, as we know from the fact that dissident lay Baptists and Quakers had to publish elsewhere. Those who *did* have their work published, like Joshua Scottow and Roger Clap, expressed a reverence for the founders of New England and reiterated the theme of "declension" that filled so many sermons. Or, like Sarah Goodhue, a church member and daughter of a deacon, they pleaded with their children to persist in fervent piety. In some instances, a clergyman intervened more directly to shape a text, as Cotton Mather did with the captivity narrative of Hanna Swarton.[90] That the clergy shared a common culture with many lay people is certain, but the history of their participation in the making of these texts also reminds us of the politics of reform and regulation over which they presided.

Learned writers in early New England commanded a broad array of genres and forms – more, undoubtedly, than among the unlearned. Within their own literary system the most important of these genres was church history, as exemplified in Eusebius's *Ecclesiastical Histories* and John Foxe's *Book of Martyrs*. William Bradford cited both in the opening pages of his history of Plymouth, and Hugh Peter had Foxe in mind when he urged in 1636 that some colonist prepare "a new book of martyrs . . . to begin where the other had left [off]."[91] Close kin to church history was the genre of "memorials" of God's wonder-working actions in the world, a genre alternatively known as "remarkable providences." (In our day, some of these collections have been wrongfully classified as diaries.)[92] Spiritual biography and autobiography, which formed an important part of the *Book of Martyrs* and Philip Stubbes's *A Christal Glasse for Christian Women* (1591), flourished among the colonists, notably in Cotton Mather's *Magnalia Christi Americana*. Some of these narratives may also be considered as examples of the *ars moriendi*, or the art of dying well, a widely selling genre on both sides of the Atlantic. Sermons and sermon-series addressed matters of doctrine, but in the main were concerned with mapping the spiritual exercises that served to awaken sinners and lead them through the oft-repeated cycle of repentance and faith. The religious lyric, though less widely practiced, appealed to Edward Taylor, who in the course of his ministry wrote hundreds of pages of lyrics that he kept to himself. Taylor also wrote elegies, as did many others, especially the Harvard-educated Benjamin Tompson (1642–1714), who became prolific in this form of verse.[93] Literary historians have proposed that the colonists broke new ground with forms like the "jeremiad" and the captivity narrative. But no one wrote plays or romances.

The power of the Protestant vernacular tradition was felt by everyone who wrote in early New England. Yet this framework goes only so far in explaining authorship and the making of literary texts among the colonists. It must be complemented by four other factors. The first we have already considered, the regulating impulse among the clergy, which prompted them to sponsor some texts for publication but not others. The other three were the role of booksellers in determining, from their vantage, what was printed and how texts were transmitted; the assumption that women, as the "weaker sex," should refrain from expressing themselves in public; and the felt pressure of alternative conceptions of writing and authorship, a pressure rooted in the enduring tension between the vernacular tradition and the cosmopolitan culture it tried to keep at a distance.

The world of commerce was slow to affect writers in New England, for books by local authors were not marketable commodities until late in the century. The possible exception was Michael Wigglesworth's *Day of Doom* (1662), which may have been issued in an edition of 1,800 copies. Wigglesworth's poem was unusual if it earned him something, for the English trade practice of providing authors with a certain number of copies of their work seems to have prevailed among the colonists. Thus the Massachusetts General Court, having paid for the publication of Norton's *Heart of N-England Rent*, ordered the printer to give him "twenty or thirty" copies.[94] The more pressing question for writers who wanted their work printed was where to find the money to pay the printer's bill. Public funds were one source; by the 1670s the civil governments in Massachusetts and Connecticut were routinely paying for the annual election sermon while also sponsoring a few substantial publications, like Morton's *New-Englands Memoriall.* Government patronage was the main reason why, before 1690, four times as many "occasional" sermons were printed as those that were pastoral or doctrinal.[95] Imprints directed at the Native Americans were subsidized by the New England Company. Within the world of commerce, London printers and booksellers affiliated with the Nonconformist community were sometimes a possibility, though the risks involved in sending a manuscript overseas were considerable. Cotton Mather, who tried harder than anyone else of his generation to secure overseas publication, suffered the experience of having manuscripts he had sent to London languish unattended; some were never published and others, when they did appear, were rife with errors.[96] Whenever he saw an opportunity, which arose most frequently with funeral sermons, Mather also asked persons of piety and wealth in the colonies or England to subsidize the costs of printing. The Boston merchant Samuel Sewall befriended a number of publications, including some he initiated himself.[97] But many manuscripts, though prepared with publication in mind, never made it through the press.

By the close of the century, booksellers in Boston were becoming more interested in publishing local texts, especially when there seemed some real possibility of quick sales. Speed was all-important in the case of sermons tied to specific events, like an earthquake or an execution; in 1717 a report on the trial and execution of pirates appeared within a week.[98] But it was as intermediaries in the making of the text itself that booksellers made their presence felt most strongly, for no concept of authorial property stood in their way. Among the first-generation ministers, a familiar experience was discovering that a bookseller in London had issued a work of theirs without asking for permission or ensuring that the manuscript being used as copy-text was accurate – a dubious assumption in any case, since some of these books were based on sermon notes taken by another person.[99] To judge from assertions in prefaces and elsewhere, the book-buying public was aware of the fluidity of tranmission, for Thomas Allen, who served briefly in the ministry in New England before returning home, vouched that a set of sermons by John Cotton were the handiwork of "a ready Writer, [who] did take those Notes from the Mouth of the Preacher." The notes that were the basis for another of Cotton's sermon series were advertised as having been "corrected by his owne hand" and sanctioned as ready for printing.[100]

But for other sermon-series the case was far different. The publishing history of Thomas Hooker's *The Poor Doubting Christian Drawn Unto Christ* is a telling example of interventions by copyists, printers, booksellers, and editors. The initial version was condemned by the editors of the second as "utterly deformed and misrepresented in multitudes of passages," yet the story continues, culminating with a London bookseller who mixed and matched the different published versions to create a hybrid of his own. When this "compiled" edition was reissued in New England at the time of the Great Awakening, its sponsor, Thomas Prince, thought that the book contained Hooker's very words "taken in short-hand by one of his auditors in England"![101] The textual history of *A Token, for the Children of New-England* (1700), which was published on this side of the Atlantic, is one of booksellers adding to or abridging the stories in successive editions, some of which lacked Cotton Mather's name on the title page.[102] As for the *errata* slips in many seventeenth-century books, these were often the doing of someone other than the author.[103]

Those who wished to see their work in print faced the constraints of patronage and trade practices. But the women who became writers had to deal with a further difficulty, the assumption, a commonplace of the times, that the female voice was properly confined to a private world. When Cotton Mather affirmed a less restrictive version of this rule in 1712, declaring that good women writers "have been Patterns of *Humility*. They have made no Noise; they have sought no Fame," he was intentionally contrasting such deferential women with those of their sex who had participated in the sectarian insurgencies of the Civil War period in mid-seventeenth-century England. In the course of those insurgencies, dozens of female radicals and visionaries had broken free of the customary hierarchies of gender and learnedness to become public speakers and writers.[104] These activists gave new life to the ancient trope of women as ever-threatening to turn things upside down, a trope reiterated in a letter from a New England minister to his sister in which he observed that "your printing of a Book, beyond the custom of your Sex, doth rankly smell," and echoed in commendatory verse prefaces (all of them by men) to Anne Bradstreet's *The Tenth Muse Lately Sprung up in America*.[105]

In the context of this trope and the private–public distinction, it is not surprising that learned men acted as the sponsors of Bradstreet and Mary Rowlandson. A brother-in-law sent a manuscript of Bradstreet's poems to England, where they were printed in 1650 without her knowledge or her name being on the title page. Mary Rowlandson entrusted the manuscript of *The Soveraignty & Goodness of God . . . Being a Narrative of the Captivity and Restauration of Mrs. Mary Rowlandson* (1682) to a yet-unidentified intermediary (possibly Increase Mather) who undertook to warrant in an introduction that the text in question had actually been written by a woman and to justify making "public" a text that had been written (as was said on the title page) "for . . . Private Use." According to her sponsor, Mrs. Rowlandson's "modesty" kept her from "thrust[ing] it into the press" until friends persuaded her that "such works of God should [not] be hid from present and future generations . . . [and] that God might have his due glory, and others benefit by it as well as herself." Yet these reasons were evidently not enough to forestall criticism, for the anonymous sponsor also asked Mrs. Rowlandson's readers to "excuse her then if she come thus into public," to pay her "vow" to "talk of God's acts, and to speak of and publish His wonderful works."[106]

A Boston bookseller reprinted Bradstreet's poems posthumously as *Several Poems Compiled with great variety of Wit and Learning, full of Delight* (1678), with additional commentary and a eulogy. This time around, however, her name was on the title page and, probably at her initiative, the collection included additional poems and revised or corrected versions of some of those which had been printed in 1650. The extent to which she took control of the second edition remains in doubt.[107] But Bradstreet had already asserted her ownership and authority as a woman in a poem that appeared in the first edition:

> I am obnoxious to each carping tongue
> Who says my hand a needle better fits,

A Poets pen all scorn I should thus wrong,
For such despite they cast on Female wits:
If what I do prove well, it won't advance
They'l say it's stoln, or else it was by chance.[108]

Whether other women who lacked Bradstreet's self-confidence confined themselves to the sphere of the home, allowing what they wrote to circulate only among friends or within a coterie, is unclear. Anonymity and manuscript publication were, in any case, practices employed both by men and women, and writers of both genders voiced the fear of being exposed in public.[109]

Nevertheless, men were clearly more privileged than women, and learned men were more privileged than those of either sex who were unlearned. These forms of hierarchy complicated the vernacular, common culture that all Puritans and Nonconformists aspired to sustain. Another source of strain was the ancient tension between separating and moderate elements within the Puritan movement, a tension aggravated in New England by the contradictory significance of isolation: Was it a good thing that the colonists were cut off from Europe, or was it necessary to overcome that isolation and partake of cosmopolitan possibilities? All of these conflicting impulses were present in Increase Mather, and the contradictions of his own career – enemy of the half-way covenant of 1662, then its strong proponent; sharp critic in the 1680s of any rapprochement with the English government, but chief advocate of a new charter (1691) that signified the end of political autonomy – are fully evident in the variety of voices he used as a writer. He signaled his awareness of two alternatives in remarking, in the preface of *A Discourse concerning Faith* (1710), a sermon-series preached "before a Popular Auditory," that he was eschewing "Scholasticall Argumentations" in order to explain things plainly to those "of the meanest Capacities." Meanwhile his aspiration to membership in the international community of the learned remained strong, leading him and a few colleagues to form a short-lived "Philosophical Society" in 1683. Mather was well aware of the possibility that literature meant not plainness and self-renunciation but artifice and fame. So was his son Cotton who, by the mid-1690s, was becoming defensive about the "meanness" of the genres and prose style he inherited from the Protestant vernacular tradition. His tone bespeaks the difficulties of sustaining an oppositional literary tradition when the reward of fame at home was weighed against the lure of pleasing an influential audience on the other side of the Atlantic. Nor was the awareness of this choice new with Cotton Mather. It had been heralded in the 1650s when Michael Wigglesworth gave a student oration celebrating the "skill" of the "orator." Naming Cicero and Demosthenes as two great practitioners of the art, Wigglesworth said nothing of the Holy Spirit. The numerous prefatory poems in Bradstreet's *Tenth Muse* and *Several Poems* commemorating her "Muse" as "Poet" and "Author" reveal a similar awareness of literature as an art form set apart from life.[110] All along, therefore, the vernacular tradition was under pressure from learned and academic understandings of style, audience, and literature. The baroque, high-style portrait painted in London in 1688 of Increase pointing to a folio, with others piled beside him, is an apt emblem of this pressure and, from another vantage, of the cultural hybridity so characteristic of the provincial. But the story of how, in eighteenth-century America, these contradictions led to a remaking of literary culture belongs to another chapter.

CHAPTER FIVE

The Atlantic World

PART ONE. THE ATLANTIC ECONOMY IN THE EIGHTEENTH CENTURY

DAVID D. HALL

BY THE CLOSE OF THE SEVENTEENTH CENTURY, all but Georgia of the English colonies on the American mainland had been founded; Delaware, long settled, became incorporated as a colony in 1701, though it remained under the control of Pennsylvania. New Netherland, initiated by a Dutch trading company in 1624, was conquered by the English in 1664 and renamed New York in honor of its proprietor, James, Duke of York. The royalist proprietors of New Jersey received their lands from James in 1664, but the western part of the colony passed within a decade into the hands of wealthy Quakers. East New Jersey was eventually purchased by a heterogeneous group of proprietors, who, like the owners of West Jersey, relinquished political control in 1702 to a royal governor. The burst of charter-granting early in the reign of Charles II also led to the founding of Carolina, where the first permanent settlement was achieved in 1670. The northern province, known originally as Albemarle, was separated off and named North Carolina in 1691. Political independence followed in 1712; in 1729, both colonies acquired royal governors. Pennsylvania was granted by the King in 1681 to William Penn, a prominent Quaker. Elsewhere in territories that would later be incorporated into the continental United States, the Spanish reestablished their presence in the Southwest after overcoming the Pueblo revolt of 1680. Early in the century, the French began to colonize Louisiana, establishing settlements at Biloxi, Mobile, and New Orleans. Here, in 1764, Denis Braud set up a printing office that was intermittently active. Another, in British Florida, was established in St. Augustine in 1783.

From an Atlantic perspective, a major aspect of the decades leading up to the Stamp Act crisis of 1765 was the ever-growing integration of the colonies into the structure of the British empire. In the 1680s, London-based administrators of this empire had devised an intercolonial political structure, the "Dominion of New England," as a means of curtailing the independence of the chartered colonies in New England. Though the Dominion collapsed as a consequence of the Glorious Revolution of 1688, the Crown pursued other means of enhancing its control. By 1730, all but two of the chartered colonies (Connecticut and Rhode Island) had royal governors, and Pennsylvania and Maryland were the sole remaining proprietorships. The task of enforcing the Navigation Acts, which regulated the shipping of "enumerated" goods from the mainland, brought an ever-growing number of customs officials and naval officers to the mainland, and their numbers also grew because of an almost uninterrupted sequence of imperial wars. Meanwhile, philanthropic agencies linked with the Church of England – the Society for the Propagation of the Gospel in Foreign Parts (SPG), and the organization known as "Dr. Bray's Associates" – were endeavoring to strengthen the Anglican presence. Other circumstances, like the founding of an intercolonial post office and the regularizing of ocean voyages, made for closer ties with the empire and among the colonies themselves.[1]

For the history of the book, the story is one of rising production and consumption. Overall, the total annual number of imprints recorded in the North American Imprints Program rose from 68 in 1700 to 798 in 1789. When newspaper issues are added in, the total for 1790 soars to slightly in excess of 8,000 (Graph 3, Appendix 1).[2] Taking a long view of this trend, we may understand it as closely correlated with demography. In the course of the century a near-doubling of the population occurred every twenty-five years, an annual rate of growth of some 3 percent that was accomplished by natural increase and immigration from Europe. The 55,000 colonists of European origin in 1670 had increased to 265,000 in 1700 and to more than two million by 1770. The federal census of 1790 indicated that, despite the disturbances of war, the population of European origins now totaled some three million. African Americans (slave and free) numbered some 310,000 in 1770 and some 759,000 in 1790. In the decades before the Revolution the fastest rate of growth occurred in the lower south (Georgia, North and South Carolina); the slowest in New England, which attracted few immigrants from outside and had a heavy out-migration.[3]

The immigrants who arrived from Europe after 1680, many of them literate in the sense of being able to read, brought new energy and needs to the book trades. Pennsylvania drew thousands of Germans, some of whom were members of religious sects that had experienced persecution in Europe. Their presence made possible a thriving trade in German-language books and, as of the 1730s, local printers and booksellers. Scotland and Ulster were the source of another major stream of immigrants, most of them an educated and religious people who almost immediately began to create churches and academies of their own and to participate in the book trades. A third influential group were French Protestants who left their native country after Louis XIV revoked the Edict of Nantes in 1685. Overwhelmingly Protestant, the population of the colonies included a handful of Catholics and, by the 1770s, as many as 1,500 Jews, most of whom were clustered in Charleston, Philadelphia, New York, and Newport.[4]

The appeal of immigration was, above all, economic, for these people arrived in a country where, after 1700, the economy was expanding at close to 3 percent a year on a long-term basis, a rate far better than the British economy was enjoying. From one decade to the next the economy went through phases of boom, inflation, and recession. Despite the downturns, per capita wealth steadily increased – most rapidly in the South and least so in New England, with the economy of the middle colonies falling between these two extremes. So did the traffic in goods within the British Atlantic economy. Although the sugar islands of the West Indies remained the most important centers of wealth within this economy, the export trade from Britain to the mainland colonies rose sharply, to the point where, by the early decades of the century, there was an "awakening appreciation that North American consumers might be as important to the empire as West Indian producers had been."[5] In keeping with the nature of the domestic economy, which produced mainly raw materials and food, the greatest share of these imports – possibly in excess of 90 percent – consisted of manufactured or processed goods.[6]

The place of books in these shipments from Europe was, in the aggregate, extremely modest compared to the colonists' need for textiles, rum, sugar, iron, glassware, and other consumer goods. Even so, the American market became an increasingly significant outlet for the British book trade. Though they were good customers of the British, the colonists also patronized local producers. Domestic production constituted a growing share – albeit a share that varied sharply by region, far higher in the northern and middle colonies than in the South – of the printed matter that circulated in the eighteenth century.[7] If newspaper issues are included in the count, the role of domestic production becomes all the greater, for by 1750, the colonists were supporting twelve newspapers and, by 1790, ninety-nine, a rate of growth (when each issue is counted as an imprint) that far exceeded the increase in book production (Graph 3, Appendix 1). Printers continued to equip their offices with presses and type manufactured in Britain, but local production of paper began in 1691 outside Philadelphia and, by the time of the Revolution, domestic output was substantial (see Part 2).

At the start of the century, Boston was the center of book production and distribution in the mainland colonies, a position it retained for several decades. An English observer remarked in 1719 that New York contained "but one little Bookseller's Shop" at a time when Boston had several, adding that "in the Plantations of Virginia, Maryland, Carolina, Barbadoes, and the Islands, [there were] none at all." But by 1770 much had changed. Boston was now being overtaken as a center of production by Philadelphia, which had some thirty bookshops (London at the same moment had 120), as the whole of New England was by printers in the mid-Atlantic colonies (Graph 2a, Appendix 1).[8] By 1790, newspaper production in this region as measured by the number of issues was twice the rate of production in New England. The new federal government was responsible for some of Philadelphia's importance as a printing center, and a sharp run-up in New York City imprints in the late 1780s was also influenced by the temporary presence of the new government. Notwithstanding the remarkable prosperity of the southern colonies as measured by wealth per capita among colonists of European descent, the overall production of books and newspapers in the area lagged well behind the rates in New England and the mid-Atlantic, a difference that would have been even greater had Charleston not been so active as a center of production, responsible for more than a third of all newspaper issues printed in the region before 1790.

The regional geography of the book trades is also apparent in the distribution of certain genres. Considering production of books and broadsides (i.e., omitting newspaper issues) for the period 1701–1790, 28 percent of domestic imprints may be classified as government-related: proclamations, orders, sessions laws, and the like. Sermons, though gradually declining in importance (the peak as a percentage of all imprints occurred in the second decade of the century) constituted another 12½ percent, and almanacs, almost 8 percent (Graphs 5a-b, Appendix 1).[9] In each of the colonies, local governments were the initial patrons of the press, which is why as much as 90 percent of the early imprints in each colony were government related. By the 1760s, this figure had fallen to 11 percent for printers in Boston and New York. Yet for those in Virginia and Maryland, government printing remained the single most important line of business. For the South as a whole during the century (1701–1790), government printing amounted to 53 percent of total book production, as contrasted with 25 percent for all of New England. Sermons provide an interesting contrast, with the Massachusetts trade alone accounting for more than half of the entire total and the southern, but 2 percent (Graph 8a, Appendix 1).

These differences of place, time, and genre start us on the road to a historically specific description of the book trade and of the role of books in politics, culture, and society, a task that requires setting aside the story of unchecked growth. The year-to-year or decade-to-decade variations in production become, instead, more interesting. These variations reveal the significance of controversies, some of them local, others international in scope, for the book trades. The near-doubling of imprints that occurred in and around 1740, a rate of change repeated between 1773 and 1775, arose out of intercolonial and transatlantic events, in the first instance the religious insurgencies known collectively as the "Great Awakening" and, in the second, the political agitation leading up to war with Britain and the *Declaration of Independence*. Wartime conditions explain the decline of production in the early 1780s to the level of the late 1760s. Not until the very close of our period did book production recover the ground that had been lost.

Lacking any adequate measure of the per capita consumption of books over time and by region, we may nonetheless suppose that, by the middle of the eighteenth century, a greater percentage of the colonists in the northern and middle colonies, and possibly in the south as well, were engaged in buying books. Even if no "reading-revolution" had unfolded before independence – an issue addressed in Chapter 11 – signs of change, including higher rates of literacy for both men and women, were accumulating by the 1760s. That the higher-end market for imported books was flourishing is suggested by the greater frequency and scale of newspaper advertisements and booksellers' catalogues, most of them hailing the arrival of imported titles (be these schoolbooks and Bibles or "new" works of fiction) and by the growing number of proposals to publish by subscription. Newspaper advertisements are perhaps the best indication of buyer interest: After a modest increase in the 1740s, they began a sharp rise in the early 1760s (Graph 6, Appendix 1). The period extending from 1762 to 1775 seems, indeed, something of a watershed, a moment when the number of colonial imprints reached a new peak, when social and circulating libraries began to multiply, and when retail advertisements became much more frequent.

Yet the book trade remained fragmented, with few means of exchanging copies between colonies or major centers of production. In this respect, the workings of the book trade mirrored the social geography of the country. On the eve of the American Revolution, more than 90 percent of the population lived in widely dispersed towns of less than 2,500 people. To be sure, these smaller communities were not all alike, for some had better connections via roads and rivers, were seats of local government, or functioned as centers for the exchange of goods. Towns that were side-by-side and of the same size could have very different "social economies" as indicated, in part, by the presence or absence of books. Thus the residents of wealthy, commercial Woodbury, Connecticut, had the means and connections to establish a social library in 1772 long before any similar event occurred in nearby Newtown, where household wealth was more evenly distributed.[10] Before the Revolution, few inland settlements were capable of sustaining specialized stores of any kind. Like most other shopkeepers, printers and booksellers congregated in the larger coastal towns where merchants, government officials, and artisans also gathered.[11] This hierarchy of scale was magnified by the difference between the coast and the "backcountry" to which an ever-growing number of colonists were moving by the late eighteenth century.[12] As for cities, by 1760 some 30,000 people lived in Philadelphia, and the growth of New York and Charleston was commensurate.

The newer modes of consumption were much more visible in these coastal towns, as were the extremes of wealth and poverty. In these same places printing and bookselling flourished. Competition between printers, which existed only in Boston before 1725, spread to Philadelphia in this decade and to New York and Charleston by the 1740s. To map the locations of printing offices in 1760 and 1790 is to discern, at a glance, both the emergence of competition and the restricted geography of the book trades (Figs. 5.1 and 5.2). This geography was being transformed in the closing decades of the century as printers and booksellers in the northern states began to move inland and to set up shop in smaller towns, a process that accelerated in the years ahead. An expanding population, together with the imperiling of coastal commerce during the war, were the keys to this dispersion; where the population was more widely scattered, as it was in the rural South, schools, libraries, printing offices, and stores remained less abundant and less widely dispersed.

Let us return to the place of politics in the book trade. Factionalism was endemic among the colonists and revolutionaries, a factionalism that, as James Madison noted in *Federalist* Paper 10, was rooted in denominational, ethnic, regional, and economic differences. Another source was the recurring fault-line of colonial politics, the conflict of interest between proprietary or imperial policies on the one hand and local interests on the other. Within each civil government, moreover, different interest groups engaged in intricate maneuvers for office and privilege. The assemblies that by mid-century existed in each of the colonies were significantly involved in the recruitment of printers and the commissioning of certain kinds of books, in part because these bodies felt that printing afforded a publicity – a means of bringing out into the open some of their deliberations and decisions – that in turn worked to curtail the power of proprietors, royal governors, and imperial administrators. Yet these officials had their own reasons for turning to the press and the book trade. Thus it happened that printers allied with royal governors issued the Stamp Act of 1765, as did printers allied with assemblies or the opposition.

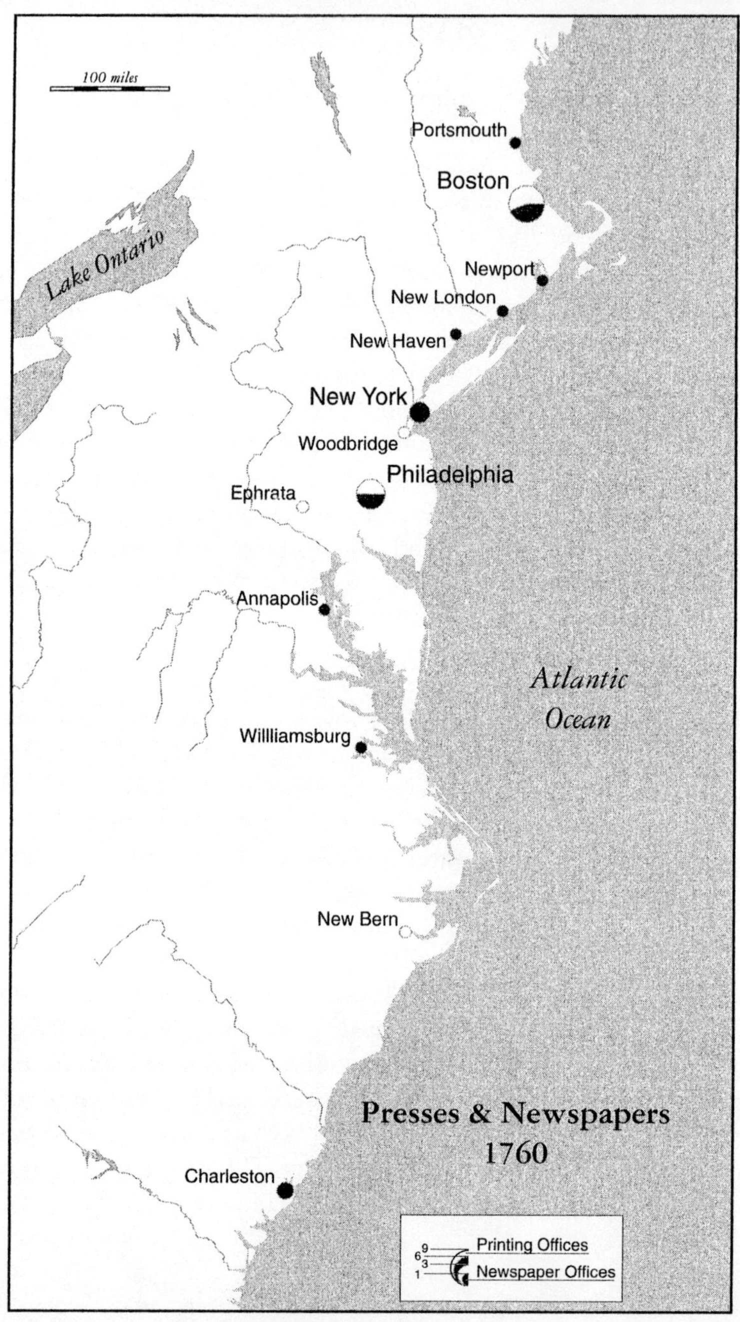

Figure 5.1. Locations of all printing offices known to be operating in December 1760, showing the ratio of those that printed a newspaper (black) to those that did not (white). Adapted from Lester J. Cappon, ed., *Atlas of Early American History: The Revolutionary Era, 1760–1790* (Princeton, N.J.: Princeton University Press, 1976), 34. Courtesy of Princeton University Press and the Harvard Map Collection.

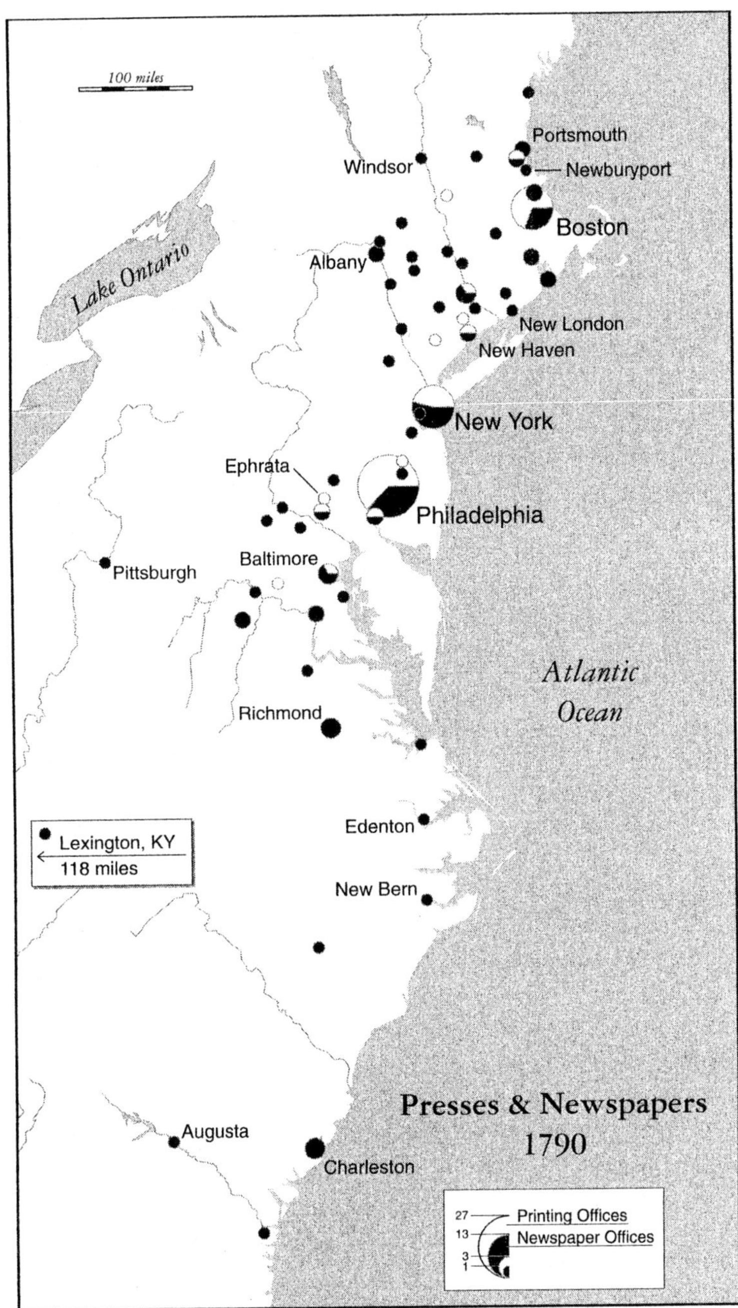

Figure 5.2. Locations of all printing offices known to be operating in December 1790, showing the ratio of those that printed a newspaper (black) to those that did not (white). Adapted from Lester J. Cappon, ed., *Atlas of Early American History: The Revolutionary Era, 1760–1790* (Princeton, N.J.: Princeton University Press, 1976), 68. Courtesy of Princeton University Press and the Harvard Map Collection.

This politics of factionalism was good for printers and booksellers because it stimulated the demand for pamphlets and newspapers. The "Keithian schism" of the 1690s translated into a flurry of seventeen imprints from William Bradford, the first Philadelphia printer, at a time when he had little else to do, and the English itinerant evangelist George Whitefield triggered a religious and social turbulence on either side of 1740 that spurred another sharp increase in production. Yet as we will see in more detail, a politics of factionalism did not always sit well with the interests of printers and booksellers, for it made them cautious lest they give offense and lose out on business, especially the profitable business of being government printer. Another possibility was being sued for libel. And, at moments like the revolutionary crisis, a stance of neutrality, which a long line of printers used to shield themselves from factionalism, ceased to be an option. Anyone who affiliated with the Loyalists risked being put out of business by a mob, like the one that descended on James Rivington's New York shop in late 1775.[13]

How the recurrent factionalism of early American politics and locality intersected with the business interests of printers and booksellers, how the technologies of speech and handwriting continued to serve the colonists well, and how the possibilities and expectations for marketing and distributing books varied from one region to another, is revealed in the ongoing history of the publication of statute law,[14] a history we tell briefly in bringing this introduction to the eighteenth century to a close.

Printed collections of statutes existed by the 1670s for Virginia and four of the New England colonies (Massachusetts, Connecticut, Plymouth, and New Haven). The colonies that came into being after 1660 were often slow to take this step, delaying, in the case of South Carolina, several decades before shifting from oral and scribal publication to print[15] or allowing, as the government of New Hampshire did, a forty-year interval to elapse between printed collections of its statutes. According to Gabriel Johnson, a royal governor of North Carolina, the effect of relying on scribal versions, together with the usual confusion about the storage and preservation of documents in archives, was that in 1736 he could not "find that there is one compleat Copy of them in any one place, neither have I yet seen two copies of [the laws] which perfectly agree." Four years later, in 1740, he reported to the assembly that every place he went he heard "complaints . . . of their wanting Copys of the Laws. Majistrates are at a loss how to decide controversies which arose amongst his Majestie's subjects, and even private persons . . . are puzzled in what manner and at what time to comply with the Law." "There is very little difference," Johnson concluded, "betwixt having no Laws at all and living under such as are impossible to come at, and are never promulgated in an authentik manner." Another nine years passed, however, before the assembly acted to secure a printed set of laws.[16] Meanwhile, governments and civil courts continued to rely on the time-honored methods of oral "publishing" and the posting of documents in public places, a method reprised by the Continental Congress, which relied on the clergy to read certain proclamations from the pulpit.[17]

No easy solution emerged to the problems of keeping printed collections up-to-date or of signaling the difference between "perpetual" and "temporary" laws. The one step that promised well was the publishing of sessions laws, as the Massachusetts government did intermittently beginning in the 1650s, New York as of 1692, and several other colonies after 1704. Imitating English practice, Lewis Timothy of Charleston paginated the sessions laws he began to print in 1736 consecutively with a collection of statute law published in the same year. Because the Crown continued to intervene and disapprove some statutes, printers ran the risk of issuing an outmoded compilation, as happened to the Philadelphia printer Andrew Bradford, who learned in 1714 that sixteen of the acts included in an edition he had just printed had been disallowed. Bradford petitioned the colony government for relief, and it bought up the entire run.[18]

Nor was it any more certain in the eighteenth than in the seventeenth century that enough buyers were on hand. The South Carolina government agreed to subsidize the initial printing of a collection of statutes, but Lewis Timothy also advertised for subscriptions, having calculated that 300 were needed to complete the financing of the project. A year later, in 1735, with a mere 48 subscribers signed up, Timothy got the colonial government to agree to buy as many copies as were needed to bring the total up to 300. The South Carolina jurist Nicholas Trott, who did the hard work of collecting and arranging the laws of his colony, declared in the preface to *The Laws of the Province of South-Carolina* (1736) that he had taken great pains with the analytical apparatus because he wanted the collection to be "plain and easy, even to the meanest Capacity" and to be "of general use to all the Inhabitants."[19] William Bladen had spoken similarly in advocating a printed edition of the Maryland laws, as had the Massachusetts government in the middle of the seventeenth century. But the modest press run of the South Carolina *Laws*, a two-volume folio, suggests a pattern of local distribution much less expansive than Trott's preface would indicate, undoubtedly because the book was beyond the means of all but a handful of Carolinians.

In those colonies where the press runs for statute books and sessions laws were of this same size, copies were printed mainly for appointed and elected members of the government. But in several of the northern colonies demand seems to have been sufficient (possibly because of traditions of distribution established in the seventeenth century) to sustain a print run of between 500 and 1,500 copies. Subscription remained the chief means of financing and distributing the laws in places such as South Carolina. In New England, on the other hand, printers and booksellers vied for the privilege of having exclusive rights to an edition, which they then sold more largely.[20]

Any form of government printing in eighteenth-century America was easily politicized, for in deciding when or whether to print an edition of the laws and what printer to use, assemblies quarreled with councils and royal governments just as printers jostled with each other for advantage. These maneuverings explain much of what happened in places like New York, South Carolina, New Hampshire,[21] and Massachusetts. In New York, the royal governor arranged the first printing of the assembly proceedings, but in Massachusetts it was the representatives in the General Court of Massachusetts who voted in 1715 to have the journals of their proceedings printed "as the best defense" of themselves after being denounced by the governor for accomplishing so little during a legislative session.[22] Published every year thereafter, the journals were not fully revealing of what went on in House business; when the Council requested in 1723 that the House end the series, on the grounds that too much was being revealed about "Public Affairs," the representatives compromised by agreeing to omit the record of certain votes from the printed version. In general, the House was reluctant to publish roll calls that indicated how each member voted. As for editions of the printed laws, the House and Council bickered through the early 1720s before agreeing on who should print a new edition, which appeared in 1726; in the interim, a London bookseller stepped in and published a collection that ended with acts passed in 1719. The bookseller Benjamin Eliot, who may have lobbied for this delay in order to work off copies that remained from the edition he had published in 1714, opposed any new printing in the 1730s for the same reason. Another edition was delayed for seven years as the two branches of the General Court contended over "the contents of the new edition" and "the method of preparing it."[23]

The details of this infighting, together with a pervasive carelessness about governmental archives and records,[24] suggest that self-interest, be it of printers and booksellers or of political bodies, outweighed any sense of obligation to the public in determining what was printed. The persistence of oral and scribal publication – practices to which the Committees of Correspondence of the 1770s returned – suggests, as well, that no direct equation can be made between the technology of printing and the emergence of a public sphere. As we carry our story forward, the particularities of this intersection between the book trades and colonial politics will loom large.

PART TWO. PRINTERS' SUPPLIES AND CAPITALIZATION

JOHN BIDWELL

COLONIAL PRINTERS SUFFERED as much from shortages of supplies as from other hardships they encountered in the distant, newly settled, sparsely populated areas where they plied their trade. Among other vexations, they had to cope with weak markets, tight credit, restive labor, poor transportation, and political interference – all serious problems but none rivaling the fundamental difficulty of obtaining basic manufacturing materials. The chronic scarcity of printing materials is one of the defining characteristics of their trade, one of the prime economic factors that serve to distinguish their operations from comparable ventures in the mother country.

Book production in the colonies responded to changing conditions of supply and demand, an economic equation that must account for the availability of resources such as paper, type, and printing equipment along with other market forces. While certain supply factors impeded the growth of the printing trade, demand factors induced Americans to supplement their stock of imported books with texts produced in their own printing shops, establishments intended to meet the religious, political, and cultural needs of their communities. Chapter 11 examines the incentives and constraints that influenced the consumption of reading matter in the American colonies, the demand side of the equation. This chapter will consider, on the other side, the economic requirements of book production in this region, ostensibly subject to the mercantilist policies of the British colonial administration, which sometimes prescribed how and where printing materials could be obtained. Despite these regulations, or because of them, American printers soon developed independent sources of supply.

Like most manufacturing concerns, printing shops contained two types of supplies, capital goods and intermediate goods. Presses, type, and other equipment usually listed among the major assets of a printing firm are considered capital goods, as are tools and accessories such as composing sticks, type cases, galleys, chases, ball stocks, and the imposing stone. Intermediate goods comprise paper, ink, bookbinding materials, and whatever else might be consumed in the process of book production. A printer had to obtain capital goods to get into business and a steady supply of intermediate goods to stay in business.

An enterprising journeyman could set up shop either by buying capital goods or by renting them. If he bought into the trade, he could raise the necessary funds either by (1) borrowing from family or friends, (2) forming a partnership with another journeyman, (3) using capital provided by a silent partner outside the trade, or (4) taking a subsidy from the government, a political group, a religious body, or some other organization that sought ready access to printing facilities. The startup costs sometimes surpassed the earning powers of printers like Zechariah Fowle, who for nineteen years never paid more than the interest on the debt incurred when he bought his press and types, apparently counting on the indulgence of his creditor, "a near relation by marriage."[25]

Even with sufficient capital in hand, aspiring master printers still had other obstacles to overcome before setting off on their own. They could not shop for their equipment in one convenient locale until the early nineteenth century, when the Philadelphia and New York trade grew large enough to support the first printers' supply houses. Instead, they had to undertake long and painful negotiations either with a European agent or with local members of the trade. If they ordered new equipment from abroad, they had to pay formidable sums in advance and at the risk of receiving the wrong goods after a punishing delay. Alternatively, they could book a passage overseas, where they could deal with suppliers directly and check the quality of their purchases, though here, too, they had to endure high costs and long delays. Or they could buy used equipment at home, providing that some was available when needed and that some other printer did not interfere.

Indeed, some printers did intervene in these transactions to quash potential competition or to exploit the scarcity of supplies. An impetuous Mathew Carey learned this lesson the hard way, having announced his first printing venture even before he had acquired the tools of the trade. This impulsive foray irked one of his Philadelphia competitors, who bid against him when the only available press in town came up for auction. Undaunted, Carey bought the press as well as other supplies he needed to get started in the printing business. His rival failed to stop him – but did succeed in slowing him down by forcing him to spend £50 currency or £30 sterling (about a third of his financial reserves) on dilapidated equipment far less serviceable than what he should have procured for that amount. In a similar predicament, Isaiah Thomas once tried to buy out a North Carolina printer who "took advantage of his situation," first by setting the price of his shop about three times its proper value and then by haggling so capriciously that Thomas finally wearied of the game and went off to seek his fortune elsewhere. In both cases the market for capital goods was so tight that even used equipment could command exorbitant prices.[26]

The cost of intermediate goods imposed an even greater burden on colonial printers. Later on in this essay I will show that their annual expenditures on paper could equal or exceed their initial investment in a printing office. The cost of other intermediate goods – ink, leather, parchment, pasteboard, etc. – was negligible in comparison to paper because these materials were more easily prepared and more often produced locally. Philadelphia printers were mixing ink made from their own lampblack in or before the 1720s, and, in the 1790s, were buying ready-made printing ink from local manufacturers at the equivalent of 1*s.* 6*d.* to 2*s.* 1*d.* sterling per pound. In 1794 Isaiah Thomas stockpiled large quantities of ink imported from England at 1*s.* 11*d.* sterling per pound as well as a small amount of "best" English ink priced at 5*s.* sterling, though he also patronized American ink makers, who charged him approximately 1*s.* 2*d.* sterling. Bookbinding tools and materials also required a minimal investment, accounting for a sixteenth of the total value of Thomas Short's printing office in 1713, a twelfth of Timothy Green II's shop in 1763, and about a thirty-third of William Rind's shop in 1773. Of course, many printers did not keep their own binding supplies but preferred to send their books elsewhere to be bound. But they all had to keep an adequate supply of paper, an essential ingredient of printed goods and a perpetual concern of the colonial printer, who was always seeking a reliable source and a reasonable price for this staple commodity.[27]

Inventories of printing shops provide valuable evidence for comparing the cost of capital goods with that of paper as well as for estimating the aggregate value of printing firms large and small, data useful for understanding how much printers were willing to pay for additional output. But this evidence has to be interpreted carefully because appraisers reckoned the value of printing equipment in different ways, depending on how their figures would be used. Inventories could be taken for several reasons: to settle an estate, to begin or conclude a partnership, to offer a printing house for sale, or merely to list what materials were in stock and to calculate their net worth along with other assets of the firm. Obviously, an estate inventory would set lower valuations on equipment than would a printer trying to sell it off at an advantageous price. Furthermore, some venerable printing outfits were so decrepit that appraisers valued them as if they were next to useless. This was the case of Anne Catharine Green's printing house, where one of the presses was "very old," all the type was worn, and various other articles were either old or broken. Nevertheless, more of these inventories survive than any other kind, they are more likely to itemize various types of equipment, and their valuations still bear comparison with other estimates, if only at the lower end of the scale.

The actual sale price of printing shops ranged significantly higher than the values assigned by estate inventories throughout the eighteenth century. Table 5.1 includes both kinds of figures, estate values as well as prices asked or paid for printing shops (Whitemarsh, Stretch, Fowle, and Saur) along with inventory amounts used either to balance the accounts of partnerships (Franklin & Hall and Fay & Williams) or to compute the total value of a

TABLE 5.1 **Valuations of printing shops, 1654–1802**

Value (Sg.)	Presses	Type (lbs.)	Name	Location	Date
£71	1		Samuel Green*	Cambridge, Mass.	1654
45	1		Marmaduke Johnson*	Cambridge, Mass.	1674
32	1		Thomas Short*	New London, Conn.	1713
52	1?		Thomas Whitemarsh	Charleston, S.C.	1731
54	1		Timothy Green I*	New London, Conn.	1757
51	1		Timothy Green II*	New London, Conn.	1763
84	1		Zechariah Fowle	Boston, Mass.	1770
76	1	1,560	John Holt*	New York, N.Y.	1785
63	1	696	I. Thomas and L. Worcester	Worcester, Mass.	1794
142	1	1,420	I. Thomas and E. Waldo	Brookfield, Mass.	1794
209	2		John Stretch	Williamsburg, Va.	1765
55	2		Jonas Green*	Annapolis, Md.	1767
102	2	1,050	William Rind*	Williamsburg, Va.	1773
34	2	2,250	Anne Catharine Green*	Annapolis, Md.	1775
165	2	7,763	Christopher Saur II	Germantown, Pa.	1778
140	2	1,578	I. Thomas and I. Thomas, Jr.	Worcester, Mass.	1794
158	2	1,630	I. Thomas and D. Carlisle	Walpole, N.H.	1794
87	2	2,670	Timothy Green III*	New London, Conn.	1796
145	2	1,000+	W. Fay and S. Williams	Rutland, Vt.	1802
192	3	4,040	B. Franklin and D. Hall	Philadelphia, Pa.	1766
911	5	7,580	Isaiah Thomas	Worcester, Mass.	1794

Notes and Sources: Valuations marked with an asterisk are based on estate inventories. The Cambridge inventories are documented in Winship, *Cambridge Press*, 165, 330; the New London inventories in Johnson, *A Checklist of New London, Connecticut, Imprints*, 443–53; and the Annapolis inventories in Wroth, *Printing in Col. Md.*, 153. For William Rind's inventory see "Old Virginia Editors," *William and Mary College Quarterly Historical Magazine* 7 (1898–1899): 9–17, and for John Holt's inventory see Victor Hugo Paltsits, *John Holt, Printer and Postmaster: Some Facts and Documents Relating to His Career* (New York: New York Public Library, 1920). The cost of Thomas Whitemarsh's "printing-house and materials" is recorded in *Account Books Kept by Benjamin Franklin*, 1:14. An advertisement for what was to have been John Stretch's printing office appeared in *The Pennsylvania Gazette*, Sept. 12, 1765. For more information about Stretch's office and for the itemized inventory of Franklin & Hall's equipment see *Franklin Papers*, 13:60–63, 105, 264, 305. The sale of Christopher Saur II's printing office is recorded in "Forfeited Estates: Inventories and Sales," *Pennsylvania Archives* (Philadelphia, 1852–1935), 6th ser., 12:865–81, 887–911. Marcus A. McCorison has transcribed the Fay & Williams inventory in "A Daybook from the Office of *The Rutland Herald* Kept by Samuel Williams, 1798–1802," *Procs. AAS* 76 (1966):395. A photocopy of Zechariah Fowle's "Articles of Agreement," October 23, 1770, for the sale of his equipment to Isaiah Thomas is in the Isaiah Thomas Papers, as are the 1794 inventories, titled "Acct. of Stock, & value of Isaiah Thomas's property in Books, Stationary, Types &c. &c. taken October 1794."

printer's assets (Thomas). Arranged chronologically, this table distinguishes between shops equipped with different numbers of presses – the traditional indication of the size of the operation, though not always very accurate because some printers retained an extra press that had long outlived its usefulness. Whenever possible, I have also calculated the total weight of type in stock, which can be correlated with other data to denote the true size of a printing business.

One-press shops appear to have cost somewhere between £60 and £85 sterling during the eighteenth century, perhaps somewhat less during the earlier part of the century, and probably somewhat more if containing new equipment. In 1731 Benjamin Franklin set Thomas Whitmarsh up in business with printing materials costing approximately £52 sterling. Adjusted for inflation, Franklin's investment was probably worth about £67 sterling in 1770, when Isaiah Thomas agreed to purchase the "Printing Types Press & Utensils" of his former master Zechariah Fowle for the equivalent of £84 sterling. In 1794 the economist Tench Coxe estimated that the startup costs of a printing business in western Pennsylvania would amount to $500, worth about £82 sterling in 1770. Tench Coxe's estimate corresponds to the price set by Zechariah Fowle but significantly exceeds Franklin's outlay earlier in the century, which ranges closer to the value an estate appraiser assigned to John Holt's printing shop in 1785, a sum equivalent to £65 in 1770 pounds sterling. Other estate inventories calculate the worth of one-press shops at even lower amounts.[28]

Information on the value of two-press shops is more elusive and less reliable. In 1766 the Franklin & Hall partnership probably owned more type and presses than any of its competitors, though most of the type was worn and one of the three presses had been "mended so often" that it could hardly function in its "shatter'd" condition. If considered an unusually large two-press shop, however, its appraised value of £192 sterling seems fairly accurate in comparison with the £209 sterling that John Stretch or his representatives had paid a year or two previously for two presses, seven fonts of type, and "every Article necessary for an immediate Entrance on the Business . . . all entirely new, having never been unpacked." The printer who appraised the equipment owned by Franklin & Hall had also inspected the "Invoice" of Stretch's shop, which he thought to be easily worth £209 sterling. Indeed, this "Complete Sett of Printing Materials" warranted such a high price because it had just been imported from England by or for Stretch, who died before it could be used. William Hunter paid an even higher price in 1753 when he bought the "Printing materials" of William Parks for £287 sterling, though in this case it is impossible to ascertain how much or what kind of equipment he was buying, or whether he was buying a stock of paper, the goodwill of the firm, or some other unusually valuable component of his predecessor's business. Predictably, the sums adduced by estate inventories range substantially below the prices set on two-press shops for commercial purposes, ranging around £150 sterling toward the end of the century. On the basis of these figures one might surmise that a two-press shop could cost between £150 and £200 during the second half of the century.[29]

Presses and types were the two most significant capital costs, representing, respectively, 29 percent and 60 percent of the capital goods investment in one-press shops and 22 percent and 64 percent of the capital goods investment in two-press shops, or nearly 90 percent overall. These costs deserve to be examined more closely because they corroborate the aggregate figures proposed here and because they help to explain why American printers sought to procure their supplies at home even though they persisted in buying them from abroad.

Americans could buy presses built by local artisans as early as 1764 but continued to order English presses as late as 1793. In that year Isaiah Thomas paid a premium price of £32 sterling for a "Mahogany Press Complete on the best Construction" as well as £21 each for "Common Demy Presses" shipped to him by a London typefoundry. Benjamin Franklin also favored mahogany presses made in England, one "made under my own Inspection with Improvements" costing £26 5*s.* sterling and a smaller one costing £12 12*s.* If given a choice, however, less affluent members of the trade sought cheaper alternatives by buying used equipment or by buying locally. A watchmaker in New Haven named Isaac Doolittle is said to have made the first presses in America, though probably as a sideline, for he and his son produced only about a dozen presses in the course of more than twenty years. In 1786 his son charged £25 currency or £19 sterling for a press of the "Common Construction," which took about five weeks to build. Some of his customers had so much difficulty raising this modest sum in hard currency that they tried to pay with bartered books and stationery, tactics that obliged him to insist on payment half in cash, half in "English Goods," which were more negotiable than printers' wares. Presses made in Hartford cost around £14 sterling in 1796. Isaiah Thomas estimated the value of ordinary printing presses at £15 to £19 sterling, approximately a quarter of the capital costs of a one-press shop.[30]

The manufacture of type demanded an investment in capital and skills far greater than that required by the construction of presses. A talented craftsman could learn the art of cutting punches and justifying matrices only after an arduous apprenticeship in one of a few European typefoundries, obscure and secretive manufactories tightly controlled by families that did not train potential competitors very eagerly. Sometimes just two or three typefoundries vegetated listlessly in printing centers as large as Amsterdam, Paris, and London, where by law no more than four were allowed during periods of the seventeenth century and even less than four were operating at various times during the eighteenth century.[31]

The precision workmanship of the punchcutter and the matrix fitter culminated in sets of justified matrices, used for the comparatively simple task of casting printing type, at that point nearly ready for sale. Among the most valuable assets of a letter foundry, matrices changed hands at high prices because they cost so much to prepare and because they might fall in the hands of unwelcome intruders in the trade who could then compete with better trained typefounders without having to master their exacting craft.

Nevertheless, some Americans succeeded in ordering or bringing matrices from abroad, most notably Christopher Saur II, who cast great quantities of pica Fraktur for a 1776 edition of the Bible, possibly intending to keep it in standing type in hopes of reprinting it cheaply and conveniently. Benjamin Franklin imported French matrices for his grandson Benjamin Franklin Bache, whose typefoundry he estimated to be worth somewhere under £600 sterling. Bache's foundry never prospered, partly because he never mastered the art of cutting punches and justifying matrices, and partly because his French matrices produced types in a style not greatly admired by American printers. Adam Mappa also lacked the requisite skills and fashionable typefaces to please his customers, though he arrived in New York with an impressive array of Dutch matrices for oriental and western fonts, said to be worth just under £2,000 sterling. No doubt others would have tried to make a living in this trade if they could have raised the necessary funds to buy matrices and if they could have bought some capable of emulating the types currently in demand.[32]

American printers could not rely on a fully equipped, completely independent local typefoundry until the establishment of the Philadelphia firm of Binny & Ronaldson in 1796. Before then some printers experimented with punchcutting, and some typefounders undertook to design as well as cast types, but none succeeded as well as Binny & Ronaldson in challenging the trade's ingrained preference for foreign wares. In 1769 an ingenious jeweler and silversmith named Abel Buell obtained a subsidy from the Connecticut Assembly to learn the whole art of typefounding, which he practiced unprofitably for a while and then fell so deeply in debt that his wife had to refund the subvention while he was hiding out in Florida to evade his creditors. He resumed the trade in 1780 with only lukewarm encouragement from printers like Isaiah Thomas, who thought that Buell's types were "much inferiour to English, and the price high." More adroit than Buell, the Scottish typefounder John Baine successfully supplied Philadelphia printers from 1787, soon after he immigrated to America, until 1790 when he died at the age of seventy-seven, by then too old to train competent successors; his grandson continued the foundry desultorily for a few years before selling out and leaving town. After working for Christopher Saur II, Justus Fox and Jacob Bay each carried on the business independently, one of them producing a roman font displayed apologetically in a newspaper, which begged the indulgence of the public in hopes "that the rustic manufactures of America will prove more grateful to the patriot eye, than the more finished productions of Europe."[33]

The European types favored by colonial printers came from English, Scottish, Dutch, German, and French foundries, each furnishing the typographic means to adopt a distinctive style of book design. A glance at the ornaments, layout, and letter forms in colonial books will reveal as many national traits as one might detect in those who printed them, immigrants or descendants of recent immigrants still retaining the speech and mannerisms of their homeland. Bibles and pious tracts printed at the Saur press declare their German origins with the *Fraktur* types of the Luther typefoundry in Frankfurt am Main. Government documents printed in New Orleans display the types and ornaments characteristic of French rococo typography. The robust letter of the Caslon foundry dominated the printing trade both in England and America, arriving first at the printing shop of Benjamin Franklin in 1738, reaching Boston a year or two later, and remaining in high esteem throughout the eighteenth century. Isaiah Thomas's 1785 specimen book of types proudly announces that his unusually large stock is "Chiefly Manufactured by that great Artist, William Caslon, Esq; Of London."[34]

But not even Caslon could quell the competition of Scottish typefoundries, which began to tap the American market around 1766. The Baine foundry in Edinburgh and the Wilson foundry in Glasgow could offer fonts of equally durable letter at a cheaper price and in the new "transitional" style heralding the strict and austere neoclassical typography that would prevail at the end of the century. The Boston printers Mein and Fleeming clearly expected to drum up business by flaunting the novel appearance of their bold-faced Baine types, "far superior to any ever brought to America." However they soon lost their competitive edge to other Boston printers like William M'Alpine and Green & Russell, who imported Wilson fonts during the 1760s. In 1771 Alexander Wilson explained to Franklin that he could undercut London prices "on Account of the cheapness of Labour here," an advantage retained as late as 1793 when his firm was said to be charging 25 percent less than the London foundries. Wilson advertised his wares by distributing type specimens in America, a tactic also adopted by Edmund Fry and John Baskerville, who informed Franklin, "I am enlarging My Foundry in Order to sell Types abroad, but first to our own Colonys."[35]

Although eager to sell overseas, British foundries rarely offered price concessions or special credit terms to their American customers, who had to pay promptly and to make their own shipping and financial arrangements through agents either at home or abroad. In 1793 Wilson charged customers the standard price of 1*s.* 6*d.* per pound for book- and newspaper-text faces in the long primer size, the same price that the Fry foundry was charging at that time and just a penny more than Wilson was charging in 1771. Over-optimistically, perhaps, John Baskerville expected Americans to pay a two- to four-pence premium over Caslon prices in recognition of the "superior Merit" of his products and to remit in advance by sending bills of exchange or notes due in three months along with their orders. Franklin and his associates usually enclosed bills with the orders they despatched to the Caslon foundry; the Fry foundry accepted bills due in a year; but it was also possible to obtain a discount for payments in cash. After paying the foundry, overseas customers had to defray the cost of shipping, insurance, wharfage, and the bill of lading, not to mention the agent's commission, all of which might amount to 30 percent of the base cost of type. Mathew Carey's agent in London received a 5 percent commission for his services in negotiating the purchase of some Wilson fonts. The New York bookseller James Rivington used his London connections to procure types for American clients, who usually paid a 25 percent down payment and the balance in cash on delivery. Benjamin Franklin and Isaiah Thomas also sold new or used fonts on the side. To my knowledge, only the Fry foundry tried to cut out the middleman, either by selling direct to favored customers like Isaiah Thomas or by arranging with a New York representative to sell their goods without charging a commission.[36]

Colonial printers had to cope with the expense of imported type as well as lengthy delays, accidents in transit, and costly misunderstandings about prices, terms, and specifications. Rather than buying new type in such difficult conditions, many printers learned to tolerate lamentably worn letter, so battered from years of constant use that it could barely produce a legible page. The Boston newspapers "perfectly blind me in endeavouring to read them," complained Benjamin Franklin. "If you should ever have any Secrets that you wish to be well kept, get them printed in those Papers." Eventually, however, compositors had to discard types that were worn beyond recognition, and then had to switch from one type size to another when sorts ran low, an expedient Isaiah Thomas spied in the *Connecticut Courant*, for years set in a dismal long primer font occasionally intermixed with pica. Another way to economize on type was to impose pages in half-sheets – for example, printing octavo gatherings in four leaves instead of eight, quartos in two leaves instead of four – thus employing half the amount of letter a certain format would ordinarily require. A two-press shop replenished at the last possible moment would still need as many as four or five fonts weighing more than a thousand pounds and costing around £80 sterling. Purchased and used sparingly, type was the most significant capital cost in a colonial printing office and the most visible indication of the extent and quality of its equipment.[37]

After paying for his equipment, the master had to purchase even more supplies, perhaps not as noticeable as the types he owned but in the long run even more expensive than all the capital goods required by his trade. In the course of a year a reasonably busy printer bought a quantity of paper worth more than the total value of the equipment in his shop. Many printers deplored the high cost of paper, and some substantiated their grievances with figures revealing how much they had to spend on it every year. John Mein claimed that in just over two years he consumed paper made in nearby Milton costing between £300 and £400 in lawful money, or between £100 and £150 sterling a year – impressive sums but not entirely trustworthy because Mein may have exaggerated his expenditures for polemical effect. In attempting to settle the accounts of the Franklin and Hall partnership, James Parker figured that this two- or three-press shop consumed domestic paper worth £4905 19*s*. 1*d*. in currency and imported paper worth at least £1385 3*s*. 4*d*. in the course of nearly eighteen years – or £214 sterling per year. Parker's estimates seemed high to Franklin, who suspected correctly that his friend may have had some difficulty interpreting his ledgers, but he confused matters even more by choosing some figures to imply that paper had cost the firm as much as £278 sterling per year while using others to arrive at the more congenial amount of £106 sterling per year. Franklin's calculations are worth noting even if they are wrong, because they represent what an experienced printer might have expected at either extreme and because they neatly bracket the sum of £214 sterling, which seems fairly reliable.[38]

We can check these figures by estimating how much paper a typical printer might have bought in a year and how much it might have cost him if he paid the typical prices in this period. If supplies were plentiful, he might have bought paper several bales at a time, each bale containing from around ten to twenty-four reams, each ream consisting of somewhat less than 500 sheets. In 1697 William Bradford bargained with the proprietors of America's first paper mill to buy printing stock at the standard price of 10*s*. currency or 6*s*. 8*d*. sterling per ream, the same price appearing in the Thomas Short inventory in 1713. Printers continued to pay this price as late as the 1740s, though of course they could pay less for very coarse grades or more for better quality or larger sizes.[39]

A typical printing office of this time would have required three or four reams a week to sustain a weekly newspaper with job printing, a modest amount of government work, and an occasional pamphlet on the side. A larger concern in a major city might have used an average of six reams a week or three hundred reams a year, still far less than the requirements of a well organized London shop like the Bowyer establishment, which consumed more than five hundred reams per press in 1731. Presses stood idle for days at a time even in the busiest American shops. And yet a colonial printer owning only one press working off only 300 reams a year and paying an average price of just 6*s*. 8*d*. a ream would have to budget for an annual outlay on paper of £100 sterling, a hefty sum easily exceeding his expenditures on equipment. Although valid mainly as a rule of thumb, this round number corroborates the estimates of John Mein and James Parker. If printers invested this amount in paper every year, then they had every reason to be concerned about its price and availability, factors of prime importance in every printer's financial affairs.[40]

Resourceful printers controlled their costs by shopping around, by seeking cheaper and more reliable sources of supply. But Americans could not forage as widely as they might like on the international market, where the most affordable printing paper could be found, because they were subject to the mercantilist policies of the British government, which decreed how and what they could trade with other nations. The Navigation Act of 1663 (15 Charles II, c. 7) and subsequent legislation required colonial merchants to buy paper from British outlets, measures designed to protect shipping interests and manufacturing endeavors in the mother country. The colonies served as a market for British manufactures as well as a source of raw materials to be used in British manufactories. As far as I can tell, the colonial authorities never tried to suppress American paper mills, but they certainly did not approve of them, and as late as 1770 it was rumored that a vindictive Parliament might try to inhibit paper manufacture in America, just as it had restrained the production of woolens, hats, and iron. Parliament did pass measures prohibiting the emigration of skilled artisans (5 George I, c. 27 & 23 George II, c. 13) as well as the exportation of machinery such as paper moulds and iron presses (26 George III, c. 89), though these laws were notoriously easy to evade.[41]

While discouraging foreign competition, the mercantilist system encouraged British exports by granting refunds or "drawbacks" on the excise duty on paper to those who could prove that they were selling it abroad (10 Anne, c. 18). In this act and the Townshend Acts, the taxes on British paper are consistently lower than the taxes on paper originating in other countries. In 1737 Parliament rescinded the drawbacks on foreign paper reexported abroad to give British manufacturers an even greater price advantage in markets overseas (10 George II, c. 27). These mercantilist regulations nourished a thriving paper industry in Britain, where previously only a few mills had been struggling to compete in a market flooded with imports from Italy, France, and Holland.

On the other side of the Atlantic, however, the Acts of Trade restricted the flow of imported paper, which could enter only through authorized channels almost exclusively controlled by British merchants. Once in a while, British papermakers attempted to deal directly with American printers, but they usually depended on their London agents to handle the export trade. And they still could not undersell foreign manufacturers, who probably paid less for labor and raw materials. Consequently, exporters of British paper generally targeted the upper end of the American market, supplying writing grades rather than printing grades, book papers rather than newsprint. The lower the price, the less profit could be gained in competition with the products of American mills and reexported foreign paper, a basic ingredient in colonial newspapers until around the middle of the century and in colonial books until after the Revolutionary War.

The colonial printing trade subsisted on Dutch, French, and Italian papers usually shipped from entrepôts in England but occasionally obtained by less orthodox means. Booksellers and drygoods merchants constantly advertised large assortments of paper "Imported in the last Ship from London" along with books, prints, and stationery supplies. How much was actually used for printing and how much actually came from London it is impossible to tell. Americans supplemented these London shipments with paper arriving by two other routes, neither very well known but both worth considering as evidence that the usual trade channels did not adequately serve this distant and demanding market.

In time of war, privateers sometimes dumped on the market a cargo of paper that they had seized from the enemy at sea, perhaps not the most lucrative of plunder but still worth selling if only at a drastic discount for ready cash. Printers welcomed the opportunity to buy "Prize Papers" at bargain prices, while their suppliers obviously did not appreciate these sudden windfalls which interrupted the profitability of their trade. Around 1711 a glut of French prize papers threatened English production so credibly that it was proposed to levy the same duty on them as on the papers regularly imported from Holland, Germany, and Genoa. Papermakers in Genoa had been shipping large quantities of ordinary printing grades to England until demand dropped off during the eighteenth century, whereupon Genoese merchants sold more of their exports in Spain, another major entrepôt for a colonial market. Vast amounts of Genoa paper show up in American imprints of the 1740s, when England was at war with Spain. In 1747 Franklin's New York associate James Parker offered to send him four or five bales of "Spanish Paper," currently selling at the incredibly low price of approximately 3*s*. sterling per ream. Almost certainly this was Genoa paper captured on a Spanish vessel and put up for sale in New York, a favorite base of operations for privateers, who sailed home in 1747 bearing paper and other spoils with a total value of £140,000. American printers liked Genoa papers because they were cheap to begin with, and liked them even more when they changed hands well below the market price.[42]

Boston merchants sometimes resorted to an even more devious means of importing paper, secretly smuggling Dutch paper straight from its country of origin in direct violation of the Navigation Acts. Merchants in other cities may have also eluded the notice of customs inspectors but not as persistently as the Bostonians, who were selling bootleg paper under the counter from the 1740s into the 1770s. Among the first to ply this illicit trade was Thomas Hancock, uncle of the famous patriot and one of the founders of the first paper mill in Massachusetts. Hancock dealt in Dutch paper regularly and legitimately until around 1737, when the repeal of the drawbacks on foreign paper drove London prices up so high that he went straight to Amsterdam for his supplies. With his new overseas suppliers he organized a clandestine triangle trade between Boston, the Caribbean, and Holland, where he obtained tea, paper, and other contraband to be sold in New England after being unloaded discreetly in unpatrolled waters off Cape Cod or Cape Ann. Another merchant smuggled tea and paper into Boston during the 1750s by arranging for his vessels to stop off in the Orkney Islands on their way from Holland in order to contrive a plausible origin for the goods he sold. Bostonians did not always succeed in hoodwinking the authorities, who sometimes confiscated paper and other merchandise suspected of being conveyed directly from Holland. But even when caught in the act, smugglers could expect lenient treatment in the colonial courts, which were more likely to condone this covert trade than to comply with unpopular legislation.[43]

Americans resorted to these unusual expedients because the import trade could not supply printing paper of the right kind, at the required price, in sufficient quantity, and at the proper time. Buying paper from British sources was just as frustrating as buying fonts of type and just as detrimental to the finished product when printers had trouble purchasing their supplies overseas. Here, too, they endured costly delays, especially if they had to order special kinds of paper for ambitious publications – such as Thomas Bacon's splendidly printed, generously subsidized, and long overdue *Laws of Maryland at Large* (Annapolis, 1765 [i.e., 1766]). In that case the customers could afford to wait, but most printing shops could not postpone the publication of jobbing work, pamphlets, and newspapers, which appeared on whatever papers were available at the time despite jarring deviations in size and quality. Colonial newspapers shrank when prices rose and changed format abruptly whenever the proprietors devised better ways to fit the text they had to print on the different sizes of paper they had on hand. Even Benjamin Franklin's *Pennsylvania Gazette* vacillated between different sizes, though like most colonial newspapers it tended to grow larger as it grew older, and to switch sizes less often after its owners started to receive regular deliveries from local manufactories.[44]

Booksellers and printers helped to finance the earliest paper mills in America, hoping that these establishments would compensate for the basic unreliability of the import trade. Founded just outside of Philadelphia in 1690, America's first paper mill belonged to a syndicate composed of the printer William Bradford, the papermaker William Rittenhouse, and several merchants in that city. Members of the book trade also helped to establish the first paper mills in Massachusetts, New Jersey, and Virginia, the only other colonies able to support papermaking ventures until the 1760s. Paper mills naturally clustered where the printing trade was strongest, in the Philadelphia area, where papermakers could count on a promising market, a rapidly developing transportation network, excellent commercial facilities, and optimum manufacturing conditions at mill sites in the surrounding countryside.

Table 5.2 shows that Pennsylvania mills greatly outnumbered those of the other colonies until the 1770s and that, even then, the paper trade was still growing faster in Pennsylvania than in any other American colony. By the 1760s Philadelphians were exporting locally made paper to other cities on the Atlantic coast, and in such quantities that it is clear that they were shipping printing rather than writing grades. Newspapers in Virginia bought so much paper from Philadelphia that one firm contracted to purchase all its newsprint from a mill outside that city.[45]

Printers were highly valued customers because they bought the single most important staple product of colonial mills: low-grade printing paper for newspapers, almanacs, pamphlets, and other cheap publications. Colonial papermakers concentrated on this sector of the market because they lacked the skills, equipment, and raw materials to manufacture better papers in competition with imported goods. They could produce wrapping paper on the side, but still could not reach a large enough market to specialize in these low-priced bulk commodities, whose returns were still too slim in relation to the cost of manufacture and transportation. Constrained both at the top and bottom end of the market, they depended on printers to buy the one product they could sell profitably, just as printers relied on them to offset the deficiencies of the import trade.[46]

Americans gained a precarious foothold in the papermaking business during the 1740s despite the Acts of Trade but nearly lost it in 1765 when Parliament passed another law designed not so much to regulate trade as to

TABLE 5.2 **American paper mills, 1690–1799**

	1690–1709	1710–1719	1720–1729	1730–1739	1740–1749	1750–1759	1760–1769	1770–1779	1780–1789	1790–1799
Pennsylvania	1	2	3	5	11	14	19	22	33	59
Massachusetts/ Maine			1	2	1	1	2	6	9	21
New Jersey					1	1	1	3	3	3
Virginia					1	1				1
Connecticut							1	3	9	12
New York							1	2	2	8
Rhode Island							1	2	3	3
Maryland								2	3	5
New Hampshire								1	1	2
North Carolina								1		1
Delaware									2	4
Vermont									1	2
Kentucky										1
Total	1	2	5	8	13	16	25	42	66	122

Sources: Partly based on Lyman Horace Weeks, *A History of Paper-Manufacturing in the United States*, 1690–1916 (1916; repr. New York: Burt Franklin, 1969) and Dard Hunter, *Papermaking in Pioneer America* (1952; repr. New York: Garland Publishing, 1981), though corrected and enlarged with data from a number of local histories, which have provided most of the statistics for the later years.

raise revenue in the colonies. If enforced as originally intended, the Stamp Act could have eliminated the trade in coarse printing paper, a calamitous side effect apparently overlooked by British authorities, who were still thinking in mercantilist terms when they drafted this legislation. They probably never considered its implications for colonial paper mills, which were more to be tolerated than encouraged in their opinion, if indeed they had any opinion about these distant, rural manufactories. Historians have also overlooked the economic consequences of the Stamp Act, perhaps because they, too, have been more concerned with the political principles at stake than with the mundane details of tax collection, the procedures actually prescribed for levying stamp duties in the American colonies.

Parliament expected the Stamp Act to operate like laws it had already implemented in the British Isles. Like the Stamp Act of 1712 (10 Anne, c. 18), the American version assessed duties on legal documents, commercial instruments, and various kinds of printed matter such as newspapers, almanacs, and pamphlets. Licenses, contracts, deeds, and bonds would not be valid without stamps indicating that the taxes had been paid. Likewise, the printed documents would have to be issued on specially marked paper priced at a certain amount above and beyond the cost of manufacture. Newspaper publishers in England paid an extra halfpenny per half-sheet until 1757, when the duty was raised to a penny, yielding average revenues of £43,140 a year. After 1757 the duty on almanacs contributed £3,000 a year. Printers and stationers obtained stamped paper in the appropriate prices and sizes from local distributors, who ordered their supplies from a central office administered by the stamp commissioners – an elaborate bureaucratic apparatus deemed capable of serving the American printing trade as well.[47]

Parliament assumed that the commissioners would employ this distribution network to prepare stamped paper for delivery overseas, though they were also given leeway to proceed "as they shall think fit." The commissioners proceeded as they knew best, by obtaining the requisite quantities from the usual sources and shipping them to the colonies in consignments weighing as much as one and a half tons. Word reached Benjamin Franklin in London that a vessel was sailing to Philadelphia laden with newsprint and other kinds of stamped paper valued at £10,000 sterling. Franklin tried to explain to the commissioners why Americans needed to use their own paper instead of imported goods, not with any great success, though the authorities did consider the possibility of allowing the colonial distributors to stamp domestic products at some later date. However, they were inclined not to grant an exception in this case since they would have to extend the same privileges to Scotland and other outlying areas where stamp duties were collected. For the moment, American printers had no choice but to accept the dictates of the stamp commissioners.[48]

Americans opposed the Stamp Act not just to protect fundamental rights and liberties but also to preserve the precious economic lifeline between the printing business and the paper trade. Printers realized that they were not the only ones who would suffer and that they would suffer even more if they did not tend their sources of supply. "If that horrid Law takes Place," David Hall warned his London correspondent William Strahan, "it will knock up most of the Printers on the Continent, and will interely ruin all our Paper-Makers." Strahan, who was paying even higher stamp duties than those proposed for America, defended Parliament's actions at first but later conceded that the colonists had valid reasons to be aggrieved, including the "manifest Injury of sending the Paper from hence ready stampt, to the total and immediate Destruction of your own Manufacture." These concerns inspired printers to take a leading part in the struggle against the Stamp Act, provoking such a resounding public outcry that it was repealed before it could be enforced.[49]

After winning this victory, Americans fought other battles in defense of the domestic paper industry. Townshend's Revenue Act of 1767 threatened papermakers less than printers, who were obliged to pay duties on various kinds of imported paper, especially foreign paper reexported to America. The heavier duties on reexported paper penalized colonial printers as much as they succored British mills, for they exacted the highest toll in that part of the trade where Americans were most likely to buy their printing supplies. And since the Townshend duties spared domestic manufactures, they might have given American paper a competitive advantage, though some Virginians complained that it had been deemed dutiable as well and had been assessed twice the usual amount when shipped from one colony to another. In fact this legislation did help colonial paper mills, if more in the political arena than in the marketplace, because it convinced printers that they needed to foster their own independent, self-sufficient sources of supply.[50]

Printers resisted the Stamp Act and the Townshend Acts by campaigning against them in print and by boycotting British goods, thus pressuring British merchants to intercede with Parliament on their behalf. They subscribed to nonimportation agreements and observed them so strictly that they drove up the price of printing paper in Philadelphia by 9*s.* a ream. Southerners also spurned the imports taxed by Parliament – with the exception of printing paper and a few other necessary articles that had to be exempted because of scarcity. Printers enthusiastically endorsed the embargo even though it was a double-edged economic sword, not only cutting into British profits but also severing their own most important lines of supply.[51]

Americans encouraged domestic manufactures as an obvious corollary of nonimportation, as the best way to achieve their political goals while minimizing their financial losses. The more easily they could buy their paper at home, the more boldly they could repudiate shipments from abroad, until the time should come when they could do without them altogether or purchase them on acceptable terms. As tensions mounted, trade declined, not just with Britain but with other countries that shipped manufactures to the colonies through British ports. The outbreak of hostilities made it even more difficult to order materials from abroad. With no relief in sight, printers had to inform the Continental Congress that it would be cheaper to import thousands of Bibles than to import the paper and type they would need to print the Scriptures in large editions.[52]

Paper shortages became so acute during the war that the provincial authorities had to requisition supplies to print government documents, circulate the news, and wrap powder and ball for muzzle-loading cartridges. The Provincial Congress of Massachusetts published its account of the conflict in Lexington on paper it had obtained from the Milton mill and delivered to Isaiah Thomas, who had recently removed his press to Worcester, farther away from the enemy but also farther from his usual sources of supplies. The government interceded in cases like this because the paper trade could not keep up with the demand and could not increase production until it could procure additional capital, equipment, raw materials, and skilled personnel. Recognizing these problems, provincial congresses subvented the repair of paper mills, subsidized the construction of new papermaking facilities, and exempted papermakers from military duty. The threat perceived in the Stamp Act and the scarcity endured during the Revolution convinced Americans that they needed to protect and enlarge the papermaking industry.[53]

Patriotic citizens could contribute to the papermaking cause in many different ways. Housewives did their part by saving rags, such a valuable ingredient of paper that official rag collectors were appointed to provision local mills in some districts. A Boston almanac advised, "when you see a Rag on the Floor or in the Street let it remind you that two new Paper Mills have lately been erected. And remember it to be a certain Truth, that with the Blessing of God, manufacturing will soon make you a rich and *independent* People." Harvard students set a good example on commencement day by donning garments made in America and propounding theses with an imprint proudly announcing that they were printed "In papyrum Miltoni in Nov-Angliâ confectam." This kind of patriotic label on printed goods reminded consumers that, by buying American, they were helping to take control of book production every step of the way.[54]

Papermakers responded to these economic and political incentives by founding new mills at every opportunity, more than doubling the number of those known to be operating in America during the 1770s and 1780s. Although they had to contend with a "Great Importation" from Europe after trade reopened in the 1780s, Table 5.2 indicates that their productive capacity grew even more quickly during the 1790s. The progress they had made greatly impressed Alexander Hamilton, whose *Report on Manufactures* (1791) noted approvingly that they could supply all the nation required and that they required no further tariff protection – unlike printers, who might benefit from a higher duty on imported books. Hamilton recommended a higher duty for the additional reason that "to encourage the printing of books is to encourage the manufacture of paper."[55]

How much credit should printers receive for the growth of the papermaking trade? It is hard to generalize on the basis of surviving business records because the most enterprising printers tend to be the best documented. Prominent members of the trade like William Bradford I, Christopher Saur I, Isaac Collins, and Isaiah Thomas either owned paper mills or invested in them. Benjamin Franklin claimed to have assisted in the foundation of no less than eighteen paper mills, either by advancing funds, bartering rags, ordering equipment, or by recruiting skilled personnel. But he should be considered a special case because he and his wife Deborah had been running a lucrative sideline in the wholesale paper trade, sometimes controlling such a large portion of the local supply that they could set prices in the Philadelphia area. In the 1740s Franklin was buying large printing demy from local mills for 15*s.* currency and selling it at 17*s.* 6*d.* to his Philadelphia competitor William Bradford III and to out-of-town customers like Jonas Green and Rogers & Fowle. But he sold the same paper at cost to his colleague in New York, James Parker, expecting his friend to return the favor sooner or later, either in kind or in some other business transaction. Likewise, he purchased fine printing foolscap for 9*s.* 6*d.* currency and sold it at 10*s.* to most of his customers with the exception of Bradford, who had to pay 10*s.* 6*d.* or 11*s.* Few printers dominated the market as noticeably as Franklin, who could insist on preferential treatment from local mills in return for the rags he supplied and the other services he provided.[56]

Printers like Franklin participated in the paper trade more as intermediaries than as investors, sometimes assisting at both ends of the manufacturing process, delivering raw materials at one end and distributing the finished product at the other. In effect they were organizing networks within the trade and with allied trades to protect their sources of supply while also aiding their friends and discomfiting their competitors. They formed similar alliances when attempting to procure type and other specialized imported goods, an intimidating prospect for those who lacked the means or the know-how to place an order overseas. In this predicament, Parker asked Franklin to negotiate for him the purchase of a new font of long primer, confessing "[I] know not well the Price, or whom to apply to, or what Quantity will do." Peripheral members of the trade depended on their better connected, more knowledgeable colleagues to deal with purveyors of printing supplies on their behalf.[57]

These supply networks extended to every printing house in North America despite dismal transportation conditions both on water and on land. The farther printers strayed from their sources of supply, the longer they waited for provisions to arrive over the bad roads and perfidious waterways that linked them to the commercial centers in eastern cities. To set up shop in Lexington, Kentucky, John Bradford bought his equipment in Philadelphia and had it conveyed first by wagon and packhorse over the Alleghenies to Pittsburgh, then on a boat down the Ohio River to Maysville, Kentucky, and, finally, from Maysville to Lexington, where his wagon lumbered over such rugged terrain that most of his type fell into pi. Once a year printers in Virginia had to order extra large quantities of paper to keep in store while navigation was closed during the winter. Although colonial printers were resourceful, they were not self-reliant, not even the elder Christopher Saur, who mixed his own ink, built his own press, and launched his own papermaking firm, just a few of twenty-six different crafts he claimed to have learned without formal instruction. Yet he, too, called on Franklin when he needed to buy bulk quantities of printing paper.[58]

And even Franklin relied on his friends in the trade and on his contacts overseas, though he is perhaps most responsible for propagating the myth of the self-reliant colonial craftsman. Franklin's *Autobiography* and kindred texts have encouraged us to view skilled artisans as stalwart individualists, who fought for their economic independence with the same indomitable spirit that roused them to win their political rights by force of arms. Lawrence Wroth, Dard Hunter, and other historians have accepted and perpetuated these notions by concentrating more on domestic manufactures than on imported supplies, emphasizing more the pluck and ingenuity of craftsmen than the structure of the trade.

Supply networks provided the printing craft not just with materials and equipment but also order and continuity. Out of necessity, American printers had to develop new ways of doing business with one another outside of the institutional infrastructure they had left behind in Europe. In its place they had to devise their own means of organization, cooperation, and mutual support. The arrangements they made to obtain paper and type influenced the formation of their trade, just as the terms of apprenticeship, the hierarchy of the guild, and the regulations of the state had shaped their profession in the Old World. If less regimented than their counterparts overseas, colonial printers were just as likely to forge alliances based on family ties, credit strategies, political alignments, and religious beliefs – but they were even more likely to strengthen their connections along the lines of supply. Networks of all kinds crystallized around their efforts to keep in stock the necessary materials of book production. They took extra care to cultivate this side of the printing business where it suffered most from the inherent disadvantages of a colonial economy, the difficulty of ordering goods from abroad, the cost of transportation, and the mercantilist prerogatives of the mother country.

PART THREE. THE IMPORTATION OF BOOKS IN THE EIGHTEENTH CENTURY

JAMES RAVEN

THE EXPORT TRADE FROM BRITAIN to its colonies in the Americas steadily advanced from the late seventeenth century, when British and European book merchants and agents began to respond seriously to book demand arising from the mainland colonies. The place of this demand within the British trade became increasingly important in the course of the eighteenth century. From 1700 to 1780, 45 percent of English book exports by volume departed for the American mainland and the West Indies.[59] During the third quarter of the century, the rate of growth of book importation easily exceeded that of the colonial population. By 1770, more books were exported annually from England to the American colonies than to Europe and the rest of the world combined, albeit with limited demand on the Continent for books in English. We are unlikely to be surprised that the importation of books from the mother country was the mainstay of bookselling in the early, sparsely populated years of colonial settlement, but that this volume should have increased rather than declined with the growth of colonial production is not so easily explained.

Given the almost complete disappearance of the business records of the London booksellers, official customs tabulations offer the fullest overall assessment of book exports.[60] Despite some recent suggestions to the contrary, customs officials had to account for total ship consignments and in these, it seems, commercial cargoes of books were not underrecorded. The summary English customs ledgers are missing for 1780–1809, but in the period of 1701–1780 that concerns us here, they survive for all but two years.[61] They do not, however, indicate how many books were conveyed. Domestic commodity export tallies give the total weight of books shipped out, together with their valuation at a standard median rate of £4 per cwt (112 lbs.). No distinction is made between bound and unbound books, and their recorded valuations as an "estimate of the first cost and value" bear no relationship to real sterling prices. Because the notional English monetary valuation was unaltered throughout the century, these tallies do at least provide confirmation of the weights recorded against each category. These weights provide the only possible basis for annual comparisons.

Certain hypothetical calculations can be made by comparing the annual English customs totals against the composition of large shipments known through surviving American invoices. Such an exercise suggests an average annual total for all book and pamphlet exports from English ports to the mainland colonies in the early 1770s of some 120,000 items, or something like 4 percent of total British annual output (or nearly 5 percent of total English annual output).[62] Although such estimates remain highly artificial, they are at least suggestive of the volume of book exports in this period. Even if it is true that some books entered unrecorded as part of general parcels or as items unworthy of record, the sheer quantity revealed by the customs ledgers must assuage doubts that surviving customs ledgers record only a fraction of total exports.[63]

These tentative calculations include allowance for the relatively small Scottish and Irish export of books before 1780. The Scottish Customs Collectors' Quarterly Account Books survive from 1742/3, providing details of books exported from individual Scottish ports, all estimated to be bound British and duty-free books. From 1755 further extant summary ledgers sent to London record imports and exports returns for Scottish ports.[64] Here, calculations of the volume of books offer problems of interpretation similar to those for the English summary ledgers, but with additional and more complex valuation differences.[65] Similar sets of summary ledgers survive for Ireland, although with yet further variation in recording practice.[66] Their significance is negligible, however, until the 1780s. Before 1778, free trade between Ireland and America was prohibited under the Navigation Acts; technically, the export of books to the colonies came under these laws.[67] The removal of remaining colonial export restrictions in 1780 and a 1783 Act of the Irish Parliament accounts for the development of book exports to America in this decade, but evidence can also be found of very modest traffic between Ireland and the colonies from the 1720s.[68] Some scholars have claimed that the Irish registers seriously underrepresent book exports. What we can say, at least, is that because of colonial restrictions the total recorded Irish exports of unbound books to America between 1760 and 1780 was a mere £1,857. Following the lifting of export and duty restrictions, nearly £10,000 worth was exported between 1782 and 1799.[69]

With some notable exceptions, for most American booksellers non-London alternatives of supply were impossible or unattractive until the final decades of the century. The total of 420 cwt. of bound and unbound British books regarded as exported to America (including the West Indies) from all Scottish ports during the period 1755–1762 represents the equivalent of 4 percent of the recorded 9,981 cwt. shipped from English ports during the same period. For reasons not entirely clear, however, tallies from Scottish customs records fail to record certain known individual shipments, while leading booksellers, such as Charles Elliot of Edinburgh in the 1770s, exported books to America from London. Certain Scots exports are therefore included in English customs summaries.[70] Imports from non-British sources are measurable with even less precision, but their overall contribution by about 1770 must have been extremely small. Even though numerically slight, these other book exports from Europe – many of them gifts to small communities – were lifelines to identity, material links to a present or past culture. Foremost amongst these were Bibles and religious works. Numerous probate documents and surviving letters document exports from Sweden, the Low Countries, and Germany to the middle colonies and Virginia.[71]

More certain are comparisons between customs volume measurements. These chart a steep rise in the proportion of total English book exports sent to America during the second half of the century. A general depression in the export trade lasted from 1744 to 1748 at the time of the War of the Austrian Succession. But after a dramatic reduction in 1756, transatlantic book traffic followed an upward trend during the Seven Years War (with some marked regional variation and a brief depression in 1762–1763). In 1750 London booksellers exported 1.2 cwt. of books to Europe and points east for every one cwt. shipped to all the American plantations, but this ratio was reversed by 1770 to 1.6 cwt. to the Americas for every one cwt. shipped east. The Revenue Act of 1767 resulted in nonimportation agreements among American booksellers, but these soon weakened and the Act itself was repealed in 1770. Before the hiatus caused by the war, America-bound shipments between 1771 and 1774 (inclusive) comprised some 60 percent of all English book exports.[72]

Annual export destinations also provide remarkable colonial comparisons. In total between 1701 and 1780 nearly a quarter of all English book exports to North America and the Caribbean went to New England (23 percent). After this the largest importers were Virginia and Maryland (recorded together, 19 percent), New York (12 percent), Pennsylvania (9 percent), and the Carolinas (8.5 percent) (See Graph 7a, Appendix 1). The volume by weight of books sent to all the islands of the West Indies also surpassed that sent to New England. Though there is evidence from subscription lists and auction catalogues for West Indian bibliophilia, plantation libraries were generally small and the predominance of the West Indies and New England shipments in the customs records probably owes more to the clerks' routine of recording only the first destination of the ship on the docket than to local demand at those destinations. In short, the quantities are so large because the northern and southern shipping routes were the most favored. Significant changes also occurred during these eighty years. The graph also shows the comparative decline in exports to New England in the second half of the century and the relative stability of book traffic to Virginia, Maryland, and Pennsylvania. Evidence of even sharper short-term fluctuations is provided by the annual English customs summaries, and are particularly illuminating for the troubled period from 1765. They suggest that book imports to New England declined by some two-thirds between 1769 and 1770, while book imports for Carolina, Virginia, and Maryland markedly increased over the four years 1768–1771. In 1770 Virginia imported more than 40 percent of all English books shipped to North America. In the Revolutionary War years, from 1775, the customs ledgers show no books imported to most of the North American colonies, but loyalist Florida leapt from importing 9.5 cwt. of books in 1775 to 84.5 cwt in 1776, suggesting an ongoing regional coastal trade to distribute books to embargoed ports. In 1779, four years before Britain abandoned it to Spain, Florida imported 53 cwt. of books from London, more than any colony save Canada and New York.[72] Until then, the northern territories did not figure largely in the summary ledgers. Newfoundland had almost no recorded book imports other then one abnormally large shipment in 1772. Nova Scotia, with imports first recorded in 1750, was more consistent but over the next twenty-five years averaged no more than 1 percent of the total weight of exports to the North American mainland. Canada, with no imports recorded before 1763, averaged about 2 percent of total exports to the mainland during the next decade, before the extraordinary circumstances of 1775 resulted in its receiving 54 percent of the total exports to mainland North America in that year.

What, then, explains the vigor and endurance of book importation to the colonies? In the first place, the expansion of the transatlantic book trade was founded on the consolidation of British trade regulation in the second half of the seventeenth century. The Navigation Acts of 1651 and 1660, together with new enforcement measures in 1696, limited colonial commerce to English and colonial vessels. This system was designed to benefit all citizens of the empire and to encourage both colonial and metropolitan initiatives. By 1700 ships built in New England undertook most of the carrying trade from the north and the Chesapeake to England and southern Europe. Under the same system, the transatlantic booktrade became advantageous to certain London booksellers and merchants, and, tentatively, a few American importers. New colonial demand for religious and secular literature was met by the increasing enterprise of London booksellers, while the extended use of London as a booktrades entrepôt also derived from booksellers' existing experience in shipping in continental editions.[74]

Increased shipment of books from Britain was an obvious consequence of the limited and unbalanced growth of colonial printing. In part the colonial trade was restrained by legal monopolies imposed in England, with patents reserved for printing rights to bibles, prayer books, psalters, and certain law books and other specialist works. In addition, basic economic considerations of cost – the expense of paper, printing equipment, and labor – also figured largely in the colonies.[75] For most of the century few provincial and colonial booksellers were able to challenge the oligopolistic dominance of London with its economies of scale, trade organization, and the use of established distributive agents. The great variable in this remained the level of discount offered to retailers by the London wholesaler. Expectations were high, with colonial booksellers and merchants demanding terms equivalent to those offered to English provincial booksellers.

The expansion in the colonial booktrades from the early eighteenth century embraced changes both in the kinds of literature being exported and the types of exporter. One early alteration was in the state of books ordered, where the increase in the number and quality of American binders reduced the demand for luxury-bound British and European publications.[76] At the same time, the export of books in cheap sheep bindings, and also, from mid-century, trade bindings, increasingly replaced unbound sheet orders in the bulk London shipments to the major colonial booksellers. A further issue central to changes in the kinds of book imported – and one often related to arguments about the later decline in imports – is the allegation that London booksellers used the colonies as a dumping ground for unwanted remainders and poor sellers. It is certain that unsaleable titles or "rum books" were sent out first by the likes of Boulter and Chiswell,[77] and later by Thomas Osborne, William Strahan, and James Rivington, among others.[78] But the evidence offsetting this argument is stronger; for example, the careful ordering of eighteenth-century colonial booksellers such as Henry Knox (who opened his London Book-Store in Boston, 1770) and Jeremy Condy, Baptist minister and bookseller, trading in Boston from 1754 to 1768.[79] Where dumping was attempted it may have been aimed more at the wholesale auctions of books, about which we still know far too little.[80]

The dynamics of the export-import trade rested with three groups: colonial traders, London traders, and colonial customers with a few general merchants like John Usher and Samuel Sewall active as importers. New England was the early center.[81] Half a century later more than a dozen London booksellers were despatching major book cargoes to colonial traders, a development well documented by the evidence for book sale and auction catalogues.[82] To local traders whose business was wholly or largely in such books can be added numerous small merchants such as John Barkley or Thomas White in Philadelphia in the 1730s, bringing in books as part of their general business.[83] During the third quarter of the century, London wholesaling booksellers pursued the American market with great zeal. As research continues on both London booksellers and American traders and customers of the period, evidence is accumulating (usually from fragmentary sources) that a very large number of the wholesalers – and almost all the familiar names – were at one time or another engaged in colonial trade. Such booksellers include the Dodsleys, the Longmans, the Rivingtons, Cadell, Millar, Nicoll, Wilson and Durham, Richardson, the Dillys, and dozens more.

Best known, of course, because of the survival of their correspondence and business papers, are the initiatives of William Strahan and his despatch of £18,000 worth of books and printing material to David Hall in Philadelphia between 1760 and 1772.[84] Typical of more modest operations were those of Thomas Osborne, who entered the colonial book trade about 1748 and sent one of his first shipments to William Parks in Williamsburg.[85] Osborne continued to receive orders from William Hunter of Williamsburg, who, from the 1750s, also bought bibles, law manuals and other books on commission from the London booksellers Samuel Birt and Thomas Waller.[86] Later evidence of the Boston trade highlights the ambition of Thomas Longman and Gill and Wright to serve as suppliers. Many books were also marked by the colonial booksellers as "sent without order."[87] Even the relatively modest trader Jeremy Condy had to return unordered books to his supplier Joseph Richardson, including some that have been shown to be London unsaleables.[88]

If this eagerness to sell (and sometimes to exploit) occasionally strained relations, a new generation of colonial booksellers responded enthusiastically to overtures from the London wholesalers. Daniel Henchman, the greatest of all the mid-eighteenth-century New England booksellers according to Isaiah Thomas, was not one of the greatest importers, but he did have books printed in London sent over in sheets and employed at least three London agents, John Rowe, Benjamin Horrocks, and Eliza Maplesden.[89] Henchman was also supplied by Thomas Longman I, and, after

Henchman's death in 1761, the London Longman connection (with the adjunct London connection of the stationers, Wright and Gill) continued with his successors and associates, including Nicholas Bowes, John Wharton, and their employee and part-successor Henry Knox, whose "London Book-store" was the third of that name.

Many of the successful ventures, and certainly the continuation of them, were the result of carefully nurtured relationships. In the absence of the financial institutions taken for granted in later years, trust between partners, as well as tolerance during financial sloughs, was essential to the conduct of business. The strongest bonds were familial, a characteristic common to many early modern trades, including printing and publishing. Other family ties continued among colonial traders, sea captains, and major bill-brokering merchants.[90] One notable feature was the commercial network of Scots booksellers and customers. Nationality was central to the personal bond of friendship and trust between William Strahan and "Davie" Hall. James Rivington's "branch" shop, opened in Boston in 1762, was kept by his Scots partner William Miller. From the commencement of his book trade in 1768, John Murray, a former sea captain, maintained far-flung customers and contacts. His transatlantic customers included a disproportionate number of Scots, notably Robert Miller, general merchant of Williamsburg, whose sisters lived in London and delivered both his orders and payment to Murray.[91] Others of the diaspora were prominent in the demanding Charleston Library Society, including James Scott, Robert Wells, and the Brisbane mercantile firm. Writing to Miller, Murray hoped such loyalties would excuse a certain commercial impertinence: "I have transmitted without order 2 copies of the Edinb. Magazine not denoting but your regard for Scotland will make you procure orders for many of them."[92]

These connections were means, among others, of helping the colonists acquire precise information about publication and availability. The next task was to set about securing a resident agent to manage the affair on the other side of the Atlantic. Both problems were faced by all commercial customer groups, whether wealthy or well-connected individuals, institutional customers (colleges, churches, libraries, and gentlemen's societies), or colonial booksellers and general merchants. From the mid-seventeenth century, prospectuses like those preserved in the Winthrop papers detailed "new books that are lately come out," together with booksellers' catalogues, including those from the great fairs of Frankfurt.[93] A century later, almost all the leading London booksellers printed catalogues of new or in-stock titles. Strahan sent his catalogues to Hall, Longman did the same for Knox, and Murray sent his to Miller in Williamsburg, "which I beg of you to shew your Friends who may perhaps order some Books from it."[94] Meanwhile, colonial traders advertised imports in newspapers. More important still, London newspapers and periodicals from the mid-eighteenth century onward provided individual and institutional customers with ever greater opportunities to read of new publications. The critical reviews, in particular, with their attempt at comprehensive notices together with extracts and criticism, were not only imports in their own right but led to exacting orders sent either to a colonial bookseller or directly to a London wholesaler or agent.

Perched on the edge of the western world, colonial customers often depended upon family and friends in London or made strategic use of journeys there to establish or revive contacts with booksellers or fellow bibliophiles. All the shipments in the Usher invoices were made through John Ive, who also managed the account of Samuel Sewall.[95] The Philadelphia library of James Logan developed from Logan's 1710 and 1723 journeys to London. Agents such as Logan's friend John Askew coordinated the financing, assembly, and dispatch of books ordered from this side of the Atlantic. From 1718, Logan's main agent was the Quaker writer Josiah Martin, and a twenty-five-year correspondence records the ups and downs of this transatlantic commerce.[96] At mid-century, the New York Society Library engaged John Ward as its London agent–bookseller, but in 1771, faced by silence from his successors, the society resolved "to find out and settle a Correspondence with some Bookseller in London who will supply the Library with such books as may be ordered from Time to Time upon the best Terms." The last condition was no small matter; breakdowns between customer and agent or bookseller were common. As Logan reminded one supplier, "Thou may therefore well excuse me for finding fault with thee as I do when thy prices are unreasonable, who have been a buyer of Books above these 50 years and are not to be put off as a common American, as thou has divers times served me, for I know a book well."[97]

Unexpected actions by booksellers and agents, or their misinterpretation of instructions, were a constant irritant. With information on the American side often imperfect, the London bookseller had to be allowed certain freedoms if he was to be effective. Indeed, the colonists sometimes selected a given bookseller because he was reputedly a person of good judgment. Surviving correspondence shows that clients, both private and commercial, resorted to vaguely stated buying mandates. Such clients had to live with the occasional unasked-for package. The New York Society Library gave prudent leave to its bookseller Ward that, "when ever he observes any Sett of Books want to be compleated, to take particular care to supply the Additional Vol."[98] Library committees that put enormous effort into the writing of "general instructions" to agents in London were rarely satisfied; the Charleston Library Society regularly dismissed its London booksellers because of their supposed inability to attend "to the spirit of the General Instructions."[99]

Yet many booksellers tried hard to keep up. Murray apologized to Miller for his failure to locate all the foreign imprints that had been requested – "at a future Period I may order what is wanting with some others [booksellers] from the Continent" – and he asked Miller to repeat orders for those he could not send "because they may be easier got at one time than another."[100] Longman and his assistant, Christopher Brown, sent elaborate explanations or letters-ahead indicating why certain ships were missed or others were chosen. Stockdale, who was summarily dismissed after only one attempt to serve the Charleston Library, fired off a letter of justification. "Many of the Articles tho' trifling in price," he wrote, "were the most difficult to procure and were only to be got by accident as they came into the trade from private persons, for this reason my Clerks and myself have traversed the streets of London from bookseller to Bookseller I firmly believe an hundred times over at least." He went on:

I have executed my instructions to the best of my Judgment and this is no trifling task, as for instance it frequently happens that a scarce book is sold by one bookseller at £14.14, and by another at £12.12 . . . , but as I have probably added Articles that you may not approve being too dear, or not wanted; should this be the case I beg that you will be so obliging as to order them sold by Public Auction, and whatever loss should there be any attending the sale I will cheerfully pay it as I would much rather put up with any reasonable loss than that the Gentlemen should think I wished to land them with Books they did not want, or that I had been imprudent in my Selection.[101]

When Charles Dilly was told that he had been elected bookseller to the society because members had been "of Opinion that Mr William Nicoll of St Paul's Church Yard their late Bookseller, had not served them with that Punctuality which the Spirit of their Society required, and which their Punctuality in Payment gave them a right to expect," his response was to decline to serve them altogether.[102] The Hall–Strahan correspondence contains many similar complaints about ambiguous instructions and unsent and unordered books.

Not least of the difficulties in ordering and receiving books was the time required to complete the transaction. The months taken to cross and recross the Atlantic added to credit difficulties and interest charges, and was a major handicap to receiving new publications and up-to-date trade information.[103] Moreover, because books were hardly the priority goods for any shipping merchant or ship's master, loading and unloading times were unpredictable. Some ships followed prearranged schedules, with full cargoes awaiting them (and additional goods such as trunks of books taken on if there was room). Others, however, advertised as being ready to carry general goods and then waited to load for a particular destination, which could sometimes also be open to negotiation. An essential issue, therefore, became the quality of the shipping information available to London booksellers and agents.

Despite these difficulties a general improvement in the efficiency of port-side procedures and inventory times is evident during the century.[104] Particularly striking was the development of greater coordination of information about ships leaving and the more exact collection arrangements, both managed through the "colonial" coffeehouses in London. The Pennsylvania Coffee House, the Virginia Coffee House, and the Carolina Coffee House were essential clearing houses for captains of ships, booksellers, customers' agents, and even colonial customers when in London. Murray, for example, left boxes for Miller at the Virginia Coffee House, and Charleston customers were usually serviced at some point by the Carolina Coffee House.[105] Sympathetic London booksellers, notably the Dillys and later John Almon and John Stockdale, offered their shops as mailing addresses for itinerant Americans in London.[106]

Even with these improvements, the rhythm of the transatlantic book trade was always subject to disruption either from the weather or because of the activity of privateers during times of warfare. As a precautionary means of dealing with these circumstances, which could easily result in the loss of cargo, colonial customers relied on double or triple copies of outgoing orders and bills of exchange.[107] Firsts, seconds, and thirds of exchange were also sent on different ships to ensure the swiftest possible delivery. Any one, but only one, of the copies could be used. For return cargoes, the other precaution available was insurance. Cheap and reliable insurance was especially important to traders such as Condy, whose capital was modest. Insurance costs and risks declined significantly as London rose to become the preeminent marine insurance center of Europe.[108] By the 1720s, rates on most transatlantic crossings had fallen to a peace-time levy of 2 percent. According to a further estimate the effective charge on insurance between 1675 and 1775 was lowered by 10 to 20 percent, with coverage increasing to within 1 or 2 percent of the loss.[109] The insurance taken out on the packages sent by Murray to Miller in Williamsburg averaged at just over 2 percent per shipment. In the same decade the insurance bill for much larger book cargoes sent by Longman to Knox was also 2 percent of total charges. Nevertheless, insurance rates remained unpredictable, and the outbreak of hostilities inevitably sent rates higher. During the war years 1757–1758 the books despatched to the New York Society Library by John Ward were covered by a policy that cost 16 percent of the total invoice. During the Revolution, British insurance rates rose again by some 23 percent.

For all parties concerned in the transatlantic book trade, however, a more significant transaction cost arose from the complexities of making payment.

Specie was the most reliable currency of credit, but it was often impossible for the colonists to provide cash. Agreements to barter or exchange like goods were relatively rare, involving both expensive negotiations with sales agents and acute problems of timing. The most common and often, indeed, the only way of securing payment to a distant supplier was by the protracted method of bills of exchange. During the century, acceptance of bills of exchange became easier. Published manuals such as Hill's *Young Secretary* helped establish common practice,[110] and a rough-and-ready standardization is evident from the surviving day books and ledgers of those engaged in book trades. In most cases, existing business or family connections provided additional security.

Methods of payment were part of the broader task of securing credit. For the bookseller advancing credit, enormous and long-running complications could ensue at the distance of 6,000 miles and four to six months between each return correspondence. In general, short-term credit was frequently used by the colonists for the purchase of British goods, and British merchants usually included a twelve-month interest charge in the price of goods shipped. Longman allowed Knox twelve months' credit on what were often very large orders. By contrast, Adrian Watkins, who held the Bible patent in Scotland, allowed only two months' credit. As a result, David Hall in Philadelphia had to pay in full (by bill of exchange bought on terms with the local drawer) before any part of the shipment arrived. After some years Watkins did extend Hall's credit to six months, and even allowed a little discount.[111] Even so, Hall considered six months' credit too short, as he could not sell all his imported cargo within that time.[112]

Also telling for London suppliers was nonpayment. In 1748 Strahan was forced to sue James Read of Philadelphia when, after three years, no payment had been received for a large consignment. Strahan eventually abandoned the attempt to recover this debt when even a power of attorney proved ineffectual.[113] When Strahan was owed over £360 three years after the death of David Hall in 1772, he found it impossible to extract payment, even though he was assured by Franklin that the Hall family business was thriving.[114] Other silences resulted from business failure or the sudden closure of a colonial shop. In May 1774 Knox received a curt reprimand from the firm of Wright and Gill about his bill outstanding for some two years.[115] He still owed Longman £1300 in 1789, fifteen years after quitting the business of bookselling. It was not until 1805 that Longman's executrix, his widow, finally received full settlement of $4,461.[116]

Matters of credit were related to the level of discount offered to retailers by London wholesaler–booksellers, and hence to the pricing of imported books in the colonies. Expectations were high, with colonial booksellers demanding terms equivalent to those offered to English provincial booksellers. The challenge of James Rivington in the 1750s, paralleling English assaults on the closed London cartels of leading booksellers, raised the stakes still higher. What for Strahan were the "low, dirty, and unwarrantable methods"[117] of Rivington were very attractive to many colonial booksellers, for he was offering 16 percent discount and a year's credit to American customers. Enticed by notions of higher profits, Hunter swapped Samuel Birt for Rivington in 1755; after visiting London in 1758, Hunter concluded that the business was fraudulent – at least according to the biased Strahan.[118] It does seem that the quality of Rivington's exports was low and that many of his consignments contained curious books.

Given the complexities of credit, shipping and insurance, the pricing of imports was a sore subject. Some customers, like Thomas Jefferson, found that they paid less for books when they ordered directly from Ireland or the Continent,[119] and some local booksellers nurtured the suspicion that their London suppliers were overcharging. In 1760, when James Rivington arrived in Philadelphia, he preyed on these suspicions, though, depending on their London connections, the locals might or might not have believed him. David Hall, a substantial bookseller whose London suppliers were exceptionally reliable, wrote the Scottish firm of Hamilton and Balfour in London, "we have got Mr. Rivington from London here, who says he can have every Thing much Cheaper than any one else; by which he will undersell us all, and get the whole into his own Hands. He says that those Booksellers we have been dealing with from this Place, have kept us all in the Dark as to the Prices, and have been picking our Pockets abominably."[120] Less well-established firms, especially in the South, who had to fork over middleman profits both to Hall and to London, may have taken a different view.

Londoners in turn urged the colonials to maintain the London prices by a surcharge. Longman gave Knox exactly the same terms as he gave provincial booksellers, but with the clear expectation that Knox would raise his prices above Longman's London retail prices. Although Knox was providing an assured outlet and able to offer unit-cost reductions on transport and the like, he was in effect held hostage to an agreed marginal rate of profit. At one point, Longman suspected Knox of breaking the agreement, a move, he argued, that "must be destructive to us both."[121] On the other hand, some American importers were able to make startling profits. At mid-century, William Hunter in Williamsburg made approximately £100 local currency per year from his cash and credit sales of imported books, with a gross profit representing a 30 percent mark-up on the wholesale cost. In the shop of his successor, Joseph Royle, some books sold for up to 60 percent more than the wholesale price charged to the colonial bookseller by the London supplier, ample compensation, it would seem, for shipping and packing costs.[122] Such profits also suggest why bibliophiles like James Logan of Philadelphia were distrustful of the booksellers' transatlantic arrangements and why well-heeled library societies attempted to maintain and, after the Revolution, to restore direct links with the London trade. Individual customers were sometimes able to offset transit costs by bargaining for the sort of "real" or trade discount prices that Rivington assured them were available in London. Bold initiatives seem to have been possible, such as that shown by a would-be client of David Hall who secured an offer from a London bookseller at prices below even those that Hall paid Strahan at discount rate.[123]

Despite these many difficulties, the export trade from Britain was flourishing on the eve of the Revolution, and, if customs records can be trusted, the outbreak of war did not entirely bring the trade to a close. The ninefold increase in books shipped to Florida from 1775–1776 presumably included those for transshipment to the newly independent states. When peace returned in 1783, trade was resumed with gusto. By the final decade of the century, the result was a far greater concentration of importing firms, now increasingly distinct from local publishers, in New York, Philadelphia, and Boston. During the 1790s the Charleston Library Society had its first, if reluctant, recourse to a Philadelphia book merchant to obtain English imprints. Leman Thomas Rede, a hack writer who had resided in the United States in 1789, observed that "they do not in North Carolina import from Europe but purchase, at an unreasonably high price, of the northern booksellers."[124]

Impressive as this continuing traffic appeared, the 1750s remained the period of fastest growth for incoming British books and print. A full explanation for the dynamics of this book traffic is still awaited, but by combining different sorts of surviving evidence, we can suggest the outlines of a trade propelled by early legal constraint, American material shortages, and the economic advantages of a London trade dominance and organization which for most of the century outweighed even the obstacles of transatlantic time and distance. Broad trends are confirmed by Graph 7b (Appendix 1), which compares the customs totals (by valuation) against annual domestic American production (by title). A ten-year moving average for both data suggests a steadily rising demand for books from 1710 to about 1730 and a plateauing in the 1730s, followed by quickening growth to 1760. Thereafter trends of imported and domestic book production diverge, with stability and then decline in imports offset by continuing growth in American printing (at least in terms of the number of titles printed), but it would be a long time before domestic production triumphed. In 1810 an American printer remarked, "For many years after the peace of 1783, books could be imported into the United States and sold cheaper than they could be printed here and indeed until 1793 nothing like a competition with English Printers and Booksellers could be maintained. The war then raging in Europe and added duty on paper made some difference but it was not until the union of Ireland and England (in 1801) that a decided advantage was ascertained to exist."[125]

What has yet to be resolved, however, is the broader cultural significance of the book import boom. Commodities they might be, but incoming books carried information and ideas. Here, signal questions about what appears to have been import-led anglicization at a time of increasing colonial tension await closer analysis of the types of literature imported, especially in comparison with American production. Such an inquiry underlines the difficulties in comparing British and European book imports with American domestic production. Not only are title-by-title comparisons affected by regional and circulation differences, but differences between the types of books printed in and exported to North America were exaggerated by the relative selling time of each type. Despite brave attempts based on the specific stocks of booksellers and libraries,[126] conclusions are as yet premature. Devotional books and practical manuals remained steady sellers, but as these were slowly displaced by American editions, the perceptions as much as the type of imported literature was altered. In the absence of local publications and reprints there had been no alternative to imported books, but even when the American presses were more active, the social valuation of imported literature remained strong. The speed of news from London and Europe had always been important and competitive, and the fashionable customer was also the customer who most expected to be able to order new things from London. The result was greater emphasis upon speciality imports, including belles lettres and novels (which so far have been given most attention[127]), but also learned literatures, periodicals, and newspapers. Importers faced the higher expectations of their customers and the self-evident requirement to receive up-to-the-minute publications in good time. "Latest print," particularly periodical publications and novels, strengthened the demand for imports but also increased the pressure upon booksellers and agents on both sides of the Atlantic. The learned periodicals and magazines became an especial trial to colonial and London suppliers, with their information about London books, their attempts at comprehensive reviewing, and above all, their tell-tale monthly masthead.

This social dimension to the import trade contributed to the evaluation of the costs and attractiveness of the imported product. Demand for British and European books had never been uniform, but was increasingly driven by particular groups and interests. As with the book boom in England, increased demand had derived proportionately more from those already active in the market and from institutions such as the proprietary and circulating libraries than from the increase in the total numbers buying books. In North America, this was paralleled in the profile of the decline of imports, where certain outstanding features remained as the more general demand for overseas print lessened. As foreign book orders declined compared to rates of domestic production, the book import trade appeared narrower, both socially and geographically.

In market terms it was largely a luxury, scholarly, and specialist community trade that survived. For those American booksellers and merchants whose business was based on the sale of small, cheap imported books, the development of the American publishing and reprint market was felt first. Given the risk of importing expensive stock that might be difficult to move, the business of most commercial American importers of the second half of the eighteenth century had indeed been grounded on the type of low-value print that was, for similar production and demand reasons, to be the leading edge of expanding American publication. The virtual collapse of both the Bible and the cheap book and almanac trade, together with the lasting export from England of high-value literature demanded by learned and public institutions, fed into the restructuring of the continuing transatlantic book business, with its revised strategies, new operators and new specialisms.

A Note on Imports and Domestic Production

Comparisons between the volume of imported books and native production face two fundamental difficulties for the colonial period. The two classes are of different kinds of books, and we know little or nothing about their relative rates of sale, which forms the only relevant basis for comparison. If the exercise is worth doing at all, one hopes that it will at least expose the numerous pitfalls attending any statistical assertion about the consumption of print in colonial America.

Government printing (session acts, legislative journals, and the like), almanacs, and broadsides were never imported, and have therefore been excluded from the count of NAIP records for 1765–1774 in the following calculation; the remainder will be designated simply "books" hereafter. Average edition sizes of "books" vary from region to region: Boston's in 1765 may be taken as about 1,000, but middle colony editions were probably smaller, and southern editions smaller still. A domestic average of 500 copies may be hazarded, but it is only a conjecture.

The rate of sale for imports must be linearly related to their rate of importation: British suppliers would not have regularly extended six months' to a year's credit otherwise, and in general we may assume that American booksellers ordered no more than they expected to sell within these periods. Nevertheless, they were often disappointed, and shipments for sale or return were not uncommon, as James Raven has shown.

American production probably operated by different rules. The *Boston Catalogue* of 1804 lists a few editions as antiquated as 1789, but most of them date from 1795 or later; from this, and a sporadic scatter of other evidence, one would assume that colonial editions stayed "in print" for an average of ten years. Assuming further that 75 percent of the copies sold in that time, and that most of the sales fell in the earlier years of publication, one might assign the following algorithm to an edition of 1,000 copies:

1st year: 250	6th year: 10
2nd year: 225	7th year: 5
3rd year: 150	8th year: 3
4th year: 75	9th year: 2
5th year: 30	10th year: 1

The sales of ten successive editions of 1,000 copies each would therefore amount to 6,510 copies at the end of the ten-year period.

Applying this algorithm to the national production of "books" recorded in NAIP for the period 1765–1774, we may compute the following totals:

Edition date	Sales (edn. = 500)	"Books" sold by 1794
1765	375.5 × 199 editions	74,724.5
1766	375 × 165 editions	61,875
1767	374 × 166 editions	62,084
1768	372.5 × 197 editions	73,382.5
1769	370 × 212 editions	78,440
1770	365 × 256 editions	93,440
1771	350 × 233 editions	81,550
1772	312.5 × 204 editions	63,750
1773	237.5 × 321 editions	76,237.5
1774	125 × 395 editions	49,375
		Total: 714,858.5

During the same period, an estimated 1,424,836 English books were imported, so that the average annual domestic sales were about half as large. NAIP records suggest a total domestic production of about 1,469,000 books (including broadsides and government documents, excluded earlier) for the same period, a total that does not include newspaper issues. There is no disguising the amount of conjecture behind this comparison, but at least it agrees with the qualitative impression of a contemporary bookseller, quoted on pages 195–96, and that is a comfort.

H.A.

CHAPTER SIX

The Book Trade in the Middle Colonies, 1680–1720

JAMES N. GREEN

PRINTING WAS EMBRACED far more readily in the middle colonies than in the Chesapeake. Though Delaware, Pennsylvania, New Jersey, and New York were occupied by the British later than Virginia and Maryland, by 1699 there were presses in New York and Philadelphia, whereas in the Chesapeake the Nuthead press had sputtered out after producing only a handful of imprints. But the introduction of printing in New York and Pennsylvania did not immediately foster a vital print culture. Until the 1720s there was never more than one printer in either town at any time; for all but a few years the press was in the hands of one family, and for all but a few months it was carefully circumscribed by religious and civil authorities, who regarded it primarily as a helpful administrative tool. For a brief moment in Philadelphia in the early 1690s there were signs of the emergence of an open and commercially viable press. Otherwise the press had a comparatively small impact on the print culture of the region before the 1720s. It produced hardly any books and only a few pamphlets, a tiny portion of the reading matter required by the inhabitants. Their book culture was largely imported from Europe, while written communication and public discourse were carried on in much the same ways as in colonies where there was no printing.

The middle colonies were carved out of the domain of New Netherland, taken from the Dutch and granted to James, Duke of York in 1664. The early English governors of this domain were receptive to the use of printing as a means of administration. The first British governor had hardly taken up his office before he made a trip to Boston in 1665, where he had a broadside printed stating the terms on which new settlers would be received in the Duke's lands.[1] In 1668 the second governor sent to Boston a request for a printer to settle in New York, but no one answered his call. Then in the 1670s a new governor, Edmund Andros, took a hard line against the introduction of printing, indeed, against any measure that threatened to undermine his authority. In 1685 the Duke of York, now King James II, affirmed this policy in a letter to yet another governor which read, "for as much as great inconvenience may arise by the liberty of printing within our province of New York; you are to provide by all necessary Orders that noe person may keep any press for printing, nor that any book, pamphlet or other matters whatsoever bee printed without your special leave & license first obtained."[2] In England the regulation of the press by the civil government had lapsed during the civil war but had been vigorously reasserted after the Restoration by the Licensing Act of 1662. In his instructions James was merely extending the spirit of the Licensing Act to England's colonies. This was not a prohibition of printing; it was a policy of control. Since there were no printers in the middle colonies to control, this policy made it virtually certain that no printer would come there without a warm invitation from the governor.

Meanwhile the Duke of York had disposed of New Jersey and Pennsylvania, which gradually came under the control of the Society of Friends. The Quakers were skilled at using the press to spread their religion. During the quarter century in which the Licensing Act was enforced by an implacable enemy of popery and dissent, Sir Roger L'Estrange, they built up a remarkably effective clandestine system of book production and distribution.[3] They naturally were eager to establish a press in Pennsylvania where their political and religious dominance would presumably enable it to operate without hindrance. When William Penn crossed the Atlantic in 1682 to explore the colony he had just been granted, he took with him the nineteen-year-old William Bradford, an apprentice to the leading Quaker printer of London, Andrew Sowle. Bradford returned to London, attained his freedom, married his master's daughter, gathered together press and type, and returned to Pennsylvania in 1685.

Bradford brought with him a letter from George Fox defining his mission: printing Friends' books and importing them from London, for the use of the faithful not only in Pennsylvania but also in New Jersey, Long Island, Virginia, Carolina, Rhode Island, Plymouth, and Boston as well. Fox desired the Friends to give him "encouragements," to arrange for each meeting to take a certain number of the books he printed and to order their books through him, "& so save you a labour of sending to England . . . a great service to you in all these places in America." In other words, they should give him plenty of business, not only to multiply Friends' books, but to allow him to make a living. Fox also desired the Friends at Philadelphia to exercise strict control over what Bradford printed and sold: "you may make an order that he shall not permit any Friend's Books among you but what Friends in the ministry do there approve of; as they do here in England."[4]

This tension between a licensed press and a commercially viable press was played out in the first thing Bradford printed. It was not a Friends' book at all but an almanac, a strictly commercial and potentially lucrative sort of publication. The author, Samuel Atkins, stated in his preface that "I having journied in and through several places, not only in this Province, but likewise in Maryland, and elsewhere, and the People generally complaining, that they scarcely knew how the Time passed, nor that they hardly knew the day of Rest, or Lords Day, when it was, for want of a Diary, or Day-Book, which we call an Almanack." Perhaps this was just an attempt to make the little forty-page book appear to be in the service of religion, or to be a way of using the technology of print to fill a real social need. But in the printer's preface, Bradford made it plain that he intended the book to make money for him. "Hereby understand that after great Charge and Trouble, I have brought that great Art and Mystery of Printing into this part of America, believing it may be of great service to you in several respects, hoping to find Encouragement, not only in this Almanack, but what else I shall enter upon for the use and service of the Inhabitants of these Parts." His preface concludes, "And for the ease of Clarks, Scriviners, &c. I propose to print blank Bills, Bonds, Letters of Attorney, Indentures, Warrants, &c. and what else presents itself."[5] Those last four words were an assertion of economic freedom that no printer in England enjoyed. The printing of almanacs was the most valuable of the privileges held by the Stationers' Company, and only certain favored members were allowed to print them. Bradford was quietly claiming the right to print not just for the Friends but for whoever would pay for his services.

For this reason or some other, Bradford's innocuous almanac was disturbing to the Friends. Fox's instructions to the Philadelphia Friends had left open the question of who was authorized to oversee the press, whether it was to be the responsibility of a civil or a religious official or body, and whether that oversight should extend only to books printed for the Friends, or to other books Bradford might print. In the absence of specific instructions, the Provincial Council decided to scrutinize the text of the almanac for anything that might be construed as bearing on their religion. They contrived to be offended by a passing but quite respectful reference to "Lord Penn." Bradford was called before the Council and ordered to efface those two words in every copy and "not to print any thing but what shall have Lycence from ye Councill."[6] At this moment Bradford had in press Thomas Budd's glowing account of Pennsylvania's commercial prospects, *Good Order established in Pennsilvania & New-Jersey*. He went ahead and finished the pamphlet. Knowing, however, that Budd had displeased the London Friends with a previous book, and perhaps fearing that the Council would be reluctant to approve this one, he published it with no place or printer noted on the title page, the same technique his master Sowle had so often used to evade the Licensing Act.

Hitherto, the Council as an agency of the civil government had exercised the power to license, but on another occasion in 1687 the Philadelphia Monthly Meeting, a religious governing body, ordered Bradford to show them anything "what may concern Friends or Truth" before he set to work. The Meeting went on to order him to collect and destroy all the copies of the almanac he had just printed because it contained some "light and airy" phrases; he was paid £4 for his loss. No copy survives.[7]

Printing for the Friends was proving to be fraught with difficulty; nor was it a very dependable source of livelihood. In 1686 Bradford printed his first two works for the Friends, a twenty-three-page epistle (Evans 405) and a four-page one (Evans 401), 100 copies; but over the next two years not a single book or pamphlet printed for them survives. They did not request him to reprint books by Friends in England, nor did local Quaker writers supply him with much copy, apart from suspect writers like Budd and, later on, George Keith. The center of Quaker printing continued to be London, where the intellectual leaders of the religion remained; no Quaker Mather emigrated to America to occupy the printers there.

The ambiguity about who was to oversee the press would have been just tolerable as long as there was no disagreement about it among the authorities. What happened next put Bradford in a much worse position: two factions appeared in the government, and one requested him to print a document which the other wished suppressed. This happened in 1689 when Penn, temporarily out of favor at court and badly in need of money, appointed the Puritan financial wizard John Blackwell as his deputy governor. The appointment was bitterly resented by the ousted Quaker deputy governor and his party. Under the revised charter of liberties Penn had granted in 1683, the powers of the governor had been diminished. To reinforce this point, the anti-Blackwell party requested Bradford to print that charter, which up to then had only been available in an official manuscript copy kept in an office in town. On April 8, 1689, he printed 160 copies of it (Evans 496) and was paid 20*s*. The sixteen-page pamphlet carried no indication of where, when, or by whom it was printed. The next day Blackwell summoned Bradford and threatened him with punishment for printing the charter without permission.[8]

Though the printing of the charter was obviously a political attack on Blackwell, the question remains why the mere printing of what was agreed to be a valid legal document should have caused so much fuss. This was not simply a question of whether the charter should be available to citizens in the form of print. The old charter *was* available in print, having been printed in London in 1682 at Penn's request. But when the charter was revised in 1683, the Council (Penn presiding) had decided not to print it because further revisions were likely.[9] In 1689 Blackwell as Penn's deputy still hoped for revisions that would restore some of the power he believed Penn had unwisely given up. That seems to be the main reason he objected to having the new charter fixed in print in its present form.

To make matters worse, Blackwell asserted, Bradford had omitted words from the new charter that changed its meaning. The governor had obviously collated the printed text with the manuscript very carefully; the bibliographer Charles Hildeburn identified just seven words in three passages omitted in sixteen pages of text.[10] None of the omissions bear directly on the governor's power; in fact two of them might be construed to diminish the Assembly's power. There is no way of determining who was responsible for the omissions or whether they were intentional or unintentional. Still, it is easy to see why they alarmed Blackwell. "Thou knows where ye Charter is kept," Bradford was told, "and those that want to know any thing, may have recourse thither. . . . It is a thing that ought not to be made publick to all the world; and therefore is intrusted in a particular person's hand whom the people confide in."[11] The existence of a printed text violated this public trust by appropriating the authority of the manuscript and in effect emending the charter.

Bradford wrote out a transcript in dialogue of the proceedings when he was summoned to appear before Blackwell, just as Penn had done in 1670 when he was tried for preaching at Gracechurch Street in London. Penn's dialogue was well known from its publication in a popular pamphlet. Bradford's transcript imitates Penn's in its dramatic form, the bullying judge contrasted with the calm, reasonable defendant.[12] These dialogues show the moral superiority of the defendant and the legal superiority of his case; they show how he stood up to the oppressor, kept his head, impressed the jury, tied the judge in knots, and got home free. In his dialogue, Bradford cast himself in Penn's role as the Quaker martyr in possession of the moral high ground; and he drove home the irony that the Friends in power in Philadelphia persecuted their own in exactly the same way they themselves had been persecuted back in London.

Bradford's language, his legal strategy, and even his very demeanor in court were copied from Penn. Like Penn, Bradford asserted the people's right to know the law as well as his own right not to give evidence against himself and to know his accusers. He declined to confess to printing the charter of liberties, though he defended, in the abstract, his freedom to undertake such a task. Noting that he had already printed the old charter in England (while working for Sowle) with Penn's approval, he claimed that, before he left for Philadelphia, the governor-to-be had proposed that he print the laws in the new colony. Accordingly, it was Penn who gave him license to print "such things as came to my hand, whereby to get my living," and Blackwell as deputy had never told him anything to the contrary. Disingenuously forgetting the reprimands he had received from the Council and the Monthly Meeting (which had happened before Blackwell had come on the scene), Bradford pleaded ignorance. He claimed he did not know that any official had been appointed "*Imprimatur*" or licenser of the press. Blackwell thundered his reply:

Sir, I am '*Imprimatur*'. . . . You should have come and askt my advice, and not have done any thing that particular parties bring to you. I have particular order from Governour Penn for the suppressing of printing here, and narrowly to look after your press. . . . I know printing is a great benefit to a country if it be rightly managed, but otherwise is a great mischief. Sir, we are within the king's dominions, and the laws of England are in force here, and you know the laws, and they are against printing, and you shall print nothing without allowance.

As it happened, Blackwell not only accepted the role of licenser of the press but also portrayed Penn as ordering the enforcement in Pennsylvania of the licensing law he had so blithely ignored in England. Then, with an irony almost too exquisite to be credible, a member of the Council at the hearing spoke up and overtly equated Bradford's position with Sowle's under the oppression of the Licensing Act: "William thou knows thy father [that is, his father-in-law] suffered much in England for printing . . . and I would not have thee bring trouble on thyself."

In reply to all this, Bradford stoutly maintained his idea of a press that was open to all parties, operating in a free market for print. This was an ideal that had not yet been realized anywhere in England or America, but which was consonant with the direction of social and cultural changes at that time. Here is Bradford's clearest statement of this idea:

Governour, it is my imploy, my trade and calling, and that by which I get my living, to print; and if I may not print such things as come to my hand which are innocent, I cannot live. I am not a person that takes such advice of one party or other. . . . If I print one thing today, and the contrary party bring me another tomorrow, to contradict it, I cannot say that I shall not print it. Printing is a manufacture of the nation, and therefore ought rather be encouraged than suppressed.[13]

Bradford's argument was not accepted by Blackwell, who made (or at least threatened to make) Bradford put up a bond of £500 to guarantee that he would print nothing without his permission. Otherwise, Bradford does not seem to have been punished. Shortly afterward, Penn relieved the unpopular Blackwell of his office.

Bradford was unrepentant, or else confident of the power of the party that was backing him, because after his appearance before Blackwell he reissued the charter from the same setting of type, but with the omitted phrases restored. This reissue appears at the end of a book called *The Excellent Priviledge of Liberty and Property being the Birth-Right of the Free-born Subjects of England* (Evans 433). It included Magna Carta and the other ancient charters comprising the English Constitution, together with a preface by Penn that acknowledges the absence of printed laws and the need for them.[14] *The Excellent Priviledge* is undated but usually ascribed to 1687, on inconclusive grounds. However, the way the type is arranged where the text was corrected makes it clear that it was printed after the offending edition of the charter, not two years before. If *The Excellent Priviledge* is reascribed to 1689, the very act of printing it at that time (i.e., after the Glorious Revolution) and in the context of Magna Carta and Penn's recommendation, takes on a new and richer meaning. It becomes not only a vindication of Bradford's right to print the charter but also a powerful statement of the connections between Penn's idea of liberty of conscience and Bradford's own idea of an open press.[15]

Meanwhile Bradford had been trying to find other ways of supporting his family besides printing for the Friends. His trade in blank forms and stationery has already been cited; he sold medicines and nostrums, and a contemporary poem alludes to his bookbinding. He also imported books, as Fox had authorized; at the end of some of his imprints he advertised numerous titles, mostly Friends' books, Bibles, and schoolbooks, but also handbooks of law and medicine. This business extended throughout the middle colonies. In the account book of one John Bowne of Flushing, Long Island, we find reference to several hundred books bought from Bradford between 1686 and 1691. Bowne resold them in his own vicinity and in nearby Connecticut and also loaned them to his neighbors from time to time.[16] Bradford had several other bookselling agents in New York, New Jersey, and Delaware.

In 1688 Bradford tried another way of making money from his press: two entrepreneurial ventures in what might be called general book publishing. The first was the 1688 *Temple of Wisdom* (Evans 447), a compilation of extracts from the works of the mystic Jacob Boehme, the pastoral (but later Puritan) poet George Wither, the metaphysical poet Francis Quarles, and the philosopher Francis Bacon. It was put together by Bradford's almanac maker Daniel Leeds. With 226 pages in small octavo, this was the first full-sized book printed in the middle colonies. It was a very odd book, with something to offend everyone, but it suggests a perceived demand for something – anything – besides a steady diet of Friends' books. It was also a risky book because of the large investment in paper and labor that it required. In

Propofals for the Printing of a large BIBLE,
by *William Bradford*.

THefe are to give Notice, that it is propofed for a large houfe-Bible to be Printed by way of Subfcriptions [a method [illegible] in *England* for the printing of large Volumns, becaufe Printing is very chargeable] therefore to all that are willing to forward fo good (and great) a Work, as the Printing of the holy Bible, are offered thefe Propofals, *viz.*

1. That it fhall be printed in a fair Character, on good Paper, and well bound.

2. That it fhall contain the Old and New Teftament, with the Apocraphy, and all to have ufeful Marginal Notes.

3. That it fhall be allowed (to them that fubfcribe) for Twe[illegible] Shillings *per Bible*: [A Price which one of the fame volumn in *England* would [illegible]oft.]

4. That the pay fhall be half Silver Money, and half Country [illegible] at Money price. *One* half down now, and the other half on the delivery of the Bibles.

5. That thofe who do fubfcribe for fix, fhall have the Seventh gratis, and have them delivered one mouth before any above that number fha[illegible] be fold to others.

6. To thofe which do not fubfcribe, the faid Bibles will not be allowed under 26 s. a piece.

7. Thofe who are minded to have the Common-Prayer, fhall h[illegible] the [illegible]hole [illegible] up for [illegible] [illegible]cribe 2[illegible] and 6 d. *per* Book.

8. That as encouragement is given by Peoples fubfcribing and paying down one half, the faid Work will be put forward with what Expedition may be.

9. That the Subfcribers may enter their *Subfcriptions* and time of Payment, at *Pheneas Pemberton*'s and *Robert Halls* in the County of *Bucks*. At *Malen Stacy*'s Mill at the Falls. At *Thomas Budds* Houfe in *Burlington*. At *John Hafting's* in the County of *Chefter*. At *Edward Blake's* in *New-Caftle*. At *Thomas VVoodrooffs* in *Salem*. And at *william Bradford*'s in *Philadelphia*, Printer & Undertaker of the faid Work. At which places the Subfcribers fhall have a Receipt for fo much of their Subfcriptions as paid, and an obligation for the delivery of the number of Bibles (fo Printed and Bound as aforefaid) as the refpective Subfcribers fhall depofit one half for.

Alfo this may further give notice, that *Samuell Richardfon* and *Samuell Carpenter* of *Philadelphia*, are appointed to take care and be affiftant in the laying cut of the Subfcription Money, and to fee that it be imploy'd to the ufe intended, and confequently that the whole Work be expedited. Which is promifed by

Philadelphia, the 14th of the 1ft Month, 1688. *William Bradford.*

Figure 6.1. William Bradford, *Proposals for the Printing of a Large Bible* [Philadelphia, 1688]. Courtesy of The Historical Society of Pennsylvania.

bearing the risk and expense of printing, Bradford was acting as the publisher of the book.

In another publishing venture of 1688 Bradford called himself the "undertaker," since the word "publisher" was not then used in its modern sense. This second venture was a folio Bible with the Geneva marginal notes, a version popular with English dissenters. Bradford printed a broadside (Fig. 6.1) proposing to publish this Bible at his own risk and expense, and to sell it for only 20*s.* (less than it would cost to import a copy), provided enough people paid half the purchase price in advance. This mode of publication was called printing by subscription, and it was just coming into use in England as a way of mitigating the financial risk of publishing large books. This project also posed a legal risk. Bible printing was a monopoly of the royal printers, but there was some doubt whether this restriction extended to Bibles with notes, and even greater doubt as to whether it extended to the colonies. To reduce both risks, Bradford formally sought the endorsement of the Meeting for his venture, but no support was forthcoming, and he never issued the Bible.

In 1690 Bradford established the first paper mill in British North America, in partnership with two rich Quaker merchants and the recently arrived Dutch papermaker William Rittenhouse. Bradford had a monopoly on the mill's output of printing paper, which was potentially a great asset, since imported paper was expensive and the supply unpredictable. Rittenhouse paper began to appear in Bradford imprints quite soon after the mill was in operation, but the use of imported paper persisted. In any case, the output of the Bradford press could hardly have kept a paper mill busy. The surviving papers of the Rittenhouse mill (long thought to be lost but acquired in 1992 by the Library Company of Philadelphia) show that the mill also produced white writing paper and coarse brown paper in considerable quantities. These papers survive in letters, legal papers, accounts, and memoranda. Bound volumes of blank writing paper were used for commonplace books, account books, music books, and the like. The product of the paper mill touched the book culture of the region at a great many more points than the printing press.[17]

Despite this diversification of his business, Bradford was dissatisfied with his prospects in Pennsylvania. Not long after the interview with Blackwell, his old master Sowle died. With a view to taking over that much more solid business, he sent his wife back to England and applied for permission for his own departure. The threat of losing their printer finally induced the Friends to make an effort to encourage him. They offered to pay him a salary of £40 a year and to buy 200 copies of everything he printed with their approval. Bradford accepted the offer and stayed on.[18]

This interlude of harmony was brief. In 1692 Bradford printed a pamphlet by George Keith, *The Christian Faith of the . . . Quakers in Rhode-Island . . . Vindicated* (Evans 600). Thus began the Keithian controversy in print. Keith was one of the foremost "publishers of the truth" within Quakerism. A close associate of Fox, Penn, and Barclay, he had come to Philadelphia in 1689 to head the school Penn was founding. The next year, partly in response to the disorder brought about by Blackwell's rule, Keith had proposed to the Yearly Meeting in Philadelphia a body of rules for church governance, including a written confession of faith and the election of elders; he also advocated more emphasis on the Bible and the historical Jesus. These proposals were too controversial for most Quakers, who believed that relying on "the light within" was the distinguishing feature of their faith. The Meeting rejected the proposals, but Keith continued to press them. Gradually he gathered support among small landholders, merchants, and artisans who may not have understood his theology but felt that the ruling party of Quakers had assumed too much power. By April 1692 Keith's followers were meeting separately and the Philadelphia Quakers were on the verge of a schism.[19]

Until the beginning of 1692 the controversy had been carried out entirely in public meetings and in the medium of manuscript minutes and epistles. But early in the year the Rhode Island Meeting, which had adopted Keith's confession of faith, requested Bradford, who supported Keith, to print a vindication of their position in the tract mentioned earlier. It was condemned by the Philadelphia Monthly Meeting, and Bradford was censured. Again Bradford was caught between two parties, each of which felt it had the authority to give him permission to print.[20]

In response a group of Rhode Island Friends, along with Keith and Thomas Budd, sent a protest to the Philadelphia Meeting in which they argued that there could be no objection to the "manner" in which the book was published, even though it had not been approved in Philadelphia, since it had been approved by their own "more antient" meeting of Friends of good judgment. Nor (of course) did they find anything wrong with the "matter" of the book. As well, they protested that disapproval by the Philadelphians would lead people to assume that the book was theologically unsound, when in fact it was exemplary:

> Certainly the friends of Rhode-Island and Else-where will think strange that so publick & faithfull a Testimony for Truth should be any way opposed by ffriends of Philadelphia. . . . The noise of its being call'd in question is too far spread abroad allready, and what the consequence will be when it comes to the ears of Christian Lodiwick, Cotton Mather & others of truth and friends adversaries, we earnestly desire you will in coolness and weightily consider. And therefore we desire . . . that you would be carefull what you do.[21]

In distinguishing so carefully between matter and manner, the Rhode Islanders seem to be replying to a charge made by the Philadelphia Meeting. Evidently the Philadelphians were at this stage just as upset by the manner as by the matter. The problem was not so much what Keith had written, or even that it had been made public in print, rather than confined to private epistles between meetings. The real problem was that because Bradford, the

Philadelphia Friends' printer, had been involved, people would assume official approval of the contents. Print misrepresented them in a way that spoken or written words never could, but Bradford's participation misrepresented them even more. For the first time, the Friends in Philadelphia truly faced the responsibility of having an acknowledged official press. The importance the Friends placed on printing had the side effect of making them painfully conscious of how they were seen by others (what will Cotton Mather think?). In the bitter print war over Keith that ensued, the Friends quarreled over doctrine, church government, and civil authority, but also over the figure they cut in the public sphere of print.

Ignoring the Rhode Islanders' plea for moderation, the Philadelphia Meeting released Bradford from his contract with them in April, just as the schism became open.[22] Now he was free to print what he wanted. Over the next few months a flood of Keithian prose streamed from Bradford's press, some seventeen imprints in all. At the same time Bradford published a number of books unrelated to the controversy – an account of the execution of a murderer (Evans 588), and a poetical description of Pennsylvania (Evans 594) – that were new departures for him in book entrepreneurship.

During the summer of 1692, the leaders of the main body of the Meeting continued to try to resolve the dispute. Respected Quakers from England were asked to mediate; hoping to mollify Keith, these outsiders rendered a judgment that found fault with both sides. Meanwhile, Keith adroitly used his exclusive control of the press to escalate the dispute into full-blown schism. His tracts became almost hysterical in their rage.[23] Bradford was accused of being a "favourer" of Keith and of refusing to print for his opponents. He replied, "The Printer hath not yet refused to print any thing for either party; and . . . he is willing and ready to print any thing for the future that G.K.'s Opposers shall bring to him."[24] He did issue a couple of exhortations against schism (Evans 591, 592), reprints of old tracts relating to English disputes, but nothing against Keith appeared in print until two years later when pamphlets on both sides began to appear in London.

Was Bradford sincere about the openness of his press? He was not an impartial observer in this conflict. He had printed Keith's pamphlets before he had become a controversial figure, and in the schism he sided with Keith. In a letter written in 1709 reflecting on the events of 1692, he called himself "Zealous in that Cause."[25] Thus his conscience probably dictated his decision to print whatever Keith asked him to, even though (as he said in that same letter) "the sale of those Pamphlets did not answer the Charge." But did he refuse to print anything opposed to Keith, as his enemies claimed? The most likely answer is that the question never arose because he was never asked to. The silence of the orthodox Friends seems to have been a deliberate policy. In 1694 the anti-Keithian Samuel Jennings stated (in a pamphlet printed in London) that "we published not a Line in Print to detect him justly of his [Keith's] notorious Falshoods against us, (hoping to have somewhat thereby kept this unhappy difference from being made more publick by us)."[26] Keith ridiculed this excuse in another London pamphlet:

They made it publick all ways imaginable (Printing excepted . . .) by causing . . . this false Judgment of theirs to be read and published against us in all the meetings; and sending Copies of it far and near . . . and over to England, which arrived before any of our printed Books; and by causing a Proclamation to be read against me in the Market Place; and many other malicious and invective Papers and Letters in Manuscript they sent out against me.[27]

Keith found this tactic of scribal publication and oral proclamation "clandestine" and "back-biting." He likened it to "Indians, that skulk behind Trees, and shoot at Men in the open Field." He did not feel that access to the press gave him an unfair advantage; on the contrary, it left him more exposed to attack. Of course, like so many of his statements, this was self-serving. Whatever the truth may have been, the Keithian controversy remains an unusual instance of the dominant party choosing not to use the press in a controversy, while the supposedly less powerful minority had what amounted to unlimited access to it.

In the fall of 1692 the Philadelphia Meeting retaliated against Keith by condemning him as an apostate and a heretic. He appealed this decision in a broadside in which almost incidentally he questioned the way certain civil magistrates (who were also among the twenty-eight religious leaders who had condemned him) had recently handled an armed confrontation with a privateer.[28] As long as Keith had confined himself to religious matters, the law was powerless to muzzle him, but by impugning the civil government, he provided his opponents with a pretext for a prosecution. Bradford was brought before a judge on a civil charge of seditious libel; later Keith was arrested as well.

Again Bradford transcribed his dialogue with the judge, and this time it was printed.[29] Here the similarities in argument and demeanor with Penn's 1670 trial are even more pronounced. Like Penn he appeared with his hat on and was rebuked by the judge. Again he asserted his right to know under what law he was being prosecuted. As in the interview with Blackwell, there was a question of whether the Licensing Act was in force in America, since the absence of an imprint was one of the pretexts for a civil prosecution. Bradford said the act had expired, but the judge pointed out that it had been revived. In a sense they were both right; the act expired in 1679, was renewed in 1685 (around the time Bradford left England), and was due to expire again in just a few months. Keith spoke up in Bradford's defense, saying that it was not clear that the act applied to the colonies, and in any case that the Quaker printers in London often did not use imprints. All this shows detailed (if not always strictly accurate) knowledge of the licensing laws.[30]

Then the hearing moved on to the more serious charge of libel. Bradford defended himself by asserting in direct contradiction to the judge that the jury was obliged to find not just whether he had printed the pamphlet but whether it was a libel; that is, the jury was to rule on law as well as fact. Bradford argued that what he had printed was not seditious because it merely raised a question about the handling of the privateer. "It is not laid down positive that they ought not to have proceeded against the privateers, but laid down by way of query for the people called quakers to consider and resolve at their yearly meeting."[31] His position had little or no basis in law, but it set a moral precedent that was recalled in almost exactly the same words by Andrew Hamilton almost half a century later at the libel trial of John Peter Zenger.

Bradford was on firmer legal ground when he argued that there was no evidence against him, since the court could not produce the type from which the pamphlet was printed. There is an old tradition that the forme of type had been brought to the jury in private, but while they were attempting to read the backwards letters, a jury member had rested it on his cane, and the type had fallen out in a jumble.[32] Whatever the reason, the type was not produced. The judge instructed the jury to rule only on the fact (whether Bradford had printed it), and without this evidence, they refused to convict him. The enraged judge punished the rebellious jury by imprisoning them along with the accused, just as the judge had done in Penn's trial. The case dragged on until April 1693 when Governor Fletcher of New York, who had been appointed governor of Pennsylvania by the Crown over Penn's objections, ruled that this was purely a religious difference, not a case of civil libel, and Bradford was released. In the process of freeing Bradford, Fletcher became acquainted with his situation and took advantage of it to issue him an invitation to come to New York to print for the Provincial Council. Bradford readily accepted.

There is no question that Bradford's press made its greatest impact in Pennsylvania during the few months when he was not under contract with the Friends. Keith leapt into that breach and made masterful use of the press to stage a paper war as virulent as anything in London, though with the difference that it was one-sided. Otherwise, the Friends made hardly any use of Bradford's press, while preventing him from publishing anything else. In his nearly nine years in Philadelphia, he had printed just fifty-four extant imprints, thirty of them in that last active year and a half. A single copy of each comprises a total of only 138 whole sheets of paper, folded in various formats.

Bradford's departure left Pennsylvania without a printer, but the faction of the Friends who dominated civil and religious government had decided they did not need or want one. When Bradford threw off the fetters of their control and poured forth books by Keith, he fully justified their fears about unlicensed printing. If they could not completely control printing, they preferred to suppress it altogether.

Bradford's New York career was rather different from his Philadelphia one in at least one respect. In Pennsylvania Bradford had posed the question of the open press and was answered firmly in the negative. In New York the question hardly even arose. There Bradford's employer was not the church but the state; his job not to disseminate truth but to print public documents, principally proclamations of the governor, laws, and the journals of the assembly. First called in 1683, the assembly originally had little power and had been abolished by King James in 1686. Then the Glorious Revolution of 1688 in England and Leisler's Rebellion in 1689 in New York changed the balance of power. The new king appointed a new governor with instructions to revive the assembly in 1691. After two busy years, it was time to print the laws.

The Licensing Act finally lapsed in 1695, but Bradford was nonetheless accountable to the governor for the books he printed because he was a salaried public employee (at £40 a year) subject to dismissal at any time. The salary was enough to make him respect the governor's opinion and to keep him from looking elsewhere for his living. Moreover, unlike the Friends, the New York government gave him plenty of work. In his first two years alone he printed twenty-four imprints for the government, including the 100-page folio volume of all the laws passed by the assembly since its reestablishment (Evans 703). In 1693 and 1694, single copies of this government work amounted to fifty-seven sheets, while nongovernment work amounted to twenty-four sheets. This level of output did not greatly increase in the period before 1720, though it did fluctuate. In 1705–1706, government printing was down to ten sheets, while nongovernment work was about the same at twenty-six sheets. In 1716–1717, government work was back up to sixty-one sheets, while nongovernment work was only eight-and-a-half sheets.

Bradford settled in to make a career as a government printer. In 1703 he became official printer for New Jersey as well, at £25 a year; later he held other posts there, including the lucrative job of farmer of the excise. He acquired considerable real estate in both colonies. In 1723 he even printed a New Jersey state document that bore a Perth Amboy imprint, though it has never been settled whether he actually had a press there. Throughout these years he had been getting much of his paper from the Rittenhouse mill near Philadelphia, but in 1728 he established another mill closer by at Elizabeth,

New Jersey, thus breaking the nearly forty years of monopoly of American paper manufacturing enjoyed by the Rittenhouse family.[33]

Bradford's relations with the various New York governors were not totally without conflict, but these conflicts were mild compared to those with the Friends in his previous job. The most serious fight he had was with the Earl of Bellomont, who succeeded Fletcher as governor. When he complained about typographical errors in Bradford's 1699 printing of the laws (and there were indeed many), the printer curtly replied that he "had nobody to correct the presse at the time he printed them." Bellomont was not pleased. Then in 1700 he instructed Bradford to print at public expense the diaries of his conferences with Indians at Albany. Evidently Bradford thought that printing private diaries was not part of his salaried job and that he should be paid for it separately. For four months he pretended he was too sick to do the job; Bellomont then relieved him of his office for neglect of duty and hired a scrivener to make "several copies" of the diaries to send to ministers of state in England, for £3 12*s.*, a price quite competitive with the cost of printing.[34] Shortly thereafter Bellomont died and the new governor, Lord Cornbury, not only reinstated Bradford but raised his salary to £75, appointed him New Jersey printer (as noted earlier), and appointed an assemblyman as corrector of the press at a salary of £30 per year.[35] Cornbury's generosity, however, was somewhat offset by the fact that he never actually paid Bradford's salary. There is no sign that he was displeased, and from time to time the money was even appropriated, but his mismanagement of the colony's finances made payment impossible. After Cornbury's death Bradford petitioned for some £540 owed him for expenses and unpaid salary dating back to his dispute with Bellomont. The cost of sending a fleet to Port Royal in 1709 further burdened the colony's finances, and Bradford despaired of ever being paid.[36] He persisted in his petitions, however, and in 1714, when the colony's finances were back in order, he was paid in full.[37] From then on Bradford seems to have been quite happy as a government printer, and his employers happy with him.

This may explain why local political or religious controversy was so strikingly absent from Bradford's nongovernment printing from his arrival in New York at least until 1720. Apart from an annual almanac or two and a handbook for clerks that went through several editions, it mostly consisted of books and pamphlets printed for various religious bodies, such as the Dutch Reformed Church, for which he printed three catechisms in Dutch (Bristol 206, 397; Evans 1350), and the Society for the Propagation of the Gospel (SPG), for whom in 1715 he printed a prayer book in Mohawk for the use of missionaries (see Fig. I.1). Bradford also published pamphlets relating to political and religious disputes in New England, which posed no risk to him, since they were distributed entirely outside the colony. In his two 1700 editions of *The Gospel Order Revived* (Evans 950, 951), a reply to Increase Mather's *Order of the Gospel*, the authors noted that they had sent their book to New York to be printed because "the Press at Boston is so much under the aw of the Reverend Author, whom we answer, and his friends, that we could not obtain of the printer there to print the following sheets." Conversely, when Francis Makemie, a Presbyterian minister based in the Chesapeake, was imprisoned by Governor Cornbury for preaching without license, his protesting pamphlets were printed in Boston (Evans 1298–1300).

For the first ten years of his New York career Bradford continued to print a steady stream of anti-Quaker, pro-Keithian works; these pamphlets were of course controversial, and Bradford himself believed they were responsible for the large numbers of New York Quakers who joined the Anglican Church. But since the Anglicans were so disproportionately powerful in New York, this printing was not the slightest bit risky; quite the contrary. Yet if printing Anglican books was safe, it was not always profitable. He claimed in 1709 that all the Keithian books he had ever published were still in print and that he had never recovered his costs. He believed that he had sacrificed the opportunity to take over his father-in-law's lucrative business as Friends' printer in London in order to support Keith, and he continued to hope for some compensation from the Anglicans.

It looked as if his efforts would finally be rewarded when, in 1706, a group of Anglican missionaries agreed to support him in publishing *The Book of Common Prayer*, a sizeable book of more than 300 pages (45 sheets) in quarto, along with the new Brady and Tate version of the psalms, which could be bound with it or sold separately. The missionaries promised to push the sale of the prayer books in their parishes, and Trinity Church advanced part of the cost of the paper without interest, promising as well to use the new psalmbook in its services. But the missionaries all died or moved away, and by 1709 he had only sold 50 copies of the prayer book out of an edition of 1,000. That year he proposed to the SPG that it allow him to sell its books for his own profit, giving back a free prayer book for every pound's worth of books he was sent. As he wrote to the SPG, Anglican books were not selling in the colonies because they were not subsidized. Merchants would not import them because they were not profitable enough ("Books will not advance in Price as other Goods do," he wrote), and the people would not buy them because they were too expensive. Friends' books, on the other hand, circulated widely because (as he well knew) they were imported by the meeting and sold "at an easy rate." Whether the SPG agreed to this proposal is not known, but in 1710 Bradford did reissue the unsold sheets of the 1706 prayer book with a new title page (the form in which all surviving copies are found) and the next year Trinity Church released him from his debt for the paper.[38]

Bradford did publish a few pamphlets on local political affairs, but they all turn out to be part of his job as government printer. For instance, his pieces on Indian affairs are official reports or petitions. The only sermons he printed were funeral sermons for a governor and a governor's wife. He also printed a couple of anonymous political pamphlets during the election of 1713 which allude to controversy, but they were written by the governor and one of his chief aides and only argue his position. The most politically volatile thing he printed was an account of Nicholas Bayard's trial for seditious libel under Governor Bellomont (Evans 1038). The trial was conducted in secrecy so no report of it would leak out, but some witnesses took notes without the court's knowledge. These notes apparently circulated in manuscript while Bayard was in prison waiting to be drawn and quartered. Bradford printed them only after Bayard's conviction had been overturned by a new governor, Cornbury, who gave permission to print.[39] The governors of New York may not have exercised control over the press as blatantly as the Quakers of Pennsylvania, but evidently they retained some of their old licensing power, and Bradford was happy to hide behind it.

Looking at the output of the New York press before 1720, one would suppose that in both church and state there was hardly any dissent or debate, public or private. Of course, that was not the case. With the arrival of Governor Hunter in 1710, New York politics stabilized as the old factions were broken up, but from 1692 to 1710 the political atmosphere in New York was "poisonous and quarrelsome," characterized by "a rapid series of policy and party reversals which pitted 'ins' against 'outs' and interest against interest, making factional strife an almost endemic condition of the colony's public life."[40] Why was none of this conflict registered in the press? In the absence of any evidence of censorship by church or state, we must conclude that Bradford exercised self-censorship by simply refusing to print anything that might have endangered his comfortable position as government printer. What about the open press, then? Bradford had defended it eloquently when his press was comparatively idle in Philadelphia, but now that he was well paid and had no competitors, it was more prudent to forget about it.

Meanwhile, the Philadelphia Friends were in no hurry to get another printer. For almost six years after Bradford left Philadelphia, no printing was done there. Several times the Friends resolved to look into getting another printer, but did nothing about it. Then in 1698 there arrived in Philadelphia from Holland one Reynier Jansen, a lacemaker who happened to have learned how to print when he was a disciple of the Flemish mystic Antoinette Bourignon, leader of a tiny radical sect called the Light of the World. At about the same time, a press and type arrived from London, and

Jansen, whose lacemaking skills were in little demand among the Friends, was put to work on it. This time, nothing was left to chance. The press and type were the property of the Monthly Meeting, and they paid the rent of the house in which it was set up. The Meeting bought a stock of paper amounting to 105 reams. A special committee of the Meeting was appointed to oversee the press. Apart from almanacs and two pamphlets in Swedish for Gloria Dei Church, the docile Jansen seems to have printed nothing without instruction, and the Meeting was careful to buy considerable numbers of whatever he printed.[41]

Between 1699 and his death in 1706 Jansen produced just forty-three imprints, an output even smaller than Bradford's. (Some imprints from the last year of his life bear the names of his sons Tiberius Johnson and Joseph Reyners.) A single copy of his entire output would contain just 129 sheets of paper, folded in various formats to yield anywhere from 4 to 24 pages per sheet.[42] The sizes of Jansen's editions are unknown, but if they averaged as high as 400 copies, which is doubtful, he would just barely have used up those 105 reams of paper in seven years. The books and pamphlets he printed were mostly anti-Keithian tracts and Quaker apologetics. Now that they had access to a press, the anti-Keithians used it to reply to the pro-Keith propaganda emanating from Bradford's press in New York.

But the Keithian controversy was losing much of its heat. The most important of Jansen's imprints was the first, the Quaker Jonathan Dickinson's 1699 Indian captivity narrative *God's Protecting Providence* (Evans 863). In addition to being a classic Quaker book, it was perhaps the most enduring literary work of the middle colonies before the age of Franklin. It is also the earliest work of the region for which payment to an author can be documented; Dickinson received fifty free copies.[43] Jansen also reprinted a primer by George Fox. He printed a few documents for the governor and assembly, including summaries of the ninety-one laws passed by the Assembly in 1700, when the whole body of laws was rewritten. But once when asked to print a militia resolution, the pacifist Friends refused the governor access to the press. The press was in the service of the church, not the state, and it was anything but open.

After Jansen's death, the Friends once again made little effort to find another printer. The next call for a printer in Philadelphia came not from the Friends but from the General Assembly, which in 1712 resolved to have the laws of the Province printed. The almanac-maker Jacob Taylor had been using the former Jansen press off and on, and he bid for the job; but William Bradford traveled to Philadelphia with his son Andrew to offer his services, and shortly thereafter Andrew was established on his own in the Quaker city. Though hired by the government, he was also on good terms with the

Friends; he leased from them the second story of their school building for his printing office.[44]

Why had the assembly chosen this moment to hire a printer? Before 1700, there was no attempt to print the laws of Pennsylvania, even when a printer was available. This was not because of a fear of print as such; in fact, one of the first laws adopted by the province stipulated that the laws already laid down by Penn should be printed and taught in the schools. The absence of printed laws was due rather to procedures and practices of law-making peculiar to Pennsylvania, which made printing the laws unfeasible. First, laws were subject to Penn's approval, which could take months when he was in England. Second, the whole body of laws had to be confirmed or repealed at each session of the assembly, and were therefore in force only until the next session.[45] This was true even when no revision of the laws was made. An effort was made to create a category of "fundamental laws" that did not need to be reenacted each session, but this only made things more complicated. Third, copies of laws could only be sent out to magistrates after they had been engrossed by the master of the rolls; but this office was held by the bitter antiproprietary Thomas Lloyd, who found it to his political advantage never to engross a single law and to disavow the laws engrossed before he was in office.[46] Consequently, there was considerable doubt as to what laws were in force, but printing the laws would only have made matters worse. It was better to do as most justices did: Ignore Pennsylvania law and rely on English law books.

The chaotic situation was first addressed by the assembly in 1700, which revised the whole law code; Penn was in the colony, so his approval was secured; and the assembly ordered the master of the rolls to have them printed, which Jansen accordingly did in 1701. In 1701 a new charter removed the need for annual confirmation of laws.[47] These changes were indirect causes of the decision to print the laws in 1712. A more direct cause was a change in the assembly itself. In the election of 1710, there was almost a complete turnover in the delegates, as Thomas Lloyd and all his supporters were defeated. The new assembly was less divided and more productive. Under Lloyd the colony's government had almost ceased to function. The new assembly set about putting it back in working order.[48] They also sought a conciliation with Penn and with his secretary James Logan, whose return to the colony coincided with the decision to print the laws. In 1713 Bradford printed the laws passed in the previous session, and in 1714 he issued a compilation of all the laws passed since 1700 in a single folio volume. He printed continuations of this periodically for decades. In 1722 he also began printing the journals and votes of the assembly. If there was a second point, besides the Keithian controversy, where the press can be said to have had a powerful effect on the culture of Pennsylvania, it was the advent of printed laws. But it seems probable that the printing of the laws was more of an effect than a cause of changes in political culture.

Having got this important government printing job for his son, William Bradford closely supervised his activities and at times worked with him as if they were partners. He frequently rode down from New York to confer with Andrew or to get paper from the Rittenhouse mill. (Andrew shared in his father's old monopoly on their printing paper.) Father and son published several books jointly: a psalmbook in 1713 (Evans 1595), and in 1716 George Petyt's English legal handbook *Lex Parliamentaria* (Evans 1850). In 1718 Andrew published a handbook for young clerks previously published by William (Bristol 556). They also cooperated in the printing of almanacs, sharing sheets for the calendar, but each printing his own lists of local court meeting dates. However, apart from these joint ventures, annual almanacs, and government printing for Pennsylvania (and also occasionally for Maryland and Delaware) Andrew printed very little before 1720. So in the middle colonies, the press came to be entirely under the control of one family working mostly in the employ of governments.

If the inhabitants of the middle colonies had had to depend on the output of their local presses for their reading matter between 1685 and 1723, they would have had a monotonous diet indeed: laws, proclamations, almanacs, and Quaker controversy. Many aspects of colonial life were not reflected in local printing, partly owing to the control exercised over the press, but largely because the market for books was so small. It did not make economic sense to print an entire edition of a book that might be of interest to only a handful of readers. The local press was by no means the only source of books; in fact, it was probably the least important one. For matters of general interest, the early colonists relied on the presses of London. It was far less risky to import a copy or two from London than to reprint a whole edition of a book.

We have already noted that William Bradford was authorized to import Friends' books and sell them up and down the eastern seaboard; he continued to act as a bookseller in New York. Without Bradford in Philadelphia the Friends undoubtedly found other ways to import the books that were such a vital part of their religious practice. In 1705 the Philadelphia Monthly Meeting even established a lending library, though nothing further is known about it.[49] Other religious bodies also imported books; in 1707 Charles XII of Sweden sent a large number of religious and school books at the request of the congregation at Gloria Dei, the Swedish church.[50] Reynier Jansen seems to have taken up as a bookseller where Bradford left off, but in a very small way. His estate inventory of 1706 includes eight unspecified bound books, seven primers (in addition to the remainder in sheets of Fox's primer which Jansen printed himself), a dozen hornbooks, a parcel of Dutch books worth £5 and another parcel worth £4 2*s*. left over from Bradford's stock of thirteen years before. He also sold stationery, blank forms, patent medicines, and notions such as buckles and spectacles. The most expensive item of stock in the inventory was 100 lb. of galls for making ink, valued at £10. This was the typical stock of a small colonial book store, though at most it may have occupied only a shelf or a trunk in Jansen's house, which was separate from his press.[51]

Jonathan Dickinson's accounts show him buying a copy of Thomas Gage's *New Survey of the West Indies* from Jansen in 1701 for 8*s*. This book was part of a consignment sent by the London booksellers Awnsham and John Churchill in 1700 at the request of William Penn, who may have felt that the stock of books in his colony needed to be replenished. The lot included 125 titles worth more than £41. Since the Churchills were the publishers of John Locke, his works were heavily represented, along with Cervantes, Milton, Algernon Sidney, Malebranche, and books on such practical subjects as surveying, agriculture, and gardening. After failing to find a ready market for these books, Penn consigned them to Jansen's book store. In 1708, after Jansen's death, Penn complained that the Churchills were still dunning him for payment.[52]

While imported books certainly enriched the reading of the middle colonies, the failure of the Churchill consignment suggests that the market for them was still quite small. Edwin Wolf in his masterful survey of the book culture of colonial Philadelphia noted an impressive number of books in the estate inventories of the first generation of settlement, but most of them were evidently brought over by immigrants, and, in general, were the basic books of the pious: a Bible or two and perhaps a few standard Quaker books, along with a scattering of books on gardening, medicine, surveying, or law. Such books routinely circulated through the community by loan, gift, bequest, or sale, transactions often recorded on flyleaves. They were valuable tools for living, and they were rare. Inventories tended to list only valuable books, so that ownership of pamphlets – an important element in the reading diet and the form in which most imported secular and popular literature appeared – cannot be quantified. Probate inventories indicate that only a tiny number of wealthy or learned men owned more than a half-dozen books, and even fewer built up what we would call libraries.[53]

The earliest extensive library in the middle colonies was that of Francis Daniel Pastorius (1651–1719), the founder of Germantown, the author of a number of books printed locally or in Germany, and the town scrivener, lawgiver, and teacher. His own catalogue (made after 1710) lists over 350 books and pamphlets in some 250 volumes, including many types of books not usually listed in estate inventories (and in fact not listed in his). For example, of the 23 folios, only 6 are bound volumes of the sort usually itemized (a German Bible, an English concordance, a Latin cosmography, etc.). The rest are religious and controversial pamphlets, including several Bradford imprints. Religion and schoolbooks make up most of the list, but here and there are glimpses of a more eclectic literary culture: a German Koran, Voigt's *Prognostica*, a Dutch play, a French guide to London, esoteric works of Agrippa and Boehme, *The Ladies Rich Closet of Rarities* (noted as "lent to Eliz. Hood") and such diversions as *Histoire amoureuse des Gaules*, *The Baccheam Magazine*, and *Speculum amatorum mundi*. Pastorius also owned some fifty volumes of manuscripts, including his own works, mostly never published (schoolbooks, German translations of Penn's works, descriptions of Pennsylvania, pastoral poetry, theological miscellanies, medical receipts), and dozens of volumes of extracts from printed books. As the law-giver of Germantown, he assembled all the laws and ordinances of Germantown in a manuscript volume that still survives (Fig. 6.2), and he also owned a few basic British lawbooks, such as two copies of Coke's *Institutes* and the popular vademecums *Conductor Generalis* and Richard Chamberlain's *Complete Justice*.[54]

Pastorius wrote in his catalogue that he had brought most of his books with him from Germany; a few he bought in America, and he borrowed others from his neighbors. The volumes of extracts must have been a part of this borrowing, the only way he had to appropriate these books, which he could not be sure of ever seeing again. That he also borrowed other people's manuscripts is suggested by one item, "A Fascicle of Several Mens Mscripts."

Among his few surviving manuscripts are two beautifully calligraphed commonplace books, the large "Bee-Hive" and the smaller "Alvearialia." In the latter is a list of seventy-five books from which he gleaned material, most of them presumably borrowed, since only four of them also appear in the catalogue of books he owned. He borrowed much more popular literature than he owned: *The Secret Life of Elizabeth and Essex*, *Visions of Quevedo*, *The Turkish Spy* (an incomplete set), *Lazarillo de Tormes* (many leaves lacking), *Amours of Madam de Maintenon*, *Pleasant Historie of Jack Newberie,* and the mildly lubricious *New Academy of Compliments* (1717). He also extracted material from several English almanacs, magazines, and "Gazettes or News-Letters" that he may have thrown or given away. Perhaps less surprising are the several works of mysticism, witchcraft, and the occult (Boehme, his English follower Jane Lead, Paracelsus, Glanville, a life of Merlin) that he owned or borrowed. The influence of the German cabbalists was widespread in Pennsylvania, from Johannes Kelpius's mystical band, the Hermits of the Wissahickon, to the writings of George Keith.[55] The assortment of writers excerpted in Daniel Leeds's *Temple of Wisdom* (mentioned earlier) seems less odd when compared with Pastorius's reading;

in fact he owned or borrowed all the same writers. In short, these lists give us a glimpse of an eclectic literary culture that Pastorius shared with his neighbors.

The rich, powerful, and learned James Logan sold his library before leaving England to become Penn's secretary, then spent the rest of his life trying to re-create in the New World an epitome of the learned culture of the Europe he had left. His library grew to be the largest in the middle colonies by the time he died in 1751, but most of his 2,200-odd books were acquired after 1720. There was no popular or mystical literature in his library. He devoted his considerable bibliographic knowledge to acquiring the best edition of every ancient writer in Greek, Hebrew, Arabic, or Latin, and of every modern philologist or scientist whose work was soundly based on the work of the ancients. He got all his books directly from London booksellers, and since no one in the colony knew more than he did about the London trade, he often helped others acquire books abroad.[56] Though Logan and Pastorius frequently loaned their books, the first formally organized public library was the 291 volumes of Anglican theology sent by the English clergyman and philanthropist Thomas Bray from 1699 to 1703 to form a parish library at Christ Church.

In sum, the reading diet of Philadelphians in the early colonial period was not confined to the output of the local press, or even to the stock of imported books in their book stores, but for most citizens it was pretty monotonous just the same, limited to the bare essentials. The situation in the other middle colonies before 1720 was probably the same. As we have seen, in the absence of book stores there were other ways the colonists obtained books, and still others remain to be discovered or can be imagined. But the scale of this trade should not be overestimated. From 1701 to 1720 British customs agents recorded book exports to Pennsylvania valued at only £800 (records are missing for two of those years), and to New York of £852. By contrast the figure for New England was £5,788, for Virginia and Maryland £2,901.[57]

The texture of print culture in both Philadelphia and New York was changed by the introduction of newspapers: Andrew Bradford's *American Weekly Mercury* in 1719 and William Bradford's *New York Gazette* in 1725. In 1719 there was just one other newspaper in the colonies, *The Boston News-Letter*, established in 1704. These newspapers circulated European news (and to a much lesser extent, colonial news) publicly for the first time, and they were a vehicle for commercial advertising. Their circulation was small, but since taverns and coffeehouses subscribed to them, and since they were often read aloud, their impact on daily life must have been considerable.

Still, their impact, at least at first, can easily be overstated. The Boston paper was devoted almost entirely to reprinting dispatches from the London press, but there was not enough room in each weekly half-sheet to print

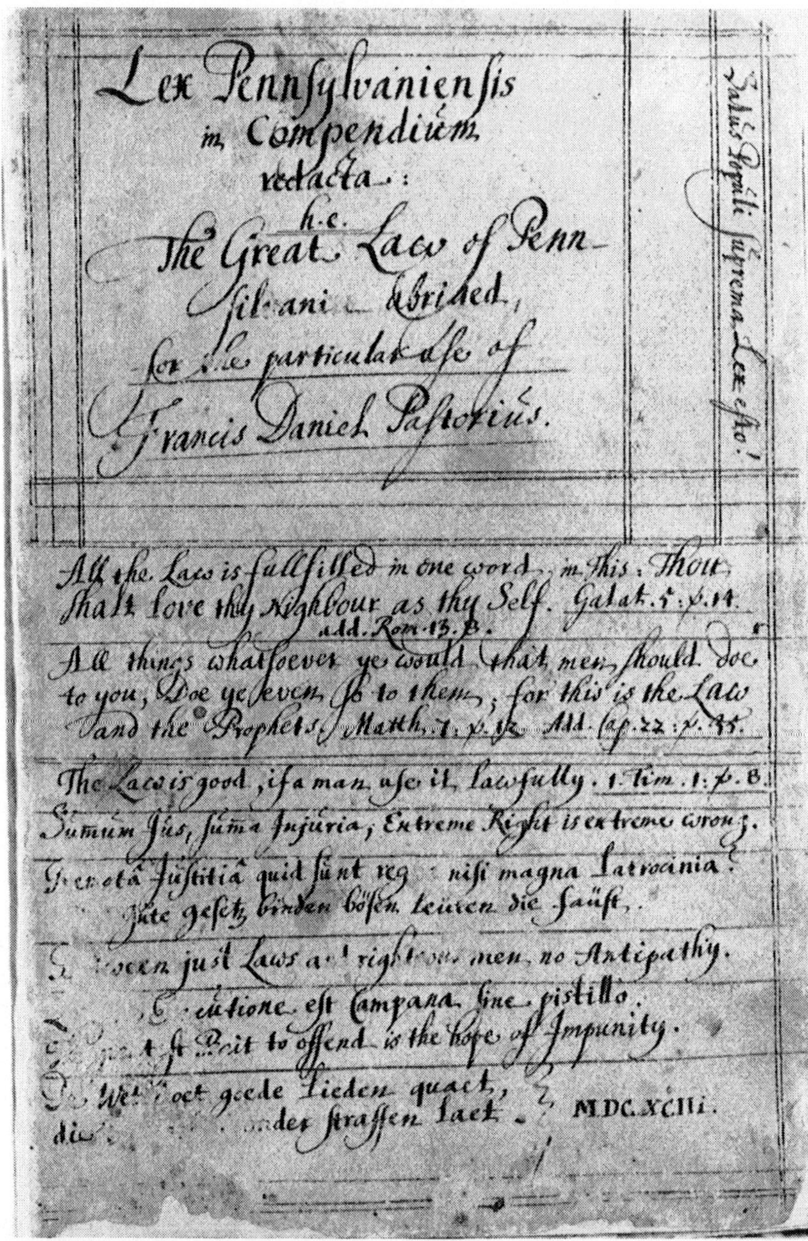

Lex Pennsylvaniensis
in Compendium
redacta:
h.e.
The Great Law of Penn-
silvani[illegible] abridged,
for [illegible] particular use of
Francis Daniel Pastorius.

Salus Populi suprema Lex esto!

All the Law is fullfilled in one word, in this: Thou
shalt love thy Neighbour as thy Self. Galat. 5. v. 14.
add. Rom. 13. 8.

All things whatsoever ye would that men should doe
to you, Doe ye even so to them; for this is the Law
and the Prophets. Matth. 7. v. 12. Add. Cap. 22. v. 35.

The Law is good, if a man use it lawfully. 1. Tim. 1. v. 8.
Summum Jus, summa Injuria; Extreme Right is extreme wrong.
[illegible] Justitia quid sunt reg[illegible] nisi magna Latrocinia?
[illegible] gute gesetz binden bösen leuten die fäust.
[illegible]ween just Laws a[illegible] righ[illegible] men no Antipathy.
[illegible] [illegible]cutione est Campana sine pistillo.
[illegible] bait to offend is the hope of Impunity.
[illegible] We[illegible] [illegible]oet goede lieden quaet,
die [illegible] [illegible]der straffen laet. MDCXCIII.

Figure 6.2. "Lex Pennsylvaniensis in compendium redacta" (1693), a manuscript abridgment of the laws of Pennsylvania compiled by Francis Daniel Pastorius for the perfomance of his duties as justice of peace in Germantown. Courtesy of The Historical Society of Pennsylvania.

them all, so the editor kept carrying them over until by 1719 he was thirteen months behind. By then it had but 300 subscribers.[58] The *Mercury* kept more up-to-date, but it was as Franklin wrote, "a paltry thing, wretchedly manag'd, no way entertaining."[59] The New York paper, after three years of publication, still did not have enough subscribers to pay for the cost to Bradford of print and paper – assuming that they kept up their payments, which many did not. "We shall loose Thirty-Five Pounds in the two years and a half," wrote William, "besides the trouble and Charge of Correspondents, collecting the News, making up Pacquets and conveying the same to those in the Country who take them."[60]

Both the Bradford papers avoided local affairs, especially political affairs, in their early years. They were as careful not to offend their employers in their newspapers as they were in the books and pamphlets they published. They pretended to be open to all parties, but in fact they preserved their commercial independence by being closed to all. They were impartial by ignoring controversy, not by airing both sides. With such a slender support, they could not afford to antagonize any faction, certainly not the government. Once Andrew Bradford ventured an opinion in his own voice; in January 1722 he mildly hoped that the General Assembly would do something to revive the local economy, the poor state of which the governor himself had recently noted. He was called before the Provincial Council, where he apologized profusely and swore that the sentence was put in by his journeyman without his knowledge; he was released, no doubt more mindful than ever of how minutely his words were scrutinized.[61] Both Bradfords had everything to lose by expressing opinions, airing controversy, even being entertaining – and they had nothing to gain as long as they were the only printers in the middle colonies.

This state of affairs was brought to an end not by the introduction of newspapers in Philadelphia and New York, but by the introduction of a second, competing printer (1723 in Philadelphia and 1726 in New York), each of whom in due course brought out a second newspaper. This effected a change in the print culture in the middle colonies profound enough to warrant one of those overly simple but still useful divisions of history into periods. The arrival of a second printer in Philadelphia marks the beginning of the age of Franklin.

CHAPTER SEVEN

The Southern Book Trade in the Eighteenth Century

CALHOUN WINTON

AT THE BEGINNING of the eighteenth century only Maryland among the southern colonies had a printer in residence.[1] Thomas Reading, an inexperienced journeyman just out of London, though able to print *All the Laws of Maryland Now in Force* in 1700 and to print a second collection in 1707 with the same title, was quite incapable, as it turned out, of distributing his products: He printed no newspaper; he sold no books. Reading's very first publishing project, a sermon by the visiting founder of the Society for the Propagation of the Gospel, Thomas Bray, was advertised on the title page as "Sold by Evan Jones." Evan Jones was a minor factotum and general merchant in Annapolis, offering books as part of his stock.[2]

Reading's example to the contrary notwithstanding, the association of printing, newspaper publishing, and bookselling would come to dominate the southern book trade in the eighteenth century. By the Revolution every mainland colony south of Pennsylvania had at least one printer and one or more newspapers (except Delaware, which after 1761 had a printer but was temporarily without a newspaper, and the Floridas, which had neither but acquired both, briefly, in 1783 during the Revolution).[3] The more populous island colonies such as Jamaica and Barbados followed suit during the same seventy-five years. By the 1770s Robert Wells in Charleston, who also operated a printing establishment, could advertise "many THOUSAND Volumes" for sale at his "Great Stationary and Book-Store, on the Bay."[4]

The careers of Robert Wells in Charleston and William Parks in Annapolis and Williamsburg together illustrate the nexus between successful bookselling, production, and imports in the southern colonies before the Revolution. The activities of the Glasgow and Maryland trading firm of Lawson and Semple, illustrate the operations of general merchants, who sold books on the side. At the zenith of their careers – Parks in the first half and Wells in the second half of the century – these men were the most important figures in the book and printing trades in the entire region, focused on the Chesapeake and Charleston, respectively. Each brought important advantages to their careers: Parks wide professional experience and Wells ethnic and guaranteed financial support. Because Parks came to an environment relatively unformed for printing, or indeed even for book buying, his problems were more fundamental than those of Wells, and more formidable. His career, then, may properly be considered first.

Already a master printer, Parks arrived in the Chesapeake in 1726, well able to establish the book and printing trades in an area where earlier attempts had seen little success. The Nutheads had barely scraped out a living, largely by printing official forms and other jobbing work. Reading, their successor, had been on salary (paid in tobacco) as public printer and had limited his brief career principally to that line of the business. Only a single example of the work of Reading's successor, John Peter Zenger, has survived, an edition of the session laws produced in 1720 before he departed for New York.[5] The title page of this unique copy also bears the inscription "Sold by *Evan Jones.*" Little had changed in twenty years. None of Parks's predecessors, apparently, had thought to establish a newspaper, begin a systematic trade in books, or analyze the political situation for personal advantage. Because Parks did all three, he became a leading figure in every aspect of the region's book and printing trades.

Parks was a native of Shropshire, and he did not come to printing through the London trade. His apprenticeship was with Stephen Bryan in Worcester. Bryan and Thomas Reading, Parks's predecessor in Annapolis, had been fellow apprentices in the large London shop of Bennet Griffin.[6] Unlike Reading, Bryan was a skillful and aggressive printer, establishing in 1710 the first newspaper in Worcester, the *Worcester Post-Man,* which still exists today. Bryan must have been a demanding master. When Parks left Bryan's shop he was able to establish a printing business of his own in Ludlow, Shropshire, where he began a newspaper, the *Ludlow Post-Man,* in 1719 and published at least one book of sermons. In Hereford he published another religious book, *Pascha,* containing long quotations in Greek and Latin. Somewhere Parks had received a respectable education. He also published in Hereford a translation into Welsh of one of John Bunyan's works.[7]

Clearly a man on the rise in provincial publishing, Parks next moved closer to London, to Reading, where in 1723 he established the *Reading Mercury,* which also continues to appear. The *Mercury* was in design, layout, and content the equal of any London newspaper then being published. Unfortunately, Parks ran afoul of the town aldermen, who effectively controlled what went on in Reading. They charged him with publishing statistics of the plague in London, thus inducing panic among the Reading citizenry who believed that the figures referred to their town.[8] Or so the aldermen alleged. Soon after the incident Parks apparently sold out his interest in the business to his partner David Kinnier: his name disappears from the masthead with *Mercury* No. 29 of January 20 1723/24. It appears that Parks may have coedited still another periodical, the *Half-penny London Journal* in London, in 1724.[9] Nothing more is known of Parks's whereabouts before he appeared in Annapolis in 1726, but for the remainder of his career Parks displayed a political acumen that may have derived from his practical, if disastrous, education in Reading.

Parks was invited to Maryland by Thomas Bordley, an attorney and member of the lower house, where he sided with the antiproprietary faction. At the authorization of the General Assembly, Bordley had been supervising the annual publication of the session laws, the *Votes and Proceedings of the Lower House of the Assembly,* printed by Andrew Bradford in Philadelphia. The invitation to Parks grew out of Bordley's efforts, which date from 1722, to secure a local printer to do this work.[10] In his role as public printer Parks would publish the votes and other proceedings of the assembly and distribute copies to various officials; like Reading, he would be compensated in tobacco.[11] His first project was a collection of the laws to replace the two earlier collections produced by Thomas Reading. The compilation, *A Compleat Collection of the Laws of Maryland,* appeared in 1727, published by subscription and sold bound. A folio volume of more than three hundred pages, the *Compleat Collection* was an undertaking of heroic proportions for Parks's single-press shop. The paper was of varying quality – obtaining good paper was always a problem in southern colonial publishing – but the binding, perhaps the work of, among others, the Philadelphia binder William Davies,[12] was respectable, and Parks's use of type ornaments and his crisp typography identify the work of a master printer. Colonial Marylanders retained and annotated their copies.

Parks merchandised his *Compleat Collection* astutely. The annual session laws, *Laws of Maryland, Enacted . . . 1727*, a pamphlet, carries an advertisement for the bound volume. The next year's collection, *Laws of Maryland, Enacted . . . 1728*, is priced at 2*s*. "to those who bought the whole Body of Laws [i.e., the *Compleat Collection*], and Two Shillings Six Pence to others." The *Laws . . . 1728* also contains (p. 30) a page of memoranda "for the Ease of those who have the Bound Books of all the Laws; that they may mark out with their Pens, those LAWS that are Repeal'd. . . ." Another advertisement follows: "ALL Sorts of useful Blanks . . . are Printed and Sold at Reasonable Rates, by *William Parks,* Printer in *Annapolis*: Where Old Books are New-Bound very cheap." Binding and jobbing work, such as the production of blank forms for business and legal use, were for Parks and every other southern colonial printer important sources of day-to-day income, sometimes almost the *only* sources of income.

Parks was by no means content to remain a binder, a public printer, and a jobbing printer of blank forms, as Reading had. He well understood the benefits of having a newspaper, both with respect to direct profits and as an adjunct to his other printing activities. He had, after all, previously worked on three, perhaps four, newspapers in Britain. In 1727 he founded the *Maryland Gazette,* the first newspaper of the mainland colonies south of Philadelphia. (The Kingston *Weekly Jamaica Courant* had preceded it in the previous decade.) In an early issue that has survived, No. 66 of December 17, 1728, we see Parks busily at work supporting through the *Gazette* his various enterprises in bookselling – among them, the *Compleat Collection*: "*Note*: There are a small Number left of the Whole Body of Laws Bound, to be Sold for a Pistole each, as usual Several Persons have waited in Expectation of having them cheaper; but they may be assur'd, that if the Price should be alter'd they will be dearer, as they grow scarcer." Parks was correct: In the decades following, the *Compleat Collection* became almost impossible to find at any price. Its scarcity, together with the ever-felt need to provide an up-to-date compilation, eventually brought about Thomas Bacon's 1765 [1766] collection, the *Laws at Large.*

Parks also ventured early into the somewhat risky but potentially profitable area of political pamphleteering, publishing in 1728 Daniel Dulany the Elder's *The Right of the Inhabitants of Maryland, to the Benefit of the English Laws.* Parks advertised the pamphlet in the *Gazette* as for sale at his "Printing-office." From the beginning, he was operating as a retail bookseller and stationer. He was prepared as well to cater as a wholesaler to the general merchant who desired to do business in bookselling. In the same *Gazette* of December 17, 1728 he advertised John Warner's *Almanack for the Year 1729.* Almanacs, as will be seen later, were a staple of the southern printer's business, with a ready market and good profit margins. No copy of Parks's first venture into the field has survived, but the *Gazette* advertisement presents the interesting continuation: "Price 6 Pence a Piece, or 4 Shillings per Dozen to those who buy them to sell again." Thus Parks offered differential pricing, 6*d.* a copy retail, 4*d.* wholesale, following the practice of the English trade, and of William Bradford in Philadelphia.[13]

Political pamphlets and the occasional literary work by such local writers as Ebenezer Cooke were financially incidental. During his first five years on this side of the Atlantic, though no accounts exist to prove it, Parks survived on public printing, binding, the almanacs, and the *Gazette,* plus the books and stationery he imported from London for resale. During a voyage to London in 1730, he evidently undertook a major transaction because he advertised in *Gazette* No. 162 (October 20, 1730) as "*Lately imported by* William Parks, *from* London" a varied assortment that provides an insight into what would sell in colonial Maryland – or what Parks believed would sell. Religious books and schoolbooks headed the list: "Bibles and Common-Prayer Books, of several Sizes, some with the Old and others with the New Version of Psalms; *Tate* and *Brady's* Psalms bound up alone, Testaments, Psalters, Spelling-Books, Primers, Horn-Books; Books of Devotion, as *Drelincourt* on Death, *Taylor's* Holy Living and Dying, [Whole] Duty of Man, Divine Entertainments, *Nelson's* Fasts and Feasts, Weeks Preparation for the Sacrament, &c." The religious selections are on the whole decidedly Protestant and Anglican; if Parks provided for his Roman Catholic readers (and he probably did), he chose not to advertise the fact. Much of the stock of 1730 consisted of schoolbooks and stationers' supplies. The advertisement specified "Grammars and Construing Books; Large and small Copy-Books, with Copies ready wrote in several curious Hands, for Youths to learn to write by; Blank Copy Books; School-Boys Peices, Pen-knives, Quills, Pens, Ink-Horns, Ink-Powder," though it also included several forms of music, prints, pictures, and "History-Books." By 1730, four or five years after his arrival in Maryland, Parks had made a good start, establishing himself as an effective public printer, a publisher of independent judgment, editor of an ongoing newspaper, and proprietor of what was in effect a bookstore and stationery shop, though conducted from the printing-office. He was ready to expand, and that is what he did.

To Virginia. Although under earlier regimes the colony had been inhospitable to printing, in the 1720s it acquired an effective royal administrator, General William Gooch, who recognized the value of having a printer resident in the colony. As early as December 1726 Parks had submitted a proposal to the Virginia General Assembly offering to print a collection of Virginia session laws similar to his *Compleat Collection* published in Maryland the following year.[14] In 1730, having presumably purchased a printing press on his voyage to England, Parks opened his printing office in Williamsburg and that year published the first poem printed in Virginia, most appropriately John Markland's *Typographia. An Ode, on Printing.Inscrib'd to the Honourable William Gooch, Esq; His Majesty's Lieutenant-Governor, and Commander in Chief of the Colony of Virginia*. Markland, a veteran of the Grub Street pamphlet wars in London and now a lawyer in Virginia, portrays the printer as the apostle of Enlightenment values:

> Happy the *Art,* by which we learn
> The Gloss of Errors to detect,
> The Vice of Habits to correct,
> And sacred Truths from Falshood to discern!

Gooch, who knew the power of the printing press without the benefit of Markland's prompting, published in 1732 an anonymous pamphlet of his own composition, which presented in dialogue form the vexed question of tobacco pricing. *A Dialogue between Thomas Sweet-Scented, William Oronoco, Planters, Both Men of Good Understanding, and Justice Love-Country, who Can Speak for Himself* became something of a Williamsburg best-seller, running to at least three editions in the year.[15]

With three important exceptions, Parks in Virginia was doing essentially what he had done in Maryland but on a larger scale: printing legislative records, editing and publishing a newspaper (he began the *Virginia Gazette* in 1736), publishing an occasional political pamphlet or item of belles lettres, issuing the collected laws of the colony (in a 1733 edition), publishing almanacs, and selling imported books and stationery at his printing office.[16] His three innovations were the operation of a book bindery on a continuing basis, the opening of a bookstore – or perhaps two bookstores – separate from his printing shop, and the building of a paper mill. Although Parks supervised the binding of manuscript records in Maryland as early as 1727, published the *Compleat Collection* bound, and advertised binding in the *Gazette* as one of the services of the printing office, it is not certain what craftsman was at hand in Maryland or Virginia. A professional bookbinder has commented that the work "reflect[s] the better practises of contemporary European craftsmen."[17] From his British experience Parks at least recognized, and demanded, quality work.

About 1742, with the *Virginia Gazette* well established and the Williamsburg region growing, Parks decided to establish a bookstore. The records of the governing body of the College of William and Mary, the President and Masters, reveal the following: "Mr Wm Parks intending to open a bookseller's shop in this Town and having proposed to furnish the students of this College with such books at a reasonable price as the Masters shall direct him to send for and likewise to take all the school books now in the College and pay 35 p.cent on the sterling cost to make it [local] currency, his proposals are unanimously agreed to."[18] At the cost of buying back the textbooks (which he no doubt planned to offer for resale in the store) Parks had in effect negotiated a textbook contract – the first in the colonies? – that would of course attract prospective buyers to his store in the form of students. Although the evidence is fragmentary, it appears that for a time at least Parks operated some kind of store in Hanover Courthouse, Virginia, perhaps to supply the needs of the Reverend Samuel Davies' Presbyterian flock. Davies, who left Virginia in 1759 to become president of Princeton, was a notably bookish pastor.[19] If Parks's enterprise was in fact a branch bookstore it would have been the first in the southern colonies.

Securing enough usable paper was a problem for printers in the Chesapeake, just as it was elsewhere in the colonies. Hugh Jones in his *Present*

State of Virginia (1724) had seen Virginia as a potential site for papermaking: "Paper-Mills I believe would answer well there; for there are good Runs of Water with Timber *for nothing* for building them."[20] Whether Parks had read Jones we do not know, but in 1742 he turned to Philadelphia, then the center of colonial papermaking, and to his professional colleague Benjamin Franklin for assistance. Perhaps Franklin suggested the enterprise. He advertised in his *Pennsylvania Gazette* of September 23, 1742 for a person capable of building a good paper mill. Conrad Schütz, the successful applicant, and a carpenter were sent off to Williamsburg and by 1744 Parks's mill was in operation and supplying Franklin paper as well as making paper for Parks's own use. Franklin, who had furnished the moulds, also shipped him thousands of pounds of rags, an essential ingredient.[21]

Who supplied Parks the books he sold that he did not publish himself? Franklin certainly supplied him some. The two printers seem to have enjoyed a close professional relationship. Parks, for example, purchased a hundred two-volume sets – a surprising quantity – of Franklin's first American edition of *Pamela,* and he received the *Pocket Almanack for the Year 1744* for 3*d.* a copy wholesale, versus the 4*d.* a copy Franklin charged Jonas Green in Annapolis for the same almanac. Of Parks's British suppliers, little is known. One who attempted to act in this capacity was Thomas Osborne of London, the well-known bookseller and employer of Samuel Johnson (knocked to the ground by Johnson one day, as readers of Boswell remember, with a folio volume). Franklin wrote his friend Strahan of this enterprise: "Mr. Thos Osborne, Bookseller of London, is endeavouring to open a Correspondence in the Plantations for the Sale of his Books: He has accordingly sent several Parcels, 1 to Mr. Parker of N York, 1 to Mr. Read here, and one to Mr. Parks in Virginia. I have seen the Invoices to Parker and Read; and observe the Books to be very high-charg'd, so that I believe they will not sell."[22] We do not know Parks's reaction to this offer, although normally unsolicited offers permitted the return of unsold books.

Parks brought formidable qualities of experience, energy, and ingenuity to the tasks of bookselling and printing, but like all the other southerners who followed those trades in the first half of the eighteenth century he found it difficult to make ends meet. When he died on a business trip to England at midcentury, his total estate barely covered his indebtedness.[23] Parks's financial practices and experience must be derived by inference from fragmentary evidence preserved here and there in newspapers, probate records, contemporary letters and diaries, and the like. The business transactions for a two-year period (1750–1752) of his immediate successor, William Hunter, and those for a similar time-span of Joseph Royle, who took over the Williamsburg enterprise when Hunter died in 1761, reveal that, even with the trade of the College of William and Mary, Parks and his successors in the Chesapeake lacked an urban base of sufficient size to support a large bookselling operation.

But Parks and his successors in Maryland and Virginia were also facing competition from stores operated by the tobacco merchants. The example of these to be used in this chapter, the Glasgow partnership of James Lawson and John Semple, is selected, though the firm was not especially large, operating as it did one and perhaps two stores in Maryland: one certainly at Port Tobacco and perhaps another at Rock Creek. (For comparison, the Cunningham partnership managed seven stores in Maryland and fourteen in Virginia.)[24] Lawson and Semple are used here because, through a legal/historical quirk, their surviving records are unusually voluminous.[25] There is no reason to believe, however, that they are in any way unrepresentative of the Scottish trade, known in Glasgow as the "tobacco lords."[26]

Fundamental to the firm's relationship with the Marylanders and Virginians who dealt with them was the direct purchase of tobacco, and, as the years passed, grain, in the colonies from those who grew the crops.[27] Thus was established a credit line on which colonial planters could draw in a variety of ways. As a contemporary observer explained to British readers, the local representatives or factors have "large quantities of all kinds of *European* and *Indian* goods, which they expose to sale in shops or houses; which in the country go under the name of *stores*."[28] The rhythm of the Lawson–Semple trade was this: Approximately twice a year a ship, owned or leased by the partners, departed Port Tobacco laden with tobacco or other commodities such as sugar and rum being transshipped. Approximately twice a year a similar ship cleared Port Glasgow for Maryland, laden with virtually anything, but always including books. At times the Lawson and Semple firm served as transportation agents for persons and materials crossing the Atlantic. When Dr. Thomas Hamilton of Maryland decided to bring out a horse from Scotland, which he insured for the enormous sum of £150 sterling, the Lawson and Semple partnership arranged the entire transaction. When the horse arrived safely they debited Hamilton's account for the bill: £51 12*s.* sterling. In that same ship was a load of books to be sold at the store: some seventy-six volumes plus ledgers and pocket books. Lawson had paid John Gilmour, bookseller at the Saltmarket, Glasgow (on the Clyde), £11 7*s.* 8*d.* for the lot.[29] Although books were never regarded as the most important part of a ship's lading, always subject to being offloaded and held for a later shipment, Lawson sent books out to Semple in every shipment of which I have seen the records.

In the same year, an uninsured shipment of books from Gilmour worth £14 6*s.* 10*d.* was lost when the ship struck an iceberg off Newfoundland and sank.[30] Yet we must look past such accidents and recognize that books were coming in from London and Scotland in some quantity. Between 1743 and 1760 the two Scottish outports of Greenock and Port Glasgow cleared 416 cwt. of books for Virginia – an average of perhaps 2,800 volumes a year.[31] Most of these almost certainly were marketed through the tobacco merchants' stores. The retail operations of the two printers, one in Williamsburg and one in Annapolis, could have accounted for only a small fraction of these totals, even if we include Parks's retail bookstore and that of William Rind in Annapolis. In 1760 the Williamsburg and Annapolis stores were still the only bookstores, as such, in the Chesapeake region. But the picture looks very different when it is recognized that the tobacco merchants' stores were also stocking books.

The workings of the bookstore in Williamsburg for the years 1750 to 1752 and again from 1764 to 1766 can be recovered through the daybooks kept by two successive owners, William Hunter and Joseph Royle.[32] Hunter and Royle were also postmasters, in the familiar colonial tradition of printers following Franklin's example, and the postal account along with stationery, bindery, and *Gazette* sales contributed substantially more in total revenues than did books. But books, in both periods, were the single largest account. Both men dealt with London booksellers, Hunter with Samuel Birt and Thomas Waller (who had supplied books to Parks) and Royle with William Johnston, and with Robert Sayer for maps and prints. Excluding almanacs, Hunter sold 2,028 copies of 355 different titles in the earlier period and Royle 1,827 copies of 395 titles between 1764 and 1766. Royle's gross revenues for selling fewer books were, however, higher than Hunter's (£1,420 to £849 in round figures) because his books sold for higher prices.[33] As the daybooks demonstrate, Hunter and Royle were essentially continuing the lines of business to which Parks had introduced them, though on a gradually expanding scale as the prosperity of the capitol increased. Yet in their work as printers they were much less active than others in the trade in northern and middle colony towns. A sheet-count of production in the years during which Hunter died and Royle took over the press (Table 7.1) indicates that, aside from the *Virginia Gazette* and the annual almanac, they did little other than government printing.[34] Taken together, the evidence of sales through the bookstore and of local production at the printing office bring home the limited scope of the market in Virginia as contrasted, say, with the market in any of the New England colonies, which in these same years were absorbing far greater quantities of cheap print (for example, almanacs) as well as printed sermons, newspapers, and the like.

Let us turn from the Chesapeake to Charleston, where after midcentury Robert Wells, a native Scotsman, facing many of the problems Parks had encountered earlier in Maryland and Virginia, evolved a number of creative solutions for them. As in Maryland and Virginia, and subsequently in North Carolina and Georgia, the civil government took the initiative in creating the first printing office in South Carolina. Here, too, as in the Chesapeake, political rivalries – in this instance between the assembly and the governor – were behind this initiative; each side sought a printer, the result being that three craftsmen arrived almost simultaneously in Charleston in 1731, one of them from faraway Massachusetts, drawn south by the promise of a large subsidy. After they died, printing in Charleston passed into the hands of Lewis Timothy and his wife, who opened their business there in 1734 with Benjamin Franklin's support.[35] Long thought to be a Huguenot, Timothy was almost certainly a Palatine German refugee.[36] The Timothys' business, continued after Lewis's death by his widow and his son Peter, centered on government printing and the *South-Carolina Gazette* but also included occasional book sales.[37]

Wells came to South Carolina from Scotland, with the assets and the responsibilities of an extended Scottish family. He had attended Dumfries Academy and then apprenticed as a bookbinder and bookseller.[38] Scotland was a major exporter of people in the eighteenth century; important among those groups seeking opportunity abroad were members of the book and printing trades.[39] David Hall, Franklin's Philadelphia partner, was a Scot as was Robert Bell, the reprinter. When Wells and his family arrived in the colony in 1752, South Carolina possessed a Scottish governor, James Glen, and had a well-established, influential Scottish community that maintained close ties with the homeland. South Carolina was then the richest of all the mainland colonies; opportunities were about and Wells quickly took advantage of them. He commenced a general drygoods business soon after his arrival – obviously he possessed financial resources of his own – and in the mid-1750s opened his "great Stationary and Book Shop on the Bay," which would become by far the largest bookselling establishment in the southern colonies. In 1757 he added a bookbindery, characteristically (and incorrectly) advertising that his was the first bookbindery in the colony. The next year he engaged another Scots printer, David Bruce, and started a printing business, with an accompanying newspaper, the *South-Carolina Weekly Gazette,* often confused with its competitor, the *South-Carolina Gazette.*

Probably encouraged by the government, Wells in 1764 inaugurated a successor newspaper to his *Weekly Gazette,* the *South-Carolina and American General Gazette,* still in competition with Peter Timothy's paper and, as of 1765, with the printer Charles Crouch's new paper, the *South-Carolina Gazette and Country Journal.* In the case of his newspaper, as in his acceptance of public appointments, Wells quite consciously aligned himself with

TABLE 7.1 **Williamsburg printing, 1760–1761**

Evans Number/Collation	Printer(s)	Sheets Per Copy
	Virginia Gazette (ed. = 1,000 copies?):[a] 104,000 sheets	
8759 (1760). fol.	W. Hunter (52 issues)	52.00
9034 (1761). fol.	W. Hunter (33 issues); J. Royle (19 issues)	52.00
	Government printing: 35,850 sheets	
o Tobacco notes, 1760–1761.	W. Hunter; J. Royle (60,000 copies?)[b]	0.125
o Receipts for import duty on slaves, 1760–1761.	W. Hunter; J. Royle (4,000 copies?)[c]	0.125
o *Procs.* (Mar. 4, Apr. 8, 10, May 19, 1760)[d]	W. Hunter (100 copies?)	0.50
o *Proc.* (Feb. 11, 1761)	W. Hunter (800 copies?)[e]	0.50
o *Speech* (1761)/Lt. Gov. Fauquier. fol.: 4 p.	J. Royle (200 copies?)	1.00
8277 *Speech* (1760)/Lt. Gov. Fauquier. fol.: [–]^2	W. Hunter (200 copies?)	1.00
8754+ Session acts (1760). fol.: A^2 B1; A^2 B1; A–B^2	W. Hunter (800 copies?)[f]	5.00
8757+ *Journal* for 1760 / H.B. fol.: pi1 A-C^2 D1; pi1 A–C^2	W. Hunter (300 copies?)[g]	7.50
9030+ Session acts (1761). fol.: C–M^2 N1; A–C^2 D1	W. Hunter (800 copies?)	14.00
9032 *Journal* for Oct. 1760–Mar. 1761 / H.B. fol.: pi1 A–^{2}A^2 ^{2}[B]1	W. Hunter (300 copies?)	25.00
9033 *Journal* for Nov. 1761 / H.B. fol.: pi1 A–F^2 G1	J. Royle (300 copies?)	7.00

a. *Press & Am. Rev.*, 113 (800 copies); but as David Rawson points out to me, the record for the 1751 edition indicates 1,000 copies.

the structure of royal influence and patronage. The short-term consequences for him were substantial; the long-term, dire. Cooperating with the royal government, particularly one headed by a Scot, must have seemed for him the self-evident course. He was named marshal of the vice-admiralty court in 1758 and vendue master, that is, public auctioneer, in 1759, both patronage appointments. On the nongovernmental side, he was elected Provincial Grand Secretary of the Freemasons in 1758. When the time came for the St. Andrew's Club – the Scottish social organization – to print a new edition of its by-laws, Wells naturally got the job and in 1762 produced an elegant docu-

TABLE 7.1 (*Continued*)

Evans Number/Collation	Printer(s)	Sheets Per Copy
	Virginia almanac (5,000 copies?):[h] 17,500 sheets	
8610 12 mo: [A]^2 B–C^6 D^4	W. Hunter (for 1761)	1.50
8868 8vo?: [A]–D^4	J. Royle (for 1762)	2.00
	Miscellaneous: 3,500 sheets	
0 Sermon / S. Davies. 8vo?: [32] p. (p. [31–2] blk.?)	W. Hunter (500 copies?)[i]	2.0
8551 8 vo: [A]–C^4	W. Hunter (500 copies?)	1.50
41028 8vo: A^4 (A1 + 1) B–G^4	W. Hunter (500 copies?)[j]	3.50
	Total sheets:	160,850

b. *Journals of the House of Burgesses of Virginia, 1758–1761*, ed. H. R. McIlwaine, (Richmond, Va., 1908), 144; for a facsimile of a specimen dated 1743, see Jack P. Greene, *Political Life in Eighteenth-Century Virginia* (Williamsburg: Colonial Williamsburg Foundation, 1986), 4.
c. *Virginia Slave Trade Statistics, 1698–1775*, ed. Walter Minchinton, C. King, & P. Waite (Richmond: Virginia State Lib., 1984), 159–63 (2,985 slaves imported, 1760–1761 inclusive). There were certainly other printed blank forms, but only tobacco notes and receipts for slave duty were specified for public printing (McIlwaine, ed., *Journals, 1752–1758* (1909), 30).
d. *Executive Journals of the Council of Colonial Virginia*, ed. B. J. Hillman, 6 (1966): 155, 157, 159.
e. Ibid., 179 (for the accession of George III). The larger number is predicated on the council's direction of copies to the 54 sheriffs and 500 or so JPs.
f. *Journals, 1758–1761*, 145 (thirteen copies of the Session acts to be sent to each of the fifty-odd county clerks; to which may be added a hundred-odd copies for the burgesses and thirteen for the Governor and Council).
g. Gregory A. and C. Z. Stiverson, "Books Both Useful and Entertaining" (Williamsburg, Va.: Colonial Williamsburg Foundation, 1977), 112, 407 (Joseph Royle sold 225 copies of the 1752 *Journal*, "most" of them to the burgesses and members of the council).
h. *Printing and Society*, 158 n., 166; Stiversons, "Books Both Useful and Entertaining," 407 (Royle sold 3,262 copies of the *Almanac for* 1765, all on credit).
i. Cf. ibid., 69 (Royle printed 500 copies of J. Camm's *Review of the Rector Detected* [1764]).
j. Dated [1759?] in NAIP and other bibliographies, but "December——, 1759" in the piece itself; as the errata states, Carter was far from the press at the time of printing, and the actual publication was probably in 1760.

H.A.

ment.[40] Wells was evidently a Scot on the move. His son William Charles recollected many years later that Wells had him wear "a tartan coat . . . and a blue Scotch bonnet" to impress on him his ethnic heritage.[41]

The principal commodity auctioned at the Charleston vendues was African slaves, but judging by the number of book auctions Wells undertook, he seems to have used the public sale of second-hand and imported books more effectively than any other southern bookseller of the period. No evidence presently suggests that Hunter in Williamsburg and William Rind in Annapolis auctioned books, though they may have done so. Charleston was a growing urban center, very self-consciously the hub of the colony, with a style neither Williamsburg nor Annapolis ever achieved. Had Wells's attempts at book auctions been failures he would not have repeated the effort. He advertised the coming sales in his newspaper, as on September 30, 1768, when the estates of "Francis Stuart, esq., deceased, and Others" were advertised for sale "by publick Outcry," with several score titles listed. Given the large inventory of the bookstore that Wells maintained, a quick return was certainly an attractive aspect of these events.

No doubt Wells drew on that inventory for his auctions (which may account for the "Others" in his advertisements). Overall, this inventory was impressive. Although his assertion (in an advertisement he printed in John Tobler's *Georgia Almanack* for 1771) that he possessed "the LARGEST STOCK and greatest VARIETY of BOOKS to be met with in all America" was undoubtedly self-serving, Wells *did* stock many books, perhaps several thousand titles at a given time. These were, until the end of his Charleston career, almost entirely imported, for Wells did little book printing. He imported from London, of course, but also ordered books from Paris and Amsterdam, or so he claimed.[42] Books imported from Philadelphia, and advertised as such, came to be an increasingly important part of his business. Wells's import trade with Scotland must have been substantial and continuing but thus far has not been documented. The mechanics of the French and Dutch trade are also not clear, but perhaps followed the example of the Lawson–Semple firm in Maryland, that is, associated with the transshipment of tobacco or other commodities to Paris and Holland. Because of his Scottish associations it seems likely that Wells had a similar arrangement with a supplier in Glasgow or Edinburgh.

Wells did not operate his business without competition; on the contrary, the conditions favorable to bookselling that had drawn him to Charleston were encouraging other entrepreneurs to compete with him. The year 1769 may be taken as representative. In January Nicholas Langford, bookseller, advertised in Peter Timothy's *Gazette* (and in Charles Crouch's *Gazette and Country Journal*) that he was departing for London to secure "a FRESH COLLECTION." Eleven months later, in the November 2 issue of the same paper, Langford reported that he had "*From* London, A Second Collection of Choice and Useful Books in polite Literature, esteemed History, &c. &c. All best Editions, and many very elegantly bound." A printed catalogue was available "at Messrs. Wilson, Coram, and Co. Mr. Tidyman's, Jeweller; and at Mr. Steven's Coffee-House and Post-Office; where all Orders he may be favoured with, will be taken care of." Langford, that is, had established a network of merchants to assist him in purveying his books. In Timothy's *Gazette* of December 21 Langford, "*Bookseller, on the Bay,*" offered subscriptions to the *London Magazine* and the *Critical Review,* and announced the sale by auction of "the major part of a Gentleman's Study."

Although 1769 was a good year, the early 1770s were even better for bookselling in Charleston and in the mainland South generally. In the three or four years before the Revolution Wells took part in elaborate reprinting and sale-by-subscription arrangements with a number of other booksellers up and down the coast. David Moltke-Hansen conjectures that Wells's participation in these practices coincided with the return of his son John from an apprenticeship with the bookseller Alexander Donaldson in Edinburgh. In 1774 Donaldson had won in *Donaldson* v. *Becket* a landmark judicial decision in which the attempts of the London booksellers to claim perpetual copyright were overturned. From Wells's point of view it may be that, as Moltke-Hansen has argued, he sent his son to Donaldson "to learn from the men responsible for some of [the] developments" in the reprint trade.[43] It was, at the least, another manifestation of his loyalty to Scotland and to the empire.

In 1774 and 1775 Wells advertised in his paper more than twenty titles of books then selling well in the English-speaking market, such as Goldsmith's *The Vicar of Wakefield.* This tracking of London publications represented an augmentation of his business; clearly, he felt that the market for such books was improving. As will be seen, William Aikman in Baltimore was experiencing the same phenomenon at the same time. Were both booksellers responding to or *creating* a new market? There is some reason to believe that they were engaged in creating a new market. For example, in 1771 Wells had proposed publishing by subscription an edition of Philip Doddridge's *Family Expositor,* explaining that the "high Price of the London Edition . . . has occasioned this Work to be less generally known than its acknowledged Merit and the great Importance of the Subjects it treats upon universally demand" (*South Carolina and American General Gazette,* December 23, 1771). Somewhere along the way the subscription process was put aside, but two years later Wells advertised (*South Carolina and American General Gazette,* December 24, 1773) as "Printed and sold by Robert Wells" an edition of the *Expositor* that seems to have been a Scottish edition, with certain additions, of the Edinburgh bookseller Alexander Donaldson and others, including E. Wilson of Dumfries, with a new title page supplied by Wells. Wells managed this undertaking successfully (remaining undetected until 1967); he may have been emboldened to repeat the process for attractive London titles in 1774 and 1775.[44]

If Wells could manage to purvey ("publish") books manufactured in Scotland or Ireland and shipped in sheets to be supplied with new title pages like the Doddridge, he might indeed be able to sell them below the agreed prices of the London market, even allowing for shipping charges, which the London booksellers would also of course have to pay on books sent for sale to America. A final determination cannot be made until more examples of these titles are found. Perhaps the most interesting aspect of the Doddridge publication is that Wells apparently believed an American imprint would promote the book better than a Scottish one.

Wells's plans for the future were defeated the following year by events at Concord and Lexington. Sensing that his identification with the royal establishment would be used against him, he departed in 1775 for London, never to return. His son John later took the printing press to British Florida.[45] Robert Wells had in his quarter-century of residence helped bring the selling of books to a level without precedent in the colonies south of Philadelphia; only twenty-eight years after Wells's departure a bookseller in Charleston – Isaiah Thomas's nephew Ebenezer – imported in a single shipment and disposed of more than 50,000 volumes, this being, Thomas asserted, "by far, the largest importation ever made into the United States."[46] Wells had demonstrated the ways in which this might be accomplished.

The last ten years before the Revolution saw the book trade begin to come of age in certain centers, not only Charleston but also Williamsburg, Baltimore, and Annapolis. The British colonies in the West Indies were also enjoying an increase in printing, publishing, and bookselling in the period.[47] Certain of these colonies had relationships with the mainland from the beginning: for example, Barbados with South Carolina and Pennsylvania. Franklin's competitor, the eccentric Samuel Keimer, emigrated from Philadelphia to Barbados and published his *Caribbeana* (1741) – a rare but important American book – through a London printers' consortium. American loyalists in the book trades, such as William Aikman of Annapolis and John Wells, son of Robert Wells of Charleston, found refuge in the West Indies during and after the Revolution.[48]

Meanwhile, the politics of the Stamp Act crisis had brought competition to Williamsburg for the first time. In 1765 Thomas Jefferson and his associates invited William Rind to set up shop in the town. Rind had served as an apprentice in Annapolis to Jonas Green, Parks's successor in Maryland, and in 1757 became Green's partner in publishing the *Maryland Gazette.* In the early 1760s he was also operating a bookstore, advertising his offerings in the *Gazette* of August 26, 1762, as "a large, entertaining, and instructive Assortment of Books." This same year he established a circulating library, apparently the first to be founded in the mainland colonies and, it seems, a premature venture, for Rind closed it down a year later and advertised that the stock would be sold at auction.[49]

Behind the invitation to Rind to come to Williamsburg lay the reality that, in a single printing center where the government provided much of the business, the political opposition had little chance of having its views aired in the press. Thus Joseph Royle refused to print the "Virginia Resolves" of

1765. As Jefferson later explained to Isaiah Thomas, "Until the beginning of our revolutionary disputes, we had but one press [i.e., Royle's], and that having the whole business of the government, and no competitor for public favor, nothing disagreeable to the governor could be got into it. We procured Rind to come from Maryland to publish a free paper."[50] By 1774 Williamsburg residents, who supported only Parks's *Gazette* in the 1730s, were reading and apparently supporting three newspapers. In these same years, Wilmington, Delaware, began to participate (as of 1761) in printing and the book trade with the arrival of James Adams. Further south, Savannah was emerging as a significant book center on the mainland, and colonists in and around the small North Carolina coastal towns of Wilmington and New Bern were buying books. The inland or up-country trade was starting in a small way in Virginia, North Carolina, and Georgia as merchants began to reach out to settlers in the Piedmont.[51]

The books procured from Glasgow and sold by the firm of Johnston and Bennehan, tobacco merchants in Piedmont North Carolina in 1770 – spelling books, schoolbooks, sermons and other religious material – bear a striking resemblance to the list Parks had published in the *Maryland Gazette* forty years earlier for a similarly unsophisticated clientele. With Whitefield's *Sermons* and Isaac Watts's *Hymns* they are, however, less specifically Anglican than the Maryland list. It is interesting to note that when Johnston and Bennehan attempted in 1773 to market a list more literary than religious – it included *Tom Jones* and *Tristram Shandy* – they had little success. It is also significant that after the Revolution, the firm recommenced using their Glasgow suppliers, John and John Alston.[52] The schoolbook trade of merchants such as Johnston and Bennehan became increasingly important as schools were founded throughout the southern colonies. Joseph Alexander, a member of the Princeton class of 1760 during Samuel Davies's presidency who married Davies' daughter Martha, perhaps also acquired at Princeton some of Davies's thirst for book learning. Ordained as a Presbyterian minister, Alexander established in 1767 a "classical school" in his parish at Sugar Creek, Mecklenburg County (present-day Charlotte), North Carolina, where he is said to have guided into the learned professions of law, medicine, and theology more than fifty young men.[53] These young men required books and presumably received them from local merchants.

In 1773 a young Scot named William Aikman began an effort with some success to pull Annapolis into the bookselling company of Charleston and Williamsburg by a combination of shrewdness, audacity, and financial resources. Aikman issued a catalogue that year of "above 12 hundred volumes" imported for his shop, "a large assortment of books, containing all the *English* classics, miscellanies, voyages, novels, plays, &c. to be sold at the *London* prices in cash only."[54] Aikman could, it seems, call on a formidable line of credit. Learning that a circulating library had been proposed in Baltimore, he inaugurated one of his own in July which included that town in its orbit by using a Baltimore merchant, Christopher Johnston, as his factor. Thus he solved the problem of access to the growing Baltimore market. The library, he informed his public, would be "upon a footing, if not superior, to any circulating library on the continent."[55]

Aikman's book advertisements emphasized the point that his customers, though paying London prices, were receiving the latest London stock: "recently published," "the last edition," and so on. When the title can be verified it appears that Aikman was telling the truth within reasonable limits of advertising license. Oliver Goldsmith's *History of Greece,* for example, was advertised in the *Maryland Gazette* on November 17, 1774 as having been just received: it was published in London that year. He also imported books published in Philadelphia, as Robert Wells in Charleston was doing at the same time. Current plays were advertised in the *Gazette* on June 23, 1774: Hugh Kelly's *The School for Wives* and George Colman's *The Man of Business,* both of which had enjoyed successful premieres in the preceding London theatre season of 1773–1774.

Aikman's own imprint appeared on at least four titles, two printed in Philadelphia and two in New York. An exceptional example of the intercolonial book trade's growing importance is the 1774 edition of John Hawkesworth's *A New Voyage, Round the World,* that is, the circumnavigations of 1768–1771. Though this elaborate subscription enterprise was largely the doing of James Rivington in New York, Aikman arranged for Rivington to issue an unknown quantity of the two-volume edition with title pages stating that the volumes were "Printed for William Aikman, Bookseller and Stationer, at Annapolis." Rivington did not name any Maryland subscribers (except for three names included under Philadelphia) in his lengthy and elaborate subscription list, which had subscribers from Quebec to Dominica. Presumably, Rivington's arrangement with Aikman was separate from those with booksellers in other colonies. Even though two volumes in length (which Aikman sold for 16*s.* currency), the text was a mere fraction of the English original, for Rivington excised three of the four travel narratives, retaining only Captain Cook's. The version printed for Aikman included a delightful, semipornographic frontispiece of Polynesian women, engraved by Paul Revere (Evans 42622). Here was an example of what American booksellers could do when they arranged the undertaking efficiently: undercut drastically the agreed prices of the London book trade, use the subscription lists they had built up, and cooperate on production, distribution, and merchandising. Robert Wells and William Aikman, Scots both, had arrived at this insight independently.

Wells and Aikman were also loyalists, and their part in the colonial book trade effectively came to an end with the gunfire at Concord and Lexington. Aikman departed for Jamaica in the fall of 1775, where, as a successful printer and bookseller, he fulfilled the promise of his brief but creative stay in Maryland. Like Wells, he had glimpsed the possibilities of an imperial bookselling network using transatlantic and Atlantic coastal resources. This was a network that, at least in the southern colonies, seemed about to come of age. The Revolution changed much of that: a national network was possible, but the imperial network that was to come, with London at its center and the dominions as consumers, would not include the mainland American colonies from Maine to Georgia.

In the 1770s the focus of the Chesapeake book and printing trade was shifting, as remarked earlier, to Baltimore. A decisive event was the arrival in the city in 1772 of William and Mary Katherine Goddard, brother and sister, with their printing press. Both Goddards were master printers and their new paper, the *Maryland Journal and Baltimore Advertiser,* would continue publication throughout the American Revolution. Mary Katherine became postmistress of Baltimore in 1775 under the new intercolonial postal system devised by her brother to replace the organization sponsored by imperial British authorities. During the Revolution, Mary Katherine had an important role not only as postmistress and editor but as printer.[56] Within thirty years of the Goddards' arrival, Baltimore became one of the leading publishing centers in the new United States.

In the years during and immediately after the Revolution, the book trade in Williamsburg was undergoing a different kind of transition. Despite the presence of competing newspapers, more booksellers were becoming middlemen or wholesalers for merchants inland, and the retail share of their business may have been declining as a percentage of the whole.[57] When Thomas Jefferson's first library burned in 1770, victim of the conflagration that destroyed his mother's house ("every pa[per I] had in the world, and almost every book"), his reaction was not to purchase books from Williamsburg but to send off an order to his booksellers in London or Scotland.[58]

About this time the Annapolis merchant firm of Wallace, Davidson, and Johnson was making book ordering easier for their clients with an arrangement unusual if not unique in the southern colonies. Joshua Johnson, one of the partners, was permanently established in London, where he would execute directly book orders for the firm's retail store in Annapolis and also orders for those assembling personal libraries or employed in the printing business. In the latter category he purchased Caslon type in 1772 and set up a separate account for Anne Catherine Green, who had succeeded her late husband as public printer in Annapolis. One London bookseller patronized by Johnson was the Fleet Street firm of John Whiston, son of the eccentric historian and mathematician William Whiston and, coincidentally, a principal foe of Alexander Donaldson in the *Donaldson* v. *Becket* proceedings.[59] Customers could be quite specific: Alexander Hanson, ordering in 1774, noted that "Second Hand Books will be for most acceptable provided they be Sound & not of the oldest & Obsolete Editions, but if such are not Conveniently to be [had] Mr. Johnson is desired to Purchase them new."[60]

Here at last was a mechanism by which readers, or at least the wealthier readers in the area of Annapolis, could have access to the books that they wanted and not merely those offered for sale by the local booksellers. The book trade for the most part was still the province of the affluent. At the lower end of the market the trade depended on the presence of newspapers, which provided advertising and other forms of merchandising support, such as notice of book auctions. Newspaper sales – and sales of advertising space – also routinely brought ready money into the printing house and book shop.[61]

Another printed medium at the lower end of the financial scale, which could take the form of a book and which was widely circulated in all economic classes, was the almanac. William Parks had been anticipated in almanac making in the Chesapeake by the Reverend Jonas Aurén, a Swedish missionary who issued an almanac in 1703, presumably in Elk River, Maryland, on the printing press he owned there. Aurén's almanac, *Noah's Dove,* no copy of which has ever been found, drew down the wrath of his fellow missionary, the Reverend Eric Björk, because Aurén was advocating sabbatarianism, that is, celebrating the Sabbath on Saturday. Aurén was also apparently a bookseller of sorts. The inventory made in 1713 at his death lists "25 Scoul bound books" and "14 Navigation books." Both entries indicate that Aurén may have conducted a school, for as Edwin Wolf has pointed out, navigation was routinely taught in the schools of this region.[62]

Sales of almanacs flourished in every southern colony for which evidence exists, sometimes in numbers that strain belief but are unquestionably accurate. For example, in 1743 Benjamin Franklin supplied Jonas Green 1,500 copies of *Poor Richard's Almanack* for 1744, with an Annapolis title page. Green must have sold them because in the following year Franklin supplied him another 1,500 copies. These were good sales figures at a time when the population of Annapolis was close to 900, and of the entire colony perhaps 120,000.[63] The costs involved in producing an almanac were easily calculated: composition and presswork, paper, overhead, and a lump-sum payment to the "philomath" who supplied the astronomical and hydrographical data. Precise figures for at least one such transaction exist, in the Williamsburg daybook of William Hunter. The entry for August 14, 1751, records expenditure of 26*s*. for composition, 42*s*. 8*d*. for presswork, £5 for paper, 11*s*. 4*d*. for "Wear & Tear," and £5 to the philomath for copy, a total of £14 costs for the entire undertaking. Cynthia and Gregory Stiverson, using the daybook, have computed total sales for this 1752 *Virginia Almanack* as £70 6*s.* 6½ *d.*, for a net of £56 6*s.* 6½ *d.*, a profit of a bit more than 400 percent.[64]

Almanacs were priced and intended for immediate sale, utilitarian publications in every sense of the word. Another variety of utilitarian document, the law and law-related book, was ordinarily published by subscription, with details of price, format, and content arranged in advance of publication. Unlike the almanac, however, these books have been preserved in greater numbers than any other genre of book produced in the colonial South. The legislature underwrote the expenses of government printing, so that the laws, session acts, proclamations, legal forms, and colonial currency (Fig. 7.1), a technically demanding job, were among the most lucrative commissions of the colonial printer. William Parks, it will be remembered, published by subscription his *A Compleat Collection of the Laws of Maryland* soon after he arrived in the colony. Six years later he printed and published, also by subscription, *A Collection of all the Acts of Assembly, Now in Force, in the Colony of Virginia.* The list of subscribers for this large folio volume includes four names from North Carolina, which did not yet have a printer.[65] In 1736 Lewis Timothy published by subscription the monumental two-volume work of Nicholas Trott, *The Laws of the Province of South-Carolina.* Within a nine-year period the three most populous colonies of the southern mainland had seen their collected laws printed and published, while the printers were also conducting weekly newspapers in which these laws were frequently discussed.[66]

The process of publishing law and law-related books by subscription may be illustrated by an example from North Carolina which is well documented, from the earliest proposal to the priced sale of a copy. Printing came late to that sparsely settled colony, but the printer who answered the North Carolina General Assembly's call in 1749 was a competent and imaginative workman. James Davis came to New Bern from Williamsburg, where he had in all probability (though no records have been found to prove it) learned his trade as an apprentice to Parks. He published the obligatory volume in 1751, *A Collection of All Public Acts . . . Now in Force and Use* and in that same year initiated the *North-Carolina Gazette.* Most ambitiously for a rural colony, he began in 1764 the *North-Carolina Magazine or Universal Intelligencer,* a weekly. The *Magazine* was an interesting miscellaneous publication, with local and foreign news, essays on religious topics and classical history reprinted from British sources, and specific, how-to-do-it articles on such practical matters as pickling meat and growing potatoes. Davis published in 1764, by subscription, *A Collection of all the Acts of Assembly,* and continued to publish and advertise in the *Magazine* the *Journal of the House of Assembly.* Ten years after he had initially advertised it as in preparation, he brought out *The Office and Authority of a Justice of Peace* (1774), with a title page on which Davis described himself as "one of his Majesty's Justices of

Figure 7.1. $50 South Carolina currency, engraved by Thomas Coram of Charleston (1757–1811), showing the obverse of one bill and the reverse of another, printed together on a single sheet, with a receipt dated August 3, 1779 (by Theodore Gaillard, Jr., one of the signers?) for 300 sheets (600 bills) of this denomination. Coram, who was born and probably trained in England, also worked as a portrait and landscape painter and drawing master. American Antiquarian Society.

the Peace for the County of *Craven*." A copy now in the North Carolina State Library, still in its original binding, was bought in 1784 for 16*s*.

The same year, the Annapolis printer Anne Catherine Green produced a volume that reflects both the continuing prosperity of the Chesapeake region and the increasing sophistication of the printing and publishing trades on the eve of the Revolution. Elie Vallette's *The Deputy Commissary's Guide* (Fig. 7.2) is essentially a guidebook on wills and inheritance, "an exceedingly

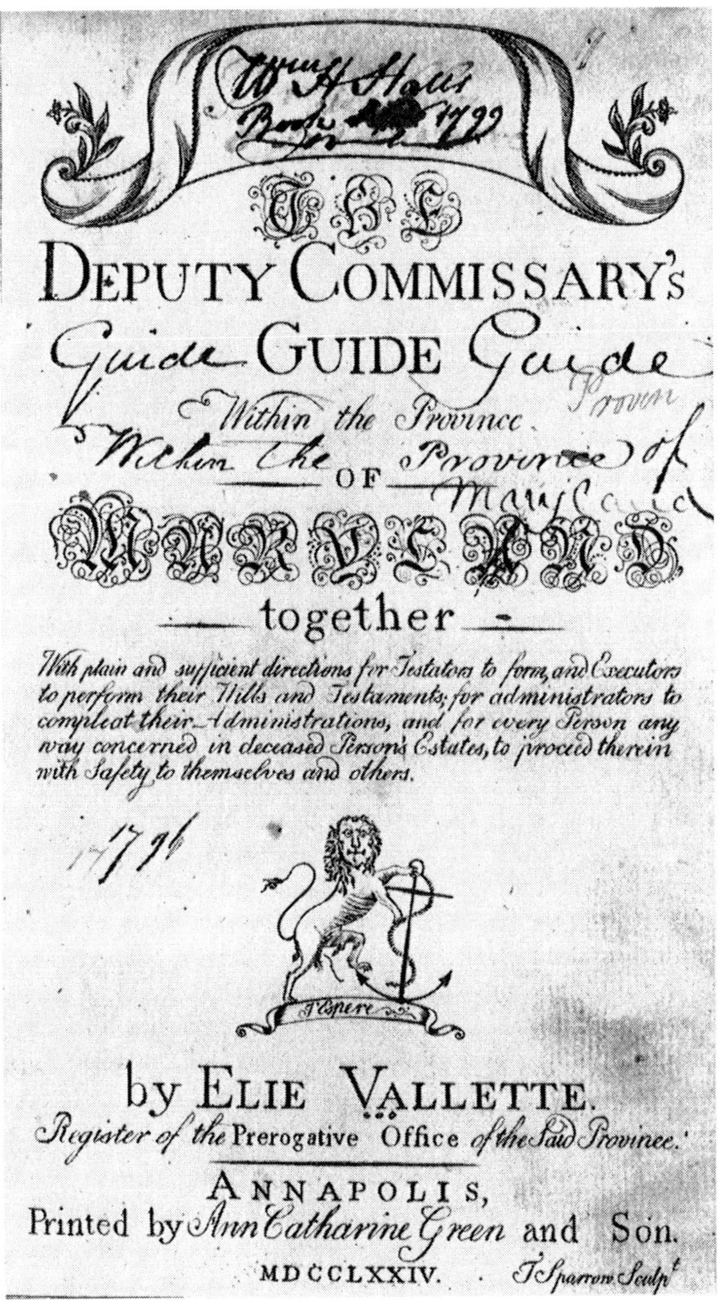

THE
DEPUTY COMMISSARY'S
GUIDE
Within the Province
OF
MARYLAND
together
With plain and sufficient directions for Testators to form, and Executors to perform their Wills and Testaments; for administrators to compleat their Administrations, and for every Person any way concerned in deceased Person's Estates, to proceed therein with Safety to themselves and others.

J'Espere

by ELIE VALLETTE.
Register of the Prerogative Office of the said Province.

ANNAPOLIS,
Printed by Ann Catharine Green and Son.
MDCCLXXIV. T. Sparrow Sculp^t

Figure 7.2. Elie Vallette, *The Deputy Commissary's Guide* (Annapolis, Md.: Ann Catharine Green & Son, 1774). Courtesy of the University of Maryland Library.

useful compilation," as Lawrence Wroth has described it,[67] directed obviously to those Marylanders who had something to bequeath. It is also a handsome volume, with a title page engraved by Thomas Sparrow, engraver and goldsmith of Annapolis, which features a stylized British lion. The Caslon type employed may have been some of that purchased by Anne Catherine Green from Joshua Johnson, noted earlier. In the *Maryland Gazette* of February 25, 1773 and other issues Green advertised a special feature for subscribers: "Every Subscriber shall have his Name and Title printed in the Title Page, in a Label adapted for that Purpose . . . provided their Signature come timely to Hand."

Anne Catherine Green's neat edition of Vallette's *Guide* also possessed at least one unusual attribute: Customers knew precisely what they would pay for a copy. This was true of subscription publication generally, of course, but subscription sales represented only a tiny fraction – though a potentially profitable fraction – of all the thousands of books sold in the southern colonies in this period. Even books published by subscription such as the *Guide* entered the retail market after subscribers had paid for their copies, but at a different price from the subscription, as the North Carolina copy of Davis's *Justice of Peace* demonstrates.

When conciliation failed in early 1776 and thirteen of the colonies declared their independence, a southern printer was importantly involved in the event. The *Declaration* was first published at various places by various printers. But the Continental Congress desired a true copy, to be signed for the record, as it were, by the "signers." Benjamin Franklin suggested the name of Mary Katherine Goddard to John Hancock. The postmistress of Baltimore supervised the publication (Evans 15650) – and in all probability composed type for the broadside with her own hands.

If much remains unclear about the mechanisms of printing and bookselling in the eighteenth-century South, it is certain that the trades had made very great progress in the seventy-seven years before Thomas Jefferson's *Declaration of Independence* was issued from Goddard's Post Office, in Market Street, Baltimore.

CHAPTER EIGHT

The Middle Colonies, 1720–1790

In the middle colonies, two different "scriptures" (see Chapter 1), drawn from the Enlightenment "civic humanism" of the English-speakers and the Pietism of the Germans and Dutch, to some degree overlapped and influenced one another. Booksellers of either ethnicity might stock some of the other's books, and both traded strongly in the South, though only the Germans enjoyed "dedicated" markets in the satellite settlements of the Shenandoah Valley and Georgia. German booksellers perforce obtained most of their stock through London, and an important share of their titles, as Heinrich Miller's 1769 catalogue suggests (see Fig. 8.6), were translated from English. Conversely, Franklin experimented with printing German (in roman type), before financing a separate office run by Anton Armbruster, and the late colonial vogue for Goethe, Kotzebue, Gessner, and other belletristic authors in German was, in part, a reflection of their popularity in English. Despite such cross-overs, however, some steady-selling German authors, like the Pietists A. H. Francke and P. J. Spener, were virtually unknown to English-speakers, and some subjects of central concern to the English, like politics, barely interested the German colonists – cultural differences that dominated their bookstocks as well, despite a common commercial and colonial position as Scotch, Irish, English, Welsh, Dutch, and German subjects of Great Britain. Their commercial, colonial, and regional connections are the only basis for yoking these two distinct scriptures in a single chapter: an "unmarked" or imperially "normal" English scripture; and an "ethnic," "other," or "minority" scripture in German and Dutch.

PART ONE. ENGLISH BOOKS AND PRINTING IN THE AGE OF FRANKLIN

JAMES N. GREEN

A NEW PHASE IN THE BOOK TRADE of the middle colonies began in the 1720s with the arrival of second printers in Philadelphia and New York. Previously, when William and Andrew Bradford had a virtual monopoly on printing in the region, the press was strictly controlled by civil and religious authorities and kept separate from the realms of commerce and politics. The Bradfords were invited into their respective colonies by these very authorities who, in doing so, were determined not to allow the press to threaten political and religious order. But by the 1720s, printing was coming to be understood as an essential element in a liberal commercial society. When Franklin and his sometime master Samuel Keimer arrived almost simultaneously in Philadelphia and when John Peter Zenger set up a competing press in New York shortly thereafter, they were at first almost unnoticed. They were not controlled by church or state but neither were they officially supported. They were left to make their living as they saw fit, to carve out places for themselves in the local ecology of print. This meant that they had to compete for business with the Bradfords, seeking out the patronage of individual consumers of print and attempting to operate their presses on a strictly commercial basis. They also attempted to compete for the patronage of church or state; but since those in power were already connected with the Bradfords, the new printers were attracted to those who were out of power. Thus the press was plunged into the realms of commerce and partisan politics to a far greater extent than it had been before. These second printers completely changed the print culture of the region.

Competition in Philadelphia: Keimer and Franklin in the 1720s

Benjamin Franklin got his first lessons in competition when he was apprenticed to his older brother James in Boston. Though the Boston trade had included two or more printers since the 1670s, until 1719 there had been but one newspaper, the *Boston News-Letter*, begun in 1704. It was published by the local postmaster, not by its printer, and it was devoted entirely to reprinting dispatches from the London press. Since there was not enough room in each weekly half-sheet to print all these dispatches, the postmaster kept carrying them over until by 1719 he was thirteen months behind and struggling along with a circulation of less than 300. In 1719 a new postmaster established a competing newspaper and employed James Franklin as printer. It turned out to be much like the other one, and Franklin was soon dismissed, leaving him free to start a third paper, completely different from the others.

Rather than merely replicating the London press, the *New-England Courant,* established in 1721, included local news and essays on controversial subjects by local writers. Useful *and* entertaining, it engaged the other newspapers in dialogue, making them more local and more entertaining, too. Many young Bostonians were inspired to write by the prospect of seeing themselves in print; one of them was James's brother and apprentice Benjamin Franklin, whose Silence Dogood essays appeared in the *Courant* in 1722.[1] Inevitably, the *Courant* offended the authorities by "boldly reflecting on His Majesty's Government and . . . the Ministry." In 1723, James Franklin was jailed and prohibited from publishing. He got around the wording of the court order by publishing under the name of his younger brother. Benjamin took advantage of this deception to escape from his apprenticeship contract, but James went to the other printers and warned them not to employ his brother. With four printers and three newspapers, Boston's printing trade was too crowded for Benjamin, so he resolved to go to New York, where there was but one printer and one newspaper. As it turned out, William Bradford had no need of a helper, so he sent Benjamin on to his son Andrew in Philadelphia, whose principal hand, the poet Aquila Rose, had just died.[2]

When the seventeen-year-old Benjamin Franklin made his now-famous entrance into Philadelphia in October 1723, he thought there was just one printer in town. Presenting himself at Andrew Bradford's (where it turned out he was not needed), he learned that a failed printer from London named Samuel Keimer had just set up the second press in Philadelphia. In London, Keimer had been a disciple of the mystical Protestant community known as the French Prophets; when he was imprisoned for debt and for printing libels and the group refused to help him, he denounced them violently in several pamphlets, embraced the Quaker faith, and emigrated to Philadelphia. When Franklin first met him, he was composing an elegy to Aquila Rose directly into type, but he had yet to print anything on his "shatter'd" press.[3]

Franklin's arrival in Philadelphia coincided precisely with the advent of a competing printer in the middle colonies; in fact he was present at the primal scene of rivalry. In Andrew's shop Franklin was surprised to see William Bradford, whom he had just left in New York, and who offered to accompany him to Keimer's. The subsequent scene is dramatized in the *Autobiography*:

> Neighbour, says Bradford [to Keimer], I have brought to see you a young Man of your Business, perhaps you may want such a One. He ask'd me a few Questions, put a Composing Stick in my Hand to see how I work'd, and then said he would employ me soon, tho' he had just then nothing for me to do. And taking old Bradford whom he had never seen before, to be one of the Towns People

that had a Good Will for him, enter'd into a Conversation on his present Undertaking & Prospects; while Bradford not discovering that he was the other Printer's Father, on Keimer's saying he expected soon to get the greatest Part of the Business into his own Hands, drew him on by artful Questions and starting little Doubts, to explain all his Views, what Interest he rely'd on, & in what manner he intended to proceed. – I who stood by & heard all, saw immediately that one of them was a crafty old Sophister, and the other a mere Novice. Bradford left me with Keimer, who was greatly surpriz'd when I told him who the old Man was.

The young witness formed a very poor impression of the men he already saw not only as competitors with each other, but with himself. "These two Printers I found poorly qualified for their Business. Bradford had not been bred to it, & was very illiterate; and Keimer tho' something of a Scholar, was a mere Compositor, knowing nothing of Presswork. He . . . was very ignorant of the World, & had, as I afterwards found, a good deal of the Knave in his Composition."[4] Soon Franklin was Keimer's pressman.

The governor of Pennsylvania, Sir William Keith, was struck by Franklin's superiority to Bradford and Keimer, and at the beginning of 1724 began to cultivate him. Keith offered to set him up on his own and to get him the public printing. He would call on Franklin while he was at work, completely ignoring Keimer, who "star'd like a Pig poison'd." Franklin was dazzled by this recognition from on high. He went to Boston to raise some working capital from his family; when he came back empty-handed in June, Keith promised to advance the money and even to send him to London to buy equipment and open accounts with booksellers and stationers. Franklin sailed at the end of 1724; the letters of credit from Keith supposedly in the captain's bag were not found on arrival. Franklin believed he had been duped, and he was stranded in London. There he met the Penn family's agent Andrew Hamilton, to whom he gave information damaging to Keith. Thereby he secured a more lasting and powerful patron.[5]

That is the story Franklin told in the *Autobiography*. It seems likely that Keith wanted to set up Franklin as the third printer in town in order to have privileged access to the press for his own political purposes. Pennsylvania was then in the midst of a political upheaval. The bursting of the South Sea Bubble had caused a severe economic depression; the surprisingly large loaves Franklin got for his last three coppers testified to the fall in local grain prices. The old merchant elite that dominated the assembly had taken no action in response to the crisis, and they were all ousted in the election of 1721. The new, somewhat more populist assembly debated such controversial measures as the use of paper money or country produce as legal tender, eventually passing a paper-money bill in 1722. Most of the old elite, including Hannah Penn's agent James Logan, were willing to give paper money a try, but they felt the bill put too much into circulation without adequate protection against depreciation.[6] Another aspect of the crisis was that William Penn had died in 1718, leaving his widow's title to the province clouded and her authority uncertain. The governor was supposed to represent the interest of the proprietor, but Keith had allied himself with the assembly and had developed more of a following among workingmen and artisans than any previous governor. All these changes passed almost unnoticed in Bradford's newspaper, though Keith did manage to get his speeches into print by ordering Bradford to print the votes and proceedings of the assembly for the first time. Keith's strategy (as it turned out) was to use the press to appeal directly to the people, to vilify Logan, and to flaunt Hannah Penn's authority. It is easy to see why he wanted a new printer.

So why did he dupe Franklin? The most likely explanation is that Keith changed his mind and decided to employ Keimer. In May 1724, while Franklin was in Boston, Keimer printed two small pieces for Keith. Yet Keith kept promising letters of credit up to the day Franklin sailed. He may have planned an elaborate deception to get Franklin out of the way, perhaps seeing that with three printers neither party could control the press. It is also possible that at the last minute Keith realized that he had no credit to give. Franklin's friend Denham said as much, though he cannot have known all the facts. It later emerged that, to secure his governorship, Keith had gone deeply in debt to a number of London merchants, including the King's printer, the very sort of man he would have asked to give credit to Franklin in the book trade.[7]

As soon as Franklin was out of the way, Keimer began to print steadily for Keith. The rivalry between the two printers burst into the open and caused a sudden explosion of print relating to the political crisis. In 1724 Keimer signaled his penchant for political extremes and his entrepreneurial spirit by reprinting John Trenchard and Thomas Gordon's Radical Whig periodical *The Independent Whig*. He published the first 20 numbers as a weekly magazine, something new in America, but finished the publication as a book of 224 pages in quarto. Then in 1725 he entered directly into local politics by printing an unauthorized version of the assembly votes in competition with Bradford's authorized one. (Keimer's version included some additional passages that might have been seen as damaging to Keith's opponents.) Later in the year, Keith's ally, Speaker David Lloyd, ejected Bradford as printer to the assembly and put Keimer in his place. At about the same time Bradford, too, began printing overtly political tracts.

It might be supposed that Bradford would print for the proprietary party and Keimer for Keith, but in fact both printers were printing for both sides. In many of these pamphlets, no printer is named, and both printers used similar type, the same small folio format, and the same page layout so that no one could tell who printed them. With one printer, there was never any doubt; with two, there was never certainty.

Rivalry between Bradford and Keimer manifested itself outside the political sphere as well. From 1725 to 1729 Keimer pirated the almanacs of Titan Leeds and Jacob Taylor, also published by Bradford. This was probably the first instance of piracy of an American text, and also the first dispute over rights to copy, since both parties claimed to have paid Leeds for the exclusive right to print his calculations.[8] However, the rivalry was most deadly where the printer's role was most traditionally fixed: printing for the Friends. In 1723, just before Keimer set up his press, Bradford had gotten the Philadelphia Friends to underwrite his publication of Willem Sewel's *History of the Quakers* by subscribing for 500 copies. But he delayed starting work, and in 1725 he backed out of the agreement. At that point Keimer announced he would do the job at a lower price, and the Friends closed a deal with him. Keimer bought new type, hired several new hands (future members of the Junto, though Franklin was then in London), and went to work. Meanwhile, Bradford arranged for his London aunt, Tace Sowle, Friends' printer, to print 500 copies and rush them to Philadelphia before Keimer had finished his work. Keimer's progress was slow because he had trouble getting enough paper. There is good reason to believe that Bradford prevailed on his old friends the Rittenhouse family (who were still the only papermakers in the colonies) to refuse Keimer's business. In any case, large amounts of paper had to be imported, a cumbersome and time-consuming process. Only by the intercession of James Logan was a supply of local paper secured. A great deal was at stake in this chess match. With some 710 folio pages and a price of 17*s.* (Keimer's offer) or 20*s.* (Bradford's), this was bigger and more expensive than any book yet printed in Philadelphia. It ended badly for Bradford; the Friends decided to stick to their bargain with Keimer, and Bradford was left with 500 unsalable copies of the London edition.[9]

Meanwhile, Franklin spent eighteen months in London (from the end of 1724 to the middle of 1726) absorbing the culture and learning the book trade of the metropolis. His prospects there were limited, however, so when his friend Denham offered to employ him as a clerk in a merchant house he proposed to establish in Philadelphia, Franklin happily returned. Keith had been dismissed as governor, but had won a seat in the assembly, which was still controlled by his allies. The pamphlet wars continued to rage, but Bradford had gotten back the government printing. When Denham suddenly fell mortally ill in the middle of 1727, Franklin went somewhat uneasily back to work for Keimer, who needed an experienced foreman to supervise the many untrained employees he had hired to work on Sewel.

Franklin quickly saw that, despite the appearance of having a flourishing trade, Keimer was deeply in debt and certain to fail. He therefore positioned himself to take his place, and then plotted to hasten his downfall. He borrowed money from the father of his coworker Hugh Meredith and ordered press and type from London; only when these arrived in the middle of 1728 did he and Meredith give notice. At the time he left Keimer, forty sheets of Sewel (nearly a quarter of the book) remained unprinted, and the Friends were getting impatient. Through the influence of a member of his Junto, Joseph Breintnall, Franklin got the Friends to transfer to his new office the job of finishing the printing. Thus his first printing job was stolen away from Keimer.

At the same time Franklin laid plans to start a second newspaper. "My Hopes of Success . . . were founded on this," he later wrote; he was perhaps the first to see that printing and editing a newspaper of his own was the best way for a printer to succeed as an entrepreneur. Bradford's *Mercury* was "a paltry thing, wretchedly manag'd, & no way entertaining; and yet was profitable to him."[10] But Keimer found out about Franklin's plan and beat him to it, publishing the first issue of the *Pennsylvania Gazette* in the last days of 1728. In a prospectus Keimer also ran down the *Mercury* ("a Scandal to the very Name of Printing . . . *Nonsense in Folio*"). He promised a better paper but did not have the wit to provide one. The *Gazette* refrained from political controversy, but it did not print much news either. Keimer filled his space by serializing Ephraim Chambers's *Cyclopedia,* starting in the first issue with a pedantic philological disquisition on the letter "A." Franklin retaliated by satirizing Keimer's paper ruthlessly in a series of letters signed "Busy-Body," which he and his friend Breintnall published in Bradford's newspaper; Keimer's circulation dropped almost to nothing, and Franklin bought the paper in the fall of 1729 for a trifle while it was still struggling through the article on "Air." Thus Franklin used one competitor's newspaper to destroy the other.[11] Around the end of 1729 Keimer sold out to his apprentice David Harry and moved to Barbados; within a year Harry had given up and followed him there.

The departure of Keimer coincided with an end to the exchange of political pamphlets that had been so brisk since 1725. The year 1729 saw half a dozen printed; in 1730 there were none. Keith left for England in 1728, Lloyd lost his seat in 1729, and the governor and the assembly were now generally in accord with the proprietor. Without controversy Keimer could not keep his business going. And yet at some level, the end of printed controversy was an effect as well as a cause of Keimer's departure. The relationship between political factions and second printers was a dynamic one. A paper war required not only a disaffected party but also two printers both willing to be drawn in. Keimer had been willing, but Franklin was not.

In Franklin's first publication as a printer and an author he adopted the even-handed, modest, and consensus-seeking posture that was to characterize not only his whole political career but also his press, and through his influence, the presses of many others over the next generation. Instead of opening his press to controversy, he used it (and his skill as a writer) to propose a solution to controversy. Paper money was still the issue of the day. By now nearly everyone agreed that it was helping the economy, but Logan's party still wanted strict limits on how much was in circulation and for how long. Franklin entered the fray with an anonymous pamphlet, *A Modest Inquiry into the Nature and Necessity of a Paper Currency,* which proposed a compromise scheme supported with arguments borrowed from European economists deftly adapted to the needs of Pennsylvania. In the *Autobiography* he wrote, "It was well receiv'd by the common People in general; but the Rich Men dislik'd it; for it increas'd and strengthen'd the Clamour for more Money; and they happening to have no Writers among them that were able to answer it, their Opposition slacken'd, & the Point was carried by a Majority in the House."[12] Franklin understated the moderation of his plan; though it called for more money, it set limits on the amount in a way that appeased Logan. As a reward his friends in the assembly got him the lucrative job of printing the money, which had previously been done by Bradford.[13] Thus Franklin invented a new way of being the second printer, quite different from Keimer's: He consciously used his press to shape the political discourse.

Competition in New York: Zenger in the 1730s

The second printer in New York was John Peter Zenger. Like Keimer and Franklin, he had to carve out a niche for himself in competition with the first printer, in this case William Bradford. As in Philadelphia, the presence of a second printer exacerbated the polarization of political parties. A former apprentice of William Bradford, Zenger set up on his own in 1726 and was struggling to keep his head above water when he launched his *New-York Weekly Journal* in 1733. The *Journal* was actually the creation of the leaders of the party that controlled the council, in particular Lewis Morris, Lewis Morris, Jr., James Alexander, William Smith, and Cadwallader Colden. Zenger was poor and uneducated; it is doubtful that he would have even thought of starting a newspaper on his own. The politician editors wrote every word of it except the advertisements and the news notices, and they conducted a lively, witty newspaper that was exceedingly popular. The *Journal* was a typical second newspaper in some respects, like Franklin's *Gazette* or his brother's *Courant,* except that it was entirely in the hands of a faction. The council was then in the midst of a power struggle with Governor William Cosby, and they had begun the *Journal* in order to have a way to attack him. Bradford was then forced to open his columns to Cosby's men because he owed his job to the governor. Thus both New York newspapers became the mouthpieces of parties, a trap that was easy to fall into when there were two newspapers, and one that Franklin worked to avoid in Philadelphia.[14]

In 1734 Cosby resolved to silence the *Journal* and had Zenger arrested for libel. The printer was brilliantly defended by the Philadelphia lawyer Andrew Hamilton, who was called in when a New York lawyer was barred. Why Hamilton was chosen and why he took the case is not known, but self-interest was paramount for him. Possibly he supported Zenger for the same reasons he supported Franklin: His own advancement depended on access to the press and on public discussion of political issues in print. He had good reason to undermine the use of the law of libel as a means of intimidating printers.[15] That was the real issue of the trial, not freedom of the press, which Hamilton never mentioned in his defense. After the Zenger trial the assumption that discussion in the press was equivalent to public discussion, even that the press was an accurate reflection of public opinion, became commonplace. Newspapers now seemed to embody public opinion as never before. Thus embodied, public opinion seemed more real and more powerful than ever.

This is not to say the New York press really did embody public opinion to any greater degree because of the trial. Zenger was now for the first time a serious rival to William Bradford; he was made public printer as a reward for his fidelity to his political patrons. As it turned out, however, Zenger lacked the energy to capitalize on his good fortune. His newspaper became studiously impartial and dull, and he printed hardly anything else. After his death in 1746, it limped along under the direction of his widow and son. Meanwhile, William Bradford, who was seventy years old at the time of the trial, continued to print his newspaper and the occasional book or pamphlet until he retired exhausted in 1744. In the wake of the Zenger trial, the New York press was weaker than ever. This was not the case with Franklin's *Gazette*.

Franklin's *Gazette* and the Strategy of the Open Press

The *Gazette* was the centerpiece of Franklin's printing business and the key to his success. As a typical second newspaper, it was livelier, more local, and better written than the *Mercury*. In one of its first issues (as Franklin later wrote):

> [S]ome spirited Remarks of my Writing on the Dispute then going on between Govr. Burnet and the Massachusetts Assembly, struck the principal People, oc-

> casion'd the Paper & the Manager of it to be much talk'd of, & in a few Weeks brought them all to be our Subscribers. . . . This was one of the first good Effects of my having learnt a little to scribble. Another was, that the leading Men, seeing a News Paper now in the hands of one who could also handle a Pen, thought it convenient to oblige & encourage me.[16]

Franklin's ability as a writer helped him carve out his niche, but it was his firm hand as an editor that kept him secure in it. He was scrupulously even-handed in his coverage of politics, and in fact he refused access to his press to many who wished him to print the sort of essays that had caused the Zenger affair.

> In the Conduct of my Newspaper I carefully excluded all Libelling and Personal Abuse. . . . Whenever I was solicited to insert any thing of that kind, and the Writers pleaded as they generally did, the Liberty of the Press, and that a Newspaper was like a Stage Coach in which any one who would pay had a Right to a Place, my Answer was, that I would print the Piece separately if desired, and the Author might have as many Copies as he pleased to distribute himself, but that I would not take upon me to spread his Detraction.[17]

The distinction Franklin made in this passage is crucial to understanding his open press policy.

An open press was open to all parties, which meant not printing anything that would make it impossible for an opponent to reply with dignity in the same columns. As an editor Franklin actively shaped his paper's content, negotiating the content of every piece with its writer, reserving the right to refuse access, not in order to abridge the liberty of the press but to preserve it from the greater repressive force of the law of libel. An open press preserved liberty of the press in another way by helping the printer succeed in business. A newspaper that was open to all parties was likely to be read by all people; one that embraced a faction would attract a few new subscribers but alienate a great many more. The open press was an economic strategy as well as a political one.

The printer who conducted an open press was far from being a "meer mechanic" (to use Stephen Botein's terms).[18] However, as the passage just quoted from Franklin's *Autobiography* shows, when he was printing a pamphlet for an author who covered all the costs and took the whole edition away with him, a printer was precisely that, a tradesman who manufactured print to the customer's specifications. In those circumstances, the press *was* like a stagecoach. This was the safety valve that made the open-press strategy work. If the printer did not want his name associated with the pamphlet, he could issue it without an imprint. Franklin's open-press policy was imitated by nearly every printer in the middle colonies. Until the very end of the colonial period, newspapers were edited by their printers, and none was in the control of a party. This policy served to keep the number of newspapers down because it discouraged factions from turning to other printers. An open press was actually more competitive because it attracted the widest support, and it helped promote a stable environment for public discourse and for business.

Franklin's Way to Wealth as a Printer

William and Andrew Bradford were the first American printers who acquired all the offices and functions later deemed necessary for success as a colonial printer: job printing, newspaper and almanac publishing, postmaster, government printer, stationer, wholesale paper merchant, book publisher, retail and wholesale bookseller. But though the Bradfords had it all, they did not make these elements cohere into a commercially viable system. Franklin duplicated or appropriated all of these practices in competition with the Bradfords and in every instance somehow expanded or improved upon them. It was he who made the system work, producing a reliable product for readers and a reliable source of income and capital for the printer.

The main financial supports of Franklin's business were the newspaper, his almanacs, and job printing; following his example, these were to be the main supports of most subsequently established colonial printers, and indeed of all printers outside the main seaport towns until well into the nineteenth century. The category of job printing subsumes many types of printing: blank business forms, single-sheet programs, announcements, advertisements, and handbills. From his records we know of at least 200 lost single-sheet items before 1748, all job printing.[19] His predecessors in Philadelphia and New York had also made part of their living from job printing, but Franklin made it a specialty. In 1730 he added a stationer's shop to his printing business and, with the help of his scrivener friend Breintnall, offered "Blanks of all Sorts the correctest that ever appear'd among us."[20]

Another source of income from his printing press was what Franklin called "book work," that is, books (or more usually pamphlets) published at the request and expense of civil or religious corporate bodies or individual authors. From 1728 to 1747 (when he retired from active involvement in the printing business) Franklin printed 432 known books, pamphlets, and broadsides, of which 241 (56 percent) can be shown by his records to have been sponsored by others.[21] None of Franklin's predecessors had produced a fraction of this output, nor, as we shall see, did his competitor Andrew Bradford. This was extremely profitable work. Franklin later wrote that he charged his customers for book work by computing the cost in wages for setting the type and printing the sheets, and then multiplied by three, adding in the cost of the paper if it was not supplied by the customer, plus a commission for securing the paper.[22]

Like the Bradfords and Keimer, Franklin printed several almanacs of different format and character, each known by the names of their compilers: For example, in 1730 he printed Jerman's *American Almanack,* which had previously been published by Bradford, and a new almanac compiled by the ingenious Junto member Thomas Godfrey. These were little pamphlets, but in 1731 he also issued Godfrey's almanac as a broadsheet. Then in 1732 *Poor Richard* for 1733 appeared, the first almanac written by Franklin. "I endeavour'd to make it both entertaining and useful, and it accordingly came to be in such Demand that I reap'd considerable Profit from it, vending annually near ten Thousand."[23] Franklin's accounts show him sending hundreds of copies as far north as Boston and as far south as Charleston.[24]

Every expansion in Franklin's business was at the expense of Andrew Bradford. In 1729 Franklin rather deviously won the job of printer to the assembly by "elegantly and correctly" reprinting a document that Bradford had printed in a "coarse blundering manner." (Andrew Hamilton used the two versions to persuade the assembly to give him the job.) We have already seen how Franklin's pamphlet on paper money helped get the job of printing paper money. Getting the postmastership away from Bradford was in the long run just as important. The postmaster controlled the source of most news as well as the means of distributing newspapers in the country. He was also able to send and receive letters at no charge, thus facilitating the flow of remittances, news, and advertising copy. Bradford was postmaster of the colony when Franklin began his business, and for years he prohibited post riders from delivering Franklin's *Pennsylvania Gazette.* Franklin was compelled to bribe the riders to keep his paper alive. The postmastership gave Bradford "better Opportunities of obtaining News," wrote Franklin, so "his Paper was thought a better Distributer of Advertisements than mine, and therefore had many more, which was a profitable thing to him and a Disadvantage to me." But Bradford was "rich and easy," and "not very anxious about his business." In 1737 the Postmaster General finally got fed up with Bradford's sloppy accounts and gave the postmaster job to Franklin. As he wrote in his *Autobiography,* "tho' the Salary was small, it facilitated the Correspondence that improv'd my Newspaper, encreas'd the Number demanded, as well as the Advertisements to be inserted, so that it came to afford me a very considerable Income. My old Competitor's Newspaper declin'd proportionably."[25]

Franklin also broke the Bradford family monopoly on the Rittenhouse family's printing paper. At first Franklin had to use imported paper in everything he printed. In 1733 he was reduced to selling half an edition of a psalmbook to Bradford just to get the paper to print it with. He must have then resolved never again to allow his supply of paper to be controlled by a competitor, since a few months later he began to set up mills of his own and thus became Bradford's rival in the paper business.[26]

Comparing the bibliography of Bradford's imprints with Franklin's, it is easy to see why Franklin thought Bradford was lazy. In the nine years from 1730 (the year Franklin took over the Pennsylvania government printing) to 1738, Bradford produced only thirty-two books and pamphlets, not counting his newspaper and an annual flurry of four to six almanacs. Franklin produced 118 imprints in the same nine years, not counting newspapers and almanacs. Not that Bradford's business declined; apart from the loss of the Pennsylvania government printing, it stayed about the same, while Franklin's expanded rapidly. The newspaper and the almanacs were not just the center of Bradford's business; lackluster as they were, they were practically his only business. The book work that made Franklin's output so rich was nearly nonexistent. Bradford managed to hold on to New Jersey's government printing by virtue of sharing it with his father; that accounted for his only big job of the 1730s, the New Jersey Acts of 1732, some 300 pages in folio, though whether printed by him or his father is not known. Of the other pamphlets he printed in those nine years, about half were replies to those printed by Franklin (many concerning Andrew Hamilton). The authors of these pamphlets probably chose Bradford simply because he was not the printer of the piece they were attacking.

The Great Awakening revived Bradford's business from 1739 to 1742 (as we shall see), and it also inspired him to renew briefly the rivalry that he had previously hardly exerted himself to sustain. In 1741 Franklin announced he was going to publish a monthly *General Magazine* on the model of the famous *Gentleman's Magazine* of London, but Bradford rushed out a competing *American Magazine* three days before, so that neither one had enough of a market to succeed. Both expired after a few issues, in Bradford's case possibly because of his declining health. He died in 1742, leaving his shop to his second wife, Cornelia. She promptly disinherited the heir, and for a time divided the family business. The octogenarian William Bradford retired at about the same time, making Franklin's victory over the Bradfords apparently complete.

Print in the Public Sphere: The Great Awakening in Pennsylvania

George Whitefield's evangelistic tour of 1739–1741 was a high point of the religious movements collectively named, much later, the Great Awakening. Whitefield's tour was perhaps the first great public event in the colonies that was mediated by, and to some degree created by, print. His own works, together with pamphlets for and against him, streamed from the presses in Boston and Philadelphia (but to a much lesser degree from New York), and the newspapers were full of him, too. His charismatic preaching was attracting crowds as large as 15,000, and his appeals for funds for his Georgia orphanage extracted huge sums from normally frugal colonists. Franklin quickly saw that the Awakening created a market for religious books: "It seem'd as if all the World were growing Religious; so that one could not walk thro' the Town in the Evening without Hearing Psalms sung in different Families of every Street." In the *Gazette*, he wrote, "No Books are in Request but those of Piety and Devotion; and instead of Songs and Ballads, the People are every where entertaining themselves with Psalms, Hymns and Spiritual Songs."[27] Accordingly, Franklin published several devotional books recommended by Whitefield, the Scottish clergyman Ralph Erskine's popular versification of part of the Scriptures, *Gospel Sonnets* (1740), Isaac Watts's *Psalms* (1740) and *Hymns and Spiritual Songs* (1741), and the seventeenth-century Nonconformist Joseph Alleine's ever popular *Alarm to Unconverted Sinners* (also 1741). All of these were good-sized books; together they represented the largest religious publishing venture the middle colonies had ever seen, except for Sewel's *History of the Quakers*. However, Sewel was underwritten by the Friends, whereas these were all published at the risk and expense of Franklin.

These devotional books were only a side-effect of the Great Awakening, dwarfed by the little mountain of books and pamphlets directly related to Whitefield and his preaching. Both Franklin and Bradford devoted the full capacity of their presses to providing reading material about the Awakening, and both saw the greatest output of their printing careers in those years. At first Bradford got the jump on Franklin and brought out pamphlet editions of several of Whitefield's sermons. But from 1740 to 1742 Franklin printed some forty-three books and pamphlets relating to Whitefield or religious enthusiasm in general; in that last year he printed nineteen pamphlets relating to Count Zinzendorf's attempt to unite the German sects. Not all of these were in Whitefield's favor, though most of them were. Bradford, whose previous output had been a fraction of Franklin's, produced nearly thirty such books, as well as an edition of John Wesley's *Hymns* printed by subscription. Again, he printed both for and against Whitefield. After Andrew Bradford died, young William Bradford became a steady publisher of Whitefield and the Presbyterian minister Gilbert Tennent.

Franklin befriended Whitefield, and got permission to collect in volume form his previously published *Sermons* and *Journals*. Franklin advertised for subscribers and got more than he had copies printed, so that he was able to sell only to those who had paid in advance or came to his shop with cash in hand. Never had there been so many auguries favorable to book publishing in America. His edition of the *Sermons* and *Journals* comprised four tiny duodecimo volumes, yet they were the largest books published in America during the Great Awakening.

Even more remarkable than the quantity of publishing that accompanied the Awakening was the skill with which print was deployed by both preachers and printers. Whitefield's versatility in this regard has been fully described, but it seems likely that Franklin, Bradford, Tennent, and Zinzendorf were quick to grasp the role that print played in the Awakening as a medium for conveying ideas, for carrying on controversy, and for publicity. The pamphlets generated by the political controversies of the 1720s were crude libels or pompous proclamations that even at the time must have been unintelligible to someone not part of the local gossip network. By contrast, the books and pamphlets generated by the Great Awakening lucidly debated all the issues, so that the entire episode on some level was represented in print and could be apprehended at a distance. Of course it was preaching that made the Awakening electrifying, but the "print version" of the Awakening was a surprisingly successful attempt to capture the power of the oratory. Whitefield, Franklin, and the rest also realized that the production, distribution, and consumption of print was a very important part of the commerce that pervaded the Awakening. There is no evidence that Whitefield or any other religious writer made a profit directly from the sales of his writing, but these books and pamphlets were an integral part of the campaign for the orphanage that netted thousands of pounds.[28]

The Great Awakening caused a spike in all the activities of the book trades in the middle colonies. Book importation, wholesale and retail bookselling, the reprinting of English books, the publishing of new books written by Americans – all increased. In these activities printers took the lead. After a few years the excitement died down, but the central position of the printer was now permanently established.

At the Center of Print Culture: The Printer as Bookseller

In the Boston of Franklin's youth, printers were at the margin of print culture. It was the booksellers who imported the print culture of England and it was they who sometimes capitalized the local publication of the works of New England divines. In the early eighteenth century when newspapers were established, postmasters were their editors and publishers, not these printers, who were still dependent on Harvard College, the government, and the church, for much of their business. The printers for the most part worked for others as mere artisans.

When Franklin made his journey to New York and then to Philadelphia in 1723, he noted that "there was not a good Bookseller's Shop in any of the Colonies to the Southward of Boston. In New-York & Philad[a] the Printers were indeed Stationers, they sold only Paper, &c., Almanacks, Ballads, and a few common School Books."[29] Before the 1720s printers in the middle colonies were only sporadically involved in the importation of books. Most books were imported by individual readers, by civil or religious organizations, or through the agency of general merchants. The Bradfords imported books from their kinswoman Tace Sowle, the Friends' printer, or through general merchants who had the necessary credit in London. The first book advertisement to appear in Andrew Bradford's *Mercury* (May 19, 1720) listed three popular religious books "Sold by Andrew Bradford and John Copson Booksellers in Philadelphia." Copson, a general merchant, was a partner in the *Mercury* in its first two years, and apparently brought to the partnership the capital and credit that Bradford either did not have or did not wish to risk.[30]

Samuel Keimer ventured boldly into bookselling not long after he established his press, and in the *Mercury* of October 15, 1724 advertised "A choice Parcel of curious and valuable Books, consisting of Poetry, Philosophy, History, Mathematicks, and Divinity of all Perswasions, most of them neatly Bound and Gilt." (Books were often imported bound, since the cost of binding in Philadelphia was so high.) Keimer also at times joined forces with a merchant when he was importing books; in 1728 and 1729 he placed advertisements jointly with John Hyndshaw, who sold not only books but also imported cloth, cutlery, and "other Merchant Goods." Hyndshaw was an artisan as well as a merchant, since he also advertised his ability to bind books neatly and to take salt water out of books, a skill useful to anyone who imported books from overseas.[31]

When Franklin set up on his own he did not at first attempt to be a bookseller, though indirectly he became a considerable importer of books when he founded the Library Company in 1731, which was in turn an outgrowth of his reading circle, the Junto. The Junto was based on the Baconian precept that knowledge is power; the Library Company was based on the facts of colonial life, that knowledge must come from books, and that the crucial books must be imported. Individually, the tradesmen members could neither have afforded such books nor obtained the credit to import them. The Library Company gave Franklin a valuable introduction to the transatlantic book trade.[32] But it was not until 1734 that he ventured into bookselling in any decisive way; his first large advertisement of imported books in the *Gazette* listed about thirty books, including many weighty tomes on navigation and medicine. Over the next few years these lists grew steadily in size, until they occupied whole columns in the early 1740s.

The Great Awakening coincided with a large increase in Franklin's bookselling as well as his printing business. The same was true for Bradford. Moreover, so great was the appetite for religious books that in those same years at least six new bookshops appeared in Philadelphia. (There was no such change in New York.) None of these new booksellers were printers. One was a schoolmaster, Alexander Annard, who probably got into the business in order to secure a supply of texts for his scholars; he also sold lawbooks and books relating to the revivals. Three of the other new booksellers were bookbinders, including Franklin's Junto associate Stephen Potts. In Europe bookbinders traditionally operated bookshops, buying books in sheets and profiting both from the binding and the retailing. The most ambitious of the new booksellers, however, was James Read, a cousin of Franklin's wife, a general storekeeper, and a next-door neighbor. In 1739 he fell under Whitefield's spell and went to London, where he made contact with Charles Wesley and the printer William Strahan, who supplied him with books. He returned in 1740, stocked his store, and began taking an active role in the revival as a trustee of the tabernacle built for Whitefield. It was through Read that Franklin made contact with Strahan and his journeyman David Hall, who was to become his partner. But as the revival waned, Read's book business slowed, and he turned to politics. His outstanding debt to Strahan was more than a hundred pounds and was never fully repaid despite half a century of dunning.[33]

None of these new booksellers stayed in the business long after the fervor of the Awakening died down. From 1740 to 1743, the annual value of imports from London to Pennsylvania had soared from two to three times its previous annual average, only to shrink back to its former size by 1747.[34] This saturation of the market left a residue of unsalable books that were disposed of in a series of auctions in the middle 1740s, one by Read, two by the bookbinder Goodwin, as well as a cut-price clearance sale by Franklin himself. The catalogue of Franklin's 1744 sale has survived, 600 volumes offered for ready money only at specially reduced prices. Most of the books were old and presumably used; some were damaged or incomplete; and there were a great many erudite Latin tomes. These were not the books the colonists read, but rather the ones they did not wish to read. The very presence of so many unwanted books suggests that the age of scarcity had ended.

Franklin's surviving accounts document his store sales in some detail, and though they record only sales on credit and give no information about cash sales, they strongly suggest that book sales accounted for only a small portion of the revenue in a colonial bookstore. By far the largest portion of his revenue from credit sales was from stationery, which included loose paper, ink, lampblack, quills, slates, bound blank books, printed forms, and parchment. The next largest source of income was newspaper advertisements at five shillings apiece. (For some reason, subscriptions to the *Gazette* at 10*s.* a year are seldom recorded in these accounts.) Next come the almanacs, with virtually all sales taking place from November to January. Book sales came last. Sometimes Deborah Franklin (who conducted the store for years) made more selling her cloth and provisions than she took in from book sales.[35]

Franklin sold books in his shop to retail customers, both Philadelphians and the multitude who periodically came to town on business or pleasure from throughout the region and across the seas. He also sold wholesale to a number of country storekeepers in the surrounding region who came to town regularly to restock the small assortments of Bibles, school books, almanacs, and stationery which they kept in addition to their regular grocery and dry goods business. Franklin also sold similar assortments to city storekeepers, as well as to bookbinders, schoolmasters, ministers, tavern keepers, itinerant peddlers, and the riders who delivered newspapers. The number of retail outlets was large, but the variety of printed matter was not. Except for a few shipments of his own publications sent to his associates in other colonies, all of Franklin's book sales were accomplished in small, face-to-face transactions. Payment was usually made in cash, though often at a much later date. Payment in goods and services was less frequent, though by no means unusual. For example, in 1735 James Johnson, a storekeeper in Allentown, Pennsylvania, paid for almanacs with 300 pounds of "neat Hogs fat," which was probably far more plentiful in his vicinity than cash.[36] In a surprising number of cases, however, no payment of any kind was ever made. All colonial merchants had to give easy credit because of the shortage of cash, and this often resulted in small debts that were impossible or not worth the trouble to collect. But page after page of unbalanced accounts in Franklin's ledgers suggest that he was extraordinarily lenient to his debtors, and that he made a policy of writing off any debt whose collection would cause resentment, no matter who the debtor was or how large the debt. Delinquent subscribers to the *Gazette* were particularly numerous. In his will Franklin left to the Pennsylvania Hospital all the debts outstanding from his printing business; even after deleting those he thought uncollectible, they came to more than £5,500. The Hospital never attempted to collect them.

The bulk of the wholesale book sales were Franklin's own publications, primarily almanacs, primers, and psalmbooks. They were sold by the dozen at a discount of usually about 25 to 30 percent. To booksellers in other regions Franklin gave a somewhat larger discount, so that they in turn could sell to storekeepers. For example, almanacs which retailed at 5*d.* were sold to storekeepers at 3½*d.*, to other booksellers at 3*d.*, and to his partners at 2⅖*d.* From late November 1736 to February 1737, he wholesaled about 2,500 copies of three almanacs (his own, Jacob Taylor's, and John Jerman's). Almost half of these (1,148) were sent out of the region (300 to Boston, 300 to his sister in Newport, 500 to his partner Timothy in Charleston, and 48 to Zenger in

New York). Another 480 were sold to storekeepers outside of Philadelphia: in Trenton and Burlington, New Jersey, Allentown, Pennsylvania, and Lewes and Newcastle, Delaware. The remaining 900 copies were sold to more than thirty-five different wholesale customers in quantities ranging from half a dozen to eight dozen. Only about thirty copies were sold on credit singly at retail price. Most retail sales were probably paid for on the spot, and no record of them survives.

Of the books Franklin imported, the only ones he sold wholesale were Bibles, Testaments, and the lower-level schoolbooks for which the demand was steady but not large enough to justify reprinting. The others, the scores of general books ordered from Great Britain in single copies, he sold retail to individuals who came to his shop or sent for them. For books of this kind he calculated his retail price in local currency in terms of a percentage "advance" over their cost to him in sterling. This markup ranged from 100 to 150 percent, depending on whether it was a wholesale or a retail transaction. Since local currency was worth about two-thirds sterling, the actual markup ranged from 33 to 66 percent. This convenient rule of thumb was used through the colonial period and beyond.[37] In advertisements he sometimes stated that imported books were to be sold only for cash with no discounts allowed. British suppliers gave him such short credit (perhaps six months from the date of shipment from London) that he could not extend credit, offer a discount for cash payment, or offer wholesale discounts to storekeepers.

At the Center of Print Culture: The Printer as Publisher

A publisher is usually defined as the entrepreneur of the book trade, the person who decides that a book is likely to be profitable, finances its printing, distributes it, and takes the risk of a loss if it does not sell or the profit if it does. The word "publisher" began to be used in this sense in the eighteenth century, though as yet no one specialized in performing this function. In the middle colonies, book publishing was usually carried on by individuals (sometimes authors) or by corporate bodies, and then never primarily for profit but rather to disseminate a good book or promote a cause. The printer was simply a craftsman working to order, not a publisher; the customer paid for the print and paper at so much per sheet and took the whole edition away to sell or give away as he pleased. At the most, he would leave a few copies with the printer to sell and credit toward the printing bill. Thus anyone could have his book published if he had the money, though the cost was not trifling. In 1740 Reverend John Thomson paid £18 2*s.* 4*d.* for paper, print, and stitching of 1,000 copies of his sixty-four-page octavo tract *An Essay upon Faith of Assurance.* The annual income of a housemaid was about £10, a clerk £25, a schoolmaster £60.[38]

In the middle colonies both wholesale bookselling and book publishing were typical sidelines of printers. The division of the trade between printers and booksellers, which was growing ever deeper in England, had no counterpart in America. In New England, as printers began to accumulate capital, they followed what became the Franklinian pattern and took over the business of book importing and publishing. After 1750 hardly any books were printed for booksellers in New England.[39]

In discussing publishing in this admittedly anachronistic way, a distinction must be made between book publishing and the publishing of newspapers, almanacs, and pamphlets. Printers did usually act as the publishers of the newspapers and almanacs, and sometimes of the pamphlets they printed, but since the cost and risk of publishing books was so much greater, very few were printed and fewer still were published by their printers. A pamphlet differs from a book in size and binding. Generally, it contains fewer sheets of paper and is issued unbound; the first distinction reduced the bookseller's investment, the second promoted sales. Since paper was the largest component in the cost of printing, and since it had to be purchased in advance of any sales, the amount of paper in a book corresponded to the capital required and to the risk the publisher ran. An issue of a weekly newspaper usually consisted at this period of a single sheet of paper folded once to make four pages, and the cost of printing it was in effect paid in advance by subscribers and advertisers. An almanac was a little unbound book, but it required hardly any more paper than a newspaper, usually a sheet and a half folded three times. A sermon or a political pamphlet could be encompassed in two or three folded sheets. Very few pamphlets exceeded six sheets, or ninety-six pages in octavo. This was about as much as most colonial printers could afford to venture from their slender capital. Publishing a bound book of ten to twenty sheets was a risk that was very seldom taken, and books of more than twenty sheets were very few indeed.

Only a handful of books of more than twenty sheets were printed by the Bradfords during the period of their monopoly, every one of them laws paid for by legislatures, except for William Bradford's disastrous 1706 quarto *Book of Common Prayer*, for which he ultimately received a subsidy from Trinity Church.[40] Fewer than a dozen other books of more than ten but less than twenty sheets can be identified, among which were their most purely entrepreneurial publications, a guide for justices of the peace, *Conductor Generalis* (1711 and 1722) and William Bradford's own handbook for clerks, *The Secretary's Guide* (perhaps as many as three editions before 1720). These were the first large books in the middle colonies printed purely for the profit of the publisher that went into multiple editions.

There was very little book publishing while the Bradfords were the only printers, but the establishment of second presses marked the beginning of an entrepreneurial book trade in general and of publishing large books in particular. Keimer's edition of Sewel's *History of the Quakers* was the largest book printed in the middle colonies before 1730; Andrew Bradford was unwilling to take it on, and Keimer was unable to finish it without Franklin's help. Keimer had already shown himself willing to act as a publisher of large books as early as 1724 when he printed the *Independent Whig*, which comprised more than thirty sheets. In 1729 he published Mary Mollineux's *Fruits of Retirement* (more than thirteen sheets), apparently at his own expense, since the next year Andrew Bradford published an edition of the same book, probably a retaliation for Keimer's pirating his almanacs and stealing Sewel. Compared with the Bradfords, he also had a healthy appetite for book work paid for by others: in 1726 and 1727 alone he printed three books of more than ten sheets, one for the assembly, one for the Friends, and one for its author.[41]

By contrast with his competitors Franklin printed books of more than ten sheets at his own risk more regularly, but still not very often: just fifteen times in his twenty-year career. Most of these books were reprints of books previously published in Britain, and many had been previously published in America as well by other printers. The books Franklin preferred to publish were those whose popularity was proven and was so great that the demand could not be met by imports. The Great Awakening created just such a demand: Eight of those fifteen books are Whitefield's works or reprints of devotional books recommended by him.[42]

Each of the other large books Franklin published tells us something about the risks of publishing in the colonies. The first book Franklin printed on his own was a psalmbook (1729), not the standard Brady and Tate version but a new one by Isaac Watts that was all the rage in London. The public rejected this innovation, and two years later, Franklin complained in his newspaper that "I have known a very numerous impression of *Robin Hood's Songs* [popular chapbook verse, no copy of an American edition of which survives] to go off in this Province at 2*s.* per Book, in less than a twelvemonth; when a small Quantity of David's Psalms (an excellent Version) have lain on my Hands above twice the Time."[43] Franklin learned his lesson; the next book of more than ten sheets he published was an edition of the old Brady and Tate psalmbook in 1733, published jointly with his rival Bradford.

Even more innovative was Franklin's edition of Richardson's *Pamela*. He began printing it in 1742, just two years after the first London edition. He must have been aware that never before had an American reprinted a popular English book so soon after its publication. He may not have realized that he had published the first modern novel. He saw it as a kind of secular *Pilgrim's Progress,* for he described Bunyan as "the first that I know of who mix'd Narration and Dialogue, a Method of Writing very engaging to the

Reader, who in the most interesting Parts finds himself as it were brought into the Company, and present at the Discourse," adding, "Richardson has done the same in his Pamela." Here, too, Franklin paid the price of being an innovator. The book was so large (seventeen sheets) and his press so occupied with the Great Awakening that it took him more than two years to finish the two volumes, by which time the demand for the book seems to have waned. In order to get it off his hands as quickly as possible he sold it not bound but only stitched, at a mere 6*s.*, about half what imported copies would have cost. He also sent 100 copies at 5*s.* to William Parks at Williamsburg and another lot to Boston. By 1748 he had only forty-four sets left in stock, but his profit on the edition must have been modest. Perhaps for this reason, no other novels were printed unabridged in America until the eve of the Revolution; given how quickly they went in and out of fashion, it was less risky to import them.

Of all Franklin's reprints, the one most emblematic of the dilemmas facing the colonial book publisher was his edition of the New Testament, supposedly printed about 1745. In England the printing of the Bible and its parts was reserved to certain licensed printers by royal patent. Even disregarding the Bible patent, an American would not want to print the Bible, because the English, the Scots, and the Dutch all produced them in such large editions at such a low price that there was no hope of competing. Moreover, it was doubtful that American readers and clergymen would have trusted the accuracy of an American Bible. But it seems Franklin did print a New Testament; in the inventory of his stock made when David Hall took it over in 1748, we find itemized "51 Testaments Philadelphia Printing." No copy of this testament is known, but one may yet turn up, since it is possible that Franklin printed it under a false London imprint so that it might escape notice then and today. Thus he may have competed with imports by camouflaging his book as one of them. It was printed on cheap brown paper to keep the cost down, yet it was still not cheaper than imported Testaments; in that same inventory "Foreign Testaments" are valued at the same 1*s.* 6*d.* He sent a large part of the edition in sheets to New York and Boston (at 10*d.* a copy), perhaps to allow it better to pass as an import.[44] Like the clandestine Boston Bibles mentioned by Isaiah Thomas, Franklin's Testament offered no real challenge to the dominance of British Bible publishers in the colonies.[45] Throughout the colonial period it was safer, easier, and cheaper to import Bibles and Testaments than to produce them locally.

All of the large books printed by Franklin were reprints of English works, except one, James Logan's translation of Cicero's *Cato Major* (1744, ten and one half sheets, Fig. 8.1). He printed it in large type on creamy paper with red ink on the title page, partly to show off his prowess as a printer – indeed

M. T. CICERO's
CATO MAJOR,
OR HIS
DISCOURSE
OF
OLD-AGE:
With Explanatory NOTES.

PHILADELPHIA:
Printed and Sold by B. FRANKLIN,
MDCCXLIV.

Figure 8.1. *M. T. Cicero's Cato Major* (Philadelphia: Benjamin Franklin, 1744), an annotated translation of *De senectute* by James Logan. Courtesy of The Library Company of Philadelphia.

the book is today reckoned the most beautiful example of the colonial printer's art – but mainly to flatter Logan and to enable his nearly blind patron to read it with ease. Franklin's goal was patronage, not profits. Logan advised him against printing it, saying "I think he must surely lose by it," and lose he did. Of the edition of 1,000, 300 were sent to William Strahan in London, with the hope of making a literary reputation for Logan in the metropolis; but Strahan lost them and never paid for them. Original American works hardly ever made a profit for either author or publisher. Just once did Franklin admit to hoping to profit from American writing, and characteristically he made a joke of it. In his preface to another Latin translation by James Logan, *Cato's Moral Distichs* (1735, three sheets) Franklin wrote, "It would be thought a Piece of Hypocrisy and pharisaical Ostentation in me, if I should say, that I print these *Distichs* more with a View to the Good of others than my own private Advantage: And indeed I can not say it; for I confess . . . I expect to sell a very good Impression."

The Integration of the Book Trade in the 1740s

Franklin was one of the first Americans to see the British North American colonies as a potential political and cultural unity. Long before he proposed the Albany Plan of Union or conceived the American Philosophical Society, he was fashioning a cooperative intercolonial network of printers. It began as early as 1731, when the South Carolina Assembly took vigorous steps to lure a printer to Charleston. Franklin's journeyman Thomas Whitmarsh was ready to set up on his own, and since the last thing Franklin wanted was another printer in Philadelphia, he encouraged Whitmarsh by making him a partner and supplying him with a press and type. In 1733 Whitmarsh succumbed to fever, and Franklin immediately sent another journeyman, Lewis Timothy, to take his place. Both partners signed contracts whereby Franklin paid a third of the expenses of the business and received a third of the income it generated. Both were primarily newspaper and job printers, but Timothy, the survivor, also sold Franklin's publications and reprinted pieces from his newspaper. In later years Franklin established similar partnerships in New York, New Haven, Annapolis, Lancaster, and Antigua. He also maintained close business ties with the widow and son of his brother James in Newport. When he became postmaster general of the colonies, he had several of these printer-partners named local postmasters, thus helping their individual businesses as well as the interactions between them. When he retired, he retained an interest in his Philadelphia office by means of a partnership with his foreman David Hall. Thus he transformed a brood of potential rivals into a sophisticated intercolonial communications network, with himself at the center.[46]

Of all the partnerships, the most strategic was the one with James Parker in New York. As early as the 1690s New York and Philadelphia were emerging as the twin commercial centers of the middle colonies. Like two ends of a magnet, they created force fields radiating out to their hinterlands and vibrating between their two poles. The collaboration between William and Andrew Bradford was a reflection of this dynamic, but in 1742 William retired and Andrew died. Franklin, having foreseen this vacuum, had already taken steps to fill it. Earlier in 1742 he had formed a silent partnership with his journeyman James Parker to operate a press in New York. (Parker had been an apprentice to William Bradford, and had run away to work for Franklin in 1733.)[47] As with his other partnerships, Franklin provided the press and type and assumed a share of the expenses and risks in return for the same one-third share of the income.[48] Like Franklin, Parker got all the government printing, ran the best newspaper, attracted most of the job printing, and in addition published the occasional book and helped Franklin distribute his publications in New York. When his partnership with Franklin expired in 1748, he continued to collaborate closely with him and his successor, David Hall. He also (courtesy of Franklin) became postmaster in New Jersey and New Haven in 1754, and in 1756 he was promoted to the post of comptroller of the whole postal system.[49]

The degree of integration of the Franklin network can easily be overstated. As we shall see in the next section, his satellite printers often turned into competitors. Nevertheless, from the 1740s to the 1760s (when more master printers began to emigrate from Britain) most of the printers in the middle colonies, with the exception of the Bradfords, rose through Franklin's network. The striking uniformity and stability of the print culture of the middle colonies in this period are probably due to this shared experience and culture. In everything from the type they used to their editorial policies, other tradesmen imitated Franklin.

Proliferation of Printers in the 1750s

Andrew Bradford had adopted his nephew William III and groomed him to take over his business, but when Andrew died in 1742, William quarrelled with his stepmother, and so for a brief time there were two Bradford shops, each with its own newspaper, in competition with each other as well as with Franklin. There was not enough business for three newspapers, and soon the widow Bradford's *Mercury* ceased publication, leaving the field to William's *Pennsylvania Journal.* After Franklin's retirement William took his place as the city's leading newspaper editor; his coffeehouse was the chief center of intelligence and literary culture in town, and for twenty years he shared rather peacefully with Franklin's firm most of the region's trade in books and printing.[50]

At least a dozen other printers established themselves at one time or another in Philadelphia and its hinterland from 1746 to 1767. That there were so many suggests an expanding market for print, but the fact that most were short-lived suggests that it was expanding less rapidly that it appeared to be. During all this time there were still just two English-language newspapers. These new printers all positioned themselves either geographically or ethnically so as not to compete directly with Franklin and Bradford: They set up in the back country, printed in German, or did both. Four of the new printers attempted to establish a press in Lancaster, the seat of a newly created county and the market town for a rich and rapidly settling agricultural region. At least three of these attempts were instigated by Franklin: James Chattin in 1751, the partnership of Peter Miller and Samuel Holland in the same year, and William Dunlap in 1754. He may also have encouraged Andrew Steuart around 1761.[51] Of the four, only the second managed to print a newspaper even briefly, and that was bilingual. All four gave up after a short time and moved to Philadelphia, where they tried to carve out new niches with varying degrees of failure. Chattin was soon reduced to a journeyman. Steuart tried to make a living by reprinting pamphlets already printed by Franklin or Bradford. He caused something of a scandal by reprinting Francis Hopkinson's poem *Science* without the author's permission, perhaps the first time an American literary work had been (as it were) pirated.[52] Soon thereafter Steuart moved to North Carolina. Henry Miller opened a successful German printing shop in Philadelphia. Only Dunlap succeeded in establishing a viable English printing business in Philadelphia.[53]

William Dunlap, a native of Ireland and an apprentice of the younger William Bradford, had the good fortune to marry a niece of Franklin's wife and therefore enjoyed the great man's patronage to a remarkable extent. Franklin turned over to him the press of the failed James Chattin in Lancaster and got substantial printing jobs for him from influential people and organizations. Then in 1757 Franklin was sent to England to serve as the province's agent, and he brought Dunlap into Philadelphia to take his place as postmaster. He also helped set him up as a bookseller with some of the old shopworn stock of James Read, another of his wife's relatives. Franklin was willing to set up a competitor with his own firm of Franklin and Hall because he believed there was now enough business for three printers in town. In 1759 he advised Hall "not to be uneasy at the Number of Printing Offices setting up in Philadelphia. The Country is increasing and Business must increase with it." Franklin wanted to be fair to both his protégés; "We [i.e., Franklin and Hall] are pretty well establish'd, and shall probably with God's Blessing and a prudent Conduct always have our Share. The young ones will not be so likely to hurt us as one another."[54] Dunlap did come to grief, not from lack of printing business but because he was incapable of keeping track of the large sums of money that passed through a postmaster's hands. In 1764 despite his pleas for mercy, Franklin removed him from the position, owing more than £1,000 to the Crown.[55]

Germans were the largest ethnic group in late colonial Pennsylvania, followed by English and Scots-Irish. At the peak of immigration in 1753, there were as many German presses and newspapers as English in Pennsylvania. The German-American press is discussed fully in a separate section of this chapter; here, it needs to be mentioned again in connection with the proliferation of printers in the back country and in Philadelphia. Christopher Saur's press was established in 1739 in Germantown, now part of Philadelphia, only a half dozen miles from the city wharves. In 1743 another German press was established in Philadelphia by Joseph Crellius. Both published newspapers. In 1745 a third German press was set up sixty miles inland at Ephrata to serve the religious community there. This was the first inland press in the colonies. From 1748 to 1758 Franklin owned a German printing office in Philadelphia run at various times by Johann Boehm and Anton and Godhardt Armbruster. One of the apprentices in the German shop was Henry Miller, whom Franklin set up briefly in Lancaster; he finally settled in Philadelphia in 1762 and began yet another German newspaper, which lasted through much of the Revolution.[56]

There were fewer new printers struggling for business in New York in the 1750s, but the competition among them was much fiercer than it ever had been in Philadelphia. There was none of the diversity of geography, ethnicity, background, and type of business that characterized the proliferation of printers in Philadelphia. In New York the new printers were primarily newspaper printers, and they were all closely associated with one another, having been journeymen of Franklin's former partner James Parker. At the beginning of the decade Parker had virtually the entire trade of New York, and his journeymen, like jealous sons or brothers, wanted a share. He tried to make them his partners in emulation of Franklin, but he failed to follow the advice of Poor Richard about overseeing your workmen, and they helped themselves to his purse, "rioting," as he later put it, "in what had cost me great Labour and Pains."[57] Parker hoped they would play Hall to his Franklin, but instead they served him worse than Franklin had ever served Andrew Bradford.

In 1750, Parker's journeyman William Weyman declared his intention of setting up a press in opposition to his master and went to London to buy his equipment. It was inevitable that another printer would soon appear, since the firms of Zenger and DeForeest were moribund, and Parker preferred to have that printer at least partly under his control. While Weyman was in

London, the last of the Zengers died; Parker bought the press and type and wrote to Weyman offering them to him on easy terms. Another of his journeymen, Hugh Gaine, was so displeased with this preferential treatment that by the same ship he ordered a press of his own from London and invited Weyman to be his partner in an independent firm. Parker countered by offering to make Weyman his foreman in a partnership expressly modeled on that of Franklin and Hall. Weyman decided to stay with Parker, and Gaine began the *New-York Mercury* in 1752, which quickly drove DeForeest's paper out of business.[58]

At just this moment three prominent Presbyterian lawyers (William Livingston, John Morin Scott, and William Smith) launched an attack on the Anglican Church for what they saw as an undue influence in politics and in the proposed King's College. They began a weekly periodical, *The Independent Reflector,* printed by Parker but edited and published by themselves. Parker thus tried to preserve his neutrality, but soon the controversy spilled over into his newspaper. The Anglicans looked about for a way to reply, and Gaine opened his columns to them, though he was bred a Presbyterian in Belfast and Parker was himself a staunch Anglican. The Presbyterians then demanded equal time in Gaine's paper. When he refused, the focus of the controversy shifted to the issue of freedom of the press, as *The Independent Reflector* decreed that "A Printer ought not to publish every Thing that is offered him; but what is conducive of general Utility, he should not refuse, be the Author a Christian, Jew, Turk, or Infidel. Such Refusal is an immediate Abridgment of the Freedom of the Press." The Presbyterians had greater popular support, and Gaine eventually compromised by allowing them to buy space in his newspaper, just as if they were placing an advertisement, for a series of essays called *The Watchtower*. Since the Zenger trial a free press was increasingly seen as a press controlled by public opinion.[59]

In 1751, Parker took the Zenger press to his native Woodbridge, New Jersey, just across from Staten Island, and by 1753 he had moved there permanently, leaving the New York office in Weyman's hands. This was the first press in that colony. Parker did the government printing and published a highly regarded monthly magazine from 1758 to 1760. In 1765 he briefly set up another press in Burlington, New Jersey (across the Delaware from Philadelphia) specifically to print Samuel Smith's voluminous *History of New Jersey* near the author's home. He found the printing business in Woodbridge "frivolous and trifling," but there was no other work in Burlington either. Both towns were too close to larger print centers; New Jersey was indeed the proverbial barrel tapped at both ends. Not until the British occupation of New York during the Revolution did newspapers appear in New Jersey or upstate New York.[60]

By their contract Weyman was supposed to render accounts to Parker monthly, but years went by without his paying a penny. He behaved as if Parker had simply given the business to him, and, like his old master, Parker was reluctant to force the payment of a debt. But by 1759 his patience was exhausted, and he appealed to a mediator for a settlement. Weyman responded by suddenly setting up on his own, leasing a press and type from DeForeest's widow. He began a newspaper with a similar title (*The New York Gazette,* compared to Parker's *The New York Gazette and Weekly Post-Boy*), arguing that the paper was really his anyway, and since he had the subscription list, he was able to convince most of the subscribers and advertisers to go with him. The circulation of Parker's paper dropped below 1,000, while Weyman's rose above 1,500. Weyman also stole the pseudonym of Parker's almanac and the public printing business that Parker had monopolized since 1743.[61]

Parker had another printing office in New Haven, which Franklin had originally set up (with a postmastership) for his nephews, and which was now run by John Holt, brother-in-law to William Hunter the Williamsburg printer and Franklin's deputy postmaster. In 1760 Parker brought Holt to New York as his partner and foreman. Holt fought to regain the place the newspaper formerly held, cutting the price of advertisements, moving the publication from Monday to Thursday to catch the Albany and Philadelphia posts, and starting a new inland postal route to Boston.[62] In the meantime Weyman's many other creditors began to press him for payment, while the popular favor he had once enjoyed was transferred to Holt. Weyman's paper faltered during the Stamp Act crisis and ceased altogether at the end of 1767. In the final issues of the *Gazette* he blamed his troubles on Franklin and Parker, whom he accused of manipulating postal regulations to hinder his newspaper's circulation. His last asset was the public printing contract, which he sold to Gaine for a year's income. He died insolvent in 1768.

Though Holt restored Parker's newspaper to favor, he paid no more attention to the terms of their partnership than Weyman had. He never even thought of paying Parker his half share of the profits from the New York office or his quarter share from New Haven (which was now a three-way partnership with Thomas Green, a scion of the ancient New England printing family). Nor did he pay long-standing debts to Franklin for the New Haven press and Post Office accounts, and to William Strahan in London and Hamilton and Balfour in Edinburgh for books, debts for which Parker was ultimately liable. Parker let things slide for years, but during the Stamp Act crisis, he began to press for payment. Holt was now very popular with the Sons of Liberty, and they paid some of his debts. When Parker finally filed suits against Holt in New York and New Haven in 1766, Holt did as

Weyman had done in 1759 and abruptly started a new newspaper of his own, taking all the subscribers with him.[63] Parker was fifty-two years old and frail, but this time he decided not to take another partner. When he resumed his paper, he had only forty subscribers. He exerted himself as never before, printing all kinds of Whiggish controversy (even a famous broadside by Alexander MacDougall which got him briefly arrested for seditious libel[64]), and he got his circulation up to 650. Holt kept pace with him in political printing, and both enlarged their papers to accommodate it, without raising the price. This competition nearly ruined them both. Weyman's death brought the number of newspapers down to three, but there was still not enough demand to support them all. Meanwhile Holt expertly evaded Parker's suits for debts which by now he had no hope of paying. He was on the verge of ruin when he was saved by Parker's sudden death in 1770. Throughout all this, Gaine was the only printer who thrived.

Convergence with England: David Hall

As printers proliferated, the quantity of print they produced increased as well, more than doubling between 1740 to 1770. Book imports in the middle colonies, while fluctuating, nearly quadrupled in this period (Graph 7a, Appendix 1). As the population and wealth of the middle colonies increased, cultural and economic ties with Britain grew stronger as well. Even as the region's print culture became more vigorous, its connections with Britain's were strengthening. Greater self-sufficiency in producing many of the most basic kinds of print went hand-in-hand with greater demand among the book-buying public for variety and luxury at the high end of the market.

The period of 1740 to 1770 was one of change in Britain as well, as the London book trade consolidated its control over the English provinces and created a national book distribution network of provincial printers and booksellers who printed newspapers but imported their books and stationery from London. The English provincial printers were in some ways similar to their American counterparts; they printed only what the London booksellers could not or would not provide them, and the books and magazines they imported from London were much the same.[65] Of course there were differences as well, such as the important role played by government printing in the colonies. The same period, however, saw the rise of a reprint trade in Scotland and Ireland that challenged the domination of London not only in these countries but even in England. The Scots also began exporting their books to the colonies in great numbers in the 1740s, and though the Irish reprinters were legally forbidden to export until 1780, their books also managed to reach America in small numbers.[66]

The book culture of Philadelphia or New York was becoming more and more like that of York or Bristol, or even of Dublin or Edinburgh from the 1730s right up to the eve of the Revolution. This convergence, which the historian Jack Greene has described in *Pursuits of Happiness*,[67] is epitomized in the improved relations between British and American booksellers. Before the 1740s the British exporters of books to America were mostly general merchants, and at least in the middle colonies, the only regular booksellers were really printers. These were two different business cultures. Printers like Franklin did not know general merchants in London, could not arrange credit with them easily, did not understand their customs, their needs and preferences, their language. Franklin did not even keep legible books, the most basic skill required of a merchant. No wonder the Bradfords' main source of books was their kinswoman Tace Sowle Raylton, the Friends' printer and a marginal figure in the London trade. No wonder the London booksellers preferred to deal with general merchants who imported books along with cloth and hardware, or with private gentlemen.

In the 1740s this relationship began to change, as American printers gained more control over the bookselling business and became more mercantile in their practices. At the same time British booksellers began to make an effort to find printers they could work with. General merchants never stopped importing the most common books – Bibles, Testaments, primers, and schoolbooks – but their share of the book market declined. The first contacts between the British and American book trades were tentative, and it is no accident that the first lasting connection was where the cultural gap was the narrowest, between the most entrepreneurial American printer and the only prominent London bookseller who was also a printer.

In 1744 Franklin heard through his wife's kinsman James Read that the London printer William Strahan had a favorite journeyman who wanted to emigrate with a view to eventually setting up on his own. Franklin was looking for another printer to set up as a partner, and he wrote to Strahan suggesting that his man, David Hall, might do. When Hall arrived in 1745, Franklin immediately took to him and decided to keep him by his side first as his foreman, later as his partner and his successor. At the same time, Franklin wrote to Strahan, whom he knew only through Hall, saying "I have long wanted a Friend in London whose Judgment I could depend on, to send me from time to time such new Pamphlets as are worth reading on any Subject (Religious Controversy excepted) for there is no depending on Titles and Advertisements."[68] This three-way friendship was the basis of the first sustained book-importing enterprise in the middle colonies.

At the beginning of 1748 Franklin retired to devote himself to scientific research and politics, activities his business and his position as a newspaper editor precluded. He turned over his shop to Hall by forming a partnership with him, much like his other partnerships. Franklin took half the profits of the printing, but whatever money Hall made from bookselling was all his own. The effect of this clause, whether intended or not, was to divert even more of Hall's energy to importing books and away from printing them.[69]

Hall's relationship with Strahan was unique because they had been boyhood friends in Edinburgh, and they shared the trade culture of printers. Strahan was at the time the only printer in London who had been successful in gaining admittance to the inner circle of copy-holding booksellers who dominated the trade. When he began sending books to Hall in 1744, he had just begun investing his printing profits in copyrights, and thus was able to supply books to Hall that he published, as well as other books that he could exchange for them, below the usual wholesale prices. Strahan also had no qualms about offering his old friend six months' credit, more than booksellers usually allowed, but the bare minimum if the importer was to have a chance to sell the books before payment was due. Hall was unfailingly prompt in payment, and Strahan was so attentive to his orders that he personally supervised their packing. They understood each other's needs perfectly, and their voluminous correspondence shows how hard they worked to accommodate each other.[70]

Strahan continued to send Hall all the newest London books, so that his bookshop was not only larger but better stocked and more cosmopolitan than it had been when Franklin was running it. However, the historian of the Hall bookshop argues that Hall's advertisements gave his stock "a superficial impression of depth. Hall preferred to have many copies of the fifty or so titles which always sold well."[71] Steady sellers still accounted for most of his business, as they had in Franklin's time. However, now there were more steady-selling titles, and he sold more of each.[72]

Hall's business records are more nearly complete than those of any other middle colonies bookseller, and they show an enormous quantity of book importing compared with what Franklin had done. Over the twenty-four years from 1748 to his death in 1772, Hall imported more than £30,000 worth of books and stationery from Strahan alone, plus some 20,000 Bibles and 3 tons of other books from Strahan's Edinburgh friends Hamilton and Balfour. He also bought smaller quantities of books from other English booksellers, and once during the Stamp Act crisis he tried smuggling books from Ireland.[73] His total imports must have exceeded £40,000 sterling, and their retail value in local currency must have been greater than £80,000. By contrast, when Hall took over Franklin's stock of books and stationery in 1748, it was valued at only £681; and his gross income from printing, including the *Gazette*, 10,000 almanacs a year, and all the government printing, was only about £28,000 local tenor, on which he got only half the profit.[74]

Considering all this, it is not surprising that Hall printed hardly any large books at his own expense. While Franklin printed fifteen books of more than ten sheets at his own risk while he was running the business, Hall printed just six in almost as many years. Of those six, one was actually at Franklin's expense, one was begun by Franklin before he retired, and two were printed by others. All appeared before Franklin left for England; without Franklin looking over his shoulder, Hall had no interest in publishing. The sort of books Franklin liked to publish, such as psalmbooks, Hall preferred to import.[75]

Hall's activity caused a sharp and permanent increase in the value of imports into Pennsylvania after 1748. Another spike in New York and Pennsylvania in 1759 and 1760 reflects new activity by several booksellers besides Hall.[76] In 1759, 2,000 volumes were sold at auction in Philadelphia by the merchant William Griffitts; Garret Noel, established as a bookseller in New York since about 1753, published a catalogue listing 500 titles for sale. Then in 1760 similar catalogues were printed in Philadelphia by William Bradford (twice), William Dunlap, and a Swiss-German sojourner named Christoph Lochner, as well as by Hall; and in New York James Rivington (whose career will be considered shortly) made his debut with a catalogue of 1,200 titles. In those two years, nine bookseller's and auction catalogues were printed in the middle colonies, almost as many as in all the previous years together (Graph 6, Appendix 1). By 1760, many London and Edinburgh booksellers were involved to some extent in the American market, and American readers and booksellers began to behave more and more like their counterparts in Britain.

James Rivington and the Opening of the Export Market

The orderly transatlantic trade in books which David Hall typified in the 1750s was disrupted in the 1760s by James Rivington. First as a London exporter, then as a transplanted American importer, Rivington used a number of strategies to wrest the trade to America away from the handful of London booksellers who controlled it. Ultimately he failed to capture that trade for himself, but he was among the first to see the American market as large and lucrative enough to be worth competing for. His aggressive methods helped open up new sources of supply and changed the way books were sold in America.

Rivington was born into the inner circle of London bookselling families, but he always put his personal entrepreneurial interest ahead of the corporate interest of his clan, and so he was cut out of the family business in 1756 at the age of thirty-two. He then invested £2,000 in the copyright of Smollett's *History of England* and made £10,000. Copyrights jointly held were still the basis of the control over the trade exercised by the London booksellers, and this spectacular success would have easily brought him back into the inner circle if he had not at the very same time sold off his other copyrights and begun a cut-price wholesale trade designed to steal away not only the English provincial trade, but that of the colonies as well.[77]

In 1755 David Hall learned that the Williamsburg bookseller William Hunter was buying books from Rivington at a discount of 16 percent off the London retail prices, plus a year's credit and the privilege of returning unsold books. Hall naturally passed this information on to Strahan, who at first could not see how a profit could be made that way. The discount alone brought the price below what Strahan himself had to pay for most books at wholesale, and even then he could not offer return privileges. Such terms, said Strahan, "were never heard of till now."[78]

But on closer inquiry in the trade, Strahan found out how Rivington could afford to offer such terms and prices and still make a profit. In a series of letters to Hall, he explained that Rivington's terms were deceptive and his prices based on unethical practices. Strahan alleged that Rivington had hired obscure printers in the provinces and in Scotland to pirate all the most popular literary properties held by the other booksellers. (Strahan cited several examples, but the offending editions cannot now be identified, perhaps because Rivington used false imprints.) Because he did not pay copy-money, because provincial labor was cheaper, and because he used inferior paper in smaller formats, these reprints were cheaper and at the same time more profitable to Rivington than the authorized editions. Second, he marked down a few of the most popular books as loss leaders to give the impression that all his prices were lower than those of his competitors. On less popular books his prices were actually higher than usual. Third, he sent books without their having been ordered, as Hall himself found when he received twenty more sets of the Smollett than he had asked for. Fourth, Rivington larded his shipments with old, unsalable books, which Strahan called "books of no price" or "waste paper books." These were probably remainders, which at this date were usually pulped. Rivington got them for little or nothing, put them in flashy new bindings, and invoiced them at their original retail prices; thus his 16 percent discount was actually a huge markup.[79] Finally, Rivington stole the customers of other booksellers by simply lying to them about how much lower his prices were.[80]

Strahan guessed that in 1757 and 1758 Rivington exported as many books as the rest of the booksellers put together, though he added the significant caveat that most of them were at his own risk – that is unordered and/or subject to return. This success, or apparent success, enraged those who had been enjoying a lucrative business with America. "This Conduct of his," wrote Strahan to Hall, "has given a general Alarm, and will determine the

Trade, I believe, to take such Measures as will render it impossible for him to undersell them, and rather to sell for no Profit at all than he should gain his ends. . . . The Booksellers are about contriving some Plan, by which they will make a difference in the Price of those Books that are sold to go abroad, and those for Home Consumption, in order to save the Trade to America from falling into the Hands of a Man who will stick at nothing to accomplish his Designs."[81] Strahan duly lowered his prices to Hall, sometimes below cost, and he offered to take back some of the books that Hall had not been able to sell.[82] More aggressively, the holders of the copyrights that Rivington supposedly pirated also planned prosecutions and reprisals.

Strahan and the other booksellers demonized Rivington for not playing by the rules of his trade, yet the fact remains that he opened up the export market to new entrepreneurial methods that were to become much more common in the years ahead. Despite Strahan's bluster, it seems clear that Rivington's prices really were lower, and that he succeeded in driving down wholesale, if not retail, prices. As his unheard-of terms became more usual, the book business became more profitable to Americans, and imported books became more plentiful. This was the greatest change Rivington wrought. His trade in remainders was a failure; William Hunter, for example, thought them "extreme dull," and they do not seem to have sold any better in America than in England. But in the 1770s and 1780s James Lackington did much the same thing with more panache and successfully challenged the London book trade.[83] Finally, Rivington's trade in piracies was a sign of the vast importance the Scottish and Irish reprint trade was about to assume in America. The copyright-holding oligarchy he had dropped out of in the 1750s was being attacked on several fronts by other maverick booksellers using methods similar to his, and in the 1770s many of the practices Strahan thought were unethical or illegal were validated by judicial reinterpretation of the copyright laws.[84] Changes in the American book trade were closely synchronized with changes in the British book trade in this period of late colonial transition.

Though he strove to meet Rivington's terms and prices, Strahan believed that his competitor's methods were fundamentally unsound, and that he would destroy himself. "It is not unlikely that he will in the End lose as much by his dirty and Scandalous Dealings as he once thought to get by it."[85] In 1760 he did indeed go bankrupt, but not for the reasons Strahan predicted. Rivington regularly attended horse races at Newmarket, and after one disastrous day he reviewed his finances, found his debts totalled £36,000, and declared himself a ruined man. As it turned out, however, his assets were almost equally large, and he emerged barely solvent from the bankruptcy proceedings. The failure seems to have been caused more by cash-flow problems than by fundamental unsoundness. At any rate, he bounced back. On the strength of his wife's £300 annuity, he purchased a stock of £3,000 and set out for America. By the end of the year he had opened a bookstore in New York and another in Philadelphia; in 1762 he started a third in Boston. He was playing the same game, only now from the other side.

In advertisements Rivington proclaimed he was "the only London bookseller in America." The fact that he could even claim to be a "London bookseller" was remarkable enough, but what did he mean by that? Partly he meant that his stock was as up-to-date as it was possible to be. For instance, on June 17, 1762, he advertised in the *Pennsylvania Gazette* "A new and excellent Novel (that cannot fail of affecting every Reader of Sensibility) called, The History of Longsword, Earl of Salisbury," a novel first reviewed in the London magazines of March 1762.[86] In other words, he was getting new novels simultaneously with their reviews in the press.

Rivington also meant that the content of his bookstores was unlike anything ever before seen in America. Where Hall seldom listed by name more than a dozen or so novels or plays in his catalogues, Rivington's pamphlet catalogue of summer 1762 consists almost entirely of "Books of Entertainment, &c." running to 782 titles. Many entries are accompanied by long editorial puffs, the most remarkable being entry 781, Rousseau's *Nouvelle Héloise,* published in English just the previous September; Rivington included an eleven-page extract from the preface. By invoking the language of sensibility, as in the puff for *Longsword,* Rivington showed that his stock was right in step with the latest literary fashion, just as his having "the genteelest Assortment of Pinchbeck Buckles ever imported from England" showed he was up to date in sartorial fashion. Hall and most of the others who ran bookstores were by comparison artisans and colonials, while Rivington was a discerning cosmopolitan: this, at least, was the image he wished to project.

Most of all Rivington meant that the prices charged in his store were lower than in other American bookstores, nearly as low, it seems, as he used to charge in London. He announced that he was better acquainted with the prices and characters of books than any American bookseller, that the booksellers of America did not know how to deal with the London trade, and that their customers were being robbed as a result. As in his London days, there was much truth to this claim. Along with the latest London books, he dealt in cheap reprints more extensively than any previous American bookseller. He even sold Irish reprints, the export of which was still illegal. (These were not advertised, but the invoice book of William and Thomas Bradford shows them buying from Rivington in 1769 what can only be Irish reprints.) His lowest wholesale price (in local currency) was a normal 100 percent advance over the cost to him in sterling, but his costs were probably lower on average because he stocked so many reprints.

Rivington did business in America almost as if there were not an ocean between him and England. This is shown most clearly by his edition of the poems of Charles Churchill. He proposed it for publication in 1766 and secured 2,200 subscriptions with no advance payment required, probably the largest such campaign yet mounted in America. The subscribers were from all over the colonies, though primarily from Virginia, Maryland, and the West Indies, with relatively few from New York, Philadelphia, and New England. (By then Rivington had closed his Boston and Philadelphia stores and was spending much of his time in the Chesapeake, so it would appear that he was overseeing the subscription drive in person.) He advertised that his edition would be in two "pocket volumes, at two dollars a set."[87] By this he meant his edition would be a duodecimo; the London edition was in two volumes octavo. Like the Scots and Irish reprinters, he intended to make his edition cheaper by issuing it in a smaller format.

Churchill was the latest literary sensation in England. He had risen from obscurity in 1761 with the satirical poem the *Rosciad*, said to be the most popular such work since Pope's *Dunciad*; but in 1764 dissipation cut short his meteoric career. In 1766 his complete works were published; this is the book that Rivington proposed to reprint.[88] When it came to getting the printing done, however, he ran into unknown difficulties, which delayed him for eighteen months. Possibly the copyright holders brought pressure on him, because in the end, instead of printing the book in America, he actually bought 2,200 copies in sheets of the authorized London octavo edition, the very one he had proposed to reprint. The only change he made was a new title page with no printer's name or place of publication, only the date, 1768.[89] This was the first time that a substantial portion of a valuable literary property had been preempted by the colonial market. (Churchill's copyrights were rumored to be worth £3,000.) That such a portion of the first collected edition of his poems was preempted by the American market is scarcely less remarkable.[90] With Rivington's edition of Churchill's poems, American and British literary culture came closer together than they had ever been before.

Robert Bell and the Beginning of a Native Reprint Trade

The British printers who emigrated to America in the 1740s and 1750s were journeymen, like Gaine and Hall. Those who began to emigrate in the 1760s were more likely to be master printers or even booksellers, and many were from Scotland and Ireland, bred to the trade of reprinting English books.

They saw America as another Scotland, part of the cultural and linguistic orbit of England, but beyond the reach of the English copyright law and the monopolizing power of the London book trade. So they tried to replicate the book trade of Edinburgh or Dublin by publishing their own reprints of English books, which would take the place of not only the London originals but also their Scottish reprints in the American market.

The most successful of this cohort of immigrant reprinters was Robert Bell of Philadelphia. Bell was born in Glasgow about 1731 and served an apprenticeship as a bookbinder. As a young man he moved to Berwick-upon-Tweed to bind for Robert Taylor, the famous piratical printer of that border town. Then in 1759 he moved to Dublin and began a new career as a bookseller, an auctioneer, and presently as a reprint publisher. He was a passionate defender of his right to reprint whatever he pleased, not only copyrighted English books but also books his colleagues in Dublin had already printed or reprinted. Here he went too far. In 1767 he reprinted a pamphlet by another notorious pirate, the Scot Alexander Donaldson, which demonstrated the legality of reprinting, and in a short preface of his own complained that certain Dublin booksellers who were in league with the London trade had "entered into a combination to distress or destroy all other booksellers that will not submit to be slaves of their usurped authoritative determinations." That same year he closed his business and moved to Philadelphia, apparently driven out of town by Irish booksellers whom he had "printed upon."

Bell established himself in Philadelphia in 1768 as a book auctioneer and immediately made an impression with his flamboyant character. His catalogues were spiced with extravagant language. They often bore headlines such as "Jewels and Diamonds, to be sold or sacrificed, by Robert Bell, humble Provedore to the Sentimentalists." Years later the printer William McCulloch recalled the demeanor of the stout impresario of the sale rooms:

> He sold his books at as exorbitant prices as he could command . . . higher at auction than in store. He was full of drollery, and many, going to his auction for the merriment, would buy a book from good humour. It was as good as a play to attend his sales at auction. There were few authors of whom he could not tell some anecdote, which would get the audience in a roar. He sometimes had a can of beer aside him, and would drink comical healths. His buffoonery was diversified and without limit. . . . When Bell was auctioneering one night, he held up, in turn, Babbington's Works, a huge folio. A clever book, said Bell, and if you have patience to go through it, you are welcome. A person, continued he, was going to the gallows, and had it left to his choice either to read Babbington through, or be hung. The fellow looked at it for some time: Well, returned he, I had rather be hung.[91]

From 1768 to 1784 he held more than fifty catalogued auctions, mostly in Philadelphia, but also in New York and Boston, to which he took tons of books by wagon during the Revolutionary War. In 1781 he was involved in the auction of perhaps the largest private library in colonial America, William Byrd of Westover's.

A faint savor of his auction patter can be sensed in the texts of his catalogues, such as this one for an out-of-town sale:

Robert Bell, bookseller, provedore to the sentimentalists, and professor of book-auctioniering in America, is just arrived from Philadelphia; with a small collection of modern, instructive, and entertaining books, which he will exhibit by auction, to the sentimentalists of the town, this evening, and to morrow evening; but no longer – At the time of the exhibition, they will then, instantaneously, either be sold or sacrificed, according to the taste of the company, by way of experiment. . . . Those who behold with their eyes, sentimental entertainment, going off reasonable, and do not improve this very great chance of purchasing the books by the assistance of the magical mallet, will probably wish in vain for such another opportunity.

Before Bell, book advertisements consisted of nothing more than a transcription of their titles; no one had ever used language to sell books in this way.

In Philadelphia Bell also revived his old business of reprinting. In 1769 he advertised for sale by subscription an edition of the new book by the eminent Scottish historian William Robertson, *The History of the Reign of Charles V,* in three volumes octavo. Hardly was this out when he published another large, prestigious book, Blackstone's *Commentaries on the Laws of England* in four volumes octavo (Fig. 8.2). In the words of Isaiah Thomas, these books were "the first fruits of a spirit of enterprise in book printing in that city." They were by far the largest books ever published at the risk and expense of a bookseller in the colonies.

Bell published both books by subscription, which mitigated but by no means eliminated the enormous risk he ran. Subscribers did not pay money in advance but were expected to pay for each volume as it was delivered, thus providing the capital for the next. For Blackstone, he promised to put the work to press as soon as he received 200 subscribers; ultimately he got almost 1,600. The elements of his advertising campaign were repeated over and over: His editions were cheaper than the imports and, because they were printed in America on American paper, they encouraged native manufactures and prevented the export of specie. The London editions of Blackstone, all quartos, sold for as much as $26.00 in Philadelphia, while Bell's octavo edition sold for $8.00. His *Charles V* cost $6.00, half as much as the

CONDITIONS.

I. BLACKSTONE's ſplendid Commentaries on the Laws of England, is to be reprinted in Four Volumes, large Octavo, page for page with the laſt Edition of the London Copy.

II. THE Work is to be printed on a fine Royal Paper, a ſize larger than this, with a handſome large margin, on the ſame Type as the Specimen annexed, and peculiar attention will be given to the correctneſs of the matter, and beauty of the letter-preſs.

III. THE Price of the Four Volumes to Subſcribers, will be only EIGHT DOLLARS, although the Engliſh Edition is ſold at Twenty-ſix Dollars.

IV. As ſoon as the names and reſidence of Two Hundred Subſcribers are collected, the Firſt Volume ſhall immediately be put to the preſs, and the whole Work will be completed ſix months after the publication of the Firſt Volume.

V. No money expected but on the periodical delivery of each Volume in neat Calf Law-Binding, Two Dollars.

VI. THIS ſplendid and expenſive Work, which will coſt above One Thouſand Pounds, can only be carried into execution under the auſpicious Patronage of the Gentlemen of the Law in America, and their liberal connections in the country, as well as the capital cities and towns on the Continent.

VII. THE names of the Subſcribers will be printed in the Fourth Volume.

SUBSCRIPTIONS will be gratefully received by the Publiſher ROBERT BELL, Bookſeller, at the late Union Library, in Third-Street, Philadelphia; and by all the Bookſellers and Printers in America.

Figure 8.2. Robert Bell, Subscription proposal [Philadelphia, 1770] for his edition of Blackstone's *Commentaries*, published 1771–1772. Courtesy of The Library Company of Philadelphia.

London edition. Much of the saving was effected simply by reducing the format and the type size, just as the Dublin reprinters did. As he wrote at the head of the list of the subscribers to *Charles V*, "this American Edition, hath been accomplished at a price so moderate, that the Man of the Woods, as well as the Man of the Court, may now solace himself with Sentimental Delight."

The subscribers' lists show the dimensions of Bell's success. He got buyers for his books in every part of North America in a period when few books were sold beyond the province in which they were printed. Of the almost 1,600 subscribers to Blackstone, more than a sixth were in New England, and almost a third were in the South. He had forty-eight subscribers in the West Indies, six in Florida, and one in New Orleans. He sold more copies in New York (355) than in Pennsylvania (317).

These books were also enterprising in the sense that they were vigorous, even defiant statements of American independence. They were key texts for those intellectuals who had protested the Stamp Act and organized the nonimportation agreements. In the early 1770s he also published James Burgh's *Political Disquisitions* in three volumes octavo and Lord Kames's *Six Sketches on the History of Man*, and he proposed for subscription but did not actually publish Hume's *History of England* and Adam Ferguson's *Essay on the History of Civil Society*. The influence of the Scottish Enlightenment in revolutionary America was magnified enormously by these publications.[92] He also reprinted essential technical works, which had hitherto always been imported, such as Cullen's *Lectures of the Materia Medica* in quarto and Abraham Swan's *Collection of Designs in Architecture* in folio with copper plates. These books can also be viewed as declarations of independence from the London book trade. The original publishers had paid dearly for their copyrights; the sum Robertson received for *Charles V* was the largest ever paid. Bell's reprints effectively shut the purchasers of the rights to copy out of the lucrative colonial market. The London publishers had no more legal recourse against Bell than they had against the publishers of the Dublin reprints; nevertheless, in a preface to the third volume of *Charles V*, Bell defended himself against the charge of piracy. The legal authority for his defense was none other than Blackstone, whose *Commentaries* he was even then starting to reprint, for that jurist held that Ireland and the American colonies were not bound by any act of Parliament unless particularly named. According to Bell:

> Surely, the precedent of the people of Ireland's reprinting every work produced in London, and the great lawyer Blackstone's authority concerning the internal legislation of colonies, are demonstrations of the rectitude of reprinting any, or

every work of excellence in America, without the smallest infringement of the British embargo upon literature. Is it not enough that their embargo prevents Americans from shipping their manufactures of this kind into Britain. Would it not be incompatible with all freedom, if an American's mind must be entirely starved and enslaved in the barren regions of fruitless vacuity, because he doth not wallow in immense riches equal to some British lords.[93]

Along with his weighty enlightenment tomes, Bell also reprinted for the first time in America the new literature of sensibility. Since Franklin's *Pamela* twenty-five years before, not a single full-length English novel had been reprinted in America. Bell did not attempt anything as large as that, but he did reprint a number of new, elegant, and short works, beginning with Johnson's *Rasselas* in 1768 and Sterne's *Sentimental Journey* in 1770. These were truly "Jewels and Diamonds" for the "sentimentalists." In the depths of war, when practically every other printer was either shut down or absorbed in politics, Bell continued in the same vein by publishing the first American editions of Thomson's *Seasons,* Young's *Night Thoughts,* Chesterfield's *Principles of Politeness,* Goethe's *Sorrows of Werther,* Moore's *Travels in Italy,* and three of Henry Mackenzie's sentimental novels, including the popular *Man of Feeling,* along with several plays fresh from London. These books made Bell the first American literary publisher.

As the printer of Blackstone, Robertson, and Burgh, Bell had a profound influence on the Revolutionary generation, but as importer and purveyor of the new literature of sensibility he had an even greater influence on the generation that followed. In Bell's language, a "sentimentalist" was someone who was blessed with the new proto-romantic capacity of sensibility, someone who could weep with Mackenzie's man of feeling or suffer with Goethe's Werther. But most sentimentalists learned to feel by reading the latest sentimental books, not by having hopeless love affairs. Once they had learned to feel, they constantly required new books to keep their emotions at a fever pitch. A sentimentalist was essentially a consumer of books, someone who required them for nourishment, someone who valued them like jewels and diamonds. Bell was their provedore, their purveyor.

As much as the books Bell published looked to the future, the way he sold them was even more an anticipation of the changes that were to take place in American society in the next quarter century. Bell sold books more aggressively and more ingeniously than any of his predecessors. The language in Bell's advertisements was unlike anything America had ever seen. As a writer his only rival in the book trade was Franklin, but Franklin used his astonishing command of the language to improve the manners and the morals of his fellow citizens, not to hawk his books. Bell was the first bookseller to use language to seduce the consumer. Bell's philosophy of bookselling was set out in a number of manifestos he wrote in defence of unrestrained book auctions when the city of Philadelphia made an attempt to license them. Auctions advanced the interests of literature, he wrote:

[N]ot only by the Distribution of Literary Works among the generality of the People, but, more particularly, by enabling the middling Class, (who cannot afford to keep large Collections of Books,) after they have had the Benefit of reading them, to exchange them for others; by which Method, a small Sum employed in the Purchase and Sale of Books, at Auctions, will keep every Individual in a Stock (with little or no Loss) sufficient to Instruct and Improve them in their Hours of Leisure, and relaxation from Business.[94]

Without auctions, he wrote elsewhere, people are condemned to read the few books they have over and over, whereas with auctions they can "immediately transform them into new acquisitions of Learning, by causing them to skip from Shelf to Shelf, and thus acquire an intimate acquaintance with NEW AUTHORS."[95] In passages like these, Bell showed a precocious insight into the revolution in reading that was getting underway. He may have been the first American bookseller to understand the mentality of extensive reading, to encourage it in his customers, and to make it the foundation of his business.

Bell anticipated not only the new mentality of extensive reading but the commercialization of every aspect of American society that was just beginning. His opposition to monopolies in publishing and auctioneering was based on a general faith in a free market. His auctions applied that principle on the microeconomic level, establishing real market values for books, neatly adjusting supply and demand, accelerating the circulation of books, and expanding the circle of readers. Bell understood the dynamics of economic growth. His contemporaries thought like mercantilists in zero-sum terms; if you sell one book, that is one book less that I can sell. Bell knew better. As early as 1774 he wrote, "The more BOOKS are sold, the more will be sold . . . For the Sale of one BOOK propagateth the Sale of another, with as much certainty as the Possession of one Guinea helpeth to the Possession of another."[96] Bell initiated thousands into the joys of extensive reading, at the same time drawing them into the nascent consumer revolution (Fig. 8.3).

Finally, Bell anticipated transformations in the way books were published in America, transformations he did not live to see unfold in the following decade. He systematically replicated the trade practices of the Scots-Irish reprinters, and he consistently reached beyond his region to a national market. Franklin and others had reprinted English books, but Bell reprinted more and bigger books than anyone ever had, and he was the only colonial printer to make this practice the focus of his business. In fact, though he had a press, he

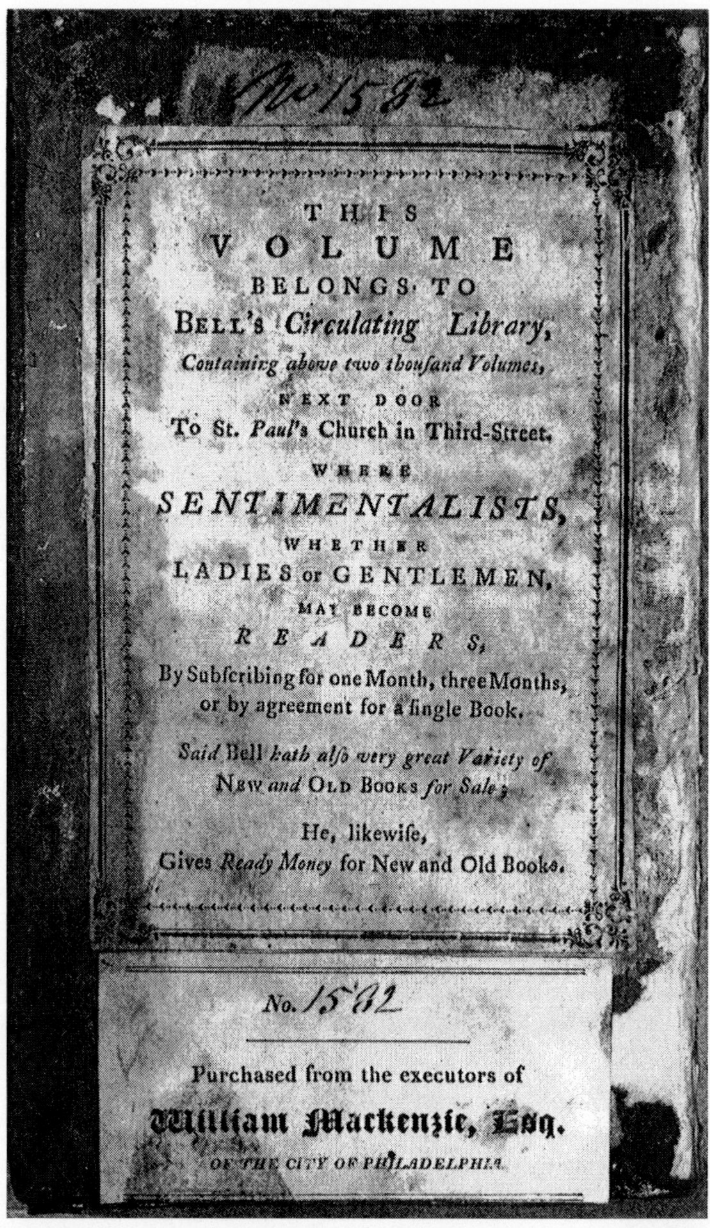

No 1582

THIS
VOLUME
BELONGS TO
BELL'S *Circulating Library*,
Containing above two thouſand Volumes,
NEXT DOOR
To St. *Paul's* Church in Third-Street.
WHERE
SENTIMENTALISTS,
WHETHER
LADIES or GENTLEMEN,
MAY BECOME
READERS,
By Subſcribing for one Month, three Months,
or by agreement for a ſingle Book.

Said Bell *hath alſo very great Variety of*
NEW *and* OLD BOOKS *for Sale*;

He, likewiſe,
Gives *Ready Money* for New and Old Books.

No. 1582

Purchased from the executors of
William Mackenzie, Esq.
OF THE CITY OF PHILADELPHIA

Figure 8.3. Bookplate of Bell's Circulating Library, Philadelphia (ca. 1775). Courtesy of The Library Company of Philadelphia.

did not print most of his large books; he hired other printers to do that for him. He was not a printer at all in the Franklinian mode; he never printed a newspaper, an almanac, or a law. Nor was he a bookseller in the David Hall mode; though he kept a bookstore, he was not much of a book importer. He was neither a printer nor a bookseller but something new: a publisher.

The Book Trade during the Revolutionary Era, 1764–1783

The colonial book trade was utterly transformed during the period that began with the Stamp Act crisis in 1764 and lasted through the peace of 1783. No longer could any printer attempt to operate on a strictly commercial basis or maintain political neutrality. The number of people involved in the book trade grew ever faster, but as entry into the trade became easier, exit was even more rapid. Many of the new players were not bred to the trade, while others were immigrants who brought new ways of doing business. As newspapers multiplied, it became common for the content to be determined by editors chosen for their political views rather than by their printers. Or, if the editor was a printer, he had to become sensitive to every change in the political winds. Once the trade in British books was curtailed by nonimportation agreements and then by war, Americans were forced to subsist on a diet of newspapers and pamphlets, most of them about the war, which they nevertheless consumed more avidly than ever before. As the printing trades became subject to the furious energies released by war, they became less coherent.

An early sign of this politicization of print was the reaction to the 1764 Paxton Rebellion, a rowdy protest by back-country Scots-Irish against the refusal of the Quaker-dominated assembly to appropriate money for defense against Indians. This episode gave rise to the largest spate of scurrilous political pamphlets since the 1720s, as well as the first American engraved political cartoons (Fig. 8.4). The feisty mood continued into the assembly election in the fall of 1764, when Franklin was lambasted for calling German immigrants "Palatine Boors." Again pamphlets and cartoons poured from the presses. This unprecedented license set the stage for resistance to the Stamp Act.

The Stamp Act established a tax on print and on paper: on newspapers, almanacs, legal forms, and advertisements in newspapers. It was an extension to the colonies of taxes that had been levied (at slightly higher levels) in England for many years. Just as Parliament believed the colonies were wealthy enough to pay for their own defense, so it assumed that the American print trade was almost as developed as that of England, and that it functioned in society in much the same way. The leaders of the resistance against the act were those who stood to lose the most by it, newspaper

Figure 8.4. "An Indian Squaw King Wampum Spies, / Which makes his lustful passions rise" [Philadelphia, 1764]; drawn and engraved by Henry Dawkins, an English engraver who emigrated ca. 1753 (d. 1786?). The Paxton Rebellion of 1764 inspired the first American political cartoons: on the left, Israel Pemberton ("King Wampum"), richest of the Quaker Indian traders, caresses an Indian woman, who is stealing his gold watch; in the middle, armed Quakers drill in ragged ranks, while a pacifist Quaker sleeps nearby; on the right, Franklin, concealed behind a curtain, orchestrates the conflict for his own advantage. Courtesy of The Library Company of Philadelphia.

printers and papermakers. They were successful precisely because American newspapers had acquired the ability to reflect and to shape public opinion.

Nonimportation agreements were an important part of this resistance, and they seriously affected book imports. David Hall and William Bradford signed the Philadelphia agreement of 1769 because their viability as newspaper editors was more important to them, but James Rivington did not, and his trade in imports was ruined.[97] In 1766 he closed his Boston and Philadelphia stores and in 1768 he petitioned for bankruptcy. In an increasingly anti-British climate, his London-style bookstore was no longer the rage.[98] The disrupted trade in part moved to other channels. Tory merchants dealing in books for the first time found different sources of supply in Britain. For example, during a second round of nonimportation in 1768 a Glaswegian merchant named William Semple advertised "a great collection of Books" that he had "Just imported in the last vessels from Glasgow, Liverpool and Ayr."[99]

David Hall supported nonimportation but was afraid to oppose the stamp tax in his newspaper because Franklin supported it. (His contract expressly forbade printing anything embarrassing to his partner.) He alone among all the American newspaper printers attempted neutrality on this issue; there were not many who would argue in favor of the act, but Hall

When Danger's threaten tis mere Nonsense
To talk of such a thing as Conscience
To Arms to Arms with one Accord
The Sword of Quakers and the Lord.
Fill Bumpers then of Rum or Arrack
We'll drink Success to the new Barrack.

Fight Dog! fight Bear! you're all my Friend
By you I shall attain my Ends
For I can never be content
Till I have got the Government.
But if from this Attempt I fall
Then let the Devil take you all.

found them and printed their views. This cost him 500 canceled subscriptions to the *Gazette* and a big drop in advertisements by the middle of October 1765.[100] When the tax took effect November 1, he ceased publication of the *Gazette* and did not resume it under his own name until after his partnership with Franklin expired in 1766.[101] His neutrality had made a powerful enemy in Joseph Galloway, who got the government printing contract transferred to his protégé William Goddard. Goddard then began *The Pennsylvania Chronicle,* which was entirely under Galloway's editorial control, and the first party-controlled newspaper in the middle colonies since Zenger's. By 1770 it had 2,500 subscribers and the *Gazette* had sunk to third place in circulation.[102] As the political stakes rose, the editing of a newspaper was becoming too important a job to leave to a mere printer.

In another sign of changing times, Rivington turned printer for the first time and began a Tory newspaper in 1773. His slavish devotion to the British and his readiness to print any rumor or slander against the patriots made him one of the most loathed men in America. Soon every newspaper in the middle colonies was either Tory or Patriot. From 1774 to 1785 twenty-five newspapers were begun in New York, twenty-two in Pennsylvania, and eight in New Jersey. The great chameleon of newspapers was Hugh Gaine's *New-York Mercury*. He kept it moderately whiggish until the British occupation, when he slipped away to Newark. There he attempted to print a patriot newspaper, but found few subscribers. When the British were about to invade New Jersey, Gaine crept back into New York and resumed his paper as a Tory.

The superintendent of the press for the British advised subsidizing newspapers because apart from "the indecent Harangues of the Preachers, none has had a more extensive or stronger Influence than the Newspapers of the respective Colonies. One is astonished to see with what Avidity they are sought after, and how implicitly they are believed, by the great Bulk of the People."[103] Rivington was named King's Printer, while Gaine was largely forgotten and forgiven by the end of the war. Rivington escaped prosecution by pretending that he had been a spy for the Americans all along. Later, both men made a living as booksellers but never again as newspaper printers. In Pennsylvania the Tory newspaper printers James Humphreys, Benjamin Towne, and Christopher Saur III were denounced as traitors after the British left Philadelphia. Saur and Humphreys fled to Nova Scotia, while Towne artfully changed his politics. Humphreys returned to Philadelphia as a bookseller in 1797.

The output of the press during the war was limited to the bare essentials; after newspapers and political pamphlets, the next largest category of print was government documents. The former colonies continued to print laws and proclamations either in their old capitals or in temporary headquarters at such places as Poughkeepsie, New York, or Lancaster, Pennsylvania. Whole printing offices were constantly being moved from one town to another at a moment's notice in order to keep the official print flowing. In many towns local authorities or self-constituted Committees of Safety churned out public notices and handbills, and where the British were in occupation, proclamations were issued on large sheets blazoned with the royal arms. The Continental Congress, constituting a new level of national government, periodically issued journals of its actions as well as numerous proclamations such as the famous one of July 4, 1776.

The number of extant American imprints reached its colonial peak in 1774–1776, reaching 1,000 in 1775, but most of these were broadsides of a half sheet or less; the *Declaration of Independence* was printed on a full sheet to underscore its exceptional importance. Edition sizes varied widely; printer's bills exist for a 1776 German address to the Hessians in 6,100 copies and a printing of a draft of the Articles of Confederation in 50 copies.[104] As the war dragged on the financial situation worsened, money and paper both became scarce, and legislators thought twice about printing even a broadside. In 1781, the worst year of the war, Congress in Philadelphia issued only ten half-sheet broadsides.

The largest public printing project of the war was the annual octavo volumes of the journals of the Continental Congress, which ranged from 300 to 800 pages or 20 to 50 sheets each. The first two volumes were printed by Robert Aitken in editions of 700 and 800.[105] Inflation raised the cost of printing to unbelievable heights; in 1779 John Dunlap and Robert Aitken submitted bills totaling over $11,000 for printing the journals. The third volume, printed by Dunlap in York, Pennsylvania in 1778, was limited supposedly to fifty copies, just enough for the legislators' own use.[106]

Legislatures understood quite well the importance of the press in governing the divided colonies and winning the war, but they resisted getting too deeply into the business of publishing. Most of their official documents reached a wider public when they were reprinted or excerpted separately or in newspapers up and down the seaboard. They counted on a deeply entrenched trade practice of reprinting for the real promulgation of their documents. Every official broadside was also printed in the newspapers. Extracts from the journals of the first Continental Congress in 1774 were reprinted at least twenty-eight times in various towns, including an edition in German, not counting newspaper printings. Steuben's *Regulations for the Order and Discipline of the Troops,* of which at least 3,000 copies were printed for the War Office in 1779, was reissued twice in a condensed form by John Dickinson for the use of the Pennsylvania militia, and was reprinted in full at least four times in Boston and Hartford in 1781 and 1782. The official printing of the *Declaration of Independence* was a broadside of about a hundred copies printed by John Dunlap. The edition was distributed among members of Congress, who saw that a copy reached every printer in their home states. The official printing was meant to ensure the authority and accuracy of scores of reprints in newspapers, magazines, broadsides, and pamphlets; it was the prototype, not the text people actually read.

Authors and Printers at War: *Common Sense*

Thomas Paine's *Common Sense* did more to move the American public toward independence than any other writing, and with numerous editions in the colonies, it was clearly the first American best-seller. It was also the first American book to make enough money for the author and the publisher to quarrel over it. Paine chose Robert Bell to publish his book on the recommendation of Benjamin Rush, who touted him as a courageous republican printer. To preserve his anonymity he did not deal directly with Bell but rather through agents who negotiated the publication on the half-profits system. Bell took all the risk, both financial and political, since only his name appeared on the title page; after the expenses of printing had been paid, Bell was to divide any profit equally with Paine. When the pamphlet proved successful, Paine decided to use his share of the profit to buy mittens for the Continental Army, and he sent his agents to settle the account and collect his money. They disputed miscellaneous charges for stitching, advertising, and so forth amounting to either £4 (according to Bell) or £14 (according to Paine's agents), and they reported to Paine that Bell was trying to cheat him. Paine chose to receive nothing rather than accept less than he figured he was due, and took his revenge by publicly (and anonymously) accusing Bell of defrauding the army of its mittens.[107]

Since there was no copyright law in America, there was now the problem of determining who had the right to print the next edition of *Common Sense*. Bell followed the Irish usage called "courtesy of the trade," whereby the printer of the first edition had that right. Following the spirit of the English copyright law, Paine felt that he had the right to his own work and that any right Bell may have had was forfeited by his failure to pay. Paine therefore published a second edition with William Bradford, and Bell retaliated by printing another unauthorized edition. For Bradford's edition, Paine wrote a new appendix specifically to make Bell's unauthorized edition inferior. Bell promptly reprinted it and offered it for free to any purchaser of his edition. Thus with some justice Bell claimed he did not try to profit from Paine's work but rather gave it away.

Common Sense was reprinted endlessly, and Paine often complained that Bell had robbed him of his profits. After the war his story was used to good effect by advocates of an American copyright law. Perhaps this dispute with Bell was inevitable since there were as yet no laws to govern the relationship between an author and a publisher, nor even any agreement on whose old-world customs should obtain in the New World. In this case Bell's antimonopoly views prevailed, and *Common Sense* was reprinted far more often and circulated far more widely than it could have been if Paine had somehow succeeded in securing his rights as an author. At least twenty-one editions of part 1 appeared in eleven different towns in 1776.

The Book Trade in War and Peace

Throughout the colonial period more people owned and read the Bible than any other book, yet no avowed American edition (in English) had ever been printed. This was widely seen as a symbol of the colonial dependence of American printers, and so in 1777 the question of how Bibles were to be printed commanded the attention of the Continental Congress. The immediate cause of the discussion was a petition from a group of Presbyterian clergymen noting that Bibles were scarce and costly since the war had halted their importation from England. Behind their petition lay the question of whether some republican analogue to the royal Bible patent was needed or its publication should be left to the realm of commerce. The committee appointed to consider the petition consulted with five printers, all of whom reported that the job could only be done economically by printing an edition of 30,000 or more, and that not enough type and paper could be had in America. Even then they estimated that the Bibles would cost more than 6*s*. a copy, two to three times what Scots Bibles cost.[108] The committee concluded that rather than import paper and type, it was better to import Bibles from Holland or Scotland and have them sent directly to the various Atlantic ports. Even without the constraint of the Bible patent, it was still cheaper and easier to import just where the demand was.[109]

The most ambitious of the printers consulted by the committee was Robert Aitken of Philadelphia, who based his estimate on an edition of 200,000. When Congress failed to act on the committee's recommendation, he printed the New Testament on his own. Still, he hesitated to print a full Bible. In early 1781 he petitioned Congress for some kind of subsidy or patent for Bible printing and, while he waited for their response, began work on the rest of the Bible. In August 1782, still without any response from Congress, he announced its forthcoming publication in a circular letter, which tellingly left a blank space where its price was to be filled in.[110] Six weeks later, Congress finally reported on Aitken's petition; heartily recommending his edition to the citizens, the government offered him no tangible support. By then, Bibles from Holland had begun to arrive in American ports. He published his edition early in 1783, just before word reached Philadelphia of the preliminary articles of peace, which signaled the resumption of imports of all sorts. At first he had charged 15*s*. a copy wholesale, but in June 1783 he lowered his price to 8*s*., and by November it was down to 5*s*.; three years later he sold as low as 2*s*. 6*d*.[111] Aitken later claimed to have printed 10,000 copies[112] though his own account books show only 2,000 sold. He also claimed to have lost huge sums, ranging as high as £4,000 in various accounts.[113] His venture was disastrous because the price of Bibles in the American market was determined by the cost of imports, not by his cost of production, margin of profit, or any factor he could control. It was as if culturally and economically America were still a colony of Great Britain.

Undeterred by Aitken's ordeal, Robert Bell could not wait to take up book publishing right where he had left off before the war. In 1784 he reprinted William Buchan's popular *Domestic Medicine* and published an important original work, Jonathan Carver's *Travels* into the new domain of the Northwest Territory. Nor was Aitken as discouraged as he pretended to be, since he reprinted Blair's *Lectures on Rhetoric* in an elegant quarto format, and even exported some of the edition to Scotland. But before the year was out, Bell died on the way to South Carolina with a load of books for auction, and postwar optimism began to evaporate as a serious depression set in. Type, paper, and money were now in such short supply that the few printers who had survived the war were barely able to continue their newspapers, much less print books. Meanwhile, British and Irish booksellers were sending over agents with consignments of thousands of pounds worth of books to be sold on any reasonable terms. Gradually those printers with access to capital or credit managed to reestablish contacts with Britain and direct the trade into their own hands; but the glut of imported books made it even harder to contemplate printing American editions.

The obstacles to American publishing seemed overwhelming. Not a single edition of the full Bible was printed in America for the rest of the 1780s, and hardly any other books of substance were published. Nevertheless the desire to establish an American publishing industry remained strong among printers because of their nationalist ideology and their entrepreneurial conviction that publishing was the way to wealth in their trade. The economics continued to be against them for the rest of the decade. Not until the 1790s were they able to realize their ambition and to bring to a belated end the colonial period in the American book trade. How they accomplished this transformation will be discussed in the next volume.

PART TWO. GERMAN AND DUTCH BOOKS AND PRINTING

A. GREGG ROEBER

GERMAN SPEAKERS AND WRITERS comprised the largest group of non-British European arrivals in the eighteenth-century mainland colonies. Almost a century beforehand, in the 1620s, the Dutch had transferred a lively language of their own. Once the founders of New Netherland surrendered their colonial enterprise to English conquest, and as migration to New York from the homeland ceased, the Dutch language in both spoken and written form became marginalized over the course of the next century. Yet trade declined more slowly, and reading from Dutch books more slowly still through the balance of the eighteenth century.[114]

The history of the book trade for these two linguistically related European peoples had much to do with settlement patterns, their numbers in relation to the dominant English speakers, and especially the timing and construction of transatlantic networks based on the German book trade. These networks were also affected by British regulations governing the importation of foreign literature. At the moment that these regulations disappeared, an important transition was occurring in the German-language book trade. Another transition took place in the aftermath of the Revolution as the longstanding fabric of international connections gave way to an indigenous but more provincial taste in German letters disseminated by a widely dispersed set of newspaper editors and booksellers. Of more importance, a gap widened between German-language secular, rational books, identified with the forces of political reform in the German states, and the Pietist tracts whose consumers were often enough supporters of reactionary monarchy in Europe. This dialectic, intensified after 1789 by disagreements concerning the revolution in France, presented German-American literary efforts and discussions centered at Philadelphia with impossible choices. By 1800 these tensions undermined a brief era of sophisticated promise in both religious and secular German-language book production and sales in North America, as we shall see.

New Netherland and the Trade in Dutch Books

The history of the German-language book *about* North America antedated the arrival of German-speakers *in* that part of the world, as Sebastian Brant's *Narrenschiff* (*Ship of Fools*) of 1494 testifies. From 1493 until the outbreak of the Thirty Years' War at least 400 known, published books sought to inform readers of German about the geography, peoples, flora and fauna, and history of the Americas. The most influential book *by* a German speaker was in Latin, Georg Bauer's (Agricola) *De re metallica* (1556), which accompanied German speakers to the Spanish mines, where they pioneered the mercury-amalgamation process. Though these economic motives for migration, and therefore the need for practical books, never vanished, the religious wars in Europe and, in their aftermath, the difficult situation of certain Protestant sects, affected the flow of emigrants to such an extent that religious books dominated the German-language trade in North America for almost the entirety of the seventeenth and eighteenth centuries.[115]

German speakers and their books appeared both in the London Company of Virginia's colony after 1607 and in substantial numbers in New

Netherland. For neither group can we accurately reconstruct the number and kinds of imported German-language books. The early migration of German speakers before 1648 came predominantly from north-German towns of the Hanseatic League and neighboring territories. The devastation wrought by the Thirty Years' War depopulated the German southwest for the better part of the next century. Its repopulation and tradition of in- and out-migration made the region the primary source of subsequent emigration to North America.

As population was restored to pre-1618 levels by the 1740s, the book trade also reemerged, but with a new emphasis.[116] This new emphasis owed much to the extraordinarily influential continental religious movement known as Pietism. In its mainstream form it demanded a reinvigoration of the state churches (Lutheran and Reformed), but the movement also produced separatist-radical spokespersons and sects. Influenced by the modes of using print that emerged during the Reformation, both groups created sophisticated trans-European networks of distribution that enabled them to flood the market with broadsides, pamphlets, and books, most of these in the form of hymnals, catechisms, devotional manuals, and critiques of social and political corruption.[117]

Beforehand, however, the arrival of German-language books in North America in the seventeenth century remained in exclusively private channels. Private distributors, often persons engaged in trade or employing ships' captains, supplied New Netherland in the seventeenth century with Dutch- and German-language books. Contrary to some accounts, the conquest of New Netherland in 1664 did not end commercial contacts for Dutch speakers in New York with their former homeland. A limited, Dutch-language literature continued to circulate well into the eighteenth century, with a brief resurgence in the midst of a religious renewal among Dutch Pietists in the 1720s.[118] German-speaking immigrants to New Netherland to 1664, comprising a third of known migrants to that colony, included Johannes Theodorus Polhemius, the first Dutch Reformed minister, who in 1655 settled in Long Island. Such persons certainly brought German books with them, but no known commercial network supplied them after their arrival. What made the demand for Dutch-language materials unusually high in New Netherland was the literacy rate, which reflected the rate in the Netherlands itself. As of 1700, perhaps 80 percent of males and 60 percent of females were fluent in written and printed forms of the Dutch language.[119]

The libraries in New Netherland were much larger than is commonly supposed. Bibles and theological or devotional literature provided the principal reading material in New Netherland households, though other forms of Dutch-language books also enjoyed an eager readership. No systematic survey exists of all surviving estate inventories, but history, geography, Dutch–English dictionaries, surveyors' handbooks, bound volumes of Dutch newspapers, and even cheap popular literature in the form of romances evidently made their way into the colony.[120] As early as 1656 one inventory reveals an extensive German-language book collection ranging from works on geography and world history to more predictable devotional tracts and the Bible. The probate inventory for the bookseller Abraham delaNoy in 1702 reveals sixty-nine personal titles as well as a commercial stock of German books in Dutch translation, imported German and Dutch versions of the Heidelberg Catechism, and Gellius de Bouma's catechism, itself an adaptation of a German Palatine commentary on the Heidelberg Catechism.[121] These ownership and distribution patterns support the conclusion that New Netherland purchasers followed Continental tastes in religious and secular literature. Cheaper books are not recorded, of course, since they had no monetary value.[122]

With the arrival of the German-speaking Mennonites at Germantown in 1683 the cross-fertilization between Dutch and Germans in both the Old and New Worlds helped to foster a fragile, personal network connecting Pennsylvania to the Mennonite community at Amsterdam. That city, which supplied Bibles, hymnals, and copies of the New Testament to New Netherland, performed the same function for Penn's colonial mixture of Dutch and German speakers. In some respects, however, the history of the German-language book in America begins with Francis Daniel Pastorius, the Frankfurt jurist and leader of the 1683 group. Fluent in seven languages, Pastorius wrote some of the earliest accounts about North America in German from personal observation. Unlike the 1618 Oppenheim pamphlet rhapsodizing on the supposed glories of Virginia (*Was die Adelspersonen und andere in Virginia für Kurtzweil haben können*), Pastorius's 1684 "Reliable Information from America" and 1692 "Brief Geographical Description . . ." were careful reports that laid the ground for his *Umständige geographische Beschreibung der zu allerletzt erfundenen Provintz Pensylvania, in denen End-Gräntzen Americæ in des West-Welt gelegen*, published in Frankfurt in 1700.[123]

Both the history of the German-language book and of German-speakers in America changed decisively with the "Palatine" or southwest German emigration that began in 1709, resumed in 1727, and peaked in 1753. German speakers now arriving in British North America came overwhelmingly from the Palatinate, Kraichgau, Württemberg, Baden-Durlach and neighboring towns and territories of the German southwest. Predominantly Lutheran and Reformed in religion, they emigrated in family groups and, by the 1770s, boasted a literacy rate that approached 90 percent. Out of their demands for printed materials sprang the dominantly religious character of both imported and North American German printed matter. Devotional and practical manuals shaped the transfer of German-language culture to North America in the course of the eighteenth century.[124]

German-Language Printing in the Colonies

The Philadelphia printer Andrew Bradford issued the earliest publication by a German colonist, Johann Conrad Beissel's *Mysterion Anomias* (1728), the first version of which may have circulated privately as early as 1725. This and other early German-language books were issued in octavo or quarto form, averaging about twenty-eight pages; they were devoted to disputes among sectarian or free-church groups or to attacks by these radicals on the clergy of the Reformed or Lutheran state churches. Thus, the essay by Georg Michael Weiss, *Der in der Americanische Wildnuß* (1729) appeared out of one such controversy. Benjamin Franklin's attempt three years later to curry favor with the emerging German-speaking population failed in the form of a newspaper but succeeded modestly in the form of the 200-page hymn collection in octavo, the *Vorspiel der Neuen Welt*.

These indigenous productions reflected the radical-Pietist flavor of early German settlement before the majority of migrants from the Lutheran and Reformed churches came to prominence after midcentury. Given shelter in the county of Wittgenstein, one of the radical sects, the Philadelphians, had issued a periodical, the *Geistliche Fama*, which, bound as a book, found its way to Pennsylvania in the 1730s. To avoid potential legal problems, one of these imprints actually lists Philadelphia as its place of publication. Other groups – for example, the Schwenkfelders – resorted to scribal production of hymnody, prayers, and treatises some of which were bound in leather for durability. Works of this genre by authors such as Christopher Schultz or Christopher Hoffman circulated privately. Only the rarest of copies survive.[125]

Pride of place among the indigenous producers and distributors of German-language books belongs to Christopher Saur. This free-church Pietist began printing a German-language almanac at Germantown, Pennsylvania, in 1738. Saur's Frankfurt connections included Heinrich Luther, who eventually provided the *Fraktur* types for Saur's press (Fig. 8.5). But Luther also knew Christoph Schütz of Homburg von der Höhe, who in 1729 had sent multiple copies of the *Geistliches Harffenspiel* to Saur for distribution among the Baptist Brethren, the radical Pietists with whom, at least briefly, Saur was affiliated.[126] Saur printed the first books in *Fraktur*, beginning with the *Zionitischer Weyrauchshügel* (1739), a compilation of Ephrata hymns written largely by Conrad Beissel. Three issues of Luther's translation of the Bible (Arndt & Eck, *First Century*, no. 47) followed in 1743. It fell to another printing office established within the radical-Pietist Ephrata community to

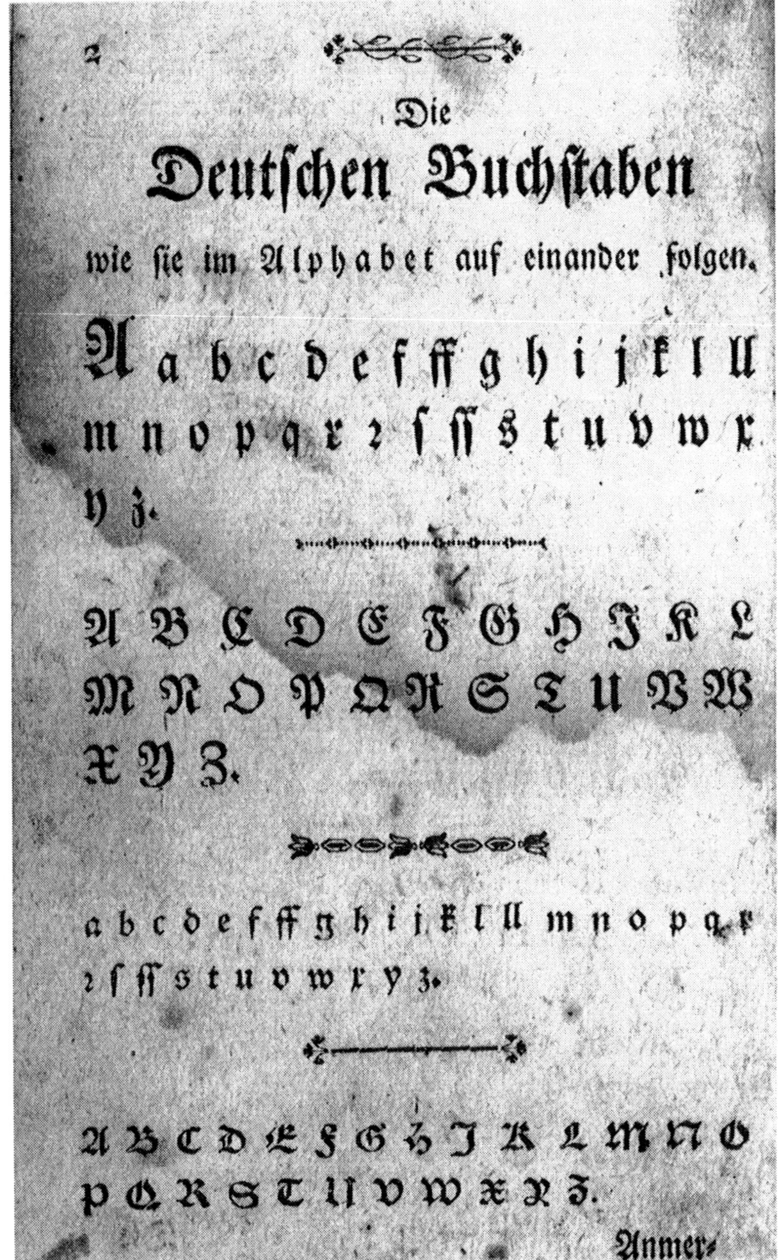

2

Die
Deutschen Buchstaben
wie sie im Alphabet auf einander folgen.

A a b c d e f ff g h i j k l ll
m n o p q r r ſ ſſ s t u v w x
y z.

A B C D E F G H J K L
M N O P Q R S T U V W
X Y Z.

a b c d e f ff g h i j k l ll m n o p q r
r ſ ſſ s t u v w x y z.

A B C D E F G H J K L M N O
P Q R S T U V W X Y Z.

Anmer-

Figure 8.5. "Die deutschen Buchstaben," from *Ein wohl eingerichtetes deutsches ABC-Buchstabir- und Lesebuch* (Germantaun, Pa.: Michael Billmeyer, 1792); this page of "A Well-arranged German ABC, Speller, and Reader" shows *Fraktur* (at the top of the page) and *Schwabacher* (the black-letter equivalent of italic) at the bottom. American Antiquarian Society.

publish in 1748 Johann Peter Miller's German translation of the Dutch Mennonite Tieleman Janszoon van Braght's classic, *Der Blutige Schau-Platz oder Martyerer Spiegel*, better known under its English title as the "Martyrs' Mirror." This last-named publication had provided a unique identity for persecuted Mennonites in Europe. Its translation into German in Pennsylvania illustrates just how different the political conditions of the New World were.[127]

Between 1728 and 1800, some 1,200 German-language titles, exclusive of broadsides, were printed within what later became the boundaries of the United States. The largest share (about a fifth of production down to 1790) was produced by the Saur press. Over the next thirty years, another 1,800 imprints paralleled the overall increase in population and the proliferation of presses into western Pennsylvania, Maryland, Virginia, and North Carolina. If North America is defined as including the present boundaries of Canada, then the list of published works would grow even longer, for by 1758 Anton Henrich had arrived in Halifax, Nova Scotia. His almanac, the *Neuschottländische Calender*, survives only for the period 1788–1801, but emigrants to Nova Scotia brought the usual copies of the German Bible and devotional manuals such as Johann Starck's prayerbook and the sermons of southwest German divines such as the Württemberg preacher Samuel Brastberger. So did their counterparts as far south as Georgia.[128]

Together with the documented numbers of indigenous printed materials – the majority of German-language imprints – the supply of books included an undocumented quantity of imports which, after the 1730s, arrived via private connections as well as through a new set of commercial networks. Those commercial networks arose in the context of a well-established link between London and a central agency of mainstream Pietism, the Hamburg–Altona depot of the Francke Foundations at Halle, in Prussia. Almost simultaneously, this network, which also used Rotterdam and Amsterdam as points of shipment to supply both Pennsylvania and Georgia German speakers at Ebenezer, the Pietist colony on the Savannah River, was challenged as secular traders, whose roots lay in German-speaking Europe from Switzerland and the German southwest to Silesia and Prussia in the east, began in the 1740s to offer their services as book traders and agents. With the appearance of Saur's almanac and newspaper by 1740, advertisements for books helped the Pennsylvania booksellers and importers to solidify their clientele's dependency on these entrepreneurs for access to European books.[129]

Under the provisions of the Navigation Acts, foreign books were considered contraband if not shipped through Britain and duties paid. But the Halle Pietists had established connections with British patrons via their membership in the Society for Promoting Christian Knowledge since 1701. Thanks to lobbying efforts carried on by the Lutheran royal chaplains to

George I in London, they persuaded British officials that books and pamphlets sent with medicines and clothing items constituted charitable gifts, not commercial goods. Sales of the Canstein Bible Institute publications were a major source of income for the Foundations, profits that in turn were systematically reinvested in other philanthropic enterprises, that is, the missions in Tranquebar and the support of pastors called to congregations in North America.[130]

The Halle Orphanage exports from 1748 to 1800 suggest the sophisticated and eclectic nature of their buyers' interests. Medical, political, geographical, and botanical texts accompanied the occasional collection of fables and odes. Priced for specific American markets in Pennsylvania and Georgia, the books epitomize the close connection between timing and types of migration that created the demand for the printed German word. Although the early Palatine migration to New York meant that the inevitable collection of hymnals, prayerbooks, and Bibles arrived with the immigrants, English authorities quickly tried to provide German-language copies of the *Book of Common Prayer* in order to wean these Lutheran and Reformed peoples from their confessional allegiances. In this, the English failed. Moreover, New York faded as a major port of entry for German imports or the seat of a German-language press, in favor of Philadelphia.

In part, the Francke Foundations were responsible for these developments. As relations between the colonial authorities and the German speakers in New York worsened in the second decade of the eighteenth century, further migrations out of that province helped rekindle the old interest in Pennsylvania among German speakers, an idea first awakened in the 1680s by the founding of the colony and William Penn's recruiting trips up the Rhine. When the Halle Lutheran Pietists were approached in the 1730s by Christopher Saur, who offered initially to be their printer, their interest in that colony heightened. Simultaneously, the Halle fathers were supporting an experiment on the Savannah River in the new colony of Georgia. By the mid-1730s, books and printed materials from Halle began arriving both at Philadelphia and Savannah, consigned in the former case to the Silesian bookseller Daniel Weisiger, in the latter to the pastors Johann Martin Boltzius and Israel Gronau.

To German speakers in Georgia, Halle sent not only the usual copies of New Testaments, devotional manuals, and tracts, but also bound volumes of German newspapers. Between 1739 and 1775 German speakers could obtain volumes of the *Preußische Nachrichten* and the *Hallesche Zeitung* in Georgia as well as astronomical calendars or Greek grammars, all ordered by the pastors or teachers who had a standing account with the orphanage at Halle. The Swiss immigrant Johannes Tobler ordered Jablonsky's *Lexikon aller Künste und Wissenschaft* by 1756. To fill out chests of books that were packed tightly and then sealed against water damage, the Halle fathers included gratis defective and unbound Bibles, or a series of religious tracts all bound together as one "book."[131] As one might expect, bindings and covers were usually simple, with many copies in *Papp-Papier*, or cardboard. Yet the 1735–1736 shipment to Weisiger included a cordovan leather copy of Rambach's *Betrachtungen* and Martin Luther's *Postille* in folio, both costing between 1 and 2 Reichstaler (i.e., 5*s.* to 10*s.*).[132]

To the Mennonite and Lutheran networks the Moravians added their own by the 1740s. With strong connections that bound Herrenhut in Saxony to Württemberg converts and cells in the Wetterau in the western part of the old Reich, the Moravians also enjoyed contacts with Dutch coreligionists and shippers. Initial book shipments that supplied the settlements of Bethlehem and Nazareth extended to the new Carolina settlements by the 1750s, although the exact numbers of books imported by the Moravians remains uncertain. To these networks, we may add collections of books gathered by individual Reformed and Lutheran congregations. For example, the Hebron (Virginia) Lutherans assembled on a trip through Germany in the late 1730s a parish library that included several hundred religious titles; a collection of a hundred titles for New York Lutherans chosen by Pastor Wilhelm Christoph Berkenmeyer had more than tripled in size by his death in 1751.[133]

The least documented dimension of German book trade and consumption for the eighteenth century centers around the small community of Roman Catholic German speakers of Pennsylvania. Certainly the German translation of the Bible by Hieronymus Emser and Johann Dietenberger was known among these Catholics. This handful of German speakers was served by a succession of Jesuit priests beginning with Theodore Schneider, a former professor of philosophy and polemics at Liège. Because Schneider built the Goshenhoppen chapel and taught school in his rectory, Catholic books in German may well have circulated in Pennsylvania before the Revolution. If so, no lists of libraries or devotional manuals seem to survive from Schneider's ministry or from that of his successor, the Württemberg-born Jesuit Ferdinand Steinmeyer. Only in 1787 does a bilingual hymnal compiled by John Aitken and printed for St. Mary's Church, Philadelphia contain a number of German hymns. By 1796, a small apologetical exchange between Roman Catholic and Lutheran clergy produced two pamphlets in addition to a sermon-pamphlet by Father Johann Nepomuck Goetz celebrating the opening of Holy Trinity church in Philadelphia. A year later, Caesarius Reuter published a controversial catechism at Baltimore in German, but these were rare exceptions.[134]

Within approximately ten years of the arrival in Pennsylvania of the first large wave of German speakers in 1727, young entrepreneurs arose to challenge this predominantly religious character of the German-language book and its networks. Book collections in the eighteenth century represented financial investments. As the young men who had arrived between 1727 and 1740 began to prosper, their interest in books as investments and a hallmark of cultural status rose, too. By virtue of the immigration patterns that emerged after 1727, Philadelphia now became the undisputed distribution center and nexus for the networks that bound German speakers to various suppliers of books and printed matter.

The advertisements placed in Christopher Saur's newspaper reveal how some dozen individuals jostled for position as book distributors and agents in Pennsylvania from the 1740s through the 1790s. Swiss Germans and descendants of Swiss migrants to the Kraichgau area southeast of Heidelberg entered the trade earlier than other German speakers. In addition to Saur, key figures in this trade included Michael Billmeyer in Germantown and Melchior Steiner in Philadelphia. Heinrich Miller, a major figure who emerged in the 1760s, helped to turn the book and print trade in a more secular direction. He began publishing his newspaper *Der Wöchentliche Pennsylvanische Staatsbote* in 1762. Soon, a series of catalogues advertising larger quantities of German books began to appear in the Pennsylvania papers. Between 1767 and 1775 six such catalogues issued by Miller and Saur, Andreas Geyer, Francis Hasenclever, Georg Christoph Reinholdt, and Christoph Lochner were supplemented by the imports of Ernst Ludwig Baisch, whose former Mannheim connections and frequent trips as an agent collecting inheritance monies guaranteed him access to the booksellers and distributors in Frankfurt, Stuttgart–Tübingen, and his native Mannheim.[135]

With the arrival of Miller, the German-language book in North America intensified its evolution from a predominantly religious-domestic offering to a more eclectic, sophisticated, and secular object. Imported books account for most of those that were secular in their subject matter; among the local productions was a legal handbook on the laws of Pennsylvania translated from the English into German by Henry Miller. Yet demand remained high for the devotional or religious literature that printers in Germantown, Ephrata, and Philadelphia were producing in such abundance, as evidenced by an inventory of stock dating from 1777, when Christopher Saur II asked the British government to compensate the Saur press for the losses he had suffered at the hands of the patriots. The list, which cannot be independently verified, included 6,000 copies of the Lutheran *Der Kleine Catechismus*, 5,000 of a psalter, 3,000 of an unspecified primer, 3,100 New Testaments, and 2,900 of *Die Ganze Heilige Schrift*, in Luther's translation – this last by far the most valuable segment of the stock, estimated by Saur as worth £1,812, whereas the primers were valued at a mere £24. The experience of Henry Miller, who in 1771 imported some 700 German- and Dutch-language titles, throws a different light on the market for secular books (Fig. 8.6). Sales were slow; like so

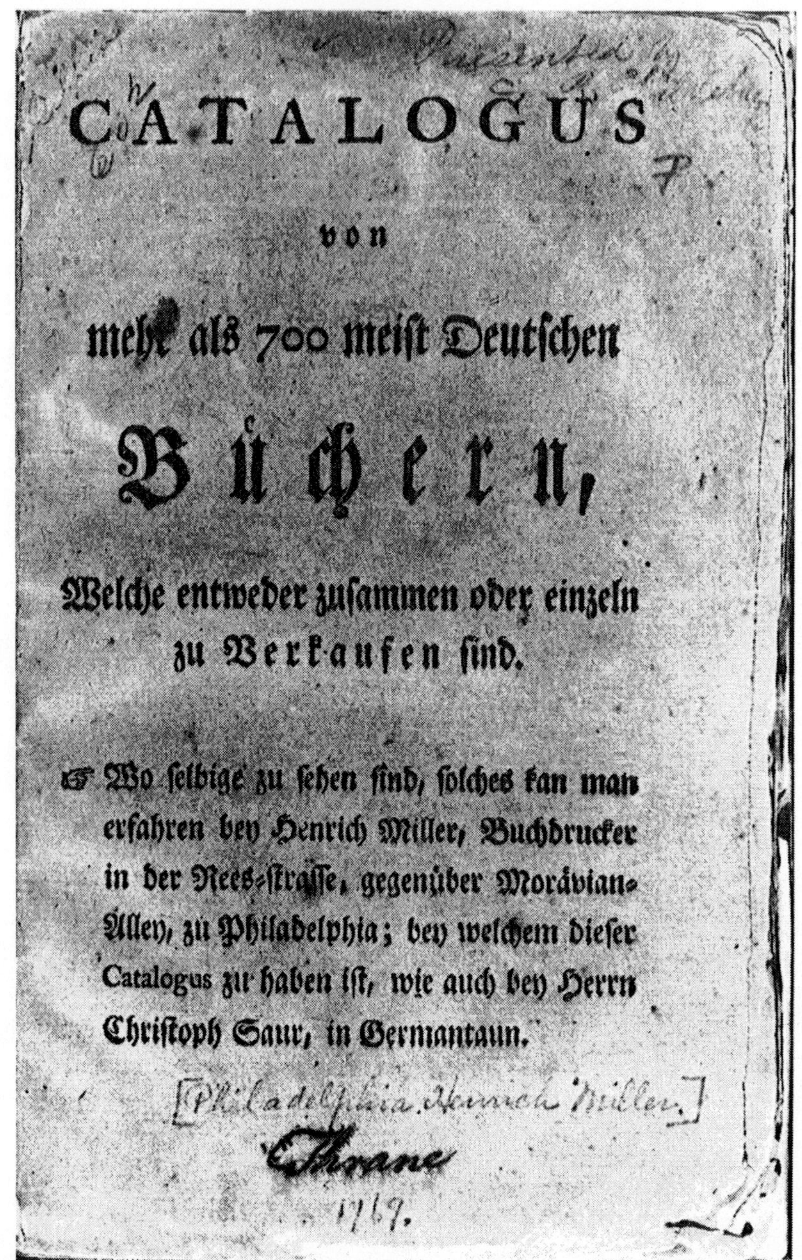

CATALOGUS

von

mehr als 700 meist Deutschen

Büchern,

Welche entweder zusammen oder einzeln
zu Verkaufen sind.

☞ Wo selbige zu sehen sind, solches kan man erfahren bey Henrich Miller, Buchdrucker in der Rees-strasse, gegenüber Morávian-Alley, zu Philadelphia; bey welchem dieser Catalogus zu haben ist, wie auch bey Herrn Christoph Saur, in Germantaun.

[Philadelphia. Heinrich Miller.]

1769.

Figure 8.6. Heinrich Miller, *Catalogus von mehr als 700 meist deutschen Büchern* (Philadelphia & Germantown: Miller & Saur, [1769?]). Miller lists 729 titles, mostly of divinity, including 157 in Latin, Greek, and/or Hebrew, 70 in Dutch, 2 in French, and one in English, "nebst allerhand englischen und deutschen Schulbüchern." Courtesy of The Historical Society of Pennsylvania.

many other booksellers in the colonies, Miller was still working off the unsold copies several years after they arrived.[136] Learned books, all of them imports and always more expensive, seem to have been especially slow moving.

The one exception may have been medical books in German, which suddenly became more available in the 1780s.[137] Within the German trade, vernacular self-help medical texts had long coexisted with the Latin-language texts intended for physicians and other learned clients. Somewhere in between lay the Pietist medical tracts produced in Halle and often sold in company with pharmaceuticals manufactured at the Francke Foundations. When the Revolution ended the production of the lower-end vernacular texts by the Saur press, importations in the 1780s and 1790s briefly filled the gap. But the possibilities for a book trade based on imported, secular German-language books would prove to be extremely limited.[138]

The Revolutionary Period

The Revolutionary crisis interrupted the book trade that had begun to flourish thirteen years earlier. Until the 1780s, the production and distribution of German-language printed materials remained almost exclusively in the hands of those entrepreneurs operating out of Philadelphia-Germantown, Lancaster, very occasionally Ephrata, Reading, and by 1778, Frederick, Maryland. This pattern, too, however, slowly began to change.[139]

Initially, once the Treaty of Paris reopened the possibility of importing German-language books, the future looked exceedingly promising. In no small part this initial possibility stemmed from the talented efforts of two Philadelphia Lutheran clerics who aggressively promoted the study of German language and literature in the context of American colleges. Johann Friedrich Kunze and Justus Christian Heinrich Helmuth would later occupy professorships in German philology at Columbia and the University of Pennsylvania, respectively. Both helped to edit the *Neue Philadelphische Korrespondenz*; Helmuth founded the von Mosheim Society in 1789 to promote the reading and discussion of German books. The pastors succeeded in sending some promising youngsters to the University of Pennsylvania, where courses in philology were taught in the German language.

Yet these efforts were undermined by the diffusion of German-language learning, books, and newspapers away from the city that had served as the center of German culture. Only a few blocks from Helmuth's parish churches of St. Michael and Zion was a 1,000-volume circulating library of German-language books, founded in 1785 by Jacob Lahn. Its presence surely abetted the objectives of Kunze and Helmut. But in 1787 Lahn decided to move his library to Lancaster. When Helmut founded the von Mosheim Society two years later, he did so in part to make up for this loss. Dedicated to promoting and disseminating serious German-language literary efforts, the society could not avoid the political controversies of the 1790s that arose out of the French Revolution, nor could it stem the flow of books and culture to the West. The first of Christian Hutter's catalogues for his bookshop at Lancaster appeared in 1798, and a catalogue of 1800 that boasted some 8,000 titles was further evidence of the dispersal of German books into the American interior.[140]

The post-Revolution years witnessed the rise of western Maryland and Virginia in addition to Pennsylvania as German-language press and book centers. Although pleas for a German press further to the south occasionally were made, no such institution arose before the printing in 1797 at Salisbury, North Carolina, of a Lutheran hymnal. Nor did a press spring into being north of Pennsylvania; though a German translation of the Constitution was published by Charles R. Webster at Albany, New York, this was a singular exception. Even the rules of the New York German Society were printed in Philadelphia, and no imprints from New York City antedate 1799. In Maryland, the career of Matthias Bartgis reflected the shift of book centers to the west. Bartgis, born in Lancaster County in 1759, learned his trade with William Bradford at Philadelphia and began publishing an almanac in Lancaster in 1777. By 1778 or 1779 he offered an almanac from Frederick, Maryland, and in 1785 began publishing the *Maryländische Zeitung* in that western town. Apparently convinced of the future of German print among western settlers, he began at Winchester, Virginia, in 1787 the bilingual *Virginia Gazette and Winchester Adviser* and, in 1789, the *Virginische Zeitung*. Another Lancaster native, Johann Gruber, who was trained in Philadelphia by the immigrant translator and publisher Carl Cist (an acronym for Charles Jacob Sigismund Thiel), copied this western shift in newspaper operations by 1795 with the publication of *Die westliche Correspondenz und Hägerstauner Wochenschrift*.

Neither the proliferation of western newspapers nor the book catalogues that newspaper publishers sometimes offered for sale should disguise the larger and more significant pattern of dispersion, provincialism, and intellectual impoverishment that brought to an end the flourishing sacred and secular offerings that had begun in the 1760s. This development cannot be accounted for without understanding the explosion in German-language books printed and distributed in Europe about America after 1776, a development that took on a more controversial meaning than at any time since the printing of the first sixteenth-century texts about the New World. To understand this pattern, let us return to the fate and content of the German book and printed material in the oldest North American center, Philadelphia, from 1783 to 1800.

German-American imprints from 1783 to 1800 remained largely the traditional hymnals, catechisms, Bibles, almanacs, ABC-books, and devotional tracts. To these genres were added medical treatises and the proceedings of various state assemblies and translations of the new Federal Constitution. Secular belles lettres, exclusively imported, included in small numbers works by Johann Wolfgang Goethe, Christoph Martin Wieland, August Friedrich von Kotzebue, and radical critics of traditional Christianity such as the ex-Pietist freethinker from Halle, Carl Friedrich Bahrdt. Astonishingly, when the new Federal Constitution was submitted for ratification, not a single book, pamphlet, or controversial treatise in German was published in all of North America debating the pros and cons of ratification. Indeed, the productions of the German-American press from 1776 to the 1790s lack any significant engagement with legal, political, or constitutional themes.

German-speakers in North America had read Thomas Paine's *Common Sense* in an elegant German translation within months of the English edition's first appearance in 1775. Only after the new Federal government came into existence, in the 1790s, did the appearance of Paine's *The Age of Reason* and the arrival in Philadelphia of radicals such as Joseph Priestley and the German observer Justus Erich Bollmann ignite a literary controversy that produced pamphlets, broadsides, newspaper essays, and even published books defending the Christian ministry and the church. Pastors such as Helmuth, Kunze, and Jakob Göring took up their pens to attack Paine, Priestley, and the French Revolution's pernicious effects upon the Christian religion in Europe and America. Helmuth in particular had identified himself from his earliest years as an educator of children and youth. It is somewhat surprising, therefore, to note that a developed children's literature did not emerge in German-American circles either before or after the Revolution.

This fact is highly suggestive of the overall pattern of language acquisition and adaptation to the dominant English-language culture. Although German migration peaked in 1753, resuming again in 1783 to perhaps 1,000 persons per year until 1800, a major shift had occurred in consumer preferences for German literature for the young. In the 1750s, Benjamin Franklin, observing German proclivities for importing books from Germany, noted as well that few German children really knew English. By 1792, it was Franklin's story of his own youth written for his son William that was translated into German and published in Berlin.[141] To be sure there are contrary examples, like the publication of catechisms, ABC primers, and inexpensive versions of the Psalms and New Testament that were made available to the young, as well as reproductions of the tales of St. Genoveva. In 1772 Miller published a basic spelling book of names for children.[142]

But Helmuth himself recognized by the 1780s and 1790s the need for a more extensive literary effort to preserve German-language readership among the young. By 1786 he had produced in unpublished pamphlet form a dialogue conversation between youths that encouraged parents to send their children to Philadelphia to take advantage of German-language schools, and, for the more advanced, German-language classical learning and the classics department at the University of Pennsylvania. Moreover, he himself composed various odes and songs to be sung by children's choirs at his parish in Philadelphia. But a letter from a young woman asking for childhood books for German girls, not the silly stories of St. Genoveva and other medieval tales, brought no results. Aside from Helmuth's efforts, German-language books for children remained a remarkably underdeveloped genre after the Revolution. Even the famous French children's text by Berquin, which itself was indebted to a German collection, Christian Felix Weisse's *Der Kinder Freund*, found no German-language translation; neither did an American imprint of Weisse's anthology appear.[143]

The period after 1783 did see a prodigious number of books and pamphlets about America written in German for German speakers in Europe. This literature emphasized American freedom (largely meaning the absence of censorship and freedom of religious opinion). But European intellectuals and correspondents such as Bollmann also firmly asserted for the German press in Europe the linkage between the secularist agenda of the French Revolution and the American event in which the German reading public had evinced such interest since 1776. Newspaper and pamphlet warfare in German in Philadelphia during the 1790s was the inevitable result.

The more elite, increasingly Federalist German printers and writers in Philadelphia, largely clerics or those critical of the French Revolution, associated themselves with Helmuth's von Mosheim Society and found themselves intellectually isolated from the secular trends within the European German-speaking literary world. Pro-Jeffersonian pamphleteers and readers pursued through the German Society of Pennsylvania a politics of rapid anglicization and cast aside any pretense of promoting the German language as a cultural, literary, religious, or political asset. To the extent that the purchasing patterns for the extensive library that still exists at the German Society of Pennsylvania can be reconstructed, it appears that the acquisition of German-language books was never a significant agenda for the society before the nineteenth century.[144] For their part, the newer presses and distributors of western Maryland, Pennsylvania, and Virginia largely avoided these controversies and persisted in issuing almanacs, ABCs, religious pamphlets, hymnals, household remedies for humans and farm animals, reprints of midwifery books, basic arithmetic and money conversion tables.[145]

Thus it was that the tastes for serious German literature that began with considerable promise in the 1760s collapsed in the new transatlantic political and ideological controversies of the 1790s. The very success of German speakers in adjusting their high rates of literacy in German to their English-speaking surroundings may have accelerated this process. Largely uninterested in the intricacies of European intellectual trends and debates, American readers of German-language books bought inexpensive medical works from Europe in the 1780s and 1790s, but not political or belletristic offerings. By default, the older domestic-religious and agrarian tastes of the pre-Revolutionary immigrant population reasserted themselves among westward-moving German-Americans. Like the Dutch, who continued to read both religious and domestic tracts into the first decades of the nineteenth-century, German speakers in North America turned away from a consciousness of the intellectual and religious ferment of late eighteenth-century Europe. With the reassertion of the religious, domestic, and private reading habits that had long characterized the readers of Dutch and German books, the history of a more sophisticated German book in particular slipped into dormancy. It would only reawaken in the context of renewed German-language settlements in the states and territories deeper in the American interior; its history belongs to the nineteenth century.

CHAPTER NINE

The New England Book Trade, 1713–1790

HUGH AMORY

THOUGH SHIPPING AND SHIPBUILDING advanced rapidly in the middle colonies, New England retained a large share of the maritime commerce of North America down to 1790, when the region was home to more than a third of the mercantile marine and half the lighthouses of the new nation. Despite this continuing orientation toward the sea – at first the Caribbean, and at the end of the period the South Seas, China, and the Pacific Northwest – Massachusetts and Connecticut also expanded internally. The early townships splintered into ever more closely packed societies, and the inland counties boomed; between 1765 and 1810, the population of Worcester County, the belly of Massachusetts, nearly doubled, and the western counties grew by 265 percent.[1] Without access to this vigorous back country, however, Boston stagnated. It had grown from 7,000 persons in 1690 to 16,382 by 1743, but by 1752, in the wake of a depression, it shrank to 15,731, where it stabilized, recovering growth only in the final decade of the century. In the meantime, its ranking in population and commerce dropped behind not only Philadelphia's and New York's, but also that of some nine provincial English cities;[2] by the end of the century, the urban population of New England had declined relatively to the countryside, from 10 to 5 percent of the whole. Other cities with access to a hinterland or cheaper commercial facilities prospered: Salem, whose population grew from 2,200 in 1692 to 7,921 in 1790; Newburyport at the mouth of the Merrimack; Nantucket, whose hinterland was the sea itself.[3]

In the period we are considering, the New England book trade developed in both size and structure. Before 1750, it was largely a Boston affair, whose fastest growing sector was bookbinding; printing elsewhere rested on government patronage and might not even extend to the production of a newspaper. In the next quarter century, all sectors of the trade expanded, but particularly imports from Great Britain, a number of printers took up bookselling, and there was modest growth in the number of country presses. The import trade crashed with the Revolution, but country presses received a considerable impetus and by 1790 were already contributing to the stocks of booksellers in Boston and other large cities. More books were printed locally in more places than in the middle colonies and the South but, apart from schoolbooks and chapbooks (no small exception), they sold nationally.

From its base in Boston, printing retraced the original embryonic skeleton of the region, along the coast and up the rivers and bays: to New London (1708) and up the Thames to Norwich (1773); to Newport (1727), and up the Narragansett Bay to Providence (1762); to Halifax, Nova Scotia (1751), Hartford (1764), Portsmouth (1756), Salem (1768), and Newburyport (1773). Exceptionally, James Parker of New York established the first press in New Haven (1754). Only the Revolution disrupted this pattern of expansion, when patriot presses dodged about the inland towns of Watertown, Worcester, Cambridge, Concord, Danvers, Attleborough, Chelmsford, Plymouth, and Rehoboth, fleeing British control of the ports; of these, only Worcester maintained a printer for more than a year or two. The earlier pattern of settlement resumed in the 1780s, extending printing up the Connecticut River from Middletown (1785) to Hanover, New Hampshire (1778), Springfield (1782) and Northampton, Massachusetts (1786), and Westminster (1781) and Windsor, Vermont (1783), as well as up the Merrimack River from Newburyport to Haverhill (1790) and Concord, New Hampshire (1789). Along the coast, new presses settled at Fairfield, Connecticut (1786) and Falmouth (1785) and Portland, Maine (1786); following the innovative example of Worcester, however, they also moved inland, to Litchfield (1784) and Danbury, Connecticut (1789), Pittsfield (1788) and Stockbridge, Massachusetts (1789), and Keene, New Hampshire (1787). In almost every case, they printed a local newspaper as well as books.[4]

Before 1760, censorship and the promise of government patronage prompted the printers' efforts to relocate. James Franklin moved to Newport after his license to operate in Boston was revoked, and he continued to print for Thomas Fleet in Boston from his new location; Daniel Fowle moved to Portsmouth after a run-in with the authorities concerning the Massachusetts Stamp Act of 1754. Bartholomew Green, Jr., was starved out of Boston and sought a fresh start in Halifax. Timothy Green reluctantly went to New London in 1714, but, as he had surmised, there was little printing to be done there, and two of his sons returned to work in Boston, from 1723 to 1752, when their father retired and they took over his shop in New London.[5] The production of print rarely rose above 3 percent of Boston's at any of these locations.

Competition from Boston and New York no doubt slowed the growth of the Connecticut trade, the most important of these provinces. New Yorkers anticipated the printers of New London in New Haven, as we have seen, and the Robertsons of Albany eliminated New Londoners in Norwich, where they published the first newspaper and drove Timothy Green IV out of business. The first regular Connecticut almanac, by Roger Sherman, began to appear in 1753; previously, the country folk made do with Leeds's *American Almanack* (1687–1746), printed in Philadelphia or New York, or with Ames's almanac, printed in Boston. Connecticut newspapers were also slow to appear. In 1762, Hugh Gaine boasted that his *New-York Mercury* was carried "to every Town and Country Village in the Provinces of . . . Connecticut and Rhode Island,"[6] and the first Connecticut newspaper only appeared in 1755, nearly half a century after printing had been established in New London. The first local newspaper of much importance was the *Connecticut Courant* (1764–1914), printed by Thomas Green and Ebenezer Watson of Hartford.[7] Nevertheless, *Rivington's New-York Gazetteer, or The Connecticut, Hudson's River, New Jersey, and Quebec Weekly Advertiser* (1773–1775) had such extensive sales in Connecticut that a band of local patriots marched to New York and destroyed Rivington's press.

Before 1770, the production of New England cities outside of Boston is best regarded as a form of "country printing," which took its lead from Boston or New York.[8] It is a sobering experience for a bibliographer to read the diary of Joshua Hempstead, a minutely detailed series of jottings about people and events in New London from 1711 to 1758, which often refers to Timothy Green and his sons, who printed there. For Hempstead, however, the father is invariably "Deacon Green," who imperturbably "Carryed on" when the preacher, Eliphalet Adams, was indisposed;[9] the silence about local imprints is deafening. Even during the 1780s, when Joseph T. Buckingham was a boy in Windham, Connecticut, colonial printing played only a minimal role in his village culture. He dwells on the "delight and instruction" he garnered from "a regular file of Almanacks, for near or quite fifty years," most of them, apparently, by Nathaniel Ames. He characterized the introduction of a printing office and newspaper in 1793 as "a memorable epoch in our village history."[10] As late as 1762, when a printing press had been operating in Newport for thirty-five years, William Goddard of Providence could protest that "it is universally acknowledged a Printer is much wanted in this Place [Rhode Island], very considerable Sums being annually sent into other Governments for Printing, to the Impoverishment of this."[11] The proliferation of country printing after 1770 should be connected with the revolutionary factionalism that found its voice in the larger cities during the 1760s, and the concurrent transformation of printers into editors. "Politics may not have created the country printer," remarks Milton W. Hamilton, "but he found his greatest activity in party service."[12]

The Boston book trade that presided over these developments was certainly larger than that of other colonies, but had never been very large – at any given time down to 1713, as we have seen, it consisted of no more than two or three printing offices and a handful of booksellers. The changing social structure of Boston in the eighteenth century had considerable consequences on the small, closely related group of shopkeepers who sold books. Family connections gradually became less important for entry to trades: the Drapers took over from the Greens, and printers like Green & Russell or Edes & Gill increasingly based their partnerships on ability and expertise. As Carol Sue Humphreys has shown, only eleven of the seventy-two apprentices who "descended" from the seventeenth-century shop of Serjeant Samuel Green actually bore his name (though four more had married into the clan).[13] Wealth became more and more concentrated in a merchant elite, leading to a more stratified society, more discriminating consumption, and more specialized forms of trade.[14]

The Great Fire of 1711, which consumed the center of Boston where most of the booksellers were located, seems to have stimulated new growth and weakened the iron grip of the Greens, who retreated to their Connecticut strongholds for the second half of the century. Thomas Fleet and Thomas Crump opened a printing office, the city's fourth, in Pudding Lane (now Devonshire Street) in 1713; James Franklin and Samuel Kneeland followed suit in Queen (now Court) Street in 1717 and 1718, respectively, so that in the seven years since the disaster (allowing for the departure of Timothy Green to New London in 1714) the number of presses had nearly doubled. New journeymen drifted into town to man the shops: Henry Coulton from Maryland and an anonymous "Irish book printer" in 1716; including the obscure James Cummins, active in 1715, the number of known printers quickly tripled.[15]

Even more striking is the no doubt related spurt in the number of bookbinders: Joanna Perry, a Boston bookseller's widow, John Eliot, Benjamin Gray, Nathaniel Belknap, and Alford Butler, Sr., all first appeared in imprints between 1715 and 1726. In the next decade or so down to 1740, they would be joined by Bennet Love, Francis Skinner (who resettled in Newport, Rhode Island, in 1731), Nathaniel Procter, John Pemberton, Martin Unwin, and Charles Harrison.[16] They worked, like the new printers, on the peripheries of the Town House (now the Old State House) where the chief booksellers had their shops: from Dock Square (in front of Faneuil Hall) along Cornhill (Washington) southwards as far as Essex Street. They would soon be reinforced by Thomas Rand, Joshua Winter, and others, and by an interesting and scrappy Scotch contingent: Andrew Barclay, John Hodgson, Walter and William McAlpine, William Lang, John Mein, and William McDuell.[17]

The growth of bookbinding in Boston is important for two reasons. First, it suggests that English and Scottish books were now being imported in sheets: the Bostonian bookseller Jeremy Condy certainly acquired much of his stock in this form, at a time when David Hall in Philadelphia was still buying his imports ready-bound.[18] Samuel Bass supplied Daniel Henchman with a goodly number of calf skins worth £18 3*s.* 7*d.* in 1741, and Joseph Bennett, a London merchant who visited Boston in 1740, praised the excellent quality of Boston veal: Calves were no longer doomed to become salt beef, it seems.[19] Second, the bookbinders were in effect retailers of sheets wherever printed – in Boston, Philadelphia, or London – and this in turn implies that booksellers like Daniel Henchman and Benjamin Franklin were wholesaling colonial imprints; *mutatis mutandis,* they were the colonial equivalents of William Bowyer, Thomas Longman, and William Strahan in London. Not surprisingly, Thomas Hancock, when he was still dealing in books, perceived the importer Thomas Cox as his greatest rival; the same pattern would reemerge in John Mein's contest with John Hancock in the 1760s. Colonial printing was no longer a mere supplement but, in a small way, a competitor to the English trade.

The difference that bookbinders made is readily observed in imprints. Driven by the need for capital, even the "principal" members of the early Boston trade, like Daniel Henchman, banded together with other booksellers, who appear by his side in imprints or on the cancel title pages of variant issues. Thus the "fifth edition" of Michael Wigglesworth's *Meat out of the Eater* (1717) appeared under five imprints, for Boone, Buttolph, Eliot, Fleet, and Henchman – nearly the entire Boston book trade of the time. Since all of these printers and booksellers were also binders, they not only shared the cost of printing but the cost of manufacturing the printed sheets into books. The incidence of shared editions dwindled after 1730, however: 87 of the 408 editions printed for Daniel Henchman were shared with other booksellers, but only 21 of these were printed after 1730, and, if we may set aside some editions of almanacs and psalmbooks in 1758–1761, only nine after 1732. It looks as though Henchman had begun to wholesale his stock to binders after 1730, instead of exchanging it with other retail booksellers on his own level. Jabez Earle's *Sacramental Meditations* is an impressive instance, printed for Henchman with three variant imprints in 1715, reprinted with two variants in 1725, and again with five in 1729. The next edition of Earle, in 1756, was printed for Henchman alone, however.

The specialization of bookbinders at the bottom of the trade had helped free Henchman from the codependency of his equals, to become "the most eminent and enterprising bookseller that appeared in Boston, or, indeed, in all British America, before the year 1775."[20] Such wholesalers were few at first, but probably included the printer Thomas Fleet, whose advertisements invite the custom of "country traders." Not all of Henchman's success belonged to his trade of bookselling, of course. His daughter

Figure 9.1. John Smibert, "Daniel Henchman," 1736. Courtesy of The Cincinnati Historical Society, Ohio.

Lydia had married another bookseller, Thomas Hancock, whose fortunes were built on Army supply contracts during King George's War. And "eminent" as Henchman was, he never donned the periwig of the merchant and professional elite, as Smibert's portrait shows (Fig. 9.1).

To judge by his surviving accounts, Henchman transacted practically none of his business directly with London or Scotland before 1750, though he certainly sold English books, some of them bought from Thomas Cox. Henchman's customers were located over a wide area, from "the Eastward" (Maine) and "Piscataway" (Portsmouth, New Hampshire, and environs), to Long Island, New York, and even Philadelphia, but inland no farther than Worcester in Massachusetts, and Hartford, Suffield, and Windham in Connecticut. He traded actively with Long Island, Connecticut, and Rhode Island, though less intensely, of course, than with his home colony. Like Jeremy Condy's, his customers lay along the coast or up rivers and estuaries and inland along post roads: Books pursued established routes of communication and commerce more readily than the potential market suggested by New England's widespread literacy.[21]

As some of the booksellers, like Henchman and Hancock, rose to be merchants, their total number, if anything, rather shrank after the fire of 1711. When Joseph Bennett described the trade in 1740, the retailers of books were considerably outnumbered by their producers:

> [A]t the Uper end of [King Street, now State Street] stands the *Town House,* or *Guild-hall;* where the Governor meets the Council, & *House of Representatives,* & the several Courts of Justice are held there also. And there are likewise walks for the Merchants, where they meet every day at one oth Clock, in imitation of the Exchange at London, which they call by the name of *Royal Exchange* too; round which there are several Booksellers Shops, & there are four or five printing houses which have full imployment, in printing, & reprinting books of one sort or other, that are brought from England and other parts of Europe.[22]

This may not seem a fair summary of the horde of sponsors named in Boston imprints, but it is accurate enough, allowing for its focus on the Town House, which elides any mention of the bookbinders.

Actually, Boston had just four printing houses in 1740, belonging to John Draper, Rogers & Fowle, Thomas Fleet, and Kneeland & Green. A fifth printer, Bartholomew Green, Jr., was associated with his brother-in-law John Draper and had issued books under his own imprint from the shop in Newbury Street both in 1725, when it was still his father's, and in 1732–1734, when Draper had taken it over. He would soon establish a new partnership with John Bushell and Bezoune Allen (another brother-in-law) at Number 2 Dock Square in 1742; Green, Bushell, & Allen renamed themselves "Bartholomew Green & Co." in 1743, when they moved back to Newbury Street.[23] The partnership dissolved only two years later, when Green went off to besiege Louisburg with the colonial forces under William, soon to be Sir William Pepperell, Bart. After Green's return, disappointed, like many of the land forces, in the profits of the expedition, he unsuccessfully petitioned the House of Representatives in 1749 for the position of doorkeeper, explaining that he had "put himself out of good Business" by the jaunt.[24] Probably Bennett counted "five printing houses" because there were five newspapers in Boston. Three of them were edited by the printers: the *Boston News-Letter* (Draper); the *Boston Evening-Post* (Fleet); and the *New-England Weekly Journal* (Kneeland). Kneeland also printed the official *Boston Gazette,* and John Bushell, possibly together with Bartholomew Green, Jr., printed the *Boston Post-Boy,* both for the postmaster, Ellis Huske. All five newspapers were weeklies, the first three printed on a half-sheet folio (two pages) in two or three columns, the last two on a half-sheet quarto (four pages) in two columns.

John Bushell is emphatically the more fascinating printer in the new partnership. He was one of the earliest (though hitherto unrecognized) wood-engravers in the colonies, preceded in New England only by John Foster and James Franklin, but far more skillful than either. The technology of the arts of the book developed more rapidly than that of printing in the eighteenth century: apart from Caslon type, there is little, technically, to choose between a 1650 colonial imprint and one a century later, but a more-than-aesthetic gulf yawns between John Foster's primitive map of New England (1677) and James Turner's chart of Nova Scotia (1750), both commemorations of military victories (Figs. 9.2a–b). Turner's indeed profits from a European mastery of hydrography and surveying to which Foster's woodcut makes no pretense, but such subjects could scarcely be communicated without an engraver's skill. Engraving is a personal, local skill, whereas most of the printer's technology was purchased ready-made. Woodcuts and engravings thus served as a kind of trademark, when entry into the market for print was uncontrolled and copyright was non-existent. The royal arms underwrote the authority of the laws, the Man-of-Signs recommended the accuracy of the almanac, a lavish banner proclaimed a newspaper's continuity, and the intricate design of colonial currency (Fig. 7.1) discouraged forgery.

Most of his engravings, including designs for colonial currency in 1737, were executed for John Draper, under whom he may have served his apprenticeship; they may be identified by the monogram IB, usually in roman but also, occasionally, cursive (Fig. 9.3). When Bartholomew Green left to fight the French and Indians, Bushell and Allen formed a brief, loose partnership with John Green (1719–1757), who had moved from his father's New London shop to Boston in 1744.[25] Bushell disappears from Boston imprints around 1750, and in 1751 something impelled Bartholomew Green, Jr., to move shop to Halifax, Nova Scotia, where a printer, two stationers, and a bookbinder had already established themselves shortly after its founding in 1749. Possibly the older printer, Herbert Jefferie, had died or moved away. Green died only a few weeks after his arrival, however, one of the many Greens whose unsatisfactory careers belie the family's reputation as a "dynasty of printers." Bushell followed him in 1752, to become the first printer in Canada whose work survives – often in debt, reportedly drunk, and yet, with the assistance of his daughter and by virtue of his skill in engraving, printer of an exceptionally elegant newspaper and of flash gubernatorial proclamations.[26]

(*text continues on page 325*)

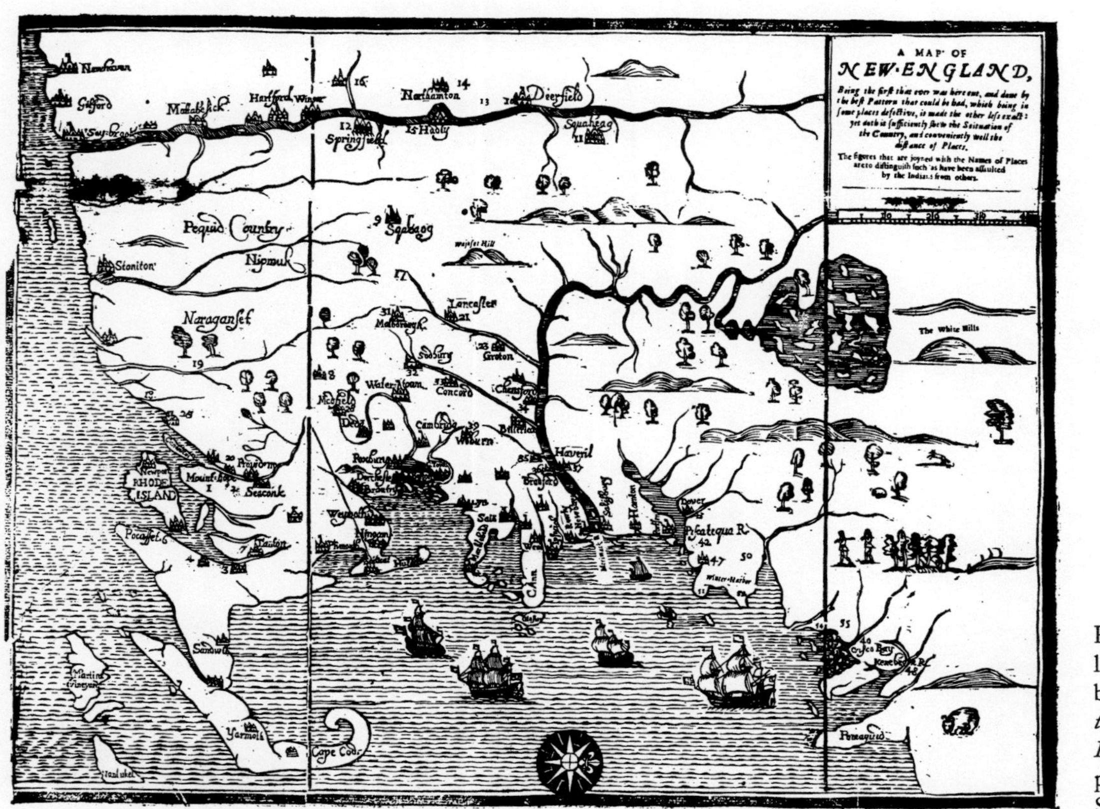

Figure 9.2a. "The South Part of Nevv England as it is Planted this Yeare, 1634," engraved by John Foster for William Hubbard's *Narrative of the Troubles with the Indians in New England* (Boston, 1677); the earliest map printed in the colonies. American Antiquarian Society.

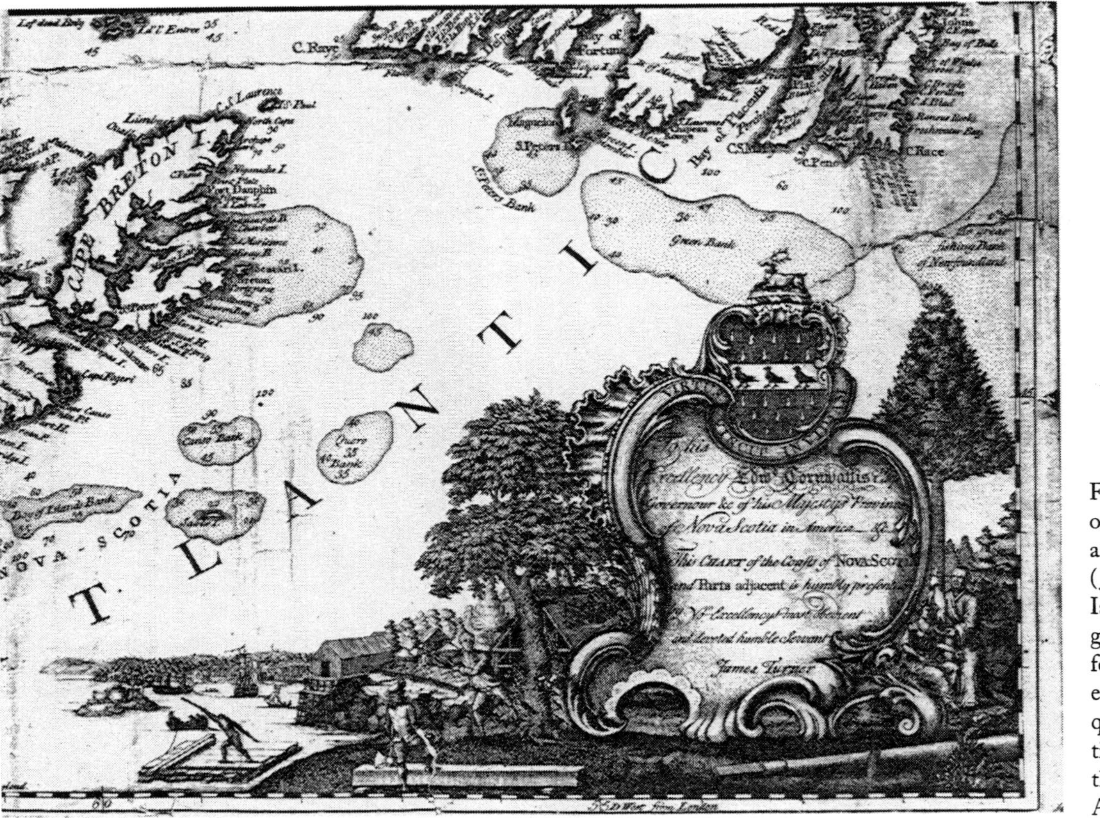

Figure 9.2b. Detail of a chart of the coast of Nova Scotia (Boston, 1750), engraved after a map in the *Gentleman's Magazine* (Jan. 1746) by James Turner (d. 1759), whom Isaiah Thomas considered "the best engraver which appeared in the colonies before the revolution"; issued to encourage emigration to Nova Scotia after the conquest of Louisburg (1745) and the foundation of Halifax (1749). The cartouche shows the progress of the lumber and fish trades. American Antiquarian Society.

Figure 9.3. The Province House and Bible; the device of John Draper, Printer to the Governor and Council, engraved by J[ohn] B[ushell]. Courtesy of the Boston Public Library.

The "several Booksellers" around the Town House that Bennett mentioned were clearly Samuel Gerrish, Daniel Henchman, and Joseph Edwards – a group that Isaiah Thomas often styles the "principal booksellers." Others in the same location who occasionally appeared in imprints were Gillam Phillips and Thomas Cox, but Phillips traded as a merchant and Cox wholesaled or auctioned off English books. Yet other Bostonians who sponsored printing were Hopestill Foster, a housewright, Thomas Hancock, who had been trading as a merchant since 1730, and John Phillips (no relation to Gillam), a merchant and stationer. Foster's shop was south of the Town House on Cornhill, Hancock's was in the North End, on Ann Street, and Phillips's was at Number 1 Dock Square, next to Green & Company. In the reign of George I, one might have counted some five Boston booksellers in addition to Gerrish, Henchman, and John Phillips: Thomas Hancock, John Edwards (d. 1725), Nicholas Boone, Nicholas Buttolph, and Benjamin Eliot – not to mention Eleazer Phillips (Gillam's cousin) in Charlestown. Other early figures who occasionally appeared in imprints were John Checkley, a shopkeeper whose publications were solely devoted to promoting the Anglican Church (he later became an Anglican clergyman), Edmund Negus, a merchant, and Robert Starkey, a shopkeeper.[27] Setting these aside, many of the earlier booksellers had already dropped out of the trade and were not replaced, or graduated to other occupations by 1730: Hancock had become a merchant, Eliot a stationer, Edwards had died, Boone had retired, and Buttolph, whose publications had never been very numerous, had nearly completed his quota.

In 1728, Daniel Henchman, Benjamin Faneuil, Gillam Phillips, and Thomas Hancock secured a patent from the General Assembly for the manufacture of paper and erected the first mill in the province, at Milton on the Neponset River. It was not very successful, and neither were two more mills on the Presumpscot and Stroudwater Rivers at Portland, Maine, operated by Richard Fry. Nevertheless, the mere predictability of a supply must have been a boon to the trade, and a subsidy from the state in 1764, together with the Stamp Act of 1765, greatly boosted native manufacture. Harvard commencement exercises (in Latin) as well as the *Massachusetts Spy* and the *Essex Gazette* (in English) duly announced that they were printed on paper made in Milton, New England. By the 1770s, there were twelve mills in New England, six of them in Massachusetts.[28] That Daniel Henchman was expanding his business and taking up wholesaling, that Thomas Hancock and Gillam Phillips were leaving bookselling for merchantry, and that Benjamin Eliot was turning into a stationer around 1730 cannot be wholly coincidental.

By 1750, Isaiah Thomas noted, the formal division of the Boston trade into printers and booksellers had dissolved: the explicit imprint "Printed, and are to be sold by Thomas Fleet" becomes the implicit "Printed by Thomas [or T. & J.] Fleet," whom we must now regard as "printer–booksellers." Rollo G. Silver posited the concomitant emergence of "bookseller–publishers" at this period or simply of "publishers" *tout court,* but the evidence for this development is less certain.[29] Silver is supported in this view by L. C. Wroth and John W. Tebbel, yet if they are right, Boston was some thirty years in advance of the London trade and perhaps fifty years ahead of the rest of the colonies.

The role of a "publisher" is not easy to define. Today it designates one who selects the texts, finances and designs the book, and normally owns or leases the copyright, yet does not write, print, nor bind the book, nor sell it to his ultimate customer the reader. None of this was true of eighteenth-century "publishers" (the term itself did not yet exist) and little of it applies to their nineteenth-century equivalents, who often printed and bound their stock in house.[30] In the eighteenth century, a "publishing bookseller," to use Isaiah Thomas's term, was one who commissioned and sold, but did not print, American production – as opposed both to printer–booksellers, who supplied their own stock, and to importers. Henchman was a "publishing bookseller," but he never "secured his manuscript" as a modern publisher might because there was no colonial copyright. Colonial "publishing" thus had rather a pathological cast, unlike anything found in England: No author, even one as eminent and voluminous as Cotton Mather, ever received a collected works; even New England's orthodoxy tended to be a canon of ideas or genres, not of any particular authors or titles. The practice of reprinting English authors, which American writers later blamed on the 1790 Federal copyright act, in fact long antedated the republic, and for one obvious reason. By the early eighteenth century, English literature had a recognized canon of "classics" that Americans shared but could not easily join. What Silver describes as "publishing" had been going on well before Henchman was born. Michael Perry and his Boston confreres in the 1690s had also secured manuscripts, contracted for printing, paid for production, and marketed their own imprints, but they did so on a retail scale, by exchanges. The innovation of the 1730s was rather the wholesaling of American printing, parallel to developments that had taken place in the English trade in the 1680s. This is a step closer to "publishing" but not quite the same thing.

English printing, indeed, had been wholesaled to the Boston trade by merchants like John Usher, as we have seen; not at all surprisingly, then, the American editions that the trade copublished in the early eighteenth century were most often of English properties. When Nicholas Boone died in 1738, Thomas Fleet, who had appraised the book-stock for his widow, seems to have bought it in and duly advertised it in the *Boston Evening Post* (June 4, 1739). The only colonial properties in a list of twenty-one named titles were Boone's own *Constable's Pocket-Book* (1710, etc.) and Ezekiel Cheever's perennial *Short Introduction to the Latin Tongue* (1709, etc.). Boone's most prominent English authors were John Flavel and John Bunyan, with three titles each; equally valuable, perhaps, were Robert Russell's *Seven Sermons,* Samuel Smith's *Great Assize,* and William Dyer's *Christ's Famous Titles* – works so familiar that their informal citations often omit the authors. "History" (i.e., fiction) was represented by a chapbook version of Flavius Josephus, *De bello Judaico.* Schoolbooks like Hodder's *Arithmetick,* and *Catonis Disticha,* and a popular manual for accountants, *The Secretary's Guide* (by John Hill? or T. Goodman?) completed this reassuringly conventional index of New England culture, which opened with the most important, "Bibles, Testaments, Psalters, Psalm Books, with Tunes or without, Primers and Catechisms," and closed with a variety of blank forms.

Though mostly by English authors, all of these works, with the possible exception of Bibles and Testaments, were reprinted in America. According to Isaiah Thomas, the first English Bible printed in America was a small quarto of seven or eight hundred copies, published "about the time that the partnership of Kneeland and Green expired." To avoid conflict with the English Bible patent, Thomas opined, it bore the false but legally mandated imprint "London: Printed by Mark Baskett, Printer to the King's Most Excellent Majesty," though it was actually printed by Kneeland and Green for Daniel Henchman "and two or three other principal booksellers." Around the same time – either before or after the Bible (Thomas's accounts in the first edition of his History conflict) – Rogers and Fowle printed a duodecimo *New Testament* of two thousand copies for the same group. Modern discussions of these editions assume that the Bible followed the Testament, because Rogers and Fowle terminated their partnership in 1750 and Kneeland and Green broke up in 1752; the Bible is accordingly dated 1752. If, however, the Testament followed the Bible, one might date both of them much earlier: the Bible in the 1730s, and the Testament after 1740, when Rogers and Fowle formed their partnership.[31]

Thomas's earlier account, however, was closer to the truth, which emerges darkly from a puzzling document in the Henchman Papers. This is a bill from Kneeland and Green charging him £8 5*s.* "To printing your part of a Book, intitled, The &c." in August 1731. A note in another hand (Henchman's?) at the foot of the page explains that the total cost of printing this enigmatic title was £382 10*s.* for 1,500 copies of 127½ sheets at £3 a sheet, and an additional £191 5*s.* "To setting up [i.e., composing] the first sheets . . . and several others" – £573 15*s.* in all; a monstrous sum, an unusually large edition, and an exceptionally expensive rate. Elsewhere in the same bill Kneeland and Green charged only 30*s.* or at most 45*s.* a sheet for 500 or 1,000 copies, and there were evidently additional charges by other printers still to come.[32] Only one book so large was conceivably worth printing without the advance sales that subscription guaranteed – the Bible; English quarto editions contained from 131 to 136 sheets, including the Apocrypha and index.[33] The enigmatic entry was part of the same scheme of deceit as the false imprint, to provide Henchman and others with legal deniability; the extraordinary charges reflected the illegality of their undertaking.

Together with his Testament, Henchman's Bible fits naturally into a pattern of ambitious projects during the second quarter of the century, when British imports, it seems, were lagging behind colonial demand: Willard's *Compleat Body of Divinity* (Boston, 1726), Willem Sewel's *History of the Rise, Increase, and Progress . . . of the Quakers* (Philadelphia, 1728), Robert Barclay's *Apology for the True Christian Divinity* (Newport, 1729), and Franklin's Testament (Philadelphia, 1745). No editions of these dimensions would surface again before the 1770s and for reasons good: Henchman was importing quantities of Scotch bibles and Testaments in the 1750s and hardly needed to print an American edition, while the later total extinction of such large and valuable properties as the 1731 Bible and both New Testaments argues their poor success.

Boone might well have stocked American Bibles, then, and Fleet's advertisement is an early token of something resembling a publisher's backlist: It can be identified as Boone's stock because he printed editions of nearly all the named titles, one of which he even wrote. More precisely, it appears to be his sheet-stock, and it is altogether likely that he had other titles, English and American, new and second-hand, that were bound, for he occasionally advertised them. Nevertheless, comparing the list with Michael Perry's inventory of 1700, one feels that the market had shifted strongly in favor of American printing. As Fleet would shortly discover, his purchase may have been unwise, for in 1740, the Great Awakening rewrote the canon of divinity: Of Boone's authors, only Russell enjoyed much of a vogue after 1730, and Boone had not reprinted the works of Bunyan and Flavel that continued in most demand.

The printed dimension of the Great Awakening has only recently begun to receive attention from its historians. George Whitefield saw the printed word as a necessary corrective to the emotionalism ("enthusiasm") his preaching had aroused: "the quintessence of enthusiasm is to pretend to be guided by the Spirit without the written word," he thought – a Quaker failing, perhaps, but Whitefield did not share it.[34] He was also concerned to direct the reading of his audiences, condemning the rationalism of Archbishop Tillotson and promoting a canon that included such early Nonconformist texts as Joseph Alleine's *Alarm to Unconverted Sinners,* as well as the dangerously broad, nonsectarian titles by "New Lights" who supported his revival. The consumerism with which he promoted the "New Lights" was matched, however, with a conservative hostility against "luxury" and the depreciated currency that oppressed New England in the 1730s and 1740s.[35]

Printers responded by reprinting such old-fashioned tirades against fancy dress as Cotton Mather's *Ornaments for the Daughters of Zion* (1691).

In a number of complex ways, Whitefield's revival reshaped both the oral present and the printed past, and it did so on a scale hitherto undreamt of. His preaching was accompanied by printed accounts of its impact, published in both England and the colonies. Whitefield's traveling companion, William Seward, returned to England in 1740 with the manuscript of the autobiography that the apostle had written on the journey over, and he printed it under the title *A Short Account of God's Dealings with the Reverend Mr. Whitefield* (June 1740) in an edition of 1,000 copies. Seward also published his own *Journal of a Voyage from Savannah to Philadelphia* in an edition of 4,000 copies for the widely dispersed community of New Lights suggested by the imprint: "London: Printed [by William Strahan]. And sold . . . at J. Oswald's. . . . Also by J. Wilson in Bristol; Gabriel Harris, Junior, in Gloucester; J. Trail in Edinburgh. . . . As also by the booksellers in New-England, New-York, Philadelphia, and Charles-Town [i.e., Charleston, South Carolina]. 1740" (Evans 4598).[36]

Daniel Henchman duly advertised his share of this edition in the *Boston News-Letter*, December 18, 1740, as sold "with *His* [Seward's] Allowance to *Him* [Henchman] of reprinting the same in case there is a Demand for more than are now transmitted him [italic reversed]," and a supply was sent to the other cities as well, but it was never reprinted. Whitefield's autobiography was another story. Under the new title of *A Brief and General Account of the Life of the Rev. George Whitefield,* Franklin and the Bradfords each published an edition in Philadelphia, and Henchman and Kneeland and Green published two editions each in Boston in December 1740 and January 1741 – six editions in a space of a few months. Since Henchman's two editions alone totalled 3,500 copies,[37] we may estimate that perhaps ten times as many copies of the work were printed in America as in England. In addition, Franklin published Whitefield's *Journals* of his voyage from England to Savannah by subscription: Benjamin Eliot in Boston subscribed for 250 sets of the *Sermons,* and Charles Harrison took 150 more; Rogers and Fowle reprinted them in 1741. Two volumes of the *Journals,* also published by subscription in Philadelphia, were equally popular: Harrison took 250 sets.[38] By publishing Whitefield's autobiography and his own *Journal* in England, Seward secured copyright, and "licensed" reprints in America, while Whitefield in Philadelphia authorized subscription editions of his *Journals* covering the remainder of their expedition and of his *Sermons,* delivered in England as well as in America.[39] Here, if you will, are "publishers," as we understand the term today, cannily coordinating edition-sizes and titles on an Atlantic scale, but it set no precedents: No more colonial editions of Whitefield's *Sermons, Journals,* and autobiography appeared after 1741.

Brief though it was, Whitefield and Seward's publishing strategy is impressive for the clear separation of speech and scripture, each of them paramount in its own domain. In the autobiography and their *Journals,* the "written" part of their oeuvre, Whitefield and Seward tried to lay down an incontestible record of his career – a "meta-sermon," forming a sort of Acts of the Apostles to Whitefield's gospel. There was undeniably a rhetorical element to all this, of course: Whitefield "innocently" revealed that he was born on December 25 in an inn, "exciting me to make good my Mother's Expectations, and to follow the Example of my dear Saviour," and he was clearly something of an artist in passive aggression, as we would call it today. Nevertheless, the controversial part of his works, and the part that his critics responded to, was resolutely oral. The *Journals,* indeed, never explained the hostility of his critics because it was simply inexplicable to Whitefield, who presents himself as a faithful adherent of his church's Thirty-Nine Articles. That he read them in the spirit in which they were written, but which his church had long agreed to ignore, is never mooted. Predictably, Congregationalists and Presbyterians in Boston and Philadelphia found him easier to take than his own, Anglican denomination in New York and Charleston.

The resulting controversy certainly galvanized the Boston trade: Even an editor like Thomas Fleet, who consistently opposed the New Lights in the *Boston Evening-Post,* was happy enough to issue editions of Whitefield's writings, as well as "impartial" counterblasts by his critics, both English and American. In 1740, "religious" printing (exclusive of the political tracts and controversy aroused by the Great Awakening) soared to more than three times the size of "government" printing (including election sermons, and other religious events that the government sponsored), whereas in 1765, it was only one and a half times as great (Tables 9.1 and 9.2). The establishment of Green, Bushell, and Allen in 1742 reflected this press of business, the "full imployment" that Bennett noted. Daniel Henchman provided the new firm with a large stock of type, worth £399 10*s.* 8*d.*, and they paid him off in publications.[40] The number of printing offices in Boston remained unchanged until 1755, when the firms of Edes & Gill and Green & Russell opened shops, and Mein & Fleeming made a seventh ten years later, importing Scottish workmen for the purpose.[41] Though a provincial Stamp Act killed off the first *Boston Gazette* and *Boston Post-Boy* in 1755, a new *Boston Gazette,* edited by Edes & Gill, and a second *Boston Post-Boy,* edited by Green & Russell, replaced them after the act had expired in 1757, and a sixth newspaper, Mein & Fleeming's *Boston Chronicle,* began in 1767. The general expansion of newspaper issues from a half to a full sheet during the French and Indian War absorbed much of this new capacity: Four offices in 1740 had printed an estimated 280,902 sheets, and some seven firms in 1765 printed 675,750, an increase of 242 percent.

Another Great Fire devastated the booksellers in 1760, but despite a general depression following the French and Indian War, the Boston trade rose again from its ruins. Booksellers, like other shopkeepers in the city, had already begun to specialize in the 1740s. Isaiah Thomas notes that Daniel Fowle printed and sold "chiefly pamphlets," and that his brother Zechariah sold "ballads and small pamphlets," while the books that Samuel Kneeland published were "chiefly on religious subjects." The most thriving and significant segment of the trade to emerge in the 1760s was the retailers of English books who bought their stock directly from Edinburgh and London, rather than from Boston merchants as heretofore or from "vendues" by English exporters like Thomas Cox. Many of the most prominent of these new booksellers were Tories and later, loyalists: Wharton & Bowes, who took over Daniel Henchman's stock; James Rivington of New York, who opened a Boston outlet in 1762 manned by William Miller; Mein & Fleeming; Cox & Berry.

The economic interests of this group were structurally opposed to those of patriot merchants like John Hancock: they undersold the trade he supplied, both because they eliminated a middleman profit by dealing directly with Great Britain, and because the Scotch and Irish "piracies" in which they chiefly dealt were cheaper than Hancock's London editions. They were especially vulnerable to any interruption of trade, since they specialized in providing the latest fashionable titles, stocked relatively small quantities of them, and bought them on short credit; hence the patriots' nonimportation agreements and embargos immediately threatened their livelihood.[42] Ironically enough, it was the rise of a social and commercial elite like the Hancocks that created most of the demand for these editions. Their politics, to judge by Mein's quarrel with Hancock, was virtually restricted to the single issue of free trade, which the patriots' measures thwarted.[43] Like most Bostonians before 1775, even including their Lieutenant Governor Thomas Hutchinson, they welcomed the repeal of the Stamp Act and viewed complete independence as indifferent, dangerous, or impractical. Scotch Presbyterians like Mein may have analogized colonial independence to Scotland's after the Act of Union (1707), but such opinions would have made them doubly detested by patriotic Bostonians, who followed John Wilkes in charging that the Scots, headed by the Earl of Bute, were plotting to enslave the free-born English and corrupt their Parliament.

The best documented bookseller of this new group was a native Bostonian, Harvard graduate, and Old Light Baptist, Jeremy Condy, but we can only speculate on what his ultimate allegiance would have been in 1775, since he died in 1768. His son, James Foster Condy, who continued the business after his father's death, removed to Haverhill during the war and died there in 1809. It is probably a mistake to divide the prewar trade into loyalist and patriot factions. "Trumpeters of sedition" like Benjamin Edes and Isaiah

Thomas there were, just as there was a "black regiment" of preachers like Jonathan Mayhew, but most of the printers, like the Fleets, preferred to be neutral, most of the newspapers continued to be open to all views, and the neutrality of ministers like Andrew Eliot or Mather Byles, however resented, did not make them government puppets. "Religious" printing continued to be important for the Boston trade, as it was for London's and Edinburgh's, but it paid all kinds of pipers.[44]

By the 1770s, the center of the Boston book trade had shifted north and west of its traditional site at the Old State House, showing strong extensions in Queen (later Court) Street and Union Street, running off Dock Square, where a number of tradesmen settled "opposite the Cornfields," now the Old Union Oyster House.[45] Printer–booksellers, whose custom now favored the trade more than private patronage, were less widely dispersed than in 1713; only a few printers, like Green & Russell, still abstained from bookselling. The print trade had also developed, beginning with the printseller William Price in 1722: Engravers like Nathaniel Hurd and Paul Revere, the copperplate printer Daniel Rea, Jr., and the japanner, glassman, and printseller Stephen Whiting and his son Stephen, Jr. The mathematical instrument makers William Williams and, a little later, Andrew Newell, sold charts, pilots, and introductions to navigation at the head of Long Wharf, where King Street began. Henry Christian Geyer was manufacturing printing ink near the Liberty Tree at the corner of Newbury and Essex Street in 1775. David Mitchelson proposed to open a type foundry in 1768 but, like other practitioners in New England, he had little success and by 1787 he had moved to New York. If he ever actually cast any type, it has not been identified.[46]

As of 1771, the Boston trade comprised eight bookbinders, seven importing booksellers (who often dealt in other "English goods" as well, like cutlery or gloves), two stationers (likewise), ten printer–booksellers, four printers, and seven firms in the print trade. Joseph Russell, besides printing with John Green, also conducted book auctions, as, occasionally, did Moses Deshon and John Gerrish.[47] Despite the growth of papermaking and patriotism, the printer–bookseller John Boyle offered imported paper of different qualities and sizes "as cheap as can be bought at the Mills," and the merchant Colborn Barrell imported "Atlas, Imperial, Royal, Medium, Demy, Foolscap & Pot, writing & printing Paper of all sorts" – a dazzling assortment beside the Milton crown and demy offered by the Fleets.[48] Stationers and importers generally had a much more valuable stock of books than printer–booksellers, worth an average of £409 as against £63 in 1771, about six and a half times as much. The annual income of printer–booksellers also ranged more widely, from £8 to £46 in 1771, as against some £20 to £46 for importers and stationers.[49] Importers and stationers were thus wealthier than the printer–booksellers, though none of them approached the Hancocks.

Their downfall began in an act of private vengeance. In 1769, John Hancock, furious at John Mein's disclosure of his surreptitious imports, alerted Mein & Fleeming's chief creditors in Edinburgh, Kincaid & Bell, and persuaded them to foreclose on Mein's debts.[50] Mein returned to London, where he wrote for the British government. The occupation of Boston by British troops under General Gage in 1774–1776 ousted patriot printers like Isaiah Thomas and Edes & Gill, and the return of the Revolutionary party to power drove out the loyalists, who resettled in Nova Scotia with the British troops when they evacuated Boston or later moved to occupied New York: Margaret Draper; John Howe, Mills & Hicks, Cox & Berry, and Andrew Barclay. Still others – Alford Butler, Jr., Benjamin and Ezekiel Russell, Joseph Snelling, and Nathaniel Coverly – set up shops outside of Boston or worked as itinerant printers. Not a few – James Foster Condy, Zechariah Fowle, Kneeland & Adams, Henry Knox, John Langdon, Timothy White – left town and trade altogether. The rapid depreciation of Continental and state currencies completed the ruin of patriots like Edes.[51] After 1775, only the Fleets remained of the pre-Revolutionary firms: Edes & Sons returned to Boston in 1780, but few names of the Boston partnerships preserved any continuity with the past. Adams & White (later Adams & Nourse), Draper & Folsom, Powars & Willis were the most important post-Revolutionary firms. Between 1776 and 1783, Boston had only two or three newspapers, which only rose to their prewar numbers with the Peace of Paris. The womb of colonial printers was finally exhausted, and Boston welcomed even alien replacements like John Norman, a Philadelphia engraver, or Robert Hodge, a New York printer. In 1786, Nathaniel Willis departed for a safari in the backlands, to Shepherdstown (West Virginia), Martinsburg (Virginia), and finally died in Chillicothe (Ohio).

The wartime divisions and antagonisms of the Boston trade began in politics, but they finished in economics. Continental and state currencies rapidly depreciated, undermining the trade's steadiest source of income: In Connecticut, the charges per sheet rose steadily from £3 15*s*. in 1776 to £67 10*s*. in 1779.[52] In Massachusetts, where two different firms had traditionally split the printing of the governor and council and the *Journals* of the House of Representatives, and where the stakes had been further enriched in 1767 by a contract for printing for the Board of Customs Commissioners, the governmental bounty ran dry with the departure of the British troops and the printing of the last House *Journals* in 1776. Revolutionary Massachusetts offered contracts for competitive bidding, and bewildering combinations of desperate printers – Edeses, Fleets, John Gill, and Powars & Willis – contended for the remains down to 1783, when the prize was finally firmly grasped by Adams & Nourse.[53]

When the dust settled, in 1790, Boston's printer–booksellers had recovered their former prosperity or more. The Federal census of that year placed them at the top of the artisan class, just below sea-captains[54] – but, of course, they were no longer the simple craftsmen that later accounts, like Wroth's, delight to celebrate. As editors of newspapers, they were professionals, though not always accepted as such; as booksellers and importers, they were traders and merchants. The movement inland to newly prospering ports like Salem and Newburyport, or to larger cities like New York, relieved patriots and loyalists, town and country printers alike from cut-throat competition, and the country produce with which some subscribers paid off the *Massachusetts Spy* or the land with which Vermont secured the services of Spooner & Green, was better pay than state or Continental currency.

The explosion of little country printing offices in the 1780s must ultimately reflect the shifting center of population, yet, as the career of Isaiah Thomas, the greatest of these country printers, shows, it was also enabled by structural transformations in Boston at the center of the trade, and it was accompanied by a radical shift in the content of country printing, whose production was no longer restricted to sermons by local preachers, local institutional or governmental publications, and "piracies" of Boston editions. The titles that poured from country presses after 1790 included reprints of recent, belletristic, popular English properties, and their distribution was typically forwarded by a regional network such as Thomas's, so that their imprints had no necessary cultural or economic connection with their place of production.

Thomas's early life, as he presents it in the *History of Printing in America*, is emblematic of the Revolution at large, the triumph of a poor apprentice over a neglectful master. Though he does not say so, the whole apparatus by which he was placed out to learn his trade had only been created in 1735, and it responded to the growing immiseration of the laboring classes in Boston (Fig. 9.4). Thomas, indeed, was luckier than most children: Only 4 of the apprentices in the 831 indentures preserved in the records of the Overseers were bound to printers; most of the poor were sent out to learn "husbandry" and "housewifery," often enough far away from their families in Boston.[55] And the political connection that Thomas would have his readers draw is not wholly fantastic, though he suppresses the evidence that makes it believable. His social background precisely parallels that of the South Boston ward boss Ebenezer McIntosh, whose command of the "rabble" proved so useful to Sam Adams and John Hancock during the Stamp Act crisis.[56]

Thomas's lowly position as "a dunghill-bred journeyman Typographer," to cite one contemptuous characterization of him, continued to affect his subsequent career.[57] The rebellious young man, who willfully broke with his master and stormed up and down the Atlantic coast defying his betters, was finally settled in the service of political factions for hire: by John Hancock, who sponsored, and Dr. Thomas Young and Joseph Greenleaf, who directed the *Massachusetts Spy* in 1771; by "several gentlemen" in Newburyport, 1773; and by Timothy Bigelow and William Stearns in Worcester, 1775. Thomas presents these employments ideologically, but the ideology was that of Hancock, Greenleaf, and Young, not of "their Man Thomas," who had contemplated moving to Bermuda in 1772 because "one of my profession here must be either of one party or the other (he cannot please both)."[58] On the whole, the Revolutionary faction served him poorly. He lost the contract of the Provincial Congress to nearer and more experienced printers: Ebenezer and Samuel Hall of Salem, who had set up shop in Stoughton Hall in Harvard Yard, and Benjamin Edes in Watertown.

The Worcester market was barely adequate to sustain his office. The circulation of the *Massachusetts Spy,* which had soared to 3,500 at the height of the pre-Revolutionary crisis, dropped to 1,200 subscriptions in Worcester, 1780, but only 150 had paid up, and his 297 customers fell into a circuit of eighty or ninety miles about town. He launched a successful almanac in 1778, but it was a country success of three to four thousand copies a year, which hardly compared to Franklin's ten thousand or Ames's fifty thousand.[59] Ironically enough, this production exactly matched that of his despised former master Zechariah Fowle: ballads, school books, chapbooks like *Aristotle's Masterpiece* and children's books like *Goody Two Shoes,* the staples that peddlers and local shopkeepers bought by the gross. This is not the production that later earned him the epithets of "the Baskerville of America" and "the Didot of the United States," the finely printed Bibles, dictionaries, and reprints of established English properties like Blackstone's *Commentaries* that flowed from his presses after 1788, when he opened a branch in Boston. But that printing, and the empire founded on it, really belongs to a subsequent volume.[60] For most of the 1780s, only Thomas's fantasy and fervid ambition distinguished him from another country knockabout, partner of Zechariah Fowle, and ballad-printer, Nathaniel Coverly, who worked in Chelmsford, Concord, Rehoboth, Plymouth, and Middleborough before finally settling in Boston in 1789. Prospectively, his patriotism, like that of most Bostonians, was mixed with his necessities; retrospectively, it became purer and served to explain both his poverty and his success. His fortune, however, was built on British properties, not on the *Massachusetts Spy,* the *Massachusetts Calendar,* and sensational attacks on his Boston elders and betters.

The proliferation of country printers in New England continued down to the 1840s, when the Boston book trade finally entered into competition with Philadelphia and New York for the national market. William Charvat has argued that the two phenomena are connected, in that the country printers preempted Boston's trade. In the mid-Atlantic region ("the New York–Philadelphia axis"), the publication of Paine's *Common Sense* (1776), of

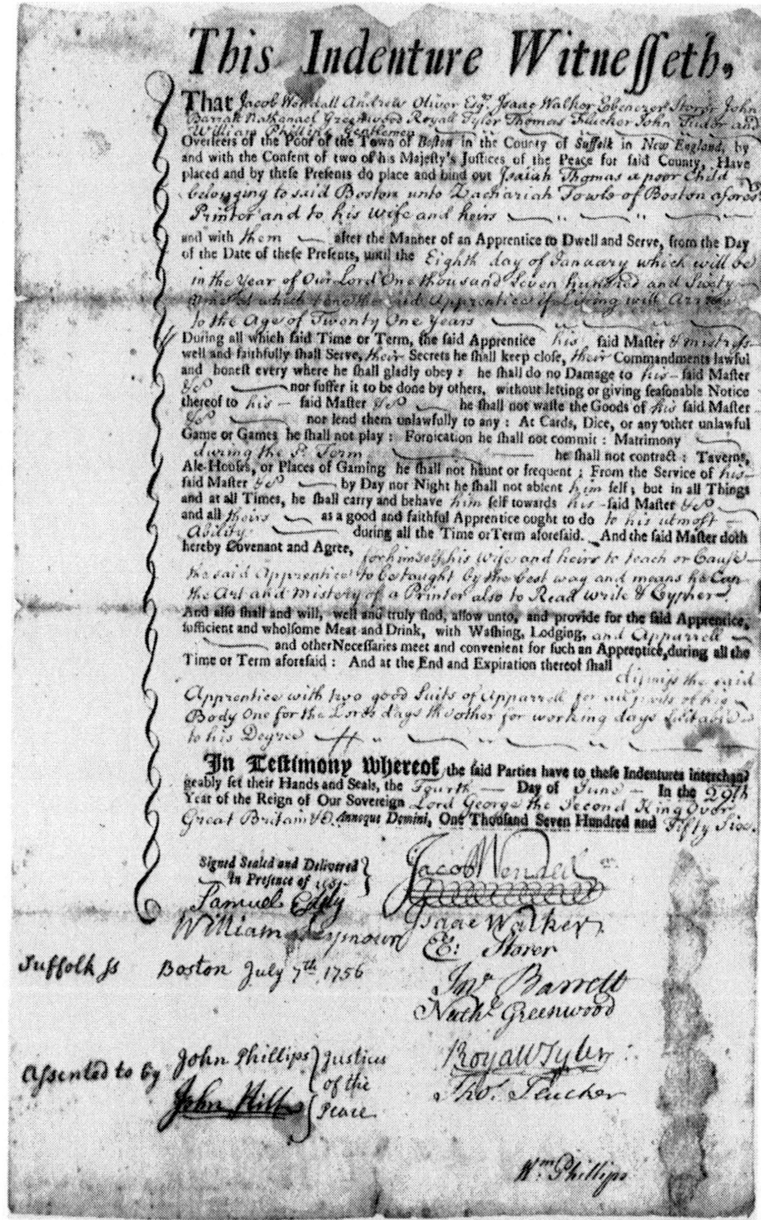

This Indenture Witneſſeth,

That Jacob Wendall Andrew Oliver Esq.r Isaac Walker Ebenezer Storer John Barrat Nathanael Greenwood Royall Tyler Thomas Flucker John Tudor and William Phillips Gentlemen Overſeers of the Poor of the Town of Boſton in the County of Suffolk in New England, by and with the Conſent of two of his Majeſty's Juſtices of the Peace for ſaid County, Have placed and by theſe Preſents do place and bind out Isaiah Thomas a poor Child belonging to said Boston unto Zachariah Fowle of Boston aforesd Printer and to his Wife and heirs and with them after the Manner of an Apprentice to Dwell and Serve, from the Day of the Date of theſe Preſents, until the Eighth day of January which will be in the Year of Our Lord One thousand Seven hundred and Sixty [illegible] which [illegible] said Apprentice if Living will arrive to the Age of Twenty One Years During all which ſaid Time or Term, the ſaid Apprentice his ſaid Maſter & mistress well and faithfully ſhall Serve, their Secrets he ſhall keep cloſe, their Commandments lawful and honeſt every where he ſhall gladly obey: he ſhall do no Damage to his ſaid Maſter &c nor ſuffer it to be done by others, without letting or giving ſeaſonable Notice thereof to his ſaid Maſter &c he ſhall not waſte the Goods of his ſaid Maſter &c nor lend them unlawfully to any: At Cards, Dice, or any other unlawful Game or Games he ſhall not play: Fornication he ſhall not commit: Matrimony during the sd Term he ſhall not contract: Taverns, Ale-Houſes, or Places of Gaming he ſhall not haunt or frequent; From the Service of his ſaid Maſter &c by Day nor Night he ſhall not abſent him ſelf; but in all Things and at all Times, he ſhall carry and behave him ſelf towards his ſaid Maſter &c and all theirs as a good and faithful Apprentice ought to do to his utmost Ability during all the Time or Term aforeſaid. And the ſaid Maſter doth hereby Covenant and Agree, for himself his Wife and heirs to teach or Cause the said Apprentice to be taught by the best way and means he Can the Art and Mistery of a Printer also to Read Write & Cypher. And alſo ſhall and will, well and truly find, allow unto, and provide for the ſaid Apprentice, ſufficient and wholſome Meat and Drink, with Waſhing, Lodging, and Apparrell and other Neceſſaries meet and convenient for ſuch an Apprentice, during all the Time or Term aforeſaid: And at the End and Expiration thereof ſhall dismiss the said Apprentice with two good Suits of Apparrell for all parts of his Body One for the Lords days the other for working days Suitable to his Degree

In Teſtimony whereof the ſaid Parties have to theſe Indentures interchangeably ſet their Hands and Seals, the Fourth Day of June In the 29th Year of the Reign of Our Sovereign Lord George the Second King over Great Britain &c Annoque Domini, One Thouſand Seven Hundred and Fifty Six.

Signed Sealed and Delivered In Preſence of us
Samuel Eddy
William Seymour

Jacob Wendell
Isaac Walker
Eb: Storer
Jno. Barrett
Nathl. Greenwood
Royall Tyler
Tho. Flucker
Wm. Phillips

Suffolk ss Boston July 7th 1756

Assented to by John Phillips, John Hill Justices of the Peace

Figure 9.4. The apprenticeship indenture of Isaiah Thomas, dated June 4, 1756, and signed by the Boston Overseers of the Poor; the counterpart that they retained, signed by Thomas's master Zechariah Fowle, is in the Boston Public Library. American Antiquarian Society.

Pope's *Essay on Man* (1790–1829), and of eighteenth-century editions of Defoe's and Richardson's novels was centralized in the main cities, whereas in New England, "scores of New England small towns" competed with Boston for these same properties. Tiny Litchfield, Connecticut, a town of some sixty-odd homes in 1804, was publishing Goethe, Pope, Goldsmith, and Gray. The printing of Royall Tyler's *Algerine Captive* in Walpole, New Hampshire, led Joseph Dennie to complain, "It is . . . extremely difficult for the Bostonians to supply themselves with a book that slumbers in a stall at Walpole"; equally unobtainable, in Charvat's opinion, were Litchfield publications, which sold only locally.[61]

The evidence he offers in support of these assertions, however, is of unequal value. In 1776, the British had just evacuated Boston, leaving the city depopulated and in shambles, and it is hardly surprising that only one edition of *Common Sense* appeared there – or that nine editions leapt from the presses of seven New England towns that were outside British control. As Dennie surmised, Walpole, a township of 1,743 inhabitants in 1800, could hardly have absorbed many copies of Tyler's novel, and in fact, it was still slumbering in its stalls in 1803.[62] Nevertheless, it was also for sale in Boston: Ebenezer Larkin and W. P. & L. Blake were both offering the *Algerine Captive* for sale in 1798, a copy somehow escaped from rural Walpole to be reprinted in London in 1802, and the edition was being offered "for general sale" throughout the United States in 1804.[63] Schoolbooks like the *Essay on Man* and heavily abridged chapbook editions of the classic English novelists sold readily enough in country stores or were peddled from door to door in the country, but new and fashionable two-volume novels like Tyler's or Goethe's needed a wider, less provincial market; it also paid the country printer to work off occasional editions of the classics in order to exchange them for proper country fare from Boston, Worcester, or Hartford. W. J. Gilmore-Lehne, in the best analysis of a New England country market to date, points out that "Only one title in seven available for sale in the Upper [Connecticut] Valley in the period 1790–1830 was published there."[64] In short, New England country printers remained "booksellers" long after their counterparts elsewhere had become "publishers."

Perhaps the most curious feature of Charvat's thesis is his *dirigiste* assumption that the true measure of a region's literary and national importance is not the absolute number of books produced there, nor even the number of books printed in its metropolis, but rather the prominence of metropolitan production compared to that of its provinces. Boston printed nine editions of the *Essay on Man* between 1786 and 1820, whereas Philadelphia and New York each printed only eight; nevertheless, Boston was weaker than the "axis," Charvat argues, because twenty-nine New England country presses in all six states printed some forty-eight editions, four of them in Windsor, Vermont, alone (population 2,211 in 1800), besides seven Vermont editions elsewhere. New York's immediate territory, moreover, was nearly as infested with country printers as Boston's. The same Malthusian scarcities that drove New England printers out of Boston and swept them up the Connecticut River from Hartford also carried them across Long Island Sound and resettled them along the Hudson River. Commercially, too, Connecticut and Vermont were closer to New York than Boston – which may also be why so few Connecticut printers moved to Maine, western Massachusetts, or New Hampshire.[65]

The statistics of the first national book-trade catalogue (Boston, 1804) speak for themselves: Of the most valuable and widely distributed literary production in America, 264 editions were printed in Pennsylvania, Delaware, Maryland, the District of Columbia, half of New Jersey and the South; 152 in New York State and the other half of New Jersey; and 299 in New England. In the metropolises alone, Philadelphia accounted for 204 editions, Boston for 172, and New York for 126.[66] The continuing importance of country printing in New England meant that a relatively high percentage of its production lay in schoolbooks and chapbooks, the properties that elevated the "plodding industry" of Hartford (as Samuel G. Goodrich called it) to rival Boston's.[67] Despite the region's many geographical, political, and economic fractures, the peculiar structure of the New England trade consolidated it into a market where the country trade extended and diversified Boston sales and production. The marketing of books in the South and West, where Philadelphia and New York were expanding, required very different strategies, which Boston would not acquire for many years, however.

TABLE 9.1 **Boston printing, 1740**

Evans Number/Collation		Printer(s)	Sheets per Copy
	Religious (ed. = 500 copies?, except as specified): 91,960 sheets.		
o	*Rules for self-examination* / J. Alleine. 8vo: [–]²	Rogers & Fowle	0.25
o	*Dialogue between a learned man and a beggar.* 8vo: A⁴	Rogers & Fowle	0.50
o	*Copy of a letter* / J. Eliot. 8vo: [–]²	Rogers & Fowle	0.25

(*continued*)

TABLE 9.1 **Boston Printing, 1740**

Evans Number/Collation	Printer(s)	Sheets per Copy
Religious (ed. = 500 copies?, except as specified): 91,960 sheets.		
0 [*Spiritual songs* / J. Mason]	Draper (1000 copies, HL)	7.25
0 [*Alarm to unconverted sinners* / J. Alleine]	Draper (2000 copies, HL)	15.50
4470 8vo: [A]–F^4 G^2	Kneeland & Green	3.25
4477 = London, 1720 ed.?		
4478 8vo: A–C^4 (C4 blk.?)	Kneeland & Green	1.50
4479 8vo: [A]–C^4 D^2	Fleet	1.75
4481 8vo: [A]–C^4	Rogers & Fowle	1.50
4482 8vo: [A]–D^4	Fleet	2.00
4483 12mo: A–Q^6	D. Fowle	8.00
4486 12mo: A–D^6 E^4	D. Fowle	2.33
4489 8vo: A–Q^4	Draper (500 copies, HL)	8.00
4490 8vo: [A]–C^4 D^2	Rogers & Fowle	1.75
4491 12mo: A–C^6	Draper (500 copies, HL)	1.50
4497 8vo: [A]–S^4 T^2	Draper	9.25
4504 8vo: [A]–D^4	Kneeland & Green	2.00
4510 8vo: [A]–F^4 G^2	Rogers & Fowle	3.25
4534 8vo: [A]–L^4 (L4 blk.?)	Draper	5.50
4561 12mo: A–I^6 K^2	Draper (500 copies, HL)	4.67
4562 8vo: [A]^2 B–E^4 ([A]1 blk.?)	Draper	2.25
4565 12mo: A^6 (A6 blk.)	G. Rogers	0.50
4595 8vo: [A]–D^4 (D4 blk.)	Kneeland & Green	2.00
4596 [1740?] = [176–?]		
4598 = London ed., also issued in Boston		
4599 8vo: [A]–E^4 (E4 blk.?)	Draper (500 copies, HL)	2.50
4614 8vo: [A]–D^4 (D4 blk.)	Draper	2.00
4625 8vo: A–C^8	Draper	3.00
4628 12mo: A–D^6 E^2	Kneeland & Green	2.17
4629 12mo: A–E^6	Draper (2000 copies, HL)	2.50
46318 vo: A–G^4	Fleet	3.50
4632 8vo: [A]–F^4	Fleet	3.00
4635 = 4633 (Philadelphia ed., also issued in Boston)		

(*continued*)

TABLE 9.1 **Continued**

Evans Number/Collation	Printer(s)	Sheets per Copy
Religious (ed. = 500 copies?, except as specified): 91,960 sheets.		
4637 8vo: A–B^4	Rogers & Fowle	1.00
4648 12mo: A–B^6	Rogers & Fowle	1.00
4659 8vo: [A]–D^4 E^2	Draper	2.25
6551 12mo: A–B^6 (not after 1740)	Kneeland & Green?	1.00
40196 12mo: A–H^6	Draper (1500 copies, HL)	4.00
40228 8vo: A–B^4	Rogers & Fowle	1.00
40229 8vo: A–B^4	Rogers & Fowle	1.00
Newspapers (ed. = 500 copies?): 71,750 sheets		
4475 *Boston News-Letter*	Draper	30.00
4476 *Boston Post-Boy*	[J. Bushell?]	26.00
4473 *Boston Evening-Post*	Fleet	33.50
4474 *Boston Gazette*	Kneeland & Green	26.50
4567 *New England Weekly Journal*	Kneeland & Green	27.50
Educational (ed. = 2,000 copies?): 35,000 sheets		
0 [*Introduction to the English Tongue* / N. Bailey]	Rogers & Fowle (advt., Evans 40188)	6.50?
0 [*English instructor* / H. Dixon]	Draper (2000 copies, HL)	9.00
4623 12mo: A–D^6	Kneeland & Green	2.00
40222 [1740?] = 1738		
Government printing: 24,442.5 sheets		
0 [Treasury warrants, Mar. 20]	Draper (100 copies, MA)	0.50
0 [Treasury warrants, Apr. 29]	Draper (100 copies, MA)	0.50
0 [Assessors' warrants]	Draper (200 copies, MA)	0.25
0 [Precepts & returns for the Assembly]	Draper (260 copies?)	0.25
0 [Constables' warrants]	Draper (380 copies, MA)	0.25
0 [Impost act, 10 January]	Draper (500 copies, MA)	2.00
0 *Oaths* [174–?]	The Boston Public Library has three editions that qualify for these two entries in NAIP: One should probably be dated September 13, 1738 (MA 246: 46); one is signed by Governor Shirley, 1746; no other editions appear in Draper's bills for printing between February 20, 1738 and November 12, 1740.	
0 [Proc.: March 8]	Draper (200 copies?)	0.50

(*continued*)

TABLE 9.1 **Continued**

Evans Number/Collation	Printer(s)	Sheets per Copy
o [Proc.: April 5]	Draper (150 copies, MA)	0.50
o Proc.: April 21	Draper (200 copies, MA)	1.00?
o Proc.: May 16	Draper (125 copies, MA)	0.50
o [Proc.: June 30]	Draper (100 copies?)	0.50
o [Proc.: June 30]	Draper (500 copies, MA)	1.00
o Proc.: September 18	Draper (200 copies, MA)	0.50
o Proc.: October 20	Draper (100 copies?)	0.50
o [Proc.: October 29]	Draper (100 copies, MA)	0.50
o [Proc. (rev. ed.): November 5]	Draper (450 copies, MA)	0.50
o [Proc.: November 6]	Draper (450 copies, MA)	0.50
4488 Funeral sermon (S. Holden) / B. Colman. 4to: [A]–D^4	Draper (430 copies, HL)	4.00
4498 Election sermon / W. Cooper. 8vo: [A]–F^4 G^2	Draper (500 copies?)	3.25
4547+ Laws (1726), pp. 693–720 [i.e., 722]). fol.: [6Z]^2 7A1 7B1 7C–7E^2 7F1 7G1 ^{2}7G^2 7H1	Draper (400 copies?)	7.50
4552 Tax act. fol.: A–B^2 C1	Draper (200 copies, MA)	2.50
4553 Proc. (Thanksgiving): October 20	Draper (200 copies?)	0.50
4554 Proc.: January 31 '1740' = 1740/1		
4555+ *Journal* for 1739–1740 / H.R.. fol.: A–2C^2 chi1 2D-2R^2 ^{2}chi1 2S–3C^2 (–E2, I2, S2, V2, Y2, 2B2, 2H2, 2O2, 2Q2, 2Z2)	S. Kneeland (300 copies?)	45.00
4597 Fast sermon / J. Sewall. 8vo: [A]–E^4	Draper (400 copies, HL)	2.50
40203 Proc.: July 17	[Draper] (100 copies?)	0.50

Psalmbooks (ed. = 2000 copies?): 22,000 sheets

4471 = 4115		
40187 8vo: A–L^8	Draper	11.00

Political and controversial (500 copies?, except as specified): 17,375 sheets

4467 4to: A–C^2	[Rogers & Fowle?]	1.50
4484 8vo: A–B^4 C^2	Fleet	1.25
4485 8vo: A–B^4 C^2	Fleet	1.25

(*continued*)

TABLE 9.1 Continued

Evans Number/Collation	Printer(s)	Sheets per Copy
4515 8vo: [A]–G^4 (G4 blk.?)	Fleet	3.50
4530 8vo: [A]–H^4	Kneeland & Green	4.00
4533 8vo: A–K^4	Kneeland & Green	5.00
4585 8vo: A–B^4	Rogers & Fowle	1.00
4587 8vo: [A]–E^4	Fleet	2.50
4600 8vo: [A]–D^4	G. Rogers (2000 copies, HL)	2.00
4602 8vo: A–B^4	Draper	1.00
4644 8vo: [A]–B^4	Kneeland & Green	1.00
4647 8vo?: [A]–D^4	G. Rogers	2.00
40190 8vo: $[-]^2$	[Fleet?]	0.25
40195 fol.: A^2 B1	[Draper?]	1.50
40197 fol.: $[-]^2$	???	1.00
Almanacs: 7,000 sheets		
4469 8vo: $[-]^8$	Draper (7000 copies, HL)	1.00
4607 = assumed from the sequence		
Miscellaneous (ed. = 500 copies?): 6,375 sheets		
4503 8vo: A–B^4	Kneeland & Green	1.00
4541 8vo: $[A]^4$ B^2	Kneeland & Green	0.75
4622 12mo: A–D^6	Draper	2.00
40188 12mo: A–S^6 (S5, 6 blk.)	Rogers & Fowle	9.00
Broadsides (ed. = 500 copies?, except as specified): 5,000 sheets		
0 *Brave Capt. Lovell /* J. Stow. half sheet	???	0.50
4525 1 sheet	[Draper] (2000 copies? cf. *Pubs. CSM* 26:12)	1.00
39802 [174–?] = [1738/50]		
40193 half sheet	[Draper] (2000 copies?)	0.50
40194 half sheet	Fleet	0.50
40198 1 sheet	???	1.00
40199 1 sheet	???	1.00
40207 half sheet	???	0.50
40209 half sheet?	[Fleet]	0.50
41097 [174–?] = [1744 or 5?]		
	Total sheets: 280,902.5	

TABLE 9.2 **Boston printing, 1765**

Evans Number/Collation	Printer(s)	Sheets
Newspapers (ed. = 1,500 copies?, apart from the *Boston Post-Boy*, whose "circulation was not extensive" [Thomas]): 290,250 sheets		
9918 *Boston Evening Post*	Fleets	54.50
9919 *Boston Gazette*	Edes & Gill	58.50
9994 *Boston Post-Boy*	Green & Russell (500 copies?)	52.50
10066 *Boston News-Letter*	Drapers	63.00
Almanac for 1766: 105,000 sheets		
9896 8vo: A–C⁴	McAlpine & Fleeming (10,000 copies?)	1.50
9897 8vo: A–C⁴	Kneeland (J.) & Adams (10,000 copies?)	1.50
10212 8vo (h.c.l.): A–C⁴	Drapers (A) / Edes & Gill (B) / Fleets (C) (50,000 copies)	1.50
Psalmbook / Tate & Brady; Watts (ed. = 2,500 copies?): 78,325 sheets		
9913 12mo: A–L¹² M⁶; A–F¹² G⁶	Kneeland (J.) & Adams	18.00
9914 12mo: A–L¹², B–C¹² D⁴ (L5, 6, 9 signed 'A2, 3, 6')	McAlpine & Fleeming	13.33
Religious (ed. = 500 copies?): 69,375 sheets		
9905 8vo: [A]–E⁴ / [F]–G⁴	Fleets / Drapers	3.50
9906 8vo: [A]–C⁴ / D–H⁴	Drapers / Fleets	4.00
9909 8vo: A–D⁴	Fleets	2.00
9923 4to: A–C⁴	Fleets	3.00
9925 8vo: A⁴ B–Y⁸ Z⁴(A1 blk.)	D. & J. Kneeland	22.00
9926 8vo: A–F⁴ (F4 blk.?)	Kneeland (J.) & Adams	3.00
9961+ 8vo: [A]⁴ B–G⁸ H² (H2 blk.?); pi⁴ A–M⁸ N–Z⁴	S. Kneeland	24.75
10007 8vo (h.c.l.): pi⁴ (–pi1) A–T⁴ [U]1 (= pi1)	McAlpine & Fleeming	10.00
10046 8vo: A–D⁴	McAlpine & Fleeming	2.00
10070 = 10071		
10071 8vo: a¹⁰ B–U⁸ W–2L⁸ 2M²	Edes & Gill	35.50
10072 8vo: [A]–C⁴	Edes & Gill	1.50
10073 8vo: [A]–E⁴ (E4 blk.?)	Edes & Gill	2.50
10119 8vo: [A]–S⁴	McAlpine & Fleeming	9.00
10163 = ghost of London ed.		
10177 8vo: pi1 A–E⁴ [F]1	Drapers	2.75

(*continued*)

TABLE 9.2 **Continued**

Evans Number/Collation	Printer(s)	Sheets
10191 8vo: A–G⁴ H²	Fleets	3.75
10204 8vo: [A]–D⁴ E²	Edes & Gill	2.25
41549 [1765?] = [1765/75]		
41550 8vo: [–]⁴	Z. Fowle	0.50
41560 12mo: A–N⁶ O²	Z. Fowle	6.75
Educational (ed. = 2,500 copies?): 38,550 sheets		
9921 16mo: [A]–B⁸	[S. Kneeland (address)]	1.00
10142 12mo: A–C⁶ D1	S. Kneeland	1.67
10179 obl. 24mo?: A–S⁸ (S6–8 blk.)	[Edes & Gill? (orns.)]	3.00
10183 8vo: A–C⁴ D²	[Z. Fowle (cf. 41542 advts.)]	1.75
10189 [1765] = [1764]		
10201 8vo: [A]–F⁴	Z. Fowle	3.00
10206 12mo: A–B⁶	Fleets	1.00
41532 8vo: A–C⁴	Z. Fowle	1.50
41542 12mo: A–B⁶	Z. Fowle	1.00
41598 12mo: A–C⁶	D. & J. Kneeland	1.50
Political and Controversial (ed. = 1000 copies?): 38,250 sheets		
9903 8vo: A–B⁴	Edes & Gill	1.00
9916 [1765] = [1733]		
9917 8vo: [–]⁸	Fleets	1.00
9930 8vo: [A]–B⁴	???	1.00
9932 8vo: pi² A–M⁴ ²M⁴	McAlpine & Fleeming	6.75
9945 8vo: [A]–B⁴ / C–D⁴	Fleets / Green & Russell	2.00
9946 8vo: A⁴ / B⁴ C²	Fleets / Green & Russell	1.25
9960 8vo: A–F⁴	Fleets	3.00
9982 4to: [A]–F⁴	Z. Fowle	6.00
9986 Stamp Act. fol.: A–F²	Edes & Gill	6.00
10068 8vo: [A]⁴ / B–E⁴ / F⁴ G²	Drapers ([A])/ Edes & Gill? (B-E) / Fleets? (F-G)	3.25
10112 8vo: [A]–C⁴	[S. Kneeland (address)]	1.50
10116 8vo: [A]–E⁴	Edes & Gill	2.50
10117 8vo: [A]–D⁴	Edes & Gill	2.00
41529 8vo: [A]–B⁴	[Kneeland & Adams (address)]	1.00
Government printing: Green & Russell, 34,000; Drapers, 10,000 sheets Proclamations (MA 254:32): £13 12*s.* @ 2*d.* a sheet = 1 ,632 sheets		
o [Proc.: April 7]	Drapers	£1 6*s.*
o [Proc.: April 13]	Drapers	£1 10*s.*
o [Proc.: July 25]	Drapers	£1 4*s.*

(*continued*)

TABLE 9.2 **Continued**

Evans Number/Collation	Printer(s)	Sheets
o [Proc.: September 6]	Drapers	£1 4s.
o [Proc.: December 18]	Drapers	£1 10s.
10060 Proc.: March 13	Drapers	£2
10061 Proc.: November 13	Drapers	£2
41562 Proc.: August 29	Drapers	£1 10s.
41563 Proc.: August 15	Drapers	£1 8s.
9732+ *Journal* for 1764–1765 / H.R. fol.: [A]–4I[2]	Green & Russell (300 copies, MA)	78.00
9964 Election sermon / A. Eliot. 8vo: [A]–G[4] H[2]	Green & Russell (750 copies, MA)	3.75
10052+ Laws (1759), pp. 481–500. fol.: 4H–4I[2] chi1 4K-4L[2] 4M1	Green & Russell / Drapers (400 copies, MA)	5.00
10055+ Temp. acts (1763), pp. 217–95. fol.: 3L–4F[2] [4G][2] 4H1	Green & Russell / Drapers (400 copies, MA)	20.50
10059 Tax act, 29 May. fol.: A1–7	Green & Russell / Drapers (400 copies, MA)	3.50
10065 Resolves, October 29 (300?)	Green & Russell (300 copies?)	0.50
10151 *Hemp-husbandry* / E. Quincy. 4to: A–D[4]	Green & Russell (450 copies, MA)	4.00
41544 Stamp Act (1759 Laws, pp. 499–520). fol.: 4M–4Q[2] 4R1	[Drapers; cf. *SB* 16: 174] (400 copies?)	5.50
41566 Treasurer's warrant, October 28	Drapers (250 copies, MA)	0.50
Miscellaneous (ed. = 500 copies?): 7,500 sheets		
o *Answer with advice* / Z.B. 12mo?: [A][4] B[2]	[Z. Fowle (address)]	0.50
10043 4to: [–][4]	Fleets	1.00
10069 8vo: A–G[4] [H][2]	Mein & Fleeming	3.75
10086 8vo: A[4] B–G[8] H–[I][4]	McAlpine	7.50
010207 8vo: A–C[4] D1	Drapers	1.75
41332 12mo: [–][6] ([–]5, 6 blk.)	???	0.50
Broadsides (tickets and labels excluded): 4,500 sheets		
9999 1 sheet	Drapers (2,000 copies; cf. *Pubs. CSM* 26:12)	1.00
10114 [1765] = [1777]		
41516 half sheet	??? (500 copies?)	0.50

(*continued*)

TABLE 9.2 **Continued**

Evans Number/Collation	Printer(s)	Sheets
41523 half sheet	[Edes & Gill (orn.); 500 copies?]	0.50
41527 half sheet	McAlpine & Fleeming (500 copies?)	0.50
41547 half sheet	[Drapers; 2,000 copies]	0.50
41555 half sheet	[Edes & Gill?; 500 copies?]	0.50
41556 half sheet	??? (500 copies?)	0.50
41559 half sheet	??? (500 copies?)	0.50
41591 No copy located		
		Total sheets: 675,250

Note: The entry "Evans 0" denotes a title that should be in Evans, either an edition recorded only in NAIP or (in square brackets) a lost edition. Items that Evans assigns to Boston that were actually printed elsewhere, printed earlier or later than the dates chosen for analysis, or never printed at all, are included in the tables, with a brief explanation for their exclusion from analysis.

The collation reconstructs the number of printed sheets and how they were folded and bound in order to make up books. Thus "8vo: [A]–E^4 (E4 blk.?)" indicates that Evans 4599 has five half-sheet gatherings, folded in four leaves each: the first gathering of Evans 4599 is unsigned, the last four are signed B, C, D, E, and in the copies examined, the last leaf of gathering E is wanting, either because the printer used it for another book or because a binder or owner removed it (blank leaves were useful as scrap paper); superscript figures indicate gatherings, on-line figures denote leaves; the pagination is considered part of the contents and ignored in this formula. The signatures "pi" and "chi" denote preliminary and intermediary unsigned leaves, respectively, whose position in the collational sequence is implied by their text. For a full explanation, see Fredson Bowers, *Principles of Bibliographical Description* (Princeton, N.J.: Princeton University Press, 1949).

Five half sheets = 2.50 sheets, recorded in the right-hand column; hence, for an edition of an estimated 500 copies, the printer of Evans 4599 would have printed a total of 1,250 sheets (included in the total of 91,960 sheets of **Religious** printing). Categories are bolded and listed in descending order of their importance, by numbers of sheets. The total number of sheets in all categories appears at the end of each table.

Key:

+ = multiple Evans numbers, listed under the first.

h.c.l. = horizontal chain-lines, uncharacteristic of the format.

HL = Daniel Henchman Ledgers; the invariable charge for printing 500–1,000 copies is recorded as 500.

MA = Massachusetts Archives (State Archives, Columbia Point, Boston, Mass.).

CHAPTER TEN

Periodicals and Politics

PART ONE. EARLY AMERICAN JOURNALISM: NEWS AND OPINION IN THE POPULAR PRESS

CHARLES E. CLARK

As a name for the usually perishable kind of writing that reports or comments upon contemporary public affairs, the term "journalism" entered the English vocabulary only in the early nineteenth century.[1] While its application to various forms of writing in the two centuries before that is therefore anachronistic in the strictest sense, a term is needed; "journalism" is handy, accurate, and understood by modern readers. Properly employed, the term refers to a literary practice as distinct from the business of publishing: A journalist writes; a publisher puts out a newspaper, magazine, or pamphlet in which works of journalism may be printed. In the days of metal type, the mechanical work necessary to that enterprise was done by a printer, whether or not he or she was also the publisher.

Obviously, it has always been possible for the same person to carry out all three of these functions – writer, publisher, and printer – as many American printers did in the eighteenth century. In England, the proprietors of several newspapers and journals called themselves "author," implying that in those cases the publisher was also the journalist. For clarity's sake, however, this discussion will maintain, as far as possible, the distinction between genres of journalism and the publications in which they were printed – though it will deal with both subjects.

Colonial Americans practiced several forms of journalism. The most obvious and most prevalent was simple news reporting, but this practice itself came in many varieties depending upon the reporter and the purpose of the report. David Paul Nord has argued, for example, that the first "news" reporting in New England is to be found in the sermons and providential histories of ministers and others who scanned and interpreted both natural and human events for signs of divine favor or disfavor and evidence of the fulfillment of prophecy.[2] A still earlier form of "news" from America was the literature of discovery, often printed in pamphlets for what one presumes was an eager European audience. Such accounts detailed encounters with natural wonders and exotic people, and in some cases conveyed optimistic reports of colonizing enterprises for which the writers sought financial and political backing.

On a more prosaic level, Europeans had long practiced the systematic reporting of what was usually called "intelligence," eventually in a standard form that profoundly influenced the content of English and American newspapers in the eighteenth century. By 1600 the supplying of political, diplomatic, commercial, and ecclesiastical intelligence, mainly by handwriting, had evolved into an actual profession. Throughout most of the seventeenth and eighteenth centuries, London "newswriters," like their somewhat earlier counterparts in Germany, France, and Italy, were being hired by country lords and gentlemen to keep them abreast of affairs at court and elsewhere in the metropolis. A few London newsletter services survived well into the era of printed newspapers; their subscribers included country printers who copied them along with printed sources into their provincial newspapers. Three colonial postmasters that we know of, and probably more, were adapting this longstanding practice to American needs at least as early as 1700 and as late as 1778.[3]

A newswriter typically reported each of his various items of intelligence, whether of court gossip, a judicial action, or a military or diplomatic report from abroad, in a terse one- or two-sentence paragraph devoid of explanation or background, since the recipient was assumed to be in need of neither. Items were always reported in the order in which the various events occurred, without regard to classification either by subject or by relative importance. Neither the style nor the content of this genre of writing, which became completely standardized before 1700, was altered by its adaptation to print. Such reports comprised the main substance of most newspapers from the official *London Gazette,* founded as the *Oxford Gazette* in 1665, to its many British and American imitators through the eighteenth century. The London bookseller Ichabod Dawks even had his *Dawks's Newsletter* printed in script-like type spread across the page instead of in columns and headed the text with a flamboyant woodcut "Sr" (Sir), thus maintaining the transparent fiction that his printed newsletter, like its manuscript predecessors, was addressed to each of its recipients individually.

While the newsletter genre can be considered a direct ancestor of most of the serious news reporting that appeared in the newspapers of the eighteenth century, it had a close relative that was not as influential in the long run. The propagandistic writing in the so-called newsbooks of the English Civil War, Interregnum, and very early Restoration eras did indeed contain news, but it was reported invariably with an entirely undisguised partisan cast, sometimes in direct response to similar publications from the other side.[4] Pamphlets such as these, whose only purpose was to wage a war of words, had little influence on the development of journalism in subsequent decades, though the adaptation of news reporting to partisan conflict resurfaced from time to time in America, most conspicuously – though neither for the first nor the last time – during the era of the American Revolution.

There were other forms of "journalism" as well. One was the belletristic essay, usually published in periodical journals established for the purpose beginning in London early in the eighteenth century. The most influential practitioners of the genre were Richard Steele and Joseph Addison, whose *Tatler* and *Spectator* set the tone for what was then called "polite" discourse about contemporary manners, morals, fashions, and politics for many decades to come. These writings were well adapted to collection in book form, and in that format became perpetuated, reaching far greater audiences over the long term than the journals in which they originally appeared. Essays by Steele, Addison, and their associates profoundly influenced the young Benjamin Franklin, who rather precociously came of age as a writer in the 1720s. Their journals also inspired a number of crude and usually short-lived attempts at American imitations, confined wholly to Boston. While these imitations of British literary journals all either failed entirely or evolved into more conventional newspapers, the literary essay promoted by the *Tatler* and *Spectator* literature became a staple, though usually only occasional, feature of most American weekly newspapers throughout much of the eighteenth century.

Another was the political essay. The highly crafted political writings of the British Whig partisans John Trenchard and Thomas Gordon in the early 1720s raised persuasive journalism to a level of respectability and lasting influence, especially among Americans of the next two generations. Their *Independent Whig* essays, which appeared weekly as a periodical pamphlet throughout 1720, and their letters signed "Cato" in the *London Journal* from 1720 to 1723, supported the revolutionary settlement of 1688–1689 against lingering Tory opposition, argued for broad religious toleration, and warned against all forms of tyranny, including restraint of the press. The antiestablishment *New-England Courant* of Boston copied several of the Cato letters as early as 1721 and another in 1722. In the 1730s, Cato's letters and American adaptations figured conspicuously in the newspaper war in

New York that resulted in the prosecution of John Peter Zenger. It was during the 1770s, however, when the Revolutionary crisis was approaching its climax, that American journalists and readers entered upon a full-scale rediscovery and adaptation of the Gordon and Trenchard literature, which more than any other single source seems to have provided the rhetorical ammunition for resistance and independence.[5]

Whether writing a literary essay, a political polemic, or a letter to one's favorite newspaper on a topic of general interest, the author of any of these journalistic genres almost always adhered to the eighteenth-century convention of anonymity. Instead of signing one's real name, the author used a pseudonym. The more literary offerings often used pen-names already familiar in English print culture, the American practice having arisen during the circulation by both sexes of scribal essays and verses within circles whose members were known to one another.[6] Political essays, again in imitation of English practice, might be signed by a descriptive phrase such as "a Freeholder" or a name borrowed or adapted from classical antiquity, as in the Cato letters. In the case of a brief newspaper letter, the signature often consisted only of a single initial. Michael Warner has suggested that this very "impersonality" of public conversation in print was assumed by its participants to constitute its validity – that the legitimacy of one's participation in the new "public sphere" of print, and of the ideas offered to the public in this way, depended upon the absence of any overt identification with a particular author.[7] Yet American pamphleteers and newspaper writers adhered with great strictness to this "polite" convention even when, as must often have happened, their real identity was obvious to most readers.

Publishing Journalism

In colonial America, journalistic writing appeared primarily in four printed formats: the incidental broadside or news sheet, the periodical newspaper, the periodical magazine, and the pamphlet. In 1685, Samuel Green, Jr., a Bostonian printer, departed from all previous colonial printing conventions to reproduce the two-month-old *London Gazette* that had reported the death of Charles II and the accession of James. From then through the end of the century, news of current affairs became an occasional part of Boston's rapidly evolving print culture, most dramatically during the rebellion against Governor Edmund Andros in Boston in the spring of 1689. One especially notable contribution was a newspaper-like sheet, printed late in 1689, entitled *The Present State of the New-English Affairs*. It contained a selection of items all concerning the progress of Increase Mather, then in England, in securing a new charter for Massachusetts. In the 1690s, Boston presses printed broadside accounts of a naval battle (1692), an earthquake in Naples (1694), and an article from London's *Monthly Mercury* entitled "The Turkish Fast." In 1700, there appeared a Boston reprint of an entire *London Gazette* with news of a new Spanish king and the coronation of a pope. In this sporadic way, the several printers of Boston supplemented the oral dissemination of news. At the same time, Duncan Campbell, a bookseller and the town's postmaster, was exchanging news of Europe and the colonies by handwritten newsletter with at least one and probably other correspondents outside Massachusetts. Soon, however, the burden of news reporting shifted to the periodical newspaper, which after one false start in 1690 became a permanent and crucially important feature of the American public sphere beginning in 1704.[8]

The introduction of the newspaper genre to Boston in 1704 was a logical, if premature, development in British publishing. It was neither a delayed imitative response to a phenomenon already well entrenched in the British Isles nor its opposite, a colonial invention in an isolated cultural climate. In 1690, Benjamin Harris, an exile from Restoration London, where he had been a bookseller and antigovernment publicist, responded to a political and military crisis in Massachusetts by adapting a London genre to local circumstances. Not until the *New-England Courant* came on the Boston scene in 1721 would the content of another American newspaper be devoted primarily, as that of Harris's paper was, to the affairs of its own town and province. The only number of his *Publick Occurrences Both Forreign and Domestick* appeared on September 25, 1690. Internal evidence – its "Numb. 1" and the publisher's printed intention to furnish a number "once a moneth" or oftener – suggests that it was intended as a serial publication, though not all modern scholars agree. Harris's bold project came to a swift end, and in five years the publisher would be back in London, putting out the second independently published newspaper after the lapse of the act that had prohibited unlicensed printing. All of these newspapers that now flourished in London were modeled after the official *London Gazette,* which had been published under Crown auspices since 1665 and was the prototype in format and essential content for the newspapers in England and America that came later.[9]

Immediately after the lapse of the Licensing Act, some printers began migrating from London to the provincial cities of England. There, probably starting in 1701 in Norwich, they printed weekly newspapers for their own cities.[10] The spread of newspaper publishing in the provinces was still in its early stages in 1704 when John Campbell enriched the provincial press by adding his *Boston News-Letter,* the first successful American newspaper.

Thus the beginning of newspaper publishing in America is best understood as part of a development that was going on simultaneously in the

British Isles. Had *Publick Occurrences* survived beyond one number – an eventuality that under the circumstances Harris, for all his brashness, had no right to expect – it would actually have been both the first independently published English newspaper and the first English provincial newspaper.[11] Viewed in this light, the long-lived *Boston News-Letter,* begun in 1704, was the fourth English provincial newspaper.[12]

Campbell had succeeded his father Duncan Campbell as Boston postmaster upon Duncan's death in 1702. Since he is known to have carried on his father's practice of sending manuscript newsletters at least to the governor of Connecticut, and probably exchanged such newsletters with some of his fellow colonial postmasters as well, the founding of the *News-Letter* is often described simply as a matter of adapting an established practice to print – a theory to which Campbell's very choice of title lends weight.[13]

However, Campbell's decision to start a newspaper, beginning with what to modern readers seems a startlingly small press run of 250, was really much more than a relatively small evolutionary step from the exchange of manuscript newsletters. It may well be that the prior practice is what made this step an obvious one to Campbell, but if anything, the occasional news broadsides of the 1680s and 1690s were more exact antecedents of the *News-Letter* than the Campbells' own scribal exchanges. The printers' broadsides, like any newspaper but unlike the limited correspondence carried on by the postmasters, had made a commodity of the news by appearing in multiple copies offered to anyone who would buy. Moreover, the chief market for the *News-Letter* would have been in its own community, not primarily the manuscript newsletters' named correspondents outside the province. Far more than either the news broadsides or the postmasters' private exchanges, however, it was the London newspapers from which the *News-Letter*'s news was mainly copied that provided Campbell's model and principal inspiration. The format of the *News-Letter* matched that of the *London Gazette* in practically every detail, right down to the "Published by Authority" that appeared under the paper's nameplate, and of course its content consisted overwhelmingly of news of Britain and Europe copied from the *Gazette* and other London prints.[14]

Campbell's announcement that the *News-Letter* was "published by authority" raises the question of the paper's exact relationship to the province government. As postmaster of Boston, Campbell was himself a public official and probably understood his one publishing activity as an extension of his official duties (and opportunities for profit) in the post office. However, he owed his appointment and his responsibility in office not to the governor or legislature of Massachusetts Bay but to the postmaster-general of England by way of the deputy postmaster-general for the American colonies. Campbell's actual behavior as publisher of the *News-Letter* suggests that the phrase "published by authority" was accurate only in the literal sense that Campbell sought and received the prior "approbation" of the governor's office for the contents of each weekly number – essentially a voluntary submission to censorship. Thus, unlike the *London Gazette* that Campbell tried so zealously to imitate, the *News-Letter* was not really an official medium of government. Campbell's repeated failure to secure a legislative subsidy for his enterprise is evidence both of the absence of official sponsorship and of Campbell's earnest effort to gain it.[15]

The *Boston Gazette,* begun by Campbell's successor in the Boston post office in December 1719, carried the designation "published by authority," which the *News-Letter* now dropped. However, there seems to have been little difference between the way the new postmaster and his several successors, each of whom in turn took over the *Gazette* with the post office until 1735, carried on publishing relations with the government and the way Campbell not only had done it while still in office but continued to do it as a private publisher until he turned ownership of the *News-Letter* over to his printer in 1722.[16] Thus in the pre-*Courant* years there was no practical difference in content between a newspaper operating with some recognized official link and one that was not; neither Boston publisher would have thought of dissenting from the proposition that ultimately it was the government, whether imperial or provincial, that controlled – and largely made – the news. Philadelphia's Andrew Bradford, who published the *American Weekly Mercury* beginning in 1719, probably operated under much the same assumption, though he did achieve greater variety in content and sources than his two earlier Boston counterparts, and in 1721 was bold enough to attack the British policy of transporting convicts to the colonies.[17] Whereas the immediate purpose of *Publick Occurrences* had been to prevent "false reports" about local matters, the chief intent of publishers like Campbell was to engage American readers in the affairs of the mother country and of Europe as seen through the eyes of London and Westminster. Exactly like the *Norwich Post* and the *Bristol Post-Boy,* the *Boston News-Letter* devoted most of its space to news copied verbatim from the newspapers of London. Most of the American newspapers that followed, with a few conspicuous exceptions, did the same thing. For neither the American publishers nor their provincial counterparts in England was this editorial decision a resort to innocuous "filler," as some historians have suggested. It was a way of overcoming the cultural and geographic boundaries that separated outlying peoples from the metropolitan center of their empire.[18] From the time of the Glorious Revolution nearly to the time of the American Revolution, the provincial people of America yearned to be more completely English – and to share as best they could in the life of the great metropolis that most of them would never see. One way to do this – the only practical way for most – was to read, and the newspapers provided the handiest and most immediate medium.

The American publishers' chief source in the earliest years, of course, was the London press. As postmaster, Campbell and his successors received bundles of the various London newspapers covering several weeks in every arriving ship that had sailed from London a minimum of six weeks earlier. During the three months of the year that winter storms closed off the North Atlantic sailing season, there were no arrivals at all and consequently the backlog of newspapers that began to arrive in March was especially large, meaning that some of the papers that came in the spring were up to five months old, reporting events that by now could have been as much as six or more months in the past. The postmaster received not only the newspapers addressed to him, but also, for appropriate distribution, those to which a very small provincial elite subscribed. Even considering the probability that some tavern owners and the proprietors of Boston's only two London-style coffeehouses in the early eighteenth century were among such subscribers, direct access to the newspapers of London would have been available to few in New England.

Thus Campbell's decision to publish an American newspaper with a comparatively small and rather arbitrary selection of what was by now very old European news was not primarily an effort to compete with the London prints themselves, but to make available some of their contents to a much wider American audience. On several occasions, in fact, Campbell advertised back numbers of the London papers for sale.[19] The *News-Letter*'s press run in its earliest years was between 250 and 300 copies per week, a figure that some historians have dismissed as tiny, leading them to conclude that the *News-Letter* could not have had much impact. However, even such a relatively small number of copies by later standards enabled far more persons, including those of non-elite status, to be drawn into an awareness and discussion of public affairs than the really tiny part of the population to which such information had been available before. The *News-Letter*, therefore, despite its small initial circulation, played a real role in the creation of a Boston, and American, public sphere.

In the three and a half decades following the first appearance of Campbell's *News-Letter*, American publishers – most of them printers – founded a total of fifteen additional newspapers, one in German, in eight mainland towns and two in the British West Indies. By this time, any printer who wished to stay in the newspaper business, according to Isaiah Thomas's estimate, needed to sell a minimum of 600 copies of his paper each week. We can take this figure, therefore, as the probable circulation of each newspaper in the highly competitive town of Boston and probably in several smaller places elsewhere. In the middle of the century, however, at least a few conspicuous newspapers exceeded that minimum significantly. William Hunter was probably printing about 1,000 weekly copies of his *Virginia Gazette* and Franklin between 1,500 and 2,000 of the *Pennsylvania Gazette*.[20] By now, the newspaper was becoming such a staple of the printing trade that more than four times as many newspaper issues, fifty-two per year in the case of most titles, were being printed as all other publications combined. This preponderance of newspapers in the print culture would become even more dramatic in the decades to come, so that by 1790, it could be said that newspaper issues had comprised 80 percent of all American publications up to that point.[21]

Most of the new publishers of these years, in keeping with the anglicizing tendencies within provincial culture generally, strove for more creative methods of involving their readers in the "polite" culture of the mother country. Beyond merely copying the news from London, publishers tried to make their newspapers actual analogues of the journals of London by adapting British formats and styles to the local community. Proclamations by the royal governor of the province and news of his comings and goings, for example, occupied the same relative places in a newspaper of Boston or New York that would be given in one of the newspapers of London to news and proclamations issuing from the royal palace. Essays on topics from marriage and fashion to religion and politics, either copied from journals like the *Spectator* and *Tatler* or written in imitation of them, began to take a prominent place in some of the newspapers.

Rarely, however, did provincial writers in this early period succeed in emulating their English models either with much grace or with great aptness to local conditions. The outstanding exception was Benjamin Franklin, whose youthful satirical "Silence Dogood" papers in his brother James's *New-England Courant* in 1722 set a brilliant new standard for American journalistic writing, even though the author was only sixteen. For all their lasting importance and the exceptional talent of their author, however, these and his subsequent writings were but one contribution to more general developments in journalism and the broadening role of print. The immediate purpose of the *New-England Courant,* which gave Franklin his first outlet, was to provide a printed opposition voice in the debate over a specific issue of local politics, the introduction to Boston of the new practice of inoculating for smallpox. This in itself was a development of great significance. On the one hand, the medium of print assumed a new role by taking up a quarrel between local factions that had heretofore been confined largely within the town's oral and probably scribal culture. On the other hand, the opponents of established authority asserted the legitimacy of their position by placing it in competition with the official view in the impersonal medium of print.[22] After the debate over inoculation died away with the epidemic that had provoked it, the *Courant* continued to represent those who opposed the traditional voices of authority in the province. In 1733, after the *Courant* had been dead seven years, John Peter Zenger's *New-York Weekly Journal* appeared in a similar role in New York under the sponsorship of a political faction opposed to the incumbent governor, William Cosby.[23]

It was not only as a political journal, however, that the *Courant* broke new ground. James Franklin and his club of fellow writers introduced to American readers the idea that a newspaper might be a vehicle of literature as well as intelligence. For a brief period in Boston, but nowhere else in pre-Revolutionary America, the literary pretensions of the *Courant* inspired subsequent attempts to publish newspaper-like journals whose organizing principle was derived from the club culture of London and which featured speculative essays and verse. Provincial conditions, however, did not permit a long life for the distinctive genre thus embodied in the *New-England Weekly Journal* during the few years after its founding in 1727, and in the *Weekly Rehearsal* from 1731 until it became the *Boston Evening-Post* under its new owner, the printer Thomas Fleet, in 1735. Not long after the youthful enthusiasm of the very few writers involved in these efforts became diverted into other channels, the papers came under the direction of their printers and assumed the look and more conventional content of what was gradually becoming the fairly standardized model of a provincial newspaper.

This experimental literary phase, however, had a marked impact on the standard product that was evolving. While neither Boston nor any other place in America possessed either a community of professional writers or a specialized reading audience sufficient to sustain any chiefly literary periodical for very long, newspaper readers everywhere had now developed a taste for speculative and imaginative essays, letters of opinion, and verse. In almost every American newspaper, these new elements in an expanded print culture now served as seasoning for the main diet of hard news.

It was these new elements that gave American newspaper publishers their first real cause for serious reflection on their proper role in the public sphere. By 1741, all but one of the dozen newspapers being published in the continental American colonies were owned by their printers. By 1755, printer ownership was universal. The printers' underlying concern in running their newspapers, of course, was assuring that this part of their printing business was turning a profit. Their most specific challenge as editors and publishers was not in the selection of news but in the treatment of readers' contributions, which could take any of several forms. One common form was a simple letter of opinion addressed to the publisher; another was an attempt at a polished essay, produced by a reader in imitation of his favorite British model. Occasionally, an aspiring local poet might submit lines for publication. At least as frequent as any kind of original contribution was an essay that a reader clipped from another source with the request that the publisher print it.

A significant portion of such contributions either addressed some local public issue such as the endemic currency shortage that afflicted all the British colonies or consisted of a more general discussion of political principles, sometimes with an implied application to local conditions. But it is a mistake to assume, as some historians have, that readers' contributions dealt invariably with political or even highly controversial topics, and that the strategies of printers in handling them were developed entirely out of political concerns. Many of these contributions, as well as much of the material that some publishers chose to print on their own, dealt with such nonpolitical topics as fashion, art, the choice of books, philosophy, and the conduct of life. Religion was another much-discussed topic, but not usually in a contentious way until the itinerary of George Whitefield in 1739–1740, when Whitefield and revivalism became "political" topics in the broadest sense themselves.

In the 1730s, publishers began to articulate their editorial policies, with particular attention to readers' contributions. Most historians who have noticed this development have emphasized the printers' desire to maintain political neutrality – thus avoiding the costly alienation either of government or of a significant segment of readers – by recourse to their own understanding of "freedom" or "liberty" of the press. In the words of Stephen Botein, "A press was 'free,' in this formulation, only if it was 'open to all parties.' A printer, in other words, should offer everyone the 'liberty' of his press, without favoring one set of opinions over the rest."[24]

Such an emphasis, while it represents one important aim of most printers (Zenger's operation of the *New-York Weekly Journal* in its earliest years being the most conspicuous exception), rests on an understanding of the colonial newspaper that is exclusively political. In fact, few printers of that era saw their role as newspaper publishers as quite such passive receptacles as this now-standard view implies. Although they were capable of resorting under criticism to the humble pose of "meer mechanic,"[25] most of them at the same time were trying on, not always comfortably, the opposite persona – that of independent gentleman with values of his own that he intended his newspaper to reflect. In every case, publishers' statements of purpose expressed not merely a desire to avoid partisanship but a positive aspiration toward moderation, fairness, and the enlightened genteel urbanity that was associated in the minds of colonials with the "polite" ideal embodied above all in Addison and Steele, the great British essay journalists of a decade or two earlier. Contributions that did not measure up, especially those devoted to what Benjamin Franklin called "private Altercation," could be and often were rejected.[26]

Americanization and Politicization

As more newspapers became published in more American cities, printers took to copying one another. Thus during the 1720s and 1730s, readers in Philadelphia, for example, became accustomed to reading scraps of news and articles of opinion from Boston, Annapolis, and Charleston. Through the printers' exchange network and the practice of mutual copying, therefore, readers began to develop a limited intercolonial "American" consciousness. At no time during those decades, however, did American content, whether produced locally or copied from another colony, come close to equalling either in measure of space or in prominence of placement the materials copied from London. Two significant changes in the character of American newspapers, one in the extent to which publishers relied on content imported from England and the other a shift by some to a more explicitly political role, took place between 1739 and 1765. The first change came in response to specific world and domestic events. The second was in part generational.

The tendency toward a somewhat heavier proportion of American content had begun in the early 1730s in New York and Boston with the heating up of factional warfare in the former and a critical stage in the Massachusetts currency crisis in the latter. This was only a preview, however, of the dramatic change in emphasis occasioned by two disparate events of 1739, a British declaration of war against Spain and the first intercolonial evangelical tour of George Whitefield.

Because much of the action in the War of Jenkins's Ear took place in the American theater and because provincial governments responded by raising both troops and money, American newspapers now paid unprecedented attention to important world events taking place in their own hemisphere and in many cases reported directly rather than in the old roundabout way through London. The trend continued as hostilities broadened into the War of the Austrian Succession and was resumed during the Seven Years' War.

Whitefield's American tour of 1739–1740 attracted even more attention while it lasted than the war, in part because of the skilled press agentry of Whitefield himself. With the enthusiastic cooperation of most newspaper publishers, Whitefield applied promotional and marketing techniques to the orchestration of what amounted to a modern evangelical crusade.[27] Newspapers thus not only reflected but contributed heavily to the American fascination with the charismatic evangelist. Thomas Fleet was attacked so vehemently for daring to challenge Whitefield's popularity in his *Boston*

Evening-Post that he was forced to print a long defense couched in the language of the "free press" ideal but also subtly lamenting a state of affairs in which it was not safe to express a minority view.[28] As Whitefield's appeal became less universal during his successive American tours, printed controversial debate over this and other aspects of the revival movement became more acceptable.

While an American reader continued to view the world partly through London eyes during the quarter century after 1740, that view was now being balanced by an increasing tendency in the newspapers to pay more attention to American events and American issues, reported and debated by Americans. This partial Americanization of content, occurring while the number of newspapers rose from thirteen to twenty-seven (plus two in the West Indies and another two in Canada), was complemented toward the end of that period by a parallel movement toward a more distinct politicization of the press. Except on the rare and usually only temporary occasions when printers had ventured into local political controversy, publishers of an earlier generation had adopted the more generalized value of "politeness" in trying to give a character to their journals and in managing the forum that they provided for readers. Their successors, working under slightly different influences, articulated a more sharply focused ideal. They were more likely to have spent their formative reading years absorbing the whiggish doctrines of the *Craftsman* and the *Independent Whig* than the *Spectator* and *Tatler* literature that had so engaged the young Benjamin Franklin. Accordingly, Benjamin Edes and John Gill, both more than a generation younger than Samuel Kneeland, from whom they bought the *Boston Gazette* in 1755, and the twenty-two-year-old William Goddard, who began the *Providence Gazette* in 1762, took deliberate steps to make their journals instruments of popular government and, as Goddard phrased it, "the Spirit of true *British* liberty."[29] While these young printers were self-consciously promoting civic virtue in New England, their contemporaries Hugh Gaine and James Parker were carrying on the New York tradition of explicit printed warfare between political factions in the *New-York Mercury* and the short-lived *Independent Reflector*, respectively, the latter a voice of the Presbyterian–Whig "New York Triumvirate" and devoted entirely to political writings. The growing politicization of the press in these years both reflected and reinforced the tendency toward popular discussion of public affairs and classical and Whig political thought, especially in the democratizing atmosphere of taverns, both urban and rural. Here newspapers and pamphlets were read aloud and their news and political essays loudly debated, tongues and the formalities of deference both loosened by alcohol.[30]

While this movement toward politicization is perhaps the most noticeable development in many American newspapers of the late provincial period, especially those founded in those years by the rising generation of printers, it is a distortion of the nature and main function of the newspapers of that era, with a few exceptions, to view them as partisan journals primarily. For a paper such as the *Independent Reflector* (and the *New-York Weekly Journal* before that) to serve as the organ of a particular party or faction was the exception rather than the rule. And although it is the political essays of the period that have attracted the most attention from historians, neither those writings nor other non-news content, despite conspicuous placement in many cases, made up the main substance of most papers. For the most part, right up until the Stamp Act, the newspapers continued to stress hard news, much of it still copied from London.[31]

The Magazine

Yet another development in English journalism inspired a further attempt at imitation by American printers. The founding of the *Gentleman's Magazine* in 1731 and its competitor the *London Magazine* in 1732 introduced a popular new British medium. In 1741, during the news-making era of King George's War and the first Whitefield tour, the two Philadelphia printers, Andrew Bradford and Benjamin Franklin, each tried to imitate the new genre. The appearance in the same week of Bradford's *American Magazine* and Franklin's *General Magazine* followed a vitriolic newspaper exchange in which Franklin accused his rival of stealing the idea of a magazine from him. The format of these first American monthly magazines, like that of their British models, was that of a pamphlet – seventy to seventy-six duodecimo pages in the case of the *General Magazine*. Like the British magazines, which had achieved popularity in part by reporting the proceedings of Parliament (sometimes thinly disguised as fiction), the two magazines carried reports of the proceedings of colonial legislatures, and in Franklin's case devoted considerable attention to the Whitefield controversy, currency, the war, and other public issues. For both Bradford and Franklin, the experiment failed; *American Magazine* lasted three months, *General Magazine* six. Their failure, however, did not prevent fifteen more attempts before 1776 to begin magazines in Boston, New York, Philadelphia, and in one case Woodbridge, New Jersey. Ten lasted a year or less, and only Boston's *American Magazine and Historical Chronicle,* a close imitation of *Gentleman's Magazine,* enjoyed a really substantial run, appearing monthly from September 1743 to December 1746.

The American reading public mainly subsisted on a diet of imported magazines until after the Revolution, when domestic titles and weekly newspapers proliferated. Seven of the fifteen magazines founded during the 1780s lasted two years or more. In most cases they moved away from a total concentration upon public affairs toward literary entertainment or essays of practical interest to certain specialized audiences. Among such audiences were female readers, children, and farmers. This was, however, only an era of experimentation for magazines, and the experiment was not a greatly successful one. The newspaper was still the staple medium for news, opinion, and even entertainment. The era of the truly successful popular magazine was still several decades in the future.[32]

Revolutionary Change

Ever since Isaiah Thomas published *The History of Printing in America* in 1810, much of the emphasis in the historiography of early American printing and journalism has been placed on the connection between the press and the American Revolution. Thomas ran his own *Massachusetts Spy*, founded in 1770, as an outspoken advocate of the Revolutionary cause, and took pains in his exhaustive survey of eighteenth-century American printers to praise those who had done the same. The broadest modern treatment of the theme is probably Arthur M. Schlesinger's 1958 monograph, *Prelude to Independence*, which stresses as Thomas did the effect of newspapers upon the movement for Independence.[33]

The effects of each upon the other, however, were reciprocal. The era of the Revolution, as much of the more recent scholarship on the subject has emphasized,[34] also affected the newspapers. The resulting transformations were, indeed, revolutionary.

One great change was in sheer numbers. American newspaper titles nearly doubled from 1763 to 1775, and more than doubled again until 1790, when 99 newspapers were being published weekly in 62 separate places. By well before this time, printing a newspaper had become essential to practically any printer who wanted to stay in business.[35] In 1755, the *Boston Gazette* and *Massachusetts Spy* were claiming circulations of 2,000 and 3,500, respectively, while in 1778 the *Connecticut Courant*, according to its publisher's figures, claimed to be printing over 8,000 weekly copies.[36] It was a true "take-off" period for the American newspaper, to be accelerated even more during the ensuing two decades so that Isaiah Thomas could list more than 350 American newspapers in the 1810 edition of his *History of Printing*.[37] One reason for the proliferation of newspapers during these years was the diffusion of the ever-growing supply of trained printers into previously unserved (and therefore noncompetitive) communities. Another was the proven role of the newspaper as the best existing instrument of a shared community consciousness, a function that took on new meaning now that the community was beginning to define itself as a nation.

The greatest reason for the proliferation, however, was the most significant journalistic transformation of the age, political partisanship. Obvious economic interests dictated a negative response among printers to the Stamp Act of 1765. Many, however, were not as ready to plunge into as strong an ideological opposition as the hotter voices of their communities thought appropriate (Fig. 10.1). David Hall, the partner Benjamin Franklin left in charge of the *Pennsylvania Gazette,* was at first inclined to discontinue the paper rather than enlist it in the fight against the Stamp Act but changed his mind under community pressure. To be accused of Toryism by his Philadelphia neighbors was now a more unacceptable risk than partisanship.[38] The Stamp Act crisis, therefore, produced a marked shift away from the pose of political neutrality and the open press ideal, even though from time to time some printers still paid lip service to both. By far the majority of printers, whether out of conviction or out of a desire to please the most outspoken segments of their communities, went on during the Revolutionary era to embrace the Patriot cause. Most striking, as Thomas C. Leonard has noticed, was the introduction of the newspaper "exposé," or the disclosure of hidden information in an effort to portray the villainy of the opposition.[39] A minority, perhaps most conspicuously the recent British emigré James Rivington of New York, took the Loyalist side. Neutrality, because the zealous on both sides associated it with the opposition – or with lack of principle – became impossible.

The American Revolution, therefore, forced newspapers to become partisans, thus bringing about a dramatic change in the fundamental nature and purpose of the newspaper press and a severe adjustment of the way in which most printers understood the ethics of their business. Many of the printers of the period no doubt were "reluctant partisans," to use Stephen Botein's phrase,[40] but partisanship nevertheless remained the most distinctive feature of the American newspaper press well into the nineteenth century.

Pamphleteering

The transformed newspaper was not the only printed medium of contention and persuasion during the Revolutionary era. While the magazine in general failed to flourish, there now began America's greatest age of pamphleteering. The pamphlet, a cheap, unbound booklet consisting of anywhere from ten to fifty or more quarto or octavo pages, had long been a staple vehicle of political and religious controversy in Britain and had figured significantly in the paper war between the Pennsylvania Assembly and the proprietary party in the 1720s. In New England it was the form in which a wide variety of current literature, most conspicuously the printed sermon, had been distributed for many decades. Unlike the newspaper, with its only

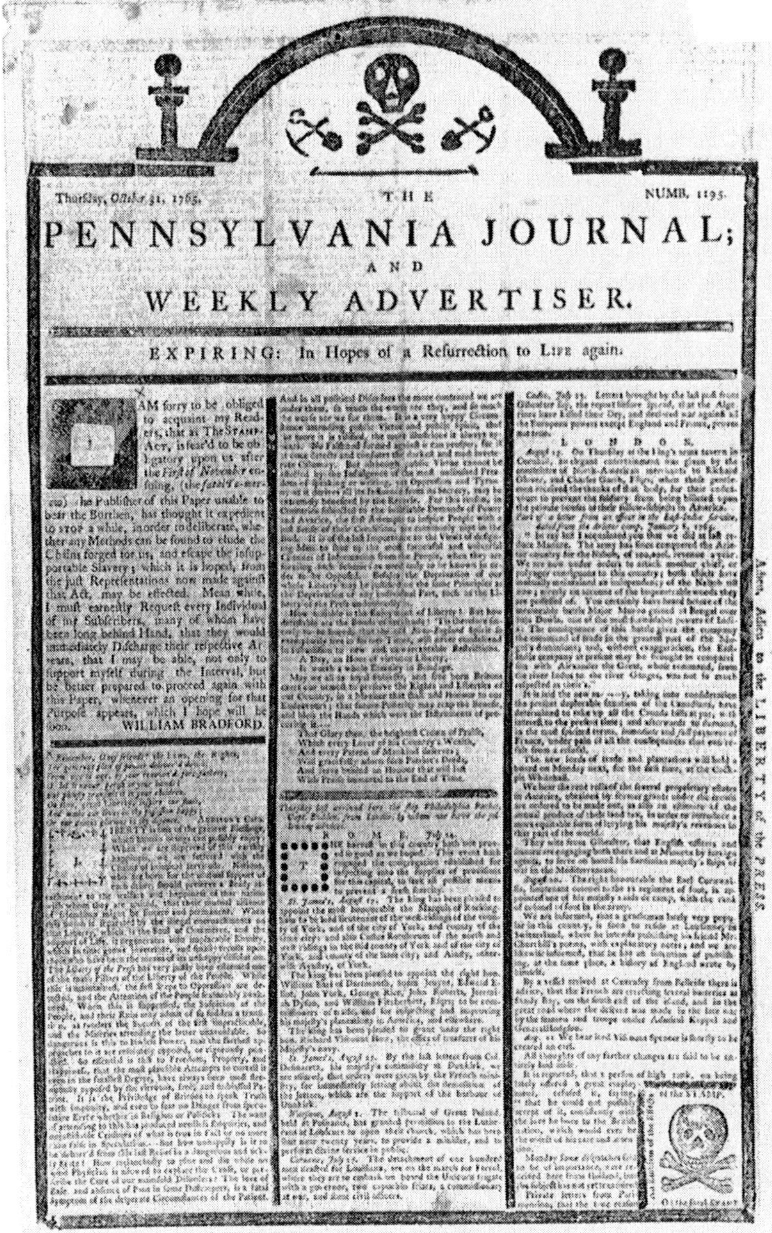

Thursday, *October* 31, 1765. THE NUMB. 1195.

PENNSYLVANIA JOURNAL;

AND

WEEKLY ADVERTISER.

EXPIRING: In Hopes of a Resurrection to LIFE again.

I AM sorry to be obliged to acquaint my Readers, that as The STAMP-ACT, is fear'd to be obligatory upon us after the *First of November* ensuing, (the *fatal To-morrow*) the Publisher of this Paper unable to bear the Burthen, has thought it expedient to STOP a while, in order to deliberate, whether any Methods can be found to elude the Chains forged for us, and escape the insupportable Slavery; which it is hoped, from the just Representations now made against that Act, may be effected. Mean while, I must earnestly Request every Individual of my Subscribers, many of whom have been long behind Hand, that they would immediately Discharge their respective Arrears, that I may be able, not only to support myself during the Interval, but be better prepared to proceed again with this Paper, whenever an opening for that Purpose appears, which I hope will be soon. WILLIAM BRADFORD.

Adieu, Adieu to the LIBERTY of the PRESS.

Figure 10.1. *The Pennsylvania Journal and Weekly Advertiser*, October 31, 1765: the banner satirizes the Stamp Act with a death's-head instead of the crown-royal stamp. American Antiquarian Society.

moderately flexible space limitations and a printer-proprietor serving as gatekeeper, the pamphlet offered an author – provided he or a supporter paid the publishing costs – the maximum freedom of personal expression and, within very generous limits, flexibility of length.[41]

Of course, a pamphlet as understood bibliographically – as a physical object – might be used as a medium for an almost unlimited variety of information and literature. However, the term will be understood here in its more restricted sense, drawing attention not so much to the pamphlet's form as to its content, a single essay or treatise invariably both topical and polemical, and usually the work of a single author wishing to make his or her case to the public. In this sense, "pamphleteering" becomes a specialized form of journalism.

Religious dissenters and other controversialists in seventeenth-century New England had sent opposition tracts to be published in London, away from the prohibitive (and punitive) restrictions of colonial authorities, and these in turn had stimulated responses, published in either England or America. Another outlet for New England writers late in the century had been William Bradford's press in Pennsylvania, but Bradford ran into trouble from local authorities when he tried to publish controversial pamphlets that struck closer to home. In the pre-Revolutionary period of the eighteenth century, the most striking instance of the potential popularity and wide audience for pamphlet literature was the narrative of the trial of John Peter Zenger, first published in 1736 and subsequently reprinted fifteen times.[42]

Between 1764 and 1776, according to one bibliographer's count, 231 separate pamphlets dealing directly with the dispute between Britain and the American colonies came off American presses. Several of these appeared in multiple editions. Thomas Paine's *Common Sense* of 1776, apparently the most widely distributed polemical essay of the era, was printed in twenty-five editions in thirteen American cities and towns, not to mention thirteen British reprints.[43] One can only assume, without proof, that "most widely distributed" translates into "most read." Certainly Paine's electrifying call for independence, cutting through the technicalities of the debate over colonial rights as it had been conducted until then, was at the very least a powerful influence in the movement for independence. The vote in the Second Continental Congress came some six months after the first edition of *Common Sense* appeared in Philadelphia.

Among other influential pamphlets published in multiple editions were two that had appeared earlier in newspapers. Bishop Jonathan Shipley's speech of 1774 opposing the Massachusetts Government Act, first published in London, was reprinted in the *Massachusetts Spy*, the *Massachusetts Gazette and Boston Weekly News-Letter*, the *Virginia Gazette*, the *New-York Weekly*

Journal, and the *Maryland Gazette* either before or during the publication of eleven American editions of the pamphlet.[44] John Dickinson's famous *Letters from a Farmer in Pennsylvania,* which appeared in seven pamphlet editions in 1768, began life as a newspaper series of twelve letters in the *Pennsylvania Chronicle* in late 1767 and early 1768. Almost every American newspaper had reprinted all or some of the series before the collected *Letters* appeared in pamphlet form.[45]

Pamphleteers of the Revolutionary era, like journalists and essayists whose work appeared in other formats, almost always adhered to the convention of anonymity. Dickinson's *nom de plume,* of course, was "A Farmer in Pennsylvania," although some editions used a frontispiece in which his engraved portrait appeared over his name with most of its letters dashed out. One of several conspicuous exceptions to the rule of anonymity was James Otis's seminal denial of Parliamentary authority over the colonies in *The Rights of the British Colonies Asserted and Proved,* which appeared in the first of five editions over the author's name in 1764.[46]

Pamphleteering thus joined newspaper journalism as a conspicuous vehicle of controversy and polemic in the ever-broadening public sphere created by print. During the Revolutionary era, both forms took on particular intensity and set precedents of rhetoric and format that American writers and printers carried forcibly into the decade after independence had been won.

The Press and the Constitution

No manifestation of newspaper partisanship in the late eighteenth century was more pertinent to the public life of the nation, nor instance of press unanimity more striking, than the eagerness with which the printers embraced the movement for the Federal Constitution. Indeed, as John K. Alexander has shown, the newspaper press entered the fray even before there was a document to debate, in effect "selling the Constitutional Convention" while it was still in progress.[47] The printed debate itself was rather one-sided. Although a few printer–publishers favored antiratification pieces such as the "Centinel," a newspaper series originating in Philadelphia, and still fewer tried to demonstrate fairness by including antifederalist writings alongside those favoring the Constitution, at least two-thirds of the newspapers made their owners' pro-ratification position plain. The federalist inclinations of the newspaper press in general is hardly surprising, since the great majority of newspapers were printed in the very urban seaports and state capitals where a "national" consciousness and a concern for the effective protection and regulation of commerce was most likely to be found.

By far the most lastingly famous entry in that debate, and perhaps the most notable newspaper series in American history, was the collection of the eighty-five essays called *The Federalist,* by which Alexander Hamilton, James Madison, and John Jay hoped to secure ratification in the crucial state of New York. Curiously, these theoretically profound articles, praised ever since by historians, political scientists, and Supreme Court justices, are not as conspicuous among the materials printed and reprinted by newspapers in most places as ratification news from their own and other states, letters on the issue from local readers, and controversial pieces much shorter and generally less sophisticated than the elegant productions of New York's "Publius." Outside of New York, one scholar has found, only sixteen newspapers and one magazine printed any of the *Federalist* papers during the ratification debates, and of the seventy-seven essays, only twenty-four made their way into print outside their home state.[48] The modern student of these writings is left to wonder whether the actual content of the printed arguments had much impact on the decisions of the various ratifying conventions. The one point on which one can be certain, however, is the indispensable role of the newspapers in *informing* their readers – first by the remarkably efficient distribution of the Constitution's text and then by keeping ratification news and debate foremost in their readers' consciousness until ratification had been accomplished and the new government installed.[49] In this decisive way, the newspapers nurtured the new republic in its infancy, providing powerful confirmation of their now unquestioned role as instruments of public – and specifically political – affairs.

PART TWO. THE SHIFTING FREEDOMS OF THE PRESS IN THE EIGHTEENTH CENTURY

RICHARD D. BROWN

THE INTENSE POLITICIZATION OF THE PRESS during the independence movement and later in the era of the Constitution and the early national government gave heightened importance to the issue of a free press and free speech. So critical did it become that when James Madison, the Speaker of the House of Representatives, prepared the Bill of Rights in 1790, the very first amendment to the Constitution guaranteed that the United States Congress would "make no law . . . abridging the freedom of speech, or of the press." Considering the earlier history of journalism in colonial America this emphasis on an unregulated press marked a departure from the past, a departure anticipated, to be sure, in the emergence of the doctrine of a free press in Britain and in the relationship, in both Britain and the colonies, between the press and a factionalized politics.

The principal British legacy to the seventeenth-century colonists was a tradition of state control intersecting with commercial privilege and monopoly.[50] The Massachusetts government did not allow the Cambridge and Boston printers to operate freely, the governor and council of Virginia thwarted the first attempt at setting up a press in that colony, and the governments in Maryland and Pennsylvania initially specified what printers could produce. As of the 1690s, the instructions royal governors received as part of their commission from the Crown gave them the authority to supervise the press and the publication of political news. Assemblies were no less willing to intervene and curtail a printer or bookseller if a book or newssheet seemed to compromise their privileges and powers.[51] Members of the trade had reason to cooperate with the government, for in each colony the surest line of business was the contract for printing sessions and statute laws, legal forms, and proclamations. To be designated "government printer" was every tradesman's goal, the consequence being that, with the exception of the occasional maverick like James Franklin, printers were pretty tame in the early decades of the century, and typically remained so in those colonies where competition was lacking.[52]

This conservatism reminds us that regulation occurred not only from outside but from within, as printers and booksellers maneuvered to gain or protect some advantage. Nor was regulation simply a matter of statutes and legal action. Every colonial assembly had to decide whether to allow its journals to be published, and, if so, what information these journals should contain.[53] This one example reminds us that the press in early America could be "controlled" by holding back information or providing it selectively. Much of that story, which also encompasses self-censorship by writers, is told elsewhere in this volume.[54] The narrative that follows has a narrower focus, to review the history of "freedom of the press" in the context of courts, civil governments, and the Revolution, and to describe how the common law of libel became an alternative to the practice of prior restraint, or licensing.

By the early eighteenth century the procedure of licensing, which in England vanished with the lapse of the Licensing Act in 1695, was also on the wane in the colonies. Joseph Dudley, the royal governor of Massachusetts between 1701 and 1716, never obeyed his instructions from the Crown to regulate the press, and efforts by various officials in the colony to suppress printed criticism of the government generally failed. By 1721, when the Massachusetts House of Representatives publicly rejected Governor Samuel Shute's proposed "Act for Preventing of Libels and Scandalous

Pamphlets, and for Punishing Authors and Publishers thereof" – Shute was seeking legislative endorsement of the customary provision in his instructions empowering him to regulate the press – the system of direct state censorship in this colony effectively came to an end. A few months later, when James Franklin began to issue the first newspaper of opinion, *The New-England Courant,* he omitted the imprimatur "Published by Authority" on the front-page masthead. In other colonies the same situation arose; although Francis Nicholson exercised his authority to deny a license in South Carolina in the 1720s and although royal governors continued for another decade to receive instructions from the imperial bureaucracy requiring them to license all printers and their publications, no one made any serious effort to do so.[55] The collapse of the licensing system made freedom of the press, in the sense of no prior restraint, a reality.

Henceforth, the possibilities for restraint were those of the English common law concerning seditious and blasphemous libel, together with assertions by legislators of parliamentary privilege. Libel was a useful weapon in the hands of those who wanted to control the press. Of the many such suits against printers[56] in the eighteenth-century colonies, we may single out the successful prosecution in Massachusetts in 1724 of John Checkley for "false and Scandalous Libel" for having published and distributed a book critical of Congregational church polity. The contentious Checkley, a defender of Episcopacy, was fined £50 and ordered to suppress the book. When he appealed the judgment, his lawyer offered the novel argument that the jury should rule not only on the *fact* of whether the offending pages were Checkley's, which was accepted legal practice, but also on the *law* as to whether they also contained "false & scandalous libel," a judgment that was the usual province of the bench.[57] This claim that the jury should rule on the law as well as the fact failed in the Checkley case, but in 1735 it would reemerge in the New York trial of John Peter Zenger.

Once regarded as a great jurisprudential landmark in the history of a free press in America, the Zenger case is now understood as having no importance as a legal precedent.[58] In its day the case had a political and ideological significance, revealing certain tendencies of American politics and anticipating the future direction of free-press policy after the Revolution. Ultimately that policy would rest on the notion, voiced by John Milton in *Areopagitica* (1644), that truth vanquishes error in a free competition and that over the long run good order and government cannot be threatened by a free press. Indeed, the free expression of opinion, and vesting the power to judge in the hands of popular juries, would come to be recognized as essential to the preservation of liberty and therefore vital in a republic. When the Zenger case began, however, no one could have anticipated such far-ranging implications. Nor were any of the principal actors libertarian republicans.

John Peter Zenger, who would suffer eight months' imprisonment, was a German immigrant who had learned the printing trade as a boy in New York City, where he later operated a small printing office. He was hired in 1734 to print a newspaper on behalf of the Lewis Morris faction of New York magnates. These men wanted to discredit William Cosby, the royal governor, and his faction, who effectively controlled the one newspaper in town, William Bradford's *New York Gazette*. The *New-York Weekly Journal*, which Zenger began to issue, was headed by two attorneys, James Alexander and William Smith, whose anonymous articles, letters, and satirical advertisements disparaged the character and policies of Cosby and his associates. Evidently, his employers were willing to put Zenger at risk of prosecution for seditious libel.

According to contemporary understanding of the law of seditious libel, as articulated by William Hawkins in his standard legal treatise of 1716, it "defames persons entrusted in a public capacity, in as much as it manifestly tends to create ill blood, and to cause a disturbance of the public peace; . . . it tends to scandalize the government, by reflecting on those who are entrusted with the administration of public affairs, which does not only endanger the public peace, . . . but also has a direct tendency to breed in the people a dislike of their governors, and incline them to faction and sedition."[59] By this definition, no reader, least of all Governor Cosby and his allies, could doubt that much of the contents of the *New-York Weekly Journal* constituted seditious libel. Appropriately, the governor had Zenger arrested and put on trial in 1735 before one of his own judicial appointees. The attorneys Alexander and Smith, who undertook Zenger's defense in hopes of using the trial to arouse further hostility to the Cosby regime, were soon outmaneuvered by the judge, who took the bold step of disbarring both of them. But the Lewis Morris faction responded to this challenge by inviting a highly respected Philadelphia lawyer, Andrew Hamilton, to represent the imprisoned printer.

Hamilton, learned, experienced, and thorough, recognized that he could never win Zenger's case with conventional legal arguments because his client could not deny public knowledge that he was the printer of the *New-York Weekly Journal*. Thereafter Cosby's judge would certainly rule that the texts in question violated the law. Hamilton concluded that his one hope was to find a way for the jury to block the conviction. Hamilton's solution, which elevated the power of the jury as an embodiment of the people's voice in government, called on the ideas of Milton and Locke and the rhetoric of the Radical Whigs John Trenchard and Thomas Gordon. Hamilton's plan, to argue that the jury could decide both the fact and the law, thus relegating the judge to merely a presiding role, was not entirely new or original. John Checkley's lawyer had tried it only a decade earlier in Massachusetts, and as far back as 1692 William Bradford, who was then the one printer in Philadelphia, had used the very same argument against a charge of seditious libel.[60] Hamilton knew that, regardless of law and precedent, where a jury was involved a way might be found. A generation earlier, in 1707, a New York jury had ruled on both the law and the fact in acquitting an itinerant clergyman for violating the law against unlicensed preaching.[61] Certainly the cases were different, but the jurymen in Zenger's trial had been selected in New York City, where opposition to Governor Cosby prevailed.

For Hamilton the key was to provide jurymen with reasons for ignoring established legal rules so that the jury itself could assume authority over judgment on the law as well as the fact. Accordingly, Hamilton appealed to the jury primarily on political grounds. He did offer some legal argument based on dubious precedents, but his main thrust was to narrow the application of seditious libel according to a Radical Whig interpretation of the English constitution. The law of seditious libel, Hamilton declared, properly protected the King of England but was never intended to shield those as distant from the throne as mere colonial officials. There must be freedom to criticize such lesser officials publicly; otherwise, the King could not correct their faults. A free press and jury trial were vital for freeholders such as the New York jurymen in order to protect the law and the constitution from greedy British placemen. Recently Zenger's *New-York Weekly Journal* had printed a passage from Trenchard and Gordon's *Cato's Letters* in which, having redefined libel as an act of public service, they argued that those who publicized anonymously the misdeeds of the government should not be punished: "The exposing therefore of publick Wickedness . . . can never be a Libel in the Nature of Things."[62] Only if criticism of magistrates was demonstrably false could it be legitimately suppressed. Hamilton's oration to the jury invited these twelve freeholders to affirm their own political stature and legitimacy by ruling Zenger not guilty on the law of seditious libel, even though no one denied the fact that he had published articles that Governor Cosby's faction deemed odious.[63] This was a winning argument in New York City in August 1735. Precisely because the jury refused to rule on the fact unless it could also rule on the law, Zenger was freed.

But the jury's decision, controverting as it did the weight of legal opinion, did not establish the principles that Hamilton had argued. Zenger's jurymen had judged his case according to the law as they believed it ought to be. Legal professionals recognized that the standing body of law said otherwise. As contemporary lawyers pointed out, only judges could properly apply the law of seditious libel; and the veracity of a libel, far from excusing it, as Radical Whigs claimed, aggravated its tendency "to scandalize the government."[64] Although the Zenger case did not immediately enlarge legal protections for the press, it did underscore the limited ability of royal officials to protect themselves by using seditious libel proceedings, especially where popular issues were being decided by juries. Fundamentally, the case left unresolved a contradiction that persisted for the rest of the century: Was it possible to combine a turbulent factionalism, which implied that power rested with the people, with the authority needed to sustain social and political cohesion – the "public good" as it had been idealized for centuries – which government by its very nature was meant to embody and maintain? This contradiction was echoed in the colonists' uncertainty about the proper role of newspapers. Were they guardians of liberty, charged with publishing (making public) "news" of the inner workings of politics? Or should newspapers avoid adding fuel to the fire of factional politics by refusing to purvey the distortions of language and fact that, in England, went hand-in-hand with a partisan press?

Given these contradictory possibilities, everyone vacillated – printers,[65] political pamphleteers, legislatures, governors. No one wanted the press to lend itself to "tyranny," yet no one wanted to surrender the hope that private conscience, partisan passions, or commercial self-interest would give way to agreement on the general good. For some printers in some cities, the underlying reality by the decade of the 1760s was an oppositional politics that they could not really avoid, a politics that also sharply limited the capacity of the party in power to succeed in prosecutions for libel; in other cities or for other printers, oppositional politics was something from which they kept their distance.[66] The outcome was not freedom of the press in any complete sense of the term, though printers, pamphleteers, and (after 1776) state governments increasingly affirmed the Radical Whig understanding of the press.

Indeed, the chief influence of the Zenger case was to publicize this view of free speech and a free press. James Alexander's *A Brief Narrative of the Case and Trial of John Peter Zenger*, first published in New York City in 1736, was reprinted in Boston later that year, and enjoyed four or five reprintings in London in 1738, a year in which Milton's century-old paean to free speech, *Areopagitica*, was first reprinted as a separate book (though Charles Blount echoed its themes at the end of the seventeenth century). Alexander's *A Brief Narrative* was issued again in London in 1752; and in 1770, when the patriot Alexander McDougall was charged with libeling the New York legislature, the case against him was dropped after his patriot friends put *A Brief Narrative* into print once more.[67] By this time, popularly oriented arguments on behalf of free speech were multiplying.

In the meantime, however, local legislatures went on using claims of "parliamentary privilege" to silence press criticism. When their own reputations or authority were at stake, legislative leaders did not worry overmuch about preserving canons of free speech or the ability of freeholders to be fully informed. In Virginia in 1749 the House of Burgesses tried to silence William Parks's *Virginia Gazette* because Parks printed a challenge to house authority issued by the Governor's Council. But when Parks explained that he had only been following the council's orders and did not himself challenge house prerogatives, the case was dropped – all without mention of free-press principles.[68] In New York, where in the wake of the Zenger episode one might have expected the earliest and fullest realization of such ideas, the appearance in 1753 of an essay "Of the Use, Abuse, and Liberty of the Press" in a monthly journal entitled *The Independent Reflector* (a title derived from Trenchard and Gordon's *Independent Whig*) illustrated the ambivalence of those who wanted a free press to serve the public interest, but not if the press was damaging to the public, which in their view constituted abuse that should be regulated. William Smith, Jr., son of one of Zenger's attorneys, asserted the freedom to criticize public evils, such as "The Roguery of Ecclesiastics" and "Corruption or Venality." Smith also proclaimed the freedom to publish anything that was "not repugnant to the Prosperity of the State."[69] But he stopped far short of the most advanced Whigs, who accepted press "abuses" as necessary evils that must be tolerated so as to assure the larger good of press freedom. On the contrary, Smith insisted that any printer who "prostitutes his Art by the Publication of any Thing injurious to his Country" was engaging in the capital crime of "high Treason against the State." Sounding more like the Zenger prosecution than the defense, Smith concluded that to invoke "the *Liberty of the Press*" in these circumstances was "groundless and trifling." Simply put, a printer whose presses operated against the "Common Good of Society . . . should be punished."[70]

From a British perspective the arguments in *The Independent Reflector* were merely the conventional rhetoric one might find in such mainstream gentlemen's magazines as *The Spectator*. More libertarian statements had appeared immediately in the wake of the republication of *Areopagitica* in 1738. In that year a periodical calling itself *Common Sense: or, the Englishman's Journal* had printed essays which connected free press principles to republicanism by arguing that if a free press was available to inform public opinion, "the Bulk of Mankind" could govern themselves. There would be abuses, to be sure, but these were mostly "trivial inconveniences," not "high Treason."[71] Governments relied on informed citizens to keep them honest, and to that end a free press was essential, even if falsehoods and calumnies were sometimes mixed in with true information. A few years later in 1742, the influential Scots philosopher David Hume implied, in a frequently reprinted essay, that a free press might even be a natural right by referring to it "as the common right of mankind."[72]

As of the 1750s the colonies' most avant-garde thinkers, such as the authors of *The Independent Reflector* or the politically radical Boston cleric,

Jonathan Mayhew, were not yet ready to claim liberty of the press as a natural right. But they were familiar with the principal British arguments, which ranged from Lord Mansfield's court rulings supporting seditious libel prosecutions to libertarian essays such as those in *Cato's Letters, Common Sense,* Hume's works, and a dozen other sources. The colonists knew as well that the British government had moved against *Common Sense,* seizing several of its issues. Before the imperial crisis of the 1760s, however, the question of a free press was peripheral to colonial public life. Only when life-and-death controversies over colonial resistance to British measures developed did the issue of press freedom become central.

In the decade from 1764 through 1774 an ideal of freedom of the press emerged as one of the central pillars of liberty, but it was not exactly the libertarian ideal. The general view that William Smith, Jr., had enunciated in 1753 – that speech that served the public interest should be protected, whereas speech against it should be suppressed – made sense to the leaders of the independence movement. In place of prosecutions for seditious libel or violation of parliamentary privilege, which governing authorities could no longer enforce, a pattern of popular censorship emerged in the context of a partisan press in colonies like New York and Massachusetts. Because patriots only suppressed printing they believed harmful to the public good, they dismissed loyalist declarations that their repressive actions contradicted invocations of press freedom.[73] As rough politics shouldered aside libertarian arguments, political polarization eliminated the middle ground for printers who wished to maintain the broadest range and greatest number of readers and advertisers by making their newspapers open to all shades of opinion. This kind of nonpartisan freedom of the press, sustained by printers in preceding decades when the political system was stable, collapsed.[74]

The idea that the purpose of a free press was to enable the many to protect themselves from the few had first appeared as far back as *Cato's Letters,* but it was Massachusetts patriots who made it a standard feature in their arguments in the 1760s and 1770s. From this perspective, although the British government's effort to silence John Wilkes by prosecuting him in London in the 1760s was an outrageous violation of Englishmen's liberties, the colonists' own intimidation of the proto-loyalist friend of government, John Mein, whose *Boston Chronicle* printed information aimed at destroying the patriots' nonimportation agreement, was acceptable. Mein had crossed the boundary separating liberty from license, so patriot Boston, some of whose leaders joined the Wilkesite Society for the Bill of Rights, made no complaint in 1769 when their foot soldiers attacked Mein's shop and threatened him physically. Indeed, after Mein fled Boston, John Hancock sought to put Mein's partner, John Fleeming, out of business by prosecuting him for debt.[75] The idea that their opponents' right to publish what patriots regarded as false, scandalous, and malicious statements should be protected was absurd from their perspective. William Smith, Jr.'s 1753 declaration that if a printer published "any Thing injurious to his Country, it is criminal" applied to Mein and Fleeming. They "should be punished"; and since they were allied to corrupt tyrannical officials, the only way to enforce true liberty of the press was to punish them by extraordinary means.[76]

In New York, as might be expected, the same way of thinking emerged as dominant, and the printer–bookseller James Rivington faced the same fate as Mein and Fleeming. As late as the 1770s this English immigrant defended the printers' version of a free press by opening his newspaper to all shades of opinion; in the middle of the Revolutionary crisis, Rivington declared himself "ready to defend the freedom of the press" in this sense of the term. But ultimately Rivington faced punishment at the hands of patriots because he printed items they deemed injurious to the country. After a commercial boycott of his shop failed to silence his press, armed patriots destroyed Rivington's types in 1775. Two years later when he returned to business, he was firmly in the British camp, both figuratively and literally, protected as he was by the British military occupation of New York City.[77]

Up and down the seacoast, popular political actors and authorities assumed the role of censor, enforcing boundaries on the press by community will, as determined by Committees of Correspondence, Safety, and Inspection (sanctioned by the Continental Congress in late 1774), state legislatures, and bands of patriots. This new approach to freedom of the press was not libertarian in Milton's sense, but it did leave room for criticism of government. Operating on the Radical Whig principle that citizens must be informed on public matters so as to serve as guardians of the public interest, patriots refused to exempt government policies and officials from being assessed in print. Consequently, although patriots closed down Loyalist-oriented printers wherever they could, their own newspapers freely criticized military operations and legislatures.[78] As long as loyalty to the American cause was manifest, criticism of government was legitimate during the war.

With the restoration of peace and the establishment of state republican governments, the doctrine of seditious libel made a comeback. Eight states had proclaimed liberty of the press in their bills and declarations of rights, and two more wrote free-speech guarantees into their constitutions; yet because states also routinely established the English common law, seditious libel was also included in their codes. Because the new governments now represented the public, attacks on government and its officials could be construed as attacks on the people as a whole. In Pennsylvania, for example, the printer Eleazar Oswald was prosecuted between 1782 and 1788 (when he was finally convicted) for making libelous attacks on his state's Supreme Court justices.[79] American jurists, still trained on Blackstone, continued to argue that the fundamental meaning of press liberty was "no prior restraint," not an unlimited freedom to criticize. It is no wonder then that wherever there were sharp political divisions, prosecutions for seditious libel arose during the 1780s, 1790s, and beyond. Most contemporary jurists and statesmen, both Federalist and Jeffersonian, saw no contradiction between the assertion in Virginia's 1776 Bill of Rights "that the freedom of the press is one of the great bulwarks of liberty, and can never be restrained but by despotick governments" and its 1792 "Act Against Divulgers of False News," which sought to regulate the press.[80] According to Leonard Levy, the leading authority on the subject, only Pennsylvania departed substantially from the common law by stating explicitly in its 1790 constitutional revision that juries would henceforth decide the law as well as the fact in libel cases, and that truth would be a defense.[81] Fifty-five years after a Philadelphia lawyer had argued these principles in Zenger's case, they were made into positive law in his state, though not in New York. Notwithstanding a political revolution that had shifted power toward freeholders, neither the truth defense – always justified because it enabled citizen freeholders to be informed – nor the authority of jurors to judge sedition, would gain explicit acceptance for a generation or longer in some states.

Considering the eighteenth century as a whole, there was no clear, consistent line of progress from censorship and repression to complete press freedom. In the seventeenth century, when the first presses were brought to the colonies, printing was being suppressed, and it was still being suppressed in the age of stereotypes and steam presses. Moreover, as Hamilton had observed, because "freedom of the press" could never be defined in a way that all could accept, it was always contested. Nevertheless, the conditions of press freedom in the seventeenth and nineteenth centuries were radically different. The eighteenth century had witnessed major changes in the boundaries, character, and agencies of suppression and censorship, the most important of them being the end of press control via government monopolies and the use of licenses. The collapse of this system in Britain in the 1690s and soon after in America made freedom of the press, in the sense of no prior restraint, a reality. Thereafter, the contest over press freedom shifted to the courts, where government prosecutions for seditious libel and breach of parliamentary privilege set effective limits on the press. The Zenger case in New York in 1735 heightened appreciation of the importance of liberty of the press as a bulwark against corrupt and tyrannical rulers, but it did not substantially enlarge the boundaries of what was permissible to say in print. At the same time, however, the logistics of post-publication censorship via court proceedings became more difficult. As the colonial economy developed and commerce grew, the demand for printing offices and newspapers multiplied. In this environment, where every printer possessed a constituency of local magnates, centralized censorship was virtually impossible.

During the Revolutionary era a pattern of "popular" censorship began. Any printer who offended powerful local interests was put out of business through extra-legal intimidation. During the war for independence, when the state was a weak, uncertain agency, this method of curtailing "the abuse of press freedom" was widely accepted. Indeed, it set a pattern of vigilante justice that would recur even after the consolidation of state and national governments in the early republic. In a representative political system local majorities tolerated few restraints when they were confronted by print they believed dangerous or licentious. As the century ended, Americans declared both their undying commitment to the freedom of the press and, when their own interests or sensibilities were challenged, their readiness to put a stop to those printers who would "abuse" that liberty.

CHAPTER ELEVEN

Practices of Reading

INTRODUCTION

DAVID D. HALL AND ELIZABETH CARROLL REILLY

WRITING OF HIS CHILDHOOD YEARS in early eighteenth-century Boston, Benjamin Franklin remembered that "from a Child, I was fond of Reading, and all the little Money that came into my Hands was ever laid out in Books." Franklin did not specify at what age he learned to read, but it was "early," for when he turned eight he spent a year in a grammar (Latin) school. Books were few in the Franklin household; the "little Library" of Benjamin's father, a tallow chandler and church deacon, "consisted chiefly of Books in polemical Divinity." To the boy's delight it also included Plutarch's *Lives*, "in which I read abundantly," and a pious uncle's manuscript sermon notes. With his own funds Benjamin bought the works of John Bunyan, which he then exchanged for "small Chapmen's Books, . . . 40 or 50 in all," by the London writer R. Burton (Nathaniel Crouch). Not until he was apprenticed to his older brother James, a printer, did Benjamin have "access to better books," some of which he borrowed from other apprentices who worked for booksellers. He was also encouraged in his reading by the generosity of a merchant "who had a pretty collection of books," a veritable "library," and allowed the young printer-in-training to borrow "such . . . as I chose to read." Yet it was by chance that he "met with an odd volume of the *Spectator*."[1]

Franklin's quest for books lends itself to three different interpretations of readers and reading in eighteenth-century America; all three will figure in this chapter. The first concerns change. By 1771, when Franklin began to write the *Autobiography*, he knew that aspiring readers in Boston, New York, Philadelphia, and Charleston were far better off than he had been in

1720: Bookstores had multiplied, social and circulating libraries had come on the scene, imports of books were rising steeply,[2] and local printers were issuing far more books and newspapers. Yet in much of rural America and perhaps for many kinds of Americans, substantial books (apart from the Bible) remained hard to come by. Looking back on his youth in pre-Revolutionary Virginia, Devereux Jarratt, who went on to become an Episcopalian minister, recalled wanting to learn something of "philosophy, rhetoric and logic" but found that "there were no books on such subjects among us." In order to learn arithmetic "he borrowed a plain book, in manuscript." After undergoing a spiritual awakening and newly eager to learn more about the Bible, Jarratt "had not a single book in the world [able to help him in this respect], nor was I able to buy any books, had I known of any for sale." Only by borrowing from "a gentleman [who lived] about five or six miles distant across the river" was he able to obtain a book on the New Testament, and only after he met a Presbyterian minister did he finally gain access to "a number of very excellent books" by the likes of Richard Baxter and Isaac Watts. Even in New England, a man who grew up in late eighteenth-century Connecticut remembered a household library that was minuscule and overwhelmingly religious compared to the world of books he knew as an adult.[3] Here, then, is a second possibility, that continuity in scale and subject matter, not change, prevailed; books, most of them concerned with religion, remained limited in number and unevenly distributed.

Colored though these recollections are by their writers' narrative designs, they remind us nonetheless that no single pattern, no one generalization, encompasses everyone who lived in British America. Many of the colonists participated in the world of books, but many others did not, constrained from doing so by the circumstances of region, race, education, income, and distribution. The surge of booksellers' advertisements and the emergence of circulating libraries in the 1760s may tempt us to entertain the assumption, seconded, it would seem, by the increasing numbers of imported books and those like almanacs, that were produced in the colonies, that on the eve of the Revolution the typical American was caught up in a new abundance of printed matter. This assumption, which is often linked with the assertion that women were becoming much more active as readers and consumers, deserves close scrutiny in its own right, but above all it must not prevent us from acknowledging the many exceptions: the African-Americans who were slaves; the colonists of European descent who remained unable to read or could not afford to buy even the cheapest forms of print; and those who were thwarted by the imperfect ways in which books were distributed from having ready access to them. North and south, east and west, the presence of books varied sharply from one community to the next. In keeping with these differences, the social and cultural hierarchies of colonial society –

hierarchies made visible in young Franklin's reliance for substantial books on merchants and, in a subsequent episode, on a royal governor – were mirrored in the presence and meaning of books.

A third conclusion to draw from the life stories of Franklin and Jarratt is that in eighteenth-century America the practice of reading was always socially and culturally mediated. Booksellers' advertisements imply the figure of the autonomous consumer encountering a choice of goods. But for Franklin and Jarratt the formative contexts in which they came to value reading were sociocultural: a family that cherished pious books, the evangelical awakenings of midcentury, and the social respect accorded learnedness, respectively. Both young men also depended on intermediaries, be these royal governors, affluent, well-placed "gentlemen," or merchants, in gaining access to a wider world of books. The story of readers and reading in eighteenth-century America is first and foremost a story of these mediations and how they shaped the act of reading.

What were the most telling forms of mediation in this century? Long-standing yet still vital institutions like the family and the congregation, Quaker Meeting, or parish remained, for many, the crucial doorway to books, settings in which family structure, ethnicity, devotional practice, and literacy overlapped. These traditional patterns held true for the German Pietists and Lutherans who relied initially on books imported from overseas, and for whom the Saur press produced such immense quantities of psalters and catechisms; the Quakers who, as in the previous century, sustained a distinctive manuscript and print culture; the Scotch-Irish Presbyterians; the "New Lights" who emerged out of the midcentury "awakenings," some of whom became Baptists; the early followers of John Wesley; the Anglicans. We may also speak of an evangelical community that, by the middle of the century, encompassed much of New England Congregationalism, middle-colony Presbyterianism, and those who were becoming Baptists or Methodists.[4] The counterpoints to a revitalized Protestantism were the emergence of a secular space marked out most visibly in gentlemen's clubs, social libraries, and literary coteries devoted to "polite" forms of culture, and the expansion of taverns, rural stores, and public performances distributing and nurtured on ballads, broadsides, and newspapers. Learned culture was also enjoying a new prosperity as more colleges and academies were founded and as Americans participated ever more vigorously in an international "republic of letters." Another social space was provided by the schools that offered instruction in the "practical arts" for artisans, clerks, aspiring merchants, sea captains, and civil administrators. As the economy expanded, the connections between commerce and the utilitarian skills of literacy and numeracy became ever more prominent.[5]

Meanwhile, booksellers and writers were addressing books to readers designated by age, gender, and income: books for "children," "ladies" and "females," "poor people" and those better off. These terms are imprecise – for they do not tell us much about which women or what age or wealth range was intended and, like the other categories we have just enumerated, they do not necessarily mark off tightly bounded, distinct spheres of reading. Within most literate, book-reading households, as within every college or social library, people read diverse kinds of books. Even as we specify the mediating structures within eighteenth-century America, we must bear in mind this fluidity of reading patterns, of which Franklin's early career as reader and author seems so emblematic. His world of print encompassed everything from chapbooks and broadsides to the classics, divinity, the *Spectator*, and, after he moved to Philadelphia and became a successful printer and journalist noted for his almanacs, the textual practices of learned culture.[6] Few colonists were this diverse or moved this easily across so many boundaries. Yet Franklin's several phases as reader and writer alert us to the multiple uses of literacy in this society.

PART ONE. LITERACY AND SCHOOLBOOKS

ROSS W. BEALES AND E. JENNIFER MONAGHAN

UNMISTAKABLY, THE RATE OF LITERACY as measured by signatures on documents increased in the course of the eighteenth century. In New England the rate of signature literacy among white men, which was 70 percent in 1710, rose to 85 percent by 1760 and reached 90 percent by 1790. Among New England white women the rate of 45 percent early in the eighteenth century steadily increased and, although theirs remained lower than male rates, women "were narrowing the gap by the close of the colonial period."[7] Advances in literacy were more substantial among urban women and those from wealthier families; by 1768–1771, 88 percent of Boston women who sold or consented to the sale of property were able to sign their names, whereas in the rural parts of Suffolk County 60 percent did so. Among widows who signed accounts of administration for their husbands' estates in three Massachusetts counties, changes in the ability to sign one's name were dramatic, rising from an overall rate of 31 percent (1690–1719) to just under 57 percent (1760–1772).[8] In Windsor, Connecticut, among women who were born in the first half of the century and who had occasion to sign deeds, between 75 and 80 percent used a signature rather than a mark.[9] In the Windsor District of Vermont, signature literacy rates were 61 percent in the years 1777–1786, 79 percent in 1787–1796, and 84 percent in 1797–1800.[10] Among women who were born in the last third of the eighteenth century and were still alive for the 1850 and 1860 censuses, virtually all native-born white women reported themselves as literate.[11] Altogether, Kenneth Lockridge's groundbreaking work and subsequent studies by other scholars demonstrate that rates of male and female literacy rose during the eighteenth century, with men approaching nearly universal rates and women making substantial advances. Because writing instruction was never begun until reading instruction was well advanced, these measures of *writing* literacy must always be understood as indicating that even greater numbers of people could read.

In other regions of eighteenth-century America, rates of signature literacy tended to be lower than in New England. According to Lockridge and Alan Tully, about two thirds of white men in Virginia and Pennsylvania were able to sign their names throughout the eighteenth century.[12] In Perquimans County, North Carolina, about two-thirds of the white male population and less than one-third of the female population were signature literate in the latter part of the seventeenth century. By the end of the colonial period, however, nearly 80 percent of the men were literate, with women remaining much as they were before. Male literacy rates in the first and last periods (77 percent in 1661–1695; 79 percent, 1748–1776) are roughly comparable with male rates in New England (60 percent in 1660; 85 percent in 1760).[13]

Immigrants brought considerable social capital to the colonies in the form of literacy. Of 2,792 male indentured servants who emigrated from London in the years 1718–1759, 69 percent were able to sign their contracts. Among women, the rate was 34 percent. The historian David Galenson has suggested that the literacy of indentured servants was "considerably higher than for the English population at large," which would mean that the American colonies benefited from the social capital invested in these people in their place of birth. German immigrants also brought significant social capital in the form of literacy. Of 24,025 male German immigrants over the age of fifteen who were required to sign loyalty oaths in Philadelphia between 1727 and 1775, 71 percent could sign their names. Not only were overall rates of signature literacy high among this cohort, they increased over time, rising from 60 percent in the 1730s to 80 percent after 1760.[14]

We may take it as a given that the rate of signature literacy among African-Americans was low, and especially among slaves in the South,[15] with a tendency for literacy to be more common among those living in the North and among free blacks in any region. Precise information is scant, but the fundamental context is readily apparent: The fear among southern whites, in particular, of a slave insurrection, together with a recurring uneasiness about the implications of Christian baptism, poisoned most attempts to introduce Christianity, let alone literacy, to those who were black, even after legislation was passed in several colonies that severed any possible link between baptism and manumission. Modest in the extreme, the possibilities for learning how to read far exceeded the possibilities for learning how to write, for no slave owner wanted slaves to be able to communicate with each other or fashion documents that could allow them to escape or move about. Many whites also questioned whether slaves had the intellectual capacity to learn to read and write. In fact, writing instruction was legally prohibited in South Carolina after 1740 and in Georgia after 1755, as was teaching how to "read writing" in Georgia as of 1770, a prohibition that did not, however, forbid instruction in reading print, especially Christian texts.[16]

Because of the continuing association between reading and religion, the history of African-American literacy is also one of philanthropic agencies undertaking to introduce slaves and free blacks to Christianity, and putting catechisms, spelling books, the *Book of Common Prayer*, and Bibles in their hands as part of this program. The most notable of these agencies were the Society of Friends (Quakers) and two groups of clergy affiliated with the Church of England, the Society for Propagating the Gospel, and Dr. Bray's Associates. The work of agents in the employ of these agencies, or of Anglican rectors who received their support, included the founding of a few charity schools in cities such as Charleston, Williamsburg, Philadelphia (with Benjamin Franklin and his wife Deborah lending a helping hand), New York, and Newport. In these schools, slave children acquired a measure of reading literacy that no southern colony prohibited.[17] Apart from these ventures, the religious awakenings of the 1740s moved some slave owners and clergy to take more seriously the task of teaching Christianity (and therefore reading) to slaves, a program Cotton Mather had urged on New Englanders – and on slaves themselves – before the turn of the century. Mather himself had participated in the founding of several short-lived charity schools for blacks.[18]

For most colonists of European descent, the household remained the most important site for preliminary instruction in how to read (Fig. 11.1). Instruction at a school, however named or constituted, became more widely available, but the children who attended often did so briefly or with many interruptions. Only in New England did a combination of proprietary and local, town-supported schools make it possible for most children – girls as well as boys – to learn to read and write and for young men in coastal towns to acquire practical training in advanced penmanship, bookkeeping, surveying, and navigation.[19] Elsewhere, the high hopes for education voiced by the founders of Pennsylvania were not realized in practice.[20] Household instruction in the middle and southern colonies, often by private tutors, was

The careful *Mother* Inſtructing her Children.

Figure 11.1. "The careful Mother Instructing her Children," engraved by Isaiah Thomas after James Turner (enlarged); from *The History of the Holy Jesus,* 10th ed. (Boston: Zechariah Fowle, 1764). Most editions of this popular book, first printed in Boston, 1745, include this little sketch (50 × 80 mm) of a wife's responsibility for her children's reading literacy. American Antiquarian Society.

complemented by church-related schools, an increase in private entrepreneurs, and, among the Scotch-Irish, by a growing number of academies. The variations from one region to the next in the type and duration of schooling, together with the persistent weakness of the Church of England in those colonies where Anglican clergy were charged with supervising parish schools, undermined most attempts to license schoolmasters or regulate what was taught.[21]

One sign that many of the colonists valued literacy, and that opportunities for schooling were widely available, was a rise in the importation of schoolbooks as well as the accelerating production of American imprints. By far the most significant increase was in works that taught introductory reading. Beginning in the mid-1730s, a new and potentially secular text was added to the traditional sequence, heavily religious, of hornbook, primer, psalter, New Testament, and Bible: the spelling book. Its spectacular growth, which accelerated after 1750, would become the defining pedagogical feature of the eighteenth century, supplanting other texts as the first book children would encounter on entering any school other than a dame school.[22]

The traditional texts, including hornbooks, continued to be used. Primers had been imported into New England since the early days of settlement. Parents in almost any colony could easily purchase a locally produced or imported copy of that quintessentially Puritan text, the *New-England Primer*, in its second Boston edition by 1690. A publishing staple, its total copies in the eighteenth century are estimated in the millions. Like all primers, it was a text used at home and in the reading schools (dame schools) run by women for the youngest children.[23] Primers were at heart denominational texts, so while the *New England Primer* remained the favorite of Congregationalists, denominations with different orientations designed their own versions, with results that sometimes blurred the line between primer and speller. Examples are the Pietist Francis Daniel Pastorius's *A New Primmer or Methodical Directions To attain the True Spelling, Reading & Writing of English* (1698) and the Quaker George Fox's *Instructions for Right Spelling* (1702), both of them printed in Philadelphia.

Meanwhile, works that were unequivocally spelling books began to appear in the colonies. Although they fall into two groups – those designed for youths and those aimed at young children – the concept of spelling was the same in each. The primary function of a spelling book was to teach its users to *read*, not merely to *spell* in our modern sense of writing a word correctly. "Spelling" in its earlier context meant naming the letters of a word aloud, one syllable at a time, in order to pronounce the entire word. Later called the "alphabetic" method because of its focus on letters as the smallest unit of instruction, it was the only approach known in the entire colonial period for decoding a text. As Isaac Watts, the English hymn-writer, described the process, children were not to guess at unfamiliar words, but were told "to spell every Word and Syllable [orally] before you pronounce it."[24] The contribution of the spelling book to this process was to make it systematic. The rationale behind the speller was that children needed explicit instruction in linking letters to pronunciations and that longer words were harder words. Spelling books therefore gave directions on pronunciation and supplied lists of words (known as "tables") that were grouped into an ever-increasing number of syllables. These were usually followed by "lessons," or some kind of connected text.

The three spelling books that successively captured the colonial market from the 1730s on – those by Thomas Dyche, Henry Dixon (in a compilation with other authors), and Thomas Dilworth – were all designed to introduce young children to reading. Dyche's *A Guide to the English Tongue*, initially published in London in 1707, was hugely popular in England and regularly imported into the American colonies. Southerners favored it, but New Englanders preferred the work of Henry Dixon. Dixon's *The English Instructor* (1728) was first reprinted in Boston in 1736. It was later incorporated, in an abbreviated form, into a uniquely American compilation titled *The Youth's Instructor in the English Tongue*, but known affectionately as "The New England Spelling Book." This work, said Isaiah Thomas (who helped his master Zechariah Fowle put an issue of 20,000 copies through the press in the late 1750s or early 1760s), was "in great repute, and in general use for many years."[25] "Collected from [Henry] Dixon, [Nathan] Bailey, [John] Owen, [Nathaniel] Strong and [Isaac] Watts," the first two parts present a shortened version of Dixon's *English Instructor*: Dixon's tables are preserved intact, as is his explication of the relationship between letters and sounds, but many of his lessons are excised. The third part draws on the other authors for practical arithmetic, offering arithmetical rules together with forms of bills, bonds, releases, bills of sale, and so on.

This omnibus approach, which incorporated writing and arithmetic for beginners as well as reading instruction, lost ground in the 1760s to Thomas Dilworth's *A New Guide to the English Tongue*, published initially in London in 1740. Benjamin Franklin was the first American to reprint Dilworth – he put out an edition in Philadelphia in 1747 – but the book did not hit its stride in America until the 1760s. At least twenty-six editions had been published by the time of the Revolution. Meanwhile, English editions were being imported into every major American port; in the six-year period 1759–1764 the Boston bookseller Jeremy Condy sold over thirty-eight *dozen* copies (almost certainly imports) to lesser merchants all over New England.[26]

After midcentury, some spelling-book characteristics disappeared while new ones emerged. Supplementary material not directly related to reading instruction vanished. Lists of "difficult Words," with their definitions, such as those that had appeared in Pastorius's *New Primmer*, were dealt with in dictionaries. The rules of arithmetic and examples of bills of lading, like those found in the *Youth's Instructor*, were eliminated as arithmetic books and self-instructional manuals became separate genres. Dilworth is a good example. There was no arithmetic instruction in his *New Guide*; instead, it all appeared in his own arithmetic, the *Schoolmaster's Assistant*.

While some authors of spellers paid lip service to the importance of the child's comprehension – Dilworth proclaimed that his tables were filled only with words that "even such as a Child may have some *Idea* of at the first Pronunciation" – none paid any attention to the child's enjoyment. In the mother country, however, a new view of education originally promulgated by John Locke was slowly infusing the eighteenth-century scene. It involved a startlingly different vision of children. In his philosophical works, Locke had introduced the notion of the *tabula rasa*, the mind as a clean slate ready to have impressions inscribed upon it through the senses. The educational corollary of this and of his political views appeared in Locke's *Some Thoughts Concerning Education* (1693), in which he advocated an education that respected the child's natural love of liberty. "I have always had a Fancy," he wrote, "that Learning might be made Play and recreation to children . . .

[that] Children may be . . . *taught to read*, without perceiving it to be anything but a Sport."[27] A London spelling book authored in 1743 by Mary Cooper, a printer's widow, and reprinted in Boston by 1750, expressed these new notions in its title: *The Child's New Play-Thing: being a Spelling Book Intended to Make the Learning to Read a Diversion Instead of a Task.*

It is difficult to exaggerate how different this little work is from the spellers that preceded and followed it. Whereas the *New England Primer* is a metaphor for Christian obedience, *The Child's New Play-Thing* is a metaphor for consumption. It opens, not with an alphabet on Calvinist themes, but on eating: "A Apple Pye/ B Bit it/ C cut it." The religious material, a mere fourth of the book, is juxtaposed with fables, one of which, in monosyllables, is about the "good Dog" Tray, who "would not hurt the least thing in the World." Thanks to his poor taste in friends, however, he shares the unenviable fate of his pal Snap, torn to shreds by the dogs Snap has antagonized. Here and elsewhere in these stories, the individual is depicted as in charge of his own fate provided he makes wise choices and sensible self-evaluations; he is not a creature of his own sinfulness or the potential victim of a wrathful God.[28] In these and other respects, *The Child's New Play-Thing* was in the vanguard of books designed to entertain children rather than preach to them. It was an early example – particularly because it was ostensibly a schoolbook – of an era that J. H. Plumb has called "the new world of children."[29]

The waves of innovation from England represented by the *Child's New Play-Thing* and by the books for children published by the London printer John Newbery from 1744 on would be channeled into children's leisure reading rather than into the schoolbook market. Late in the century, an entirely American product captured the audience for reading instructional texts. As the Revolutionary war came to a close, the young and ardently patriotic Noah Webster, a graduate of Yale College, novice schoolteacher, and aspiring lawyer, penned the first version of his spelling book, designed as an improvement on Dilworth's. In 1783 he offered it to the public as "a mite [thrown] into the common treasure of patriotic exertions." Four years later, reorganized and retitled the *American Spelling Book*, it was already on its way to becoming *the* work that would teach American children to read (and, not incidentally, to pronounce words in a uniform manner); it would successfully fight off all challengers for almost forty years. Long on tables and short on lessons, the *American Spelling Book* preached a strict moral code. At this early moment in his life Webster seems to have been theologically moderate; the moral lessons in the text of 1783 and subsequent editions were carefully nondoctrinal, and a sentence about behaving in church acknowledged the very un-Puritan practice of kneeling.[30]

In mediating the experience of learning how to read, the spellers and primers most in use among the colonists continued to associate literacy with religion or morality. But learning how to read, and especially learning how to write and figure, were also utilitarian, ever more appropriate to the kind of economy and society that America was becoming as of 1776. Half of the white population in this society were under the age of twenty, a demographic circumstance that helps put into perspective the strong demand for schoolbooks and their disciplining function. In this same society, assumptions about race and gender continued to affect who became literate, and at what level. Yet women were gaining ground and, and as a consequence, becoming a greater presence, both real and symbolic, in the world of books.

PART TWO. CUSTOMERS AND THE MARKET FOR BOOKS

ELIZABETH CARROLL REILLY AND DAVID D. HALL

THE DIFFICULTIES IN THE WAY OF ESTABLISHING how many white Americans in the eighteenth century owned or used books are many, and the quantitative evidence we are about to present must not be regarded as authoritatively comprehensive. Did a greater share of Americans participate in the world of books, in keeping with the greater percentage who were becoming literate? Did those who read continue to prefer the same genres as in the seventeenth century, or switch to other kinds of books? Fiction looms large as the test case: in a century that witnessed "the rise of the novel" in English and Continental literary culture, were Americans abandoning "dreary Days of Doom" for gothic romances, as the American writer Royall Tyler said they were in his end-of-the-century novel *The Algerine Captive* (1797)?[31] Contrary to his self-serving observation, the evidence we are about to review does not suggest any major transition in reading preferences. As the preceding chapters on the book trades have shown, in the first six decades of the century the kinds of books local printers and booksellers chose to issue show little signs of change. These tradesmen were unwilling to risk much capital on books of any size. Although more persons were able to read, those who patronized booksellers were mainly persons of wealth, for substantial books remained too expensive for people of middling and lower social status to buy. The great exception to this rule was the cheap print – almanacs, broadside ballads, chapbooks, psalters, primers, spellers, unbound sermons, and pamphlets dealing with sensational events – that, as incidental purchases, many persons could afford and that the book trade issued in edition sizes (or totals from a number of editions) which sometimes mounted into the tens of thousands. Only in the new and still just barely visible milieu of the circulating library, and perhaps in a handful of bookstores, did fiction begin to outnumber other genres.

Several kinds of book passed through the hands of readers during their lifetimes. Estate inventories indicate that a majority of testators owned books at the time they died.[32] Some 60 percent of inventories recorded in Maryland between 1700 and 1776 included one or more books.[33] The most comprehensive study, encompassing some 7,500 inventories from two Tidewater counties in Maryland and another two in Virginia, considers books as among the "amenities" (linens, knives and forks, pictures, silverplate, etc.) that appeared in households in much greater numbers in the decades before the outbreak of war. Compared to the level of book ownership achieved in the previous century, the figures for St. Mary's County indicate a doubling by the 1770s among persons in the lowest wealth cohort (from 19 to 44 percent), with the increases coming after 1740; among the wealthier colonists, ownership remained at about the same level as before, with books in nearly three fourths of these households. In another Tidewater county the figures are even higher: 66 percent by the 1770s for those in the lowest cohort, with ownership being almost universal for those at the highest end of the scale. Yet in two other counties no clear pattern of growth is visible.[34] A similar study of the influx of consumer goods among the people living in southern New England shows that people in the middling and higher ranks were not acquiring books (of the kind they would retain) at the same rate as they were buying tableware. Moreover, the books these people owned remained overwhelmingly religious. Still another inventory study from a mix of rural and urban areas in post-revolutionary Virginia – the data extends beyond our period – shows that 50 percent or more of white Virginians who lived in rural areas did not own books at the time of their decease; although books were somewhat more prevalent among townspeople, it may be more pertinent to note that, when titles are specified among the rural inventories, the subject matter is invariably religious and that fully a fourth cite only the Bible.[35] For Marylanders and, we may suppose, for Americans in general, the typical household library was tiny in size; of the inventories studied by Joseph Wheeler, three fourths contained fewer than ten books (when titles are specified, these are usually the Bible, Bayly's *Practice of Piety*, and the like); those with twenty or more comprised but 3 percent of all collections.[36] End-of-the-century inventories in a Connecticut town show much the same pattern, with no more than a quarter containing other than a Bible or psalter.[37]

Bookstore studies confirm this picture in one respect but modify it in another. Thanks to sales records kept by two different bookstores, Jeremy Condy's in Boston and the store in Williamsburg maintained successively in the 1750s and 1760s by William Hunter and Joseph Royle, we know who came to these shops, what kinds of books they wanted, and how many copies they purchased. Some 565 customers' names appear in the day books recording credit purchases at the Williamsburg shop over a four-year period (1750–1752; 1764–1766). All but twelve of them men (many of whom were surely buying books for others in their household to read), the great majority of these customers bought but three books or less during these years; a minority (182) of gentry, burgesses, and members of the council bought four or more, though of this group only a handful bought in any quantity at all.[38]

In Boston as in Williamsburg, the most visible customers were affluent and learned men who could afford to buy books imported from overseas. Condy, who went into business as a bookseller around 1754, kept a record of 600 customers who bought from him on credit in the 1750s and 1760s. Perhaps more than any other document from the period, his account book is sharply revealing of the patronage of educated men. A quarter of the 600 were Harvard students; half of the rest had been educated at Harvard, and half of these were ministers. The rest, be they Harvard graduates or not, were physicians, scholars and teachers, lawyers, men with military titles, and merchants. Nineteen artisans and a few women listed as "widow" appear in the book, but usually as providers of goods and services to Condy. The common purchases of the Harvard students, particularly of Locke's *Essay on Human Understanding*, Robert Dodsley's *Preceptor*, and Nathan Bailey's *Dictionary*, show that they were seeking books required by their tutors. College reading also accounts for the largest orders of imported books: ninety-six of the English Nonconformist Philip Doddridge's *Rise and Progress of Religion in the Soul*, seventy-six of Locke's *Treatises of Government*.[39]

The pattern of sales in Condy's store seems to prevail elsewhere, as we have already seen in the case of Hunter and Royle. Most of the books (counted by the number of titles) in these stores came from Britain, most were expensive, and most were available in very small quantities. From a stock that ranged over 295 titles, Royle sold only 1,827 copies. When Henry Knox of Boston was ordering books from London in the 1770s, a characteristic request was extremely modest: three orders for Locke's *Treatises of Government* (for a total of twenty copies); four each of Richardson's *Charles Grandison* and *Pamela*, and two of *Clarissa Harlowe*. Over the course of four years Knox imported about 500 copies of novels spread out over 100 different titles; the most popular was Henry Mackenzie's *The Man of Feeling*, which he ordered a dozen times for a total of twenty-two copies.[40] Like other urban booksellers in the 1760s, David Hall in Philadelphia advertised a large number of different titles from England but ordered them only in small quantities and seldom reordered.[41]

The newspaper advertisements and booksellers' catalogues that became more frequent in the 1760s are a deceptive mirror of consumer demand.

David Hall ordered and advertised more than 1,600 titles over a twenty-four-year period (1748–1772), the largest percentage of them in literature. As noted already, the number of sales per title was extremely modest. Yet these advertisements and catalogues suggest that a certain number of the colonists were eager for news about the latest and most fashionable books which the London book trade was purveying. Catalogues and advertisements were a principal vehicle for this information, and English magazines another. Condy and Knox sold more copies of *The Gentleman's Magazine*, *The London Magazine*, and similar periodicals than any other genre of print, dispatching a large portion of them to gentry and clergymen who lived outside Boston. Booksellers sometimes quoted from the notices of new fiction in these magazines, as William Rind did in the *Maryland Gazette* of September 20, 1762, borrowing a comparison of Rousseau's *La Nouvelle Héloise* with *Clarissa*. The short-lived American versions of these magazines, such as *The American Magazine and Historical Chronicle* (1743–1746), weighed in with monthly features like "A Catalogue of the Newest Books." Booksellers' catalogues, some of them imported and others issued locally, were another major source of information. When Thomas Jefferson drew up a list of books in 1771 as recommended reading for a young cousin, he relied on the catalogue of Thomas Waller, a London bookseller.[42]

Let us look more largely at the kinds of books that bookstore customers preferred. In Williamsburg, the subject matter most in demand during the span of time Hunter was in charge (1750–1752), as measured by the number of copies sold, was religion (54 percent of the total, with Anglican works of devotion, sermons, and the Presbyterian minister Samuel Davies's *Miscellaneous Poems* [1751] among the better-selling titles), lawbooks and statutes (almost 16 percent, including a 1751 session laws printed in an edition of 1,000), schoolbooks, and belles lettres (a total of ninety-four copies of this last). Under Royle for the years 1764–1766, no single category dominated; belles lettres slightly exceeded grammars and rhetorics, law-related items, geography and travel, religion, and Latin schoolbooks, in that order. For the most part, these were imported books, for Royle printed even less than Hunter.[43] Of the stock that Hall ordered from abroad or printed in Philadelphia, religion, history, medicine, and the law trailed literature among the books he *advertised*, and Hall was not always sure he could sell more books on religion; on one occasion he remarked to his London supplier William Strahan that "Divinity is a most dull Article here. Send no more," and on another asked, "Why have you sent six sets of Tillotson?" Yet in the space of five years (1760–1765) he ordered 450 copies of Robert Russell's *Seven Sermons*, a book initially printed in England near the close of the seventeenth century, much reprinted in relatively inexpensive editions, and of great interest to the common reader in the colonies.[44]

This tantalizing glimpse of a larger audience for books is enhanced by our knowledge of other items Hall was issuing in large quantities: *Poor Richard's Almanack*, a primer, and a catechism, together with imported Bibles (he ordered at least 10,000) and schoolbooks. As in his case, so in that of other booksellers and printers the quantities in circulation of almanacs and chapbooks (some, like the almanac, always printed locally, others a mix of imported and local production) paint a picture of the book market that contrasts with the customer studies we have been citing. These quantities alert us to the material and cultural realm of cheap print. The boundaries of cheap print encompassed books of a format and sometimes of a length that could be sold for very little: books in small type, with narrow margins; unbound chapbooks;[45] broadside ballads (a speciality of the Boston printer Nathaniel Coverly); and "small books for book pedlars," the speciality of Zechariah Fowle, another Boston printer–bookseller of these pre-Revolutionary years, whose careless shop practices were memorably recalled by his one-time apprentice Isaiah Thomas.[46] Many chapbooks or other kinds of cheap books were produced overseas; in the 1770s Henry Knox was importing thousands of chapbooks costing *2d.* wholesale from the London trade, some of them copies of children's books issued by the London bookseller John Newbery, others abridged versions of novels such as Samuel Richardson's *Pamela* and *Clarissa Harlowe*.[47] These books were distributed not only through bookstores such as Henry Knox's or Hall's but also through a far-flung network of country peddlers and general stores.[48] In the back country of North Carolina, William Johnston's Little River store offered dozens of Bibles, psalters, and Testaments along with books by Bunyan and George Whitefield and little histories and spelling books. A general store at Elkridge Landing, Maryland included chapman's books, single sermons, Bibles, and books for children among its goods.[49]

As the range of titles suggests, cheap print was not confined to any particular subject or genre. As had long been true within the trade, printers could squeeze everything from novels and adventure tales to the Bible, captivity narratives, and evangelical treatises into a format that, because less paper was used and copies were invariably sold unbound or with blue-gray paper covers, allowed the price to fall well below the cost of most bound, imported books. Knowing very well that price mattered, booksellers intentionally issued some books in differing formats, as James Rivington did in 1774 with an edition of James Hervey's *Meditations among the Tombs*, one version of which, "in a "neat 12° volume," he offered to Henry Knox at *2s. 6d.* wholesale in sheets, the other, a shortened version "sewed in strong paper," he anticipated selling for a single shilling ("New York Currency") to "poor people . . . who cannot afford to buy the whole at once and Pedlars will sell great numbers of it." "Inexpensive" is, like everything else, a relative term, but in eighteenth-century America it may properly designate a retail price that ranged from 1 or 2*d.* to a high of a shilling (12*d.*).[50] One further observation is in order: notwithstanding Rivington's awareness of "poor people," cheap print does not designate a category of customer, for bookstore records and diaries reveal that chapbooks appealed to readers in every social milieu. A single illustration must suffice, a Harvard student who bought from Condy books that cost a pound or more along with chapbook stories that cost 1½ *d.* each.[51]

Almanacs are the best-documented and most pervasive aspect of the trade in cheap books, a trade, however, that was much more active in the middle and New England colonies than in the South. Indispensable as calendars and pocket memoranda books, almanacs were carried by every bookseller as well as by many general merchants. Ordinarily illustrated by cheap, reusable, and highly conventional woodcuts, they occasionally sported topical engravings subvened by political faction (Fig. 11.2a–b). Thomas Legate, a storekeeper in Leominster, Massachusetts, distributed enough of the yearly almanacs of Isaac Bickerstaff and Nathaniel Low to supply every household in and around his town. On the side of production, the annual edition sizes were greater than for any other form of print. Customers in New England annually bought more than 60,000 copies of Nathaniel Ames's almanacs in the 1760s. In Williamsburg, Hunter and Royle sold far more copies of the local almanac – between 4,000 and 6,000 a year, priced at 7½ *d.* – than of any other title. Franklin was issuing some 3,500 annually in the mid-1730s, but at the peak of his career the total rose to 10,000, priced at 4*d.* or 6*d.* each. When his partner–successor David Hall rendered the accounts of the firm in 1765, he noted that, during a fourteen-year period (1752–1765), it had printed 141,257 copies and another 25,735 as pocket almanacs.[52] By this time almanacs, which remained eclectic in their contents, often included abridged stories and excerpts of poetry by the likes of Alexander Pope.[53]

The very range of texts that qualify as cheap print – not only those we have cited already, but also texts intended to amuse or to promote powerful religious emotions, like *The Second Spira*[54] – stands in the way of identifying the presence of particular reading communities – that is, those distinctive clusterings of reader preference which flow from deeper patterns of culture and which serve to reveal certain structures of mediation. For evidence that leads in this direction, we may turn back to the printing office that Parks had founded and that Hunter and Royle ran after his death. Other than the almanac, few locally printed books emerged from this office, for demand was scant and distribution not easy to arrange. These restrictions did not hold, however, for a book of poems, sold bound, that Hunter published in 1751. Written by the Presbyterian minister Samuel Davies, who came to

Juſt publiſhed,

Embelliſhed with four Plates, neatly engraved, viz. The Boſton Maſſacre, The four Seaſons, with the Twelve Signs of the Zodiack.---The King of Denmark.---Jonathan Weatherwiſe.

Price 22s. 6d. Old Tenor the Dozen, and ſeven Coppers ſingle.

Printed on much larger Paper than Almanacks commonly are,

The Maſſachuſetts Calendar,

OR AN

ALMANACK

FOR

The Year of our LORD 1772,

From the CREATION, according to Prophane Hiſtory, 5722,
According to the Sacred Scriptures, 5674,

Being BISSEXTILE or LEAP-YEAR:

CALCULATED FOR

The Meridian of BOSTON, New-England, Lat. 42 Deg. 25 Min. North.

By PHILOMATHES.

CONTAINING,

The Lunations,
Eclipſes,
Planets Places,
Aſpects,
Judgment of the Weather,
Feaſts and Faſts of the Church,
Courts,
The riſing, ſouthing, and ſetting of the Seven Stars,
Sun and Moon's riſing and ſetting.
Time of High Water,
Moon's Place,
Clock's Equation,
Ephemeris, &c.
Vulgar Notes for 1772,
Names and Characters of the Twelve Signs, Seven Planets, and Five Aſpects,
The Parts of the Body that are governed by the Twelve Signs,
Roads, &c.

ALSO,
Several ſelect Pieces, viz.
On Liberty and Government,
Thoughts on Government,
On the Culture of Silk,
Man of Pleaſure,
Woman of Pleaſure,
Jonathan Weatherwiſe's Prognoſticks,
A Table of Intereſt on an entire new Conſtruction; reviſed and corrected by Mr. JOHN LEACH, Teacher of the Mathematicks in Boſton,
POETRY, viz.
The Difference between To-Day and To-Morrow,
Of Time. Of Pride. Of Vice.
Reflections on Time, &c.
On the Boſton Maſſacre,
On the King of Denmark,
On the Twelve Signs,

BOSTON,
Printed and ſold by ISAIAH THOMAS, in Union-ſtreet, near the Market.

Figure 11.2a. [Isaiah Thomas,] Advertisement (Boston, [1771]) for *The Massachusetts Calendar for 1772*, "embellished with four plates, neatly engraved, viz. The Boston Massacre, The four seasons, . . . The King of Denmark [&] Jonathan Weatherwise." American Antiquarian Society.

Figure 11.2B. "The BLOODY MASSACRE perpetrated in King-Street, *BOSTON*" [Boston, 1770], pirated by Paul Revere from Henry Pelham and sold for 8*d.* (4*d.* less than Pelham's engraving); the barracks on the right is renamed "BUTCHER'S HALL." Revere also engraved a smaller, less graphic, relief-cut version, published in the *Massachusetts Calendar* and reused in some broadsides on the Boston Massacre. American Antiquarian Society.

Virginia in the late 1740s, *Miscellaneous Poems, Chiefly on Divine Subjects* found an immediate market among his fellow Presbyterians, most of them immigrants from northern Ireland or Scotland, who were flooding into upland Virginia. One of these Scots, the founder of a Presbyterian settlement, bought 200 copies and three other Presbyterians, including Davies, bought another 111. In these same years Davies was ordering thirty-six copies of a book printed in far-off Boston, Jonathan Edwards's *Freedom of the Will.*[55]

Thus did the convergence of ethnicity, religious affiliation, and the Great Awakening of the 1740s, a religious insurgency in which George Whitefield played a large part (Fig. 11.3), manifest itself in Virginia. Elsewhere, too, this insurgency played itself out in patterns of reading, as it did even in the liberal confines of Harvard College, where a tutor observed in his diary, "There is a new face upon things. [Solomon] Stoddard and [Thomas] Shephard [sic] are the Books now." Suddenly, out-of-print sermons and long-lasting steady sellers by Nonconformists and seventeenth-century New England divines were being reissued in edition sizes that easily ran to 2,000 copies, the quantity Daniel Henchman of Boston arranged to have printed in 1742 and 1743 of three different works of devotion, one of them Thomas Shepard's *Sound Believer*.[56] Demand fell off somewhat after 1745, but the reading community that asserted its preferences so strongly in the 1740s remained a major presence up to the Revolution and beyond.

One measure of its influence is the frequency with which certain *titles* were reprinted. Barring catechisms, hymn books, schoolbooks, and parts of Bibles, these steady sellers were devotional or evangelical in nature. The seventeen printings of Robert Russell's *Seven Sermons* (to which must be added the copies David Hall and others were importing), the fourteen of the Nonconformist Thomas Wilcox's *A Choice Drop of Honey*, the twenty-five between them of two Nonconformist manuals on how to prepare for the Lord's Supper, the fourteen of Samsom Occom's execution sermon – such works were the staple reading matter of many middling and, no doubt, some upper-income Americans.[57] Another of these texts was *An Account of the Life of . . . David Brainerd*, Jonathan Edwards's spiritual biography, much of it based on Brainerd's journal, of a young college student who became a missionary to Indians in New Jersey. Published with a list of 1,953 subscribers, the *Life* was frequently reprinted and, in a redaction subsequently made by John Wesley, sold for relatively little.

Thanks to the diary of Nicholas Gilman, the Congregational minister in Durham, New Hampshire, we can see the evangelical reading community in action on a local scale. Hearing in 1739 of the revivals taking place in the middle colonies, he responded by seeking out books that conveyed news of the awakenings. In a single month (January 1740) he read four of Whitefield's publications; at the end of that month he bought 26*s*. 6*d*. worth of "small books" at Daniel Henchman's Boston bookstore, presumably new editions of steady sellers from the seventeenth century, for in his diary he noted reading two of Thomas Shepard's books and sermons by such English Nonconformists as John Flavel, James Jennings, and Matthew Henry. Meanwhile he was also gathering up copies of magazines and newspapers that specialized in reporting on the transatlantic revivals. He shared his ever-growing library of evangelical reading matter with parishioners who gathered at his house to

An ELEGIAC

POEM,

On the DEATH of that celebrated Divine, and eminent Servant of JESUS CHRIST, the late Reverend, and pious

GEORGE WHITEFIELD,

Chaplain to the Right Honourable the Countess of HUNTINGDON, &c &c.

Who made his Exit from this transitory State, to dwell in the celestial Realms of Bliss, on LORD's-Day, 30th of September, 1770, when he was seiz'd with a Fit of the Asthma, at NEWBURY-PORT, near BOSTON, in NEW-ENGLAND. In which is a Condolatory Address to His truly noble Benefactress the worthy and pious Lady HUNTINGDON,---and the Orphan-Children in GEORGIA; who, with many Thousands, are left, by the Death of this great Man, to lament the Loss of a Father, Friend, and Benefactor.

By PHILLIS, a Servant Girl of 17 Years of Age, belonging to Mr. J. WHEATLEY, of BOSTON:--And has been but 9 Years in this Country from Africa.

HAIL happy Saint on thy immortal throne!
To thee complaints of grievance are unknown;
We hear no more the music of thy tongue,
Thy wonted auditories cease to throng.
Thy lessons in unequal'd accents flow'd!
While emulation in each bosom glow'd;
Thou didst, in strains of eloquence refin'd,
Inflame the soul, and captivate the mind.
Unhappy we, the setting Sun deplore!
Which once was splendid, but it shines no more;
He leaves this earth for Heaven's unmeasur'd height:
And worlds unknown, receive him from our sight;
There WHITEFIELD wings, with rapid course his way,
And sails to Zion, through vast seas of day.

When his AMERICANS were burden'd sore,
When streets were crimson'd with their guiltless gore!
Unrival'd friendship in his breast now strove:
The fruit thereof was charity and love
Towards *America*-----couldst thou do more
Than leave thy native home, the *British* shore,
To cross the great Atlantic's wat'ry road,
To see *America's* distress'd abode?
Thy prayers, great Saint, and thy incessant cries,
Have pierc'd the bosom of thy native skies!
Thou moon hast seen, and ye bright stars of light
Have witness been of his requests by night!
He pray'd that grace in every heart might dwell:
He long'd to see *America* excell;
He charg'd its youth to let the grace divine
Arise, and in their future actions shine;
He offer'd THAT he did himself receive,
A greater gift not GOD himself can give:
He urg'd the need of HIM to every one;
It was no less than GOD's co-equal SON!
Take HIM ye wretched for your only good;
Take HIM ye starving souls to be your food.
Ye thirsty, come to this life giving stream:
Ye Preachers, take him for your joyful theme:
Take HIM, "my dear AMERICANS," he said,
Be your complaints in his kind bosom laid:
Take HIM ye *Africans*, he longs for you;
Impartial SAVIOUR, is his title due;
If you will chuse to walk in grace's road,
You shall be sons, and kings, and priests to GOD.

Great COUNTESS! we *Americans* revere
Thy name, and thus condole thy grief sincere:
We mourn with thee, that TOMB obscurely plac'd,
In which thy Chaplain undisturb'd doth rest.
New-England sure, doth feel the ORPHAN's smart;
Reveals the true sensations of his heart:
Since this fair Sun, withdraws his golden rays,
No more to brighten these distressful days!
His lonely *Tabernacle*, sees no more
A WHITEFIELD landing on the *British* shore:
Then let us view him in yon azure skies:
Let every mind with this lov'd object rise.
No more can he exert his lab'ring breath,
Seiz'd by the cruel messenger of death.
What can his dear AMERICA return?
But drop a tear upon his happy urn,
Thou tomb, shalt safe retain thy sacred trust,
Till life divine re-animate his dust.

Figure 11.3. [Phillis Wheatley,] *An Elegiac Poem on the Death of that Celebrated Divine George Whitefield* (Philadelphia: William Goddard, 1770). One of many broadside editions of this popular piece. Courtesy of The Historical Society of Pennsylvania.

hear him read aloud from these sermons and reports; others borrowed books, as when "Mother Thing took home Edwards on Northampton" (Gilman's copy of Edwards's *Narrative of Surprizing Conversions*).[58]

Notwithstanding the extensiveness of these practices, other colonists participated in different or competing interpretive communities. The urban, elite women and men who shared manuscript poetry in literary coteries and salons; the governor of Massachusetts who joined with others of his status to create a reading circle; the naturalists, doctors, and amateurs of science, or "natural philosophy" who at meetings of the American Philosophical Society for the Promotion of Useful Knowledge passed around copies of the *Philosophical Transactions* or perhaps of Benjamin Franklin's letters on electricity; the people who, in singing schools or societies in New England, were rehearsing tunes and melodies, some of which were written by local psalmodists; the undergraduates at colleges up and down the coast who formed literary clubs with private libraries devoted mainly to belles lettres – these are but a small number of sharply focused reading communities. Not only did these circles or coteries prefer different kinds of books from those that evangelicals sought out, several of them also embodied an emerging form of sociability characterized by politeness and "refinement."[59]

Meanwhile, women in mid-eighteenth century and Revolutionary America were playing a greater role as readers. Ever more literate, though still excluded from some circles, they found themselves increasingly courted by booksellers and writers who sensed a new audience for their work among the "ladies" or "fair sex" whom they addressed in poetry, sermons, essays on moral conduct, newspaper advertisements, and booksellers' catalogues. English writers and the English trade were acting on these possibilities during the first third of the century. Not until after midcentury, however, did American booksellers begin routinely to single out women in their advertisements or catalogues, as John Mein of Boston was doing in the 1760s. And not until the closing decades of the century did American booksellers and writers begin to issue books and periodicals linked to gender: for example, *The Ladies' Magazine; and Repository of Entertaining Knowledge* (1792–1793). In these same years, a female-education movement emerged, its premise being that young women should receive training in academic subjects rather than being limited to schooling in the domestic arts. This period also saw the founding of gender-specific private societies devoted to reading. Yet the long-lasting assumption that women's virtue was best preserved apart from learnedness and, in particular, apart from certain kinds of books, died hard. Some of those who justified the new activity of women – most prominently, Benjamin Rush of Philadelphia – drew on the ideology of republicanism. But many who welcomed the participation of women continued to insist on some form of difference and, explicitly or by implication, made it clear that women's reading should be constrained, as Rush himself did in critiquing fiction.[60] Another new current at midcentury was a recognition of children as readers who deserved or should be addressed through a distinctive set of publications. Signaled in some of the spellers that the colonists imported from overseas and signaled, as well, in the English bookseller John Newbery's pocket books for children, this movement would not take hold in America until after 1800.[61]

Young or old, men or women, the importance of active consumers for the book trades and, more generally, the importance of the reading they did for the cultural and intellectual life of the colonies and new republic, was immense. Yet our warning against any exaggeration of the place of reading in everyday life bears repetition. Notwithstanding the rise in the rate of literacy, the growing abundance of cheap print, and what seems to have been a rising standard of living for many Americans, the situations in which ordinary people *needed* books other than almanacs, or framed their sociability around the practice of reading, remained few. Cost continued to be an obstacle; a substantial fraction of the colonists could not afford to buy books with any regularity.[62] Distribution remained another barrier, for as Devereux Jarrett discovered in Virginia at midcentury, certain sections of the country were poorly served by the book trade. A minister in North Carolina who published a collection of his sermons in 1788 remarked in the preface that "so affectingly scarce are good books, among the common people of these southern states, since the late war, that this little piece may compose the whole library in some houses its author has called at."[63] Did he ignore the presence of books he would not have deemed "good"? Possibly; yet the tiny quantities of books preserved in most book-owning households (as indicated by probate inventories) and, at the other end of the scale, the relative wealth and superior status of the customers who bought from Condy and the Williamsburg bookstore, are a strong demonstration of social circumstances – wealth, gender, education, and region – that both limited and sustained the practice of reading.

Let us look one more time at the kinds of books that people in the eighteenth century preferred to buy or borrow and read. Were we to generalize about the taste of all those who participated in reading communities, the emphasis would fall on a cluster of genres which, in the context of the times, were understood as providing guidance on the conduct of a moral life. Works of history figured prominently in this cluster, as did evangelical steady sellers. That in the final three decades of our period (1760–1790), Pope's *Essay on Man* and Lord Chesterfield's *Letters to His Son* were among the most frequently reprinted titles in America is indicative of this preference. So are the two books most frequently requested from the Harvard

College Library between 1773 and 1782 by faculty and neighboring clergy, David Hume's *History of England* and Philip Doddridge's *Family Expositor.* Another cue is the vogue of Richardson's *Pamela*, which made its way even into the Stockbridge, Massachusetts household of Jonathan Edwards.[64]

These preferences and, as we will see more fully in the final section of this chapter, the framing of fiction as offering moral instruction, stand in the way of any narrative of secularization or "the rise of the novel" as sketched by historians of reading in Europe. The subject matter or genre classifications of the books listed in booksellers' catalogues tell us otherwise; fiction constituted a mere nine percent of the total,[65] and Thomas Newton's *Dissertations on the Prophecies* (1758), a book by an English minister explicating the prophetic parts of Scripture, appeared more often in bookseller and library catalogues than did "Enlightenment" texts or, for that matter, *Pamela*. The percentage of "secular" books in probate inventories, always modest save in the estates of professional men, seems to have gradually increased, but the largest share of books retained at death remained those dealing with religion.[66] As for book advertisements, for the first half of the century they showed little change in reading taste.[67] At the Little River store in Orange County, in upland North Carolina, customers made their conservatism painfully clear to local merchants who tried to introduce novels and dictionaries imported from Glasgow; not a single copy of the new books sold, while Bibles, hornbooks, psalters, and books by John Bunyan did.[68] The fissures in American culture and therefore in reading preferences ran along doctrinal or denominational lines, as Condy knew in catering to readers who welcomed certain liberalizing currents within English Nonconformity and New England Congregationalism, and as Hunter and Royle knew in catering either to Anglicans or, in the instance of Davies's *Miscellaneous Poems*, to Presbyterians.[69] Only in the history of social and circulating libraries can we detect the early stages of a "reading-revolution" the full force of which would unfold after 1800.

PART THREE. LIBRARIES AND THEIR USERS

ROSS W. BEALES AND JAMES N. GREEN

PEOPLE WHO NEEDED BOOKS but could not afford them frequently borrowed from other individuals (a minister or community leader, as Franklin and Jarrett did), or from stocks of books kept in places such as taverns and general stores.[70] In the course of the century, book borrowing also became formalized via a new institution, the social library. Privately owned and sponsored, these libraries were nonetheless "public" in the distinctively eighteenth-century sense of being a space where civic, religious, and commercial values converged and overlapped.

At the outset of the century, when English observers were commonly remarking that books were in scant supply, philanthropic agencies associated with the Church of England took on the task of multiplying the number of libraries in the colonies (Fig. 11.4). The Anglican minister Thomas Bray was responsible for this initiative, which arose after Bray was appointed Commissary of the Church of England in Maryland in 1698. Learning that most Maryland parishes were very short of clergy (as were many parishes elsewhere), Bray reasoned that he could more easily recruit candidates from England for the ministry if they were guaranteed an adequate supply of books. Thus came into being his scheme of "parochial" libraries, collections of relatively modest size and scope (numbering two or three hundred books, almost entirely religious, some new and others old, and strongly Anglican in flavor), paid for by English donors and shipped by the dozens to the colonies during the next seven decades. Ostensibly private in being designated for the benefit of clergy, these libraries were often made available to lay persons. Bray supplemented these collections with larger shipments, termed "provincial," to capital towns like Annapolis and Charleston; in the course of time, the Charleston books were absorbed into the Charleston Library Society. Other philanthropic ventures included the books sent out to Georgia by benefactors and trustees of that colony, most of whom were members of Dr. Bray's Associates; one such gift in 1733 comprised 187 copies of Richard Allestree's *The Whole Duty of Man* and 186 copies of the Bible. Drawing on these and other connections, George Whitefield gathered some 1,200 books for Bethesda, his orphanage-turned-college in the same colony.[71]

Of little importance in the long run, though surely making more books available in inland towns where no bookstores could exist, these philanthropic collections were later eclipsed by two other kinds of libraries: the social or subscription and the circulating. In 1731, Benjamin Franklin and his fellow members of the Junto in Philadelphia established the first social library in America, which he would hail in retrospect as "the Mother of all the N American Subscription Libraries now so numerous." Franklin had a point, though he also exaggerated; almost simultaneously, four such libraries were being founded in Connecticut.[72] Subscription libraries shared a common organization and mode of operations. This pattern involved the local initiative of individuals who pledged funds, selected officers and appointed a librarian, decided on what books to acquire for their members' uses, established hours and rules for borrowing, and found a suitable room to house

Figure 11.4. Bookplate of The Society for Propagating the Gospel, removed from their gift. The society presented a copy of Epictetus, *Dissertationes*, ed. John Upton (London, 1741) to Harvard with the same plate in 1765. American Antiquarian Society.

the collection. Each of the original subscribers of the Union Library Company of Philadelphia, organized in 1746, paid three pounds to "form a joint Stock for the Purchasing a Collection of useful Books." The group limited its membership to 100 in a partnership that was to last 100 years. The members selected a treasurer and five directors, along with a clerk who would act as librarian, who was to be present at the library room once a week for two hours. Nonmembers were allowed to borrow books by giving their note to the clerk, "with a penalty of double the Value of the Book, or Set of Books," and with the understanding that the books would be returned "undefaced." The library's first published catalogue (1754) listed 317 books.[73]

Invariably, social libraries acted through agents to purchase books in England. The founders of the library in Salem, Massachusetts, commissioned Jeremy Condy, who was going to England for other reasons, to act on their behalf. Armed with a list of titles and given discretionary funds for additional purchases, Condy was to buy second-hand volumes if possible and to obtain octavos rather than folios or quartos. All books were to be bound, and among them the tragedies, the comedies, and the farces were to be bound by themselves. In the case of books about which there was any question of "good repute," Condy was to use his own judgment. Not in this instance, but in the assembling of other collections, the category of belles lettres loomed large, comprising nearly a quarter of all titles in four Pennsylvania collections.[74] Subscription libraries spread with some rapidity. With these institutions in mind, by 1766 it was claimed that Pennsylvania "had distinguished herself in her attention to public Libraries, there not being less than four in the Metropolis, and in almost every Town of Note, one." More precise figures are available for New England, where at least fifty-one social libraries were established between 1733 and 1780.[75]

The circulating libraries that appeared in several colonies in the 1760s – William Rind's in Annapolis, which quickly failed, may have been the first – offered new opportunities for extensive reading to a somewhat different spectrum of readers. The first so-called circulating library was created in London in 1742, the year after Richardson's *Pamela* was published, and in both England and America such libraries would become associated with novel-reading. (In Britain, such libraries had been preceded by rental and subscription libraries.) Usually the customer paid a fixed sum per year or per week for the privilege of taking out one book at a time. It was cheaper to pay by the year (usually about a pound), but the non-elite and cash-poor readers who made up the bulk of the customers almost always paid by the week at sixpence. Since these libraries were usually open six days a week and books could be exchanged daily, anyone who had the time could read up to six volumes, a penny a volume. These arrangements meant that circulating libraries were well situated to appeal to readers who had spending money but not capital and to women. These libraries bought the latest and most popular books, expecting them to be read to pieces and replaced by yet newer books. The Boston bookseller John Mein, who opened a circulating library in 1765, advertised its stock in a published catalogue. "History, Poetry, Novels, &c." comprised the largest category, with a numbered list of more than 650 volumes (only 14 percent were novels); "Livres Francois," most of them novels, was the second category, with "Divinity" in third place with about 220 volumes.[76]

A close review of one example is revealing. In 1769 the venerable Bradford firm in Philadelphia opened a circulating library under the direction of twenty-two-year-old Thomas Bradford. A register of books borrowed for the year running from December 3, 1771, to December 14, 1772, says a great deal about this library and its users. The register lists about 20 to 25 transactions a day, which adds up to some 7,000 for the entire year. In the absence of a catalogue, the approximate number of books in the library can be inferred from the fact that each title was given a number and that the highest is 300. Since so many works were in sets, the total number of volumes was much larger. The collection also included multiple copies of popular works, like Henry Brooke's novel *The Fool of Quality*. In a sample month (April 1772), women borrowed nearly as many books as men, though men borrowed more books per visit. Forty-seven individuals (twenty-five men, twenty-two women) borrowed more than five books in the month. Three men were absolutely voracious; buying two shares apiece so they could exchange two books a day, these readers each borrowed twenty-one books in the month.

The ledger confirms to a surprising degree the common assumption that fiction and circulating libraries went hand in hand. The two surviving catalogues of colonial circulating libraries, for Boston and Annapolis, show that fiction accounted for 14 percent and 25 percent of the holdings, respectively; by 1783 the Annapolis library was 42 percent fiction. But almost two-thirds of the Bradford collection was fiction (none of it printed in America), and the *rate of circulation* for the genre was also much higher. Out of 617 books borrowed in April 1772, an astonishing 86 percent were fiction, while plays and verse were another 7 percent, leaving only 7 percent nonfiction.

Who used the library? Its patrons cannot readily be identified by occupation or income level, but their gender is self-evident. Considering the limits on women's participation in the public arena, it would seem surprising if they participated even half as much as men. The Bradford register shows just the opposite, a near equality in numbers of borrowers by gender: 53 percent male, 47 percent female in April 1772. Men tended to borrow more books; reckoned by transactions, the figures are 55 to 45.[77]

The avidity of the Bradford library patrons is startling, and the shift in taste is equally remarkable. For the moment, however, these circumstances were a sign of things to come. Like several others of its type, the library folded on the eve of the Revolution, and although social libraries continued to flourish, it was not until the 1790s and beyond that any of these institutions entered a phase of explosive growth. The deeper change, under way since the late seventeenth century, was in theories of the moral self that impinged on what people wished to read and how they approached certain texts.

PART FOUR. MODALITIES OF READING

ELIZABETH CARROLL REILLY AND DAVID D. HALL

THE MATERIALITIES OF EVERY TEXT – the quality of paper, the spacing of the lines of text, the nature of the binding (if bound at all) – that passed through people's hands in eighteenth-century America conveyed how it should be read. These materialities spanned a range that encompassed, at one extreme, coarsely printed execution broadsides and, at the other, Franklin's edition (1744) of James Logan's *Cato Major*, printed on specially imported paper with widely spaced margins and a two-color title page (Fig. 8.1). We see these hierarchies in action when the Boston merchant Samuel Sewall gave away books, for he sometimes specified a distinctive style of paper or binding as a means of enhancing the value of the gift and of calling attention to the importance of the text itself.[78] By the mid-eighteenth century an increasing number of books included illustrations, some of good quality and perhaps newly made for a particular book, others showing evidence of wear and tear because of being second-hand or reused.[79]

Certain though it is that these aspects of the physical book affected the practice of reading, how they did so is almost impossible to specify. Was the practice of reading also affected by the difference between publications which were issued on a regular schedule, such as monthly periodicals and weekly newspapers, and those (the great majority) which were singular or intermittent? And what influence on reading did the catchwords "new" or "latest" in booksellers' advertisements have on the experience of reading? Did the increasing frequency of these catchwords after 1760 indicate that reading was being caught up in the rhythms of cosmopolitan literary fashion or those of an emerging consumer culture? Here, too, we can only suggest that *some* eighteenth-century readers (like those, perhaps, who thronged the Bradford circulating library in Philadelphia) were becoming accustomed to new kinds of regularities that anticipated the prominence of serial publication – including the serial publication of novels – in the nineteenth century.

Where we are on firmer ground is in discerning the regulating aspects of prefaces addressed "to the reader" and the rules that governed how books were classified into genres. Every text contains an "implied reader," be it the person in need of spiritual guidance or transformation to whom almost every sermon was addressed or the figure of the citizen that "Publius" constructed in the opening pages of the *Federalist Papers*. Often these opening statements indicted *bad* reading, juxtaposing, in the case of the *Federalist Papers*, the unstable, naive person swayed by "passion" with the judicious man of reason. Some of these figures were long-lasting. Others were new, like the reader moved by "sentiment." As for genres and how they were represented or understood, the starting point, as always, was a hierarchy of value. These hierarchies varied from one interpretive community to the next; no evangelical would have accorded civil history the importance that it had for Thomas Jefferson, nor he the Bible or other "sacred" genres (church history, psalmody, sermons, poetry that employed the rhetoric of the religious sublime, the lives of exemplary Christians) that meant so much to evangelicals. Other than the emergence of explicitly secular and genteel versions of these hierarchies, the most interesting development in mid-eighteenth-century America was a new uncertainty about the genre of the novel: was it worthless, as moralists had so often declared, or could it be understood as a legitimate means of moral instruction? A single text, Samuel Richardson's *Pamela* (1741), opened the way to reconsidering the place of fiction in "good" reading, and in keeping with this change, to the emergence of sentimentalism as a ground on which religious and secular modalities of reading were able to converge.

The most pervasive framework of meaning in eighteenth-century America was not new but old, the nexus between reading and the inner self that Protestants had taken over from the middle ages and refashioned in the sixteenth and seventeenth centuries. For Hannah Heaton, a farm woman and evangelical Christian living in North Haven, Connecticut, the experience of reading John Bunyan's autobiography, *Grace Abounding to the Chief of Sinners*, amounted to an act of inward, spiritual identification, as recorded in her journal: "his tryals & temptations altho not exactly like mine yet in the nature alike." This experience of (self)discovery happened anew when she read Jonathan Edwards's *Life of David Brainerd*: "ah methinks I had fellowship with him." For Heaton and other evangelicals, Bunyan was meaningful because his prose was akin to the Word of God, imitating its plainness and power in being able to transform the heart or inner self, and reiterating the great narrative structures of repentance, pilgrimage, and redemption. Within this literary tradition the Bible remained foundational, the one book that evangelicals felt they must master and pass on to their children because it offered the priceless gift of life everlasting. For many, it remained a transparent, "speaking" book. "I was filled with a pineing desire to see Christs own words in the Bible," wrote the Connecticut farmer Nathan Cole in his spiritual autobiography:

> . . . and I got up off my bed being alone; and by the help of Chairs I got along to the window where my bible was and I opened it and the first place I saw was the 15th Chap.: John – on Christ's own words and they spake to my heart and every doubt and scruple that rose in my heart about the truth of God's word was took right off; and I saw the whole train of Scriptures all in a Connection, and I believe I felt just as the Apostles felt the truth when they writ it, every leaf line and letter smiled in my face: I got the bible up under my Chin and hugged it; it was sweet and lovely; the word was nigh me in my hand, then I began to pray and to praise God.[80]

Cole's assumption that printed texts were transcriptions of the Word as speech was acted out in the oft-repeated experience among "New Light" lay men and women of hearing Scripture passages "dart" into their heads as they went about their daily business. When a traveler from Scotland turned up in Virginia in 1743 with a book based on shorthand notes of sermons George Whitefield had preached in Glasgow, the interchangeability of speech and writing was demonstrated anew as neighbors gathered to "hear" them read aloud.[81]

Always, the Protestant vernacular tradition was prescriptive, censuring "idle" kinds of reading and demanding that the practice be not "cursory but searching." The lay men and women who took such advice to heart could be moved, at moments of felt crisis, to purge their households of certain books, as happened in New London, Connecticut, in 1742 when, at the urging of a young minister, some of the townspeople disposed of vanities and bad books in a bonfire. Always, as well, the Protestant tradition could easily turn into a critique of learnedness not unlike what the Quakers and other radicals in mid-seventeenth-century England had voiced. Hermon Husbands, a North Carolina farmer who described in his spiritual autobiography how he came to spurn "Fictitious" chapbooks and to prefer Whitefield's writings, insisted that all the "Doctors of Divinity" in the world were of less weight than "the inward and sensible inspirations of the Holy Spirit" that enabled him to understand the Bible. To affirm this spirit-centered radicalism was to pass beyond or outside of the regulating hierarchies that ordinarily prevailed within the Protestant tradition; "they find [in the Bible] new chapters, new psalms, new histories, because they see them in a new light," Jonathan Edwards remarked of his parishioners, and though in this instance he spoke approvingly, he and many other moderates were shocked by the bonfire in New London.[82]

Because of this reaction, which rippled widely outward from the evangelical community, and because in religious as in secular intellectual circles, many of the colonists were influenced by John Locke's critique of "enthusiasm," the modalities of reading in eighteeenth-century America encompassed the moderating temperament of those who advocated the mechanism of "reason." The distance from religious ecstasy that many readers preferred is epitomized in a customer's request for a copy of Bunyan's *Pilgrim's Progress*, which Hannah Heaton had also read with kindred fervor and sense of identification. Writing in 1773 to Henry Knox at his Boston bookstore, Andrew Oliver, a Harvard graduate and man of wealth, asked for a list of books, adding at the end that "I forgot to set down [Bunyan] . . . which, the Divinity aside, I admire as an Allegory. If you have a handsome edition of it by you with Cutts please send me one, if not, to write for it." These specifications – a stylish ("handsome") artifact and a firmly literary classification (allegory, not divinity) of the text, not to mention the aspect of status (the ability to afford an imported copy) – turned Oliver's experience of owning and, no doubt, of reading *Pilgrim's Progress* into something very different from Heaton's.[83]

The appeal of reason, which Locke had urged in *The Reasonableness of Christianity* (1695) as a means of sorting through and evaluating Scripture, was several-fold. As had Locke before him, Benjamin Franklin regarded reason as a natural faculty that, when properly used, led to toleration and agreement, whereas the outcome of unregulated passion was conflict and authoritarianism. In keeping with this belief, Franklin urged that Americans read the sermons of the Anglican minister and archbishop John Tillotson, a Latitudinarian who became something of a beau ideal among theological moderates and liberals for having embraced "charity." (George Whitefield complained in 1740 that Harvard undergraduates were too fond of him!) Another body of texts that abetted the training of reason were the classics (the child who relished Plutarch's *Lives* liked them still); yet another was history, which Jefferson, who shared much of Franklin's way of thinking, recommended as the basic reading stuff of elementary education. Like the evangelicals, secular rationalists and theological moderates construed reading as a means of self-construction. But in their scheme the subjectivity fashioned through the act of reading was keyed to the disciplining of the passions and especially, a curbing of religious "enthusiasm." Those who gained this mastery of themselves were free not in the same manner as Bunyan's pilgrim, for whom freedom depended on the liberating movement of the Holy Spirit, but in being able to participate in public service and to differentiate truth from "superstition."[84]

Yet from another vantage, Jefferson and Franklin shared with evangelicals an expectation that reading drew on a wholly different faculty or aspect of the self. Using older language, evangelicals termed this faculty the "heart" or the "affections," whereas Franklin and Jefferson referred to it as "sentiment" or "feeling." Either way, the term pointed to a modality of reading the mark of which was an inward, emotional response to certain patterns of language and/or narrative themes. This modality arose within "sentimentalism," a new literary movement in the eighteenth century that was manifested in the fiction and poetry of (among others) Oliver Goldsmith, Edward Young, James Hervey, and James Thomson. In *Miscellaneous Poems,* Samuel Davies evoked Thomson as one of his models, and Benjamin Franklin had Thomson's *Seasons* in mind when he wrote his London bookseller in 1745 asking for a "dozen copies" of anything Thomson had recently written, adding that the "charming poet has brought more tears of pleasure into my eyes than all I ever read before." Tears were an almost universal response among the readers of sentimental fiction and poetry, though their meaning varied; for the more religious, they were less a sign of "pleasure" than of the seriousness and sublimity of certain themes. Hervey's widely marketed *Meditations among the Tombs* was, like Richardson's *Pamela,* a book that greatly pleased the readers in Jonathan Edwards's household, Edwards himself observing that he found in it a satisfying convergence of the "evangelical and [the] polite."[85] Notwithstanding the differing uses of sentimentalism, it was meaningful to many eighteenth-century readers because it seemed to offer a tempered, more "natural" form of religion – or to say this differently, to function as a hybrid category where the religious and the secular were melded into one.[86]

Within the context of sentimentalism, some forms of fiction became sanctioned as a means of moral formation. Advising his cousin Robert Skipwith in 1771 on what to read in a letter enclosing a list of some 148 recommended titles – the list was deliberately limited to books considered "improving and amusing" for a young man "who understands but little of the classicks and who has not leisure for any intricate or tedious study," as his cousin described himself – Thomas Jefferson was especially intent on explaining why plays and novels, two genres that conventionally were considered merely "fiction" and "entertainment," were rightly to be understood as richly instructive of the "moral rule[s] of life." "The entertainments of fiction are useful as well as pleasant," Jefferson wrote, going on to explain:

> . . . every thing is useful which contributes to fix in us the principles of practice or virtue . . . in the instance of which we speak, the exercise being of the moral feelings, produces a habit of thinking and acting virtuously. We never reflect whether

the story we read be truth or fiction. . . . We neither know nor care whether Lawrence Sterne really went to France . . . or whether the whole [Sterne's *Sentimental Journey*] be not a fiction . . . The spacious field of imagination is thus laid open to our use, and lessons may be formed to illustrate and carry home to the mind every moral rule of life. Thus a lively and lasting sense of filial duty is more effectually impressed on the mind of a son or daughter by reading King Lear, than by all the dry volumes of ethics and divinity that ever were written.[87]

For Jefferson as for many others, reading thus became a means of developing or exercising the moral sentiment. The nexus between reading and morality was, it seems, almost inescapable. Yet the moralists who encouraged the practice also fretted about its possibilities for leading people astray. In particular, they fretted about women, for in their thinking it was a fact of nature that the female sex was more vulnerable than the male – more given to emotional excess, more apt to allow illusion to cloud the workings of reason, and more impressionable, as though the female *tabula rasa* were more radically a blank slate than the unformed self of males.[88] Paradoxically, these assumptions lent themselves to a positive prescription, that all readers should be as "natural," as capable of sentiment and feeling, as women readers were. The ideal reader was curiously androgynous, someone who, like Franklin, was moved to tears or flights of rapture by the act of reading certain texts – or texts a certain way.

These assumptions complicated the act of reading as it was undertaken by actual women in eighteenth-century America. They could not escape – indeed they embraced – the principle that reading was a road to virtue. Nor could they avoid the moralizing of the clergy and other learned men about the vulnerability of their sex. Much of this moralizing focused on the form of novel known as the "romance," which by definition defied common sense. But the pleasure women experienced when reading fiction was the real problem. Could this pleasure serve the end of virtue, as Jefferson proposed to his cousin, or was it both sign and cause of women's weakness, abetting the excess of feeling that threatened fragile reason? And should women worry even more because booksellers were marketing magazines and books especially for their "entertainment"? Was the woman who read sentimental novels becoming the prototype of a new kind of consumer, someone passively manipulated by the sales pitch of newness and novelty?[89]

These questions did not trouble Hannah Heaton, who spent her free moments reading Bunyan, Watts, Alleine, and Foxe's *Book of Martyrs*. Nor were they troubling to many other women who moved beyond the Protestant vernacular tradition into the new world of the novel. This was the case with two high-status clergymen's daughters, Esther (Edwards) Burr and Sarah Prince, who corresponded with each other in the 1750s about what they were reading. For both women, virtue was the ultimate ideal, and both agreed that reading Richardson's *Pamela* or Hervey's *Meditations* benefitted their moral education. In Burr's letters to Prince, she rehearsed the plot of *Pamela* in ways that bespoke a sense of shared identity: "Pray my dear, how could Pamela forgive Mr. B all his Devilish conduct so as to consent to marry him[?]" So, too, she argued that sentiment or feeling was morally useful, a means of developing the right kind of self. To be stirred by feeling, to read in order to experience the pleasure of sentiment, was not to escape but to pursue the road to virtue that enlightened men so much admired and tried themselves to follow. Moreover, reading and writing prompted friendship and conversation, both of which were regarded by Sarah Prince, Esther Burr, and many of their contemporaries (men and women) as modes of moral improvement.[90]

Were the moralizers who feared the consequences of the romance wrong about women, or had they done their work too well? The historical evidence in our period allows no clear answer to this question, and the ambiguities present in mid-eighteenth century America would endure – indeed, intensify – far beyond our period as women became ever more active as readers and, increasingly, as writers of fiction.

CHAPTER TWELVE

Learned Culture in the Eighteenth Century

DAVID D. HALL

As in the seventeenth century, so in the eighteenth, learned men and, for the first time, women[1] in the colonies participated in distinctive forms of sociability, the most consequential of them a transatlantic system of exchange. At the outset of the new century the difficulties of doing so were considerable. New books arrived in a haphazard manner, and there was little intercolonial intellectual life. But by midcentury a thickening of connections in two directions, up and down the coast and across the Atlantic, was occurring. Meanwhile, the local possibilities for learning were becoming more abundant as, for the first time, medical schools came into being and as more colleges were founded; by 1770, five new institutions of higher learning had joined the three that existed at the beginning of the century: the College of New Jersey (Princeton), King's College (New York), the College of Philadelphia, the College of Rhode Island, Queen's (New Brunswick), and newly founded Dartmouth. In keeping with the greater possibilities for receiving a college education and with the overall prosperity of the colonies, the number of students matriculating at these institutions almost tripled between the 1740s and the 1770s.[2] Building on these accomplishments, transatlantic and intercolonial scientific collaboration was realized more fully than ever before in studies of the transit of Venus in 1769. Encouraged by advice from astronomers in England, teams of learned men in Philadelphia, Newport, Providence, and Boston essayed to perform a complicated series of measurements.[3]

In this effort, as in the patronage and practice of learned culture more generally, the clergy found themselves working side-by-side with civil administrators, lawyers, physicians, merchants, "gentlemen," and naturalists.[4] The world of the learned also encompassed a certain number of artisans whose participation was in keeping with a relatively open-ended social structure and an understanding of learnedness that extended to the practical arts of surveying, navigation, and arithmetic. In Benjamin Franklin's Philadelphia, the issues deemed important by college-educated clergy did not dominate social and intellectual life, as they did in New England for all of the seventeenth and much of the eighteenth centuries. Franklin and his allies thought of knowledge as something "useful" that was ascertained by experiment. It followed that knowledge was best advanced by allowing a certain liberty or openness of inquiry. Not only, therefore, did learnedness become more in evidence in mid-eighteenth-century America, it also involved a new ethos and, as we will see, new sites of cultural production.

Even in its stronger and more prosperous condition, however, learned culture in the colonies continued to depend on patronage from overseas.[5] In the early decades of the century, these forms of patronage helped offset the seeming loneliness of intellectual life. Writing to an English correspondent in 1706, William Byrd II lamented that the possibilities in America for making "natural inquirys" were not being realized, since "we have not some people of skil and curiosity amongst us." Thomas Brattle's assertion in 1703 that "I am here [in Boston] all alone by myself" was echoed by the Scots Quaker James Logan of Philadelphia, who endeavored to relieve his solitude by building up a remarkable library.[6]

In this context the significance of some 800 books destined for Yale College that arrived unexpectedly in Connecticut in September 1714, the result of solicitations made by Jeremiah Dummer, a native New Englander living in England and acting as agent for Massachusetts, was all the greater. Recalling, in his old age, the circumstances of learnedness in Connecticut in the early part of the century when "there was no such thing as any books of learning to be had in those times under a 100 or 150 years old such as the first settlers . . . brought with them," Samuel Johnson, who had been a youthful tutor at the college when the books turned up, emphasized the impact of the Dummer books and, as well, of a single book he came upon by chance: "accidentally lighting on Lord Bacon's . . . *Advancement of Learning* (perhaps the only copy in the country and nobody knew its value) he immediately bought it and greedily fell to studying it." After Johnson converted to Anglicanism, was reordained in England, and returned to Connecticut, he found another patron in the person of Governor William Burnet of New York, who (as Franklin was discovering about the same time) "had a large library, and delighted very much in communicating both his knowledge and his books." But the most exciting moment of patronage came in 1729 when Johnson learned that the English philosopher and Anglican George Berkeley had arrived in Newport, where he would stay for nearly two years. Hastening to Newport to meet Berkeley in person, Johnson was "admitted to converse freely on the subject of [Berkeley's] philosophical works, and presented with the rest which he had not seen, and to an epistolary correspondence upon them and any other parts of learning." As Berkeley was leaving, he performed yet another kindness by giving Johnson "many very valuable books." Berkeley also donated books and funds to Yale College.[7]

The role that Dummer and Berkeley played in these years was replicated many times over in the course of the century by other learned men in England, Ireland, and Scotland. Of the many who did so, in a sequence that extends back into the seventeenth century,[8] two stand out as having an unusual significance for intellectual life in the colonies: Peter Collinson (1694–1768) and Thomas Hollis of Lincoln's Inn (1720–1774). Collinson, a member of the Royal Society and wealthy Quaker merchant engaged in transatlantic trade, carried on an extensive correspondence with aspiring men of science in America, providing them with books and periodicals and transmitting their reports to the society for publication in its *Philosophical Transactions.* After he began a correspondence in 1741 with Cadwallader Colden, a native Scotsman educated in medicine who emigrated to the colonies in 1710 and became surveyor-general of New York, Collinson found a London publisher for an expanded version of Colden's *History of the Five Indian Nations,* encouraged him in his botanical interests, and forwarded copies of Colden's speculative treatise on gravity, initially published in New York in 1745, to other learned men throughout Europe. It was to Collinson that Franklin dispatched a series of letters reporting his experiments with electricity, letters published in the *Philosophical Transactions* and, at Collinson's initiative, turned into a book that was rapidly translated into French and German. It was also Collinson who in 1736 sent James Logan the earliest version of Linnaeus's *Systema naturae,* an event that led to an exchange of letters between Logan and Linnaeus; to the publication, at Linnaeus's urging and via yet another intermediary, a Dutch botanist, of Logan's botanical experiments, issued in Latin as *Experimenta et Meletemata de Plantarum Generatione* (Leyden, 1739), and to the international recognition and financial support mobilized for the young Pennsylvania naturalist John Bartram that enabled him to pursue a career as naturalist-collector within the framework of the Linnaean scheme of classification.[9] One of Bartram's English correspondents was the naturalist Mark Catesby, whose fieldwork in the Carolinas in the 1720s was supported by another group of patrons.

Thomas Hollis was the third person of this name to become a benefactor of the colonists. His great uncle Thomas Hollis (1659–1731), a successful merchant and Baptist who came to know Increase Mather at the end of the seventeenth century when Mather was in London lobbying in behalf of Massachusetts, began to donate books to Harvard College in 1719, distributed dozens of copies of the library catalogue of 1723 to potential donors, and provided funds to endow professorial chairs in divinity (1721) and mathematics (1727). Hollis seems to have delighted in thinking that a "free and

Catholic air" prevailed in the New-World Cambridge, which, he was assured, welcomed "Protestants of every Denomination" whereas Old-World Oxford and Cambridge still excluded Nonconformists. Tolerant of theological differences, he urged the same policy on the recipients of his gifts, suggesting to a minister in Boston in 1725 that "if there happen to be some books not quite Orthodox [in those he was sending], in search after truth with an honest design dont be afraid of them. A publick library ought to be furnished . . . with Con as well as Pro – that students may read, try, judg – see for themselvs and beleive upon Argument and just reasonings of the Scripture. Thus saith Aristotle, thus saith Calvin, will not now pass for proof in our London disputations."[10]

Religious toleration was also strongly favored by Thomas Hollis of Lincoln's Inn, but his particular passion was to abet a "Spirit of Liberty" embodied in the "republican" or "Radical Whig" tradition. To this end Hollis employed his considerable wealth subsidizing reprints and distribution of selected titles, "to disperse as widely as possible, over the world, books on liberty by the great English writers and by classical and European authors as well." Along the way, he corresponded with certain moderate or "catholic" clergy in Boston who, like Hollis himself, were abandoning the doctrines of the Westminster Confession and who shared his hostility to the scheme for establishing a bishopric of the Church of England in the colonies. When he learned in 1764 that fire had destroyed the Harvard College Library, Hollis, who had already donated books, redoubled his efforts, contributing over the next several years "between two and three thousand volumes, most of them carefully selected and specially bound" and soliciting other contributions. Disaffected by the actions of the British government that provoked the Revolutionary crisis, Hollis did much to encourage colonial political writers and publicists of events such as the Boston Massacre to stand fast in their defense of "liberty."[11]

For another group of Americans, the important connections were with Nonconformist and evangelical circles in England and Scotland. In the late seventeenth century, a handful of the New England clergy were corresponding with Nonconformists such as Richard Baxter.[12] In the early decades of the new century a younger group of ministers – notably Benjamin Colman, who went to England after graduating from Harvard in 1692 before returning to become the first minister of Boston's Fourth (Brattle Street) Church – began to correspond with the likes of Isaac Watts. But the crucial moment in the history of this network occurred during the 1740s when evangelicals on both sides of the Atlantic eagerly shared reports of the spiritual awakenings, or revivals, that broke out in Scotland, England, and the colonies.[13]

The earliest of these reports, written by Jonathan Edwards, a young minister in Northampton, Massachusetts, in the form of a letter to Colman, described a revival that occurred in his congregation in 1734–1735. Colman shared some of Edwards's narrative with an English Nonconformist minister, who asked if Edwards would prepare a fuller account, which he did. With Colman acting yet again as intermediary, this longer letter was edited by Isaac Watts, and printed in London under the title by which it has been known ever since: *A Faithful Narrative of the Surprizing Work of God in the Conversion of Many Hundred Souls in Northampton* (1737). Within a year it had been reprinted in Edinburgh and, in translation, in Germany and the Netherlands; extracts were published in the *Glasgow-Weekly-History,* one of several periodicals that sprang up in the early 1740s for the purpose of spreading such reports, the American equivalent being the Boston-based *Christian History* (1743–1744), in which Edwards published a narrative of a subsequent revival in his congregation.[14]

Edwards was soon receiving letters from orthodox Scottish clergymen with whom he discussed theological issues of the day, among them the validity of the revivals and the threat of anti-Calvinist "Arminianism." Edwards came to depend on his correspondents for information about (to cite a typical request, made in 1748) "the best books that have lately been written in defence of Calvinism." In response, the Church of Scotland minister John Erskine, among others, forwarded him books that he was unable to obtain in New England. Meanwhile, Edwards's sermons, essays, and treatises were routinely being published or reprinted in Britain. Immediately after Edwards's death, Erskine broached the possibility of a Scottish edition of yet-unpublished work, a possibility partially realized in 1774 when he oversaw the first printing of a manuscript he had been sent, *A History of the Work of Redemption,* a collection of sermons Edwards had preached in 1739.[15] Similar networks were important to other writers and religious communities – notably, the Anglicans who were sustained by voluntary societies like the SPG and the Presbyterian clergy who emigrated from Scotland and Ireland or who graduated from the College of New Jersey. Samuel Davies participated in this network as a fundraiser in Britain in 1753–1755 for the College of New Jersey, of which he served briefly as president before dying in 1761 at the age of thirty-six.[16] During Davies's lifetime, London and Scottish booksellers issued more of his sermons, or did so sooner, than American booksellers; after his death, an English admirer oversaw the publication in London of a five-volume edition of sermons (1766–1771), making Davies probably the first colonial writer to be honored in this fashion.

Edwards, Franklin, Davies, and Bartram – these examples also remind us that the traffic in intellectual goods was two-way, for there was much about America and Americans that interested European men of learning. So, too, in telling this story of patronage, exchanges, and the making of American writers, we must not overlook the importance of learned emigrants, some here temporarily as royal governors or as naturalist-collectors, and of colonists who returned after having earned degrees abroad.[17] The migration of university-trained physicians from Scotland was crucial to the development of medicine and medical societies in the colonies, and the presence of colonists with medical degrees from Edinburgh enabled John Morgan, himself an Edinburgh graduate, to found a medical school in Philadelphia in 1766.[18] Lawyers trained at the Inns of Court also became a significant presence, especially in the southern colonies and states. Some of these men had listened to William Blackstone's lectures at Oxford and, when Robert Bell of Philadelphia issued an eight-page prospectus soliciting subscriptions for the first American edition of the *Commentaries* (1771–1772), the response was an outpouring of 1,600 orders, a level of demand in keeping with the interest many of the colonists showed in owning books pertaining to the law.[19]

By these various routes the colonists were made increasingly aware of a new understanding of learnedness and knowledge that emerged in Europe in the late seventeenth century. John Locke, Pierre Bayle, and other architects of this new framework proposed that all men of learning, be they Catholic or Protestant, Jew or Christian, believer or skeptic, belonged alike to a "republic of letters." This republic embodied a rule of service or exchange: learned men willingly assisted one another. Occurring across confessional, political, and national boundaries, these exchanges were meant to be regulated by an ethic of "civility." Another leading principle was that traditional methods of ascertaining truth, or of assembling the parts of knowledge into a whole, were inadequate or misguided. Deeming these older methods "scholastic" and abstract, the reformers argued that the one sure method of advancing human knowledge, of adding to the sum of learnedness, was experience or experimentation. Such knowledge was "useful" – that is, of service to the public in forming virtuous citizens and in leading to "improvement." One other circumstance was crucial: In order for the pursuit of truth to flourish, the modes of censorship and control that church and state traditionally exercised had to give way to a situation of free inquiry. This argument expanded into an idealization of printing as an instrument of liberty; only when it was emancipated from "arbitrary" authority, only when printers and writers were allowed "freely" to "examine" all forms of knowledge, would truth come to prevail. By midcentury, when the French *philosophes* came to the fore, the republic of letters – we may note, a republic depending on the instrumentalities both of printing and of correspondence – took on a larger significance as a "public sphere" where, in contrast to the underground or covert forms of exchange and production necessitated by the absolutism of the French monarchy, the work of critical reason could proceed in the open.[20]

The colonists absorbed these assumptions about the "republic of letters" from an eclectic array of sources – Francis Bacon, John Locke and publications of the Royal Society, English Nonconformity and the dissenting academies to which it gave rise, certain Scottish reformers, political radicals such as Thomas Hollis. Another vehicle for these ideas was a cluster of periodicals that served as the instruments of enlightened politics and learning and that transformed the imaginary community of a "republic of letters" into something visible and concrete.[21] The earliest was the *Journal des Sçavans* (1665), followed by (among others), the Leipzig-based *Acta Eruditorum* (1682), Pierre Bayle's *Nouvelles de la République des Lettres* (1684; published in the Netherlands in order to escape the system of censorship in France), the English *History of the Works of the Learned* (1699), and *Republick of Letters* (1728). These periodicals alerted their readers to new books, commonly by providing extended extracts or summary reviews; accordingly, as Norman Fiering has observed, they may be regarded as "an important ramification of the entire systemization of bibliographical culture" in the age of printing. Harvard College ordered the *Acta Eruditorum* in 1698 using funds acquired from the sale of duplicates, Bishop Berkeley's gift in 1733 to Yale of over a thousand volumes included a thirty years' run, and two men with the means to buy all the books they wished, James Logan and William Byrd II, owned, respectively, forty-six and forty-three volumes of the same periodical.[22]

These and similar compendia – for example, *The Young Students Library* (1692), a 480-page folio recapitulating the contents of four of these periodicals, Ephraim Chambers's *Cyclopaedia; or Universal Dictionary* (1728), and Bayle's *Dictionnaire historique et critique* (1695–1697; an English translation was published in the 1730s) – were immensely helpful to provincials unable to afford very many learned books, yet anxious to remain in touch with currents of thought.[23] Thus it was that Samuel Johnson relished the *Republick of Letters,* in which he also published an essay on the "Study of Philosophy," and that Jonathan Edwards kept a running "Catalogue" of books he had heard of and wanted to read, based in part on his browsings in the eighteen volumes of the *Republick of Letters* owned by a local ministers' association.[24] Though less specifically devoted to learnedness, the *Gentleman's Magazine* (1731–1907) and others of its kind also attracted a wide readership in the colonies and sometimes published material that originated in America. Beginning in 1741, printers in the colonies began to publish their own magazines, the contents of which depended heavily on these European compilations.[25]

As reiterated in the colonies, the characteristic themes of the republic of letters were appropriated by more liberally minded clergy to justify intellectual freedom *vis-à-vis* theological orthodoxy and by politicians who warned (rhetorically) that their opponents were tyrants in the making.[26] These same themes were also voiced by printer–educators such as Franklin, by most of the men involved with the new colleges that came into being after midcentury, and by the founders of the American Philosophical Society who, in an Act of Incorporation in 1780, spoke of "Societies of liberal and ingenious men uniting their labours, without regard to nation, sect or party, in one grand pursuit." In the agitation that led up to the Revolution some of these themes acquired a larger significance, merging with the "republicanism" on which the colonists drew in defending the sovereignty of the colonies against the authority of the King and Parliament. In a series of essays John Adams published in 1765 in the *Boston Gazette,* Adams, having averred that the (white male) colonists enjoyed a near-universal literacy – "A native of America who cannot read and write is as rare . . . as a Comet or an Earthquake" – proposed that the "art of printing" should "be easy and cheap and safe," conditions that would enable "any person to communicate his thoughts to the public." Like a latter-day John Foxe, Adams extolled the "freedom of thinking, speaking and writing" in America, which he contrasted with the "Yoke of Bondage" that prevailed in countries "of Romish superstition, [where] the Laity must not learn to read." These themes resonated anew in Thomas Jefferson's vision of an educated citizenry as the bulwark of republican society.[27]

Within the more limited sphere of learnedness, the practical importance of these themes was in their bearing on the fellowship of the learned, the curriculum of the colonial college, the contents of libraries, and book collecting. In several coastal cities civil administrators, royal governors, clergy, lawyers, doctors, artisans, and merchant–gentlemen collaborated in founding learned societies that complemented the clubs and salons where a new literary culture was also being fashioned.[28] In 1728 Colden suggested to the Scots physician William Douglass, who had settled in Boston, that learned men should enter into some kind of organization, with Boston as its headquarters; nothing came of the idea. A local "Society for the promotion of Knowledge and Virtue by a Free Conversation" was organized in Newport in 1730. Thanks to the generosity of the merchant Abraham Redwood, the society established its own library in 1747. The first independent subscription library able intentionally to deploy its funds to provide newer works of learning, most of them in the sciences, was the Library Company of Philadelphia; because Franklin and its other founders were, strictly speaking, not learned men themselves, they asked James Logan to advise them on what books to buy.[29] In 1743, Franklin, not yet a scientist himself but strongly moved by the vision of "useful knowledge," proposed in a broadside that the men in and around Philadelphia who were already collaborators in the study of natural history proceed to organize a learned society. This they did, naming the new body the American Philosophical Society.

Franklin's sense of collaborative possibilities also led him to imagine a new monthly or quarterly periodical, which he tentatively entitled *American Philosophical Miscellany*.[30] His hopes in this regard were not fulfilled, while the society quickly petered out. But in the 1760s two new learned societies were organized almost simultaneously in the city; when they merged in 1769 the organization, which aspired to an intercolonial membership, carried the name of the American Philosophical Society for Promoting Useful Knowledge. Immediately it undertook to issue *Transactions*, of which the first quarto volume, largely devoted to reports on the transit of Venus and illustrated with copperplate engravings, appeared in 1771. Proud of this accomplishment, the society dispatched copies to other learned organizations throughout Europe, as it did again when a second volume was published in 1786. As the Revolution was drawing to a close, a group of Bostonians founded in 1780 another intercolonial learned society, the American Academy of Arts and Sciences.[31]

Some of the men active in organizing the Philosophical Society were also involved in planning the College of Philadelphia. The Scottish Anglican William Smith, the first president, had caught Franklin's eye after having written *A General Idea of the College of Mirania* (1753). Franklin had already devised a plan for a school in which English was the prevailing language, the classical languages were not required, and instruction was to focus on history.[32] Smith had encountered similar reforms at Aberdeen, where the medieval arts program had been jettisoned and the curriculum reorganized around mathematics, history, moral philosophy, and the sciences. The scheme he put in place at the new college turned out to be a mixture of the old and the new. Yet here and elsewhere in the colonies – at the College of New Jersey after the Scots minister John Witherspoon took charge in 1765, and even at Yale during the presidency of Thomas Clap, an ostensible conservative – the curriculum embodied a greater emphasis on mathematics and other sciences, belles lettres, and history; in the languages, Hebrew faded away as a requirement, a modern language (French) was introduced, and English displaced Latin as the primary language of instruction.[33] The most dramatic transformation occurred at William and Mary, where, as a consequence of legislation drafted by Thomas Jefferson in 1779, the chairs devoted to theology and rhetoric were abolished and new positions created in the fields of "the laws of nature and of nations," "history, civil and ecclesiastical," and the "modern languages."[34]

The transformation in college libraries was less dramatic, perhaps because the colleges depended so much on the generosity of donors. Dummer, Berkeley, and Isaac Watts for early Yale,[35] the Hollises for Harvard, a series of royal governors for the College of William and Mary and of Anglican clergymen for King's – the generosity of these and other patrons was the story up and down the coast. Never assembled according to any master plan and weighted toward older books in theology and Biblical commentary,[36] these collections gradually came under the influence of the "catholic" spirit of the republic of letters and the newer understanding of "useful" knowledge. These ways of thinking are evident not only in the tilting of collections policy toward acquisitions in mathematics, history, the practical arts and the physical sciences, but also in President Samuel Davies's preface to the College of New Jersey's printed library catalogue of 1760, issued, like others in the eighteenth century, as a means of soliciting further donations. President Davies argued that, since knowledge was "boundless and variegated," an "extensive" library would "enable [students] to investigate Truth thro' her intricate Recesses; and to guard against the Stratagems and Assaults of Error." He revealed some of the priorities of the republic of letters when he admitted that, as constituted in 1760, the library contained "but few modern Authors, who have unquestionably some Advantage above the immortal Ancients," and that the "Defect" in the collections was "most sensibly felt in the Study of Mathematics, and the Newtonian Philosophy." The Congregational clergyman Ezra Stiles, who became president of Yale in 1777, had an even more expansive vision of the ideal library in a country that had recently declared its independence; writing to one of his peers in 1780, he proposed that American colleges should "collect & embrace the Literature of the Universe."[37]

When warfare ended in 1781 and the colleges began to rebuild or restore collections that had been dispersed or damaged, Americans turned anew to the London trade. The Harvard printed catalogue of 1790 suggests the changing nature of acquisitions. Its predecessor of 1723 was essentially a catalogue of rare books, half of them in foreign languages (chiefly Latin), but by 1790 the subject matter had widened to include agriculture, architecture, and the experimental sciences, and, although "Theologia" comprised half of the collection, newer books in history, politics, medicine, and the law were significantly represented. By this year, moreover, the two upper classes of undergraduates were entitled to borrow books, a privilege they acquired in the 1760s. Yale was admitting all students to the library by the 1750s, though freshmen and sophomores were allowed to borrow only a short list of books specifically designated for this purpose. It may well be that little use was made of the more academic or learned portions of a library such as Harvard's; the charging records suggest as much, as do a separate, shorter catalogue published in 1773 and a Harvard tutor's personal checklist of books he owned and lent to people like John Adams.[38]

The newer tastes in reading matter were embodied more fully in the collections assembled in the second half of the century by subscription and social libraries. Starting afresh, and with funds of their own to expend on purchases, the organizers of these libraries shared in common a preference for "modern Authors," as the principals of the New York Society Library wrote their London supplier in 1754. A decade later, the library was described as "a large well chosen collection of the most useful modern books," whereas a clergyman's collection that had passed into public ownership was characterized as containing "very valuable, antient, curious, and rare books." The nearly 300 books purchased by the Library Company of Philadelphia and listed in its earliest printed catalogue (1741) were, with but three exceptions, in English; by subject matter, a third pertained to history, with literature and science accounting for an additional half. Theology was represented by only about twenty-five books; except for the works of Alexander Pope, belles lettres were almost absent. The intention of the organizers of this and other society libraries was that they should "be for the use of the publick," which in practice meant that nonmembers were, in some instances, admitted as readers.[39]

Change was also manifested in the categories that came into use for classifying books. The European intellectuals who, like Francis Bacon, sketched such a system of categories, thought of their scheme as demonstrating that knowledge cohered into a whole. The vision of a "Philosophical Catalogue of books," a means of "systematic arrangement" which would serve to demonstrate the "extensive mutual relations" among the branches of knowledge, persisted throughout the eighteenth century. In the long history of attempts at making such a catalogue, Bacon's own tripartite scheme of Memory, Imagination, and Reason was a new departure, for it broke with the medieval division of the arts into the trivium and quadrivium and gave as much or greater emphasis to "human" and "natural" sources of knowledge as to divine revelation.[40] His, however, was not the scheme used in arranging books in libraries such as Harvard's, where the shelf-order began with Bibles and their commentaries. When Thomas Clap reorganized the books at Yale in 1743, he arranged them into twenty-five subject categories correlated with the sequence of study Samuel Johnson had outlined in *An Introduction to the Study of Philosophy* (1743), a sequence designed to give students "a General Idea or Scheme of all the Arts and Sciences and the several things which are to be known and learnt." In evoking the unity of all knowledge, the Yale catalogue depended on the concept of knowledge as a unifying "circle" or "encyclopedia" that Johnson affirmed in his *Introduction*.[41] That Clap had to list some books under as many as five separate headings underscores the complex relationship between the contents of books and *all* schemes of subject cataloguing. Bacon's scheme returned to the fore in the classifications that the Library Company used in a catalogue of 1789 and that Thomas Jefferson adopted for his books. Famously, Jefferson eschewed any entry for metaphysics and, in the classification scheme for the collection he sold in 1815, which prevailed for the rest of the century as the system of the Library of

Congress, placed religion under jurisprudence, which itself was a subcategory of philosophy.[42]

Learned men had long used other techniques for organizing knowledge – commonplacing for one, schemes of logic for another. In the *Manuductio ad Ministerium* (1726) Cotton Mather sketched a method of commonplacing and reaffirmed the importance of syllogistic reasoning as a means of achieving certainty. For the first few decades of the century the curriculum at Harvard and Yale required students to read William Ames's *Marrow of Theology*, an early seventeenth-century textbook that employed syllogisms and the Ramean system of dichotomies.[43] But the trend in logic-teaching under way in England by the late seventeenth century was to assert that no "scholastic" method yielded absolute certainty and to affirm the importance of "reason" or common sense. Translated into academic practice, this trend eventually undermined the exercise, a requirement for all master's students at Harvard and early Yale, of preparing a comprehensive synopsis in the form of axioms. For Johnson, the transition occurred with a bang in 1715 when, after having prepared, in Latin, the mandatory "System of Arts" or "Encyclopedia," he became "wholly changed to the New Learning." Some years later he denounced the project of drawing up "a little system of all parts of learning" as "nothing else but a curious cobweb of distributions and definitions."[44] Nonetheless, disputations remained a common practice at most colleges, broadsides listing topics of debate at commencement continued to appear, and the practice of commonplacing enjoyed a longer life – Jefferson, for one, stored extracts from his reading in commonplace books – though there was little consistency in how these notebooks were used.[45]

Even as learned books were becoming more readily available in libraries and as textbooks in logic, Hebrew, Latin, astronomy, mathematics, and philosophy were, for the first time, being printed in the colonies, men of learning and their merchant and professional allies continued to build large collections of their own. Compared to seventeenth-century private libraries, a smaller share of these books were in foreign languages or the format of folio and a larger share unbound pamphlets published in the colonies.[46] Bookplates came into wider use (Fig. 12.1), and, in a handful of instances, collectors arranged for distinctive bindings.[47] Pamphlets, which individually had little value and often were not listed in catalogues of academic or learned libraries, were sometimes bound together; only in our century have these volumes commonly been unbound and redistributed.[48] Other than by descent within families, few means were available for preserving any of these collections. James Logan, who owned, in the strictest sense of the term, the most "learned" of all early eighteenth-century collections (the great majority were in Latin; see Fig. 12.2), specified that his books would become a permanent

(*text continues on page* 426)

Figure 12.1. Bookplate of John Chandler, Jr., engraved by Nathaniel Hurd (1729–1777). Hurd, like Paul Revere, was trained as a silversmith, but he also engraved prints, trade cards, and especially bookplates; Chandler, a Worcester Tory, fled to London in 1776, where he died in 1800. American Antiquarian Society.

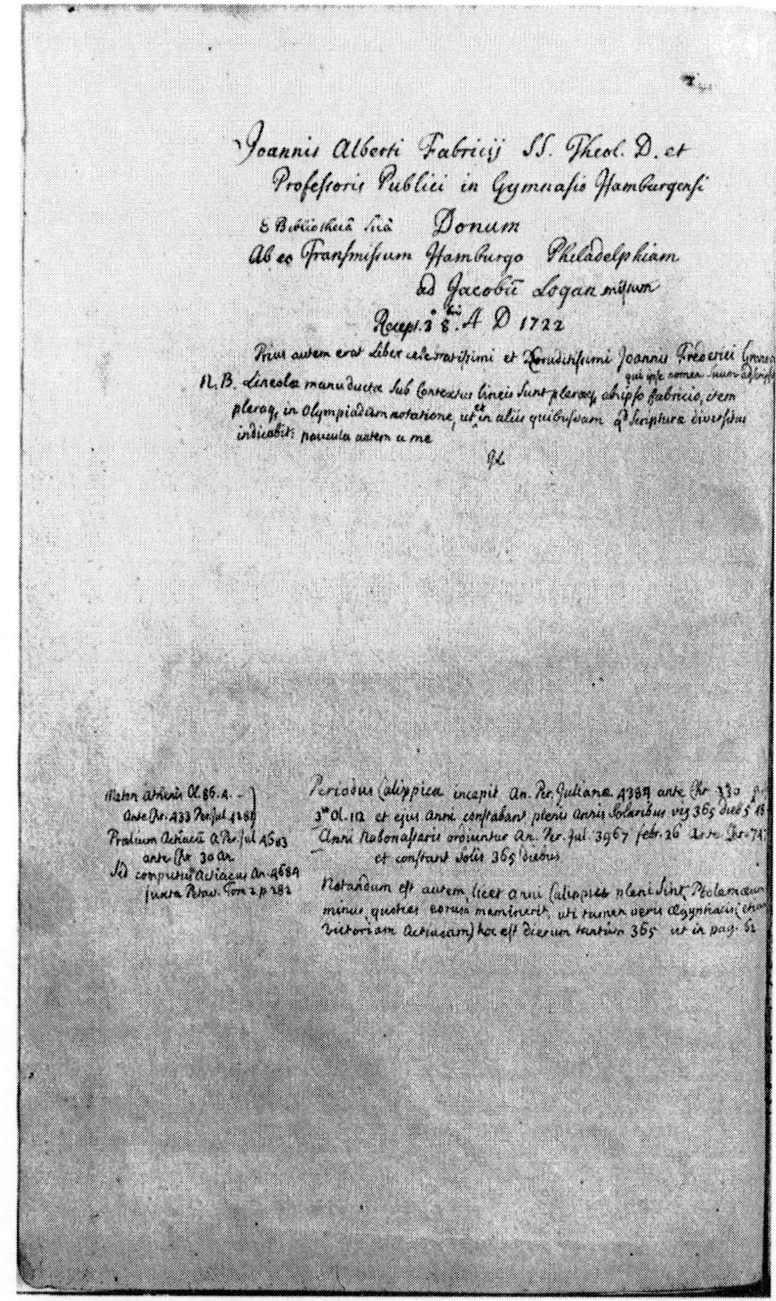

Joannis Alberti Fabricij SS. Theol. D. et
Professoris Publici in Gymnasio Hamburgensi
e Bibliotheca sua Donum
Ab eo Transmissum Hamburgo Philadelphiam
ad Jacobū Logan missum
Recept. 3° 8bris A D 1722

Figure 12.2. Ptolemy, *Almagest* (Basileæ: Apud Ioannem VValderum, 1538); the *editio princeps*, presented by the distinguished bibliographer Johann Albert Fabricius to James Logan of Philadelphia; formerly belonging to the Dutch classical scholar Jacobus Fredericus Gronovius, with his signature on the title page. Courtesy of The Library Company of Philadelphia.

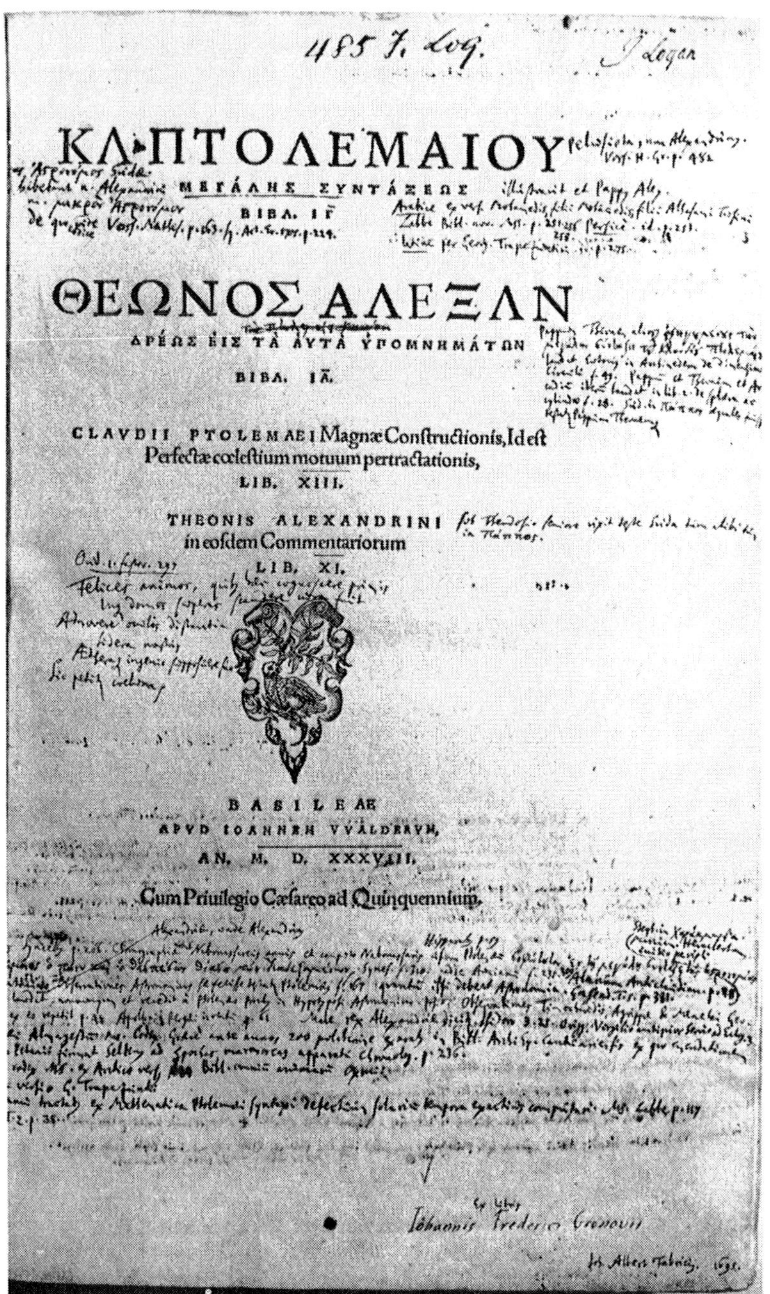

485 J. Log.

J Logan

ΚΛ. ΠΤΟΛΕΜΑΙΟΥ

ΜΕΓΑΛΗΣ ΣΥΝΤΑΞΕΩΣ

ΒΙΒΛ. ΙΓ

ΘΕΩΝΟΣ ΑΛΕΞΑΝ

ΔΡΕΩΣ ΕΙΣ ΤΑ ΑΥΤΑ ΥΠΟΜΝΗΜΑΤΩΝ

ΒΙΒΛ. ΙΑ.

CLAVDII PTOLEMAEI Magnæ Constructionis, Id est
Perfectæ cœlestium motuum pertractationis,
LIB. XIII.

THEONIS ALEXANDRINI
in eosdem Commentariorum
LIB. XI.

BASILEAE
APVD IOANNEM VVALDERVM,
AN. M. D. XXXVIII.

Cum Priuilegio Cæsareo ad Quinquennium.

Ex libris
Iohannis Frederici Gronovii

Figure 12.2. *Continued*

institution, the Loganian Library, housed in a building for which his will provided the funds. More commonly, collections were dispersed by sale at auction. This was the fate of another great private library in eighteenth-century America, the one William Byrd II (1676–1744) assembled at Westover, his plantation in Virginia. Byrd's 3,500 books, some of them legacies from his father, reflected the tastes of a Virginian who spent much of his early life in England, where he learned Latin, Greek, and several modern languages and moved in the circles of the Royal Society, the theatre, and the coffeehouse. Returning to Virginia in 1705, Byrd decided to house his books in a separate building designed for that purpose. In subject matter the collection was strong in plays (more, it seems, than any other library in colonial America), natural history, travel, the law, medicine, the classics,[49] architecture,[50] and a category Byrd named "Entertainment, Poetry, Translations &c." In 1778, one year after the death of William Byrd III, who had willed that it be sold to cover his "Just Debts," the entire library passed into the hands of an ironmaker, who eventually turned the books over to Robert Bell in Philadelphia for sale by auction.[51]

Yet the story is not entirely one of losses, great as these were. Certain far-seeing men, moved by a feeling for the history of their colony or province, began to collect books and documents and to write about the past. Aside from Cotton Mather, the earliest and in many respects the most remarkable of these early collectors was Thomas Prince, a minister in Boston who "may well be called the Father of American bibliography." Entering Harvard College in 1703, Prince began as a youth – moved, it seems, by the example of the great English antiquarian Robert Cotton – to seek out New England books, aspiring, as he put it, to amass "every Book, Pamphlet, and Paper, both in Print and Manuscript" that might "have any Tendency to enlighten our History." Into his hands came a host of treasures from the seventeenth century, a collection he named the "New-England Library," part of which was dispersed or destroyed during the wartime British occupation of Boston, part of which was dispersed at country auctions in the nineteenth century.[52] His successors included Ezra Stiles and Thomas Hutchinson, who, "inclined" by "the repeated destruction of ancient records and papers, by fire in the town of Boston," undertook to write a three-volume *History of the Colony and Province of Massachusetts-Bay* (1764–1774) based on manuscripts passed to him by inheritance or preserved by Prince and the Mathers.[53] Historians and antiquarians in Virginia were collecting historical documents by midcentury, but it was Jefferson who outdid his contemporaries in amassing manuscript and printed sources, on which he drew in asserting the rights of the colonists. Eager to collect copies, printed or handwritten, of sessions laws and statutes, Jefferson retrieved one set from a tavernkeeper, who was using the sheets as waste paper.[54]

Two Baptists, Morgan Edwards and Isaac Backus, deserve recognition for their attentiveness to manuscript sources.[55] The Revolutionary crisis inspired Ebenezer Hazard to begin collecting the "state papers" that he finally published in the 1790s. Matters strictly bibliographical went unattended, though Cotton Mather's son Samuel prepared a list of his father's publications on which modern bibliographers have relied. Early in the century, an Anglican bishop, White Kennett, compiled *Bibliothecæ Americanæ Primordia* (1713), the earliest English-language bibliography of books relating to America. Inevitably, there were lapses in knowledge. Thomas Bacon, who prepared a new edition of the laws of Maryland, published in 1766, did not know of Bladen's edition of 1700 and regarded his own disbound copy of the 1708 laws as the only one in the colony.[56]

This attention to local culture had little significance for the practice of authorship within the social world of the learned. Participating, as they did, in a transcolonial and transnational system of exchange, the central sites for which were London and Edinburgh, any of the colonists who aspired to publish within the republic of letters had, by definition, to depend on British patrons and the British book trade. Thanks to the networks in natural history and natural philosophy, naturalists and "natural philosophers" found it relatively easy to publish abroad, as Logan, Colden, and Franklin were doing at midcentury. The network of Nonconformity was the avenue for Colman, Edwards, Charles Chauncy, and Davies; Anglicans depended on a third set of connections. Locally, the patronage of an organization or civil government continued to make the difference in whether sermons were printed or merely preached.[57] But by the middle of the eighteenth century, publishing by subscription, a method of seeking advance orders that became popular in England in the 1670s, was opening up new possibilities linked to the growing numbers of the learned and their allies. The earliest work of learning to be financed in this manner, Samuel Willard's lectures on the Westminster Catechism, published almost twenty years after his death by a coalition of Boston booksellers as *A Compleat Body of Divinity* (1726), attracted some 630 persons whose names were listed at the back of the volume. Thereafter, colonial printers and booksellers frequently issued proposals for titles to be published in this manner.[58]

Notwithstanding the larger audience for learned books, the risks to printers and booksellers were real, as Franklin discovered when he printed Samuel Johnson's *Noetica,* having received Johnson's advice that the book would sell 200 copies in New England. In 1754, not long after the book had appeared, Franklin expressed his disappointment to Johnson in a letter that says much about expectations on both sides of this transaction and much, as well, about the awareness among authors and printer–booksellers of the problematic fate of learned books in a provincial marketplace."I think you ought not to be, as you say you are," Franklin wrote a disappointed Johnson,

vexed at your self that you offered your Noetica to be printed; for the Demand for it in this part of the World has not yet been equal to the Merit of the work, yet you will see by the enclosed Newspaper, they are reprinting it in England, where good Judges being more plenty than with us, it will, I doubt not, acquire a Reputation, that may not only make it extensively useful there, but bring it more into Notice in its native America.

Averring that, "For my own part, I knew too well the Badness of our general Taste, to expect any great Profit in Printing it," Franklin admitted that he had assumed "it might sell better than I find it does, having struck off 500, and not dispos'd of more than 50 in these Parts." According to the terms of their agreement, Franklin had expected Johnson to meet any costs that were not covered by sales. Reminding him of this point and recalling Johnson's optimism for sales in New England, Franklin added that he would not insist on being reimbursed.[59]

The amiability of Franklin's letter should not deceive us into thinking that the ancient quarrel between writers and booksellers was absent in the colonies. As James Logan remarked tersely, booksellers were "great sharpers." Apart from feeling that booksellers were always out for gain, learned writers had to reckon with the consequences of surrendering control of their text to intermediaries who, as often as not, "carelessly" reworked it at will. Edwards's *Narrative of Surprizing Conversions,* his posthumous *History of the Work of Redemption,* Franklin's letters on electricity, the London edition of John Adams's *Dissertation on the Canon and Feudal Law* – these and other texts were altered, sometimes for political reasons, in the course of passing through the hands of editors and booksellers. Few had the opportunity either to read proofs or to issue a corrected edition, as Franklin was able to do in 1764 when he took fresh copies of his letters to England and oversaw the printing of the fourth London edition. One instance is illustrative: long after he had died, James Logan's name disappeared from overseas editions of his translation of Cicero's *De Senectute,* to be replaced by Franklin's![60]

These circumstances remind us that eighteenth-century writers remained dependent on certain forms of patronage. To be sure, the social sites of the republic of letters – the philosophical and professional societies, the new periodicals, some of the colleges – provided supportive ground for persons who concerned themselves with medicine, law, the natural sciences and, to a lesser extent, philosophy. In the main, learned writers did not have to worry about selling what they wrote. Yet patronage remained imperative if a book were to be published or access gained to expensive, learned books, and as writers in early America realized again and again, patronage carried with it certain prerogatives. The good news was that, in deciding how and where to publish, men of learning in the colonies did not have to worry about being censored. Clandestine publishing, as evidenced by false imprints, under-the-table booksellers' catalogues, and editions published outside the boundaries of a political jurisdiction, was a prominent feature of the Continental book trade, and especially of books in French, but not of the American. To be sure, pamphlet writers during the Revolutionary crisis, who published initially in newspapers, rarely signed their work, preferring anonymity or pen names in keeping with a well-established practice that arose as a means of shielding agitators and critics from the wrath of the faction in power.[61] Self-censorship does not seem to have played as large a role in the eighteenth century as it had in the seventeenth, though as a journeyman printer in London Franklin had second thoughts about publishing his argument for "necessity" and destroyed most of the edition. Others who, like Franklin, entertained rationalist or liberal interpretations of Christianity felt a sense of caution; some early critics in New England of the doctrine of original sin preferred anonymity, and for some thirty years the Boston minister Charles Chauncy shared a manuscript critique of the doctrine of limited atonement only with a handful of trustworthy intimates, who nicknamed it "the pudding." Chauncy seems to have been more concerned with the popular reaction to his heterodoxy than with how his peers would respond.[62]

But the major task may have been to regulate – in effect, to censor – the opinions and effusions of the laity. Moderates and evangelicals joined in denouncing the "enthusiasm" of the lay insurgencies unleashed by the Great Awakening, linking them with the "Antinomianism" of the 1630s. The impulse to control these insurgencies led Jonathan Edwards to eliminate many of the more fervent passages in David Brainerd's journal, a task he also undertook with his wife Sarah's narrative of spiritual experience.[63] Regulation was also much on the minds of the men with degrees in medicine and law. In private and sometimes in public, they liked to satirize the figure of the blacksmith-turned-doctor or other such amateurs in medicine, theology, and the law, even as they acted to extend their own authority. This process is clearly visible in the course of reading John Adams set himself in the 1760s and in how, thereafter, he introduced learned references – in one instance, to a book he alone had read, or so he estimated – into arguments he was making in court.[64]

The absence of overt censorship and the ideology of "civility" and "free inquiry" – circumstances that were severely compromised during the Revolution – were therefore relative and in some sense class-specific. Yet as practised by the learned, these conditions did not wholly exempt their sphere from conflict and resistance. Each shipment of books from overseas, each new learned emigrant, was a means of transposing to the American mainland the debates and disagreements that (to cite but one example) were pervasive within the Church of Scotland in the eighteenth century. Intra- and inter-denominational rivalries, some of them provoked by the anti-Calvinist liberalism that emerged within English Nonconformity and even in New England by midcentury, were exacerbated by the practices of itinerancy and pulpit exchange, especially as embodied in the charismatic figure of Whitefield, and by the Anglican missions, which were premised on the assumption that Nonconformist clergy were not properly ordained. Political factionalism, with its links to economic and social privilege, extended into the Revolutionary crisis and the debates between radicals and moderates over the proper form of "republican" government.[65] Conflict and resistance were also rooted in the assumption that those who commanded distinctive ways of learning and a distinctive body of knowledge were properly the authoritative interpreters of the "book of nature" and the book of God's revelation. Having come to regard nature as a system ordered by natural laws, learned men deployed their authority against the lore, now deemed "superstitious," of prodigies and portents.

But the most persistent tensions were rooted in the nexus of religion and culture. Did the new versions of learnedness undermine religious orthodoxy, as defined by the Westminster Confession? Were "civility" and "politeness" compatible with the "plain style" of vernacular, oppositional Protestantism? Did the modes of the republic of letters serve to distance the clergy even further from the people? Was the Bible still self-authenticating, or was it to be approached through the instrument of "reason" and understood as a historical document?

Some Congregational, Presbyterian, and Baptist clergy and their allies were alarmed by the style and substance of the republic of letters. In 1722 Cotton Mather complained to the Overseers of Harvard College that the students were reading "plays, novels, empty and vicious pieces of poetry" instead of "books of divinity, as have . . . the spirit of the Gospel in them," a complaint Whitefield renewed in the 1740s. Edwards and his colleagues in the Hampshire Association discovered this problem first-hand in 1735 when a young ministerial candidate fresh out of Harvard admitted to preaching that the light of nature was sufficient to learn the truth about God, an idea he gained from reading an English Deist.[66] No wonder, then, that in 1759 Thomas Clap refused a donation from a Baptist merchant in Newport who asked that all books, whether deemed orthodox or erroneous, "be available to students." Previously, Clap had purged the library of the sermons of Samuel Clarke, an Anglican minister who seemed too inclined toward rationalism. Another approach was to mount an intellectual offensive against unorthodox and liberalizing tendencies. In the school for ministers that Joseph Bellamy ran for many years in Bethlehem, Connecticut, he insisted that his students "read the most learned and acute opposers of the truth," the better to comprehend "the fallacy of the most specious reasonings in these writers."[67]

The larger issue concerned cultural style and cultural politics. Was it possible to reconcile the secular and cosmopolitan themes of the republic of letters with the modalities of piety and opposition that had been crucial to the Protestant vernacular tradition? Did learning always serve to distance ministers from the laity, or was it possible to sustain a common culture despite the schisms and insurgencies that erupted after 1740? Thomas Clap preferred a middle ground where new and old were reconciled, but he also rejected the argument, which he criticized in *The Religious Constitution of Colleges* (1754), that "the only Design of Colleges, was to teach the Arts and Sciences; and that Religion, is no part, of a College Education."[68] The Baptist Isaac Backus went further, arguing in the same year that a college education all too often introduced young men to the "corrupt principles" of "rank" Arminianism and that being "internally called by the Spirit of God" was better than learnedness in enabling a minister to interpret the Bible. Preachers first and writers second, evangelicals such as Backus, David Brainerd, and Samuel Davies continued to regard speech and writing as transformative practices modelled on the action of the Holy Spirit and the "humble" language of Scripture. "I was . . . enabled to open divine truths and explain them to the capacities of my people in a manner beyond myself," Brainerd noted of a sermon he had preached. Not surprisingly, these men were also attracted to the prophetic books of the Bible. In these matters of style and literary practice, therefore, most evangelicals tried to sustain a fusion of learnedness, orality, performance, and the Bible. This fusion, though not identical with popular religion, remained closely related to it. Even so, there was room for disagreement on how far evangelicals should go in opposing "worldly" culture or in allowing learnedness to come between them and the people. Thus Ezra Stiles urged Clap to accept the Baptist donation "in the name of 'that generous and equal Liberty for which Protestants and Dissenters have made so noble a Stand.'" Reiterating a fundamental rule of the republic of letters, Stiles argued that any blow against liberty meant that "Truth may be extinguished," for the one sure way of overcoming error – even error as extreme as Deism – was "to come forth into the open Field and dispute this Matter on even Footing."[69]

Yet the evangelicals who warned against the tendencies of the times knew whereof they spoke. Some of the "gentlemen" who stocked their libraries with the latest London magazines were, indeed, unsympathetic to the concept of religious orthodoxy. In the society libraries that sprang up along the coast, books and reading were linked to entertainment or pleasure; as James Logan remarked of his own practice, reading was not a devotional exercise but a "Diversion" that "serves me agreeably, to spend my vacant hours." Far less interested in the Bible and disinclined to reiterate its phraseology, an evangelical practice they found ludicrous, these men regarded Whitefield as a comic, vulgar figure. For themselves they preferred Anglicanism or some form of "natural" religion. Among the more advanced, the narrative and rhetorical traditions embodied in the Bible were ceasing to be credible, as Jefferson indicated in *Notes on the State of Virginia,* where he argued in favor of "natural causes" and the "laws of nature" over against the traditional story of the Flood.[70] That by 1730 more college graduates were moving into occupations other than the ministry, a trend that accelerated as the century wore on, suggests that evangelicals had reason to worry about the convergence of intellectual and social forces in the making and sustaining of learnedness.[71]

The persons of this new persuasion were no less censorial than the evangelicals and no less political in seeking cultural authority. Their concerns were two: to hold in check the pressure for religious orthodoxy and, in the arena of affairs of state, to avoid "popular" excitement lest "the people" get out of hand. The ethos of the republic of letters, with its themes of civility, reason, and free inquiry, was an excellent weapon in the struggle against orthodoxy, though in the long run an even better weapon was the argument that religious belief was something "private," which should not be allowed to impinge on the realm of the "public."[72] When it came to dealing with the unruliness of the *vox populi,* however, the line of defense was different, for the political elite in early America was never comfortable with the mobilizing and libertarian implications of using print to address the people.[73] The pamphlets of the Revolutionary period are revealing of this defence, which in part was stylistic. As literary documents they are "essentially decorous and reasonable"; premised on the assumption that calm deliberation is the proper mode of dealing with political questions, they rely on anonymity and a range of learned references (chiefly to classical and early modern history) to establish a tone or stance in keeping with this assumption. In these respects the pamphlets were far less accessible or public than the sermons preached by evangelicals to heterogeneous audiences, a difference that became startlingly evident when Thomas Paine's *Common Sense* (1776), which employed a different set of rhetorical strategies addressed to common folk, achieved an "uncommon frenzy," and far outsold every other pamphlet of the period.[74]

Behind the seeming unity of learned culture in eighteenth-century America lay, therefore, two different versions of learnedness and two different schemes of cultural politics: one of them the forms of civic and polite culture closely linked with social privilege and embodied in practices and institutions deemed "useful," "free," and cosmopolitan; the other, a form of culture centered on religious orthodoxy, embodied both in regulating and in reaching out to the people (whether literate or illiterate, black or white), and still retaining a sense of opposition to "the world." A third framework of meaning should be added to this schema: an expansive vision of learnedness, articulated especially during the Revolutionary period, as a means of advancing "liberty" and thereby of fulfilling the promise of a republican America. Were the ideal conditions of liberty and virtue to prevail, as many contemporaries thought they would in the newly independent country, it was possible to imagine that learned men in America would some day become leaders in the world of ideas. So reasoned a member of the Princeton faculty, who speculated in a letter of 1787 to Benjamin Rush that the time would come when American scholarship would rival and surpass that of Europe.[75]

The history of learned books and writing in eighteenth-century America is, in large measure, a history of these differing versions of learnedness and the conflicts that arose out of their intersection. But the history of learned culture is also one of negotiation in and around these conflicts as old boundaries were modified by the ethos of the republic of letters. No war broke out between religion and science; many who were orthodox continued to fraternize with others who thought differently. Ezra Stiles was perhaps the quintessential moderate who had friends in almost every camp. A portrait painted of him in 1771, when he was a minister in Newport, is an apt emblem not only of the man but of the middle ground on which so many others stood. Stiles specified the books he wanted in the picture: a "preaching Bible" in his right hand and, behind him, a shelf of folios indicating "my Taste for History," which for Stiles encompassed "the Roman Empire," the early centuries of Christianity, and the history of the Jews before and after the coming of Christ. On a second shelf were "Newton's Principia, Plato, Watts, Doddridge, Cudworths Intellectual System; & also the New Engld primaeval Divines Hooker, Chauncy, Mather, Cotton."[76] Thus were reconciled, from one man's vantage, the centuries leading up to his own and, within his times, natural philosophy and revealed religion. The love of reading, the pride in achieving intellectual harmony and in being a member of the republic of the letters – all these were captured in an image that may fittingly close this account of learned culture in eighteenth-century America.

CHAPTER THIRTEEN

Eighteenth-Century Literary Culture

DAVID S. SHIELDS

THE PHRASE "LITERARY CULTURE" came into use in England during the 1830s when critics began questioning the adequacy of the terms "genius" or "tradition" in explaining how communicative manners formed within societies and nations. Since then, the idea of literary culture has changed profoundly; now, at the end of the twentieth century, it has become divorced from considerations of manners. It speaks, instead, of the ethnic, class-bound, gendered qualities of written discourses. This chapter takes up questions of ethnicity, class, and gender, yet also revives Romantic criticism's interest in the formation of manners. Furthermore, it recovers the self-understandings of writers and readers before "literary culture" denominated the institutional dynamic of written communication. It recalls the finer social, economic, religious, political, and linguistic discriminations made by preromantic critics when describing literary commerce. Resurrecting these categories will dramatize the extent to which the literary culture of Anglo-Americans during the eighteenth century operated on premises largely unfamiliar to us, and not easily comprehensible.

Historians have long wondered why, during the English Restoration, literate persons began to reflect so extensively upon the circumstances of the production, reception, and evaluation of literature. All concur that the disruption in England of customary institutions of literary patronage during the Commonwealth, particularly that of the court and the aristocracy, and the creation of a host of new institutions (coffeehouse, postal service, newspaper, political parties, and periodical press among them) made the circumstances of literary communication particularly visible to the educated classes. The new range of possibilities opened up in the writings of the mid-seventeenth century was not foreclosed by the Restoration and the Stuart project of reestablishing court, aristocracy, and control of the public prints. Attempts to quash the discursive liberties of the coffeehouse failed. The campaign against religious dissent faltered, for few hearts and minds were won back from Nonconformity; some dissenters simply relocated in the colonies. Royal efforts to manage the affairs of state occasioned the coalescence of an opposition, the Whigs, who used political conversation societies (Green Ribbon clubs) and scriptoria to circumvent the control of the press.

Because of the unsettled character of social and political institutions – because of the contest between restoration and innovation – the audience for certain writings became a question rather than a presumption. Long prefaces sprouted, as introductions ceased being simply a patron's payment in praise. Prefaces called readerships into being, prospected new identities for traditional groups, or drew disparate constituencies into common cause.[1] The Glorious Revolution exacerbated this already volatile situation by permitting the emergence of Grub Street, the speculative market for print that came into existence in London about 1690. The lapse of the Licensing Act in 1695 removed the most obtrusive state mechanism for the exercise of prior restraint upon the creation of new communities of opinion.

The volatility of eighteenth-century literary culture can be discerned in the number of groups invoked by writers as audiences. In British America, the community represented in books was not necessarily the society of the learned, society-at-large, the empire, the nation, the public, or the republic of letters. It might be "friends," or "Christian brethren," or imaginary families, or the private society of clubs, or partisans of theological or political causes. Yet over the course of the century, printed books increasingly invoked more spacious forms of society. If one were to single out the most conspicuous historical development in colonial literary culture as manifested in books, it would be the expansive projection of discursive communities – groups identified by distinctive manners and matters of communication.

Traditionally, students of print in America have visualized the history of the book progressively, seeing increasing identification of the writer or reader as "an American,"[2] a tale of the continental growth of patriot solidarity as settlers resisted crown prerogatives and metropolitan impositions. On the contrary, the metropolis *imposed* an aggregate "American" identity upon the colonies, and the colonies resisted this aggregate identity, each insisting upon its distinct chartered privileges, material character, and commercial potential. Meanwhile, Whitehall stressed *its* need to combine neighboring governments for a common defense and an efficient common scheme of trade and government. Just as post-Union metropolitans in Britain sought to subsume Scots, Welsh, and Irish loyalties in the myth of Britannia, so they proposed an imperial American identity for the dominions in the western hemisphere. John Oldmixon's frequently reprinted *The British Empire in America* (1708) proposed that the American plantations possessed a general, commercial character. An image of an Indian maiden bearing a cornucopia of commodities, cribbed from Spanish imperial iconography, soon came to symbolize this identity.

The term "American" came into general use in the same decade, being taken up by cosmopolitan colonials such as Cotton Mather and Jeremiah Dummer, particularly in their transatlantic addresses to Britons. Later, it was taken up by intellectual brokers looking for metropolitan and intercolonial readerships for periodicals. William Bradford's *American Weekly Mercury* (1719–1749), the *American Magazine and Historical Chronicle* (Boston, 1743–1746), Provost William Smith's *American Magazine or Monthly Chronicle* (Philadelphia, 1757–1758), and the *New American Magazine* (Woodbridge, N.J., 1758–1760) were inaugurated upon the most imperial of occasions – war – and sought continental and transatlantic readerships for their reportage of the hemispheric struggle.[3] Most failed to survive to the coming of peace. Until the projection of an American identity in the patriot writings of the Revolution, Americanness remained tenuous and occasional. Other communities (that of a colony, for instance) were inscribed more conspicuously in provincial writings. Indeed, recent investigations find that colonial literary culture did not evolve as a simple consolidation of national identity but through a process of ramification. In British America the diversity, particularity, and generality of readerships increased simultaneously.

The growth of these new communities in British cities and in British America can be correlated with the creation of new literary genres and the transformation of traditional forms. In London, new genres emerged following the Restoration – the novel, the periodical essay, the anecdote, the news story, the town eclogue, the court ballad, the toast, the screed, the mock-political speech, and the dialect poem. All were imported into the colonies. Old genres – the epigram, the Anacreontic, the convivial song, the vision, the familiar letter – developed new applications. Often these forms operated instrumentally, promoting sociability, consolidating group identities, or pointing out and celebrating occasions. The second most powerful development in literature during the provincial era (1690s–1760s) in America was the increasing popularity of ephemeral forms of writing. The eighteenth century was the period when occasionality, immediacy, and triviality were deemed agreeable features of writing.

Literary works with these traits lent themselves to becoming consumer items, provided they were brought to market in a timely fashion. The print market did not give rise to this literature of shared pleasure. Belles lettres (or "polite letters" as it was "Englished") had its birth in the face-to-face conversation of the court and of private society. Its manners and matters were taken over by persons attempting to create new readerships and pools of subscribers for books and periodicals.

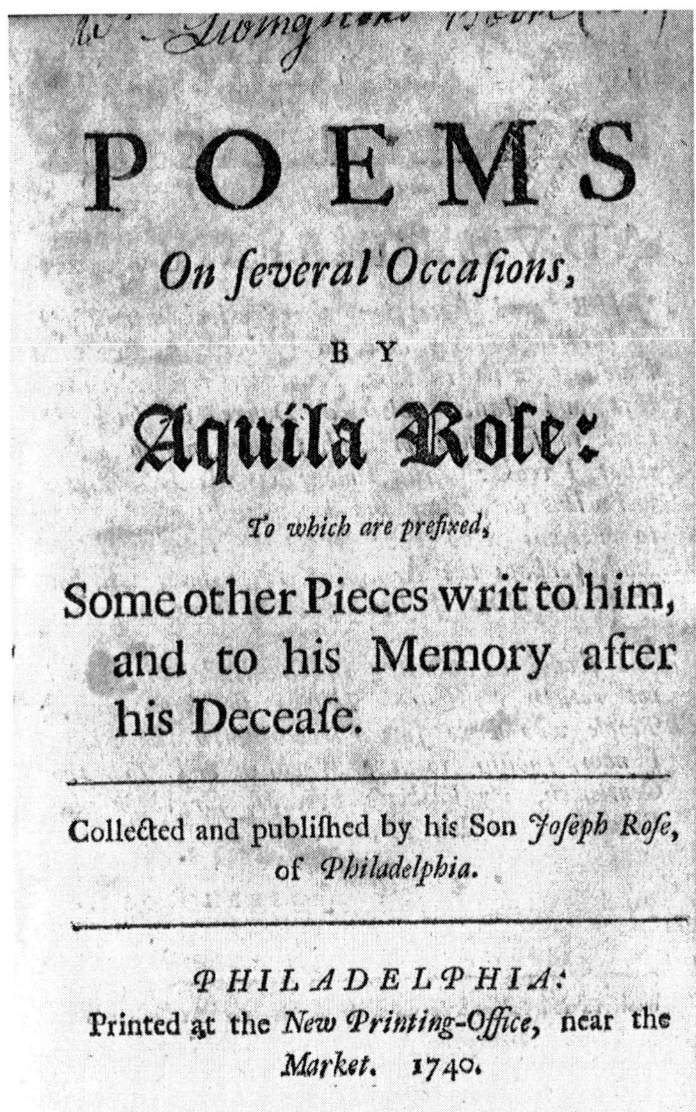
POEMS
On ſeveral Occaſions,
BY
Aquila Roſe:
To which are prefixed,
Some other Pieces writ to him, and to his Memory after his Deceaſe.

Collected and publiſhed by his Son Joſeph Roſe, of Philadelphia.

PHILADELPHIA:
Printed at the New Printing-Office, near the Market. 1740.

Figure 13.1. Aquila Rose, *Poems on Several Occasions* (Philadelphia: [Benjamin Franklin,] 1740). Sailor, printer, clerk, ferryman, and the laureate of Sir William Keith's administration, Rose was the presiding genius of the belletristic coterie whose productions form an appendix to the poems; Franklin succeeded him as a journeyman in Samuel Keimer's printing office. Courtesy of The Houghton Library, Harvard University.

Sponsored by colonial executives and peopled by merchant and planter families, the polite world came into being in the American port cities early in the eighteenth century. The creation of a beau monde in the colonial metropolises had a political point: By establishing a space of polite sociability, conspicuous display, and amusement, imperial administrators and politicians in Boston, Newport, New York, Trenton, Philadelphia, Annapolis, Williamsburg, Charleston, Savannah, and Kingston suggested that the empire's promise to improve subject territories by instituting civility and the "arts of peace" was being fulfilled. Nevertheless, attempts to import the trappings of state literary culture, particularly any form of court patronage, proved difficult.

Poems on Several Occasions, by Aquila Rose (Philadelphia, 1740) (Fig. 13.1) is a useful book through which to approach colonial literary culture, for it reveals the difficulties attending the importation of certain features of the metropolitan scene. While Benjamin Franklin may have urged Aquila's son, Joseph, to collect and publish his father's works in order to give an orphaned young man some certification of his place in the genteel world, the imprint was no vanity issue intended for free distribution, nor was it a project that required an advanced subscription to insure its printing. *Poems on Several Occasions* was a trade book that presumed a market for polite letters. This market had formed recently and remained somewhat unsettled. In 1739, Franklin had published Eliza Rowe's poem, *The History of Joseph,* in an edition of approximately 500 copies, half of which remained unsold by 1743.[4] His lack of success may have been due to the availability of cheaper English editions. Rose's poems, a local production, did not suffer from competition with London or Dublin imprints. Nevertheless, offering an edition of the verses of a local virtuoso sixteen years dead was a novelty, particularly since Aquila Rose had never offered his verses for sale during his brief career in the early 1720s.

As apprentice to printer William Bradford, Aquila Rose had access to Bradford's press and could have issued vanity sheets, like those the bookseller Jacob Tonson produced for the members of London's Kit Kat Club or Franklin produced in 1730 for his friend George Webb and the benefit of "Batchelor's Hall." Rose did not. Presumably, manuscript served his purposes better than print. Possessing fair copies of a writing in an author's hand advertised a personal connection between writer and reader. During the 1720s, scribal publication served the end of personal access to persons with talent, power, and place.[5]

What made verses that were so personal and occasional in the 1720s saleable commodities in the 1740s? The printed volume supplies an answer, for it contained something absent from the manuscripts circulated by Aquila Rose in the coffeehouses and polite parlors of Philadelphia, the story of the author's life. Recounted in a long prefatory verse memoir entitled, "To the Memory of Aquila Rose, Deceas'd" (unsigned but probably written by scrivener Joseph Breintnall), that life had powerful cultural resonances.[6] For the first time in British America, a writer was rendered a character in a romance and his works were presented as illustrations.

Lives of artists are an early modern phenomenon. During the 1690s in England the genre emerged with Anthony à Wood's *Athenæ Oxonienses* (1691–1691), Gerard Langbaine's *An Account of the English Dramatick Poets* (Oxford, 1691; continued by Charles Gildon in 1698), and John Toland's *The Life of Milton* (London, 1699) driving this development. The individual's career (vocation was the issue) had to contain or point to some larger narrative.

Rose's story combined a tale of thwarted love with another of a young man's rise in the world from a low condition. Jilted by his love, Rose turned vagabond sailor in order to forget. On a voyage to the New World he contracted a life-threatening disease. While recuperating in Philadelphia, he attracted the attention of some townsmen: "They courted him, and he delighted them: / Soft in Discourse, and easy of Access, / Thankful his Mind, persuasive his address, / The learn'd approved his Wit, the unlearn'd admir'd, / And docile Youths to his regard aspir'd." The group that formed around Rose (their poems also appeared in the volume) included the prothonotary of the New Castle court, David French, almanac maker and surveyor general Jacob Taylor, scrivener Joseph Breintnall, and judge Richard Hill. These new friends secured Rose a place in William Bradford's printing office. There he attracted the notice of Lieutenant Governor William Keith, who enlisted Rose as laureate of his administration. In exchange for the accolades Rose heaped on his regime, Keith secured for Rose posts as clerk of the assembly and proprietor of the Schuylkill ferry. Soon thereafter, Rose found a new love, married, and fathered Joseph before taking a chill in the waters of the ferry and dying.[7]

This story confirmed one of the fondest wishes of literate youths of modest means, that one's wit might win one friends, patron, place, and income. The 1720s were the heyday in the Anglo-American world of tales of patrons elevating meritorious literary youths into power. The careers of Jonathan Swift, Joseph Addison, and their friend, Governor Robert Hunter of New York, were known to every periodical reader in British America.[8] In the American colonies, however, no established hereditary aristocracy existed to sponsor an efficient scheme of patronage. Its place was taken by a transient group of imperial placemen, most of whom had accepted executive positions in the New World in order to generate income for themselves, not to dispense cash and favors to likely young men. Governor William Keith, though typically greedy, was nevertheless constructing the semblance of a court. His "free and easy way of living" much ingratiated him with persons (including Quakers) in Pennsylvania.[9] In order to give a semblance of splendor, Keith knew that he needed a court poet to celebrate the occasions of his rule. A laureate could inject the element of state ceremony ("officiousness") that elevated courtliness above mere sociability.

The prime requisite for a laureate was an ability to praise. Rose's encomium "To Richard Hill, Esq;" demonstrated his expertise. Judge Hill, an old warrior turned civil servant, inspired a lively appreciation in the style of a court wit:

SAY, Hill, what Pow'r could make a man like thee,
Brought up in Wars and Tempests on the Sea;
Unknown to fear; or fly the daring Foe;
At once the Bravery of the Sword forego?
Some heav'nly Force, has, by a powerful Charm,
Unstrung thy Sinews, and restrain'd thy Arm;
Shewn thee what Joys from peaceful Virtues rise;
That lift to Heav'n, and scale the distant Skies:
When Blood and Horror, and the Lust of Fight,
Lead to the Shades of everlasting Night,
Whilst thus retir'd, our Country's Friend you prove,
In all the Social Arts of Peace and Love.

This tale of martial valor overtaken by the "powerful Charm" at work in the "Social Arts of Peace and Love" personalized one of the potent stories animating European culture during the previous century, the narrative of the civilizing process. It was *the* central story of the royal courts: masculine valor ceased to be the means to eminence when the court embraced politeness, amiability, and stylishness in conduct and conversation.[10]

Rose's panegyric limned the ideals of civility so aptly that it inspired "An Encomium to Aquila Rose, on his Art in Praising." Written by Joseph Breintnall and included among the club poems at the rear of Rose's *Poems,* it also commended a second poem (now lost) celebrating Robert Allen. More materially, the panegyric attracted the notice of Keith, who recognized the advantage of a poet who could commend without grovelling. Rose fell easily into the role of the regime's laureate, composing a set of works lauding the governor's negotiations with the Indians at Conestoga.[11] In the court poem, "To his Excellency Sir William Keith, Bart. on his journey to Connestogoe, and Treaty with the Indians there," Rose proclaimed, "To Indians thou shalt a Lycurgus be, / Who Ages hence shall almost worship thee." In a companion piece meant to illustrate the spread of Anglo-American civility to the frontier, Rose wrote a paean "To J[oh]n C[artled]ge, Esq; on his Generous Entertainment of Sir William Keith, and his Company, at Conestogoe":

we found
A House capacious, and a fertile Ground:
Luxurious Dishes grac'd the loaded Board,
With all the Bounties of rich Nature stor'd.
The flowing Cups with sprightly Liquor smil'd
And pleasant Talk the running Hours beguil'd.

These poems circulated in manuscript among the coteries that made up the governing classes of Pennsylvania. Like the manuscript of Governor Hunter's closet drama "Androboros" or the political verses of Governor Lewis Morris in New Jersey, Rose's verse was intended only for the eyes of the select groups that constituted polite society.[12] Access to such texts marked one's membership in circles of consequence in the province.

Holograph manuscripts radiated an aura of human connection because of the personality of an author's hand, a personality that provided an immediacy absent from print. Yet their scarcity made them vulnerable to the ravages of time, changes in taste, and alterations in society. In an editorial preface Aquila's son Joseph noted that "many of his best Pieces were lent out, after his Decease, by my Mother, to persons who forgot to return them." A scant fourteen verses appeared in the collection. (The paucity of the surviving works dramatizes the extent to which the book features the story of Rose's life rather than his works.) The perishability of manuscripts was a general problem; consider Rose's friends and contemporaries in Philadelphia. In the 1760s, David French's manuscripts were rescued by John Parke from "oblivion, through the obliterating medium of rats and moths, under the sequestered canopy of an antiquated trunk."[13] Those of Rose's poetic rival, Henry Brooke, have survived in a single posthumous collection made by his friend, the Reverend William Becket of Lewes Town.[14] Two brief lyrics remain from Joseph Breintnall's vast store of manuscript plays, poems, and satires.[15]

Rose's manuscripts, none of which survive, were imperiled by circumstances other than the vulnerability of the medium. The mortality of panegyric, particularly court panegyric, was notorious. Praise was cheap because it was so abundant and because occasions for praise clotted the calendar. As governors departed (as Keith was forced to do in 1728), the cults of personality they sponsored and the praises they inspired became moot. So long as manuscript court literature was restricted to panegyric, it was evanescent. Yet laureates had larger uses. Authors who mastered dispraise and could argue convincingly about the issues of the day could be useful to those in power. Court poems began to be printed when controversy made praise of the executive a matter of polemic. Thus Francis Harrison's appreciations of Governor William Cosby of New York appeared in the *New York Gazette* when the governor was being reviled by James Alexander and Lewis Morris in the pages of Zenger's *New-York Weekly Journal.*[16]

During the 1720s, the publication in print of state odes and elegies began in Pennsylvania, Massachusetts, and New York, marking an increase in the cultivation of civic ceremony and occasion by provincial courts. Rose's memorialist, Joseph Breintnall, inaugurated the Pennsylvanian literature with a broadside, *The Death of King George Lamented in Pennsylvania* (1728).[17] Mather Byles established himself as the state oracle of Massachusetts with *A Poem on the Death of His late Majesty King George, of Glorious Memory* and *A Poem Presented to His Excellency William Burnet, Esq; on his Arrival at Boston, July* 19, 1728.[18] Francis Harrison contributed "An Elegy upon His Excellency William Burnet, Esq; who departed this Life Sept. 7th, 1729 Aetat 42," as the first New York civic elegy.[19] Had Rose survived five more years, he, rather than Joseph Breintnall, would have been the first publishing civic bard of Pennsylvania.

In Virginia, John Markland supplied the most elaborate commentary upon print's transformation of patronage, panegyric, courts, civility, and publicity. His 1730 ode on printing, *Typographia* (Evans 3298), addressed to William Gooch, Lieutenant-Governor of Virginia, has long been a datum in histories of early American printing and intellectual culture. Its message, however, had less to do with the progress of learning and the rise of civilization than historians have supposed. Michael Warner has observed how it celebrated the power of exemplary virtue and the potency of pattern captured in writing.[20] Yet *Typographia* also had a local political point; it told how the press perfected imperial rule, so that "Where GOOCH administers, AUGUSTUS reigns." Print extended the power of the law, while "blotted manuscripts" obscured law's dominion. Inviting more readers to participate in the cult of Gooch's authority, print (and the printed poem) served both his rule and his fame. It also perpetuated the fame of the celebrator, for such officious praise is marked by the poet's declaration of his name, preserving it for posterity.

Only one man in British America published poems under his name bearing the title "laureate," and he perhaps in jest: Ebenezer Cooke of Maryland. Dubbed laureate by Thomas Bordley, the speaker of the Maryland Assembly, Cooke received no emolument from his office, which seems to have been a mock honor recognizing his burlesque of the colony, *The Sot-Weed Factor.*[21] Cooke, however, employed the title only on serious state poems, such as his 1726 broadside, *Mors Omnibus Communis: An Elogy on the Death of Thomas Bordley* (Evans 39843).[22] His public satires, *Sotweed Redivivus* (1730) and *The Maryland Muse* (1731), were signed "E. C. Gent" and "E. Cooke, Gent." Social rank was the matter that needed clarification when wit was exercised in public. In England the poet laureate was a member of the royal household, appointed for life and supported by the public exchequer.[23] But Cooke was politically aligned with the forces fighting the Maryland proprietary. Bordley, his patron, was Governor Calvert's nemesis in the assembly. Bordley, not one of the Calverts, named Cooke state oracle. The Calverts' poetic champion was the Annapolis Latin master, Richard Lewis.[24] Even though no British American held a formal laureateship in the colonies – no civil list was rich enough to support ceremonial offices – civic poets in the colonies, beginning with Benjamin Tompson, performed most of the functions of a laureate: marking occasions of state, memorializing an executive's great deeds, and speaking as the voice of the public in ceremonies of greeting or leave-taking.[25] These volunteer laureates wrote with an eye to patronage.[26] Whether the favors granted these spokesmen were dispensed by partisans of the assembly or members of the executive was immaterial.

Executives were not alone in cultivating young men of ability. Party bosses and speakers of legislative assemblies also recompensed talent with place. The signal political development of the eighteenth century, as Jack Greene has revealed, was the consolidation of power in the colonial assemblies. They acquired it in an unceasing conflict with proprietors and governors.[27] In elections, in salary disputes and legislative contests (often about public credit), political bosses – Elisha Cooke in Massachusetts, James Alexander in New York, Andrew Hamilton in Pennsylvania, Thomas Bordley in Maryland, John Mercer in Virginia – countered the exercise of prerogative. In these efforts they claimed the authority of the voice of the people, and, to ensure this claim, cultivated public opinion by every possible means – songwriting, speechifying, pamphleteering, forming popular associations, and (if the opposition controlled sufficient resources, as in 1730s New York) bankrolling a newspaper. Popular party bosses understood the value of literary aptitude in the task of molding public opinion.[28] Leaders of the popular party placed a premium upon wit and rhetorical skill, not praise.

In this respect, the path that Aquila Rose took to preferment differed from that of his would-be replacement in Bradford's printing office. Like Rose, Benjamin Franklin obtained the secretaryship of the Pennsylvania Assembly. When courtly blandishment did not win Franklin a patron (Franklin counted his run-in with Governor Keith one of the misadventures of youth, a lesson in crediting the promises of poseurs in power), he turned to publishing a closely argued essay on paper money. It caught the eye of Andrew Hamilton.[29] Hamilton cultivated Franklin for his skill as a controversialist. When Hamilton won election as speaker of the assembly, he engineered his protégé's appointment as public printer in 1730, then as clerk in 1736.

While Rose and Franklin pursued different paths to preferment, their destination was the same, the office of secretary to the assembly. In literary *and* in political culture, the role of the secretary was crucial, bringing four shillings a day, a rate only a little below that of a representative. Rose and

Franklin kept minutes of the proceedings, which were reviewed by committee, and prepared the text for publication or entry into the body's official records. At times they assisted in the formulation of language for legislation. We can best approach some sense of the potentialities for power residing in the secretary's office by considering the governmental stations that retain the designation: those of cabinet officials, such as the secretary of state or secretary of defense. In these modern posts, the articulation of policy and the administration of executive orders are the paramount operations. This was also the case in the eighteenth century when cabinets first came into being. Then it was by means of letters that both the articulatory and administrative tasks were performed – through diplomatic correspondence, written orders, treaties, and position papers.[30] Given the necessity of verbal skill in these matters, one understands Sunderland's rationale for elevating Joseph Addison to a political secretariat. Because of the transatlantic character of colonial governments, the dependence of rule and civil order upon writing was nearly absolute.

Among the American colonies, Georgia owed most to its secretaries. Only James Logan's influence in Pennsylvania when he served as the secretary of the proprietors approached the power of the secretary of Georgia in the 1730s.[31] The colony came into being in 1732 as a result of a philanthropic publicity campaign run by James Oglethorpe and mainly composed by the Board of Trustees' secretary, Benjamin Martyn. Through the 1730s, the residents of Georgia had no legislature of their own, for the London-based board presumed that many of the colonists were sturdy beggars and poor folk needing habituation to industry in the workhouse of the wild. The president administered the board's directives, while the secretary recorded intelligence on local affairs, ensured the dissemination of board directives, and informed the board of happenings in the colony. The transmission of intelligence became a particular concern in the later 1730s because of the emergence of an opposition, "the clamorous malcontents" who challenged the conditions of rule.

Surveyor and planter William Stephen was appointed secretary of the colony in 1741 on the basis of dispatching his journal recording the political agitations in Savannah. Two entries from his journal provide a graphic portrait of an opposition literary culture operating to form public opinion without benefit of a press:

> Friday. January 5. 1738. Much Talk about Town of an anonymous Letter said to be found in the Street, supposed to be dropt with Design, and directed to the General; full of such Politicks as were now in Fashion among us. . . .
>
> Saturday. January 6. 1738. Having a strong Inclination to get a Sight of this anonymous Letter (if possible) which was so much talked of; I thought the likeliest Place to come at any Knowledge about it, would be among our Gentry at

the nightly Club. . . . I had not sat long, before I was made sensible, that one who had the Custody of the Letter, was as ready to shew it me, as I was to see it: Wherefore calling me aside into another Room in Privacy, he pulled it out of his Pocket, told me what he had got, and asked me to hear him read it; which he did: It was very long, and filled two or three Sheets of Paper in a loose Hand; the Stile was copious and flowing, attempting a Sort of Panegyrick on the General . . . After much haranguing on that Part, and a great deal of Tautology in setting for the miserable Disappointment of the Landholders here . . . , it was very easy from many circumstances to discover, that he who read it was the Author (viz. Mr. Hugh Anderson).

As these entries reveal, public opinion in 1730s Savannah was the opinion of landholders – the nascent gentry. It was institutionalized socially in a tavern club and discursively in manuscript remonstrances and satires. Stephen styled the club "a little Assembly" of malcontents who met at an unlicensed public house. The "little Assembly's" membership was composed of Scotsmen, "but promiscuous also, and open to any that would come, in the Manner of a Coffee-House."

The heyday of the coffeehouse had already passed in England by the 1730s, yet it retained its symbolic association with faction, free-thought, and public controversy. The coffeehouse was promiscuous not only in terms of membership but of opinion. Each coastal city in North America had at least one coffeehouse, which served as a commercial venue and news center. Ever since Charles II's attempted repression of the London coffehouses in 1668, the authorities had viewed these centers of political debate and commerce with suspicion. Stephen's characterization of the club in Savannah as being "in the Manner of a Coffee-House" carried with it the usual disapprobation. Like the denizens of the political coffeehouses of the Restoration, the Georgia malcontents aspired to a broader influence upon public sentiment than that exerted by conversation and rumor; such forms depended upon the familiarity among speakers for effect. They composed manuscripts "fixed to the most publick Places, abusing the Magistrates in the most gross Terms, and throwing some scandalous Reflexions upon others also." In July 1738, the Georgia grand jury presented these pasquinades to the local justices as attempts to disturb the peace.

The malcontents' campaign had one difficulty: No local body could alter the circumstances of government. There being no elections, there was little to be gained by forming the mind of an electorate. Countering the publicity of the Board of Trustees with satire may have had some cathartic effect, yet it had no influence on the board's instructions or its representations to would-be recruits to the colony. Moreover, this mode of criticism ran the risk of prosecution in the court, an institution of government that did perform locally. Consequently, the malcontents removed to Charleston, where a press was located. There they provided the most powerful transatlantic fusillade in the campaign being waged by the government of South Carolina against its rival to the south. Hugh Anderson (he of the anonymous letter), Dr. Patrick Tailfer, and David Douglas published *A True and Historical Narrative of the Colony of Georgia in America* in 1741 (Evans 4816). Carolina's London agent saw that a second edition was printed in London in December. It told how the colonists credited the Edenic publicity of the board, left for the New World, and discovered a country in ruin by reason of misgovernment. Various promises from Secretary Benjamin Martyn's publicity campaign were reviewed and burlesqued. By 1743 the malcontents' deconstruction of official publicity had thwarted recruitment to the colony so well as to force an alteration of its constitution.

The role of writing in Georgia's politics marked an extreme. During the eighteenth century no other colony in British America, apart from Canada during its garrison government, operated without a elective assembly. No other colony was so much a creation of print publicity or so vulnerable to charges of misrepresentation. While every colony had to address the metropolis, Georgia's political literature was pitched entirely to the British ear. Elsewhere, every colony that possessed an elective assembly developed a controversial literature addressed to a local public. As Michael Warner has shown, printing transformed legislative controversies over tobacco policy in the Chesapeake colonies, monetary policy in Massachusetts, and the exercise of prerogative in New York from personal power clashes into contests in which "the people" were represented. Print permitted the emergence of publics.[32]

Pamphlet wars first erupted in British America during the 1720s. They were perceived by contemporaries familiar with the broader world of letters as being a local manifestation of metropolitan paper wars. During the reign of Queen Anne, print fueled a series of public disturbances over the Church of England, the succession, and the conduct of the war. Conflict in the prints provoked disorder in the streets, with mug clubs and artisan cabals burning Nonconformist meetinghouses and destroying property. Ned Ward's *Vulgus Britannicus*, an early literary anatomy of "the mob," linked the activity of the press with the political disorders hatched by the urban lower orders. While public mayhem had been a calculated feature of urban politics since the 1680s, when "scowering" became a favored pastime of disaffected Tories (see Thomas Shadwell's 1691 play, "The Scowerers"), it was practised by upper-class youths. The agitations during the reign of Queen Anne were more deserving of being styled the riot of the *mobile vulgus*. Ned Ward, a pioneer Grub Streeter, was well positioned to comment. A Tory, Ward found the disorders disturbing even when the lower orders were rioting on behalf of the Tory martyr, Sacheverell. Ward recognized that new forces were being unleashed that would not be restrained by the old mechanisms of authority that Tories cherished.

In British America similar connections were drawn among the press, disorder, and the aspirations of the lower classes. In 1733 or 1734, Archibald Home, the third son of Sir John Home, Bart., circulated a satire in a coffeehouse in New York City. Burlesquing one of the "popular" genres engendered by the press, the criminal biography, it can be read as an elitist's commentary on the political turmoil in New York excited by John Peter Zenger. In an echo of Horace's Satires 1.8, it begins, "I am Sprung from a good Stock in Germany; my Father was cutt down in the Flower of his Age to furnish out a Gibbet which in my Twentieth Year had like to have proved my Fate also, but that I with Several more of my companions was purchased and carried to London by an English Merchant," who shipped him to America "in the Quality of a Hand-spike," where he then became "the Main Beam of a Printing-Press from which I weekly squeez'd such black putrid Venom that I was thought a Common Nuisance," descending at last to "become a Pillory or a Whipping post."[33]

Latin tags marked the satire as a learned production, cuing the elite audience intended for the text. The mock memoir stigmatized the political street disturbances of sailors and artisans, linking them to the press's poisoning of the peace with its "black putrid venom."[34] One poisoner, Lewis Morris, who sponsored the vilification of Governor Cosby in Zenger's *New-York Weekly Journal*, thought so highly of this piece of mockery that he sought out the author, making Home secretary of New Jersey after Morris became its governor.

Whether or not sailors could read Zenger's paper or venomous pamphlets mattered little; someone in the dram houses could read it for them. What mattered was that print was reaching a popular audience in coastal cities, an audience that would grab the hand spike and threaten those of different opinions. Furthermore, this force had to be reckoned with by the powers that were, because it meant a threat of violence stood behind expressions of displeasure by the *vox populi*. The dramatic point of Aquila Rose's capacity to speak to both the learned and the unlearned made him valuable to Governor Keith, for Keith believed the polls were the key to maintaining power, and numbers of the unlearned possessed the franchise. Keith organized and proselytized a following, forming a gentlemen's club *and* a "leather-apron" club to make demonstrations during elections. Rose could speak to both, yet his ambition was to be numbered among the former.

The primacy of learning in colonial literary culture may be adduced from the arrangement of Rose's *Poems on Several Occasions*. The book was organized by genre; first place was granted to his imitations of Ovid's elegies of Scythian exile, since "learning" in its basic sense meant a reading knowledge of the classics. By 1720, it had come to mean something broader, an acquaintance with reputable letters, ancient and modern. Yet the priority of ancient wisdom was widely acknowledged, so much so that literary history has characterized the era as "the age of neoclassicism" or "the Augustan age" of letters. Archibald Home's posthumous manuscript poetry collection, dating from 1744, followed Rose's book in its arrangement by genre and the priority given neoclassical imitations. Ovid loomed large in Home's learning, supplying the basis for four of the five most elaborate neoclassical imitations. An exile of empire, Ovid loomed large in the symbolic imagination of many American colonists, and Rose's circle in particular. All of the surviving works of Rose's club-mate, David French, were translations of Ovid's *Tristia* or Anacreon's Odes.[35] Henry Brooke travestied Ovid in his ballad of commercial misadventure, "The New Metamorphosis" (1702).

This fascination with Ovid's elegies of Scythian exile arose out of the provincial situation of cosmopolitan intellectuals who understood themselves as living in rude backwaters, a situation framed by the feeling that they mediated the center with the periphery, the high with the low, the familiar with the strange, the civil with the wild, the past glory with the present rudeness. The learned operated as a priesthood of durable truth, proclaiming ancient wisdom for successive ages. The learned were not bound by nationality or by the present moment. They were an international community that tied the living to the dead.[36] Books performed a similar function, spanning space and time. It is not surprising that the learned understood themselves to have been speaking libraries, persons who vivified the dead letter. When a learned person died, society suffered because the conversation lost a quality of dynamism brought by wide and weighty reference. Obituaries formulaically regretted the loss of the virtuoso who "from his great and extensive Reading had a great Fund to entertain in Conversation."[37]

Why did learning become identified with an ability to "entertain in Conversation?" The reason lay in the demand by polite society that learning not be confined to the colleges, but injected into polite conversation to give it sense and weight. To keep learning from sinking under its own weight, it had to be worn lightly, refurbished by eloquence, or couched in wit. Learning unleavened with wit was pedantry. Politeness without learning was chatter, the fashionable agreeableness of Sir Sprightly Surface or Mr. Dapper.[38] Paradoxically, as critics of polite society bemoaned the eclipse of the college by the coffeehouse and learning by "trifling News and Chat," "Learning" became a contested term in the American colleges. At Harvard, the conflicts were played out in the pages of the *New England Courant* and through the formation of student societies. In the *Courant* a paper war erupted concerning the Harvard plain style of writing elegies, stimulated by *Pitchero-Threnodia*.[39]

The issue of learning served to define communities within the student bodies. Evangelical modernists formed prayer societies on the model set out by Cotton Mather in *Bonifacius* (1710) and *Religious Societies* (1724).[40] These groups made praying and the performance of good works in society at large their chief concerns. The counterweight to these societies were the learned fellowships – at Harvard, the 1721 "Tell-Tale" circle,[41] the 1728 Philomusarians and the 1746 Phinphilinici,[42] or "Fifth Day Club," organized in November 1746, at Yale the Linonians, at William and Mary the FHC Society and later Phi Beta Kappa,[43] at the College of New Jersey the Cliosophical Society, at King's College the King's College Club.

The Philomusarians explicated their program in detail. Their declaration can serve as a general gloss upon the projects of these undergraduate societies:

To be Brief, Vice is Now Become Alamode & Rant Riot & Excess is Accounted the Heigth of Good Breeding & Learning – In Order Therefore to Stem That Monstrous Tide of Impiety & Ignorance wch is Like to Sweep All Before it & for Our Mutual Advantage & Emolumt The Subscribers Have Thought fitt to Engage In The Following Combination As We are Sensible That Next to Religion Learning Claims the precedency.[44]

Here, religion and learning were differentiated. Learning had links with friendship, good breeding, conversation, and civility, but was opposed to fashionability, riot, excess, ignorance, and impiety.[45] The Philomusarians framed their project in the 1690s rhetoric of the Whig reformers of manners. Yet they suffused it with concern for precedence in social and intellectual hierarchies, an interest that smacked of mercantile cosmopolitanism and, perhaps, Anglicanism.

The linkage between Anglicanism, liberty of intellectual inquiry, and books was a cultural commonplace.[46] When orthodox Calvinists criticized Harvard, they charged it with being enticed by the culture of the New Babylon, London, imported in print and consumer goods.[47] These criticisms were not unfounded. Student groups like the authors of "The Tell Tale," a Harvard manuscript of 1721, began parroting speculative theologians by asking "whether there be any standard of truth." President John Leverett enacted a student ranking scheme based on the courtly model, recognizing social precedence rather than piety, Christian zeal, and academic merit.[48] Yale came into existence in response to perceptions that Calvinist rigor at Harvard was being sacrificed for something more liberal and temperamentally, if not in fact, Anglican. Yet Yale, too, would suffer a crisis in 1722 when the effects of Anglican books became evident in the apostacy of the college rector and some of the faculty and trustees. Timothy Cutler, Samuel Johnson, and John Checkley became notorious in the annals of American religion as the apostates who consolidated episcopacy in New England. At William and Mary the rhetoric of the FHC Society was no different than that of the cosmopolitan societies at Harvard, Yale, or the College of New Jersey.[49]

Over the course of the eighteenth century, the great controversy in higher education was the ordering of educational priorities. Franklin and others of his mind challenged the primacy of classical knowledge in the curriculum, desiring the elevation of vernacular study of the business of life. The conservative force maintaining the primacy of classical studies was the sons of the elite. The major beneficiaries of higher education, they saw classical learning as an unambiguous marker of elite status and, accordingly, tended to resist any alteration of the curriculum. Schoolmasters, too, proved a constraining force. The masters and ushers of grammar and writing schools viewed themselves as agents for learned culture. The staff of South Grammar School (later the Boston Latin School) from 1700 to 1750 boasted Ezekiel Cheever (1615–1708) author of a standard *Short Introduction to the Latin Tongue*, Robert Treat Paine (1731–1804) comic poet and signer of the *Declaration of Independence*, Nathaniel Gardner, Jr., the major neoclassical poet to have emerged in New England in the generation after Mather Byles and the Reverend John Adams.[50] It was Gardner, "a fine Classick Schollar, a Man of Wit and Humour," who captured in Latin verse the aspirations and travails of those who labored at classic learning.[51] His long witty epistle to John Beveridge about teaching Latin at the Boston School is learning incarnate, chock full of witty echoes of school poets and ironic avowals of the worth of the ancients.

> Qui formet pueros paucis schola nostra monebo.
> Paeniteat tantum versare modosque loquendi
> et genus et nomen, quaecunque et Lillius egit.
> Majus opus moveam interdum, et majora laborem!
> Interdum doceam quid turpeque quidque decorum,
> quo sit amore parens, sacrum quo numen amandum,
> quae neglecta quidem et pueris senibusque nocerent.
> Est tantae molis pueriles fingere mentes![52]

For those who had no Latin, an encounter with a text like this reminded one of his or her exclusion from the learned world.

Until late in the eighteenth century, learned networks in natural history promoted an ethic of gentlemanly sociability. Before the triumph of a discourse of natural history dependent upon Linnean schematic, the ideal form of report leavened description with classical reference, theological wit, or narrative.[53] The literariness of William Bartram's *Travels in the Carolinas, Georgia and Florida* (1791) was no novel efflorescence of romantic sensibility so much as a latter-day manifestation of the gentlemanly style of natural history reportage found in works such as Griffith Hughes's *Natural History of Barbadoes* (London, 1750) or the letters of John Custis to Peter Collinson (1734–1746), a correspondence that the Virginian styled as the friendly communication of "we Brothers of the Spade."[54] Occasional learned women, such as Jane Colden and Susanna Wright, injected their observations into the talk of this transatlantic brotherhood.[55]

Over the course of the century, learning became less a marker of gender and more one of gentility. Its social significance could exceed its worth as edification. Schoolmasters in British America exploited their connection with learning to raise their standing in the world. Richard Lewis, the master of the Latin School in Annapolis and correspondent to the Royal Society, used his 1728 translation of Holdsworth's *Muscipula, sive Kambromyomachia*, a comic narrative poem about the battle between the ancient Welsh and the mice, to announce the reign of civility in Maryland and establish his place as its spokesman.[56] The names of the subscribers printed in the volume identified the colony's friends of learning. "It shall appear from the subsequent List, that the smallest Attempt to cultivate polite Literature, in MARYLAND, has been received with . . . ample Testimonies of Candor and Generosity." Lewis, modestly and disingenuously, cast his own role as that of an accidental stimulus "to a generous Disposition in the Province, to encourage Learning." He was the most accomplished neoclassical poet who published in British America and, with James Grainger of St. Kitts, the most famous.[57] His works appeared in the metropolitan magazines and newspapers, oft-times under his proper name.

It was not unusual among the learned to publish one's name (or a Latinized version of it if an international readership were envisioned) on the title page of a book. Only with the creation of a genteel society in which learning and politeness operated as status markers did the names of the readers/subscribers enjoy similar publicity.[58] Lewis was supremely conscious that his was the first volume in Maryland to publicize the existence of a provincial community of polite learning. The list of subscribers is informative regarding status: The 148 men (no women) were identified by professional tags for military officers and ship captains (19), physicians (9), and ministers (2). The remaining 118 subscribers were distinguished by property, 20 being designated esquires, that is, holders of heritable estates, while the remaining 98 (merchants, tradesmen, shipwrights, and factors for the most part) bore "Mr.", the common title of courtesy prefixed to the surname of a man not entitled to be addressed as Sir or Lord, and lacking official or professional standing. Lewis took pains to indicate that "I have not the Pleasure of a Personal Acquaintance with many of them." That is, the community described in the subscription list was truly a society of the learned, for it was fundamentally constituted in print, not in conversation. This community of readers operated more in terms of a culture of politeness than of learning. The subscribers may not have had personal dealings with Richard Lewis, but they did among themselves, for these were the principal actors in Maryland's civil and commercial life.[59] Having a metropolitan lustre of civility bestowed upon them by being named as friends of polite learning identified them as the beneficiaries of the *translatio studii.* They perform not simply as the great men of a small colony, but as actors in the great imperial dissemination of the "arts of peace."

The Mouse-Trap is a useful work through which to understand the difference between learning and polite learning. Edward Holdsworth's Latin original, reprinted on the left page, was learned;[60] it was a Latin work intended for the delectation of the academic brotherhood. Lewis's English rendering was polite learning; it rendered the beauties of a Latin text available in English to amuse a nonacademic society with an interest in learning. The polite qualities of ease, pleasantness, correctness, and sociability were featured in the performance. Most importantly, the purpose of the writing was not illumination, memorialization, or documentation, but amusement or "entertainment."

Polite learning was the classical foundation of belles lettres or "polite letters." Indeed, the print market for polite letters was not built on romances, plays, or even poems on affairs of state, but on the great translations, beginning with Brome's Horace (1666), and institutionalized as a central literary project in the English-speaking world by Dryden's Ovid (1680), Juvenal (1697), and Virgil (1697), L'Estrange's Aesop (1692–1699), Pope's *Iliad* (1715–1720) and *Odyssey* (1725–1726), Ambrose Philip's Anacreon and Sappho (1713), Addison's Anacreon (1735), and a host of other works. Some of the writers engaged in this enterprise came to British America. The Reverend James Sterling, translator of Musaeus's *Loves of Hero and Leander* (London, 1728), moved from Dublin to Maryland. Some residents in America undertook their own projects.[61] James Logan's translations, *Cato's Moral Distichs* (1735) and *M. T. Cicero's Cato Major, or his Discourse of Old-Age* (1746), and John Parke's *The Lyric Works of Horace* (1786) were distinctive for being American products published in a provincial market flooded with London and Dublin translations. More often, translations were undertaken as projects of self-cultivation (an adult's extension of school exercises) or for the delectation of coteries of like-minded lovers of learning. The Reverend Thomas Chase (ca. 1703–1780), graduate of Eton and St. John's College, Cambridge, translated Silius Italicus' hexameter *Punica* into two volumes of heroic couplets while serving as rector of St. Paul's in Baltimore.[62] One person who certainly read the approximately 14,000 lines of poetry was his boon companion and fellow cleric, the Reverend Thomas Cradock. Cradock was the quintessential practitioner of polite learning, translating Martial's epigrams, writing a closet drama, "The Death of Socrates," and composing the "Maryland Eclogues," a witty satire on the manners of Maryland in imitation of Virgil's Eclogues.[63] Cradock's writings apparently circulated in Annapolis's polite circles as well as in those of Baltimore.

Becoming known as a renovator of ancient learning had several attractions. An elegant translation vested a writer with double authority: the uncontested authority of the classical original and that of his or her modern eloquence. When Pope's *Iliad* made the poet the brightest celebrity of the era, a colonial poet enthused, "Hast in thy English so preservd his [Homer's] Flame, . . . / Sure no presuming Critic more will boast / Of Modern Bards, and Homer's glory lost."[64] The hard question for the modern critic was whether the English translator was the proper vessel for the ancient fire. A work's quality was measured by its capture of an ancient glory in an alien tongue. Indeed, a task of criticism was to determine whether the genius of an ancient original had been correctly and vividly rendered in English. If one were successful, like Pope, one spoke with a double luminosity; if one were unsuccessful, like many a schoolchild in Ezekiel Cheever's classroom, the merit of the original prevented the exercise from eliciting the total contempt of the critic.

Eloquence was a writer's distinctive contribution in neoclassical writing, and the warrant of his or her status as an author. Current discussions of authorship, following Foucault, have made much of the birth of authorship in the state's recognition and coercive treatment of writers challenging its power.[65] Certainly, attempts to discover the speaking subject behind the anonymous or pseudonymous text in order to discipline it for its libel, treason, or blasphemy marked the forcible emergence of the author in the West. Yet authorship also emerged in tension with literary tradition as well as the state. In the name of eloquence, individuals presumed to voice improvements over the ancient wisdom, or to propose that which had not yet been considered. They sought to make their names great by doing so. These risked the rhetorical power of the critic, who spoke as avatar of critical wisdom, whether Cicero's stylistics, Aristotle's formal analytics, or Longinus' psychology.

The emergence of criticism in literary conversation outside of schools marked the maturation of a public literary culture. The ideal of polite learning stood warrant for the emergence of an instructor, corrector, and censor outside of the classroom. In London and Paris during the latter half of the seventeenth century, intellectuals exploiting the fashion for philosophy assimilated the figure of the philosopher to that of the critic, thereby disassociating criticism from malediction, satire, and polemic. The philosopher's work, encompassing both academic inquiry and public discourse, bridged the chasm between society and the schools. John Dryden stood as the first of the self-called critics in England. His reign as the grand marshal of English letters was exercised from his second-floor chair near the fireplace at Will's coffeehouse. It depended upon his success in the theater, his published prefaces, his wit in conversation, his personal charisma, and his official character. In British America, this complex organization of literary culture was maintained, with print and manuscript reenforcing the dominion of charismatic virtuosi over genteel circles within society and projecting it into a larger world. This was Aquila Rose's story, and Archibald Home's, and Richard Lewis's. In Home's rise to the role of archpoet and spokesman for New Jersey's polite literary culture we see the importance of his function as critic as well as paragon of politeness (Rose) or master of learning (Lewis).

Abigail Streete Coxe, a member of Home's Trenton coterie, anatomized Home's importance for the circle of lovers of polite learning in an elegy on Home's poetry, published in *The Pennsylvania Gazette*.[66] The elegy demonstrated that Abigail Coxe had achieved sufficient mastery under Home's tutelage to speak for the Trenton circle. Four members of the circle had composed elegies; hers was the only one permitted to reach print. Coxe's elegy was neoclassical, employing the usual equipment of the genre – the weeping muses, the bays, the wreath-strewn hearse. Its neoclassicism operated not only on the level of ornament but as a component of the argument, for neoclassicism's retention of ancient truth provided the model of literary greatness conceived as the durability of meaning:

> Great Judge of Number's! when he Struck the lyre,
> 'Twas Attic Harmony, and Roman Fire;
> Anacreon's Ease; Gay Horace' Sprightly Art;
> And Ovid's melting Language of the Heart;
> But (like Roscommon) Chaste; He scorn'd to use
> The pert, low Turn and prostitute the Muse[.]

What did the canvas of classical names mean other than that Home manifested peculiar versatility as an artist? In a sense the names stood surety over the idea of literary memory itself. The ability of the great names of antiquity to remain alive, to merit recitation, opened a possibility that others might enjoy futurity as well. Since the sociable desideratum of agreeableness was no longer pertinent to the dead, fame became the sole issue in literary reception. Only by manifesting in one's works the qualities of harmony, fire, ease, sprightliness, and passion that had preserved classical art could the archpoet of New Jersey join the exalted company of the memorable dead. Coxe insisted that Home's poetry qualified for such exaltation.

The one modern quality admixed to the atavistic conjunction of Home's art was "Roscommon's chastity." Coxe alluded to Wentworth Dillon, Earl of Roscommon, whose *Essay on Translated Verse* (1684) set out the critical standards by which classical imitations were judged. Reacting to the profanations of Grub Street, Roscommon proscribed the obscenity and pornography that had been elements of classic poetry. Roscommon and Addison had promulgated propriety in subject as well as correctness in diction and metrics. Coxe's phrase, "prostitute the Muse," bespoke a genteel suspicion of the burgeoning literary market where value was measured in sales. She alluded to Home's pointed disinclination to print his verses. Besides Roscommon, Coxe named another master of neoclassical correctness when she stated her aspiration as an elegist: "O! Lend such Notes as fell from Tickell's Tongue, / When he the best of Friends and Poets Sung." By citing Thomas Tickell's elegy addressed "To the Earl of Warwick on the death of Addison" as her model, Coxe revealed her literary learning and taste, for, as Samuel Johnson would later observe, there existed no "more sublime or more elegant funeral poem to be found in the whole compass of English literature."[67] Reciting the totemic names of the masters and proceeding from the examples of their masterpieces, Coxe demonstrated her full membership in the belletristic world (a transhistorical world made available to Trenton by print as well as the tutelage and example of Home).

Two great names were conspicuously absent from Coxe's list: Virgil and Pope. The place of the Roman oracle of the expanding empire was taken by Horace, the celebrant of achieved civility. The selection was significant. Unlike many poets of the British empire in America, Home cared little for the physical work involved in transforming the New World into a civilization. He did not conceive the poet to be a eulogist for the planter-hero of the georgic or the merchant-hero of the mercantilist epic. Rather, the poet's fiat, like Amphion's song, called civilization into being. Civilization was constituted wherever and whenever a poet spoke.

Alexander Pope's absence from the list of the great is more curious, particularly since his death took place so close to that of Home. One suspects the anxiety of influence. Pope's rise to power in the metropolis imported the charismatic organization of the British literary club into print: the authority of Ben Jonson at the Apollo Club or John Dryden at the brotherhood at Will's coffeehouse. In so doing he consolidated the print market of authorial celebrity. Once installed as archpoet of the metropolis, Pope emasculated his rivals by the malediction of his *Dunciad* – a curse empowered by the distribution networks of the booksellers. Richard Lewis provoked the archpoet's wrath for his claim that the glories of nature in the New World defied the capacity of art to represent it, earning an extended rebuke and refutation.[68] Philadelphian James Ralph saw his career as a poet in the metropolis snuffed out by Pope when he presumed to criticize Pope in *Sawney*. After Pope delivered his curse in a later edition of the *Dunciad*, the booksellers dropped Ralph, forcing him to become a political hack and historian.[69] Power was concentrated in Pope's name and in the metropolitan market of which he was the focus. In a curious and definitive way Pope rendered irrelevant the efforts of Home and his kind. No army of Amphions was needed in the provinces when the Archpoet spoke his civilizing word in the New Rome.

From the 1740s onward, the manuscript commerce that colonial virtuosi plied in the cause of gentility slowly waned, increasingly obviated by the print culture that Pope brought to fullness.[70] By 1744 an intelligent poet such as Coxe sensed the change in the framework of literary valuation that had occurred. Her anxiety was justified in the long run. By the time that American literary history came into being in the 1790s, Home had gone into that limbo of forgetfulness where, with the exception of Franklin, Mather Byles, James Grainger, and Phillis Wheatley, every provincial American litterateur would eventually languish. In the short term, however, Home enjoyed a posthumous influence shared only by Richard Lewis of his generation. As critic and teacher, Home's aesthetic practice had instructed the work of his followers. The manuscripts of his *Poems on Several Occasions* dramatized the instruction in an appendix featuring the coterie's verse. Lines and phrases improved by Home were underscored. Home's verse likewise appeared as the product of a process of critical correction. Earlier versions of lines appeared in footnotes to dramatize the polish and precision of his finished work. Home's authority lay in his avidity to manifest in poetry the qualities of eloquence, taste, and correctness.

Home's circle was the rarest sort of elite cultural formation in British America, a coterie whose membership was determined not by ethnicity, gender, politics, or religious denomination, but by property and an attraction to the sister arts. It included Jews, Huguenots, Presbyterians, and Anglicans of both sexes in nearly equal number. It was also unusual in that writing, rather than conversation or sociable diversions, bound the group together. Indeed the society existed to fashion the writings; the writings for the most part did not operate as instruments to enliven society. The distinctiveness is particularly apparent when we read Dr. Alexander Hamilton's descriptions of the importance of conversation to the Hungarian Club of New York City, another circle to which Home belonged.[71] The project of Home's circle was to create an aesthetic consensus in art, not to use art to promote sociability or good-fellowship. This point deserves particular notice because by far the bulk of belles lettres composed in Europe and the colonies had an instrumental function. It might be used to ornament the conversation of private society; or to project a playful identity for a club; or to aid courtship; or to lend the pleasures of wit and ease to argument. Only rarely did the idea of fashioning literary artifacts of self-substantiating beauty (a hypostatizing of the ancient rhetorical ideal of eloquence) operate as the governing aesthetic of a colonial circle.

When Home died in 1744, Abigail Coxe collected his poetry, organizing the manuscript to show the growth of Home's art to mastery (Fig. 13.2). She arranged the verse by genre, with the long classical imitations first and the songs and social verse composed when he first arrived in New York in the 1730s last.[72] To read the manuscript back to front is to trace a rough chronology of Home's poeticizing. For Home's coterie, the manuscript operated as a model for self-cultivation, a descent from Parnassus that began at the top to show the steps by which mastery was achieved.

The beginning pages of Home's manuscript suggested the goal of elite aesthetic aspiration in British America, while the closing leaves marked out the starting point of poetic practice: songs and convivial wit. Songs were popularized in British cities by a number of means. Ballads were performed by itinerant singers in the streets of the cities and the singers sold printed broadside texts of the pieces they performed. Often the tunes were traditional and local ballad bards (John Dommett in Pennsylvania or Tom Law in Massachusetts) fashioned texts suited to the news, the politics, or the fashions of the moment. Law's ballad of the Norridgewock Indian fight, *The Rebel's Reward* (1724) followed the best metropolitan marketing strategy, sporting a lurid woodcut illustration of Captain Harmon's troops gunning down the Indians to boost sales.[73] Like most ballads, it bore a headnote indicating the tune to which the singer should fit the words, in this case, "All you that love Good Fellows." The popularity of certain tunes enabled writers with political agendas to disseminate opinion quickly. If the songs themselves had political associations, so much the better. David Humphrey's "The Lamentable Story of two Fatherless & Motherless Twins which Lately appeared in ye City of N—w-Y—k who for their Prophetick Cries were Condemn'd to be burnt by ye Common Hangman which was Accordingly Executed &c," a ballad on the public burning of Zenger's *New-York Weekly Journal* and an antiproprietary ballad composed by Lewis Morris, stirred Whiggish fervor by being sung to "Great William Our Renowned King."[74]

Song tunes and texts were disseminated by a number of means. Primary among them was performance. The itinerant acting companies in the colonies sang the hits featured in repertoire plays such as Centlivre's *Busybody,* Farquhar's *Beaux Strategem, Recruiting Officer,* and *The Constant Couple.* If

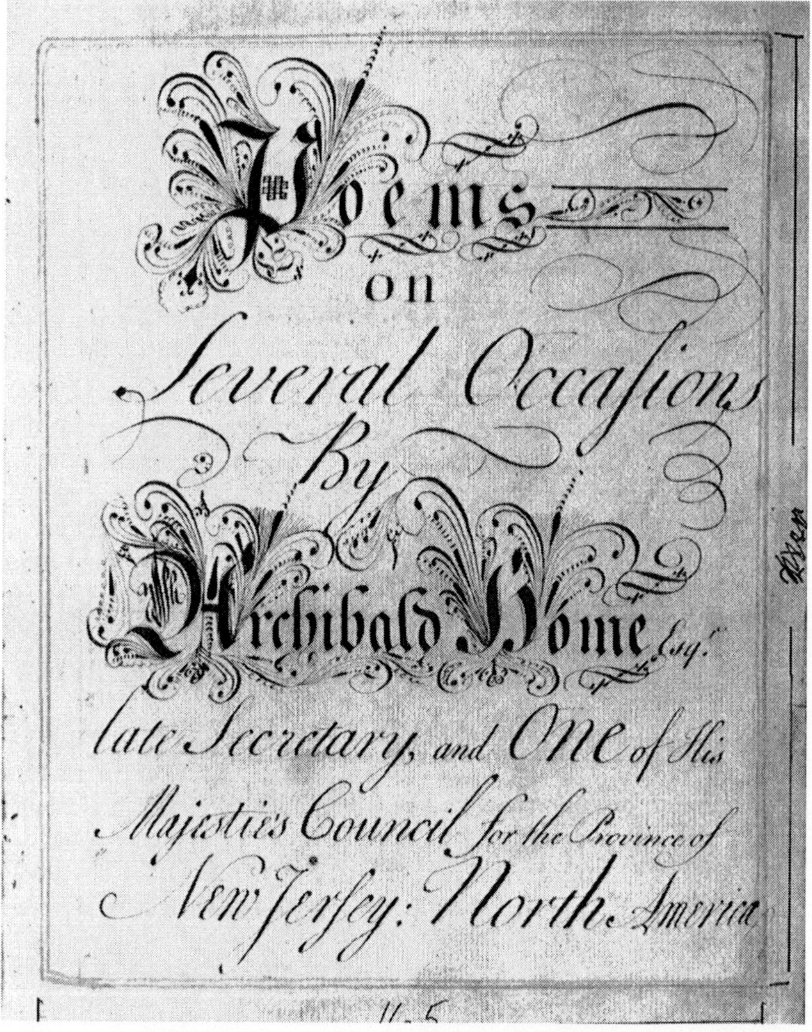
Poems
on
Several Occasions
By
Archibald Home Esqr.
late Secretary, and One of His
Majesties Council for the Province of
New Jersey: North America

Figure 13.2. Archibald Home, *Poems on Several Occasions* [Ms., ca. 1750]. The masterpiece of British American manuscript publication: Copies circulated both in Great Britain and the colonies. Courtesy of the University of Edinburgh Library (Laing Mss.)

sufficient local talent existed in a city to gather an orchestra, a company might stage the greatest well-spring of English songs, the ballad opera. In 1752 Annapolis, for instance, performed Colley Cibber's *Damon and Philida* (1729), Charles Coffey's *The Female Parson* (1730) and *The Devil to Pay* (1731), and Henry Fielding's *An Old Man Taught Wisdom* (1735).[75] By mid-century, theatrical songs and compositions intended for parlor performance were being published in the widely circulated periodicals. During the 1740s and 1750s, the *Gentleman's Magazine* averaged ten songs a year. Imported copies of plays, purchased by members of the gentility, also supplied texts and sometimes music of the London hits.

Eventually the demand for printed lyrics and music grew sufficiently large to create a market for songsters, books devoted entirely to collecting popular ballads, theatrical songs, lyrics, catches, and merry ditties, and in 1795 in Philadelphia, a periodical, *The Songster's Magazine.* As with virtually every category of literary composition, the song lyric developed an increasingly ramified sense of the social circumstance of use. By century's end, songbooks were marketed to specific audiences with particular needs: *Songs and Lullabies of the Good Old Nurses* (1799), *Songs for the Amusement of Children* (1790), *Songs, Naval and Military* (1779), *The Merry Companion* (1798), and *The Patriotic Medley* (1800).

Convivial wit had its life in the face-to-face encounters of people in society, yet printing increasingly supplied a stock of jests, anecdotes, riddles, tales, and table talk for use in conversation. Again, the theater, particularly Restoration comedy, generated models for sociable wit and witticisms. Among the colonial gentility a distinction began to be made around 1700 between jest (a coarser, lower sort of humor, suited to masculine company) and wit (a memorable and ingenious fitting of language to thought, suitable for repetition in mixed company). Henry Brooke, upon his arrival in Pennsylvania in 1702, made the development of a literary culture of wit his principal task.[76] In Enoch Story's inn in Philadelphia, the tavern at Newcastle, and Cartridge's coffeehouse, Brooke in speech and poems "writ in company" demonstrated the politeness and ingenuity of wit while militating in works like "A Discours Upon Jesting" against the crudity of low humor. Though his campaign did not halt the dependence of masculine conversation upon jokes and jests (as the ample literature of jestbooks attests), it envisaged a new public in the city taverns and coffeehouses. He pioneered a style of polite conversation in public places that was inviting to women. Indeed, Brooke was distinctive in Pennsylvania for seeking to incorporate women into the exchange of wit and sense.

"Politeness," as the historian Lawrence Klein has indicated, was a discursive and behavioral mode designed for heterosocial arenas.[77] In England it had consolidated itself in the penumbra of private society around the royal court and in the spas. Neither court nor spa existed in America, so the creation of polite society, polite manners, polite conversation, and polite letters consolidated when and where it found champions: sometimes around the demi-courts of colonial governors (such as Sir William Keith), or in city taverns (such as Gignilliat's Long Room in Charleston) and assembly rooms, or in the parlor society of merchant families. It was this last that saw the emergence of the two principal institutions of women's literary conversation, the tea table and the salon.

Both institutions had become consolidated in European metropolises and in the republic of letters by the end of the seventeenth century. In Britain, the tea table became particularly associated with the formation of a women's sphere and the articulation of women's opinion. By the 1690s, when the quarrel of the sexes became one of the cultural crises promoted by Grub Street, female opinion was typically represented as emanating from London's tea tables. Indeed, the decade's great summary refutation of masculine slanders, *The Challenge* (1697), presented itself as a systematic effort by the network of metropolitan tea tables to answer by letter every point of contention in the quarrel, topics having been assigned to certain circles for discussion and composition.[78]

Grub Street recognized that a women's interest had become sufficiently organized to constitute a discrete market. Titles began to appear addressed exclusively to ladies. Spearheading this initiative was John Dunton, recently returned from New England. Having been impressed with the literacy and character of New England's women, he paid metropolitan women the respect of preparing for them *The Women's Dictionary* (1694), the first lexicon recognizing women's distinctive placement in language. Thereafter books, magazines (most notably the *Female Spectator*), manuals, and even the occasional almanac spoke to a generalized women's audience. These materials were often written by men in an effort to discipline female behavior. Against this literature for females sounded the opinion generated by the tea table.[79] Indeed, the most eloquent of English women's vehicles of opinion was Eliza Haywood's 1724 essay series, entitled *The Tea Table.*

In the major port cities of British America the tea table was well established as a cultural force by the 1720s. It became the center for the assertion of a feminine interest defined by a consumerism tied to metropolitan fashion, a will to project women's presence in public places such as courtrooms, inns, gardens, and wharves, and a exercise of judgment over the reputations of persons in society, enforced by the dissemination of scandal and gossip.[80] As a discursive institution, it was more oral than literary, although it did give rise to one scribal masterwork, the journal of Sarah Kemble Knight composed for and read to her circle in Boston, and a scattering of printed defenses against male censures floated in newspapers.[81] In Boston, New York, Philadelphia, and Charleston, periodicals debated the cultural meaning of the tea table. Often the rhetoric of a crisis between the sexes (borrowed from the 1690s Grub-Street exchanges) pervaded these discussions, creating a social sensation designed to sell papers. The *New-England Courant*, for instance, made tea-table manners one of the controversies that tweaked sales during the early 1720s.[82] More than inoculation, the Yale apostasy, the abilities of Harvard scholars, and the machinations of the government, the tea-table squibs appealed to a women's readership.

The tea table's association with gossip and surface made it a controversial institution among women. For one thing, it made the participation of men in the conversation a problem, for the persons attracted to the tea table tended to be creatures of surface – fops, would-be beaux, and lovers of scandal. Typical of the superficial masculine types obtruding on the notice of the tea-table set was the facetious beau who in 1754 addressed an open letter to Charleston's tea tables, desiring "to see the Ladies of Charles-Town walking the Streets, without concealing the Charms of a fine Countenance under a sable Mask. However, should Fashion, a Fear of being thought singular, or any other Motive, induce a Lady to appear with a Mask, let it rather serve to adorn her Hand than to conceal the Beauties of her Face."[83] No profound philosopher, he. A counterideal of polite conversation to tea-table gossip was projected by Elizabeth Magawley in Philadelphia, Jane Turell in Boston, and Abigail Coxe in New Jersey: Sense rather than scandal should be the predominating mood of conversation.[84] Sensibility rather than malice should inform fellow-feeling. These female champions of sense and sensibility also favored written over oral communication on the theory that the cultivation of sense depended upon the inquiry into durable truths, matters worthy of preservation in writing.

During the 1750s, elite women in British America began organizing salons. The salon was a heterosocial coterie that met in the home of a hostess who superintended the conversation. The more literary of the salons – those of Annis Boudinot Stockton at Morven in Princeton, Elizabeth Graeme Fergusson at Graeme Park in Horsham north of Philadelphia, Hannah Simons Dale at Daughterdale in Charleston – operated according to the literary conventions of the aristocratic court culture, adopting neoclassical nicknames and exchanging verses, familiar letters, and journals.[85] The bulk of literary production circulated in manuscript. Until the 1780s, members of the salon world published items in print only occasionally. Of the 120 surviving poems of Annis Boudinot Stockton ("Emelia"; Fig. 13.3), Carla Mulford has discovered printed versions of 21.[86] Two appeared in the 1750s, one in the 1760s, one in the 1770s, thirteen in the 1780s, and four in the 1790s. Mrs. Stockton was distinctive for the frequency of her appearance in print.

It is instructive to consider Stockton's career in print. With the exception of an elegy appended to Samuel Stanhope Smith's funeral sermon for her husband, Richard Stockton, the poems appeared exclusively in magazines or newspapers.[87] In two instances the publications may be fugitive; a recipient of

Figure 13.3. "Annis Boudinot Stockton" (1736–1801), by an anonymous American painter. Courtesy of the Princeton University Art Museum; gift of Mr. and Mrs. Landon K. Thorne, for the Boudinot Collection.

a manuscript may have forwarded it to an editor who printed it without the author's permission. In every other instance, Stockton appears to have put pieces in the hands of editors whom she favored – Samuel Nevill of *The New American Magazine*, James Trenchard of *The Columbian Magazine*, Mathew Carey of *The American Museum*, David Austin of *The Christian's, Scholar's and Farmer's Magazine* – for several pieces appear in series in a given periodical.

Her most significant projection into print were four poems printed in the *Gazette of the United States*, the newspaper of record for the Washington administration. Her ode "To the President of the United States" (*Gazette,* May 13, 1789), and "The Vision," an ode "inscribed to General Washington, a short time after the surrender of York-Town," were the most conspicuous attempts by the literary organ of state to project a mystique about Washington along the lines of traditional court odes. The officiousness of these public poems provoked the ire of radical republicans, who saw the trappings of monarchy being draped upon Washington. The *National Gazette*, organ of the Jeffersonian democratic-republicans, inaugurated a campaign against birthday odes and ceremonies, linking them with titles, Alexander Hamilton's formation of a national bank, and Martha Washington's levees.

In truth, Stockton's renovation in print of the old music of court panegyric to a new governmental circumstance was a much more baldly public project than that engineered by Martha Washington in her "Republican Court." Martha Washington's continental network of salons radiating from her Friday-evening drawing room maintained the oral bias of private society.[88] The Republican Court came into being to institute a practice of polite conversation flexible enough to enable social civility around the new national government. It hybridized a new continental style of urbane social conduct that married the manners of European gentility with the morals of post-Revolutionary American republicanism.[89]

Stockton in 1789 had hosted a salon for more than thirty years and had herself presided over governmental society when Congress and President Elias Boudinot came to Princeton in 1783. She knew intimately the powers and limitations of a discursive culture based on sociability. Her venture into the world of print in the pages of a newspaper that aspired to a continental readership and conveyed the authority of state was a calculated projection of her woman's voice into the new discursive space opened up by nationhood. The price of her venture was the derision of male critics and politicians. The projection of an officious, courtly, genteel female voice into public challenged the increasingly uncivil and sensationalist writing of the press. It was not a challenge many women were willing to undertake. Stockton, however, possessed the worldliness, the familiarity with public life, the verbal fluency, and the zeal to enter the lists. Her final public poem, "Impromptu on Reading the Several Motions Made against Mr. Hamilton," attempted to seize the rhetoric of patriotism both for women and for the Federalist cause. In a headnote she disavowed a political program: "I am no politician, but I *feel* that I am a patriot, and glory in that sensation."[90] Even republican ideology allowed that patriotism was a passion worthy of feminine cultivation. Patriotism, like piety and domesticity, were terms of such broad scope that they permitted much in their name. Federalist culture did not find politeness and patriotism inimical. Women could avow both in public.

At the same time Stockton was being installed as the Washington administration's volunteer laureate in the pages of the *Gazette of the United States*, Philip Freneau, the poet/editor of the *National Gazette*, made himself into the nation's antilaureate. Whereas Stockton used that crucial device of early modern patriotism, a national myth linked to the person of the leader, and projected it through a central authoritative medium as the means of promulgating a national spirit, Freneau nominated another figure as the central person cementing national culture, "The Country Printer." Freneau vested this figure with no mystique. He was not the noble leader, national savior, political genius, cultural father:

> Fame says he is an odd and curious wight,
> Fond to distraction of this native place
> In sense not very dull nor very bright,
> Yet shows some marks of humour in his face
> One who can pen an anecdote, complete,
> Or plague the parson with the mackled sheet.[91]

The printer's village newspaper was the glue that bound the locals to the world. Gleaned from the thrice-weekly stagecoach stops, news "welcome alike from Christians, Turks, or Jews" made the world a theater of sensation, telling of "Monarchs run away; / And now, of witches drown'd in Buzzard's bay." In the 1790s back country of the United States, news was still very much tidings of the world of wonder that it was at the beginning of the eighteenth century.[92]

If facts and fanciful prodigies intermingled in rural news, this did not gainsay its value or the importance of the printer as a cultural agent. His press, according to Freneau, stirred the town during the Revolution and educated the countryside in their rights. In the post-Revolutionary era, the village paper was the material register of the workings of the country, connecting the represented to the representative, the governed to the governor.

Freneau's portrait of a country printer was well observed. Though an editor in the nation's metropolis at the time of the poem's composition, he had the broadest experience of conditions in the western hemisphere of any writer or publisher in the early republic. His periodic ventures as a merchant and ship captain had taken him from Maine to the Indies, from the Carolina backcountry to the great cities of the continent.[93] He was the first American author to turn his back completely on the literary culture of sociability and conduct his entire communication with readers through the medium of print. His commercial experience disposed him to see the tides of taste in terms of the working of markets. In a meditation on the country printer's types, he noted that at one time they had printed "Erskine's *Gospel Treat*, / Tom Durfey's songs, and Bunyan's works complete." But times have changed, and "from this press no courtly stuff is read / But almanacks and ballads for the Squire, / Dull paragraphs in homely language dress'd / The pedlar's bill, and sermons by request." The uncourtly staples of the country printer's trade in the 1790s were, of course, the basic business for most job printers throughout the provincial era. Courtly belles lettres circulated in manuscript, while almanacs, newspapers, printed forms, ballads, and sermons were the stuff of print.

Freneau's country printer was a writer, generating grist for his newspaper and copy for his almanac. The printer as man or woman of letters was an eighteenth-century possibility. Yet a capable printer was a busy person, and to the extent he could enlist others to provide material, the greater the advantage to the printer. The more an imprint depended upon market differentiation to attract buyers, the more literary or technical skill mattered. The case of almanacs is instructive. The minimal almanac – the "sheet almanacs" printed in January for display in public houses and shops – needed only clarity of design to be competitive. Regular almanacs needed more – the mystique of the Man-of-Signs, tables of court days, useful essays, chronologies, proverbs, prophecies, recipes, or verses that gave an imprint an extra edge in the market.[94] Literary skill by the 1720s mattered. When Aquila Rose was establishing himself as the court poet of Pennsylvania, his friend and club companion, Jacob Taylor, was the most widely read poet of the province, for his almanac brought his art before the broadest regular readership to be had in North America.[95]

In a competitive market, literary skill mattered, especially when accurate astronomical calculations became commonplace. In "The Diarists," a Philadelphia satirist of 1735 (perhaps Elizabeth Magawley or Joseph Norris) critiqued the regional almanacs and their makers, including Benjamin Franklin, whose *Poor Richard's Almanack* had just premiered. This heretofore unremarked poem is the most important comment upon market competition, the circumstances of authorship, and the "most popular of prints" that survives from the early eighteenth century. In 211 lines the critic differentiated among the abilities in calculation, mystification, prose, and verse of Jacob Taylor, Daniel Leeds, John Jerman, Benjamin Eastbourn, Thomas Godfrey, Sr., Titan Leeds, and John Hughes.

Of Benjamin Franklin's entry into the lists the satirist observed,

> But who could be so mad to think,
> A Printer should appear in Print,
> And so much Sense and Judgment lack
> To write himself an Almanack;
> And should attempt to be, Jove bless us!

A mungril Son of bald Pernassus?
Perhaps he thought the Artists dead,
And knowing well they scarce had Bread;
What by Experience he hath found,
'Twas treading on forbidden Ground:
And since he found he could not please,
Hath left himself and World at ease:
And will, e're write another Page,
I hope, turn [Andrew] on a Stage.[96]

The satirist's wish, of course, proved futile. The printer proved to be the greatest almanac-maker of all, and precisely because he had a theatrical sense of character and the world.

Franklin's adoption of personae was a metropolitan strategy for attracting notice. A truism of Grub-Street practice was that persons whose livelihood most depended on print sales needed the flexibility of numbers of persons through which to speak. Multiple pseudonyms (as opposed to the single pen-names that belletrists employed in the sociable world) graced the works of journalists in print. Among eighteenth-century American almanac-makers, pseudonymity followed English patterns, with "Bickerstaff," "Father Abraham," and "Timothy Trueman," folk figures of English print culture, making transatlantic appearances. The favorite borrowed persona was that of the "poor" man – a demotic everyman whose common sense and ordinary travails rendered him both sympathetic and comic. Poor Robin was the English ancestor, with Poor Richard Saunders, Poor Will (William Birkett), the American Poor Robin (James Franklin, Sr.), Poor Job (James Franklin, Jr.), and Poor Roger More, who later transmogrified into Poor Thomas More.[97] The only indigenous front for an almanac was "Father Tammany," Father Abraham's Indian counterpart, whose legend emerged out of the mock-myths of the Philadelphia fishing companies.

"Diarists" who could afford the vanity of publishing under their own name usually had a calling that did not depend on vending publications. Daniel Leeds and John Jerman were farmers, Thomas Godfrey a glazer, Jacob Taylor, Benjamin Eastbourn, and John Hughes surveyors. Of other famous almanac-makers Nathaniel Ames was a physician and tavern-keeper, Nathaniel Low a physician, Benjamin West a college professor of mathematics at Brown, Nehemiah Strong a professor of mathematics at Yale, and Benjamin Banneker a farmer.[98] All shared a philomathic talent for calculation. To varying degrees they possessed some of the other arts that made up a man of parts. There were until very late in the century no "female" almanacs, though women were regularly addressed in essays, verses, and moral sentences beginning at midcentury.[99]

Besides almanacs, ballads, and printed forms, the staple of the country printer was the sermon "by request." Underwritten by a congregation, society, militia, or well-heeled parishioner, request sermons constituted a shadow subscription market, minimizing the risk of financial loss for the publication. Recent inquiries into the social history of reading have made much about the organization of reading circles, social libraries, and magazine clubs in the latter half of the eighteenth century.[100] Yet all of these came after the several sorts of groups which sponsored the printing of "sermons by request." The requesting body had usually heard the text performed orally. Particularly in New England, as we have seen, provincial councils, ministerial associations, militia companies, congregations, relations of the departed, or Masonic lodges might print the performance that enlightened or comforted them.[101]

The forms and rhetorics of occasional sermons were highly formalized because they were tied to established social rites – election days, civic fasts, militia musters, ordinations, funerals, St. John's day celebrations. An audience rewarded performances that fulfilled or exceeded its expectation. The performers to some extent were interchangeable. As long as the speaker/writer was a minister of good standing in theological harmony with the group being addressed, he would serve. Speakers at annual events were rotated. A minister spoke in his official capacity, so his name and pulpit appeared on the title page. If the artillery company sermon one year proved substandard, it would not be printed. If it roused the Christian militancy of the assembly, it was. Certain ministers became virtuosi at occasional sermonizing. Reverend Jason Haven (1733–1803) of Massachusetts was a specialist, having published by request a round robin of sermons delivered before the governor, the artillery company, ordination ceremonies for three ministers, a funeral, special occasions at Dedham, Stoughton, Needham and Boston, and a day of thanksgiving for the colony. He was also favored with a request to publish by that less public form of Christian community, the "religious society" or "private meeting," the eighteenth-century form of conventicle.[102] This institution arguably prompted the greatest creative flowering of Christian literature in the colonial era.

Whereas the conventicle was a heterosocial gathering of Christians who lived in proximity with one another and often belonged to the same congregation, the newer form of private gathering, which Cotton Mather named "religious meetings," were further discriminated by age, gender, race, and sometimes profession.[103] While young men's prayer meetings were not unusual at Harvard or the English colleges throughout the seventeenth century, by the 1680s in Massachusetts and Connecticut they had begun to form outside of the academy. Shortly thereafter, all-women meetings came into existence. In his diary for 1706, Cotton Mather noted, "It may be, I am the only Man in the World, that has preached unto such an Auditory."[104]

That the organization of Christian sociability underwent a gender segregation at the same time the coffeehouse and tea table had enacted a similar separation in society at large is a matter of historical interest. The change was registered in an increase in sermons and discourses directed at young men and young women as separate audiences.[105]

Like the secular sodalities in the metropolis, Christian meetings began to be organized in terms of shared interests. The emergence of singing circles, promoted by Thomas Walter and the champions of the new hymnody of the early 1720s, should be understood as a development out of conventicle practice into the new social forms of the eighteenth century.[106] One danger of the meetings was their tendency to concentrate on matters peculiar to a group, drawing them away from a general orthodoxy. For this reason spokesmen for orthodoxies felt a particular need to regulate the new forms. Cotton Mather, cognizant of the institutional transformation taking place around him, attempted to legislate the change, publishing shortly after his visit to the women's prayer group, *Private Meetings Animated and Regulated* (Boston, 1706). Another difficulty lay in the attraction of the meetings to the culture of pleasure encouraged in institutions of secular sociability. Benjamin Colman's *The Government and Improvement of Mirth* (Boston, 1707) sought to forestall in Boston the creation of a society grounded upon wit. Nevertheless, there were advantages in the new forms of organization and the new emphasis upon particular projects. Sectarian division might be overcome in groups more intent on performing a good work than on debating the theological reasons behind it. Mather's *Bonifacius* celebrated the work of "reforming societies" – circles that organized for the suppression of disorders in public. First formed in London during the 1690s by "[v]irtuous men of diverse qualities and persuasions" – "Persons High and low, Con and Non con" – they checked profanity and incivility in the workplace, places of resort, and the street. "The report of the societies flew over the seas; the pattern was followed in other Countries." Mather's sometime rival, Benjamin Colman, joined him in promoting the cause, preaching in 1716 *A Sermon for the Reformation of Manners*. Their willingness to see the performance of good works in society as gracious, regardless of their theological rationale, opened up a space in British-American Christian culture for benevolism. The world of charitable societies, abolitionist circles, humane societies, and societies for encouraging industry and employing the poor exfoliated from practical Christianity's concern with reform.

Among the cosmopolitan holders of pulpits in the coastal cities of British America, an appreciation of the ecumenical potentials of reformed societies developed. Some recognized the cultural development as an antidote to the pathology of Protestantism – schism. In British America, schism remained a problem; the political and cultural circumstances promoted the impulse of bands of Christians to conceive of themselves as the saving remnant. At the same time that some were reaching across denominational boundaries to form communities committed to projects of good will, others indulged the ancient impulse to set up independent fellowships possessing an exclusive revelation of God's plan. Christian reform during the eighteenth century ramified into an aggregate of sects, denominations, and societies.

Denominationalism – the coexistence of a variety of distinct religious societies, each claiming comprehensive authority, each possessed of a confession, a distinct ecclesiology, doctrine, and religious practice – developed when sectarianism operated in political spaces that had legislated tolerance. Not every colony in British America legislated tolerance, so denominationalism came into being first in those settlements that made tolerance an enticement to come over: Rhode Island, Pennsylvania, Maryland, South Carolina, and Georgia. Toleration begat competition, and a controversial literature pitting doctrine against doctrine, rite against rite. This controversial literature can be analyzed rhetorically in terms of audience. One body of writings was addressed primarily to one's sect, confirming members in their faith and practice; rival tenets and practices were treated derisively, as ludicrous superstitions or as expressions of human vanity. The vast Reformation literature of anti-Catholicism was ancestor to such discourse. Dissenting satires on the Church of England were a more immediate progenitor. A second body of writings addressed adherents to rival creeds and sought to show them the error of their ways. The bulk of the publications of Baptist Isaac Backus and Calvinist Samuel Hopkins took this tack.[107] Admonitions alternated with avowals of love and concern. A third body of writings spoke "rationally" to a general Christian public, seeking truths and principles recognizable to all who confessed Jesus as Savior. This antisectarian rhetoric of "rational Christianity" would become the discursive marker of Deism and can also be seen in the work of Anglicans such as Reverend Samuel Johnson and Provost William Smith in Pennsylvania.[108]

The evangelical movement may be defined culturally in terms of manners. Evangelicalism understood the work of reformation as a spiritual regeneration that inspirited the manners of society with piety. Evangelicalism attacked polite manners and polite Christianity (the latitudinarian Episcopacy of the Yale apostates and cosmopolitan congregationalism of Reverend Mather Byles and Reverend John Adams) as worldliness. It denied the polite understanding of the reformation of manners as the spread of civil graces through the beau monde. Those who in the name of politeness gave themselves over to the vainglory of fashionable display, the levity of wit, the consumption of luxurious goods, and the idleness of dancing and gaming, were confronted with the terrors of divine judgment. Gilbert Tennent and Samuel Finley were the most caustic of the beau monde's judges; even George Whitefield indulged in attacks on ballroom dancing in Charleston.

In effect, the evangelical reformation of manners challenged the ethic established by the governing classes and gentilities of the colonies, declaring that the empire was providing the civilizing "arts of peace" and the material wealth of a global empire of the seas. Such a confrontation of polite worldliness and pious other-worldliness was ensured the widest sort of literate interest because the great constituencies of written culture were involved: the "people of the book," colonial civil servants, merchants, elite women, and tradesmen. Every vehicle of communication was enlisted in the contest, including the innovations in publicity that James Oglethorpe had worked out in the campaign to reform English prisons in the 1720s and that he and Benjamin Martyn fine-tuned in the Georgia colonization project. Newspaper campaigns, correspondence networks, orations at mass meetings, the creation of cults of personality about principal figures, the use of verse and song to support the cause, the cultivation of a utopian discourse, the repeated appeals to the public – all became armaments in revivalist publicity.

This publicity resembled earlier modes of Christian reform in that it was transatlantic and operated through oral, manuscript, and printed media. What was novel about the literary activity of the revival was its expansion of print vehicles. Its champions published the first religious periodical in British America, Thomas Prince, Jr.'s *The Christian History* in 104 issues from March 5, 1743 to February 23, 1745. It greatly popularized spiritual diary-keeping, as exemplified in the best-seller that Jonathan Edwards constructed from the diary of David Brainerd, *An Account of the Life of David Brainerd* (Boston, 1749). Whitefield's *Journals*, published by Franklin, adapted a form associated peculiarly with the Quakers and made it a general characteristic writing of itinerant evangelists, such as James MacSparran and Robert Rose.

The revivals expanded a Christian women's literary culture that had been forming since the emergence of the women's prayer meetings in the 1690s. The Old Light critique of female emotionalism at revival meetings made women's reception of evangelical discourse a matter of controversy. The networks of women's prayer meetings supplied a feminine community where an evangelical solidarity might be expressed. On a regional basis, at least, an exchange of manuscript diaries, letters, and notes took place. It is difficult to determine the scope and influence of these communications. Isolated texts, such as Esther Edwards Burr's letter-diary prepared at Princeton for Sarah Prince and the women's prayer meeting at Old South Church in Boston, suggest the mechanisms by which women's opinion was formed in discursive institutions other than the tea table and the salon. Burr's manuscript was understood by both its writer and its reader as a public document. Other letters to Sarah Prince, which they called "privacies," were periodically burnt,[109] though Burr briefly considered printing them, before Prince forbade it. As the editors of Burr's journal have argued, a powerful precedent for printing the epistolatory communication of a group of Christian women was Elizabeth Singer Rowe's *Letters, Moral and Entertaining, in Prose and Verse* (London, 1729–1733).

A distinctive feature of evangelical women's literary culture is evident in Burr's diary, the explicit interest in polite letters. Burr and Prince savored Richardson's novels. They employed neoclassical pen-names during moments of playfulness. The young poetess Annis Boudinot was welcomed into their network. Burr cherished the engaging and sociable character of politeness, yet knew that it permitted a worldly-mindedness and obsession with surface that tainted tea-table society: "This day had a company of young Ladies from Trenton to dine and drink Tea – poor vain young creatures as stupid as horses. It would be casting Pirls before swine to say any thing about relegion before them." To enable religion, morality, and entertainment to concurrently enliven social intercourse was the discursive project of these women. The project differed from the polite Christianity championed by the Old Lights Mather Byles and Reverend John Adams in its foreclosure of wit from the conversation. It differed from the rigorism of masculine evangelicals typified in the diary in the character of "Mr. [John] Ewing," a tutor at the College of New Jersey, and later Provost of the College of Pennsylvania. "Speaking of Miss Boudanot I said she was a sociable friendly creature. A Gentleman seting by joined with me, But Mr Ewings says – she and the Stocktons are full of talk about Friendship and society and such stuff – and made up a Mouth as if much disgusted. . . . He did not think women knew what Friendship was." Attacks on the pleasure-seeking of the beau monde moved easily in the thought of the Mr. Ewings of British America to justifications for restricting women to the domestic roles prescribed in the Book of Proverbs, and for denying them access to public spaces, learning, and the pleasures of society.

In one instance, evangelical women's culture and the transatlantic networks of Reformed Christian publicity converged: in the publication and promotion on the eve of the Revolution of Phillis Wheatley's *Poems on Various Subjects, Religious and Moral* (London, 1773) (Fig. 13.4). The role of the Countess of Huntingdon (a central cog in the transatlantic evangelical community) in bringing forth Wheatley's poetry is recognized in the volume's dedication. Wheatley's celebration of politeness, the power of the imagination, and Reformed Christianity marked her art as an analogue

Figure 13.4. Frontispiece portrait of Phillis Wheatley, in her *Poems on Various Subjects* (London: Printed by A. Bell, and sold by Messrs. Cox and Berry, Boston, 1773): visible "proof" of a seven-day wonder, a black woman writing (the printer added an affidavit from her Boston master, attesting her authorship). American Antiquarian Society.

to that of Esther Edwards Burr, Annis Boudinot Stockton, and Hannah Griffitts.

Burr's diary and Stockton's poetry alert us to the existence of a civic sorority, a discursive community of women that understood its literary transactions to be public well before the American Revolution. Recent scholarship reveals that this civic sorority articulated its identity and interests in manuscript, in letters, journals, and poetry. It promoted an ideology similar to that of the English bluestockings – that is, it championed sense over wit, sensibility over unfeeling judgment. It sought the improvement of manners, the formulation of a style of civic probity. Friendship and Society, Religion and Philanthropy comprised its ethic. It sought to construe feminine domesticity in such a way that it did not preclude access to public arenas. By the Revolution the writings of certain women in the Delaware Valley – Susanna Wright, Elizabeth Graeme Fergusson, Sarah Morehead, Eliza Powel, Annis Boudinot Stockton, and Hannah Griffitts had gained wide currency in manuscript. The commonplace book of Milcah Moore is one repository of this American women's literature.[110] These women and their project should be considered the grounds upon which the Republican Court and other experiments drew in forming a women's cultural domain in the early republic.

The growth of schools and the formalization of readerships were two important conditions permitting the expansion of print markets. School texts had long been staples of the book trade. The great innovation of marketing in the eighteenth century was preparing works for the various arenas of private society that came into being throughout colonial America. The model for this development lay in the specialized publishing that grew up around law and medicine in the sixteenth century, and trade in the seventeenth. Late in the seventeenth century the metropolitan coffeehouses further articulated communities of interest that would be served – groups interested in natural history, politics, antiquities, agriculture, manufactures (the *Tatler's* organization of its intelligence in terms of the specialties of various coffeehouses mirrored the development.) Certain of these communities of interest formalized their identities, becoming chartered societies or corporations. Others remained private societies predicated on the performance of public projects. Others formed gentlemen's clubs, sodalities that maintained an in-camera exclusivity in order to protect a liberty of conversation. We have already seen how the coffeehouse was the cultural space in which a public opinion independent of state management emerged. It also was the venue for the creation of many of the discursive institutions of the British empire.

Because of the coffeehouse's association with commerce, it was the haunt of persons engaged in the business of trade – ship captains, merchants, jobbers, factors, tradesmen, placemen, and planters. Every major port city in the empire had its coffeehouse or "exchange tavern." Because the ship captains carried the transatlantic mail and bore the latest intelligence from the recent stops on their itineraries, the coffeehouses became the center for the latest news. They formed the distribution nodes of the imperial postal system (so much so that persons maintained postboxes at coffeehouses– in effect, their business addresses). They also constituted both the reception and dissemination point of news.[111]

The need to insulate one's liberty to form opinions about state and church drove the institutionalization of friendly society within the coffeehouse.[112] Rules insured the secrecy of conversation, the integrity and exclusivity of the membership, and the liberty of expression. The privacy of private society insured that it could communicate with great honesty; as Shaftesbury had declared, the refinement of thought required a conversation in which ideas had to withstand the clash of untrammeled opinion; indeed of "total raillery."[113] The exhilaration of such liberty became in itself an end of communication. Some of the most extravagant, audacious, and unaccountable works of British American literature were club writings meant for the delectation of the select brotherhood (Fig. 13.5). Dr. Alexander Hamilton's History of the Ancient and Honorable Tuesday Club, the archives of the Schuylkill Fishing Company, and the Minute Books of the Homony Club burlesque the officious worlds of church and state with a humor and candor unmatched by anything then in print.[114] These are profoundly collaborative writings, expressing the consensus of a group of writers/speakers/actors.

Projecting societies, too, depended upon the privacy of their deliberations; a circle such as Franklin's Junto legislated practices of secrecy and mutual aid. Such groups had two modes of discourse: esoteric, for in-camera deliberations and the formulation of policy; and exoteric, for publishing abroad. From the 1720s national societies – the Sons of Saint Patrick, the St. Andrew's Societies, the Sons of St. George, St. David's Societies – formed in colonial metropolises to aid recent immigrants from the British Isles. Charitable bodies followed, such as the Planters' Society and the Winyah Indigo Society of South Carolina, designed for the support of local schools. By the end of the century a panoply of voluntary societies covered the continent, maintaining records, publishing constitutions, papers, advertisements, and debates. These include societies for the promotion of useful arts, antislavery societies, organizations for the relief of widows and orphans, social insurance clubs, agricultural reform groups, and even a "Society for Political Inquiries."[115]

One form of voluntary association has always been recognized as important to the formation of early American literary culture, the social library. Subscription clubs kept collections of books at a central locale available for the use of members. They were a town phenomenon, and an activity prosecuted by those classes of persons who saw literature as a means to improvement in society. Social libraries were not reading clubs so much as information depots and financial institutions that mitigated the cost of owning books. While their history, collections, and subscription practices cannot be

Figure 13.5. "Comedy or Club," and "The Comic orchestrum," an illustration by Dr. Alexander Hamilton in his *History of the Tuesday Club* [Ms., ca. 1752–1754], showing the role played by humor, appetite, and the arts in club life. Courtesy of The John Work Garrett Library of the Johns Hopkins University.

treated here, one point must be broached. Institutionally, the social and subscription libraries supplied what local conversation did not: classical texts, learning from the universities, professional treatises, law books, histories, travel narratives, approved European authors and critics, the fashionable London plays, and systematic or apologetic divinity. Matter from these books had to be vivified by being put into local discourse. Social libraries thus existed in a symbiotic relationship with other forms of private society where conversation reigned; subscribers held concurrent membership in multiple groups. The pattern of institutional doubling was widespread: The Library Company of Philadelphia with Franklin's Junto, the Redwood Library with Newport's "Society for the Promotion of Virtue by Free Conversation," the Charleston Library Society with the South Carolina Society, the New York Society Library with the King's College Club.

This portrait of literary culture in British America has emphasized the social organization of literary production and reception. I have suggested the variety and complexity of discursive institutions, and related their conduct to oral, manuscript, and printed modes of communication. An understanding of the performative world of the early American man of letters or *femme savante* aids in determining the rhetorical strategies of writings, the implied readerships found in texts, types of self-presentation (the use of pseudonyms, pen-names, titles, or proper names), and sheds light on various devices used by booksellers in marketing books and periodicals. I have taken care to discuss literature in the expansive manner of the eighteenth-century, not restricting it to belles lettres, and have attempted to touch on the cultural situation of the spiritual journal, familiar letter, witticism, satire, state ode, religious tract, denominational polemic, social song, news story, secretarial report, state instruction, club writing, neoclassical imitation, novel, and sermon. Following recent historians of the public sphere, the social spaces in which these forms operated are viewed in light of a range of discursive communities, not in light of a simple dichotomy of public and private. Indeed, a central point of this account is that the communication (whether oral, manuscript, or printed) of "private society" must be viewed as "publication." I have touched upon state schemes of patronage, the role of political oppositions, Christian denominations, conventicles, religious meetings, and a variety of forms of private society to give a preliminary sense of the institutional forces at play in literary culture. Given the emphasis here upon the conditions prevailing during the colonial era, I have not treated the question of the professionalization of the literary vocation. In British America, letters could support someone if it won him a patron and a place or franchise. Only after the Revolution could an anonymous readership of book or magazine purchasers supply sufficient income for someone to subsist upon.

Afterword

HUGH AMORY AND DAVID D. HALL

WARFARE WAS NOT GOOD FOR PRINTERS AND BOOKSELLERS, whose livelihoods after 1775 were disrupted by inflation, partisan pressures, shortages of paper, and the collapse of intercolonial and transatlantic trade.[1] The production of books fell in half during the second half of the seventies – from a peak, however, that had much to do with the rapid growth of newspapers and an explosion of proclamations, and other public documents (Graph 1B, Appendix 1). The fall in imported books was no less sharp. Yet stability was returning by the mid-1780s, production began to rise, especially in the number of newspapers, and the import trade resumed in full force (Figures 5.1 & 5.2). After independence no less than before, readers in the new republic continued to depend on books printed overseas for much of their reading matter. Colleges regrouped and began to rebuild their libraries, the American Philosophical Society managed to issue the second volume of its *Transactions* (1786), and though warfare and the collapse of the imperial establishment weakened denominations such as the Anglicans and ended their philanthropic outreach, others, like the Methodists, began to fashion a structure of conferences and ministries.

In this interim period before the adoption of the Constitution in 1789, the most important development was a movement in favor of copyright – though the native booktrade itself had little use for the law, since British properties were free for the taking, and few American titles were likely to be reprinted. The initiative for copyright was rather authorial, beginning in Connecticut with the petitions of the composers William Billings (1772) and Andrew Law (1781) for protection of their songbooks, but it was a petition to the state legislature from Noah Webster, a native son, requesting "a law to secure to me the copy-right" of his yet unpublished *Grammatical Institute*, that prompted the passage in January 1783 of a general "Act for the Encouragement of Literature and Genius." Declaring that "every Author should be secured in receiving the Profits that may arise from the Sale of his Works," the act specified that any author of an unpublished manuscript or map should have "the sole Liberty of printing, publishing and vending" it within the state for a period of fourteen years, renewable for another term of fourteen years, the same period allowed by the British copyright act of 1710. Well aware of fears of monopoly that John Milton, among others, had voiced in the seventeenth century, the Connecticut legislature added a provision that others might reprint a text if the original owner abused his privilege by setting too high a price on his work. Two months later, the Continental Congress passed a resolution authorizing a committee "to consider the most proper means of cherishing genius and useful arts through the United States by securing to the authors or publishers of new books their property in such books," and in May it endorsed the committee's recommendation that the states should grant authors or publishers a term of fourteen years, renewable once, for "any new books not hitherto printed." By the end of the eighties, nine states, including Connecticut, had enacted such laws, and in 1790 the national government followed suit, superseding the state acts and providing authors such as Webster – who had traveled from state to state seeking protection for his speller – nationwide security for their intellectual property. In contrast to British practice, where copyright originated in trade privileges, the federal law limited literary rights to native authors and residents in the United States. Even as late as 1820, booksellers rarely used the act except to protect schoolbooks and other frequently reprinted, commercially valuable titles.[2]

The distinctiveness of the 1790 statute prompts a larger question: did trade practices in a newly independent America vary from trade practices in Britain, or is the story essentially one of continuity? We want to address this question from two angles: first, by recalling the main lines of development within the trade during the decades leading up to 1776; and second, by comparing the distribution of subscribers to Robert Bell's edition of Blackstone's *Commentaries* (1771–1772) with the sources of the imprints listed in *A Catalogue of All the Books Printed in the United States* (Boston, 1804), the first American trade catalogue, compiled by the Boston bookseller Edward Cotton.

Looking back from the vantage of 1776, we can identify five structural features that had emerged by the mid-eighteenth century. The first, strongly emphasized by James N. Green (Chapter 8), is competition between printers in the same town once a second shop was opened. A second is the thickening of commercial connections between booksellers in London and those in the colonies, in keeping with the ever-enlarging market for imported books; hence the importance of Wells in Charleston, Hall in Philadelphia, Rivington in New York, and Condy and Knox in Boston. A third is the emergence of entrepreneurial publishing alongside the publications sponsored by civil governments, churches, denominations, and cultural or philanthropic agencies. A fourth is the regional and interregional wholesale trade that Franklin initiated through his partnerships and that the Boston printer–bookseller Daniel Henchman began to develop in the 1740s. A fifth is the singular growth in newspapers; as the sheet count at the end of Chapter 9 reveals (Table 9.1), newspapers had become the largest single item of production in the Boston trade by 1765, a trend that was accelerating throughout the colonies on the eve of the Revolution.

The timing of these developments varied from one region to the next, and some occurred by fits and starts; after all, competition of a kind in the New England trade dates back to the 1660s when the two Cambridge printers, Samuel Green and Marmaduke Johnson, contended against each other. These developments chiefly characterized the urban trade, not country or small-town printers and booksellers, since before the Revolution, most towns had but a single printer. Even among urban booksellers, few carried on a significant business in imports; as the Englishman Leman Thomas Rede noted in his 1789 survey of the American trade, "Northward of New York, there are [no importers] of any consequence – not even in Boston; or, southward of Baltimore; not even in Charlestown."[3] Developments were uneven, moreover, since production could vary abruptly and considerably, as in William Bradford's flurry of imprints growing out of the controversy prompted by George Keith, the short-lived boom in Whitefieldiana in Philadelphia and Boston in 1740, or the phenomenal reprintings of Paine's *Common Sense*. There were also short- and long-term phases within the imperial and colonial economies, and the scale of printing and bookselling between the South, on the one hand, and New England and the middle colonies, on the other, varied widely.

To think about these features in the context of British trade practices is to be reminded, once again, of the difference sketched in Chapter 1 between a "colonial" and a "provincial" relationship with England. By the mid-eighteenth century there was much about American printers and booksellers that made them seem near-twins of the trade between the English provinces and London. Yet there were also marked differences. The Americans thrived by ignoring the system of privileges or copyrights that stood at the very center of the London trade and its relations with provincial printers and booksellers. The irony is that American printers and booksellers rarely "pirated" each other's imprints, and that when they did – as with Nathaniel Ames, Jr.'s almanacs and Andrew Stewart's reprinting of Francis Hopkinson's *Science* (1762)[4] – the authors, not the booksellers, protested. The trade, indeed, had little use for authors like the popular schoolbook writer Jedidiah Morse, who insisted on cash for his labors instead of the customary fifty or a hundred "free" copies; Isaiah Thomas called them "Morseish," defined as someone who "loves money and knows how to get it." Instead of copyright, the trade preferred to rely on its customary "courtesies" by which, as in Ireland, overprinting a title that had already entered the market was deemed unethical.[5]

A second, related difference concerned editions of major literary figures. By the early eighteenth century, a literary canon had formed in England. The consequences for the book trade were twofold: certain literary properties appreciated in value, and the authoritative transmission of texts came to interest both writers and booksellers. No such canon emerged for colonial American writers – indeed, no such canon exists to this day. Consequently, no colonist could expect a premium for his or her writings, much less an authoritative edition, and piracy was pointless. A third, though again related, difference concerned censorship and regulation. The welter of political jurisdictions in the colonies, together with local factionalism and the relative weakness of the imperial establishment, meant that eighteenth-century Americans were relatively free to write and publish what they wished. This is not to deny the importance of self-censorship or of the partisanship of 1776, but the French Revolution was a veritable "revolution in print" because it swept away an elaborate system of state regulation, whereas the American had no such significance.[6] With their independent legislators and royally appointed governors, the model that the colonists rather emulated was the kingdom of Ireland – and perhaps they never felt more "provincial" than after they had left the empire.

Victory in the struggle for independence entailed, if not exactly censorship, certainly a kind of *damnatio memoriae*, seen to more advantage from a point of time beyond our period.[7] "America," once an imperial system extending from the Caribbean to Canada, now was silently appropriated to the United States. Booksellers in the 1790s aligned their Bibles with the Revolution by styling them the "First American" or even "First Worcester" edition and paraded the accuracy of their text and the sumptuousness of their format, paper, type, and illustrations, whereas the candles of the occasional pre-Revolutionary edition were hidden under bushels of false imprints. Noah Webster added to the many inconveniences of the Atlantic Ocean by changing the spelling of "English" and announcing that his mother tongue was "American." Before the Peace of Paris (1783), American readers of Isaac Watts's popular *Divine Songs* rejoiced that they were born on "British ground"; afterwards, on "Christian ground." At the request of the Congregational churches of Connecticut, Joel Barlow rewrote Watts's metrical version of the Psalms "to make them more adaptable to singing in the United States" by removing or revising analogies between Israel and Britain.[8]

The perspective on the colonial past after 1790 also had a positive aspect, however. Thus when Edward Cotton looked back upon our period in 1804, he could exult that "Twenty years since, scarcely a book was published" in the United States, by which he meant that American imprints had rarely been wholesaled outside of the city where they were printed, whereas by 1804, this practice was routine.[9] By his day, too, the center of the new nation's book trade had shifted from New England to the middle Atlantic states. Possibly Boston remained a stronger contender in terms of domestic production than New York, but Philadelphia outstripped them both in the 1790s. It was the Philadelphia booksellers who organized the earliest American trade fair (1801), and the innovative practices of their leading bookseller, the Irish-American Mathew Carey, stand in sharp contrast with the traditionalism of Isaiah Thomas.[10] In all three places, however, the texts of choice for reprinting were British.

Another kind of evidence is provided by a comparison of the distribution of the subscribers to Robert Bell's edition of Blackstone's *Commentaries* (Philadelphia, 1771–1772) with the imprints listed in Cotton's *Catalogue of All the Books Printed in the United States.*[11] Blackstone's *Commentaries* was preeminently a "book of general sale," the announced subject of Cotton's Boston *Catalogue*: he omits "local and occasional tracts," notably Latin, French, German, and Dutch titles (except for schoolbooks, grammars, and dictionaries), local laws (except for those of Massachusetts, of course), and sermons and controversial theology. Of the 707 "Miscellaneous" (but mostly literary) titles in his *Catalogue,* 502 were printed in Philadelphia (204), Boston (172), or New York (126); the remainder were distributed among forty-three places, among which only Albany (12), Baltimore (20), Exeter (New Hampshire) (10), Hartford (13), Newburyport (15), and Worcester (32) attained double-digit respectability. These imprints stretched along the Atlantic seaboard and up rivers, from Hallowell (Maine) to Norfolk and Petersburg (Virginia) and inland as far as Chambersburg (Pennsylvania), but distribution southwards was notably sparse. Bell's subscribers were far more widely scattered, from Bermuda, Dominica, and the British West Indies, to the Floridas and Nouvelle Orléans, to Nova Scotia, and Québec. He had substantial southern sales: 68 copies in North Carolina, 149 in South Carolina, and 177 in Virginia alone.

From a total of 1,587 copies, Bell sent only 65 to subscribers outside the future thirteen states, a sign, among others, that the mainland book trade with the West Indies remained quite modest. "Every gentleman [going to the West Indies] almost takes out his own library with him," Rede would note in 1789, "and what books may be wanted are generally sold in the store of merchants who import them from England with their other goods."[12] Still, Bell's list breathes the air of an extended empire and Cotton's *Cata-*

logue celebrates the unity and uniformity of a republic. What is most impressive is surely the absence of sectarian and ethnic minority interests among Cotton's books. Just as their technology encouraged the first printers in Europe to seek an international, Latin, religious market, so, in America, it forwarded the English language and secular European culture, the "books of general sale." Print culture is generalizing (like any mass medium), and one surprising consequence of American independence from the British Empire was to reinforce the anglicization of print that culturally was a strong feature of the pre-war decades.

One measure of this anglicization is the proliferation of American editions of British authors after the Revolution. Any count of such editions must wrestle with various bibliographical and historical criteria, and the checklist compiled by Samuel J. Rogal is inadequate in some respects, for he defines eighteenth-century "British literature" strictly (omitting, for example, Bunyan, Milton, and Southey), he includes editions attested only by advertisements or hearsay, and he omits many religious writers (e.g., James Hervey) and dramatists (e.g., Kane O'Hara) as well as hymnals and psalters such as Watts's *Divine Songs*. Corrected to omit Evans entries that may be advertisements of British exports, this checklist records 133 editions down to 1749, 163 from 1750–1774, and 982 in the final quarter of the century.[13]

Paradoxically, some post-Revolutionary authors blamed the trade's preference for British literature on the new copyright statutes, which made American properties more expensive. Not quite consistently, they also held that republican chic lay in anonymity and collaborative authorship, for which the obvious models were the United States Constitution and the *Federalist Papers*.[14] The new national scale of commerce in books also militated against the author's market, however. So long as the trade remained local, a single prestigious author like Cotton Mather might dominate it, but the wider post-colonial market diluted any single author's audience and relegated his production to the commercially less alluring "local and occasional tracts." The plight of the American author after the Revolution reflects, in a way, the maturation of the colonial trade.[15]

Nonetheless, for some friends of the United States, like Thomas Paine, the copyright laws were an important symbol of future greatness. In an essay of 1782 addressed to European intellectuals, Paine argued that "literature" flourished only when and where the rights of authors were protected.[16] We leave to Volume two in this series the outcome of Paine's prophecy, but for us it may serve as a closing reminder that trade practices reflect broader political and cultural factors. At the outset, we identified one of these as a deference to European high or cosmopolitan culture, a cultural cringe that, as we noted in the Introduction, has cast its long shadow over bibliography and book history almost to the present day. National independence heightened the ante, at least among the learned and the more cosmopolitan of literati; thus the poet Philip Freneau insisted in 1788 that "we [who] had spirit to humble a throne, / Have genius for science inferior to none." But Freneau also knew that independence did not automatically end the anglicization that had been so marked a feature of colonial culture before 1776: "Can we never be thought to have learning or grace / Unless it be brought from that horrible place / Where tyranny reigns with her impudent face[?]"[17]

For many Americans, the appropriate answer to Freneau's challenge continued to be some version of Protestantism, be it radical or mainstream, orthodox or moderate. Out of the Reformation had come frameworks of meaning for literacy, reading, writing, and printing, and the persistence of these frameworks – indeed their reinforcement via evangelical movements of the middle and late eighteenth century – is strongly evident in the titles that American booksellers chose most often to reprint and in the authors (most of them British Nonconformists, such as Isaac Watts) whose work remained the longest in print during the eighteenth century (Appendix 2). The high rate of literacy that had become social fact among white males and females in the northern and middle colonies by the time of the Revolution, and that John Adams had idealized in his *Dissertation on the Canon and Feudal Law*, was another legacy of Protestantism, as was the importance of the sermon in the larger universe of print (Appendix 1, Graph 5b).[18]

The ever-growing number and circulation of newspapers also underlines increasing popular participation in politics and an integration of regional separatism in an imperial and, later, national consciousness. On the eve of the Revolution, a contemporary attempted to explain to an English correspondent why the patriot cause was becoming so powerful among the colonists:

> They are a well-informed, reasoning commonalty, too, perhaps the most of any on earth, because of the free intercourse between man and man that prevails in America. Their free access to courts of law . . . ; their frequent and free elections, which give occasion for candidates to scan each other's principles and conduct before the tribunal of the people, together with the freedom and general circulation of newspapers, and the eagerness and leisure of the people to read them, or to listen to those who do.[19]

Here was literacy of an unusually participatory kind, which this observer linked with the structure of politics and, in turn, with a widely circulating form of print, the newspaper. One episode of great importance in the radicalization of the Revolutionary movement (though few at that very moment were thinking ahead to independence) was the extraordinary diffusion of the "Virginia Resolves" of 1765. On May 30, 1765, a divided House of

Burgesses passed four resolutions against the then-pending Stamp Act but rejected two or three others as too extreme. Joseph Royle, the only printer in Virginia, refused to publish the Resolves, but in faraway Rhode Island, the *Newport Mercury* printed six of them in its issue of June 24, whence they were copied by other newspapers up and down the coast, always in a manner that made it seem that the Virginians had asserted the "sole and exclusive Right and Power" to levy taxes on themselves. Elsewhere in the colonies, this challenge to the sovereignty of Parliament was promptly imitated by legislatures that thought they were merely repeating the Resolves.[20] That a single printed source could have so much effect – an effect far greater than that of the letters dispatched from Virginia recounting the Burgesses' action – dramatizes the impact of printing in general and of newspapers in particular to political movements in late eighteenth-century America, whether this consciousness operated in colonial assemblies or in mobs.

Still another network of connections was rooted in commerce. For merchants, artisans, clerks, and lawyers, printing was a utilitarian means of producing the quantity of forms, paper money, and statute laws on which commerce and credit depended. In the late seventeenth century, the Maryland Assembly had acknowledged the benefits of the newer technology in remarking on the confusion that prevailed "afore there was printing," and the author of the preface to *All the Laws of Maryland Now in Force* (1700) had reinforced this distinction in hailing their first printed collection of laws as a means of making them more widely known not only to magistrates and jurists but also to ordinary people.[21] The proliferation of handbooks addressed to young clerks or secretaries, together with the growth of newspaper advertisements, were other signs of how literacy and printing were becoming ever more utilitarian within the intersecting worlds of commerce and government.[22]

The relationship between print and culture in pre-Revolutionary America may also be cast in terms of political and social ideologies: "republicanism" or for some historians, a proto-democratic shattering of elitist hierarchies that, it has been argued, pervaded much of print culture in the pre-Revolutionary decades.[23] Within "republicanism," print took on the meaning of an instrument of "liberty," a means of making "public" the antilibertarian strategies of would-be tyrants. This conception is epitomized in the *Independent Reflector*, in the eventual fame of the Zenger affair, and in Thomas Hollis of Lincoln Inn's patronage of a "Library of Liberty."[24]

It must be said, however, that the details of the story we have told in *The Colonial Book in the Atlantic World* do not easily fit within the framework of democratization, for the contradictions are too many. Print represented *both* authority *and* nonconformity, the imperial center *and* the colonial periphery, the voice of the clergy *and* that of the laity, the loyalist *and* the revolutionary: how could it not, when all these different interests used it? The Boston mob and the Boston press worked through speech and print to oppose Thomas Hutchinson, and he used both to answer them; that characteristic colonial product, the sermon, was both oral *and* printed; manuscript, printing, *and* oral tradition combined in the construction of a colonial "literature" that was far more than the sum of its component "letters." Education both elementary and advanced involved not only manuscript commonplacing and printed texts, but also memorization and oral recitation. Thus, contrary to the prediction of Plato's wise Egyptian Thamus, writing did not make memory superfluous, any more than the computer has introduced a "paperless revolution" today. On the contrary, writing and, later, printing multiplied the number of things to remember, and the great Rococo librarian Antonio Magliabechi, who carried the entire catalogue of the Laurenziana and his own 30,000 volumes in his head, knew and remembered more than wise Thamus could ever have imagined.

All too often, the profile of the printer's twenty-six little lead soldiers outlines an oversimplified "typographic man" or returns, some twenty-two centuries after their invention, as yet another *nova stella* in the fixed firmament of a Gutenberg Galaxy; but the uses of print are far too complexly and deeply embedded in their time and culture for such technological (or even cultural) reductionism, as we have tried to show in this volume.

A Select Bibliography

HUGH AMORY

1. Generalities

For some of its most distinguished proponents, "the history of the book" has seemed to offer an escape from the sterile rigors of "bibliography" and the anal retentiveness of "rare book rooms." G. Thomas Tanselle's *The History of Books as a Field of Study* (Chapel Hill, N.C.: Hanes Foundation, 1981) offers a useful corrective to this misconception. In his otherwise valuable survey of the major scholarship, *A Bibliographic History of the Book: An Annotated Guide to the Literature* (Metuchen, N.J.: Scarecrow Press, 1995), Joseph Rosenblum omits the analysis and enumeration of the books themselves, on the one hand, and studies of authorship, reading and copyright on the other – a simplification perhaps imposed by limited space, but that poorly responds to the cross-disciplinary complexity of the field. Current work on the history of books and libraries is indexed through the annual *Bibliographie der Buch- und Bibliotheksgeschichte* (1982–), covering an international range of monographs, articles, and reviews in many languages each year. The chief Anglo-American journals concerned with the history and bibliography of early British America are the *Library* (1889–), *PBSA* (1904–), *SB* (1949–), *BNYPL* (1904–), *HLB* (1949–), *Procs. AAS* (1843–), and *WMQ* (1892–).

Isaiah Thomas's *History of Printing in America,* 2 vols. (Worcester, Mass. 1810) is still the single best introduction to the history of the early American book. His account of publications ends in 1775, but the biographies of printers and booksellers continue well beyond, and are of primary importance. The abridged edition by Marcus A. McCorison (1970; reprinted New York: Weathervane Books, [1975]), based on the corrected text of 1874, contains useful notes and corrections from later research; Rollo G. Silver's "Aprons instead of Uniforms: The Practice of Printing, 1776–1787," *Procs. AAS* 87 (1978): 111–94 fills out the remainder of our period.

An annual series of conferences edited by Robin Myers and Michael Harris (1979–) has done much to connect the minutiae of bibliographical investigation with wider cultural and historical concerns. Collections of essays specifically concerned with American book culture are *Printing and Society in Early America,* ed. William L. Joyce et al. (Worcester, Mass.: American Antiquarian Society (AAS), 1983), and *The Press and the American Revolution,* eds. Bernard Bailyn and John B. Hench (Worcester, Mass.: AAS, 1980); their contributions are not separately noticed in the following. The social and political position of colonial printing and bookselling in New York, Philadelphia, Boston, Newport, and Charleston is well described by Carl Bridenbaugh in his *Cities in the Wilderness: The First Century of Urban Life in America, 1625–1742* (New York: Ronald Press Co., 1938) and *Cities in Revolt: Urban Life in America, 1743–1776* (New York: Knopf, 1955); see also Stephen Botein, " 'Meer Mechanics' and an Open Press: The Business and Political Strategies of Colonial American Printers," *Perspectives in American History* 9 (1975): [125]–225, and, for urban artisans, Gary B. Nash, *The Urban Crucible: Social Change, Political Consciousness, and the Origins of the American Revolution* (Cambridge, Mass.: Harvard University Press, 1979), On the economic background, John J. McCusker and Russell R. Menard, *The Economy of British America, 1607–1789,* 2nd ed. (Chapel Hill: University of North Carolina Press, 1985; reprinted with supplementary bibliography, 1991), is the most authoritative recent treatment.

Bookselling remains a neglected subject: see James Gilreath, "American Book Distribution," *Procs. AAS* 95 (1985–86): 501–83, reviewing the literature. For special forms of publication, see Robert B. Winans, *A Descriptive Checklist of Book Catalogues Separately Printed in America, 1693–1800* (Worcester: AAS, 1981), and Donald Farren, "Subscription: A Study of the Eighteenth-Century American Book Trade" (D.L.S. thesis, Columbia University, 1982). Winans is preparing an index of newspaper advertisements that list five or more titles, and Farren is working on a bibliography of American imprints sold by retail subscription. The long-projected CD-ROM index to British subscription lists, in preparation by Professor F. J. G. Robinson at the University of Newcastle-upon-Tyne, will yield a harvest of colonial subscribers as well. The largest corpus of print published by subscription was, of course, newspapers.

The literature on imprints is superbly surveyed in G. Thomas Tanselle, *Guide to the Study of United States Imprints,* 2 vols. (Cambridge, Mass.: Belknap Press, 1971). The on-line North American Imprints Program (NAIP), accessible through the Internet, has superseded many of these inventories, particularly lists of a single printer's production or the imprints of a single city, which are only noticed here when they are part of more discursive accounts. At the level of a state or region, however, or even for a major city over any extended period, the material becomes too complex to consult efficiently on-line, and it is usually too abundant to be worth printing out. Editions of which no copy is known to survive and unique copies in private hands or in archives will usually not appear in NAIP but are often recorded in printed lists, moreover. For all these reasons, printed authorities should continue to be useful for research. Despite its title, NAIP does not cover Canadian imprints, and it does not include newspapers or periodicals.

For the British context of colonial printing, and for the identification of titles in colonial library catalogues and inventories, the best place to begin is the on-line union catalogue of ESTC, which ultimately aims to cover every monograph (i.e., any publication that is not a serial) printed in Great Britain and her colonial possessions, or in English anywhere, from 1474 to 1800. For an approach by subject and for the diffusion of colonial texts in Great Britain, the chronologically arranged compilation of R. C. Simmons, *British Imprints relating to North America, 1621–1760: An Annotated Checklist* (London: British Library, 1996) is based on the ESTC and may be more convenient to use. In his introduction, Simmons surveys the related printed reference works – STC, Wing, and *European Americana* – in which the researcher may broaden or deepen his or her inquiry; it will be quite a while before ESTC completely incorporates the data of these resources.

BIBLIOGRAPHIES

Evans, Charles. *American Bibliography,* 13 vols. Chicago: The author, 1903–1955 (completed by Clifford K. Shipton through 1800; with *Index* (v. 14, 1959) and *Supplement* (1970) by Roger P. Bristol. Evans includes newspapers and periodicals, excluded from Bristol).

Shipton, Clifford K., and James E. Mooney. *National Index of American Imprints through 1800: The Short-Title Evans*, 2 vols. [Worcester, Mass.]: AAS, 1969 (serves at once as a revision of Evans and Bristol, and as a guide to the monographs reproduced in the microform series, *Early American Imprints, 1639–1800*).

Tremaine, Marie. *A Bibliography of Canadian Imprints, 1751–1800*. Toronto: University of Toronto Press, 1952 (covers newspapers as well as monographs, with signature collations, and brief biographies of the printers; serves as a guide to the monographs reproduced in the microform series, *Canadian Imprints, 1751–1800*).

BIOGRAPHIES

Dzwonkoski, Peter, ed. *American Literary Publishing Houses, 1638–1899* (*Dictionary of Literary Biography,* vol. 49, pts. 1–2), 2 vols. Detroit, Mich.: Gale Research Co., 1986 (uneven, but often the only recent account).

NARRATIVE HISTORIES & DISCURSIVE BIBLIOGRAPHICAL ACCOUNTS

Bercovitch, Sacvan, ed. *The Cambridge History of American Literature,* Volume One: *1590–1820*. Cambridge: Cambridge University Press, 1994 (with an extensive list of literary and theoretical authorities).

Gaskell, Philip. *New Introduction to Bibliography,* 2nd impression, corr. New York: Oxford University Press, 1972 [i.e., 1974] (the best account of the technology).

Gundy, H. Pearson. *Canada* (The Spread of Printing: Western Hemisphere). Amsterdam: Van Gendt & Co., 1972.

Parker, George L. *The Beginnings of the Book Trade in Canada.* Toronto: University of Toronto, 1985, chap. 1.

Silver, Rollo G. *The American Printer, 1787–1825*. Charlottesville: University Press of Virginia, [1967] (a better-documented account of trade practices than Wroth).

Wroth, Lawrence, C. *Colonial Printer,* 2nd ed., rev. & enl. 1938; repr. Charlottesville, Va.: Dominion Books, 1964 (the classic account; covers the history of printing in the territory of the United States from the beginning to 1800. Wroth's chief source, Joseph Moxon's *Mechanick Exercises* (1677), described London practices that colonials may or may not have observed).

a. Copyright

Bugbee, Bruce Willis. *Genesis of American Patent and Copyright Law.* Washington, D.C.: Public Affairs Press, [1967].

Feather, John. *Publishing, Piracy and Politics: An Historical Study of Copyright in Britain.* London: Mansell, 1994.

Kaplan, Benjamin. *An Unhurried View of Copyright.* New York: Columbia University Press, 1967 (legal history; makes the vital point that copyright exists to protect publishers, not authors).

Rice, Grantland S. *The Transformation of Authorship in America.* Chicago: University of Chicago Press, 1997.

Wills, Elizabeth Carter, ed. *Federal Copyright Records, 1790–1800*, with introduction by James Gilreath. Washington, D.C.: Library of Congress, 1987.

Woodmansee, Martha, and Peter Jaszi, eds. *The Construction of Authorship: Textual Appropriation in Law and Literature.* Durham, N.C.: Duke University Press, 1994.

b. Bookbinding

Students of early bookbinding have tended to concentrate on the decoration of bindings rather than on their structure and function; hence they have provided more information on book ownership and ateliers than on trade history. The cost of books, their distribution, and the intellectual and social contexts in which they were read, however, were profoundly dependent on their binding.

French, Hannah Dustin. "Early American Bookbinding by Hand." In *Bookbinding in America,* ed. Hellmut Lehmann-Haupt. 1941; repr. with supplement, New York: R. R. Bowker, 1967 (includes a list of American bookbinders by cities).

Spawn, Willman. "The Evolution of American Binding Styles in the Eighteenth Century." In *Bookbinding in America, 1680–1910*: From the Collection of Frederick E. Maser. Bryn Mawr, Pa.: Bryn Mawr College Library, 1983.

c. Prints

BIBLIOGRAPHIES

Hamilton, Sinclair. *Early American Book Illustrators and Wood Engravers, 1670–1870*, 2 vols. Princeton, N.J.: Princeton Library, 1958–1968.

Lewis, Benjamin. *Guide to Engravings in American Magazines, 1741–1810*. New York: New York Public Library, 1959.

Means, Mary Elizabeth "Early American Trade Cards." (M.A. thesis, University of Delaware, 1958).

Newman, Eric P. *The Early Paper Money of America*, 3rd expanded ed. Iola, Wisc.: Krause Pubs., 1990 (covers the currencies issued by the Continental Congress and the thirteen original states, together with Florida, Louisiana, Vermont, and the North-West Territory down to 1800, with facsimiles and bibliographical references).

Wheat, James, C., and C. F. Brun. *Maps and Charts Published in America Before* 1800: *A Bibliography*, rev. ed. London: Holland Press, 1978.

NARRATIVE HISTORIES & DISCURSIVE BIBLIOGRAPHICAL ACCOUNTS

Boston Prints and Printmakers, 1670–1775. Boston: Colonial Society of Massachusetts, [1973].

Dolmetsch, Joan D., ed. *Eighteenth-Century Prints in Colonial America: to Educate and Decorate*. Williamsburg, Md.: Colonial Williamsburg Foundation, 1979.

Morse, John D., ed. *Prints in and of America to 1850*. Charlottesville: University Press of Virginia, [1970].

Reilly, Elizabeth Carroll. *A Dictionary of Colonial American Printers' Ornaments and Book Illustrations*. Worcester, Mass.: AAS, 1975.

Tooley, R. V. *The Mapping of America*. London: Holland Press, 1980.

d. Music

Britton, Allen P., Irving Lowens, and Richard Crawford. *American Sacred Music Imprints, 1698–1810: A Bibliography*. Worcester, Mass.: AAS, 1990.

Lowens, Irving. *A Bibliography of Songsters Printed in America before 1821*. Worcester, Mass.: AAS, 1976.

2. Printing Supplies and Equipment

C. William Miller presented the first systematic account of imported supplies in his admirably thorough introduction to *Benjamin Franklin's Philadelphia Printing* (cited under "Middle Colonies," Section 6). The identification of the sizes, qualities, and watermarks of the paper used to print American books, however, is still in its infancy. Isaiah Thomas corresponded avidly about supplies, dispatched detailed orders for type and presses to English firms, and kept scrupulous inventories of his shops in Worcester and vicinity. Some of these documents have been published in Clifford K. Shipton's *Isaiah Thomas: Printer, Patriot and Philanthropist, 1749–1831* (Rochester, N.Y.: Leo Hart, 1948), but many more deserve to be examined in greater detail. Another abundant, but neglected, source of information is the Registers of Exports and Imports (see "Imported Books," Section 3).

Bidwell, John, introduction, *Early American Papermaking: Two Treatises on Manufacturing Techniques,* reprinted from James Cutbush's *American Artist's Manual* (1814). New Castle, Del.: Oak Knoll Books, 1990.

Hunter, Dard. *Papermaking in Pioneer America.* 1952; repr., New York: Garland Publishing, 1981.

Leonard, Eugenie Andruss. "Paper as a Critical Commodity During the American Revolution." *PMHB* 74 (1950): 488–99.

Weeks, Lyman Horace. *History of Paper-Manufacturing in the United States, 1690–1916.* 1916; repr. New York: Burt Franklin, 1969.

Wroth, Lawrence C. *Abel Buell of Connecticut: Silversmith, Type Founder and Engraver,* 2nd ed., rev. and enl. Middletown, Conn.: Wesleyan University Press, 1958.

3. Imported Books

The Registers of Imports and Exports of Foreign and Colonial Merchandise have been published in a microfilm edition by W. E. Minchinton and C. J. French, *Customs 3, 1696–1780 in the Public Record Office, London* (East Ardsley, Wakefield: EP Microfilm, 1974). The Registers record imports and exports to and from London and the "outports" separately, and further divide exports into three series, of (a) English manufactures, (b) Foreign goods "out of time" (exported to England), and (c) Foreign goods "in time" (reexported elsewhere). Shipping returns from the different colonies, with occasional references to packages of books, survive in PRO CO 5 series, with many gaps (there are no extant returns for Pennsylvania and Connecticut). On the American end, there are a few colonial booksellers' invoices and customer records, such as those of Henry Knox or Jeremy Condy, and, in some cases, correspondence between colonial and English booksellers, customers, or agents, notably between William Strahan and David Hall of Philadelphia, between the Charleston Library Society and its booksellers, and in the letter books of John Murray I.

Barber, Giles. "Books from the Old World and for the New: the British International Trade in Books in the Eighteenth Century." *Studies on Voltaire and the Eighteenth Century* 151 (1976): 185–224.

Ford, Worthington Chauncey. "Henry Knox and the London Book-Store in Boston, 1771–1774." *Procs. MHS* 61 (1927–1928): 225–303.

———. *The Boston Book Market, 1679–1700*. Boston: Club of Odd Volumes, 1917, 88–152; with corrections and additions by Roger Thompson, *Procs. MHS* 86 (1975): 67–78 (on the records of the Boston bookseller John Usher).

Harlan, Robert D. "David Hall's Bookshop and Its British Sources of Supply." In *Books in America's Past: Essays Honoring Rudolph H. Gjelsness*, ed. David Kaser. Charlottesville: University Press of Virginia, 1966.

Kinane, Vincent. " 'Literary Food' for the American Market: Patrick Byrne's Exports to Mathew Carey," *Procs. AAS* 104 (1994–1995): 315–32.

McDougall, Warren. "Copyright Litigation in the Court of Session, 1738–1749, and the Rise of the Scottish Book Trade." *Edinburgh Bibliographical Society Transactions* 5:5 (1988): 2–31.

———. "Scottish Books for America in the Mid 18th Century." In *Spreading the Word: The Distribution Networks of Print 1550–1850*, eds. Robin Myers and Michael Harris. Winchester and Detroit, Mich.: St. Paul's Bibliographies, 1990.

Raven, James. *London Booksellers and American Customers: Transatlantic Community, Literary Conduits, and the Charleston Library Society, 1748–1811*. Columbia: University of South Carolina Press, 2000.

Zachs, William. *The First John Murray and the Late Eighteenth-Century London Book Trade.* Oxford: Oxford University Press, 1998.

4. Indian Books

Alphabetization, print, and script mediated between the colonists and the Indians in two ways: as representations by Europeans for Europeans of Indian culture or of European culture to the Indians; and as expressions of Indian culture by the Indians themselves. European and Indian languages, as well as pidgins, served to carry on either relationship.

BIBLIOGRAPHIES

Clancy, James Thomas. "Native American References: A Cross-Indexed Bibliography of Seventeenth-Century American Imprints Pertaining to American Indians." *Procs. AAS* 83 (1974): 287–341.

DePuy, Henry F. *A Bibliography of the English Colonial Treaties with the American Indians.* 1917; repr. New York: AMS Press, 1971.

Pilling, James C. *Bibliographies of the Languages of the North American Indians*, 9 pts. in 3 vols. 1887–1894; repr. New York: AMS Press, 1995 (Algonquian and Iroquoian parts).

NARRATIVE HISTORIES & DISCURSIVE BIBLIOGRAPHICAL ACCOUNTS

Amory, Hugh. "The Trout and the Milk: An Ethnobibliographical Talk." *HLB*, n.s., 7 (1996): 50–65 (on two fragments of European print found in seventeenth-century Indian graves).

Axtell, James. "The Power of Print in the Eastern Woodlands." *WMQ*, 3rd ser., 44 (1987): [300]–9.
Boyd, Julian P., ed. *Indian Treaties Printed by Benjamin Franklin, 1736–1762*. Philadelphia: Historical Society of Pennsylvania, 1938.
Goddard, Ives, and Kathleen J. Bragdon, eds. *Native Writings in Massachusett*, 2 vols. Philadelphia: American Philosophical Society, 1988.
Kellaway, William. *The New England Company, 1649–1776*. 1961; repr. Westport, Conn.: Greenwood Press, 1975.
Murray, David. *Forked Tongues: Speech, Writing, and Representation in North American Indian Texts*. Bloomington: Indiana University Press, 1991.
Peyer, Bernd C. *The Tutor'd Mind: Indian Missionary-Writers in Antebellum America*. Amherst: University of Massachusetts Press, 1997.
Sturtevant. William C., ed. *Handbook of North American Indians*, vol. 17: *Languages*, ed. Ives Goddard. Washington, D.C.: Smithsonian Institution, 1996, 158–84 (alphabetization) and 275–89 (native graphics).

5. The Northeast

The chief surviving New England bookseller's archives are Daniel Henchman's accounts, 1713–1760, divided between the Boston Public Library and the Harvard Business School, Jeremy Condy's account book, 1758–1770, and Isaiah Thomas's papers, 1754–1831, at the AAS. For an introduction to Henchman's records, see William T. Baxter, *The House of Hancock: Business in Boston, 1724–1775* (Cambridge, Mass.: Harvard University Press, 1945) and Rollo G. Silver, "Publishing in Boston, 1726–1757: The Accounts of Daniel Henchman," *Procs. AAS* 66 (1957): [17]–36; for Thomas's, see James N. Green, "The Rise and Fall of Isaiah Thomas's Bookselling Network," an AAS seminar paper presented October 24, 1996. The rich resources of New England probate inventories and court records have hardly been scratched. A neglected, authoritative manuscript source is Isaiah Thomas's list of American imprints through 1775 (at the AAS). His assignment of Boston books with false or anonymous imprints (adespota) was *not* incorporated in Samuel F. Haven's bibliography, appended to the *History of Printing in America*, 2nd ed. (1874), the ancestor of Evans and haunted source for many bibliographical "ghosts." The ongoing construction of a Boston trades index at the Massachusetts Historical Society has great promise, and one hopes the commercial distribution of books will eventually attract the attention of a business historian.

BIBLIOGRAPHIES

Alden, John Eliot. *Rhode Island Imprints, 1727–1800*. New York: R. R. Bowker, 1949.
Bates, Albert C. *Connecticut Statute Laws: A Bibliographical List of Editions . . . to 1836*. [Hartford, Conn.: Acorn Club], 1900.

Ford, Margaret Lane. "The Types of the Franklin Press of Rhode Island, 1727–1763, with Addenda to Alden's *Rhode Island Imprints.*" *PSBA* 82 (1988): 83–95.

McCorison, Marcus A. *Vermont Imprints, 1778–1820*. Worcester: AAS, 1963 (with two *Additions and Corrections* ([Worcester, Mass.]: AAS, [1968] & [1973]) as well as various updatings in *Procs. AAS* 84 (1975): 402–04; 94 (1984–1985): 343–56; and 101 (1991–1992): 375–89).

Tapley, Harriet S. *Salem Imprints, 1768–1825*. Salem, Mass.: Essex Institute, 1927 (covers all aspects of the book trade there, from printing to social and private libraries and auctioneers).

Whitmore, William H., ed. *Bibliographical Sketch of the Laws of the Massachusetts Colony from 1630 to 1686*. Boston, 1890 (corrected but by no means superseded by John D. Cushing's *Bibliography of the Laws and Resolves of the Massachusetts Bay, 1642–1780* (Wilmington, Del.: M. Glazier, in cooperation with the Massachusetts Historical Society, 1984)).

BIOGRAPHIES

Brown, H. Glenn and Maude O. *A Directory of Printing, Publishing, Bookselling and Allied Trades in Rhode Island to 1865*. New York: New York Public Library, 1958 (lists 125 names, 1727–1783).

Franklin, Benjamin V. *Boston Printers, Publishers, and Booksellers, 1640–1800*. Boston: G. K. Hall, 1980 (adds little to earlier authorities except vital statistics and counts of editions from the American Antiquarian Society's Printers' File; the contributions by MaryAnn Yodelis Smith, on Loyalist printers, and by John B. Hench, on Thomas Adams, may be particularly recommended, however).

Littlefield, George E. *Early Boston Booksellers, 1642–1711*. 2 vols. Boston: Club of Odd Volumes, 1900.

———. *The Early Massachusetts Press, 1638–1711*. 2 vols. Boston: Club of Odd Volumes, 1907.

NARRATIVE HISTORIES & DISCURSIVE BIBLIOGRAPHICAL ACCOUNTS

Harris, J. Rendel, and S. K. Jones. *The Pilgrim Press: A Bibliographical and Historical Memorial of the Books Printed at Leyden by the Pilgrim Fathers*. 1922; rev. ed. by R. Breugelmans, Nieuwkoop: De Graaf, 1987.

Humphrey, Carol Sue. *"This Popular Engine": New England Newspapers during the American Revolution, 1775–1789*. Newark: University of Delaware Press, 1992 (chaps. 1–4 are the best account of New England bookselling).

McCorison, Marcus A. "John Mycall – The Ingenious Typographer of Newburyport." *Printing History* 17 (1995): 25–40.

McMurtrie, Douglas C. "The Royalist Printers at Shelburne, Nova Scotia." *American Book Collector* 2 (1932): 359–61; 3 (1933): 40–[44].

Morison, Samuel Eliot. *The Puritan Pronaos*. 1936; repr. with corrections as *The Intellectual Life of Colonial New England*. New York: New York University Press, 1956.

Robertson, Marion. "The Loyalist Printers: James and Alexander Robertson." *Nova Scotia Historical Review* 3:1 (1983): [83]–93.

Silver, Rollo G. "Financing the Publication of Early New England Sermons." *SB* 11 (1958): 168–78.

———. "Government Printing in Massachusetts, 1751–1801." *SB* 16 (1963): [161]–200.

———. "Government Printing in Massachusetts-Bay, 1700–1750." *Procs. AAS* 68 (1959): [135]–62.

Stewart, J. J. (John James). "Early Journalism in Nova Scotia." *Collections of the Nova Scotia Historical Society* 6 (1888): [91]–122.

Winship, George Parker. *The Cambridge Press, 1638–1692*. Philadelphia: University of Pennsylvania Press, 1945 (discursive, covering the production of the Eliot Tracts as well as Cambridge printing).

6. Middle Colonies

The secondary literature on the history of printing in the middle colonies before 1720 is sparse and antiquated. After 1720, the scattered articles by Robert D. Harlan on David Hall and by Beverly McAnear on New York printers (listed in Tanselle, under "Generalities," Section 1) are the equivalent of book-length studies. Joseph Felcone's forthcoming New Jersey bibliography will be patterned on Miller. A complete edition of Franklin's account books by J. A. Leo Lemay will supersede George S. Eddy's extracts, *Account Books kept by Benjamin Franklin,* 2 vols. (New York: Columbia University Press, 1928–1929). David Hall's still-unedited papers are at the American Philosophical Society in Philadelphia, 1745–1775. The only other major sources, apart from the books themselves, are the *Papers of Benjamin Franklin,* ed. Leonard W. Labaree and W. J. Bell, Jr. (New Haven, Conn.: Yale University Press, 1959–), now nearing completion; the Bradford Papers at the Historical Society of Pennsylvania, which sketchily document newspaper circulation, book imports, and a lending library, all at the very end of the period; and the wastebook and ledger of Robert Aitken, 1771–1802, at the Library Company of Philadelphia.

BIBLIOGRAPHIES

Hildeburn, Charles R. *A Century of Printing: The Issues of the Press in Pennsylvania, 1685–1784,* 2 vols. Philadelphia, 1885–1886 (still worth consulting for its notes).

Miller, C. William. *Benjamin Franklin's Philadelphia Printing, 1728–1766: A Descriptive Bibliography*. Philadelphia: American Philosophical Society, 1974.

BIOGRAPHIES

Brown, H. Glenn and Maude O. *A Directory of the Book-Arts and Book Trade in Philadelphia to 1820*. New York: New York Public Library, 1950 (listing 434 names or firms down to 1790).

McKay, George L. *A Register of Artists, Engravers, Booksellers, Bookbinders, Printers and Publishers in New York City, 1633–1820*. New York: New York Public Library, 1942 (listing some 206 names or firms down to 1790).

NARRATIVE HISTORIES & DISCURSIVE BIBLIOGRAPHICAL ACCOUNTS

De Armond, Anna Janney. *Andrew Bradford, Colonial Journalist.* Newark: University of Delaware Press, 1949.

Riewald, J. G. *Reynier Jansen of Philadelphia, Early American Printer.* Groningen: Wolters-Noordhoff, 1970 (with imprint bibliography).

Sher, Richard B. "Charles V and the Book Trade." In *William Robertson and the Expansion of Empire,* ed. Stewart J. Brown. Cambridge: Cambridge University Press, 1997), 164–95 (on Robert Bell's reprints).

Wall, Alexander J. Jr. "William Bradford, Colonial Printer." *Procs. AAS* 73 (1964): [361]–84.

Wallace, John William. *Address delivered at the Celebration by the New York Historical Society . . . of the Two Hundredth Birthday of Mr. William Bradford.* Albany, N.Y., 1863 (incorporates some essential documents).

Wolf, Edwin, 2nd. *The Book Culture of a Colonial American City: Philadelphia Books, Bookmen, and Booksellers.* Oxford: Clarendon Press, 1988.

7. The Chesapeake to the Caribbean

Because of the continuing flow of books, printing materials, and printers from Pennsylvania southwards, the *Franklin Papers* and the papers of David Hall (see "Middle Colonies", Section 6) are a mine of information that touches on virtually every one of the southern mainland colonies. Otherwise, the chief surviving southern colonial bookseller's archives are the daybooks of William Hunter, 1750–1752, and Joseph Royle, 1764–1766, at the University of Virginia, Charlottesville. These sources may be pieced out by the claims of loyalist printers submitted to the Exchequer after the Peace of Paris, in the Public Record Office, London, Series I, A.O. 12 (a transcript) and II, A.O. 13 (the original petitions).

BIBLIOGRAPHIES

Daniel, Betty Jane. "Georgia Imprints, 1763–1799: A Study of the Form and Subject Matter of the Early Printing in Georgia" (M.A. dissertation, Emory University, 1952).

Gould, Christopher, and Richard Parker Morgan. *South Carolina Imprints, 1731–1800: A Descriptive Bibliography.* Santa Barbara, Calif.: ABC – CLIO, 1985 (lists "dubious" as well as genuine imprints, whether or not a copy is known to survive, and reissues of British editions; the signature collations, however, omit format, and thus provide little more information than the paging).

Handler, Jerome S. *Guide to Source Materials for the Study of Barbados History, 1627–1834.* Carbondale: Southern Illinois University Press, 1971 (covering books, newspapers, and manuscripts printed in or relating to Barbados, arranged chronologically in three sequences; with a *Supplement* (Providence, R.I.: John Carter Brown Library, 1991)).

McMurtrie, Douglas C. *Eighteenth Century North Carolina Imprints, 1749–1800.* Chapel Hill: University of North Carolina Press, 1938 (corrections and additions by William S. Powell, *North Carolina Historical Review* 35 (1958): 50–73).

Torrence, W. Clayton. *A Trial Bibliography of Colonial Virginia,* 2 vols. Richmond: Virginia State Library, 1908–1910 (covering Williamsburg imprints chronologically, together with books by Virginians and relating to Virginia from 1608 to 1776; with useful annotations).

Wheeler, Joseph Towne. *The Maryland Press, 1777–1790.* Baltimore: Maryland Historical Society, 1938.

Wroth, Lawrence C. *A History of Printing in Colonial Maryland 1686–1776.* [Baltimore, Md.]: The Typothetae of Baltimore, 1922 (supplemented by some broadsides announced in his "The St. Mary's City Press: A New Chronology of American Printing," *MdHM* 31 (1936): 91–111).

LIBRARY CATALOGUES

De Renne, Wymberley Jones. *A Catalogue of the Wymberley Jones De Renne Georgia Library at Wormsloe, Isle of Hope near Savannah, Georgia,* 3 vols. Wormsloe: priv. pr., 1931, vol. 1 (listing books about Georgia as well as imprints; the library itself was sold to the University of Georgia in 1938).

Swem, Earl G. *Virginia Historical Index,* 2 vols. Roanoke, Va., 1934–1936 (limited to the holdings of the Virginia State Library).

NARRATIVE HISTORIES & DISCURSIVE BIBLIOGRAPHICAL ACCOUNTS

Cave, Roderick. *Printing and the Book Trade in the West Indies.* London: Pindar Press, 1987.

Cometti, Elizabeth. "Some Early Best Sellers in Piedmont, North Carolina." *Journal of Southern History* 16 (1950): [324]–37.

Cundall, Frank. *A History of Printing in Jamaica from 1717 to 1834.* Kingston: Institute of Jamaica, 1935 (with biographies of printers and a checklist of imprints).

Davis, Richard Beale. *Intellectual Life in the Colonial South, 1585–1763,* 3 vols. Knoxville: University of Tennessee Press, 1978 (covering, *inter alia,* material in English archives).

Lemay, J. A. Leo. *Men of Letters in Colonial Maryland.* Knoxville: University of Tennessee Press, 1972.

Moody, Robert E., and Charles C. Crittenden. "The Letter-book of Mills & Hicks . . . [1781–1784]." *North Carolina Historical Review* 14 (1937): 39–83.

Powell, William S. "Patrons of the Press: Subscription Book Purchases in North Carolina, 1733–1850." *North Carolina Historical Review* 39 (1962): [423]–99 (with index of the Carolinian subscribers and a list of the colonial editions to which they subscribed).

Swan, Bradford F. *The Caribbean Area* (The Spread of Printing, Western Hemisphere). Amsterdam: Van Gendt & Co., 1970.

Winton, Calhoun. "The Colonial South Carolina Book Trade," *Proof* 2 (1972): 71–87.

———. "English Books and American Readers in Early Florida." In *Eighteenth-Century Florida and the Revolutionary South,* ed. Samuel Proctor. Gainesville:

University Presses of Florida, 1978 (only three books and a newspaper were printed in Florida before 1790).

Wright, Louis B. *The First Gentlemen of Virginia.* 1940; repr. Charlottesville: University Press of Virginia, 1964.

8. German- and Dutch-Language Books

The history of both Dutch- and German-language books in North America remains a largely underdeveloped field of inquiry, especially for imports. The progress of the New Netherland Project headed by Gehring, and the on-going recovery of evidence on the Dutch book trade is best followed through the essays in *De Halve Maen*, published by the Holland Society of New York.

BIBLIOGRAPHIES

Arndt, Karl John Richard, and Reimer C. Eck. *The First Century of German Language Printing in the United States of America,* 2 vols. Göttingen: Niedersächsische Staats- und Universitätsbibliothek Göttingen, 1989 (supersedes Seidensticker, except for broadsides, reserved for a 3rd vol.).

Edelman, Hendrik. *The Dutch Language Press in America: Two Centuries of Printing, Publishing, and Bookselling.* Nieuwkopp: De Graaf, 1986.

Seidensticker, Oswald. *The First Century of German Printing in America, 1728–1830.* 1893; repr. Millwood, N.Y.: Kraus Reprints, 1980 (with supplements by Wilbur H. Oda, in the *Pennsylvania Dutchman* 4 (1953–54)).

NARRATIVE HISTORIES & DISCURSIVE BIBLIOGRAPHICAL ACCOUNTS

Cazden, Robert E. *A Social History of the German Book Trade in America to the Civil War.* Columbia, S.C.: Camden House, 1984.

Christoph, Peter R., Kenneth Scott, and Kenn Stryker-Rodda, eds. *Kingston Papers,* trans. Dingman Versteeg. (New York Historical Manuscripts, Dutch), 2 vols. Baltimore, Md.: Genealogical Pub. Co., 1976.

Dolmetsch, Christopher L. *The German Press of the Shenandoah Valley.* Columbia: University of South Carolina Press, 1984.

Gehring, Charles T. "Documentary Sources Relating to New Netherland." In *Colonial Dutch Studies: An Interdisciplinary Approach,* eds. Eric Nooter and Patricia U. Bonomi. New York and London: New York University Press, 1988.

Roeber, A. Gregg. *Palatines, Liberty, and Property: German Lutherans in Colonial British America.* Baltimore, Md.: Johns Hopkins University Press, 1993).

Sommer, Frank H. "German Language Books, Periodicals, and Manuscripts." In *Arts of the Pennsylvania Germans,* ed. Catherine E. Hutchins. New York: W. W. Norton & Co., 1983.

Waldenrath, Alexander. "The Pennsylvania-Germans: Development of Their Printing and Their Newspress in the War for American Independence." In *The German Contribution to the Building of the Americas: Studies in Honor of Karl J.*

R. Arndt, eds. Gerhard K. Friesen and Walter Schatzberg. Worcester, Mass.: Clark University Press, 1977.

9. Journalism

The Readex Corporation's microform edition, *Early American Newspapers, 1704–1820* remains indispensable for many purposes. For any account of the size of the sheet, format, supplements, and layout, however, one must still turn to the original copies, or to the observations that Isaiah Thomas dispersed in his *History of Printing in America.*

BIBLIOGRAPHIES

Adams, Thomas R. *American Independence: The Growth of an Idea.* Providence, R.I.: Brown University Press, 1965 (covering pamphlets originating in the British colonies, and the only account of colonial editions of British authors).

———. *The American Controversy: A Bibliographical Study of the British Pamphlets about the American Disputes, 1764–1783,* 2 vols. Providence, R.I.: Brown University Press, 1980 (covering pamphlets originating in Great Britain).

Ayer, Mary Farwell. "Check-List of Boston Newspapers, 1704–1780," with a "Bibliographical Note" by Albert Matthews, *Pubs. CSM* 9 (1907) (an essential companion to Brigham).

Brigham, Clarence S. *A History and Bibliography of American Newspapers, 1690–1820,* 2 vols. 1947; repr. with additions and corrections, Hamden, Conn.: Archon Press, 1962 (a monument of meticulous research, but rather a checklist than a history or a bibliography; indexed by E. C. Lathem, *Chronological Tables* (1972); for chronological and geographical conspectuses, see also Lester J. Cappon et al., *Atlas of Early American History: The Revolutionary Era, 1760–1790* (1976)).

Gimbel, Richard. *Thomas Paine: A Bibliographical Check List of Common Sense.* New Haven, Conn.: Yale University Press, 1956.

NARRATIVE HISTORIES & DISCURSIVE BIBLIOGRAPHICAL ACCOUNTS

Brigham, Clarence S. *Journals and Journeymen: A Contribution to the History of Early American Newspapers.* Philadelphia: University of Pennsylvania Press, 1950.

Clark, Charles E. *The Public Prints: The Newspaper in Anglo-American Culture, 1665–1740.* New York: Oxford University Press, 1994.

Leonard, Thomas C. *The Power of the Press: The Birth of American Political Reporting.* New York: Oxford University Press, 1986.

Mott, Frank Luther. *American Journalism: A History of Newspapers in the United States . . . 1690–1940.* New York: Macmillan, 1941.

———. *History of American Magazines,* Vol. 1: *1741–1850.* 1938; repr. Cambridge, Mass.: Belknap Press, 1957.

Steele, Ian K. *The English Atlantic, 1675–1740.* New York: Oxford University Press, 1986 (on communications between England and her colonies and their immact on colonial "news").

Warner, Michael. *The Letters of the Republic: Publication and the Public Sphere in Eighteenth-Century America.* Cambridge, Mass.: Harvard University Press, 1990 (theoretical).

10. Freedoms of the Press

Alexander, James. *A Brief Narrative of the Case and Trial of John Peter Zenger, Printer of The New York Weekly Journal* [1736], 2nd ed., by Stanley N. Katz. Cambridge, Mass.: Belknap Press, 1972.

Brown, Richard D. *The Strength of a People: The Idea of an Informed Citizenry in America, 1650–1870.* Chapel Hill: University of North Carolina Press, 1996.

Davidson, Philip G. *Propaganda and the American Revolution, 1763–1783.* Chapel Hill: University of North Carolina Press, 1941.

Duniway, Clyde Augustus. *The Development of Freedom of the Press in Massachusetts.* 1906; repr. New York: Burt Franklin, 1969.

Jones, J. R., ed. *Liberty Secured? Britain before and after 1688.* Stanford, Calif.: Stanford University Press, 1992.

Levy, Leonard W. *Legacy of Suppression.* 1960, rev. & enl. as *The Emergence of a Free Press.* New York: Oxford University Press, 1985.

Schlesinger, Arthur M. *Prelude to Independence: The Newspaper War on Britain, 1764–1776.* 1958; repr. Boston, Mass.: Northeastern University Press, 1980.

Smith, Jeffrey A. *Printers and Press Freedom: The Ideology of Early American Journalism.* New York: Oxford University Press, 1988.

Treadwell, Michael. "1695–1995: Some Tercentenary Thoughts on the Freedoms of the Press." *HLB,* n.s., 7 (1996): 3–19.

11. Literacy, Reading, and Learned Culture

BIBLIOGRAPHIES

Adams, Thomas R. *The Non-cartographical Maritime Works Published by Mount and Page: A Preliminary Handlist.* London: Bibliographical Society, 1985.

Davis, Donald G., and J. M. Tucker. *American Library History: A Comprehensive Guide to the Literature.* Santa Barbara, Calif.: ABC–CLIO, 1989.

Holmes, Thomas J. *Cotton Mather: A Bibliography of His Works,* 3 vols. Cambridge, Mass.: Harvard University Press, 1940.

Karpinski, Louis. *Bibliography of Mathematical Works Printed in America through 1850.* Ann Arbor: University of Michigan Press, 1940.

Nash, Ray. *American Writing Masters and Copybooks: History and Bibliography through Colonial Times.* Boston: Colonial Society of Massachusetts, 1959.

Norton, Arthur O. "Harvard Text-books and Reference Books of the Seventeenth Century." *Pubs. CSM* 28 (1933): 361–438.

Rink, Evald. *Technical Americana: A Checklist of Technical Publications Printed [in America] before 1831.* Millwood, N.Y.: Kraus International Pubs., 1981.

Weiss, Harry B. "American Chapbooks, 1722–1842: A Preliminary Check List." *BNYPL* 49 (1945): 587–96.

Welch, D'Alté. *A Bibliography of American Children's Books Printed Prior to 1821.* [Worcester, Mass.]: AAS, 1972.

LIBRARY CATALOGUES

Bond, William H., and Hugh Amory, eds. *The Printed Catalogues of the Harvard College Library, 1723–1790.* Boston: Colonial Society of Massachusetts, 1996 (facsimiles, with index-concordance).

Cushing, John D, et al., eds. *Catalogue of Books in the Massachusetts Historical Library: An Annotated Edition of the 1796 Catalogue of the Massachusetts Historical Society.* Boston: The Society, 1996.

Hayes, Kevin J. *The Library of William Byrd of Westover.* Madison, Wisc.: Madison House, in cooperation with the Library Company of Philadelphia, 1997.

Sowerby, E. Millicent. *Catalogue of the Library of Thomas Jefferson,* 5 vols. Washington, D.C.: Library of Congress, 1952–1959 (and see, for omissions, Douglas L. Wilson, "Sowerby Revisited: The Unfinished Catalogue of Thomas Jefferson's Library," *WMQ,* 3rd ser., 41 [1984]: 615–28).

Wolf, Edwin, 2nd. *The Library of James Logan of Philadelphia, 1674–1751.* Philadelphia, Pa.: Library Company of Philadelphia, 1974.

NARRATIVE HISTORIES & DISCURSIVE BIBLIOGRAPHICAL ACCOUNTS

Chartier, Roger, ed. *Histoires de la lecture: un bilan de recherches.* Paris: Institut Mémoires de l'édition contemporaine, 1995.

Cremin, Lawrence A. *American Education: The Colonial Experience, 1607–1783.* New York: Harper & Row, 1970 (with an extensive bibliography).

Fiering, Norman. *Moral Philosophy at Seventeenth-Century Harvard.* Chapel Hill: University of North Carolina Press, 1981.

Hall, David D. "Readers and Reading in America: Historical and Critical Perspectives." *Procs. AAS* 103 (1993–1994): 337–57.

———. *Worlds of Wonder, Days of Judgment: Popular Religious Belief in Early New England.* New York: Knopf, 1989.

Hayes, Kevin J. *A Colonial Woman's Bookshelf.* Knoxville: University of Tennessee Press, 1996.

Hindle, Brooke. *The Pursuit of Science in Revolutionary America, 1735–1789.* Chapel Hill: University of North Carolina Press, 1956.

Lockridge, Kenneth A. *Literacy in Colonial New England: An Inquiry into the Social Context of Reading in the Early Modern West.* New York: W. W. Norton, 1974.

Love, Harold. *Scribal Publication in Seventeenth-Century England.* 1993; repr. as *The Culture and Commerce of Texts,* Amherst: University of Massachusetts Press, 1998.

Morison, Samuel Eliot. *Harvard College in the Seventeenth Century,* 2 vols. Cambridge, Mass.: Harvard University Press, 1936.

Nash, Ray. "A Colonial Writing Master's Collection of English Copybooks." *HLB* 14 (1960): 12–19 (on the archive of the Boston writing master Abiah Holbrook at the Houghton Library).

Reilly, Elizabeth Carroll. "Common and Learned Readers: Shared and Separate Spheres in Mid-Eighteenth-Century New England." (Ph.D. dissertation, Boston University, 1994.

Spufford, Margaret. *Small Books and Pleasant Histories: Popular Fiction and Its Readership in Seventeenth-Century England.* London: Methuen, 1981.

Stowell, Marion Barber. *Early American Almanacs: The Colonial Weekday Bible.* New York: Burt Franklin, 1977.

Tadmore, Naomi. " 'In the even my wife read to me' ": Women, Reading and Household Life in the Eighteenth Century." In *The Practice and Representation of Reading in England,* eds. James Raven, Helen Small, and Naomi Tadmore. Cambridge: Cambridge University Press, 1996.

Wolf, Edwin, 2nd. "Great American Book Collectors to 1800." *Gazette of the Grolier Club,* n.s., 16 (1971).

12. Literary Culture

Literary culture has been studied in terms of its constituent institutions, its social and political functions, and its framing of authorship, intellectual property, and literary work in eighteenth-century America. Bibliographies are limited here to poetry, its most characteristic colonial expression.

BIBLIOGRAPHIES

Jantz, Harold S. "The First Century of New England Verse." *Procs. AAS* 53 (1944): [219]–523 (covering appearances in manuscript as well as print).

Kaiser, Leo M. "A Census of American Latin Verse, 1625–1825." *Procs. AAS* 91 (1981–1982): 197–299 (mostly manuscript, with notes on the history of publication).

Lemay, J. A. Leo. *A Calendar of American Poetry in the Colonial Newspapers and in the Major English Magazines through 1765.* Worcester, Mass.: AAS, 1972.

Stoddard, Roger E. *A Catalogue of Books and Pamphlets Unrecorded in Oscar Wegelin's* Early American Poetry, 1650–1820. Providence, R.I.: Friends of the Library of Brown University, 1969 (with "Further Addenda," *PBSA* 65 (1971): 169–72, "More Addenda," *Procs. AAS* 88 (1979): 83–90, "Fourth Addenda," *Procs. AAS* 90 (1980–1981): 387–90, "Fifth Addenda," *Procs. AAS* 100 (1990–1991): 251–53 and "Sixth Addenda," *Procs. AAS* 107 (1997–1998): 389–93).

Wegelin, Oscar. *Early American Poetry,* 2nd ed., rev. & enl., 2 pts. New York: Peter Smith, 1930 (covering separate editions of poetry by writers "born or residing" in continental British North America, wherever printed, 1650–1820).

NARRATIVE HISTORIES & DISCURSIVE BIBLIOGRAPHICAL ACCOUNTS

Brown, Richard D. *Knowledge Is Power: The Diffusion of Information in Early America, 1700–1865.* Oxford: Oxford University Press, 1989.

Conroy, David W. *In Public Houses: Drink & the Revolution of Authority in Colonial Massachusetts.* Chapel Hill: University of North Carolina Press, 1995.

Daly, Robert. *God's Altar: The World and the Flesh in Puritan Poetry.* Berkeley: University of California Press, 1978 (with a bibliographical essay on literary criticism).

Mulford, Carla. *Only for the Eye of a Friend: The Poems of Annis Boudinot Stockton.* Charlottesville: University Press of Virginia, 1995.

Richards, Jeffrey. *Theater Enough: American Culture and the Metaphor of the World Stage, 1607–1789*. Durham, N.C.: Duke University Press, 1991.

Shields, David S. *Civil Tongues and Polite Letters in British America.* Chapel Hill: University of North Carolina Press, 1997.

Sommerville, Wilson. *The Tuesday Club of Annapolis (1745–1756) as Cultural Performance.* Athens: University of Georgia Press, 1996.

Stoddard, Roger S. "Poet and Printer in Colonial and Federal America: Some Bibliographical Perspectives." *Procs. AAS* 93 (1982–1983): 265–361.

APPENDIX ONE

A Note on Statistics

HUGH AMORY

THE FIGURES IN THIS APPENDIX derive from the North American Imprints Program (NAIP), an on-line machine-readable database maintained by the American Antiquarian Society. Historically, NAIP may be regarded as a revision of the *American Bibliography* of Charles Evans (1903–1955) and its supplement by Roger P. Bristol (1970), both of them cumulated and corrected in the *National Index of American Imprints* (1969) by Shipton and Mooney. All of these, in different ways, are national retrospective listings of American imprints down to 1800, for the most part in American libraries. In general, NAIP is fuller, more accurate, and much more accessible than any of its precursors: As of June 16, 1997, it contained about 2,866 records of items "not in Evans or Bristol," of which 1,162 were printed after 1790.

Bibliographers have often exaggerated the numbers of lost editions by compounding books, whose losses may be reliably estimated, with job printing. Thus L. C. Wroth, generalizing from the Franklin–Hall ledgers for 1760–1765, estimates that only 1 out of 4.7 pieces that they printed survives today (*Col. Printer,* 216), a conclusion that is widely repeated. The researches of C. William Miller have now reduced the ratio to only 1 in 3, but fundamentally, the whole way of posing the inquiry is mistaken. That there was a vast sea of printing in addition to the production of books is undeniable, but we can never estimate its extent until we can match the records with the survivors. It is essentially impossible to date job printing outside of the context of a manuscript archive, and we can rarely assign it to a printer because most eighteenth-century colonial printers used the same types (by 1760, generally Caslon). Thus it is often the case that more ephemera survive than we can positively identify in our records. With the possible exceptions of seventeenth-century printing and the South, it seems unlikely that more

(*text continues on page* 514)

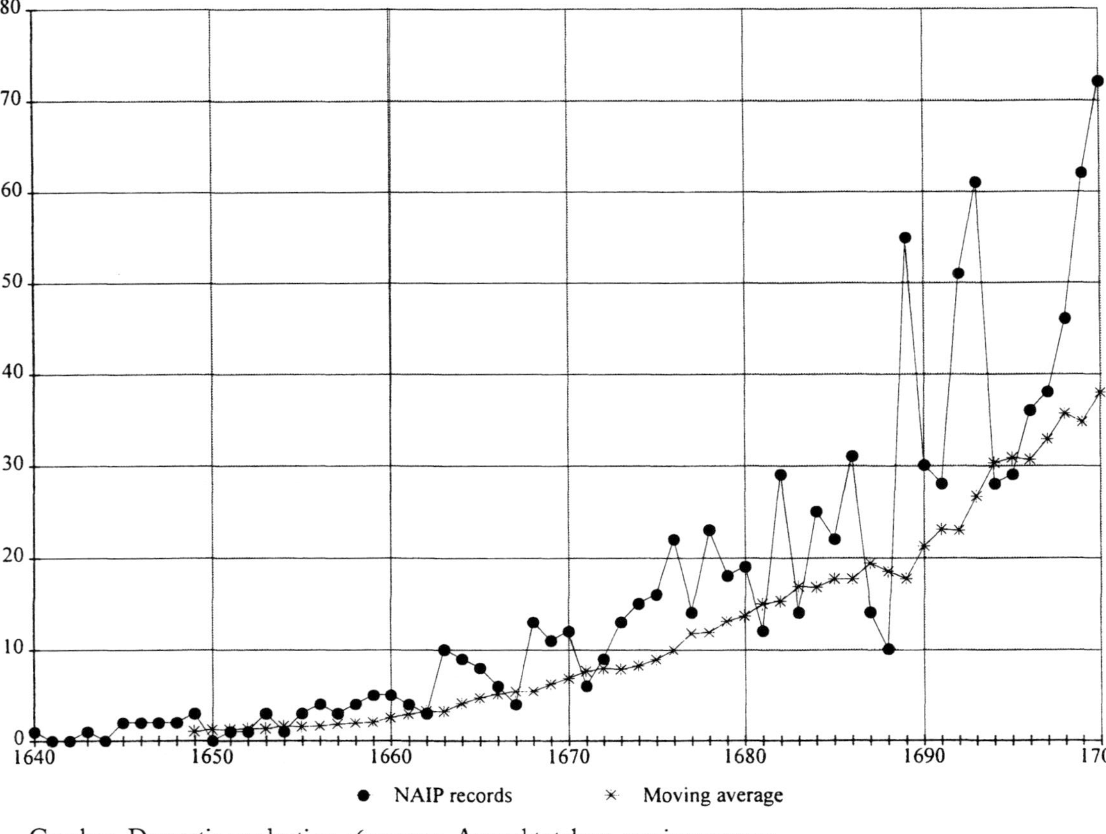

Graph 1a. Domestic production, 1640–1700. Annual totals vs. moving average.

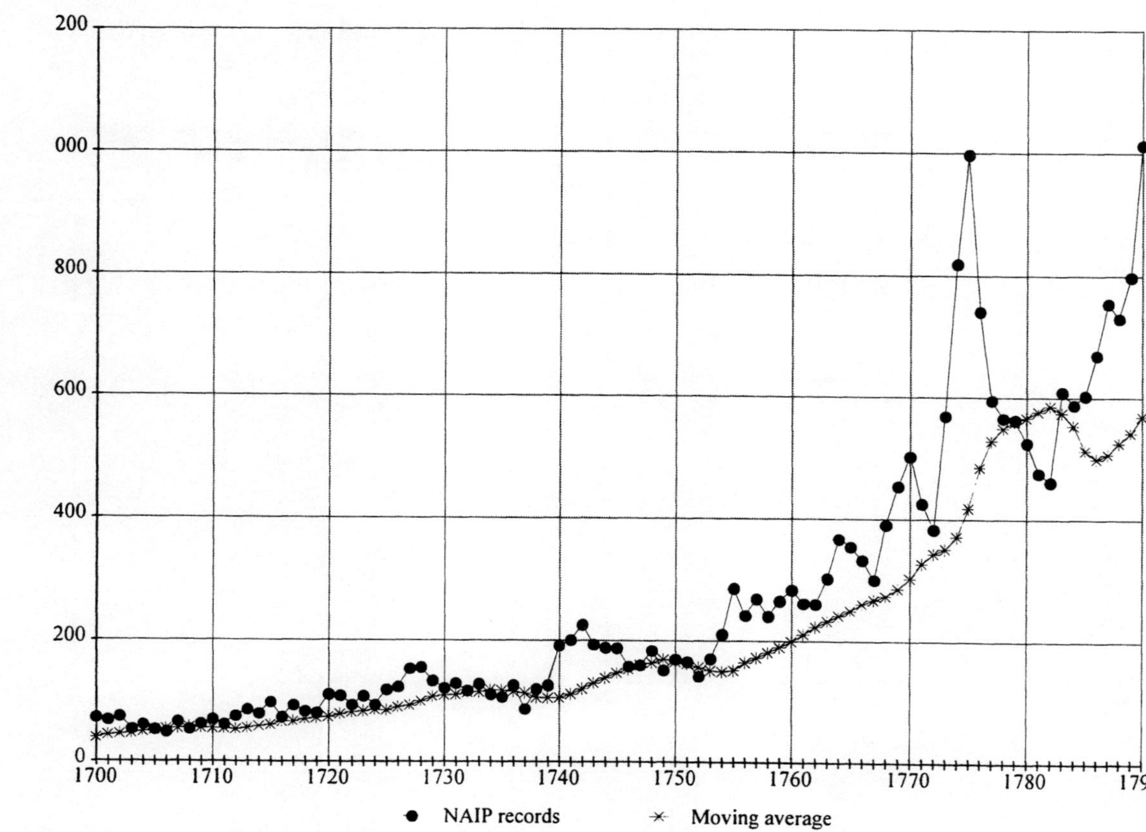

Graph 1b. Domestic production, 1701–1790. Annual totals vs. moving average.

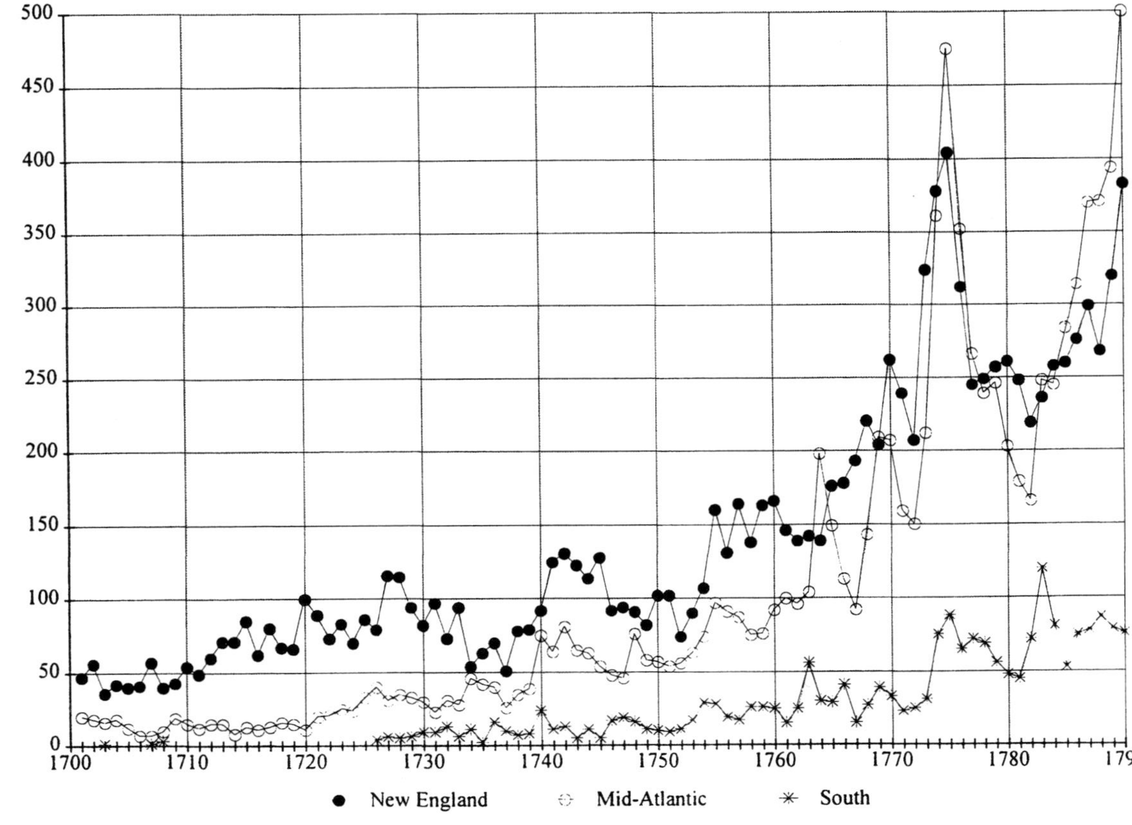

Graph 2a. Regional production, 1701–1790. Annual totals.

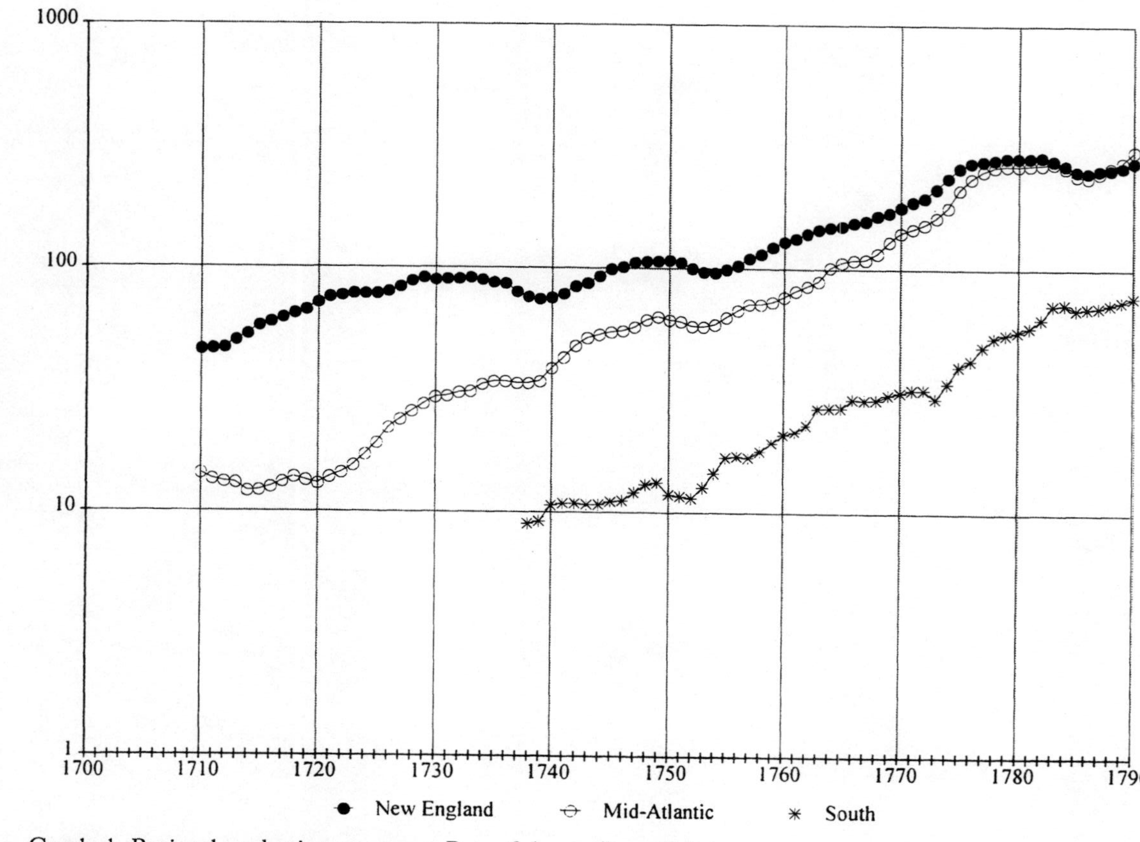

Graph 2b. Regional production, 1701–1790. Rate of change (log scale).

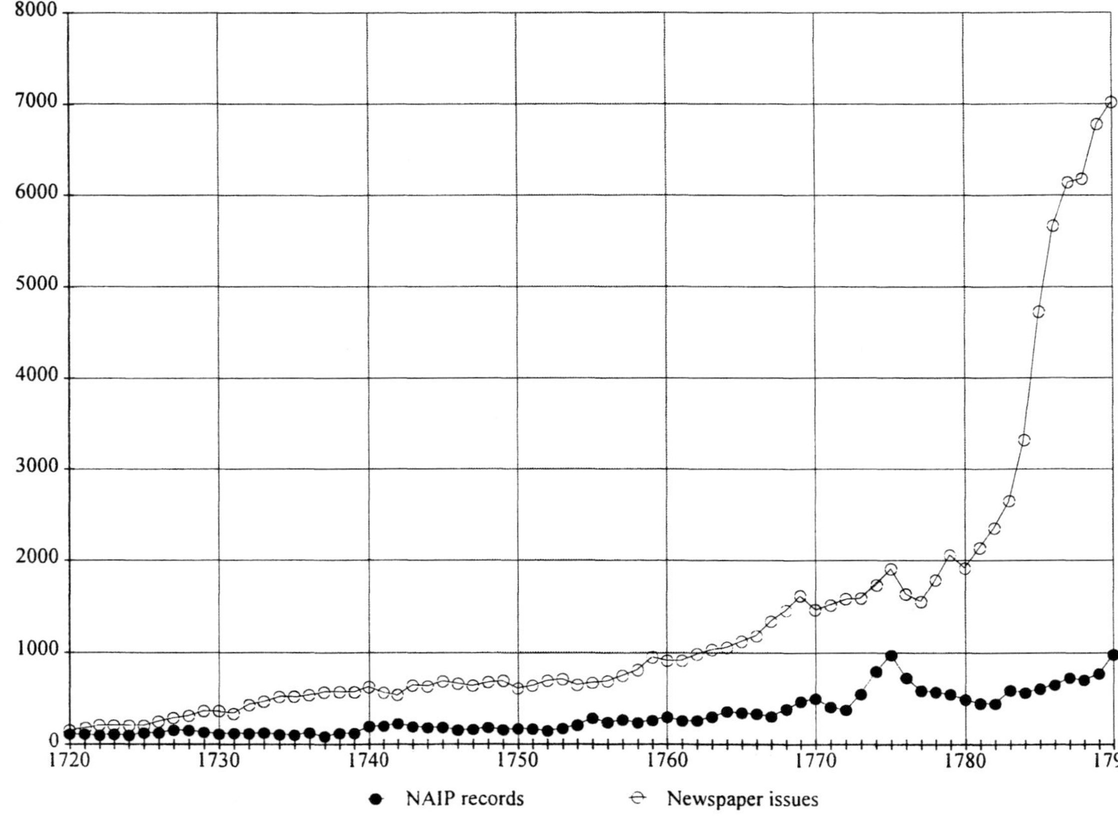

Graph 3. NAIP records vs. Newspaper issues. Annual production, 1720–1790.

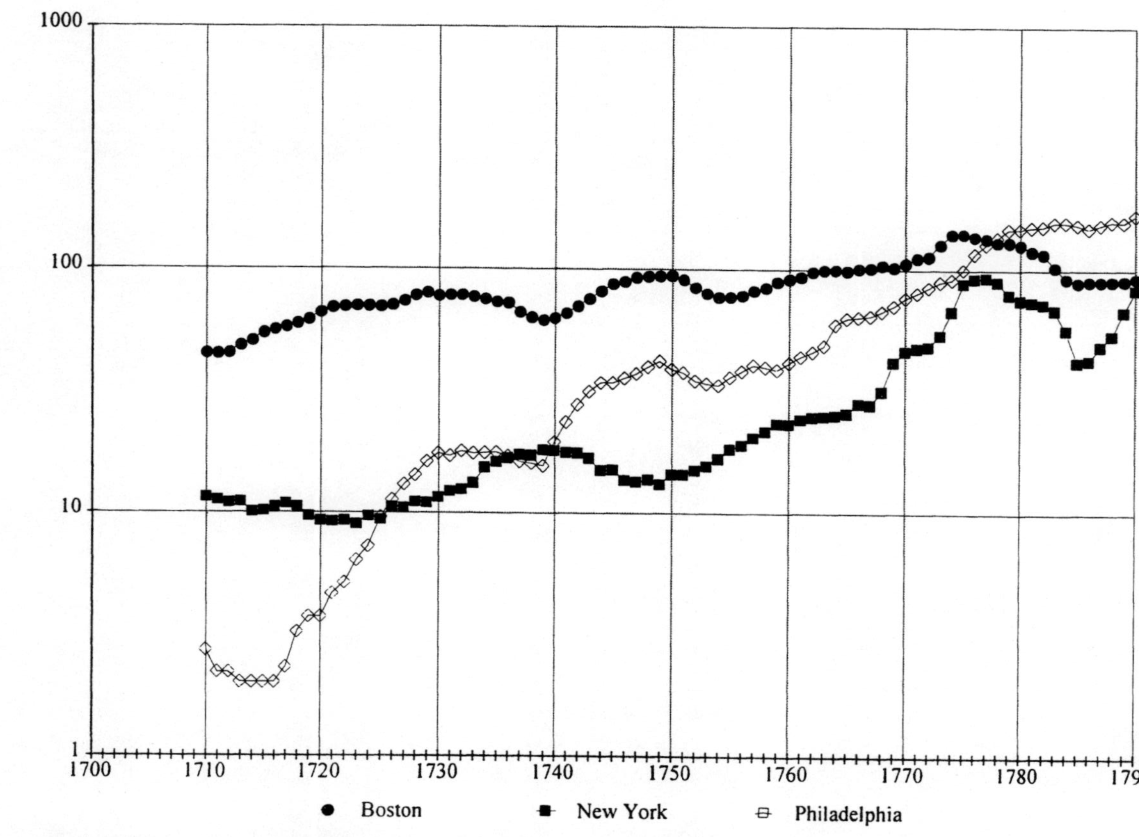

Graph 4. Boston, New York, Philadelphia. NAIP records, 1701–1790 (log scale).

Genre	All regions	MA	CT	RI	NH	VT	ME	N.E.	NY	NJ	PA	DE	Mid-Atlantic	MD	VA	NC	SC	GA	South
Government printing	**7182**	1931	590	504	271	76	0	**3372**	1180	230	1183	102	**2695**	325	365	122	195	108	**1115**
Sermons	**3192**	2067	476	79	60	20	3	**2705**	138	21	252	11	**422**	13	17	3	24	8	**65**
Almanacs	**1977**	506	196	98	34	7	3	**844**	273	38	594	55	**960**	38	75	0	57	3	**173**
Poetry	**1854**	853	223	65	26	12	1	**1180**	156	14	453	3	**626**	26	9	0	13	0	**48**
Booksellers' advertisements	**1227**	559	38	24	6	0	0	**627**	168	8	374	14	**564**	10	14	0	9	3	**36**
Juvenile/schoolbooks	**1085**	543	100	32	11	4	3	**693**	83	10	289	6	**388**	1	1	0	2	0	**4**
Academic dissertations	**323**	194	92	12	0	0	0	**298**	2	3	18	1	**24**	0	0	0	1	0	**1**
Prayers & prayer books	**313**	116	20	7	4	1	2	**150**	23	2	130	4	**159**	2	2	0	0	0	**4**
Hymnals	**254**	114	25	6	2	1	0	**148**	11	4	87	1	**103**	2	0	0	1	0	**3**
Psalmbooks	**253**	187	10	1	2	0	0	**200**	16	3	33	0	**52**	1	0	0	0	0	**1**
Satires	**201**	64	12	12	0	0	0	**88**	42	0	65	1	**108**	1	1	2	1	0	**5**
Plays	**111**	31	5	4	0	1	0	**41**	16	0	53	0	**69**	1	0	0	0	0	**1**
Subscribers' lists	**110**	29	16	2	1	0	0	**48**	17	4	33	1	**55**	2	3	1	1	0	**7**
Playbills	**103**	1	0	0	0	0	0	**1**	6	0	18	0	**24**	78	0	0	0	0	**78**
Maps	**72**	12	7	0	0	0	0	**19**	24	3	23	1	**51**	0	0	0	2	0	**2**
Captivity narratives	**71**	36	13	0	0	2	0	**51**	3	0	16	1	**20**	0	0	0	0	0	**0**
Novels	**38**	9	3	0	0	0	1	**13**	2	0	22	1	**25**	0	0	0	0	0	**0**
Dictionaries	**28**	20	0	0	0	0	0	**20**	0	0	8	0	**8**	0	0	0	0	0	**0**
Total records in NAIP, 1640-1790	**25404**	9295	2288	1221	498	154	18	**13474**	3333	452	5775	247	**9807**	704	630	161	464	164	**2123**

Graph 5a. Leading genres, by place, 1640–1790.

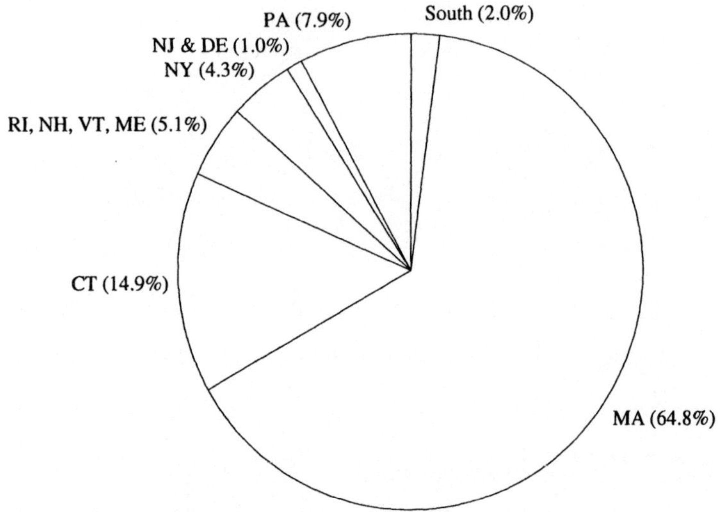

Graph 5b. Sermons. By place of publication, 1640–1790.

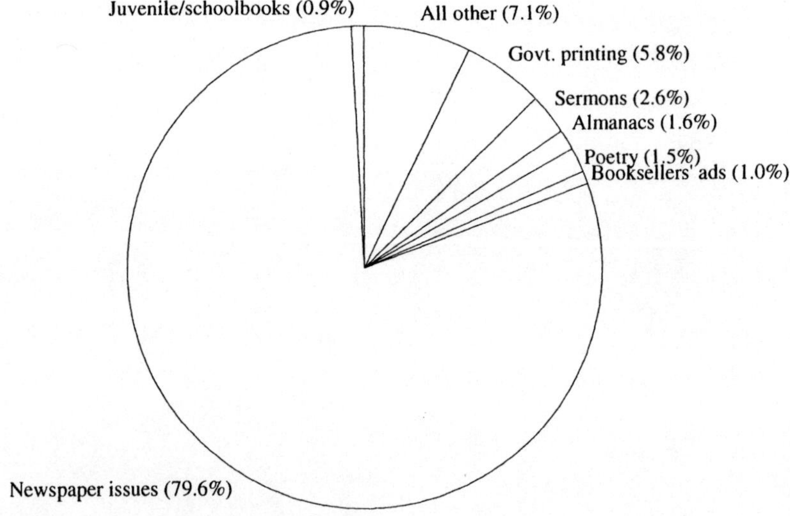

Graph 5c. Leading genres, 1640–1790. NAIP & newspapers.

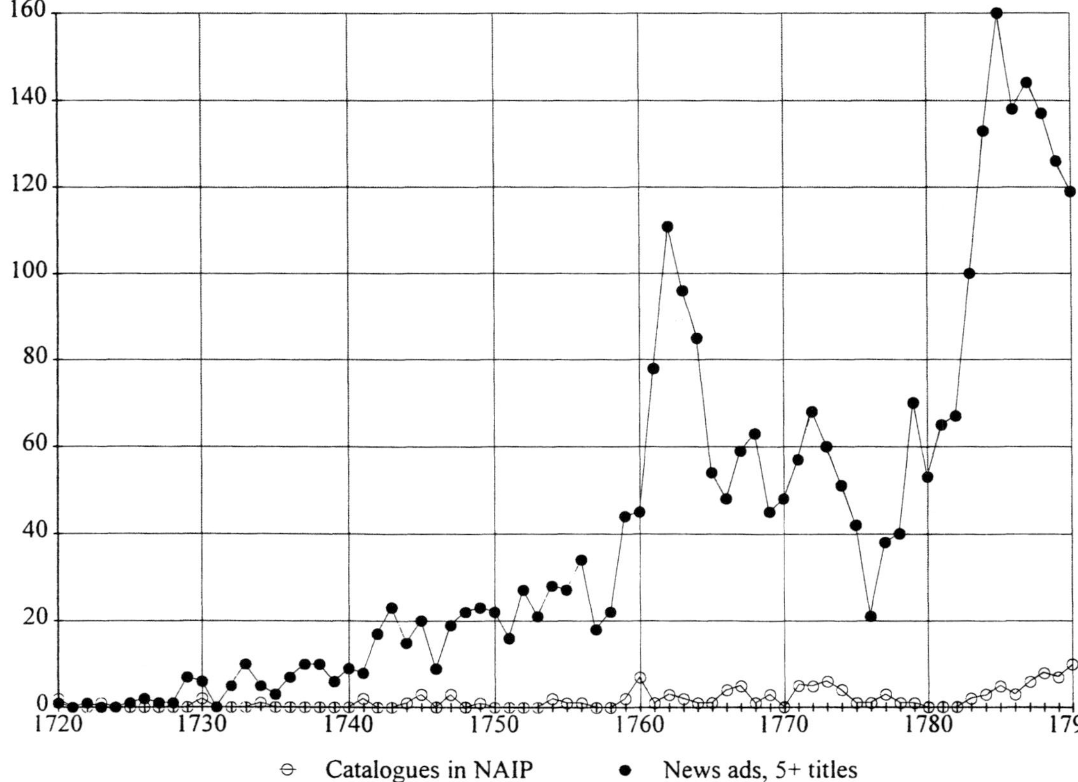

Graph 6. Booksellers' catalogues and advertisements, 1720–1790.

	1701-1750	*Percentage*	1751-1780	*Percentage*	1701-1780	*Percentage*
British West Indies	23,192	*31.7*	28,577	*20.7*	51,769	*24.5*
New England	21,498	*29.4*	26,700	*19.3*	48,198	*22.8*
Virginia & Maryland	12,794	*17.5*	28,067	*20.3*	40,861	*19.3*
New York	5,575	*7.6*	19,384	*14.0*	24,959	*11.8*
Pennsylvania	5,906	*8.1*	12,705	*9.2*	18,611	*8.8*
Carolina	4,161	*5.7*	13,774	*10.0*	17,935	*8.5*
Canada	0	*0*	3,253	*2.4*	3,253	*1.5*
Nova Scotia	14	*0*	2,371	*1.7*	2,385	*1.1*
Georgia	62	*0.1*	1,895	*1.4*	1,957	*0.9*
Florida	0	*0*	1,190	*0.9*	1,190	*0.6*
Newfoundland	0	*0*	440	*0.3*	440	*0.2*
Totals	73,202	*100*	138,356	*100*	211,558	*100*

Graph 7a. Exports of books from London to North America and the B.W.I., 1701–1780.

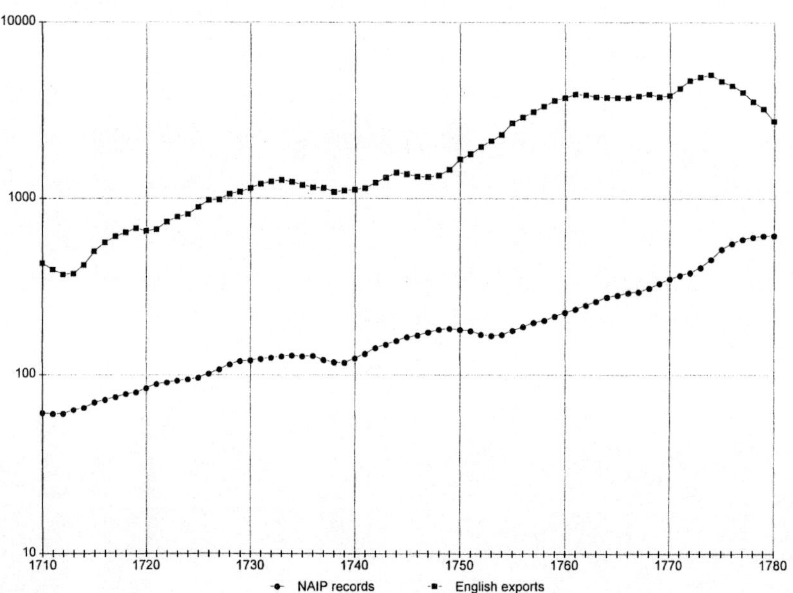

Graph 7b. NAIP records vs. English exports, 1710–1780. Rate of change (10-year moving average).

than 10 percent of the books printed in America have perished without a trace; to adjust this figure by the feeble survival of lottery tickets and colonial currency (little of it surviving in libraries anyhow) is absurd.

NAIP indeed was never intended to provide reliable and useful statistics of printing or publication; like any union catalogue, it was designed as a tool for locating copies and answering questions about their contents.

G. Thomas Tanselle rightly concludes that, though the data of such union catalogues may give some "suggestive" measure of relationships, their absolute value is of little worth ("Some Statistics on American Printing, 1764–1783," in *Press & Am. Rev.*, 321). Even in assessing relationships, everything depends on our unit of measurement. Professor Tanselle, reckoning in entries, concludes that 15.9 percent of the 1765 Massachusetts production was printed for the government; reckoned in sheets, however, it was only 6.5 percent (see Chapter 9, Table 9.2, above). Entries (i.e., records) cannot be equated with books, since a single book may have more than one record, and a single record may cover more than one book; and any consistent treatment of books and ephemera is impractical, given the haphazard formation of the library collections on which NAIP is based. In another effort to measure the importance of print in colonial culture, Mary-Anne Yodelis used the number of pages as her index ("Who Paid the Piper?" *Journalism Monographs* 38 [1975]), and hence concluded that religious patronage was far more important than that of the numerous Massachusetts governmental agencies from 1765 to 1775. Her unit assigned religion a disproportionate share of the pie, however. Government printing was generally in folio (4 pages to a sheet), whereas sermons and psalmbooks were usually in octavo or duodecimo (16–24 pages), and printers reckoned their charges in sheets. In pages, government printing totalled only 11.5 percent of religious production (including psalmbooks) in 1765; in sheets, it swells to 32 percent.

Based on records, like Professor Tanselle's, our statistics may be a better measure of modern American library economy, collection policies, and cataloguing practices than of books. Partially to compensate for such distortions, we have eliminated "analytics" (records of a part of a book) from our reckoning and supplement the monographic records in NAIP with a count of newspapers from Brigham. These are here counted as fifty-two records a year – as opposed to the single record a library would assign each distinct title, or the annually cumulated entry of 52 issues given by Evans. Our procedure may exaggerate the importance of newspapers, since no issue is (mathematically) allowed to perish, multivolume monographs count as one book, and a half-sheet newspaper issue is essentially equivalent to a broadside. A whole-sheet issue, such as became the norm in the 1760s, is equivalent to an almanac, but edition runs of almanacs were vastly larger than those of newspapers. Nevertheless, any measure of printing that ignores newspapers is bound to be unrealistic.

The statistical problems sketched here are too complex to resolve in a note, and unfortunately there are still no generally accepted procedures for dealing with them. For the moment, our figures should be seen as a provisional, highly conjectural measure of production; their precision should not be mistaken for accuracy.

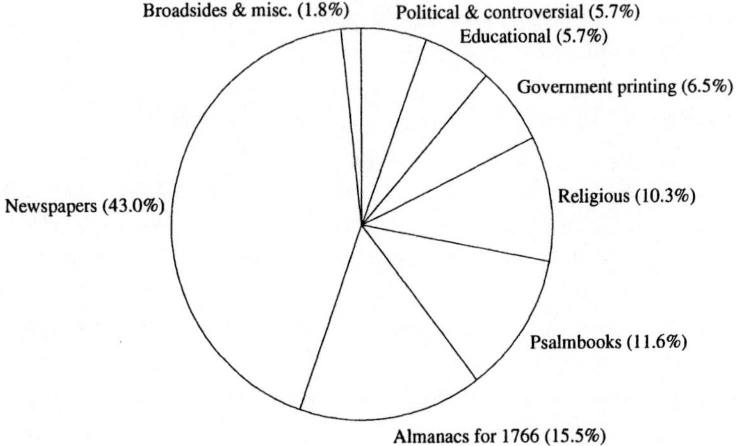

Graph 8a. Boston printing, 1765. Genres, by sheets.

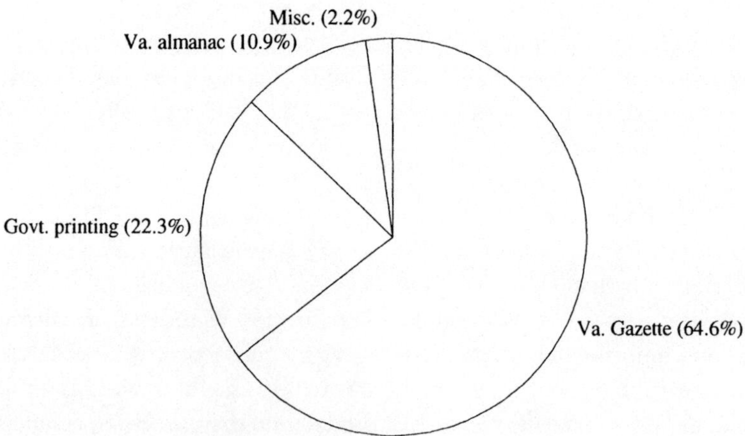

Graph 8b. Williamsburg printing, 1760–61. Genres, by sheets.

1701-1710	*NAIP records*	*% of all works of personal authorship for decade*	*% of all NAIP records for decade*
Cotton Mather (1663-1728)	95	26.91	15.83
Increase Mather (1639-1723)	29	8.22	4.83
George Keith (1639?-1716)	12	3.40	2.00
Benjamin Wadsworth (1670-1737)	12	3.40	2.00
Caleb Pusey (1650?-1727)	7	1.98	1.17
Solomon Stoddard (1643-1729)	7	1.98	1.17
Benjamin Colman (1673-1747)	5	1.42	0.83
1711-1720			
Cotton Mather (1663-1728)	129	23.33	15.23
Benjamin Wadsworth (1670-1737)	42	7.59	4.96
Increase Mather (1639-1723)	36	6.51	4.25
Benjamin Colman (1673-1747)	25	4.52	2.95
Michael Wigglesworth (1631-1705)	9	1.63	1.06
T. (Thomas) Goodman	7	1.27	0.83
Samuel Moodey (1676-1747)	7	1.27	0.83
1721-1730			
Cotton Mather (1663-1728)	96	12.77	7.95
Benjamin Colman (1673-1747)	26	3.46	2.15
Thomas Foxcroft (1697-1769)	19	2.53	1.57
Thomas Prince (1687-1758)	11	1.46	0.91
Jabez Earle (1676?-1768)	10	1.33	0.83
John Webb (1687-1750)	9	1.20	0.75
John Flavel (1630?-1691)	9	1.20	0.75
1731-1740			
George Whitefield (1714-1770)	45	6.52	3.60
Benjamin Colman (1673-1747)	20	2.90	1.60
Jonathan Dickinson (1688-1747)	12	1.74	0.96
William Cooper (1694-1743)	10	1.45	0.80
Thomas Prince (1687-1758)	9	1.30	0.72
Israel Loring (1682-1772)	8	1.16	0.64
Gilbert Tennent (1703-1764)	8	1.16	0.64
Jonathan Edwards (1703-1758)	7	1.01	0.64
1741-1750			
George Whitefield (1714-1770)	35	3.50	1.91
Gilbert Tennent (1703-1764)	33	3.30	1.80
Jonathan Edwards (1703-1758)	17	1.70	0.93
Isaac Watts (1674-1748)	17	1.70	0.93
Charles Chauncy (1705-1787)	15	1.50	0.82
Jonathan Dickinson (1688-1747)	13	1.30	0.71
Nicolaus Ludwig, Graf von Zinzendorf (1700-1760)	12	1.20	0.66
Nathaniel Appleton (1693-1784)	11	1.10	0.60

Graph 9. Leading authors, 1701–1790, by decade.

1751-1760	*NAIP records*	*% of all works of personal authorship for decade*	*% of all NAIP records for decade*
William Smith (1727-1803)	14	1.43	0.61
Jonathan Mayhew (1720-1766)	11	1.12	0.48
Benjamin Franklin (1706-1790)	10	1.02	0.44
Aaron Burr (1716-1757)	8	0.82	0.35
Charles Chauncy (1705-1787)	8	0.82	0.35
Thomas Prince (1687-1758)	7	0.72	0.31
Nathaniel Appleton (1693-1784)	7	0.72	0.31
1761-1770			
John Dickinson (1732-1808)	18	1.14	0.52
Isaac Hunt ca. 1742-1809)	15	0.95	0.43
Isaac Watts (1674-1748)	14	0.89	0.40
Charles Chauncy (1705-1787)	13	0.83	0.37
Joseph Bellamy (1719-1790)	12	0.76	0.34
Samuel Davies (1723-1761)	12	0.76	0.34
Jonathan Mayhew (1720-1766)	12	0.76	0.34
1771-1780			
Thomas Paine (1737-1809)	53	2.41	0.85
John Leacock (1729-1802)	40	1.82	0.64
Isaac Watts (1674-1748)	29	1.32	0.47
Anthony Benezet (1713-1784)	18	0.82	0.29
Jonathan Shipley (1714-1788)	17	0.77	0.27
Thomas Dilworth (d. 1780)	15	0.68	0.24
Samson Occom (1723-1792)	14	0.64	0.22
1781-1790			
Noah Webster (1758-1843)	34	1.33	0.50
Thomas Dilworth (d. 1780)	30	1.17	0.44
Isaac Watts (1674-1748)	27	1.06	0.40
Benjamin Rush (1746-1813)	18	0.70	0.27
Anthony Benezet (1713-1784)	12	0.47	0.18
Robert Dodsley (1703-1764)	11	0.43	0.16
Philip Morin Freneau (1752-1832)	11	0.43	0.16

Graph 9. Continued.

APPENDIX TWO

A Note on Popular and Durable Authors and Titles

DAVID D. HALL AND RUSSELL L. MARTIN

THANKS TO A MACHINE-READABLE DATABASE, the North American Imprints Program (NAIP), we can answer the question, What books and authors did American printers and booksellers choose to publish most often or most persistently, as measured by the frequency of authors' names within each decade, and for the entire period 1640–1790, by the frequency by which specific titles were reprinted? Like every other question we approach quantitatively, this one begs certain matters of attribution and classification: authored books that had no author's name on the title page and that may be catalogued as authorless (e.g., Benjamin Franklin is not listed as the author of *Poor Richard's Almanac* in NAIP); authored books over which the putative author had no control or that gradually became something of a hybrid (certain editions of Isaac Watts; for other examples, see Chapter 4). Another difficulty is comparing unauthored texts, like the Constitution and the *Declaration of Independence* (which, as a broadside, may belong in a different category from bound or unbound books) with those by authors. The data that follows cannot take account of edition sizes, that is, of the number of *copies* put into circulation. Were we able to do so the relative weighting of authors and titles would change considerably: For example, the press run of a single edition of Isaac Watts's *Hymns and Spiritual Songs* equaled the press run of four or five Cotton Mather sermons. The information we provide does show the relative importance of durability over time, as contrasted with prominence in a particular decade (George Whitefield, so prominent in the 1740s, sinks into insignificance thereafter.) Here, the most instructive comparison is between the bestselling books and most popular authors up to 1760, and those for the period 1761–1790.

Do schoolbooks properly figure in the history of authorship? If so, the most durable American writer was Ezekiel Cheever, whose Latin grammar was reprinted every single decade before 1790, and the most reprinted title (ninety-two known editions) was the *New England Primer*, an authorless book. Yet if all the editions of the Bible and parts of the Bible (including paraphrases of the Psalms) are counted together, this category (or "title") is hands-down first, with a total of 340 entries (133 of these were printed more than once). The distinction between American and European authors did not matter to the colonists and, given the multitude of possibilities for interpreting American, has not figured in our calculations.

Of the 3,519 authors identified in NAIP, the vast majority (2,073) are represented by a single NAIP record and another 543 by two. At the other end of the spectrum, Cotton Mather stands in lonely splendor (335 records). Other leading authors in NAIP for the period 1701–1790 include Isaac Watts (ninety-eight entries – excluding his version of the psalms), George Whitefield (ninety-eight), Benjamin Colman (eighty-six), Increase Mather (seventy-four), Benjamin Wadsworth (sixty-two), and Thomas Paine (fifty-six). As for durability, the number of authors reprinted three decades or more declines in a remarkably symmetrical pattern: 211 for three, 84 for four; 46 for five, 24 for six, 9 for seven, 2 for eight and 1 (our schoolmaster) for nine. Isaac Watts and John Bunyan were the two authors who appeared at least once over eight decades. (See Appendix 1, Fig. 9, for a list of popular authors, by decade.)

A closer look at titles at various points in time provides a sharper sense of cultural change. To 1730, for example, the most frequently printed work was the *Bay Psalm Book,* with 24 editions, beginning with the first of 1640. After 1730, the *Bay Psalm Book* declined in popularity, with seven editions from 1731 to 1760 and only one after 1761. Other psalmbook (metrical psalms) supplied the constant demand, however. Tate and Brady was published four times in America before 1730, with fourteen editions in the years 1731–1760, and forty-three editions from 1761 to 1790. The authorized version of the Psalms had a similar rise in popularity: three surviving editions before 1730; seventeen from 1731 to 1760; and twenty from 1761 to 1790. Isaac Watts' version of the Psalms was first printed in 1729, with eleven editions from 1731 to 1760, and thirty-eight from 1761 to 1790.

Of the fifty works that appeared in two or more printings to 1730, the vast majority were on religious themes. After Biblical texts, the leading title in this period was Jabez Earle's *Sacramental Exercises* (eleven editions), followed closely by the Westminster Assembly's *Shorter Catechism* (ten editions), the sermon collection *Three Practical Discourses* (eight), Matthew Henry's *Communicant's Companion* (seven), and Robert Russell's *Seven Sermons* (seven).

A list of the reprinted titles from 1731 to 1760 conforms to the previous pattern, with religious works dominating as before. Martin Luther's translations of the New Testament (1745 and 1755) and the Psalms (1746 and 1759) were added to the rolls of biblical texts printed in the colonies – fifty-four editions of the Psalms in this period. The Westminster Assembly's *Shorter Catechism* (fifteen editions) was joined by Luther's *Kleine Katechismus* (five) and Watts' *First Sett of Catechisms and Prayers* (three). The dominant personality in print, however, was George Whitefield, whose *Journal* (twelve) and *Short Address to Persons of All Denominations* (five) were printed and circulated widely. Among schoolchildren, the *New England Primer* held sway (twelve).

The great shift in publishing patterns took place, as one might expect, in the years surrounding the Revolution. Religious and instructional works continued to dominate, but these steady sellers were joined by a lively and influential stream of political works on the questions of the day. Not only was the reprinting of political pamphlets a new phenomenon, but the pace at which such titles were issued from the press was a signal change as well. That twenty-seven editions of Thomas Paine's *Common Sense* were printed up and down the seacoast, all within the space of one year (1776), must have been as revolutionary for printers and readers as Paine's essay was for the cause of independence. Similarly, Jonathan Shipley's *A Speech Intended to Have Been Spoken on the Bill for Altering the Charter of the Colony of Massachusetts Bay* appeared in twelve editions in 1774, in Boston, Philadelphia, Lancaster, Pa., New York, Hartford, Salem, Mass., Newport, and Williamsburg.

More literary fare included *The Oeconomy of Human Life,* attributed to Robert Dodsley, reprinted six times from 1731 to 1760 and fifteen times from 1761 to 1790. Alexander Pope's *Essay on Man* was first printed in the colonies in 1747 and was reprinted thirteen times to 1790. Abridgements of *Robinson Crusoe* were the most reprinted "literary" work of all: One American edition appeared in 1757 and another in 1774, thirteen more editions were printed from 1784 to 1790, with an additional twenty-nine editions forthcoming in the last decade of the eighteenth century.

APPENDIX THREE

A Note on Book Prices

RUSSELL L. MARTIN

"An entire monograph could be written on the prices of books in the eighteenth century." So wrote Clarence Brigham in 1951, and despite all the work on printers, bookselling, and book distribution done since Brigham's day, no such comprehensive study yet exists, no doubt because the study of book pricing is a complex field of investigation. Part of the difficulty in dealing with book prices is the complicated state of colonial currency. Each colony issuing paper money had its own monetary system that fluctuated in value in relation to pounds sterling and in accordance with inflationary and deflationary phases of the economic cycle. The best guide to these matters is John J. McCusker, *How Much Is That in Real Money? A Historical Price Index for Use as a Deflator of Money Values in the Economy of the United States* (Worcester, Mass.: American Antiquarian Society, 1992). Another difficulty is coping with differences of formats: was a book being sold unbound or bound and, if bound, in what kind of material? Booksellers and customers (Robert Skipwith, Thomas Jefferson's brother-in-law, is a good example) were quite aware of how the presence or absence and quality of binding affected price. Underlying all book prices was the quality and quantity – that is, the number and size of sheets – being used. (Here, the information in Chapter 5 on the kinds and pricing of paper is pertinent.) Using Franklin's Poor Richard almanacs as a guide – one-and-a-half sheets, retailing at 5 to 6*d.* each – for the mid-eighteenth century, a single printed sheet of ordinary quality paper, in an unbound format, sold at retail for 3 to 4*d.* It is not automatically the case that the greater the length of a text *in words,* the higher the price, for the simple reason that more words could be accommodated on a page if a printer chose to reduce the margins and use a smaller type size. In this regard it is instructive to compare different printed versions of a steady seller – say, Bunyan's *Pilgrim's Progress* or

Russell's *Seven Sermons* – some of which compressed these texts into a remarkably small compass. (Information on this practice, and on book prices in general, is contained in Elizabeth Carroll Reilly, "Learned and Common Readers: Shared and Separate Spheres in Mid-Eighteenth-Century New England" [Ph.D. dissertation, Boston University, 1994]). The valuations in probate inventories and library catalogues are generally of second-hand books in uncertain condition, and the estimates of the valuators are chiefly useful for indicating their sense of the *relative* worth of the books they were appraising.

These several circumstances render almost meaningless any price series over time. In lieu of such a series, which we gave up trying to construct, we can point to several useful sources of data. According to Robert B. Winans, fourteen American booksellers' catalogues issued by 1790 contain retail prices for books, for a grand total of 10,845 entries. Book catalogues published in newspapers, to which a forthcoming checklist by Winans will provide a guide, are another major source of information. Books were advertised in other books as well; NAIP cites 1,189 such advertisements up to 1790. Some of these advertisements include prices – for example, the list of "Books Printed for, and Sold by Benjamin Harris, at the London-Coffee-House in Boston" at the end of Cotton Mather's *A Companion for Communicants* (Boston, 1690). Printers and booksellers sometimes indicated a price on the cover of an unbound book. NAIP contains 2,198 records for such books to 1790, with prices in pounds, shillings, and pence, and another thirty records for books with prices printed in dollars and cents. On the whole, these were inexpensive books, many of them almanacs.

Book prices bear on the social history of a culture: What could people afford to buy? Principals in the mid-eighteenth century book trade, like James Rivington and Benjamin Franklin, assumed that "the common people" lacked the means to buy bound, imported books. (See Chapter 11 and *Franklin Autobiography*, 1397.) Further information is provided in Cynthia Z. and Gregory A. Stiverson, "The Profitablity and Affordability of Books in Eighteenth-Century Virginia," in *Printing & Society*. The countervailing rule is that many people of middling or modest means managed to own a Bible, a psalter, a schoolbook or two, and each year's almanac.

Notes

Introduction

1. *Md. Arch.* 4:269.
2. Volume 2 of this series will take up the topic of printed images. Richard Crawford ably describes one branch of music publishing in his "Introduction" to Allen P. Britton, Irving Lowens, and Richard Crawford, *American Sacred Music Imprints, 1698–1810: A Bibliography* (Worcester, Mass.: American Antiquarian Society, 1990).
3. Harry Y. Gamble, *Texts and Readers in the Early Church: A History of Early Christian Texts* (New Haven, Conn.: Yale University Press, 1995).
4. Mark U. Edwards, Jr., *Printing, Propaganda, and Martin Luther* (Berkeley and Los Angeles: University of California Press, 1994), chap. 1; Gerald Strauss, *Luther's House of Learning: Indoctrination of the Young in the German Reformation* (Baltimore, Md.: Johns Hopkins University Press, 1978).
5. William Haller, *Foxe's Book of Martyrs and the Elect Nation* (London: Jonathan Cape, [1963]), 118; *The Actes and Monuments of John Foxe*, ed. Stephen R. Cattley, 8 vols. (London, 1837–41), 3:719–20 (hereafter cited as *Book of Martyrs*). The myth lived on; John Foster, a seventeenth-century Boston almanac writer and printer, included the invention of printing in "A Chronology of very memorable things" that begins with the creation of the world: *An Almanack of Cœlestial Motions for the Year of the Christian Epochs, 1679* (Boston, 1679).
6. Charles M. Andrews, *The Colonial Period of American History*, vol. 4, *England's Commercial and Colonial Policies* (New Haven, Conn.: Yale University Press, 1938).
7. Peter Fraser, *The Intelligence of Secretaries of State & their Monopoly of Licensed News, 1660–1688* (Cambridge: Cambridge University Press, 1956).
8. Alfred W. Pollard, ed., *Records of the English Bible: The Documents Relating to the Translation and Publication of the Bible in English, 1525–1611* (Oxford: Oxford University Press, 1911), 164.
9. Adrian Johns defines and describes the practice thus expansively in *The Nature of the Book : Print and Knowledge in the Making* (Chicago, Ill.: University of Chicago Press, 1998), 160–68.

10. Michael Treadwell, "1695–1995: Some Tercentenary Thoughts on the Freedoms of the Press," *HLB*, n.s., 7 (1996): 3–19, recapitulating in part the argument of Raymond Astbury, "The Renewal of the Licensing Act in 1693 and its lapse in 1695," *Library*, 5th ser., 33 (1978): 296–322.
11. Paul F. Grendler, *The Roman Inquisition and the Venetian Press, 1540–1605* (Princeton, N.J.: Princeton University Press, 1977); Lucien Febvre and Henri-Jean Martin, *The Coming of the Book: The Impact of Printing, 1450–1800*, trans. David Gerard (London: Verso, 1984), 245; Robert Darnton, *The Forbidden Best-Sellers of Pre-Revolutionary France* (New York: Norton, 1995); Keith L. Sprunger, *Trumpets from the Tower: English Puritan Printing in the Netherlands, 1600–1640* (New York: E. J. Brill, 1994).
12. Annabel M. Patterson, *Censorship and Interpretation: The Conditions of Writing and Reading in Early Modern England* (Madison: University of Wisconsin Press, 1984); Christopher Hill, "Censorship and English Literature," *The Collected Essays of Christopher Hill*, vol. 1, *Writing and Revolution in 17th Century England* (Amherst: University of Massachusetts Press, 1985), 32–71.
13. This paragraph is indebted to John J. McCusker and Russell R. Menard, *The Economy of British America, 1607–1789* (Chapel Hill: University of North Carolina Press, 1985); for labor systems see esp. chap. 11.
14. Graham Pollard and Albert Ehrman, *The Distribution of Books by Catalogue from the Invention of Printing to A.D. 1800* (Cambridge: Roxburghe Club, 1965).
15. Margaret Spufford, "The Pedlar, the Historian and the Folklorist: Seventeenth-Century Communications," *Folklore* 105 (1994): 13–24.
16. Lisa Jardine, *Worldly Goods* (London: Macmillan, 1996), esp. chap. 3; alternatively, the consumer revolution may be dated from the eighteenth century, as Neil McKendrick, John Brewer, and J. H. Plumb argue in *The Birth of a Consumer Society: The Commercialization of Eighteenth-Century England* (Bloomington: Indiana University Press, 1982).
17. S. H. Steinberg, *Five Hundred Years of Printing*, 2nd ed., rev. (Harmondsworth: Penguin Books, 1961), 74.
18. See Chapter 3.
19. Edwin Wolf, 2nd, *The Book Culture of a Colonial American City* (Oxford: Clarendon Press, 1988); Clifford K. Shipton and James E. Mooney, *National Index of American Imprints through 1800: The Short-Title Evans*, 2 vols. (Worcester, Mass.: American Antiquarian Society, 1969); G. Thomas Tanselle, "Some Statistics on American Printing, 1764–1783," in *Press & the Am. Rev.*, 319–20.
20. John Clive and Bernard Bailyn, "England's Cultural Provinces: Scotland and America," *WMQ*, 3rd ser., 11 (1954): 200–13; Carole Shammas, "English-Born and Creole Elites in Turn-of-the-Century Virginia," in *The Chesapeake in the Seventeenth Century: Essays on Anglo-American Society*, ed. Thad W. Tate and David L. Ammerman (Chapel Hill: University of North Carolina Press, 1979), 274–96.
21. Elizabeth L. Eisenstein, *The Printing Press as an Agent of Change: Communications and Cultural Transformations in Early Modern Europe*, 2 vols. (Cambridge: Cambridge University Press, 1979).

22. Walter J. Ong, *The Presence of the Word: Some Prolegomena for Cultural and Religious History* (Minneapolis: University of Minnesota Press, 1981); Ong, *Orality and Literacy: The Technologizing of the Word* (London: Methuen, 1982).
23. Claude Lévi-Strauss, "A Writing Lesson," *Tristes Tropiques,* trans. John Russell (New York: Criterion Books, [1961]), an argument carried over into Michel Foucault, *The Order of Things: An Archaeology of the Human Sciences* (New York: Pantheon Books, 1971), and from thence into works such as Jonathan Goldberg, *Writing Matter: From the Hands of the English Renaissance* (Stanford, Calif.: Stanford University Press, 1990).
24. As Edwards argues in *Printing, Propaganda, and Martin Luther*; see also Jean-Francois Gilmont, ed., *La Réforme et le livre: L'Europe et l'imprimé (1517–v. 1570)* (Paris: Editions du Cerf, 1990).
25. Alvin B. Kernan, *Printing Technology, Letters, and Samuel Johnson* (Princeton, N.J.: Princeton University Press, 1987), 49; Robert Steele, *A Bibliography of Royal Proclamations of the Tudor and Stuart Sovereigns,* 2 vols. (Oxford: Oxford University Press, 1910), 1:xxii; Katharine F. Pantzer, "Printing the English Statutes, 1484–1640," in *Books and Society in History,* ed. Kenneth E. Carpenter (New York: R. R. Bowker, 1983), 70; see also D. R. Woolf, "The 'Common Voice': History, Folklore, and Oral Tradition in Early Modern England," *Past and Present* 120 (1988): 26–52. For a thoroughgoing critique of this and similar arguments about the "power of writing" within contemporary literary criticism, see Harold Love, *Scribal Publication in Seventeenth-Century England* (Oxford: Clarendon Press, 1993); Johns, *Nature of the Book.*
26. In *The English Atlantic 1675–1740: An Exploration in Communication and Community* (New York: Oxford University Press, 1986), Ian K. Steele proposes (p. 260) that an "oral culture" prevailed in the colonies before 1740. For another, divergent proposition see Jack P. Greene, "Paine, America, and the 'Modernization' of Political Consciousness," *Political Science Quarterly* 93 (1978): 75 (a reference provided by Michael Schudson).
27. Sandra M. Gustafson, "Performing the Word: American Oratory, 1630–1860" (Ph.D. dissertation, University of California, Berkeley, 1993).
28. This closing point is persuasively demonstrated in Keith Thomas, "Literacy in Early Modern England," in *The Written Word: Literacy in Transition,* ed. Gerd Baumann (Oxford: Clarendon Press 1986), 97–131.
29. Jürgen Habermas, *The Structural Transformation of the Public Sphere,* trans. Thomas Burger and F. Lawrence (Cambridge, Mass.: MIT Press, 1989).
30. Michael Warner, *The Letters of the Republic: Publication and the Public Sphere in Eighteenth-Century America* (Cambridge, Mass.: Harvard University Press, 1990); Grantland S. Rice, *The Transformation of Authorship in America* (Chicago, Ill.: University of Chicago Press, 1997), chap. 2; Michael Schudson, "Was There Ever a Public Sphere? If So, When? Reflections on the American Case," in *Habermas and the Public Sphere,* ed. Craig Calhoun (Cambridge, Mass.: MIT Press, 1992), 143–63. See also Mary Beth Norton, *Founding Mothers & Fathers: Gendered Power and the Forming of American Society* (New York: Knopf, 1996), 20–24, where the gender aspects of the distinction are considered. We return to this question in Chapters 10 and

12, and the discussion in Chapter 13 of manuscript literary production is also pertinent.

31. Alain Viala, *Naissance de l'écrivain: sociologie de la littérature à l'âge classique* (Paris: Editions de Minuit, 1985); Mark Rose, *Authors and Owners: The Invention of Copyright* (Cambridge, Mass.: Harvard University Press, 1993).
32. See Chapters 4 and 13. In Volume 2 of this series, Meredith McGill will carry this story further.
33. Roger Chartier, "Du livre au lire," in *Pratiques de la lecture,* ed. Roger Chartier (Marseilles: Editions Rivages, 1985), 80–85; Chartier, *The Order of Books: Readers, Authors, and Libraries in Europe between the Fourteenth and Eighteenth Century,* trans. Lydia G. Cochrane (Stanford, Calif.: Stanford University Press, 1994), chaps. 1 and 2.
34. For a rethinking of these categories as they pertain to the German reading public, see Hans Erich Bödeker, "D'une 'Histoire litteraire du lecture' à l'histoire du lecteur: bilan et perspectives," in *Histoires de la lecture,* ed. Roger Chartier (Paris: IMEC, 1995), 93–124.
35. The concept of exchange is richly developed in Richard White, *The Middle Ground: Indians, Empires, and Republics in the Great Lakes Region, 1650–1815* (Cambridge: Cambridge University Press, 1991).
36. Foster, *An Almanack . . . for 1679*; Edmund S. Morgan, *American Slavery, American Freedom: The Ordeal of Colonial Virginia* (New York: W. W. Norton, 1975), 98–101.
37. David J. Weber, *The Spanish Frontier in North America* (New Haven, Conn.: Yale University Press, 1992), chap. 4; Eleanor B. Adams and Frances V. Scholes, "Books in New Mexico, 1598–1680," *New Mexico Historical Review* 17 (1942): 226–70; Bernardo P. Gallegos, *Literacy, Education, and Society in New Mexico, 1693–1821* (Albuquerque: University of New Mexico Press, 1992).
38. Weber, *Spanish Frontier,* 94, 98, 104.
39. James Axtell, *The Invasion Within: The Contest of Cultures in Colonial North America* (New York: Oxford University Press, 1985), chap. 11.
40. Hall, *Narratives Md.*, 124, 137; Robert Emmett Curran, J. T. Durkin, and G. P. Fogarty, *The Maryland Jesuits, 1634–1833* (Baltimore: Maryland Society of Jesus, 1976), 13.
41. Victor Egon Hanzeli, *Missionary Linguistics in New France: A Study of Seventeenth- and Eighteenth-Century Descriptions of American Indian Languages* (The Hague: Mouton, 1969), chap. 4.
42. Henry S. Burrage, ed., *Early English and French Voyages . . . 1534–1608* (New York: Scribner's, 1906), 237, 391. The New England Puritans' fears of contamination or "indianization" are skillfully evoked in John Canup, *Out of the Wilderness: The Emergence of an American Identity in Colonial New England* (Middletown, Conn.: Wesleyan University Press, 1990), chaps. 3–5.
43. Alexander Brown, *The Genesis of the United States,* 2 vols. (Boston, 1891), 1:53; for the outcome, see W. Stitt Robinson, Jr., "Indian Education and Missions in Colonial Virginia," *Journal of Southern History* 18 (1952): 152–68.
44. Cotton Mather voiced a typical and much-reiterated contempt, *Magnalia,* 1:572–73.

45. Lawrence A. Cremin, *American Education: The Colonial Experience, 1607–1783* (New York: Harper & Row, [1970]), chap. 11; Margaret Szasz, *Indian Education in the American Colonies* (Albuquerque: University of New Mexico Press, 1988), chaps. 5 and 6; John Heckewelder, *A Narrative of the Mission of the United Brethren among the Delaware and Mohegan Indians* (Philadelphia, 1820); Sydney V. James, *A People among Peoples: Quaker Benevolence in Eighteenth-Century America* (Cambridge, Mass.: Harvard University Press, 1963), chap. 6.
46. Charles L. Cohen, "Conversion Among Puritans and Amerindians: A Theological and Comparative Perspective," in *Puritanism: Transatlantic Perspectives on a Seventeenth-Century Faith,* ed. Francis J. Bremer (Boston: Massachusetts Historical Society, 1993), 233–56; and see Chapter 4.
47. William Kellaway, *The New England Company, 1649–1776* (London: Longmans, 1961), 123–25; W. W. Tooker, *John Eliot's First Indian Teacher and Interpreter, Cockenoe-de-Long Island and the Story of his Career from the Early Records* (New York, 1896); Winship, *Cambridge Press,* 167; Jill Lepore, "Dead Men Tell No Tales: John Sassamon and the Fatal Consequences of Literacy," *American Quarterly* 46 (1994): 479–512.
48. Winship, *Cambridge Press,* 157, chaps. 8–10, 15; Kellaway, *New England Company,* 137 and chap. 6; Wilberforce Eames, "Early New England Catechisms," *Procs. AAS* 12 (1897): 128–30. Thomas Mayhew, Jr. wrote a catechism that was never printed.
49. Winship, *Cambridge Press,* 175; Roger Williams, *Christenings make not Christians* (1645), quoted in Canup, *Out of the Wilderness,* 158. As a nineteenth-century antiquarian fluent in Algonquian observed, "That [the colonists] did not always succeed in giving the precise meaning at which they aimed, or that the rules of Indian grammar were often violated, is not to be wondered at." J. Hammond Trumbull, *Notes on Forty Algonkin Versions of the Lord's Prayer* (Hartford, 1873), 5; these difficulties are abundantly illustrated in Trumbull's analysis of his forty texts. The history of efforts to describe any of the native languages is too complicated to be retold in these pages, but see Hanzeli, *Missionary Linguistics.*
50. Mather, *Magnalia,* 1:546; Canup, *Out of the Wilderness,* 64–73.
51. Hugh Amory, *First Impressions; Printing in Cambridge, 1639–1989* (Cambridge, Mass.: Harvard University Press, 1989), 41–42.
52. Winship, *Cambridge Press,* 158; Axtell, *The Invasion Within,* 184–85. Kellaway, *New England Company,* chap. 7, provides the best account of this transition.
53. *Mass. Records,* 3:100; James P. Ronda, "Generations of Faith: The Christian Indians of Martha's Vineyard," *WMQ,* 3rd ser., 38 (1981): 369–94; Morison, *Harv. Coll.,* chap. 17; Kellaway, *The New England Company,* 115.
54. The entire story, including passages from Occom's autobiography (pp. 23, 24, 36, 51), is told with admirable precision in William DeLoss Love, *Samson Occom and the Christian Indians of New England* (Boston, 1899).
55. As J. Hammond Trumbull notes, "An elegy in Latin verse and an epigraph in Greek . . . composed by Eleazer, 'Indus Senior Sophister,' of Harvard College in 1678, are preserved in [Cotton] Mather's *Magnalia Christi Americana* (London, 1702), bk. iii. ch. xxvi." Trumbull, "The Indian Tongue and Its Literature as Fashioned by Eliot and Others," in *The Memorial History of Boston,* ed. Justin Winsor, 4 vols. (Boston, 1880–1881), 1:477 n.

56. Love, *Samson Occom,* chap. 10.
57. This section also ignores the literary genres (e.g., captivity narratives) the colonists employed in writing about their encounter with Indians and the wilderness. But see the bibliography in R. W. G. Vail, *The Voice of the Old Frontier* (Philadelphia: University of Pennsylvania Press, 1949).
58. Brown, *Genesis,* 2:791–92; James Axtell, *After Columbus: Essays in the Ethnohistory of Colonial North America* (New York: Oxford University Press, 1988), chap. 6.
59. Ives Goddard and Kathleen J. Bragdon, eds., *Native Writings in Massachusett,* 2 vols. (Philadelphia, Pa.: American Philosophical Society, 1988), 16. The extensive historical and bibliographical notes in Julian P. Boyd, ed., *Indian Treaties Printed by Benjamin Franklin, 1736–1762* (Philadelphia: Historical Society of Pennsylvania, 1938), provide a superb account of the oral, performative, ritualized, and political aspects of treaty-making. See also Lawrence C. Wroth, *An American Bookshelf, 1755* (Philadelphia: University of Pennsylvania Press, 1934), 94–99.
60. Trumbull, "Indian Tongue," 471–72, 477; E. Jennifer Monaghan, "'She loved to read in good books': Literacy and the Indians of Martha's Vineyard, 1643–1725," *History of Education Quarterly* 30 (1990): 493–521. Trumbull also suggests, as do Goddard and Bragdon (*Native Writings,* 1:19) that local dialects may have become more like each other thanks to the presence of a printed version of one of them.
61. Hugh Amory, "The Trout and the Milk: An Ethnobibliographical Talk," *HLB,* n.s., 7 (1996): 50–65. Goddard and Bragdon, *Native Writings in Massachusett,* argue that the acquisition of literacy did not fundamentally alter the communicative practices or world view of the Indians, who continued to rely in certain contexts on oral recitation.
62. Francis Jennings, *The Invasion of America: Indians, Colonialism, and the Cant of Conquest* (Chapel Hill: University of North Carolina Press, 1975), chap. 14. Arnold Krupat, "On the Translation of Native American Song and Story: A Theorized History," in *On the Translation of Native American Literatures,* ed. Brian Swann (Washington, D.C.: Smithsonian Institution Press, 1992), 4: "All English translations from Native language performances cannot help but place themselves in relation to Western conceptions of art (literature) or of (social) science as they inevitably privilege *either* the Sameness of Native American verbal expression . . . *or* its Difference, in forms committed to scientific authenticity and accuracy." See also David Murray, *Forked Tongues: Speech, Writing and Representation in North American Indian Texts* (Bloomington: Indiana University Press, 1991).
63. Goddard and Bragdon, *Native Writings,* 1:31–43.

Chapter 1. Reinventing the Colonial Book

1. "art": Samuel Ampzing, *Beschryvinge ende lof der stad Haarlem in Holland* (Haerlem: A. Rooman, 1628), 376; cited in Samuel Palmer, *A General History of Printing* (London, 1732), 3, Thomas, *Hist. Printing,* 3, and Lawrence C. Wroth, *Col. Printer,* 3. "artful venture": Karl Schorbach, ed., "Die urkundlichen Nachrichten über Johann Gutenberg," in *Festschrift zum*

funfhundertjährigen Geburtstage von Johann Gutenberg, ed. O. Hartwig (Mainz, 1900): 162. "spinning wheel": Wroth, *Col. Printer*, 3.

2. Stephen Botein, "Printers and the American Revolution," in *Press & Am. Rev.*, 11–57.
3. Rollo G. Silver, "Benjamin Edes, Trumpeter of Sedition," *PBSA* 47 (1953): 248–68; and his "Aprons instead of Uniforms: The Practice of Printing, 1776–1787," *Procs. AAS* 87 (1977): 111–94.
4. Benedict Anderson, *Imagined Communities: Reflections on the Origin and Spread of Nationalism*, rev. ed. (London: Verso, 1991).
5. Reinhard Wittmann, *Geschichte des deutschen Buchhandels: ein Überblick* (München: C.H. Beck, 1991), 24, 36.
6. Ibid., 25, 75.
7. Ibid., chap. 4.
8. Sentiment in favor of English soared after King Philip's War, but the first primer in English for Indian use only appeared in 1720. William Kellaway, *The New England Company, 1649–1776: Missionary Society to the American Indians* (London: Longmans, 1961), 142; and chap. 9.
9. [Leman Thomas Rede], *Bibliotheca Americana* (London: J. Debrett, 1789), 19; Willi Paul Adams, "The Colonial German-Language Press and the American Revolution," *Press & Am. Rev.*, 208. See generally, Robert E. Cazden, *A Social History of the German Book Trade in America to the Civil War* (Columbia, S.C.: Camden House, 1984), chap. 1; and Howard Mumford Jones, *America and French Culture, 1750–1848* (Chapel Hill: University of North Carolina Press, 1927), 175–200.
10. John Feather, *Publishing, Piracy, and Politics: An Historical Study of Copyright in Britain* (London: Mansell, 1994), chap. 3. For the Scotch commerce with the colonies, see Chapter 5.
11. Timothy Green, letter, April 20, 1773 (Massachusetts Historical Society, Huntington Papers); photocopy in the Book Trades Collection (Mss.), American Antiquarian Society, Worcester, Mass.
12. STC (2nd ed.) 13918.5; and see Tamara P. Thornton, *Handwriting in America* (New Haven, Conn.: Yale University Press, 1996), 5. Only a fragment survives of the first edition, and none of later editions, attested only by advertisement.
13. Perry Miller, *The New England Mind: From Colony to Province* (Cambridge, Mass.: Harvard University Press, 1954), 6.
14. Michael Warner, *The Letters of the Republic: Publication and the Public Sphere in Eighteenth-Century America* (Cambridge, Mass.: Harvard University Press, 1990), chap. 4.
15. John Bidwell, "American History in Image and Text," *Procs. AAS* 98 (1988): 246–302, includes a bibliography of the more important of these facsimiles, 1817–ca. 1911.
16. Michael J. Walsh, "Contemporary Broadside Editions of the Declaration of Independence," *HLB* 3 (1949): 31–43; for the historical background, see also Pauline Maier, *American Scripture: Making the Declaration of Independence* (New York: Knopf, 1997).
17. Donald Farren, "Subscription: A Study of the Eighteenth-Century American Book Trade" (D.L.S. dissertation, Columbia University, 1982); e.g., the

1736 South Carolina Laws (Evans 4080), and the 1752 Virginia Laws (Evans 6941).

18. J. E. Alden, "John Mein, Publisher: An Essay in Bibliographic Detection," PBSA 36 (1942): 199–214; Mary Pollard, "The First American Edition of *The Vicar of Wakefield*," in *Treasures of the Library, Trinity College, Dublin*, ed. P. Fox (Dublin, 1986), 123–30; *Boswell's Life of Johnson* (Oxford: Oxford University Press, 1952, repr. 1957), 62; D. H. Borchardt & W. Kirsop, *The Book in Australia: Essays towards a Cultural & Social History* (Melbourne: Australian Reference Publications in association with the Centre for Bibliographical and Textual Studies, Monash University, 1988), 80.
19. My account of the company follows the standard history of Cyprian Blagden, *The Stationers' Company: A History, 1403–1959* (Cambridge, Mass.: Harvard University Press, 1960).
20. Gerald D. Johnson, "The Stationers versus the Drapers: Control of the Press in the late Sixteenth Century," *Library*, 6th ser, 10 (1988): 1–17; David McKitterick, *A History of Cambridge University Press*, vol. 1, *Printing and the Book Trade in Cambridge, 1534–1698* (Cambridge: Cambridge University Press, 1992) gives the best account to date of the import trade.
21. A. W. Pollard and G. Redgrave, comps., *A Short-title Catalogue of Books Printed in England, Scotland, and Ireland, and of English Books Printed Abroad, 1475–1640*, 2nd ed., by W. A. Jackson, F. S. Ferguson, and Katharine F. Pantzer. 3 vols. (London: Bibliographical Society, 1976–91) – later cited as STC – vol. 3 (indexes); R. B. McKerrow, *A Dictionary of Printers and Booksellers in England, Scotland and Ireland, 1557–1640* (London: Bibliographical Society, 1910). By contrast, some two hundred sixteenth-century printers and booksellers are known in provincial France; H. J. Martin & Roger Chartier, eds., *Histoire de l'édition française*, 4 vols. ([Paris]: Promodis, 1982–86), 1:353.
22. John Barnard, "Some Features of the Stationers' Company and its Stock in 1676/7," *Publishing History* 36 (1994): 5–38; Blagden, *Stationers' Company*, 106–7. McKitterick, *Cambridge University Press*, chaps. 8 and 9; Harry Carter, *A History of the Oxford University Press: Volume I, to the year 1780* (Oxford: Clarendon Press, 1975), 33.
23. Michael Treadwell, "Lists of Master Printers: The Size of the London Printing Trade, 1637–1723," in *Aspects of Printing from 1600*, ed. R. Myers and M. Harris (Oxford: Polytechnic Press, 1987), [141]–74; Blagden, *Stationers' Company*, 120.
24. J. A. Cochrane, *Dr. Johnson's Printer: The Life of William Strahan* (Cambridge, Mass.: Harvard University Press, 1964), 34.
25. Stephen Parks, *John Dunton and the English Book Trade: A Study of his Career with a Checklist of his Publications* (New York: Garland, 1976), no. 27.
26. Edward Arber, ed., *The Term Catalogues, 1668–1709 A.D.*, 3 vols. (London: The editor, 1903), 1:xii.
27. John Barnard and Maureen Bell, *The Early Seventeenth-Century Book Trade, and John Foster's Inventory of 1616* (Leeds: Leeds Philosophical and Literary Society, 1994), 33; John Feather, *The Provincial Book Trade in Eighteenth-Century England* (Cambridge: Cambridge University Press, 1985), 45–46; on Usher, see further Chapter 3.

28. Philip Gaskell, *A New Introduction to Bibliography,* 2nd impression, corr. (New York: Oxford University Press, [1973]), 178–9.
29. Norma Hodgson and Cyprian Blagden, eds., *The Notebook of Thomas Bennet and Henry Clements (1686–1719): with Some Aspects of Book Trade Practice* (Oxford: University Press, 1956), 86 ff.; Terry Belanger, "Booksellers' Sales of Copyright: Aspects of the London Book Trade, 1718–1768" (Ph.D. dissertation, Columbia University, 1970).
30. Michael Treadwell, "1695–1995: Some Tercentenary Thoughts on the Freedoms of the Press," *HLB,* n.s., 7 (1996): 3–19; Sheila Lambert, "State Control of the Press in Theory and Practice: The Role of the Stationers' Company before 1640," in *Censorship and the Control of Print in England and France, 1600–1910,* ed. R. Myers and M. Harris (Winchester: St. Paul's Bibliographies, 1992), 1–32.
31. On provincial sales, see John Feather, *Provincial Book Trade,* 37–43, who rather underestimates their importance (Jan Fergus and Ruth Portner, "Provincial Bookselling in Eighteenth-Century England: The Case of John Clay Reconsidered," *SB* 40 [1987]: 147–63); John Pendred, *The Earliest Directory of the Book Trade (1785),* ed. G. Pollard (London: Bibliographical Society, 1955). Cf. the complaints of Sir William Boothby about Michael Johnson's binding (Lichfield), James L. Clifford, *Young Sam Johnson* (New York: Oxford University Press, 1961), 67; a typical seventeenth-century bookseller, John Foster, did binding (Barnard & Bell, *Early Seventeenth-Century Book Trade,* 55–96), but his eighteenth-century counterpart, Ellen Feepound, evidently did not (Feather, *Provincial Book Trade,* 125–29).
32. Feather, *Provincial Book Trade,* 56; interestingly, Johnson uses the Dillys as his hypothetical distributor. For their colonial connections, see L. H. Butterfield, "The American Interests of the Firm of E. and C. Dilly, with their Letters to Benjamin Rush, 1770–1795," *PBSA* 45 (1951): 283–332.
33. Bennet & Clements, *Notebook,* 97–98.
34. John Dunton, *The Life and Errors of John Dunton* (London, 1705); Winans, *Book Catalogues,* nos. 6, 12, 41, etc.
35. Alexander Pope, *The Dunciad* [(A): bk. I, l. 200], ed. James Sutherland, 3rd ed. (London: Methuen, 1963), 86. Sutherland overlooks the innuendo, which did not, however, escape Benjamin Franklin, *Franklin Papers,* 3:13.
36. Donald Wing, comp., *Short-Title Catalogue of Books Printed in England, Scotland, Ireland, Wales, and British America, and of English Books Printed in Other Countries, 1641–1700,* rev. ed. by J. J. Morrison and C. W. Nelson. 3 vols. (New York: Modern Language Association of America, 1982–94), nos. E123, E123A–C, and M1101–3 (incorrectly described as separate "editions"). Fugill's issue remains unassigned in Wing, though correctly assigned to Hull in the catalogue of Trinity College Library, Dublin (1864–87), its only location; see C. W. Chilton, *Early Hull Printers and Booksellers* (Kingston-upon-Hull: City Council, 1982), 8–9. On Cripps, sometimes confused with his homonymous father of Oxford, see Paul Morgan, "The Oxford Book Trade . . . c. 1611–1647," in *Studies in the Book Trade in Honour of Graham Pollard* (Oxford: Oxford Bibliographical Society, 1975), 85.
37. *Boston News-Letter,* May 19/26, 1726.
38. Ford, *Boston Book Market,* 13.

39. John Lancaster, "The Transatlantic Printing History of Joseph Priestley's Discourses relating to the Evidences of Revealed Religion, 1794–1799," in *Essays in Honor of James Edward Walsh on his Sixty-Fifth Birthday*, ed. R. G. Dennis and H. Amory (Cambridge, Mass.: Goethe Institute and Houghton Library, 1983), 221–30; see also Robert Wells's reissue of a Scottish piracy of Doddridge's *Family Expositor* (1771), discussed in Chapter 7, p. 237.
40. George S. Eddy, ed., *Account Books Kept by Benjamin Franklin: Ledger "D", 1739–1747* (New York: Columbia University Press, 1929), 53, 70; John B. Hench, "Massachusetts Printers and the Commonwealth's Newspaper Advertisement Tax of 1785," *Procs. AAS* 87 (1977): 208.
41. Ian K. Steele, *The English Atlantic, 1675–1740* (New York: Oxford University Press, 1986), 132–33.
42. Lawrence C. Wroth, "Evans's American Bibliography, a Matrix of Histories," in Charles Evans, *American Bibliography, 1693–1729* (Boston: Goodspeed, 1943); for further discussion, see Appendix 1.
43. Feather, *Provincial Book Trade*, 14.
44. *The Charlemagne Tower Collection of American Colonial Laws* ([Philadelphia]: Historical Society of Pennsylvania, 1890) is the most convenient bibliography of these laws. *An Abridgement of All the Laws in Force in Her Majesty's Plantations* (1704) was the latest title to be printed by the trade at large.
45. John Clive and Bernard Bailyn, "England's Cultural Provinces: Scotland and America," *WMQ*, 3rd ser., 11 (1954): 200–13.
46. Cf. Carole Shammas, *The Pre-industrial Consumer in England and America* (Oxford: Clarendon Press, 1990), 268; the earliest citation for "bookstore" in the *OED* is Boston, 1763.
47. Lawrence C. Wroth, "The Book Trade Organization in the Colonial Period," in *The Book in America: A History of the Making and Selling of Books in the United States*, 2nd ed., by H. Lehmann-Haupt (New York: Bowker, 1951), 46–59. Thomas notes that before 1750, New England "printers did but little on their own account" (*Hist. Printing*, 213). Wroth also distinguishes booksellers who financed book-printing as "publisher–booksellers," but given the exchange of sheets, the absence of copyright, and indeed of a "public," the difference is nominal.
48. Thomas, *Hist. Printing*, 360 (perhaps satirically). Cf. John Alden, "Pills and Publishing: Some Notes on the English Book Trade, 1660–1715," *Library*, 5th ser., 7 (1952): 21–37; Feather, *Provincial Book Trade*, 83 ff.
49. William T. Baxter, *The House of Hancock: Business in Boston, 1724–1775* (Cambridge, Mass.: Harvard University Press, 1945), esp. chap. 2; George F. Dow, comp., *Arts and Crafts in New England, 1704–1775* (Topsfield, Mass.: Wayside Press, 1927), s.t. "Fabrics," 156–62; advertisements in the *Independent Chronicle* of Boott & Pratt, June 3, 1784, and of William Allen, May 13, 1784. Edwin Wolf, 2nd, notes the activity of mercers in the Philadelphia book trade, *The Book Culture of a Colonial American City* (Oxford: Clarendon Press, 1988), 64.
50. Miller, *Franklin's Philadelphia Printing*, nos. 293, 338; Willman Spawn, "The Evolution of American Binding Styles in the Eighteenth Century,"

in *Bookbinding in America, 1680–1910: From the Collection of Frederick E. Maser* (Bryn Mawr, Pa.: Bryn Mawr College Library, 1983), 32–33.

51. *New England Courant,* Nov. 30/Dec. 7, 1724; the only surviving copy is mutilated; for the minimal impact of the "Company," see Thomas, *Hist. Printing,* 213.
52. Margaret Lane Ford, "A Widow's Work: Ann Franklin of Newport, Rhode Island," *Printing History* 12 (1990): 15–26; Thomas, *Hist. Printing,* 94, 128 n.; "William McCulloch's Additions to Thomas's History of Printing," *Procs. AAS* 31 (1921): 174; and cf. C. K. Shipton, *Procs. AAS* 61 (1951): 229–30, conjecturing that a woodcut signed "P. F." is by Pompey Fleet. For Franklin's career, see his *Autobiography.*
53. Silver, *American Printer,* chap. 1.
54. *Boston News-Letter,* June 18/25, 1716.
55. Holmes, *Cotton Mather,* 523–25.
56. Cf. M. A. McCorison, "The Wages of John Carter's Journeymen Printers, 1771–1779," *Procs. AAS* 81 (1971): 273–303.
57. Silver, *American Printer,* 65; H. Glenn Brown and Maude O. Brown, *A Directory of the Book-Arts and Book Trade in Philadelphia to 1820* (New York: New York Public Library, 1950).
58. Thomas, *Hist. Printing,* 592 n.
59. Isaiah Thomas, Isaiah Thomas Papers, Box 11, vol. 1 (folio), t.-p. verso, American Antiquarian Society, Worcester, Mass.
60. Bentley, cit. Rollo G. Silver, "Financing the Publication of Early New England Sermons," *SB* 11 (1958): 173; Gaskell, *New Introduction,* 161; Rollo G. Silver, "Government Printing in Massachusetts-Bay, 1700–1750" *PBSA* 68 (1958): 135–62, and "Government Printing in Massachusetts, 1751–1801"; Miller, *Franklin's Philadelphia Printing;* Christopher Gould and R. P. Morgan, *South Carolina Imprints, 1731–1800: A Descriptive Bibliography* (Santa Barbara, Calif.: ABC–CLIO, 1985), no. 100 n.
61. The Houghton Library has a copy of the Mecom issue, not in NAIP.
62. Thomas, *Hist. Printing,* 141 (Mecom), and 124 (Ames: 60,000); Isaiah Thomas Papers, Box 11, vol. 1 (Ames: 50,000)
63. For the bibliography of the *Pietas et Gratulatio,* I am indebted to Roger E. Stoddard; details will appear in his forthcoming revision of Wegelin.
64. O. M. Dickerson, "British Control of American Newspapers on the Eve of the Revolution," *NEQ* 24 (1951): 458.
65. "William McCulloch's Additions," 109; Thomas, *Hist. Printing,* 266. The surviving 'colonial' presses are all of imperial size; see Philip Gaskell, "A Census of Wooden Presses," *Journal of the Printing Historical Society* 6 (1970): 1–32; and his *New Introduction,* 123. Their dating, however, is often questionable.
66. For English printing, 1716–1776, see *The Bowyer Ledgers,* ed. Keith Maslen and John Lancaster (London: Bibliographical Society, 1991); and cf. "The Present Current Prices of Paper," Nov. 1, 1785, and John Carter's "Account Book No. 1" (photocopy of the original in the Rhode Island Historical Society), both in the Book Trades Collection, American Antiquarian Society, Worcester, Mass. The sizes of paper varied considerably, as did their names: the measurements in the text follow the table in Gaskell, *New Introduction,* 73–5; see also John Bidwell, "The Size of the Sheet in America: Paper-

Moulds Manufactured by N. & D. Sellers of Philadelphia," *Procs. AAS* 87 (1977): 299–342.

67. Blagden, *Stationers' Company,* 45; Dunton, *Life and Errors,* 344; Robert D. Harlan, "David Hall's Bookshop and its British Sources of Supply," in *Books in America's Past,* ed. David Kaser (Charlottesville: University Press of Virginia, [1966]), 6; Cochrane, *Dr. Johnson's Printer,* chap. 6.
68. Roger E. Stoddard, "The Use of Mourning Wrappers in New England, with a Note on Mourning Papers in English Books at Harvard," *HLB* 30 (1982): 96–98.
69. Spawn, "American Binding Styles," 35; *New England Weekly Journal,* July 3, 1739.
70. The earliest printed colonial wrapper known to me is on the Houghton Library copy of Evans 40301 (1743); see also William A. Jackson, *HLB* 1 (1952): 313–21; Graham Pollard, "Booksellers' Binding," *TLS* (Mar. 10, 1932): 176.

Chapter 2. The Chesapeake in the Seventeenth Century

1. Contemporary comments on this situation may be found in *The Reverend John Clayton: A Parson with a Scientific Mind,* ed. Edmund and Dorothy Berkeley (Charlottesville: University Press of Virginia, 1965), 4; Henry Hartwell, James Blair, and Edward Chilton, *The Present State of Virginia, and the College,* ed. Hunter Dickinson Farish (Williamsburg, Va.: Colonial Williamsburg, Inc., 1940), 4–5, 12; Robert Beverley, *The History and Present State of Virginia,* ed. with an introduction by Louis B. Wright (Chapel Hill: University of North Carolina Press, 1947), 57–58.
2. Hening, *Statutes,* 2:517.
3. M. T. Clanchy, *From Memory to Written Record: England, 1066–1207* (Cambridge, Mass.: Harvard University Press, 1979).
4. *A Complete Collection of all the Laws of Virginia now in Force* (London, [1684?]), 128. Excellent historical reviews of recordkeeping in Maryland may be found in the essays in Elisabeth Hartsook and Gust Skordas, *Land Office and Prerogative Court Records of Colonial Maryland* (Publications of the Hall of Records Commission No. 4 [State of Maryland], 1946, repr., Baltimore: Genealogical Publishing Co., 1968).
5. *Md. Arch.* 41: deeds (4), bill (4), inventory (5), warrant (18), indenture (19), accounts (19), bond (28), writ (38), receipt (41), patent (51), survey (52), bill of sale (75). Wesley Frank Craven describes the recording of land titles in *The Southern Colonies in the Seventeenth Century, 1607–1689* (Baton Rouge: Louisiana State University Press, 1949), 277–80.
6. The scope of this archive at the level of a colony secretary is indicated in a Maryland document of 1673, "A list of Records belonging to the Secretaryes Office." *Md. Arch.* 15:32–34.
7. *Md. Arch.* 1:488 (1663). In 1639 the Maryland government had ordered each court to "keep a book of Record" for land titles (*Md. Arch.* 1:61–62), although it called for the written record to be supplemented with oral publication, ordering the registrar of deeds to "proclaime and publish the said Claime . . . and such proclamation shall be Continued and renewed in open Court once at least in every year for three years." On the preservation of property boundaries through collective memory rather than through

written deed, see Darrett and Anita Rutman, *A Place in Time: Middlesex County, Virginia, 1650–1750* (New York: W. W. Norton, 1984), 122. The time-honored method of claiming land via turf and twig was also employed in the colonies: *Md. Arch.* 49:xii.

8. *Md. Arch.* 41:197.
9. *Md. Arch.* 2:133; 13:448; Hening, *Statutes,* 2:147; see also David D. Hall, *Cultures of Print: Essays in the History of the Book* (Amherst: University of Massachusetts Press, 1996), 103.
10. Hall, *Narratives Md.,* 20. For a parallel reading aloud of "the printed Coppy of the fundamentall Constitutions lately sent here by the Lords proprietors" in South Carolina, see *Journal of the Grand Council of South Carolina,* ed. A. S. Salley (Columbia: Historical Commission of South Carolina, 1907), 1:71.
11. John Smith, *Works (1608–1631),* ed. Edward Arber, 2 pts. (London, 1895), pt. 1:150, and see Chapter 6, for more on charters and their authenticity.
12. Robert Steele, *A Bibliography of Royal Proclamations of the Tudor and Stuart Sovereigns,* 2 vols. (Oxford: Clarendon Press, 1910), 1:xxxi. The equation of proclamations with statute law ended in 1641 with the abolition of the Star Chamber.
13. "Wyatt Papers," *WMQ,* 2nd ser., 7 (1927): 247, 249; *Calendar of Virginia State Papers and Other Manuscripts, 1652–1781, Preserved in the Capitol at Richmond,* ed. William P. Palmer (Richmond, Va., 1875); see also Hall, *Cultures of Print,* 107.
14. Alexander Brown, *The Genesis of the United States,* 2 vols. (Boston, 1890), 1:493.
15. Hall, *Narratives Md.,* 224–25, 227, 237, 238, 240, 243–44.
16. *Narratives of the Insurrections, 1675–1690,* ed. Charles M. Andrews (New York: Scribners, 1915), 32–33, 35; Wilcomb Washburn, *The Governor and the Rebel* (Chapel Hill: University of North Carolina Press, 1957), 64, 103–07; Edmund S. Morgan, *American Slavery, American Freedom: The Ordeal of Colonial Virginia* (New York: W. W. Norton, 1975), 273; Hening, *Statutes,* 2:429–30; *Journals of the House of Burgesses of Virginia,* ed. H. R. McIlwaine, 13 vols. (Richmond: Virginia State Library, 1905–15), 2:115. This paragraph abbreviates a much richer story of communications by rumor, gossip, and proclamation that may be followed in Washburn, *Governor and the Rebel* and John Davenport Neville, comp., *Bacon's Rebellion: Abstracts of Materials in the Colonial Records Project* (Jamestown, Va.: Jamestown Foundation, [1976?]), which includes materials found in Egerton MS 2395 (British Museum).
17. Katharine F. Pantzer, "Printing the English Statutes, 1484–1640: Some Historical Implications," in *Books and Society in History,* ed. Kenneth E. Carpenter (New York: R. R. Bowker, 1983), 69–114.
18. Agencies of the Crown also imposed certain obligations of recordkeeping; over time, these obligations expanded, and the colonists were also requested to send over a better quality of records. See, e.g., Hening, *Statutes,* 2:512; Philip A. Bruce, *Institutional History of Virginia in the Seventeenth Century,* 2 vols. (New York: G. P. Putnam's Sons, 1910), 1:403.
19. Hening, *Statutes,* 2:512; Clayton Torrence, *Old Somerset on the Eastern Shore of Maryland* (Richmond, Va.: Whittet & Shepperson, 1935), 62.

20. Early on, it sometimes happened that county clerks went to Jamestown to copy acts of the assembly. See, e.g, Charles B. Cross, Jr., *The County Court, 1637–1904: Norfolk County, Virginia* (Portsmouth, Va.: Printcraft Press, 1964), 30.
21. Thomas Jefferson collected a number of these county compilations, some of which also formed the basis of Hening's *Statutes.* E. Millicent Sowerby, comp., *Catalogue of the Library of Thomas Jefferson,* 5 vols. (Washington, D.C.: Library of Congress, 1953), 2:242. In 1634, when counties were set up, Virginia had eight; in 1660 the number had risen to seventeen, and by 1700 reached twenty-three.
22. Hening, *Statutes,* 2:147–48.
23. Petition to the Council for Foreign Plantations (July 22, 1662), Colonial Office 1/16 at folio 18, Public Record Office, London; reference supplied by Warren Billings, text to appear in his edition of *The Papers of Sir William Berkeley* (Richmond: Virginia Historical Society, forthcoming).
24. Hening, *Statutes,* 2:189, 247.
25. Ibid., 2:340 n.
26. Almost certainly, Buckner's initiative was related to the complex political situation in Virginia, which included considerable agitation over the right of the crown to negate laws passsed by the assembly limiting the production of tobacco; Hening, *Statutes,* 2:501–02, 560–63.
27. *Executive Journals of the Council of Colonial Virginia,* ed. H. R. McIlwaine, 3 vols. (Richmond: Virginia State Library, 1925), 1:493; Wroth, *Printing in Col. Md.,* 1–2; *The Papers of Francis Howard, Baron Howard of Effingham, 1643–1695,* ed. Warren M. Billings (Richmond: Virginia Historical Society, 1989), 42. In 1690 the Crown instructed Howard that "No printer's press is to be used without the Governor's leave first obtained." Wroth, *Printing in Col. Md.,* 2.
28. *Journals . . . Burgesses,* 2:201–03.
29. Hening, *Statutes,* 1:v. Of the copies that I have examined, six include handwritten additions: a copy formerly owned by Edmund Andros, who served as royal governor in Virginia in the 1690s, presently in the library of the Virginia Historical Society; a copy formerly owned by William Byrd II, subsequently acquired by Thomas Jefferson and now in the Library of Congress; three copies in the Library of Virginia, one of them formerly belonging to Nathaniel Bacon, Senior; and a copy at the New York Public Library, which has other contemporary manuscript material bound in. The copy in the Charlemagne Tower Collection (Historical Society of Pennsylvania) was Robert Beverly's and includes manuscript additions, including legal forms; the same collection includes a copy of the laws of 1662 with additions on blank pages extending to October 1677 (information I owe to Brent Tarter). Neither the John Carter Brown Library nor the Harvard Law School copies of Purvis contain blank pages. In some copies the blank pages were bound in as issued, for the watermark is the same throughout.
30. *Md. Arch.* 2: 54–55; see, e.g., *Md. Arch.* 57:448. At this time Maryland had seven counties.
31. *Md. Arch.* 2:542–550; 1:468; Hening, *Statutes,* 1:vi.
32. *Md. Arch.* 2:543.

33. Wroth, *Printing in Col. Md.*, chap. 2; Wroth, "The St. Mary's City Press: A New Chronology of American Printing," *MdHM* 31 (1936):91–111; *Md. Arch.* 20:449; 19:306, 370. The insurgents' "Declaration of the reason and motive for the present appearing in arms" was issued scribally and printed some weeks later. *Md. Arch.* 8:101–7.
34. *Md. Arch.* 19:466–67; 24:22, 60, 83, 198; Wroth, *Printing in Col. Md.*, 17–18, 23; information provided by Calhoun Winton, who also has studied what seems to be the sole surviving complete copy, located in the Niedersächsische Staats- und Universitätsbibliothek at Göttingen. As the revised code of 1699 was being completed and with a printing press on hand, the assembly nonetheless ordered that the statutes be issued in handwritten multiple copies on "large Royall Paper": *Md. Arch.* 22:558.
35. From the dedication to Nathaniel Blakiston, quoted in *MdHM* 5 (1910): 187.
36. Wroth, *Printing in Col. Md.*, 227; J[ohn]. Markland, *Typographia: An Ode on Printing* (Williamsburg, Va., 1730), 10.
37. Warren M. Billings, "English Legal Literature as a Source of Law and Legal Practices for Seventeenth-Century Virginia," *VMHB* 87 (1979): 403–17; Francis S. Philbrick, "Prefatory Note," in *County Court Records of Accomack-Northampton, Virginia, 1632–1640*, ed. Susie M. Ames (Washington, D.C.: American Historical Association, 1954), xi, remarking on the near-complete absence of legal terminology in local court records.
38. *Md. Arch.* 2:543; Hartwell, Blair, and Chilton, *Present State of Virginia*, 40, 43; Lois Green Carr and David William Jordan, *Maryland's Revolution of Government 1689–1692* (Ithaca: Cornell University Press, 1974), 15–16, 21; and chap. 1.
39. Susie M. Ames, *Reading, Writing, and Arithmetic in Virginia, 1607–1699* (Williamsburg, Va.: 350th Anniversary Celebration Corporation, 1957), 38; David B. Quinn, ed., "A List of Books Purchased for the Virginia Company," *VMHB* 77 (1969): 347–60; William S. Powell, "Books in the Virginia Colony before 1624," *WMQ*, 3rd ser., 5 (1948): 177–84. The subjects I deal with in this section are discussed at much greater length in Richard Beale Davis, *Intellectual Life in the Colonial South*, 3 vols. (Knoxville: University of Tennessee Press, 1978).
40. Richard Shelford, who may have been a schoolmaster, died on board ship en route to Virginia in 1708. He had in his effects six Testaments, six psalters, twelve primers, and six hornbooks. Middlesex County Will Book [A], 1698–1713, 207–8 (reference provided by Darrett and Anita Rutman).
41. Richard Beale Davis, "The Literary Climate of Jamestown Under the Virginia Company, 1607–1624," *Toward a New American Literary History: Essays in Honor of Arlin Turner*, ed. Louis J. Budd et al. (Durham, N.C.: Duke University Press, 1980), 36–53 (quotations: 37, 41, 49–50, 51–52); Louis B. Wright, "The Classical Tradition in Colonial Virginia," *PBSA* 33 (1939): 85–97.
42. Jon Butler, ed., "Two 1642 Letters from Virginia Puritans," *Procs. MHS* 84 (1972): 107.
43. *Recs. Va. Co.*, 1:589; 4:271; *Calendar of State Papers, Colonial Series, America and West Indies 1681–1685*, ed. J. W. Fortescue (London, 1898), no. 1329; *WMQ*, 1st ser., 4 (1895): 15. The 1683 donation included, as well, thirty-nine

copies of the *Book of Common Prayer,* the Homilies, the Canons, the Thirty-Nine Articles, and the "Tables of Marriages." In the mid-1680s further donations of books for religious services and instruction were provided by the Crown to several mainland colonies and those in the West Indies. Philip S. Haffenden, "The Anglican Church in Restoration Colonial Policy," in *17th-Century America: Essays in Colonial History,* ed. James Morton Smith (Chapel Hill: University of North Carolina Press, 1959), 188.

44. *Recs. Va. Co.,* 1:575, 3:506–07.

45. A number of probate inventories are cited in Wyndham Blanton, *Medicine in Virginia in the Seventeenth Century* (Richmond, Va.: Garrett and Massie, 1930), 89–92.

46. Hening, *Statutes,* 2:246. In 1661 the York County court, "finding it very necessary that a Statute booke be provided for the Courts use," sought to acquire the English statutes "out of England the next Shipping"; the acquisition cost 450 pounds of tobacco. York County Deeds, Orders, and Wills 3:125, 134 (hereafter, DOW), transcript, Department of Historical Research, Colonial Williamsburg Foundation.

47. George Thorpe to Sir Edwin Sandys, May 15, 1621 in *Recs. Va. Co.,* 3:447; *William Fitzhugh and His Chesapeake World, 1676–1701: The Fitzhugh Letters and Other Documents,* ed. Richard Beale Davis (Chapel Hill: University of North Carolina Press, 1963), 110–11, 124, 363–64. See also A. G. Roeber, *Faithful Magistrates and Republican Lawyers: Creators of Virginia's Legal Culture, 1680–1810* (Chapel Hill: University of North Carolina Press, 1981), 57–58. Thorpe's request is usefully analyzed in Powell, "Books in the Virginia Colony," 181–82.

48. Bruce, *Institutional History,* 1:440–41. Bruce's several chapters (13–16) on books contain much information not carried over into this narrative.

49. Calculations for St. Mary's County provided by Lois Green Carr; James Horn, *Adapting to a New World: English Society in the Seventeenth-Century Chesapeake* (Chapel Hill: University of North Carolina Press, 1994), 320–21. For comparable figures embracing several Maryland counties, see Gloria L. Main, *Tobacco Colony: Life in Early Maryland, 1650–1720* (Princeton, N.J.: Princeton University Press, 1982), 169, 242. My own calculations in this and the succeeding paragraph are based on transcriptions of surviving inventories from St. Mary's County (1658–1676; Maryland Hall of Records, Annapolis; provided by Lois G. Carr), York County (1637–1684, Department of Historical Research, Colonial Williamsburg Foundation), and Surry (provided by Kevin Kelly, Colonial Williamsburg Foundation). Probate inventories survive for only a limited fraction of the colonists; in the case of York County it may dip to 30 percent or less, the estimate given by Ronald Grim, "The Absence of Towns in Seventeenth-Century Virginia: The Emergence of Service Centers in York County" (Ph.D. dissertation, University of Maryland, 1977), 108.

50. This point is emphasized by George K. Smart, "Private Libraries in Colonial Virginia," *American Literature* 10 (1940): 33–34.

51. Horn, *Adapting to a New World,* 320–21, provides comparative data for one English region. For New England, see Chapter 4.

52. A woman of some means, Sarah Willoughy, owned two Bibles in quarto, a Latin Bible and two Testaments when her inventory was taken in 1674;

WMQ, 1st ser., 3 (1894–1895):44–45. A fifth of planters' inventories in Lower Norfolk County "explicitly mentioned Bibles"; Horn, *Adapting to a New World,* 402.

53. Hugh Stamford, DOW 3:23; though it is misleading to single out any one inventory as typical, Thomas Deacon's (1648; York County) is surely indicative: "A Bible, the practice of piety, a testament & a small parcell of other bookes all old." *WMQ,* 1st ser., 3 (1895): 181.

54. Historians of early Virginia have exaggerated the presence of "Anglican" books among these inventories; see Hall, *Cultures of Print,* 121 n. 68.

55. In seventeenth-century Maryland, "only a handful of men, probably fewer than 5 percent of all free white adult males, owned reading matter other than these [Bibles, psalters, etc.], such as sermons and moral treatises, or books on medicine, mathematics, history, and the law." Main, *Tobacco Colony,* 244.

56. *Md. Arch.* 4:75–76; Ames, *Reading,* 55 (for an inventory with twelve manuscripts); the "list of writings in a Red Trunke" inventoried after the death of James Stone of York County in 1648 specified six separate account books (DOW 2:377); Davis, ed., *Fitzhugh,* 82.

57. In *Bookbinding in Colonial Virginia* (Williamsburg, Va.: Colonial Williamsburg, 1966), C. C. Samford and John M. Hemphill II note (p. 1) the presence of an English bookbinder in Lower Norfolk County, Virginia, in the 1640s, but it is very unlikely that he practiced his craft in the colony.

58. Middlesex County Will Book [A], 1698–1713, 55–76 (a transcription provided by Ann Smart Martin). Another Middlesex merchant, Robert Dudley, whose will is dated November 1701, had three hornbooks and one primer and three other books (Middlesex County Will Book G, Order Book No. 3, p. 105); information provided by Darrett and Anita Rutman. English hornbooks, small single-sided sheets printed with the alphabet and a few sentences or syllables, are described in Margaret Spufford, ed., *The World of Rural Dissenters, 1520–1725* (Cambridge: Cambridge University Press, 1995), 72–73.

59. St. Mary's County Inventories; DOW 5:113–14, possibly an inventory of goods left on account in Virginia by London merchants.

60. DOW 4:230; *The Old Dominion in the Seventeenth Century: A Documentary History of Virginia, 1606–1689,* ed. Warren M. Billings (Chapel Hill: University of North Carolina Press, 1975), 192–98. Newell's network of trade relations is described in Grim, "Absence of Towns," 164–71. No books: in York County, Edward Phelps (1679), DOW 6:111, though his inventory included 15 quires of "white writing paper"; Edward Lockey (1667), DOW 4:191–92. It is suggestive that the store of Robert Slye of St. Mary's City contained one paper book, ten inkhorns, five and one half reams of paper, and but two "printed" books. St. Mary's County inventories.

61. Inventory of John Sampson, Rappahannock County, *Deeds, Etc.* No. 6, p. 62 (microfilm, Department of Historical Research, Colonial Williamsburg Foundation); alluded to in Ames, *Reading,* 34, this inventory was traced for me by Kevin Kelly. No valuation was given for the law books; the store contained two Bibles and perhaps another eight books.

62. Horn, *Adapting to a New World,* 158.

63. Kenneth A. Lockridge, *Literacy in Colonial New England: An Inquiry into the Social Context of Literacy in the Early Modern West* (New York: W. W. Norton, 1974), chap. 2; see also Bruce, *Institutional History,* 1:450. Based on the York County court records, my rough count of the ratio of marks to signatures among women is 3:1. Amandus Johnson, *The Swedish Settlements on the Delaware, 1638–1664,* 2 vols. (Philadelphia: Swedish Colonial Society, 1911), has data on literacy among Swedes (1:28) and Finns (1:31). No evidence is available on the literacy of African-Americans in the Chesapeake, who numbered some 10,000 by the end of the century; the presence of Christian language in the wills of free blacks suggests a measure of literacy. T. H. Breen and Stephen Innes, *"Myne owne Ground": Race and Freedom on Virginia's Eastern Shore, 1640–1676* (New York: Oxford University Press, 1980), 87–88.

64. DOW 3:68.

65. See, e.g., DOW 4:12, for a mother willing a daughter her "Church Bible" (1665). There is also evidence to suggest that, in willing books to the next generation, fathers assigned far more books to sons than to daughters, and sometimes provided *only* for sons; when gifts and bequests were made to wives and daughters, these were typically Bibles and books of devotion. See, e.g., *William Fitzhugh,* ed. Davis, 379; will of John Catlett, *VMHB* 3 (1895): 64; will of Samuel Baylly, *VMHB* 8 (1901): 422; for contrary examples, *VMHB* 5 (1897): 183 and, most interestingly, Thomas Teackle's legacies of learned books, including Greek and Latin lexicons, to his two daughters: Anne Floyd Upshur and Ralph T. Whitelaw, "Library of the Rev. Thomas Teackle," *WMQ,* 2nd ser., 23 (1943): 301–03.

66. Margaret Spufford, "First Steps in Literacy: The Reading and Writing Experiences of the Humblest Seventeenth-Century Spiritual Autobiographers," *Social History* 4 (1979): 407–35; and see Chapter 4.

67. Edward Neill, *Virginia Carolorum: The Colony under the Rule of Charles the First and Second, A.D. 1625–A.D. 1685* (Albany, 1886), 119; Rutman and Rutman, *Place over Time,* 158–61; *VMHB* 9 (1901): 80.

68. Lois G. Carr, "The Foundations of Social Order: Local Government in Colonial Maryland," in *Town and County: Essays on the Structure of Local Government in the American Colonies,* ed. Bruce C. Daniels (Middletown, Conn.: Wesleyan University Press, 1978), 80, 83; Carr, "County Government in Maryland," 622; Blanton, *Medicine in Virginia,* 88–90; Bruce, *Institutional History,* 1:450.

69. For references in wills by parents, see especially "Isle of Wight County Records," *WMQ,* 1st ser., 7 (1899): 221, 222, 236, 241, 244, 248; Rosemary C. Neal, *Elizabeth City County, Virginia Deeds, Wills, Court Orders, Etc., 1634, 1659, 1688–1702* (Bowie, Md.: Heritage Books, 1986), 86, 88. See also Edgar W. Knight, *A Documentary History of Education in the South Before 1860,* 5 vols. (Chapel Hill: University of North Carolina Press, 1949), 1:53–55.

70. William Stevens Perry, ed., *Historical Collections Relating to the American Colonial Church,* 5 vols. in 4 (Hartford, 1870), 1:283, 288, 300 and passim (twenty-nine clergy returned such reports, out of forty-five parishes); Ames, *Reading,* 16. Davis, *Intellectual Life,* chap. 3, overstates both the percentage of literacy and the number of schools.

71. Jon Butler, "Thomas Teackle's 333 Books: A Great Library on Virginia's Eastern Shore, 1697," *WMQ*, 3rd ser., 49 (1992):449–91; Calvert Inventory, Testamentary Papers, Maryland Hall of Records; *WMQ*, 1st ser., 3 (1894–95): 133–34; Bruce, *Institutional History*, 1:419; *WMQ*, 1st ser., 2 (1893–1894): 169–74, subject analysis from Bruce, *Institutional History*, 1:426; Ames, *Reading*, 39.
72. St. Mary's County Inventories; *WMQ*, 1st ser., 8 (1899–1900): 18; Louis B. Wright, "The Gentleman's Library in Early Virginia: The Literary Interests of the First Carters," *HLQ* 1 (1937): 2–61.
73. *WMQ*, 1st ser., 8 (1899–1900): 237; *WMQ*, 1st ser., 3 (1894–1895): 44–45.
74. *WMQ*, 1st ser., 3 (1894–1895): 246; *William Fitzhugh*, ed. Davis, 379; Main, *Tobacco Colony*, 163.
75. *Recs. Va. Co.*, 2:506–07. Powell, "Books in the Virginia Colony before 1624," brings together much information on the ordering of books, and what was available.
76. Blanton, *Medicine in Virginia*, 90; Neill, *Virginia Carolorum*, 406; Augusta B. Fothergill, *Wills of Westmoreland County, Virginia 1654–1800* ([n.p.]: Appeals Press, 1925), 80, 97; Noel Currier-Briggs, *Virginia Settlers and English Adventurers: Abstracts of Wills*, 3 vols. (Baltimore: Genealogical Pub. Co., 1970), 1:401; and see in general Bruce, *Institutional History*, 1, Chap. 13.
77. John and Nesta Ewan, *John Banister and His Natural History of Virginia 1678–1692* (Urbana: University of Illinois Press, 1970), 131, and, in general, chap. 11: "Books of Banister's Bearing His Signature"; *William Fitzhugh*, ed. Davis, 124, 233; Bruce, *Institutional History*, 1:434.
78. Ewan and Ewan, *John Banister*, 134; *William Fitzhugh*, ed. Davis, 286, 288, 353; *The Calvert Papers* (Maryland Historical Society Fund Publication No. 28, 1889), 236; see also 244–50.
79. Lawrence C. Wroth, "The First Sixty Years of the Church of England in Maryland, 1632–1692," *MdHM* 22 (1916): 4 (Claiborne was seeking to recruit a minister); Bruce, *Institutional History*, 1:432 n.; *William Fitzhugh*, ed. Davis, 271, 333, 341; Ewan and Ewan, *John Banister*, 51–52; *The Correspondence of the Three William Byrds of Westover, Virginia, 1684–1776*, ed. Marion Tinling (Charlottesville: University of Virginia Press, 1977), 61. See also Elizabeth Donnan, "Eighteenth-Century English Merchants: Micajah Perry," *Journal of Economic and Business History* 4 (1931): 74, 75.
80. See, e.g., *The Vestry Book of Kingston Parish, Mathew County, Virginia*, trans. C. G. Chamberlayne (Richmond, Va.: Old Dominion Press, 1929), 2.
81. Described in Hall, *Cultures of Print*, 143–47.
82. Louis B. Wright, "Pious Reading in Colonial Virginia," *Journal of Southern History* 6 (1940): 389; *VMHB* 3 (1895): 64; *WMQ*, 1st ser., 17 (1909): 271; *William Fitzhugh*, ed. Davis, 101 n.
83. T. A. Birrel, "Reading as Pastime: The Place of Light Literature in Some Gentlemen's Libraries of the 17th Century," in *Property of a Gentleman: The Formation, Organisation and Dispersal of the Private Library, 1620–1920*, ed. Robin Myers and Michael Harris (Winchester, Eng.: St. Paul's Bibliographies, 1991), 113–31. Like the argument concerning "Anglican" culture, the kindred assertion of "gentlemen's" libraries and readers severely distorts the uses of literacy in the Chesapeake. But see the inventory of Captain Thomas Cocke (1697), *WMQ*, 1st ser., 4 (1895–1896): 15.

84. Louis B. Wright, "The Purposeful Reading of Our Colonial Ancestors," *ELH* 4 (1937): 85–111.
85. John Melville Jennings, "Notes on the Original Library of the College of William and Mary in Virginia, 1693–1705," *PBSA* 41 (1947): 242; Hartwell, Blair, and Chilton, *Present State of Virginia,* 68–69.
86. *Recs. Va. Co.,* 1, 247, 248, 421; Jennings, "Notes on the Original Library," 239–67. The information in the succeeding paragraph also comes from this essay, which is incorporated into Jennings, *The Library of the College of William and Mary in Virginia, 1693–1793* (Charlottesville: University Press of Virginia, 1968). A catalogue of Nicholson's books, based on a manuscript inventory of 1695, is included in Jennings's essay.
87. A full listing of these texts lies beyond the scope of this chapter. To cite but a single example, Thomas Mathew's narrative of Bacon's rebellion, written after the turn of the century at the request of Robert Harley, remained in manuscript in the Harleian library until it somehow passed into the book trade and thence into the hands of Thomas Jefferson. Howard Mumford Jones, *The Literature of Virginia in the Seventeenth Century* (1946; repr. Charlottesville: University Press of Virginia, 1968), 107 n. 23; much useful information on such manuscripts is provided in this short study as well as in Davis, *Intellectual Life.*
88. Francis Berkeley, Jr., Introduction to John Rolfe, *A True Relation of the State of Virginia* (New Haven, Conn.: Yale University Press, 1951), 24–25.
89. Colonel John Catlett to Thomas Catlett, April 1, 1664 (Colonial Williamsburg Foundation Library Transcripts, 1); Neill, *Virginia Carolorum,* 315.
90. James Grant Wilson, *A Maryland Manor* (Maryland Historical Society Fund Publication No. 30, Pt. 2 [Baltimore, 1890]), 32. Herrman claimed that he had expended £200 sterling on the map.
91. Davis, *Intellectual Life,* 1:12. For a thoroughgoing critique, see William Spengemann, *A New World of Words: Redefining Early American Literature* (New Haven, Conn.: Yale University Press, 1994), chap. 2.
92. The several such incidents include *Md. Arch.* 1:427–31; Davis, *Intellectual Life,* 1354. John Hammond "fixed my name" to *Leah and Rachel* (London, 1656) to "prevent the imputation of a libeller." Hall, ed., *Narratives Md.,* 307.
93. *The Complete Works of Captain John Smith (1580–1631),* ed. Philip L. Barbour, 3 vols. (Chapel Hill: University of North Carolina Press, 1986), 1:5–6, 124; Smith, *Works,* ed. Arber, 1:1–4. Whether the Virginia Company deliberately sponsored this publication is unclear.
94. *Recs. Va. Co.,* 1, 451–52; Smith, *Works,* ed. Arber, 1:622. I accept the argument of David Quinn that the "Smith" who came before the Company was not John, the explorer, but John Smyth of Nibley. Quinn, "List of Books," 352.
95. Smith, *Works,* ed. Arber, 1:cxxvi.
96. Ibid., 275–77. The many misgivings this practice aroused in authors and patrons are described in H. S. Bennett, *English Books & Readers 1603 to 1640* (Cambridge: Cambridge University Press, 1970), chap. 2; Phoebe Sheavyn, *The Literary Profession in the Elizabethan Age* (Manchester: Manchester University Press, 1909), chap. 1. See also Franklin B. Williams, *Index of Dedications and Commendatory Verses in English Books before 1641* (London: Bibliographical Society, 1962). Another complicating circumstance was the

high-risk game of being a court favorite and its implications for authors such as Smith, who removed a reference to Sir Walter Raleigh from his *Overall Historic Map of Virginia* (1612) after Raleigh was beheaded. Smith, *Complete Works,* ed. Barbour, 1:150 n. 5.

97. George Alsop, *A Character of the Province of Maryland* (1666), quoted in Moses Coit Tyler, *A History of American Literature during the Colonial Time,* 2 vols. (New York, 1897), 1:67.
98. [Alexander Whitaker], *Good Newes from Virginia* (London, 1613), sig. A2 recto.
99. Hall, *Narratives Md.*, 307. Closer to Smith in time, the author of *Newes from Virginia: The Lost Flocke Triumphant* (London, 1610), declared, "Reader: Thou dost peradventure imagine that I am mercenarie in this busines, and write for money (as your moderne Poets use) hyred by some of those ever to be admired adventurers to flatter the World. No; I disclaim it." Brown, *Genesis of the United States,* 1:421.
100. *The Discoveries of John Lederer,* trans. William Talbot (London, 1672), sig. A2 recto, verso; J. W. Saunders, "The Stigma of Print: A Note on the Social Bases of Tudor Poetry," *Essays in Criticism* 1 (1951): 139–64.
101. Smith, *Works,* ed. Arber, 1:178.
102. *William Fitzhugh,* ed. Davis, 326–27, 345–49. Fitzhugh may have known that authors who wrote for the theater were relatively well paid.
103. Adrian Johns, *The Nature of the Book* (Chicago, Ill.: University of Chicago Press, 1998), chap. 7, esp. pp. 459–65.
104. Raymond P. Stearns, *Science in the British Colonies of America* (Carbondale: University of Illinois Press, 1970), chap. 6; Michael Hunter, *Science and Society in Restoration England* (Cambridge: Cambridge University Press, 1981), 36, 41, 49–50, 52, and chap. 3; Ewan and Ewan, *John Banister,* chap. 5.
105. The text is included in *Narratives of the Insurrections,* ed. Andrews, 47–98. The much-disputed questions of authorship and distribution are addressed in Jones, *Literature of Virginia,* 108 n. 25, and in W. H. Ward, "'To Caesar Friend or Foe?' The Burwell Papers and Bacon's Rebellion," in *Essays in Early Virginia Literature Honoring Richard Beale Davis,* ed. J. A. Leo Lemay (New York: Burt Franklin, 1977), 73–90. My account leans toward Jones's interpretation. Alsop's work is described in J. A. Leo Lemay, *Men of Letters in Colonial Maryland* (Knoxville: University of Tennessee Press, 1972), 48–69.
106. [John Grave], *A Song of Sion* ([London], 1662).

Chapter 3. Printing and Bookselling in New England, 1638–1713

1. Perry Miller, *The New England Mind: The Seventeenth Century* (Cambridge, Mass.: Harvard University Press, 1954), ix. Among the historians who have qualified this assertion of unanimity is, of course, Miller himself, in his sequel, subtitled *From Colony to Province* (1953).
2. Hugh Amory, "A Bible and Other Books: Enumerating the Copies in Seventeenth Century Essex County," in *Order and Connection: Studies in Bibliography and Book History,* ed. R. C. Alston (Cambridge: D. S. Brewer, 1997), 17–37.

3. Winship, *Cambridge Press,* 294; Ford, *Boston Book Market,* 116, 121, 139; Roger Thompson, *Sex in Middlesex: Popular Mores in a Massachusetts County, 1649–1699* (Amherst: University of Massachusetts Press, 1986).
4. Benjamin Lynde, Diaries, Nov. 4, 1687, Massachusetts Historical Society, Boston, Mass. On Quaker books, see *Mass. Records,* 4, pt. 1: 278.
5. Michael Treadwell, "1695–1995: Some Tercentenary Thoughts on the Freedoms of the Press," *HLB,* n.s., 7 (1996): 3–19.
6. Winship, *Cambridge Press,* 283, 317.
7. Ibid., 179; Bernard Bailyn, *The New England Merchants in the Seventeenth Century* (Cambridge, Mass.: Harvard University Press, 1955).
8. My count, differing somewhat from NAIP (which does not, of course, record lost editions), for reasons given in Appendix 1.
9. The Bay Psalm Book, the Eliot Indian Bible, and the various colonial Laws will usually be cited by uniform title in roman, not by their actual titles, e.g., *The Whole Book of Psalms* (or, *The Psalms, Hymns, and Spiritual Songs*), *Mamusse Wunnutupanatamwe,* etc.
10. William S. Reese, *The Printer's First Fruits: An Exhibition of American Imprints, 1640–1742* (Worcester, Mass.: American Antiquarian Society, 1989), no. 11; Sidney E. Berger, "Innovation and Diversity Among the Green Family of Printers," *Printing History* 12 (1990): 7; and cf. Thomas Goddard Wright, *Literary Culture in Early New England, 1620–1730* (New Haven, Conn.: Yale University Press, 1920), [82].
11. Elizabeth C. Reilly, *A Dictionary of Colonial American Printers' Ornaments and Illustrations* (Worcester, Mass.: American Antiquarian Society, 1975), no. 849; that is the same ornament as Robert Steele, *A Bibliography of Royal Proclamations of the Tudor and Stuart Sovereigns* (Oxford: Clarendon Press, 1910), "The Royal Arms as on Printed Proclamations" (2:497–540), no. 22. The colonial printer cut out Charles's initials and replaced them with William's, in black-letter type.
12. William C. Kiessel, "The Green Family: A Dynasty of Printers," *NEHGR* 104 (1950): 81–93; Mass. Archives 58:135 (State Archives, Columbia Point, Boston, Mass.).
13. Thomas, *Hist. Printing,* 86–87.
14. See generally Winship, *Cambridge Press*; and for the later history of the press, William Kellaway, *The New England Company, 1649–1776: Missionary Society to the American Indians* ([London]: Longmans, 1961).
15. Winship, *Cambridge Press,* 266, 269.
16. Hugh Amory, *First Impressions: Printing in Cambridge, 1639–1989* (Cambridge, Mass.: Harvard University, 1989), 61–63, is an attempt to account for the use of this paper stock.
17. Bond and Amory, *Harvard Catalogues,* xxvii.
18. Bradford F. Swan, *Gregory Dexter of London and New England, 1610–1700* (Rochester, N.Y.: Leo Hart, 1949); Winship, *Cambridge Press,* 72.
19. Ibid., 30; Hugh Amory, *Steven Day's First Type* (Cambridge, Mass., 1989); Thomas, *Hist. Printing,* 54.
20. David Cressy, *Coming Over: Migration and Communication between England and New England in the Seventeenth Century* (Cambridge: Cambridge University Press, 1987), chap. 1.

21. *Some Correspondence between the Governors . . . of the New England Company in London and the Commissioners of the United Colonies in America* (London: Spottiswoode, 1896), 62, trans. pp. 64–65.
22. See Amory, *First Impressions,* for the laws.
23. Morison, *Harv. Coll.,* 345; Francis Jennings, *The Invasion of America: Indians, Colonialism, and the Cant of Conquest* (Chapel Hill: University of North Carolina Press, [1975]).
24. John Dunton, "Letters Written from New-England," ed. W. H. Whitmore, *Publications of the Prince Society* 4 (1867): 57; Winship, *Cambridge Press,* 226, 228.
25. Ibid., 320.
26. Cf. a bill from John Usher to Governor Bellingham, 1668, including items purchased from his father in 1662–1663. *Mass. Archives,* 100:158.
27. Samuel Abbot Green, *John Foster: The Earliest American Engraver and the First Boston Printer* (Boston, 1909); Sewall, *Diary,* "Sewall's Imprints": 1108–11; order to pay Ratcliffe 9*s*. for government printing, 1675, *Mass. Archives* 100:305; S. J. (ed.), "Letters of Chief Justice Sewall," *NEHGR* 9 (1855): 287–88.
28. Benjamin Harris, *Publick Occurrences* (Boston, 1690); William Kellaway, "Marmaduke Johnson and a Bill for Type," *HLB* 8 (1954): 224–27.
29. Duniway, *Freedom of the Press,* 60.
30. Ibid., 64.
31. Littlefield, *Boston Printers,* 2:31–2, 47, 52.
32. Jeffries Papers, 1:122, Massachusetts Historical Society, Boston, Mass.; these engravings are Reilly, *Dictionary of Colonial Ornaments,* nos. 871 & 931.
33. William H. Whitmore, *A Bibliographical Sketch of the Laws of the Massachusetts Colony from 1630 to 1686* (Boston: Rockwell & Churchill, 1890), 128–38; Jeffries Papers, 1:101.
34. Bartholomew Green's printing bill, October 20, 1690, Mass. Archives, 58: 137; Winship, *Cambridge Press,* 328; Thomas's account of Green is based on the obituary in the *Boston News-Letter,* Jan. 4, 1733.
35. *DAB,* s.n. Green, Bartholomew.
36. Thomas, *Hist. Printing,* 90.
37. Samuel Eliot Morison, *The Intellectual Life of Colonial New England,* 2nd ed. (Ithaca, N.Y.: Cornell University Press, 1956), 199–208.
38. Mather, *Diary,* 1:472.
39. Thomas, *Hist. Printing,* 311.
40. Ibid., 296.
41. Rollo G. Silver, "Financing the Publication of Early New England Sermons," *SB* 11 (1958): 175–78.
42. Edmund S. Morgan, *The Puritan Family: Religion and Domestic Relations in Seventeenth-Century New England,* new ed., rev. & enl. (New York: Harper & Row, 1966), 173.
43. Michael Zuckerman, *Peaceable Kingdoms: New England Towns in the Eighteenth Century* (New York: Knopf, 1970).
44. Cotton Mather, *What Should Be Most of All Tho't Upon* (Boston, 1713), pref.
45. Wilberforce Eames, "Early New England Catechisms," *Procs. AAS* 12 (1898): 76–182. He lists a ghost of John Davenport's lost "shorter catechism"

(Cambridge, 1650?) under Roxbury (by "Samuel Danforth"), and for Norris, see R. J. Roberts, "A New Cambridge, N.E., Imprint: The Catechisme of Edward Norris, 1649," *HLB* 13 (1959): 25–28.

46. Cotton Mather, *Work upon the Ark* (Boston, 1689), intro., sec. 11.
47. On Pembroke's litigation, see Alicia C. Williams, "Plaintiff/Defendant Guide to Suffolk County (Mass.) Common Pleas," *The Mayflower Descendant* 35 (1985): 153–54; 36 (1986): 50–51, 180; 40 (1990): 192–93; 41 (1991): 45, 197; 42 (1992): 166; on Wheeler, see Holmes, *Cotton Mather,* 2:453 (Evans 793, a lost title), 3:973; and Evans 796.
48. Sewall, *Diary,* [495]; on this practice generally, see George Selement, *Keepers of the Vineyard: The Puritan Ministry and Collective Culture in Colonial New England* (Lanham, Md.: University Press of America, 1984), chap. 4.
49. Mather, *Diary,* 1:548; 2:135.
50. Ford, *Boston Book Market,* 108–20; George E. Bowman, "Governor Thomas Prence's Will and Inventory, and the Records of His Death," *The Mayflower Descendant* 3 (1901): 203–16.
51. Ford, *Boston Book Market,* 86–87.
52. Hugh Amory, "Under the Exchange: The Unprofitable Business of Michael Perry, a Seventeenth-Century Boston Bookseller," *Procs. AAS* 103 (1993): 31–60.
53. Richard R. Johnson, *Adjustment to Empire: The New England Colonies, 1675–1715* ([New Brunswick, N.J.]: Rutgers University Press, 1981), 355–56.
54. "The Mather Papers," *Coll. MHS,* 4th ser., 8 (1868): 493; H. R. Plomer, et al., *A Dictionary of the Printers and Booksellers . . . in England, Scotland and Ireland from 1668 to 1725* (Oxford: Bibliographical Society [of London], 1922).
55. John Dunton, *The Life and Errors of John Dunton* (London, 1705), 127–28.
56. Suffolk County (Mass.) Common Pleas, Record Book (Oct. 7, 1707), p. 67 (Mass. Archives).
57. Mather, *Diary,* 2:242; and cf. 283.
58. Winship, *Cambridge Press,* 293.
59. Ibid., 239.
60. Hannah D. French, "Bookbinding in the Colonial Period, 1636–1783," in *Bookbinding in America,* ed. Hellmut Lehmann-Haupt (Portland, Me.: Southworth-Anthoensen Press, 1941), 8–47.
61. Hall, *Worlds,* 48; Sylvester Judd, *History of Hadley* (Springfield, Mass.: H. R. Huntting & Co., 1905), 61. Eleazar Phillips was the first Massachusetts bookseller to appear in an imprint outside Boston (Charlestown, 1715).
62. Harriet S. Tapley, *Salem Imprints, 1768–1825* (Salem, Mass.: Essex Institute, 1927), 163–71.
63. See pp. 111–12; and cf. Gloria L. Main, who uses books as an "index of amenity" in "The Distribution of Consumer Goods in Colonial New England: A Subregional Approach," *Annual Proceedings of the Dublin Seminar for New England Folklife* 12 (1989): 165.
64. [Benjamin Colman], *Some Reasons and Arguments Offered to the Good People of Boston . . . for the Setting Up of Markets* (Boston, 1719); the regulations appointing market days on Thursday (1633) and on Tuesday, Thursday, and Saturday "and no other days" (1696) were apparently not enforced.

65. Cf. Draper's bill for "the &c.," 1731, reprinted in Rollo G. Silver, "Publishing in Boston, 1726–1757: The Accounts of Daniel Henchman," *Procs. AAS* 66 (1956): 32; discussed in Chapter 9.
66. Ford, *Boston Book Market,* "Lists no. I–V": 88–150.
67. Ibid., 21.
68. "Samuel Sewall," *Sibley,* 2:336; Littlefield, *Boston Booksellers,* facsim. at 2:188: the list includes thirteen copies of Increase Mather's *Ichabod* (1702) and 3 copies of Samuel Willard's *Truly Blessed Man* (1700).
69. Giles Barber, "Books from the Old World and for the New: The British International Trade in Books in the Eighteenth Century," *Studies on Voltaire and the Eighteenth Century* 151 (1976): 185–224.
70. B. J. McMullin, "Joseph Athias and the Early History of Stereotyping," *Quærendo* 23 (1993): 184–207.
71. Ford, *Boston Book Market,* 8 n. 2, and cf. Chiswell's remarks on cheap Dutch-printed English bibles, p. 85.
72. Ibid., 151.
73. Diary of Michael Wigglesworth, New England Historic Genealogical Society, Boston, Mass.
74. Matt B. Jones, "Notes for a Bibliography of Michael Wigglesworth's 'Day of Doom' and 'Meat out of the Eater,'" *Procs. AAS* 39 (1929): 77–84; the older theory, that three colonial editions have been lost, still survives in the *DAB.*
75. Sewall, *Diary,* 174.
76. These incunables were four commentaries on Peter Lombard's Sentences (Goff A–481, B–928, H–287, and G–718); the *Polychronicon* by Ranulf Higden and the *Nuremberg Chronicle* by Hartmann Schedel (Goff H–268 and S–367); William of Ockham's *Decisiones super Potestatem Summi Pontificis* and the *Epistolæ* of Pope Pius II (Goff O–7a and P–722).
77. Amory, "Bible and Other Books."
78. Morison, *The Intellectual Life of Colonial New England,* 142.
79. *The Journal of John Winthrop, 1630–1649,* ed. R. S. Dunn, James Savage, and L. Yeandle (Cambridge, Mass.: Harvard University Press, 1996), 570; "The Mather Papers," 285; facsim. of Sewall's bookplate in Littlefield, *Boston Booksellers,* at 1:111.
80. Wroth, *Col. Printer,* 224.
81. Winship, *Cambridge Press,* 19.
82. Charles Evans, "Oaths of Allegiance in Colonial New England," *Procs. AAS* 31 (1921): 377–438; and cf. Sewall, *Diary,* 319, for a multiple swearing-in.
83. Ford, *Mass. Broadsides*; the 1679 warrant is Bristol B50 (trimmed to the type area, but originally a half-sheet, probably with manuscript signatures, as in later such documents).
84. Winship, *Cambridge Press,* 110.
85. *Mass. Records,* 4, pt. 1:422; for the apportionment of the rate, ibid., 3:28. *Watertown Records* (Watertown, Mass., 1894–1939), 1:68, 75.
86. Ford, *Boston Book Market,* 13; Albert C. Bates, *Connecticut Statute Laws: A Bibliographical List of Editions* ([Hartford, Conn.]: Acorn Club, 1900), [11].
87. *Watertown Records,* 1:121; 2:115.
88. Zechariah Chafee, Jr., ed., "Records of the Suffolk County Court, 1671–1680," *Pubs. CSM* 29–30 (1933): xxviii–xxxv.

89. To supply the place of the lawbook, the Dominion used Wingate's abridgment and Dalton: Jeffries Papers, vol. 1: 64, 71.
90. Johnson, *Adjustment to Empire,* 287, 293–94. Even the legislators found revision of the earlier compilation puzzling on occasion (*Mass. Records,* 4, pt. 2:468–69).
91. Peter Fraser, *The Intelligence of the Secretaries of State & Their Monopoly of Licensed News, 1660–1688* (Cambridge: University Press, 1956).
92. Richard D. Brown, *Knowledge Is Power: The Diffusion of Information in Early America, 1700–1865* (New York: Oxford University Press, 1989), chap. 1.

Chapter 4. Readers and Writers in Early New England

1. *A Parte of a Register* [Edinburgh, 1593], passim.
2. William Haller, *The Rise of Puritanism* (New York: Columbia University Press, 1938).
3. *Records of the English Bible: The Documents Relating to the Translation and Publication of the Bible in English, 1525–1611,* ed. Alfred W. Pollard (Oxford: Oxford University Press, 1911), 41–44; Barbara Kiefer Lewalski, *Protestant Poetics and the Seventeenth-Century Religious Lyric* (Princeton, N.J.: Princeton University Press, 1979), 39 and passim; John N. King, *English Reformation Literature: The Tudor Origins of the Protestant Tradition* (Princeton, N.J.: Princeton University Press, 1982), 212–18; Tessa Watt, *Cheap Print and Popular Piety, 1550–1640* (Cambridge: Cambridge University Press, 1991), chap. 2 and passim; Hall, *Worlds,* chap. 2; Edwin Haviland Miller, *The Professional Writer in Elizabethan England* (Cambridge, Mass.: Harvard University Press, 1959), 54–55; Sharon Achinstein, *Milton and the Revolutionary Reader* (Princeton, N.J.: Princeton University Press, 1997), 114.
4. John Dod and Robert Cleaver, *A Godly Forme of Houshold Government* (1630), quoted in Stephen Foster, *The Long Argument: English Puritanism and the Shaping of New England Culture, 1570–1700* (Chapel Hill: University of North Carolina Press, 1991), 76; and for an excellent overview of the literary campaign, see pp. 85–92. In *Cheap Print and Popular Piety,* Tessa Watt emphasizes the overlap between pious and commercial motives.
5. "Puritanism" is a word I use hesitantly, since it implies a narrower scope of commitment and practice than I wish to evoke.
6. Morison, *Harv. Coll.,* 1:36; King, *English Reformation Literature,* 16–17, 138–44. See also Barbara A. Johnson, *Reading Piers Plowman and The Pilgrim's Progress: Reception and the Protestant Reader* (Carbondale: Southern Illinois University Press, 1992), a reference I owe to Carol Acree Cavalier.
7. My narrative scants the disagreements within New England over policies like the half-way covenant. These disagreements had direct consequences for literary patronage and production, as in the choice of ministers to deliver the election-day sermon in Massachusetts. For an authoritative history of this politics, see Foster, *The Long Argument.*
8. Williston Walker, *The Creeds and Platforms of Congregationalism* (New York, 1893), 369; Lawrence Sasek, *The Literary Temper of the English Puritans* (Baton Rouge: Louisiana State University Press, 1961), 59–61; King, *English Reformation Literature,* chap. 2; *Records of the English Bible,* 40, 167; John R.

Knott, Jr., *The Sword of the Spirit: Puritan Responses to the Bible* (Chicago, Ill.: University of Chicago Press, 1980), 34, 40, 167; Achinstein, *Milton,* 72–73.

9. Its impact on Nonconformity after 1662 is described in N. H. Keeble, *The Literary Culture of Nonconformity in Later Seventeenth-Century England* (Leicester: Leicester University Press, 1987), chap. 3; see also Keith L. Sprunger, *Trumpets from the Tower: English Puritan Printing in the Netherlands, 1600–1640* (New York: E. J. Brill, 1994).
10. Thomas Cartwright, *A Confutation of the Rhemists Translations* (Leyden, 1618), sigs. B3, C5, quoted in Peter Lake, *Moderate Puritans and the Elizabethan Church* (Cambridge: Cambridge University Press, 1982), 288. But see Foster, *Long Argument,* 84–85.
11. *Mass. Recs.* 2:6–7, 203; *Conn. Recs.* 1:520–21, 544–55; 2:307–8; 3:9; *New-Haven's Settling in New-England, and Some Lawes for Government* (London, 1656), 32.
12. The customary method of learning how to read is more fully described in Hall, *Worlds,* chap. 1; see also Chapter 11. E. Jennifer Monaghan calls attention to the exclusion of women from some writing schools: "Literary Instruction and Gender in Colonial New England," in *Reading in America: Literary and Social History,* ed. Cathy N. Davidson (Baltimore, Md.: Johns Hopkins University Press, 1989), 53–80; I have also drawn on a work-in-progress by Monaghan on seventeenth-century school laws. In 1654 the Massachusetts government urged selectmen "not to admitt or suffer any such to be continewed in the office or place of teaching . . . that have manifested themselves unsound in the faith or scandalous in theire lives." This resolution, which was occasioned by worries about religious dissent, did not lead to a system of licensing teachers like that which existed in England. *Mass. Recs,* 4, pt. 1:182–83.
13. Kenneth Lockridge, *Literacy in Colonial New England: An Inquiry into the Social Context of Literacy in the Early Modern West* (New York: W. W. Norton, 1974), 14–27; in a little-noticed passage (p. 14) Lockridge assumed that the ability to read was much more widespread than the ability to write. See also Hall, *Worlds,* 32–34; and for the use of scriveners by those unable to write, David Cressy, *Coming Over: Migration and Communication between England and New England in the Seventeenth Century* (New York: Cambridge University Press, 1987), 217–20. For one methodological issue, and a finding of only 50 percent male literacy, see Ralph J. Crandall and Ralph J. Coffman, "From Emigrants to Rulers: The Charlestown Oligarchy in the Great Migration," *NEHGR* 131 (1977): 1–27, esp. p. 9. Using jury records, Jennifer Monaghan has found a rate of male signature literacy that approaches 90 percent (unpublished research); research such as hers, done across the life cycle and using records other than wills, tends to indicate a higher rate of signing literacy.
14. *Mass. Recs.* 4, pt. 2:395–96; 5:240–41; *Watertown Records, Comprising The First and Second Books of Town Proceedings* (Watertown, Mass., 1894), 102–115, 128 (references I owe to Jennifer Monaghan); *Records and Files of the Quarterly Courts of Essex County, Massachusetts,* 9 vols. (Salem, Mass.: Essex Institute, 1912–1975), 4:212–13; "Middlesex Statistics. 1680," *NEHGR* 5 (1851): 171–73; *Conn. Recs.* 2:307–08. Geraldine J. Murphy, "Massachusetts

Bay Colony: The Role of Government in Education" (Ph.D. dissertation, Radcliffe College, 1960), recounts town and colonial government actions (and to a large extent, inactions) in regard to school laws.

15. *Watertown Records,* 121; Paul Leicester Ford, *The New-England Primer: A History of its Origin and Development* (New York: Dodd, Mead, 1897), [8].
16. Charles Lloyd Cohen, *God's Caress: The Psychology of Puritan Religious Experience* (New York: Oxford University Press, 1986), 164; Elizabeth Lee-Hood has made similar calculations (unpublished seminar paper, Harvard Divinity School).
17. Hall, *Worlds,* 45; *Mass. Recs.* 3:204; and see 5:243.
18. Larzer Ziff, "Upon What Pretext? The Book and Literary History," *Procs. AAS* 95 (1985): 304.
19. Hall, *Worlds,* 31–38; Deborah Keller-Cohen, "The Web of Literacy: Speaking, Reading, and Writing in 17th- and 18th-Century America," in *Literacy: Interdisciplinary Conversations,* ed. Deborah Keller-Cohen (Cresskill, N.J.: Hampton Press, 1994), 155–76.
20. Solomon Stoddard, *The Defects of Ministers Reprov'd* (1724; 2nd ed., Boston, 1747), 15–17.
21. Samuel Whiting, *Abraham's Humble Intercession* (1666), quoted in Matthew Brown, "Orbits of Reading: The Presence of the Text in Early New England" (Ph.D. dissertation, University of Virginia, 1996), 35.
22. *The Actes and Monuments of John Foxe,* ed. Stephen Cattley, 8 vols., (London, 1851), 8:754; Mather, *Magnalia,* 2:145. See also Lewalski, *Protestant Poetics,* chap. 5.
23. *The Apologia of Robert Keayne,* ed. Bernard Bailyn (New York: Harper Torchbooks, 1964), 28; see also *The Diary of Michael Wigglesworth 1653–1657,* ed. Edmund S. Morgan (1951; repr., New York: Harper Torchbooks, 1965), 101.
24. See, e.g., the diary of John Tuck, cited in Joseph Dow, *History of the Town of Hampton, New Hampshire,* 2 vols. (Salem, Mass., 1893), 2:1017 (a reference I owe to Douglas Winiarski). See also David Cressy, "Books as Totems in Seventeenth-Century England and New England," *Journal of Library History* 21 (1986): 92–106.
25. *Thomas Shepard's Confessions,* ed. George Selement and Bruce C. Woolley, *Pubs. CSM* 58 (1981) 184, 63. I am indebted to Elizabeth Lee-Hood's seminar paper for these and other references.
26. Mary Rowlandson, *The Soveraignty and Goodness of God* (1682), repr. in *Puritans among the Indians: Accounts of Captivity and Redemption, 1676–1724,* ed. Alden T. Vaughan and Edward W. Clark (Cambridge, Mass.: Harvard University Press, 1981), 41, 51, 46.
27. Hugh Amory, " 'A Bible and Other Books': Enumerating the Copies in Seventeenth-Century Essex County," in *Order and Connexion,* ed. R. C. Alston (Cambridge: D. S. Brewer, 1997), 22; Thomas Shepard, *Eye-Salve* (Cambridge, Mass., 1673), 50; *Journal of the House of Representatives of Massachusetts, 1715–1717* (Boston: Massachusetts Historical Society, 1919), 113, 214; *Conn. Recs.* 5:436, 529–32. This situation may be a consequence of the colonists' inability to replenish the stock of books brought over in the 1630s; see Chapter 3.

28. Hall, *Worlds,* 247–51; Amory, " 'A Bible and Other Books,' " 17–37; Gloria L. Main, "The Standard of Living in Southern New England, 1640–1733," *WMQ,* 3rd ser., 45 (1988): 133–34.
29. *NEHGR* 33 (1879): 183; Thomas J. Waters, *Ipswich in the Massachusetts-Bay Colony,* 2 vols. (Ipswich, Mass.: Ipswich Historical Society, 1905), 1:50. Certain books that Henry Dunster willed to his wife are cited in Jeremiah Chaplin, *Life of Henry Dunster, First President of Harvard College* (Boston, 1872), 305.
30. *Records and Files of the Quarterly Courts of Essex County,* 3 (1913):65; "Plymouth Colony Libraries 1627: A Report" (Unpublished paper, July 1971, Research Department, Plimoth Plantation). The process of dispersion and transmittal is also touched on in Julius H. Tuttle, "The Libraries of the Mathers," *Procs. AAS* 20 (1910): 169–356.
31. Ford, *Boston Book Market,* 175, 179; Rollo G. Silver, "Publishing in Boston, 1726–1757: The Accounts of Daniel Henchman," *Procs. AAS* 66 (1956): 30–31; Charles F. Heartman, *The New England Primer Issued Prior to 1830* (New York: R. R. Bowker, 1934), xx.
32. *The Notebook of the Reverend John Fiske,* ed. Robert G. Pope, *Pubs. CSM* 47 (1974): 198–200; see also Winship, *Cambridge Press,* 59–60.
33. See page 98.
34. Mather, *Magnalia,* 1:454; "Mather Papers," *Coll. MHS,* 4th ser., 8 (1868): 247; Mather, *Diary,* 1:548, and e.g., 368, 566. A fuller discussion of ministry-distributed books appears in George Selement, *Keepers of the Vineyard: The Puritan Ministry and Collective Culture in Colonial New England* (Lanham, Md.: University Press of America, 1984), 63–73.
35. C. H. Walcott, *Concord in the Colonial Period* (Boston, 1884), 128 (1672); Franklin B. Dexter, "The First Public Library in New Haven," *Papers of the New Haven Colony Historical Society* 6 (1900): 301–13; Michael J. Canavan, "The Old Boston Public Library, 1656–1747," *Pubs. CSM* 12 (1911): 116–32. See also "The First Public Library in Rhode Island," *Publications of the Rhode Island Historical Society,* n.s., 4 (1896): 227–31.
36. Hall, *Worlds,* 48–51; Selma L. Bishop, *Isaac Watts's Hymns and Spiritual Songs (1707): A Publishing History and Bibliography* (Ann Arbor, Mich.: Pierian Press, 1974). The many adaptations and reprintings of these steady sellers may be followed in David A. Currie, "Cotton Mather's *Bonifacius* in Britain and America," in *Evangelicalism: Comparative Studies of Popular Protestantism in North America, the British Isles, and Beyond, 1700–1900,* ed. Mark A. Noll et al. (New York: Oxford University Press, 1994), 73–89; William Haller, *Foxe's Book of Martyrs and the Elect Nation* (London: Jonathan Cape, 1963), "Appendix"; and, above all, Johnson's history of editions of *Pilgrim's Progress* in *Reading Piers Plowman.*
37. Thomas Goddard Wright, *Literary Culture in Early New England, 1620–1730* (New Haven, Conn.: Yale University Press, 1920), 136; Ellen Starr Brinton, *Books by and about the Rogerenes* (New York: New York Public Library, 1945); Mather, *Magnalia,* 1:492.
38. Ford, *Boston Book Market,* 139; see also Wright, *Literary Culture,* 120–23; Shepard, *Eye-Salve,* 31; Urian Oakes, *New England Pleaded With* (Cambridge, Mass., 1673), 40; Mather, *Diary,* 2:242; Hall, *Worlds,* 55. For the kinds of books

being objected to, see J. L. Gaunt, "Popular Fiction and the Ballad Market in the Second Half of the Seventeenth Century," *PBSA* 72 (1978): 1–13.

39. Roger Thompson, *Sex in Middlesex: Popular Mores in a Massachusetts County, 1649–1700* (Amherst: University of Massachusetts Press, 1986), 87; Samuel Eliot Morison, "The Reverend Seaborn Cotton's Commonplace Book," *Pubs. CSM* 32 (1935): 320–52; and for peddlers and their stock, see Chapter 3.

40. Walker, *Creeds and Platforms,* 236; William G. McLoughlin, *New England Dissent, 1630–1933: The Baptists and the Separation of Church and State,* 2 vols. (Cambridge, Mass.: Harvard University Press, 1971), esp. chap. 5.

41. *Mass. Recs.* 4, pt. 1:29–30; Mather, *Magnalia,* 1:492.

42. *Mass. Recs.* 4, pt. 2:62, 73; 5:4.

43. Duniway, *Freedom of the Press,* chaps. 4 and 5; Ford, *Mass Broadsides,* 57–58; Sibley, 1:311–15. Having written a sharp critique of Puritan orthodoxy, the Quaker Peter Folger "set [his] Name / to what I here insert, / Because to be a Libeller, / I hate it with my Heart." Folger, *A Looking-Glasse for the Times* (1676; [n.p.], 1725), 15.

44. A putative book-burning in Harvard Yard is reviewed in Morison, *Harv. Coll.,* 2:497–98.

45. Julius H. Tuttle, "Writings of Rev. John Cotton," in *Bibliographical Essays: A Tribute to Wilberforce Eames* (Cambridge, Mass.: privately printed, 1924), 363–80; "Winthrop Papers," *Coll. MHS,* 4th ser., 7 (1865): 269; *Winthrop Papers* 4:183; Mary Jane Lewis, "A Sweet Sacrifice: Civil War in New England" (Ph.D. dissertation, State University of New York, Binghamton, 1986); Grantland S. Rice, *The Transformation of Authorship in America* (Chicago, Ill.: University of Chicago Press, 1997), 55. The anti-Puritan mood of the 1630s led some of Winthrop's correspondents to use cipher, and shorthand was employed by an occasional colonist as a means of secrecy. For other examples of self-censorship or uneasiness, see Sewall, *Diary,* 1:382, Hall, *Wonders,* 60–61.

46. Holmes, *Cotton Mather,* 3:1236; *Narratives of the Witchcraft Cases 1648–1706,* ed. George Lincoln Burr (New York: Scribners, 1914), 169–70, 187.

47. Thomas Hutchinson, *The History of the Colony and Province of Massachusetts-Bay,* ed. Lawrence Shaw Mayo, 3 vols. (Cambridge, Mass.: Harvard University Press, 1936), 1:192 n; Walker, *Creeds and Platforms,* 304; Michael G. Hall and William L. Joyce, "The Half Way Covenant of 1662: Some New Evidence," *Procs. AAS* 87 (1977): 108; Jonathan Mitchell and Richard Mather, *A Defense of the Answer and Arguments of the Synod met at Boston* (Cambridge, Mass., 1664), sig. A2 recto.

48. See John Morgan, *Godly Learning: Puritan Attitudes towards Reason, Learning and Education, 1560–1640* (Cambridge: Cambridge University Press, 1986).

49. *New Englands First Fruits* (London, 1643), 13–16; "The Lawes of the Colledge . . . [1655]," in "Harvard College Records, pt. 3," *Pubs. CSM* 31 (1935): 327–39; Richard Warch, *School of the Prophets* (New Haven, Conn.: Yale University Press, 1973), chap. 8; D. De Sola Pool, "Hebrew Learning Among the Puritans of New England Prior to 1700," *Publications of the American Jewish Historical Society* 20 (1911): 31–83.

50. David D. Hall, ed., *The Antinomian Controversy, 1636–1638: A Documentary History* (Middletown, Conn.: Wesleyan University Press, 1968), 213; H. S. Bennett, *English Books and Readers, 1603 to 1640: Being a Study in the History of the Book Trade in the Reigns of James I and Charles I* (Cambridge: Cambridge University Press, 1970), 90–91.
51. Winship, *Cambridge Press,* 43–44, 89.
52. Copy at Houghton Library, Harvard University.
53. Mather, *Magnalia,* 1:144–45, 149; Norman Fiering, "Solomon Stoddard's Library at Harvard in 1664," *HLB* 20 (1972): 256–59. William Perkins explained how to make a commonplace book in *The Arte of Prophecying,* included in *The Workes of . . . William Perkins,* 3 vols. (London, 1608–1631), 2:651. Some manuscript examples may more properly be considered "personal miscellanies," a term suggested by Harold Love. See, e.g., George Lyman Kittredge, "A Harvard Salutatory Oration of 1662," *Pubs. CSM* 28 (1935): 1–24.
54. Mather, *Magnalia,* 2:144–45; *Pubs. CSM* 31:335; Morison, *Harv. Coll.,* 1:155, citing a number that survive. The Hoar letter is reprinted in ibid., 2:639–44. See also Elizabeth Eisenstein, *The Printing Press as an Agent of Change* (New York: Cambridge University Press, 1979), 102.
55. Arthur O. Norton, "Harvard Text-Books and Reference Books of the Seventeenth Century," *Pubs. CSM* 28 (1935): 361–438; a rare listing of a student-owned collection is Fiering, "Solomon Stoddard's Library." A number of other title pages containing multiple student signatures may be found in Morison, *Harv. Coll.*
56. William B. Sprague, *Annals of the American Pulpit: Trinitarian Congregationalists,* 2 vols. (New York, 1857), 1:179; Alfred C. Potter, "Catalogue of John Harvard's Library," *Pubs. CSM* 21 (1920): 190–230, supplemented by Henry J. Cadbury, "John Harvard's Library," *Pubs. CSM* 34 (1940): 353–77; *John Winthrop's Journal "History of New England",* ed. James K. Hosmer, 2 vols. (New York, Scribner's, 1910), 2:18.
57. A large number of inventories survive, some of which have been published with full bibliographical descriptions of the titles that appraisers recorded. Inventories without annotation are printed in Wright, *Literary Culture*; others are listed in the bibliography to Perry Miller and Thomas H. Johnson, *The Puritans,* rev. ed., 2 vols. (New York: Harper Torchbooks, 1963), 2:807–11. I am also indebted to Mary Rhinelander McCarl's transcription of Jonathan Mitchell's inventory (1668), with bibliographical annotations. My analysis of the Latin/English ratio is based on the Mitchell and Samuel Lee inventories (as analyzed by Ford, *Boston Book Market,* 5), and on a sample of the books that survive from the Mathers' library (AAS). The comparison with sixteenth-century inventories is based on Elisabeth Leedham-Green, *Books in Cambridge Inventories,* 2 vols. (Cambridge: Cambridge University Press, 1986).
58. Samuel Eliot Morison, "The Library of George Alcock, Medical Student, 1676," *Pubs. CSM* 28 (1935): 350–57.
59. Lists of logic books transmitted in this manner may be found in Rick Kennedy, ed., *Aristotelian and Cartesian Logic at Harvard, Pubs. CSM* 67 (1995): xi–xii; see also note 69.

60. "Mather Papers," 76–77; *Winthrop Papers,* 3:131, 151, 158; "Correspondence of Several of the Founders of the Royal Society with Governor Winthrop of Connecticut," *Procs. MHS* 16 (1878): 206–51; Morison, *Harv. Coll.,* 1:154 n.
61. Mather, *Magnalia,* 2:88; Michael G. Hall, *The Last American Puritan: The Life of Increase Mather* (Middletown, Conn.: Wesleyan University Press, 1988), 129. Notable among these donations are the numerous gifts Samuel Sewall made to Edward Taylor; these may be traced in the "Letter-book of Samuel Sewall," *Coll. MHS,* 6th ser., 1–2 (1886–1888), 1:253, 274, 374–375, 413. Wright, *Literary Culture,* chap. 7, has much information on ordering not carried over into this account.
62. *The Library of The Late Reverend and Learned Mr. Samuel Lee* (Boston, 1693); see Winans, *Book Catalogues,* for subsequent sale catalogues.
63. As indicated in the shop inventory of Duncan Campbell: Littlefield, *Boston Booksellers,* 136.
64. Mather, *Diary,* 1:368, 548, 532; Tuttle, "The Libraries of the Mathers," 269–356, includes a listing Increase made in 1664 of his books, which by this early date numbered nearly 1,000.
65. Samuel Eliot Morison, *The Founding of Harvard College* (Cambridge, Mass.: Harvard University Press, 1935), chap. 19; Morison, *Harv. Coll.,* chap. 15; Bond and Amory, *Harvard Catalogues,* xxv–xxx.
66. *The Light Appearing More and More towards the Perfect Day* (1651), repr. in *Coll. MHS,* 3rd ser., 4 (1834): 128.
67. John Norton, *The Orthodox Evangelist* (London, 1654), 256. Much can be learned about how a minister drew on his library from the careful annotating of Edward Taylor's writings, based on what he owned: *Edward Taylor's "Church Records" and Related Sermons,* ed. Thomas M. and Virginia L. Davis (Boston, Mass.: Twayne, 1981). See also *The Poetical Works of Edward Taylor,* ed. Thomas H. Johnson (New York: Rockland Editions, 1939), 201–29; Kester Svendsen, *Milton and Science* (Cambridge, Mass.: Harvard University Press, 1969), chap. 1: "The Compendious Method of Natural Philosophy: Milton and the Encyclopedia Tradition."
68. "Winthrop Papers," *Coll. MHS,* 3rd ser., 10 (1849): 70–71 (hereafter cited as "Winthrop Papers" [1849]); Samuel Eliot Morison, "The Harvard School of Astronomy in the Seventeenth Century," *NEQ* 7 (1934): 3–24; "Correspondence of Several of the Founders of the Royal Society with Governor Winthrop of Connecticut."
69. R. S. Wilkinson, "The Alchemical Library of John Winthrop, Jr. (1606–1676) and his Descendants in Colonial America," *Ambix* 11 (1963): 139–86. Some thirteen manuscript copies of Morton's *Compendium Physicae,* each prepared by a different student, have been identified (*Pubs. CSM* 30 (1940):xxxiii–xxxvi). But see I. Bernard Cohen, "The Compendium Physicae of Charles Morton, 1627–1698," *Isis* 33 (1942):657–71.
70. Holmes, *Cotton Mather,* 2:729–35; manuscript at Massachusetts Historical Society.
71. Walker, *Creeds and Platforms,* 368–69; Knott, *Sword of the Spirit,* 17; *The Geneva Bible: A Facsimile of the 1560 Edition* (Madison: University of Wisconsin Press, 1960), sig. 4r.

72. Winthrop, *Journal,* 1:179; Richard Bernard, *The Faithful Shepherd* (London, 1609), chaps. 6–8.
73. Hall, ed., *Antinomian Controversy,* 264, 336; Edward Johnson, *The Wonder-Working Providence of Sions Saviour* (1654), ed. J. Franklin Jameson (New York: Scribner's, 1910), 127.
74. Michael Metcalfe, Ms., New Hampshire Historical Society (a text I owe to Douglas Winiarski); Isaac Backus, *A History of New England, with Particular Reference to the Denomination of Christians called Baptists* (Boston, 1777), 223–24, 493; *Records of the First Church in Charlestown, Massachusetts, 1632–1789* (Boston, 1880), iv.
75. Peter Pratt, *The Prey taken from the Strong* (New London, 1725), 15.
76. Foxe, *Actes and Monuments,* 7:314.
77. Bernard, *Faithfull Shepherd,* 94; Johnson, *Wonder-Working Providence,* 127–28, 227; Winthrop, *Journal,* 2:225. See also Keeble, *Literary Culture,* chap. 5.
78. Hall, ed., *Antinomian Controversy,* 380–81; Winthrop, *Journal,* 2:225. See, in general, Lyle Koehler, *A Search for Power: The "Weaker Sex" in Seventeenth-Century New England* (Urbana: University of Illinois Press, 1980). That excessive learning weakened mental balance was a judgment applied as well to men who were "scholars."
79. Jonathan Mitchell, "A Modell For the Maintaining of Students & fellows . . . at the College in Cambridge," *Pubs. CSM* 31 (1935): 309–11.
80. Winthrop, *Journal,* 2:36–37; *Winthrop Papers,* 3:345; Charles Chauncy, *Gods Mercy shewed to His People in Giving Them a Faithful Ministry and Schooles of Learning* (Cambridge, Mass., 1655); *New Englands First Fruits,* 13–14; Morison, *Harv. Coll.,* 1:145. The wider context is sketched in Morgan, *Godly Learning,* chap. 4.
81. Hall, ed., *Antinomian Controversy,* 213; Charles Chauncy, *Antisynodalia,* quoted in Walker, *Creeds and Platforms,* 226 n; Henry Dunster Will, Probate Records, Middlesex County, Mass.
82. "The Countryman's Apocropha," in [John Richardson], *An Almanack . . . for . . . 1670* (Cambridge, Mass., 1670); *Narratives of Witchcraft Cases,* 174; Henry Newman, "A Postscript," *Non Cessant Anni . . . Harvard's Ephemeris* (Cambridge, Mass., 1690).
83. John Norton, *Responsio ad Totam Questionum Syllogen* (London, 1648); Kuno Francke, "The Beginning of Cotton Mather's Correspondence with August Hermann Francke," *Philological Quarterly* 5 (1926): 193–95; see also Hall, *Last American Puritan,* 217–18.
84. "Winthrop Papers" (1849): 71.
85. *Winthrop Papers,* 3:282 n.
86. One version of Anne Bradstreet's prose meditations survives in her own hand (Stevens Memorial Library, North Andover, Massachusetts) and another in the hand of her daughter (Houghton Library, Harvard University).
87. Johnson, *Piers Ploughman,* 187; Nathaniel Morton, *New-Englands Memoriall* (Cambridge, Mass., 1669), sig. a1 verso; John Ward Dean, *Memoir of the Rev. Michael Wigglesworth,* 2nd ed. (Albany, N.Y., 1871), 64–65, and see also Wigglesworth's entries (pp. 81–84) as he was writing *Meat out of the Eater*

(1669); *The Works of Anne Bradstreet in Prose and Verse,* ed. John H. Ellis (Charlestown, Mass., 1867), 4.

88. John Dane's Narrative, 1682," *NEHGR* 8 (1854): 147–56 (more of his text remains in manuscript at the New England Historic Genealogical Society); Harold S. Jantz, "The First Century of New England Verse," *Procs. AAS* 53 (1943): 486. Holmes's autobiography is published in full in *Baptist Piety: The Last Will and Testimony of Obadiah Holmes,* ed. Edwin S. Gaustad (New York: Arno Press, 1980); Goodhue's is printed in Waters, *Ipswich,* 1:519–24; Browne's text is partially quoted in *NEHGR* 2 (1848): 45. "Commonplace Book of Benjamin Franklin (1650–1727)," *Pubs. CSM* 10 (1904–1906): 191–205. The ploughman trope is described in Johnson, *Piers Ploughman.*
89. Cotton Mather, *Memorable Providences, Relating to Witchcrafts and Possession* (Boston, 1689), 45; for a tart response to such criticism, see Jantz, "First Century," 269.
90. Lorrayne Carroll, " 'My Outward Man': The Curious Case of Hannah Swarton," *EAL* 31:1 (1996): 45–73.
91. Winthrop, *Journal,* 1:179.
92. Hall, *Worlds,* chap. 2.
93. Some of this verse, together with information on how it was copied into private journals and put to use, is gathered in *Handkerchiefs from Paul, being Pious and Consolatory Verses of Puritan Massachusetts,* ed. Kenneth B. Murdock (Cambridge, Mass.: Harvard University Press, 1927). See also Jantz, "First Century," 219–508, and for the longer tradition, Ola E. Winslow, *American Broadside Verse From Imprints of the 17th & 18th Centuries* (New Haven, Conn.: Yale University Press, 1930).
94. *Mass. Recs.* 4, pt. 1:381; Wright, *Literary Culture,* 125; and see Chapter 3 for a reappraisal of Wigglesworth's sales. The son of the Hartford minister Samuel Stone alleged in a court hearing that, after his father's death, a manuscript "Body of Divinity, in a catechetical way" had been sold for "sixty pounds," but to whom and why, is unclear. Nor was the book ever printed. Winship, *Cambridge Press,* 53.
95. Harry S. Stout, *The New England Soul: Preaching and Religious Culture in Colonial New England* (New York: Oxford University Press, 1986), 333 n. 7.
96. Wright, *Literary Culture,* 125; Holmes, *Cotton Mather,* 3:975; D. N. Deluna, "Cotton Mather Published Abroad," *EAL* 26 (1991): 145–72; Chester N. Greenough, "A Letter Relating to the Publication of Cotton Mather's Magnalia," *Pubs. CSM* 26 (1927): 296–312, a document instructive about the difficulties of overseeing proof.
97. *Selected Letters of Cotton Mather,* ed. Kenneth Silverman (Baton Rouge: Louisiana State University Press, 1971), 76–77 and passim. In general, see Rollo G. Silver, "Financing the Publication of Early New England Sermons," *SB* 11 (1958): 163–78.
98. Silver, "Publishing in Boston," 19; Samuel Abbott Green, *John Foster: The Earliest American Engraver and the First Boston Printer* (Boston: Massachusetts Historical Society, 1909), 26–28.
99. Even in the case of a manuscript that a preacher reviewed or carefully prepared himself, the written version undoubtedly differed substantially from the spoken, as Increase Mather remarked in his preface to *The Wicked Mans*

Portion (Boston, 1675); see also Bennett, *Books and Readers*, 115–16, and Winfred Herget, "The Transcription and Transmission of the Hooker Corpus," in *Thomas Hooker: Writings in England and Holland, 1626–1633*, ed. George H. Williams et al. (Cambridge, Mass.: Harvard University Press, 1975), 253–70.

100. Tuttle, "Writings of Rev. John Cotton," 363–80.
101. *Thomas Hooker: Writings*, ed. Williams et al., 147–51; the editors extend this analysis to other texts in this collection.
102. Holmes, *Cotton Mather*, 3:1103–14.
103. "Reader, The Old Plea, The Authors absence from the Press, being stil in force, occasions the further desire of this, viz. that before thou readest thou wilt with thy pen mend these following faults." William Adams, *The Necessity of the Pouring out of the Spirit* (Boston, 1679), sig. A4 verso; after listing some errata, the printer added that he was responsible for a number of spellings.
104. Cotton Mather, *Awakening Thoughts on the Sleep of Death* (1712), quoted in Pattie Cowell, "Early New England Women Poets: Writing as Vocation," *EAL* 29 (1994): 104; Phyllis Mack, *Visionary Women: Ecstatic Prophecy in Seventeenth-Century England* (Berkeley: University of California Press, 1992); and see Chapter 2.
105. *The Copy of a Letter Written by Mr. Thomas Parker . . . to His Sister, Mrs. Elizabeth Avery* (London, 1650), 13.
106. Rowlandson, *Soveraignty*, 317, 320–21.
107. As is noted in *The Complete Works of Anne Bradstreet*, ed. Joseph R. McElrath, Jr. and Allan P. Robb (Boston: Twayne, 1981).
108. *Works*, ed. Ellis, 101.
109. Some of the details for other New England writers are provided in Cowell, "Early New England Women Writers." I follow Margaret J. Ezell's argument about the relation between gender and these practices; see, in particular, her analysis of "Patterns of Manuscript Circulation and Publication," *The Patriarch's Wife: Literary Evidence and the History of the Family* (Chapel Hill: University of North Carolina Press, 1987), chap. 3. In some settings, anonymity was deemed "libellous," but in others, as when Cotton Mather availed himself of the practice (two-thirds of his publications were anonymous), it was acceptable both to authors and readers as a sign of self-renunciation or because contemporaries knew how to recognize the presence of a particular writer.
110. Increase Mather, *A Discourse concerning Faith* (Boston, 1710), xvii; Mather, *Magnalia*, 2:154; Dean, *Memoir of Wigglesworth*, 39–45.

Chapter 5. The Atlantic World

1. Ian K. Steele, *The English Atlantic, 1675–1740: An Exploration of Communication and Community* (New York: Oxford University Press, 1986), Pt. 2; Arthur Pierce Middleton, "The Chesapeake Convoy System, 1662–1763," *WMQ*, 3rd ser., 3 (1946): 182–207; Jack P. Greene, *Pursuits of Happiness: The Social Development of Early Modern British Colonies and the Formation of American Culture* (Chapel Hill: University of North Carolina Press, 1988).
2. These numbers, which are derived from NAIP, do not correspond with what was actually printed, for reasons that are explained in Appendix 1, "A

Note on Statistics"; the qualifications expressed in that note also pertain to the other statistics and percentages in this chapter, all of which were calculated from NAIP.

3. John J. McCusker and Russell R. Menard, *The Economy of British America, 1607–1789* (Chapel Hill: University of North Carolina Press, 1985), chap. 10; Evarts B. Greene, *American Population before the Federal Census of 1790* (New York: Columbia University Press, 1932), 118.
4. A. S. W. Rosenbach, *An American Jewish Bibliography* (Baltimore, Md.: American Jewish Historical Society, 1926).
5. McCusker and Menard, *Economy,* 39 n. 5.
6. Ibid., chap. 13.
7. See the "Note on Imports and Domestic Production," at the end of Chapter 5 for discussion of the relative proportions of imported and locally printed books in the American market.
8. Daniel Neal, *The History of New England . . . to 1700,* 2 vols. (London, 1747), 2:225; *Franklin Autobiography,* 1379; Carl Bridenbaugh, "The Press and the Book in Eighteenth-Century Philadelphia," *PMHB* 65 (1941): 1–30.
9. As is pointed out in Appendix 1, however, these totals do not coincide with production as measured by sheets, in which case government printing as a share of total work might fall by half or more.
10. Edward S. Cooke, Jr., *Making Furniture in Preindustrial America: The Social Economy of Newtown and Woodbury, Connecticut* (Baltimore, Md.: Johns Hopkins University Press, 1996). A careful study of the three-tiered geography of Massachusetts in the 1780s reveals that, of a total of 323 towns, 54, most of them located in the eastern part of the state, "controlled" the production and distribution of information. Van Beck Hall, *Politics without Parties: Massachusetts, 1780–1791* (Pittsburgh, Pa: University of Pittsburgh Press, 1972), chap. 1. *Atlas of Early American History,* ed. Lester J. Cappon (Princeton, N.J.: Princeton University Press, 1976), includes useful maps showing the locations of libraries, colleges, medical societies, medical schools, and the like; see also Jesse H. Shera, *Foundations of the Public Library: The Origins of the Public Library Movement in New England 1629–1855* (Chicago, Ill.: University of Chicago Press, 1949), 257.
11. Carole Shammas, *The Pre-Industrial Consumer in England and America* (Oxford: Clarendon Press, 1990).
12. See, in general, Gregory H. Nobles, "Breaking into the Backcountry: New Approaches to the Early American Frontier," *WMQ,* 3rd ser., 46 (1989): 641–70.
13. Thomas, *Hist.Printing,* 508.
14. The intersection of political factionalism and the book trades is described as well in Chapters 7, 8, 9, and 13.
15. Douglas McMurtrie, "The First Decade of Printing in the Royal Province of South Carolina," *Library,* 4th ser., 13 (1932–33): 425–52.
16. Mary Lindsay Thornton, "Public Printing in North Carolina, 1749–1815," *The North Carolina Historical Record* 21 (1944): 182–83; this vacuum opened the way for a commercial product, a compendium issued in 1704 by a London printer for the benefit of merchants trading with the colonies: *An Abridgment of the Laws in Force and Use in Her Majesty's Plantations* (London, 1704).

17. See, e.g., Nicholas Trott, *Laws of the Province of South Carolina* (Charleston, 1736), 111; *The State Records of North Carolina,* ed. Walter Clark, 26 vols. (Goldboro, N.C., 1886–1905) 23:175, 177; and a list of fees (234–40) allowed for preparing handwritten documents; *The Papers of William Penn,* ed. Richard and Mary Dunn, 5 vols. (Philadelphia: University of Pennsylvania Press, 1977–), 2:16; A. G. Roeber, *Faithful Magistrates and Republican Lawyers: The Creation of Virginia Legal Culture, 1680–1810* (Chapel Hill: University of North Carolina Press, 1981), chap. 3; *Journals of the Continental Congress, 1774–1789,* ed. Worthington C. Ford and Gaillard Hunt, 34 vols. (Washington, D.C.: Library of Congress, 1904–1937), 11:474–81.
18. *The Earliest Printed Laws of Pennsylvania, 1681–1713,* ed. John D. Cushing (Wilmington, Del.: Michael Glazier, 1981), viii.
19. McMurtrie, "First Decade," 440–42; Trott, *Laws of the Province of South-Carolina,* v–vi. Trott added, "of use" so that everyone "may readily give Obedience to the same; in which . . . not only their Duty, but also their Safety and Happiness doth consist" (p. vi).
20. *State Records of North Carolina,* 23:113; Albert H. Hoyt, "Historical and Bibliographical Notes," *Procs. AAS* (April 1876): 89–104; Rollo G. Silver, "Government Printing in Massachusetts-Bay, 1700–1750," *Procs. AAS* 68 (1958): 135–62.
21. Hoyt, "Historical and Bibliographical Notes."
22. *Journals of the House of Representatives of Massachusetts, 1715–1717* (Boston: Massachusetts Historical Society, 1919), vii; 44–45. Not until 1771 did the House of Commons agree to have its journal printed.
23. Silver, "Government Printing"; Robert Zemsky, *Merchants, Farmers, and River Gods: An Essay on Eighteenth-Century American Politics* (Boston, Mass.: Gambit, 1971), 241–42.
24. Alison G. Olsen, "Eighteenth-Century Colonial Legislatures and Their Constituents," *Journal of American History* 79 (1982): 550 n. 13, 547 n. 9.
25. Thomas, *Hist. Printing,* 163.
26. Mathew Carey, *Autobiography* (Brooklyn, N.Y.: Research Classics, 1942), 11–16; Thomas, *Hist. Printing,* 161–62.
27. For the cost and availability of printing ink, see C. William Miller, *Franklin's Philadelphia Printing,* xxv; Hellmut Lehmann-Haupt et al., *The Book in America,* 2nd ed. (New York: R. R. Bowker, 1951), 21; Rollo G. Silver, "The Costs of Mathew Carey's Printing Equipment," *SB* 19 (1966): 100. The inventories of the printing shops belonging to Isaiah Thomas, Thomas Short, Timothy Green II, and William Rind are cited in Table 5.1.
28. Tench Coxe, *A View of the United States of America* (1794; repr. New York: Augustus M. Kelley, 1965), 389. The real money values used here for comparison purposes are based on the composite price indexes in John J. McCusker, "How Much Is That in Real Money? A Historical Price Index for Use as a Deflator of Money Values in the Economy of the United States," *Procs. AAS* 101 (1991): 297–373. Currency figures have been converted to sterling using exchange rates tabulated by McCusker in *Money and Exchange in Europe and America, 1600–1775: A Handbook* (Chapel Hill: University of North Carolina Press, 1978).
29. "Report of Executors of Estate of William Parks, the First Printer in Virginia," *WMQ,* 2nd series, 2 (1922): 202–09.

30. Thomas Green to Isaiah Thomas, June 10, 1786, Isaiah Thomas Papers, American Antiquarian Society, Worcester, Mass.; Clifford K. Shipton, *Isaiah Thomas: Printer, Patriot and Philanthropist, 1749–1831* (Rochester, N.Y.: Leo Hart, 1948), 86; *Franklin Papers* 29:598.
31. Talbot Baines Reed, *A History of the Old English Letter Foundries,* ed. A. F. Johnson (London: Faber and Faber, 1952), 120–23.
32. Gustav Mori, "Der Buchdrucker Christoph Sauer in Germantown," *Gutenberg-Jahrbuch* (1934): 229; "William McCulloch's Additions to Thomas's History of Printing," *Procs. AAS* 31 (1921): 150; Rollo G. Silver, *Typefounding in America, 1787–1825* (Charlottesville: University Press of Virginia, 1965), 11–17, 31–36.
33. Isaiah Thomas to George Goodwin, Oct. 19, 1780, photocopy in Isaiah Thomas Papers; Silver, *Typefounding in America,* 3–11; Wroth, *Col. Printer,* 104–08; Lawrence C. Wroth, *Abel Buell of Connecticut: Silversmith, Type Founder & Engraver* (Middletown, Conn.: Wesleyan University Press, 1958).
34. John Bidwell, "Some Caslon Ornaments in Some American Books," *Printing History* 4 (1980): 21–25.
35. *A New Version of the Psalms of David* (Boston, [1767?]), advertisements, 19; John Mein, *A State of the Importations from Great-Britain into the Port of Boston, from the Beginning of Jan. 1769, to Aug. 17th 1769* (Boston, 1769), 53; Silver, *Typefounding in America,* 115; *Franklin Papers* 18:68 and 20: 375.
36. Silver, *Typefounding in America,* 109–20; Edmund Fry to Isaiah Thomas, August 16, 1786 & "Acct. of Stock . . . taken October 1794," Isaiah Thomas Papers.
37. *Franklin Papers* 30:514; Wroth, *Col. Printer,* 268–72; Thomas, *Hist. Printing,* 308; *Connecticut Courant,* Dec. 22–29, 1772.
38. *Boston Chronicle,* Aug. 14–17, 1769; *Franklin Papers* 13:91–92, 97–98, 114–15.
39. James Green, *The Rittenhouse Mill and the Beginnings of Papermaking in America* (Philadelphia, Pa.: The Library Company of Philadelphia and Friends of Historic Rittenhouse Town, 1990), 11; Hazel A. Johnson, *A Checklist of New London, Connecticut, Imprints, 1709–1800* (Charlottesville: Published for the Bibliographical Society of America by the University Press of Virginia, 1978), 444; *Account Books Kept by Benjamin Franklin,* ed. George Simpson Eddy, 2 vols. (New York, 1928–1929), 2:21, 32, 65.
40. *Franklin Papers* 3:154; Keith Maslen, *An Early London Printing House at Work: Studies in the Bowyer Ledgers* (New York: Bibliographical Society of America, 1993), 143.
41. *Virginia Gazette* (Rind), April 19, 1770. The first Massachusetts paper mill provoked unfavorable comment in the Board of Trade, quoted in Timothy Pitkin, *A Statistical View of the Commerce of the United States of America* (1816; repr. New York: Augustus M. Kelley, 1967), 4–5.
42. Richard Parker, *Proposals Humbly Offer'd to the . . . House of Commons, for Raising Forty Thousand Pounds* (London, 1711?); Charles-Moïse Briquet, "Papiers et Filigranes des Archives de Gênes, 1154 à 1700," *Briquet's Opuscula* (Hilversum: Paper Publications Society, 1955), 186; Miller, *Franklin's Philadelphia Printing,* xlii–xliii; James G. Lydon, *Pirates, Privateers, and Profits* (Upper Saddle River, N.J.: Gregg Press, 1970), 154.

43. W. T. Baxter, *The House of Hancock: Business in Boston, 1724–1775* (Cambridge, Mass.: Harvard University Press, 1945), 69–71, 85–94; John W. Tyler, *Smugglers and Patriots: Boston Merchants and the Advent of the American Revolution* (Boston: Northeastern University Press, 1986), 30, 163, 231; *English Historical Documents: American Colonial Documents to 1776* (New York: Oxford University Press, 1969), 372–76.
44. Wroth, *Printing in Col. Md.*, 107–10; Thomas, *Hist. Printing*, 336–37; Arthur M. Schlesinger, *The Colonial Merchants and the American Revolution, 1763–1776* (New York: Atheneum, 1968), 211.
45. Miller, *Franklin's Philadelphia Printing*, xlv; *American Museum* 7 (1790): 137–41 and 8 (1790): 9–10, 114–15; *Virginia Gazette* (Purdie & Dixon), March 22, 1770; *Virginia Gazette* (Pinkney), April 13, 1775; *Virginia Gazette* (Dixon & Hunter), Jan. 13, 1776.
46. John, Lord Sheffield, *Observations on the Commerce of the American States*, 6th enl. ed. (London: Printed for J. Debrett, 1784), 42–43.
47. Edward Hughes, "The English Stamp Duties, 1664–1764," *English Historical Review* 56 (1941): 234–64.
48. *Franklin Papers*, 12:171, 190, 233–34; *Pennsylvania Gazette*, Oct. 31, 1765, Nov. 14, 1765.
49. Robert D. Harlan, "David Hall and the Stamp Act," *PBSA* 61 (1967): 20, 35.
50. *Virginia Gazette* (Purdie & Dixon), August 3, 1769.
51. Robert D. Harlan, "David Hall and the Townshend Acts,"*PBSA* 68 (1974): 34; Schlesinger, *Colonial Merchants*, 137, 521.
52. E. B. O'Callaghan, *A List of Editions of the Holy Scriptures and Parts Thereof, Printed in America Previous to 1860* (Albany: Munsell & Rowland, 1861), xix–xx.
53. Silver, "Government Printing"; Eugenie Andruss Leonard, "Paper as a Critical Commodity During the American Revolution," *PMHB* 74 (1950): 488–99; John Hancock to Joseph Warren, April 26, 1775, Isaiah Thomas Papers.
54. *Edes and Gill's North-American Almanack* (Boston, 1770), A6[r]; *New-York Journal*, August 4, 1768.
55. "Commonwealth of Massachusetts . . . The Petition of the Subscribers, Manufacturers of Paper," Nov. 1, 1785, Book Trades Collection, American Antiquarian Society, Worcester, Mass.
56. *Account Books Kept by Benjamin Franklin*, 2:16, 20–21, 25, 28–29, 45–46, 65, 94, 111, 123.
57. *Franklin Papers*, 3: 173.
58. John Clyde Oswald, *Printing in the Americas* (New York: Gregg Publishing Company, 1937), 310–11; *Virginia Gazette* (Purdie), Dec. 29, 1775, Dec. 6, 1776.
59. See Giles Barber, "Books from the Old World and for the New: the British International Trade in Books in the Eighteenth Century," *Studies on Voltaire and the Eighteenth Century* 151 (1976): 219–24; Giles Barber, "Book Imports and Exports in the Eighteenth Century," in *The Sale and Distribution of Books from 1700*, ed. Robin Myers and Michael Harris (Oxford: Oxford Polytechnic Press, 1982): 94; and James Raven, "The Export of Books to Colonial North America," *Publishing History* 42 (1997): [21]–49.

60. Public Record Office, Cust 3, Ledgers of Imports and Exports, 1697–1780. Tallies for exports to the Americas exclude continental European books (recorded under "foreign goods") numbers of which are not significant.
61. PRO Cust 3/1–79. A volume for 1805 has recently been acquired privately. Cust 11, Ledgers of Exports of Foreign and Colonial Merchandise, runs from 1809 to 1899. In the period when no English customs ledgers survive, certain American customs records exist from 1789. These are very incomplete, however; none survive for Boston, for example.
62. Details are given in Raven, "Export of Books to Colonial North America"; and James Raven, "I viaggi dei libri: realtà e raffigurazioni," in *Gli spazi del libro nell'Europa del XVIII secolo,* ed. Maria Gioia Tavoni and Françoise Waquet (Bologna: Pàtron Editore, 1997), 47–85.
63. The most recent claim of underrepresentation is based on a misreading of Barber's customs tabulations. An average shipment to Knox in 1771 represents about 1.5 percent of the total imports to New England in that year. For a rough comparison of imports and domestic production, 1765–1774, see the "Note" at the end of this chapter.
64. Scottish Record Office, Edinburgh, E504 series, Customs Collectors' Quarterly Account Books, and SRO RH2/4 and RH20, copies of PRO Cust 14/1a, 1b, 2, 3, 4, 5–13b, Ledgers of Imports and Exports, Scotland 1755–1763, 1764–1775, 1775–1780, 1779–1782, 1781–1784, and a series 1785–1800. See Warren McDougall, "Scottish Books for America in the Mid-18th Century," in *Spreading the Word: The Distribution Networks of Print 1550–1850,* ed. Robin Myers and Michael Harris (Winchester and Detroit, Mich.: St Paul's Bibliographies, 1990), 21–46; and McDougall, "Copyright Litigation in the Court of Session, 1738–1749, and the Rise of the Scottish Book Trade," *Edinburgh Bibliographical Society Transactions* 5: 5 (1988): 2–31. I am grateful to Warren McDougall for assistance in locating and interpreting the SRO ledgers.
65. See McDougall, "Copyright Litigation," 17 n. 53.
66. PRO Cust 15/1–140, Ledgers of Imports and Exports, Ireland, 1698–1829; with copies of some of these in the National Library of Ireland, Dublin, MSS 353–72, Customs House ledgers 1764–1815.
67. 15 Car. II, c. 7 (1663); amended, 23 Car. II, c. 26 (1670/71).
68. 20 Geo. III, c. 10; 23 & 24 Geo. III, c. 9, Ireland. The occasional official pre-1780 entries are contrary to the continuing ban on book exports in the customs officers' manuals; see Mary Pollard, *Dublin's Trade in Books, 1550–1800* (Oxford: Oxford University Press, 1989), 137.
69. Pollard, *Dublin's Trade in Books,* 142, graph 2. It has been suggested that because customs officers concentrated on the major items of export only, Irish customs records underrecord books by a factor of ten, Vincent Kinane, "'Literary Food' for the American Market: Patrick Byrne's Exports to Mathew Carey," *Procs. AAS* 104 (1994): 321, although another historian claims that the records "serve as an acceptable general indication of the extent of trade," L. M. Cullen, *Anglo-Irish Trade, 1660–1800* (Manchester: Manchester University Press, 1968), 218; cf. Richard Cargill Cole, *Irish Booksellers and English Writers, 1740–1800* (London: Mainsail, 1986), 49; Kinane, "'Literary Food'," 316.

70. Calculations are taken from sources given in Note 64. For examples of regular Scots book exports included in general shipments and via London, see Chapter 7.
71. Raven, "Export of Books to Colonial North America"; and see Chapter 8, Part 2.
72. For 1771–1779 inclusive (including the American import exclusions of the war years) a total of 9,876 cwt. of books were exported to the American plantations compared to a total of 14,570 cwt. to Europe and the east. Although given as "English" totals, some London merchants clearly exported goods (including books) manufactured in Scotland and other regions of Britain. James F. Shepherd and Gary M. Walton, *Shipping, Maritime Trade, and the Economic Development of Colonial North America* (Cambridge: Cambridge University Press, 1972), 38, fig. 3.2.
73. PRO Cust 3/79, fols. 63, 64v, 67v, 69v.
74. Bernard and Lotte Bailyn, *Massachusetts Shipping, 1697–1714: A Statistical Study* (Cambridge, Mass.: Belknap Press, 1959); McCusker and Menard, *Economy of British America,* 46–50.
75. See Chapter 5, Part 2, for the cost of supplies, and Chapter 1.
76. Hannah D. French, "Early American Bookbinding by Hand 1636–1820," in *Bookbinding in America: Three Essays,* ed. Hellmut Lehmann-Haupt (Portland, Me.: Southwold-Anthoensen, 1941), 3–127; and Willman Spawn, "The Evolution of American Binding Styles in the Eighteenth Century," in *Bookbinding in America, 1680–1910,* ed. John Dooley and James Tanis (Bryn Mawr, Penn.: Bryn Mawr College Library, 1983), 29–36.
77. See Chapter 3.
78. Stephen Botein, "The Anglo-American Book Trade before 1776: Personnel and Strategies," in *Printing and Society,* 74–79.
79. See Elizabeth Carroll Reilly, "The Wages of Piety: The Boston Book Trade of Jeremy Condy," in *Printing and Society,* 83–131.
80. Elizabeth Carroll Reilly, "Common and Learned Readers: Shared and Separate Spheres in Mid-Eighteenth-Century New England" (Ph.D. dissertation, Boston University, 1994), 183 n. 11.
81. See Chapter 3.
82. Winans, *Book Catalogues,* xviii, table 1; 4, no. 2.
83. Edwin Wolf, 2nd, *The Book Culture of a Colonial American City: Philadelphia Books, Bookmen, and Booksellers* (Oxford: Clarendon Press, 1988), 38–39.
84. British Library, Add MSS 48800, fols. 113, 129, 145, 146, 149; American Philosophical Society, Hall Papers and Hall Letterbook (hereafter APS HP).
85. Lawrence C. Wroth, *William Parks: Printer and Journalist of England and Colonial America* (Richmond, Va.: William Parks Club, 1926), 25.
86. Cynthia Z. Stiverson and Gregory A. Stiverson, "Colonial Retail Book Trade," in *Printing and Society,* 146–47, 154.
87. Henry Knox Papers, Massachusetts Historical Society, Boston, Mass. (hereafter HKP), 1:43, 99, 117 Longman to Knox; 1:131 Wright and Gill to Knox; Botein, "Anglo-American Book Trade," 72.
88. Jeremy Condy Account Book, American Antiquarian Society, fol. 57 [1761].
89. Papers of Daniel Henchman, 1689–1761, 3 reels: day books, ledgers and miscellaneous papers. The archive is most conveniently available as a whole on microfilm at the American Antiquarian Society.

90. James Raven, *London Booksellers and American Customers: Transatlantic Community, Literary Conduits, and the Charleston Library Society, 1748–1811* [hereafter *LBAC*] (Columbia: University of South Carolina Press, 2000), introduction.
91. Archives of John Murray Ltd., Albemarle St., London (hereafter JML), Letterbooks, 1765–1802, 12 vols. (hereafter LB); Day book, 1768–1773 (hereafter DB); and Account book, 1769–1780. JML LB 3, Murray to Robert Miller of Williamsburg, Aug. 17, 1772. I am grateful to Virginia Murray and William Zachs for their assistance here.
92. JML LB 4, Murray to Miller, Dec. 5, 1773.
93. Examples from the Winthrop papers and the collections of the Massachusetts Historical Society, cited in Thomas Goddard Wright, *Literary Culture in Early New England, 1620–1750* (New Haven, Conn.: Yale University Press, 1920), 25–61.
94. JML LB4, Murray to Miller, March 26, 1773 (relating to DB fol. 353).
95. "The Letter-Book of Samuel Sewall," *Coll. MHS,* 6th ser., 1–2 (1886–1888) 1:271–72, Sewall to Ive, June 13, 1702.
96. Edwin Wolf 2nd, ed., "James Logan's Correspondence with William Reading, Librarian of Sion College," in *Homage to a Bookman: Essays on Manuscripts, Books and Printing,* ed. Hellmut Lehmann-Haupt (Berlin: Gebr. Mann, [1967]), 209–19.
97. Logan to John Whiston, July 27, 1748, Letterbook, 1748–1750, Historical Society of Pennsylvania, 5–6.
98. New York Society Library Archives, NYSL First Minute Book, fol. 32–33, Mar. 27, 1758.
99. James Raven, "Gentlemen, Pirates, and Really Respectable Booksellers: Some Charleston Customers for Lackington, Allen & Co.," in *The Book-trade and its Customers, 1450–1900: Historical Essays for Robin Myers,* ed. Arnold Hunt, Giles Mandelbrote, and Alison Shell (Winchester: St. Paul's Bibliographies, 1997), 247–64.
100. JML LB 4, Murray to Miller, July 1, 1773; JML LB 4, Murray to Miller, Dec. 5, 1773.
101. *LBAC,* letter 53, Stockdale to Charleston Library Society, Sept. 14, 1792.
102. *LBAC,* letter 38, McCall to Charles Dilly, Jan. 14, 1786.
103. For shipping circuits, see Steele, *The English Atlantic,* and on the book trade, Raven, *LBAC.*
104. Shepherd and Walton, *Shipping, Maritime Trade,* 87–88.
105. JML DB, fol. 384, record of invoice July 1, 1773.
106. L. H. Butterfield, "American Interests of the Firm of E. and C. Dilly with the Letters to Benjamin Rush, 1770–1795," *PBSA* 45 (1951): 288–332; Eric Stockdale, "John Stockdale of Piccadilly: Publisher to John Adams and Thomas Jefferson," in *Author/Publisher Relations during the Eighteenth and Nineteenth Centuries,* ed. Robin Myers and Michael Harris (Oxford: Oxford Polytechnic Press, 1983), 63–87.
107. Among many early examples, "Letter-Book of Samuel Sewall," 1:300, Samuel Sewall to Sir William Ashhurst, July 21, 1704.
108. A. H. John, "The London Assurance Company and the Marine Insurance Market of the Eighteenth Century," *Economica,* n.s., 25 (1958): 126–41; and see also Clive Trebilcock, *Phoenix Assurance and the Development of British*

Insurance: Vol. 1, 1782–1870 (Cambridge: Cambridge University Press, 1985), esp. chap. 5.

109. Shepherd and Walton, *Shipping, Maritime Trade,* 89.
110. In 1703, "Thomas" [John] Hill's popular *Young Secretary's Guide* was republished in Boston. (It reached a twenty-seventh edition in London, 1764.)
111. Robert D. Harlan, "David Hall's Bookshop and Its British Sources of Supply," in *Books in America's Past: Essays Honoring Rudolph H. Gjelsness,* ed. David Kaser (Charlottesville, Va.: University Press of Virginia, 1966), 13.
112. David Hall Papers, American Philosophical Society, Philadelphia, Pa., (hereafter HPS HP), Hall to Strahan, Sept. 27, 1750, Oct. 7, 1755.
113. Robert D. Harlan, "William Strahan's American Book Trade, 1744–76," *Library Quarterly* 31 (1961): 238.
114. Ibid., 243–34.
115. HKP 1:104, Wright and Gill to Knox, March 24, 1774.
116. HKP 18:158; 20:26, 99; 23:158; 26:71,144; 27:138; 28:166; 34:65,173; 35:57.
117. HPS HP, Strahan to Hall, July 11, 1758.
118. Ibid; J. A. Cochrane, *Dr Johnson's Printer: The Life of William Strahan* (London: Routledge and Kegan Paul, 1964), 84.
119. E. Millicent Sowerby, "Thomas Jefferson and his Library," *PBSA* 50 (1956): 217–18.
120. HPS HP, Hall to Hamilton and Balfour, Dec. 22, 1760, cit. Leroy Hewlett, "James Rivington, Loyalist Printer, Publisher, and Bookseller of the American Revolution, 1724–1802: A Biographical-Bibliographical Study" (D.L.S. dissertation, University of Michigan, 1958), 19–20.
121. HKP 5:244, Longman to Knox, July 21, 1773.
122. Stiverson and Stiverson, "Colonial Retail Book Trade," 163–65 (some allowance has to be made for fluctuating Virginian currency, however).
123. APS HP, Hall to Strahan, Mar. 21, 1752.
124. Stuart C. Sherman, "Leman Thomas Rede's *Bibliotheca Americana* [1789]," *WMQ,* 3rd ser., 4 (1947): 347; Rede's account was later plagiarized by Henry Lemoine in 1796.
125. Charles L. Nichols, "The Literary Fair in the United States," in *Bibliographical Essays: A Tribute to Wilberforce Eames,* ed. G. P. Winship (Cambridge, Mass., 1924), 85; see also the "Note" at the end of this chapter.
126. Including Wolf, *Book Culture*; Raven, *LBAC*; and Kevin J. Hayes, *The Library of William Byrd of Westover* (Madison, Wisc.: Madison House, 1997).
127. Robert B. Winans, "Bibliography and the Cultural Historian: Notes on the Eighteenth-Century Novel," in *Printing and Society,* [174]–85.

Chapter 6. The Book Trade in the Middle Colonies, 1680–1720

1. Douglas C. McMurtrie, *A History of Printing in the United States: Middle and South Atlantic States* (New York: R.R. Bowker, 1936), 133. The broadside is Evans 98.
2. Ibid., 134.
3. Edwin B. Bronner and David Fraser, *William Penn's Published Writings, 1660–1726: An Interpretive Bibliography* (Philadelphia: University of Pennsylvania, 1986), 49–86.
4. McMurtrie, *History of Printing,* 407.

5. Samuel Atkins, *Kalendarium Pennsilvaniense, or, America's Messinger: Being an Almanack for the year of grace, 1686* (Philadelphia, 1685), 3–5.
6. McMurtrie, *History of Printing,* 2.
7. Charles R. Hildeburn, *The Issues of the Press in Pennsylvania, 1685–1784,* 2 vols. (Philadelphia, 1885), 1:8; Alexander J. Wall, Jr., "William Bradford, Colonial Printer: A Tercentenary Review," *Procs. AAS* 73:2 (1963):363.
8. John William Wallace, *An Address delivered at the Celebration by the New York Historical Society . . . of the Two Hundredth Birthday of Mr. William Bradford* (Albany, N.Y.: J. Munsell, 1863), 50; *The Frame of the Government of the Province of Pennsilvania* [Philadelphia, 1689].
9. *Minutes of the Provincial Council of Pennsylvania* (Philadelphia, 1852), 1:72–74.
10. Hildeburn, *Issues of the Press,* 1:13.
11. Wallace, *Address,* 51.
12. The manuscript in the New-York Historical Society is transcribed in Wallace, *Address,* 49–52; and cf *The People's Ancient and Just Liberties Asserted...* (London, 1670).
13. Wallace, *Address,* 50, 51.
14. The preface is signed "Philopolites" and is attributed to Penn by Bronner and Fraser. It reads in part, "I know this Country is not furnished with Law Books & this being the Root from which all our wholesom English Laws spring. . . . I have ventured to make it publick . . ." (p.[3]). Penn is referring to local printed laws rather than to British statutes, casebooks, or commentaries, though the latter were certainly scarce in Pennsylvania in the first years of its settlement. For law books owned by an early Germantown magistrate, see the discussion of Pastorius's library (pp. 220–22). Edwin Wolf found that some of the largest private libraries recorded in early Philadelphia estate inventories belonged to lawyers. See, for example, that of John Guest, chief justice of the Supreme Court of Pennsylvania, brought over by Penn in 1699, died 1708: 53 works, more than half legal, including Coke's *Institutes,* reports of cases in Chancery and other courts, Edmund Wingate's *Abridgment of all the Statutes,* Charles Molloy's *De Jure Maritimi et Navali,* and (reflecting the importance of trade with the West Indies, two copies of the *Laws of Jamaica. The Book Culture of a Colonial American City: Philadelphia Books, Bookmen, and Booksellers* (Oxford: Clarendon Press, 1988), p.133.
15. Bronner and Fraser were the first to point out (*William Penn's Published Writings,* 5:332–33, 364–65) the nearly identical settings of type in the two printings of the charter, and they noted that *The Excellent Priviledge* had to have been printed before the separately printed charter, but still they hesitated to change the long-accepted dating of the two imprints. *The Excellent Priviledge* is usually ascribed to 1687 on the basis of an advertisement in Bradford's almanac of that year stating that a book of that title was "in the press." There is no other evidence that it was actually printed that year. The advertisement also states that the book will include *A Guide for the Grand and Petty Jury,* which does not appear in *The Excellent Priviledge* as published. The advertisement fixes only an earliest possible date. On the other hand, the separately printed charter was attested in court as having been printed on April 8, 1689. Since *The Excellent Priviledge* was printed after the separate printing, I conclude that it was printed after the Blackwell hear-

ing. This makes better sense in any case, since no mention was made in the hearing of an earlier American printing of the charter, and indeed Blackwell's condemnation of Bradford would not make much sense if it had already been readily available in print. Furthermore, an invoice of books sold by Bradford to John Bowne of Long Island on May 29, 1689 includes "1 doz: Liberty and Property."

16. Gerald D. McDonald, "William Bradford's Book Trade and John Bowne, Long Island Quaker, as his Book Agent, 1686–1691," *Essays Honoring Lawrence C. Wroth* (Portland, Me., 1951), 209–22.
17. James N. Green, *The Rittenhouse Mill and the Beginnings of Papermaking in America* (Philadelphia, Pa.: Library Company, 1990) 5–10, 19–22.
18. Wall, "William Bradford," 365.
19. Gary B. Nash, *Quakers and Politics: Pennsylvania, 1681–1726* (Princeton, N.J.: Princeton University Press, 1968), 144–61; Ethyn Williams Kirby, *George Keith, 1638–1716* (New York: Appleton-Century, 1942), 39–53.
20. Hildeburn, *Issues of the Press,* 1:22–23.
21. "To the Monthly or Quarterly Meeting of ffriends in Philadelphia 1691/2," Parrish Family Papers, Historical Society of Pennsylvania.
22. Wallace, *Address,* 63.
23. Nash, *Quakers,* 148; Kirby, *George Keith,* 68.
24. Bradford's advertisement in George Keith, *A True Copy of Three Judgements Given forth by a Party of Men, called Quakers at Philadelphia, against George Keith and his Friends* [Philadelphia, 1692], 16.
25. William Bradford to John Chamberlayne (secretary of the Society of the Propagation of the Gospel), New York, September 12, 1709, in Beverly McAnear, "William Bradford and the Book of Common Prayer," *PBSA* 43 (1949): 104.
26. Samuel Jennings, *The State of the Case . . . betwixt the People called Quakers . . . who remain in unity; and George Keith* (London, 1694), 24.
27. George Keith, *A Further Discovery of the Spirit of Falshood & Persecution in Sam. Jennings* (London, 1694), 28.
28. George Keith, *An Appeal from the Twenty-eight Judges to the Spirit of Truth* (Philadelphia 1692). It appeared first as a broadside and was twice reprinted as a pamphlet that same year.
29. George Keith, *New-England's Spirit of Persecution Transmitted to Pennsilvania* [Philadelphia, 1693], 10–11, 32–37.
30. Raymond Astbury, "The Renewal of the Licensing Act in 1693 and its Lapse in 1695," *Library,* 5th ser., 33 (1978): 296–97.
31. Keith, *New England's Spirit of Persecution,* 34.
32. Thomas, *Hist. Printing,* 354.
33. Wall, "William Bradford," 372–73.
34. Wallace, *Address,* 73. In 1705 Bradford charged the New York government £3 10*s*. for reprinting one act of Parliament and £1 15*s*. each for printing two New York acts; cf. Stauffer collection, 31:2410, Historical Society of Pennsylvania.
35. Ibid., 76; I. N. Phelps Stokes, *The Iconography of Manhattan Island* (New York: Dodd, 1915–1928), 4:433.
36. McAnear, "William Bradford," 106.
37. Wall, "William Bradford," 369.

38. McAnear, "William Bradford," 101–10.
39. Stokes, *Iconography,* 4:434.
40. Patricia U. Bonomi, *A Factious People: Politics and Society in Colonial New York* (New York: Columbia University Press, 1971), 78.
41. J. G. Riewald, *Reynier Jansen of Philadelphia, Early American Printer* (Groningen: Wolters-Noordhoff, 1970), chaps. 4 and 6.
42. Ibid., chap. 7, "A Bibliographical Catalogue of Jansen Imprints."
43. Ibid., 115, citing minutes of the Philadelphia Monthly Meeting.
44. Anna Janney DeArmond, *Andrew Bradford, Colonial Journalist* (Newark: University of Delaware Press, 1949), 9–10.
45. *The Statutes at Large of Pennsylvania in the Time of William Penn,* comp. Gail McKnight Beckman (New York: Vantage, 1976), 173 (cap. 191).
46. Joan de Lourdes Leonard, "The Organization and Procedure of the Pennsylvania Assembly, 1682–1776, II, The Legislative Process," *PMHB* 72 (1948): 391–96.
47. Leonard, "Organization and Procedure," 393.
48. Nash, *Quakers,* 306 ff.
49. Wolf, *Book Culture,* 33.
50. C. A. Weslager, "The Swedes' Letter of William Penn," *PMHB* 83 (1959): 91.
51. Riewald, *Reynier Jansen,* 198–200.
52. Wolf, *Book Culture,* 9–12.
53. Ibid., 19–28.
54. Marion Dexter Learned, *The Life of Francis Daniel Pastorius* (Philadelphia, 1908), 255–57, 274–84; Wolf, *Book Culture,* 4–8.
55. Elizabeth W. Fisher, "'Prophesies and Revelations': German Cabbalists in Early Pennsylvania," *PMHB* 109 (1985): 299–333.
56. Edwin Wolf, 2nd, *The Library of James Logan* (Philadelphia: Library Company, 1974), xvii–lvii.
57. Giles Barber, "Books from the Old World and For the New: British International Trade in Books in the Eighteenth Century," *Studies on Voltaire and the Eighteenth Century* 151 (1976), 219–24. Customs clerks recorded only the first destination of a ship, and since northern and southern shipping routes were favored, these records probably understate the quantity of books ultimately destined for the middle colonies.
58. Thomas, *Hist. Printing,* 219.
59. Franklin, *Autobiography,* 1363.
60. *New York Gazette,* no. 137, June 17, 1728.
61. De Armond, *Andrew Bradford,* 12–14.

Chapter 7. The Southern Book Trade in the Eighteenth Century

1. The events leading up to the establishment of this press are narrated in Chapter 2.
2. Jones, though not a printer, attempted to enter the publishing business as an intermediary for the printing of session laws. Wroth, *Printing in Col. Md.,* 39–45.
3. The existence of the *Wilmington Courant* in 1762 is, as Evald Rink says, "still shrouded in doubt." *Printing in Delaware 1761–1800* (Wilmington, Del.:

Eleutherian Mills Historical Library, 1969), 16–17. For the early newspaper and book trade in Florida, see Calhoun Winton, "English Books and American Readers in Early Florida," in *Eighteenth-Century Florida and the Revolutionary South,* ed. Samuel Proctor (Gainesville: The University Presses of Florida, 1978), 110–21.

4. John Tobler's *Georgia Almanack for 1771*, verso of title page.
5. The existence of this unique imprint, *The Acts and Laws of the Province of Maryland,* was reported by Sarah M. Sartain, "A Lost Imprint of Peter Zenger," in *An Occasional Bulletin of the Virginia Historical Society,* 50 (June 1985): 5–7. I am indebted to Gregory A. Stiverson for this reference.
6. For Reading and Bryan, see Donald F. McKenzie, *Stationers' Company Apprentices, 1641–1700* (Oxford: Oxford Bibliographical Society, 1974), entries 1803 and 1798. For Parks, see Ian Maxted, *The British Book Trades 1710–1777* (Exeter: The author, 1983), entry 0246.
7. There is no satisfactory treatment of Parks's early career, which is here put together from examination of the publications mentioned, from the ESTC, from Lawrence Wroth, *William Parks, Printer and Journalist* (Richmond, Va.: William Parks Club, 1926), which has itself been superseded by Wroth's own later work, and from Llewelyn C. Lloyd, "The Book Trade in Shropshire," *Transactions of the Shropshire Archaeological and Natural History Society* 48 (1936): 91,152–56.
8. Reading Corporation Diary 1721–1726 in Berkshire Record Office R/Acal/19; *The Reading Mercury, or Weekly Entertainer* for July 8 and July 29, 1723. Michael Treadwell has pointed out to me in a letter that Parks's partner David Kinnier also had newspaper experience, having completed his apprenticeship in 1722 with Mathew Jenour, who printed the London *Flying-Post*. Parks was, however, distinctly the senior partner and it was against him that the wrath of mayor and corporation was directed.
9. William L. Mitchell, "William Parks of LONDON?," *Factotum* 40 (December 1995): 4.
10. A local schoolmaster agreed to take on the job but then withdrew. *Md. Arch.* 34:365, 450, 613; 35:406–08.
11. Wroth, *Printing in Col. Md.*, 60–63; *Md. Arch.*, 35:477.
12. Compare University of Maryland copy (shelfmark: KFM 1225.2 1727) with the illustration of Davies' binding of a 1730 Philadelphia book in *Bookbinding in America 1680–1910,* ed. John Dooley and James Tanis, introduction by Willman Spawn (Bryn Mawr, Pa.: Bryn Mawr College Library, 1983), 43. The blind-tooling appears to be identical with that employed on the *Compleat Collection*. Spawn has informed James Green that there were at least two other binders at work on various copies of the edition, suggesting that the work was done in "several batches, over time": personal communication to me from Green of October 25, 1995.
13. I am indebted to James N. Green for the information on Bradford's practice.
14. *Executive Journals of the Council of Colonial Virginia,* ed. H. R. McIlwaine, Wilmer L. Hall, and Benjamin J. Hillman, 6 vols. (Richmond: Virginia State Library, 1925–1966), 4:125. I am indebted to John Hemphill, II, for this reference, which corrects Wroth.

15. Susan Stromei Berg, *Eighteenth-Century Williamsburg Imprints* (New York: Clearwater, 1986), 5:5.
16. For information on Parks in Virginia, in addition to that already cited, see James A. and Mary Caperton Bear, *A Checklist of Virginia Almanacs, 1732–1850* (Charlottesville: University Press of Virginia, 1962); and William H. Castles, Jr., "The 'Virginia Gazette,' 1736–1766" (Ph.D. dissertation, University of Tennessee, 1962).
17. C. Clement Samford and John M. Hemphill, II, *Bookbinding in Colonial Virginia* (Charlottesville: University Press of Virginia, 1966), 22.
18. "Journal of the Meetings of the President and Masters of William and Mary College," *WMQ*, 1st ser., 2 (1893):51.
19. "Old Virginia Editors," *WMQ*, 1st ser., 7 (1898):11.
20. Hugh Jones, *The Present State of Virginia* (London, 1724), 132.
21. Miller, *Franklin's Philadelphia Printing*, xliii–xliv.
22. *Franklin Papers* 3:322. On Osborne, who was employing Johnson just at this time, see Thomas Kaminski, *The Early Career of Samuel Johnson* (New York and Oxford: Oxford University Press, 1987), 177–84.
23. Wroth, *William Parks*, 27.
24. J. H. Soltow, "Scottish Traders in Virginia, 1750–1775," *Economic History Review* 12 (1959–1960): 85. Soltow does not discuss Lawson and Semple.
25. Lawson and Semple became embroiled in a lawsuit; the suit rose to the highest jurisdiction on the civil side, the Court of Session. The firm's records were received as evidence and have remained in public custody of the Court and then of the Scottish Record Office. They have recently been indexed in Court of Session Productions 96 (C.S 96).
26. The basic work on these firms is J. M. Devine, *The Tobacco Lords* (Edinburgh: John Donald, 1975). Devine uses the Lawson/Semple records but does not refer to their part in the book trade. Warren McDougall quotes briefly from them in "Scottish books for America in the Mid-18th Century," in *Spreading the Word*, eds. Robin Myers and Michael Harris (Winchester: St. Paul's Bibliographies, 1990), 21–46.
27. Important discussions of the trade are found in Jacob M. Price, *Capital and Credit in British Overseas Trade: The View from the Chesapeake, 1700–1776* (Cambridge, Mass.: Harvard University Press, 1980); Soltow, "Scottish Traders in Virginia," 85; and Emory G. Evans, "Planter Indebtedness and the Coming of the Revolution in Virginia," *WMQ*, 3rd ser., 19 (1962): 511–33.
28. John Mair, *Book-keeping Methodiz'd*, 6th ed. (Dublin, 1760), 332.
29. Scottish Record Office (SRO), Edinburgh, C.S. 96/1186, pp. 106, 169, 170, 203.
30. SRO, C.S. 96/1186, Daybook, Glasgow, pp. 52, 63, 65, 101–102, 160, 169; 96/1197 (not paginated), letters under dates of 19 March, 22 July, 1 August, and 31 August 1761.
31. Scottish customs records, which I have not verified, quoted in Warren McDougall, "Scottish Books for America," 24; and see Chapter 5, Section 3.
32. Nothing is known of the provenance of these daybooks (Alderman Library, University of Virginia). Cynthia Z. Stiverson and Gregory A. Stiverson analyze them in "The Colonial Retail Book Trade: Availability and Affordability of Reading Material in Mid-Eighteenth-Century Virginia," in

Printing and Society, 132–173. Susan Stromei Berg has also used them as a basis for "Agent of Change or Trusted Servant: The Eighteenth-Century Williamsburg Press" (M.A. thesis, College of William and Mary, 1993). The daybooks are analyzed in further detail in Chapter 11.

33. Stiverson and Stiverson, "Colonial Retail Book Trade," 146, 151–52.
34. The interested reader should compare this sheet count with the one for Boston printers provided in Chapter 9, and related figures in Chapter 8.
35. Douglas C. McMurtrie, "The First Decade of Printing in the Royal Province of South Carolina,"*Library*, 4th ser., 13 (1932–1933): 425–52.
36. *Detailed Reports on the Salzburger Emigrants Who Settled in America*, ed. George Fenwick Jones, 18 vols. (Athens: University of Georgia Press, 1968–1995), 1:57: "The printer, named Timotheus, is also a German." The evidence for Timothy's German ancestry is summarized in G. F. Jones, "Printer Lewis Timothy: French or German Ancestry?" *Carologue: A Publication of the South Carolina Historical Society* 12 (1996): 27.
37. Still the basic source for information on the Timothys is Hennig Cohen, *The South Carolina Gazette, 1732–1775* (Columbia: University of South Carolina Press, 1953), 233–48.
38. For Wells, see my essay "The Colonial South Carolina Book Trade," in *Proof* 2 (1972): 71–87; and David Moltke-Hansen, "The Empire of Scotsman Robert Wells, Loyalist South Carolina Printer–Publisher," unpublished paper. I am most indebted to Moltke-Hansen for allowing me to use and quote from his important paper.
39. Moltke-Hansen, summarizing the emigration of Scots in the book trades, ibid., 1–14, estimates that three times as many Scots as Londoners established themselves in book and printing trades in America before 1800.
40. Christopher Gould and Richard Parker Morgan, *South Carolina Imprints 1731–1800* (Santa Barbara, Calif.: ABC–CLIO, 1985), no. 203, who do not locate a copy; however, the John Carter Brown Library, Brown University, has one.
41. William Charles Wells, *Two Essays . . . with a Memoir of his Life* (London: Archibald Constable & Co., 1818), viii–ix. I am indebted to Moltke-Hansen for this reference.
42. *South-Carolina Gazette*, May 21, 1754.
43. Moltke-Hansen, "The Empire of Scotsman Robert Wells," 36.
44. Gould and Morgan, *South Carolina Imprints*, no. 367; for *Donaldson* v. *Becket*, see John Feather, *The Provincial Book Trade in Eighteenth-Century England* (Cambridge: Cambridge University Press, 1985), 4–11.
45. Winton, "English Books and American Readers in Early Florida," 110–21.
46. E[benezer]. S. Thomas, *Reminiscences of the Last Sixty-five Years, Commencing with the Battle of Lexington*, 2 vols. (Hartford, Conn., 1840), 2:25.
47. Roderick Cave, *Printing and the Book Trade in the West Indies* (London: Pindar Press, 1987). See also Hensley C. Woodbridge and Lawrence S. Thompson, "The Beginning of Printing in the Spanish Antilles," *Printing in Colonial Spanish America* (Troy, N.Y.: Whitston Publishing Co., 1976), 114–20.
48. Wells left Florida after the British evacuation in 1784 and began publishing the *Bahama Gazette* in New Providence, the Bahamas. See Winton, "English Books and American Readers," 121.

49. Wroth, *Printing in Col. Md.*, 85; David Kaser, *A Book for a Sixpence* (Pittsburgh, Pa.: Beta Phi Mu, 1980), 3.
50. Thomas, *Hist. Printing*, 1:336 n.
51. Rink, *Printing in Delaware*, 9–23.
52. Elizabeth Cometti, "Some Early Best Sellers in Piedmont North Carolina," *Journal of Southern History* 16 (1950): 324–37.
53. James McLachlan et al., *Princetonians: A Biographical Dictionary*, 5 vols. (Princeton, N.J.: Princeton University Press, 1976–1991), 1:299–300.
54. *Maryland Journal and Baltimore Advertiser*, October 30, 1773.
55. *Maryland Gazette*, November 11, 1773. Joseph T. Wheeler, "Booksellers and Circulating Libraries in Colonial Maryland," *MdHM* 34 (1939): 117–27.
56. Joseph Towne Wheeler, *The Maryland Press, 1777–1790* (Baltimore: Maryland Historical Society, 1938), 1–18.
57. David A. Rawson, "'Guardians of their Own Liberty'": The Social and Political Context of Printing and Reading in Virginia, 1750–1820" (Ph.D. dissertation, College of William and Mary, 1997).
58. *The Papers of Thomas Jefferson*, ed. Julian P. Boyd et al., 23 vols. (Princeton, N.J.: Princeton University Press, 1950–) 1:34, 51–52. Jefferson evidently (ibid., 61) ordered books in 1770 from Thomas Waller, bookseller of London, and Benson Fearon (not identified). He "pressed them both most earnestly to lose not a day in sending them."
59. Order book, Wallace, Davidson, and Johnson, Chancery Papers, Maryland State Archives, Annapolis: Whiston's son-in-law had taken over management of the firm in 1766. Much useful information on the Annapolis firm is to be found in *Joshua Johnson's Letterbooks, 1771–1774*, ed. Jacob M. Price (London: London Record Society, 1979), the text of which is derived, however, principally from the first of two letterbooks. Johnson set up a system for supplying Mrs. Green with publications and supplies (p. 20). Edward C. Papenfuse, *In Pursuit of Profit: The Annapolis Merchants in the Era of the American Revolution, 1763–1895* (Baltimore, Md.: Johns Hopkins University Press, 1975), 38.
60. Maryland Archives, Private Accounts 1507–1519. Maryland Hall of Records, Annapolis.
61. Robert Barrow, "Advertising in the Colonial American Newspapers" (Ph.D. dissertation, University of Virginia, 1967), passim.
62. Björk's response to Aurén's almanac, which provides evidence of its existence, is *A Little Olive Leaf Put in the Mouth of that (So Called) Noah's Dove* (New York: William Bradford, 1704). Aurén's probate inventory, which lists his printing press and type as well as the books cited, is Maryland Hall of Records, Cecil County Inventories, Box 2, Folder 77. I am indebted to Dr. Richard Hulan of Arlington, Virginia, for this reference and for guidance on Aurén's career. For navigation in the schools, see Edwin Wolf, 2nd, *The Book Culture of a Colonial American City* (Oxford: Clarendon Press, 1988), 71–72.
63. C. William Miller, "Franklin's *Poor Richard* Almanacs: Their Printing and Publication," *SB* 14 (1961): 111.
64. Stiverson and Stiverson, "Colonial Retail Book Trade," 165–66.
65. The North Carolina subscribers in Halifax are identified in William S. Powell, "Patrons of the Press: Subscription Book Publishing in North Carolina, 1733–1850," *North Carolina Historical Review* 39 (1962): [423]–499.

66. David Moltke-Hansen, "Newspapers in Colonial South Carolina Legal History," in *South Carolina Legal History,* ed. Herbert A. Johnson (Columbia: Southern Studies Program, University of South Carolina, 1980), 260.
67. Wroth, *Printing in Col. Md.,* 245; the signed copy is in the New York Public Library, Rare Books Division, call no. Broadsides ++1777.

Chapter 8. The Middle Colonies, 1720–1790

1. Thomas, *Hist. Printing,* 110–12, 215–26, 232, 234–42.
2. Franklin, *Autobiography,* 1330–31.
3. Ibid., 1331.
4. Ibid., 1330–31.
5. Ibid., 1333, 1343–45.
6. Frederick B. Tolles, *James Logan and the Culture of Provincial America* (Boston, Mass.: Little, Brown, 1957), 113–14, 124–26; Gary B. Nash, *Quakers and Politics: Pennsylvania, 1681–1726* (Princeton, N.J.: Princeton University Press, 1968), 332–35; David Haugaard, "Sir William Keith," in *Lawmaking and Legislators in Pennsylvania: A Biographical Dictionary,* vol. 2, *1710–1756* (Philadelphia, 1997).
7. For Keith's debts, see *The Case of the Heir at Law and Executrix of the Late Proprietor of Pennsylvania* (Philadelphia, 1726), Evans 2735, probably published by Andrew Hamilton.
8. Thomas, *Hist. Printing,* 364–65; Stephen Bloore, "Samuel Keimer," *PMHB* 54 (1930): 266–67; C. Lennart Carlson, "Samuel Keimer, A Study in the Transit of English Culture to Colonial Pennsylvania," *PMHB* 61 (1937): 378–80.
9. Miller, *Franklin's Philadelphia Printing,* 1–2; Franklin, *Autobiography,* 1362.
10. Franklin, *Autobiography,* 1363.
11. Ibid., 1364. Keimer printed a pamphlet, now lost, but which was evidently some kind of reply to the "Busy Body" papers, called *A Touch of the Times* (Evans 3174). Its imprint read "New Printing Office," Franklin's address, and instructed the hawkers to get it there. Franklin issued a disclaimer in the *Mercury,* April 24, 1729.
12. Ibid., 1368.
13. Ibid. It seems Franklin misremembered that Bradford printed the money that year, but Franklin got the job of printing the next issue in 1731 and was paid £100 for it. But his point remains valid, that the contract was a reward for his services. See *Franklin Papers,* 1:141.
14. Livingston Rutherfurd, *John Peter Zenger: His Press, His Trial, and a Bibliography of His Imprints* (New York: Dodd, Mead, 1904); James Alexander, *A Brief Narrative of the Case and Trial of John Peter Zenger,* ed. Stanley Nider Katz (Cambridge, Mass.: Harvard University Press, 1972); *"Mr. Zenger's Malice and Falshood" Six issues of the New-York Weekly Journal, 1733–34,* edited with an introduction and afterword by Stephen Botein (Worcester, Mass.: American Antiquarian Society, 1985).
15. Hamilton's enthusiasm for Zenger's cause may also have sprung in part from Andrew Bradford's bitter and personal attacks on Hamilton in the *Mercury,* so ably answered by Franklin. A conviction would help William Bradford a great deal by removing his only rival. Franklin left no comment

on the trial, though he did sell dozens of copies of the *Narrative* of the trial printed by Zenger (*Franklin Papers,* 2:127); and in the *Gazette* (March 30, 1738) he reprinted a strongly pro-Zenger essay from *The Craftsman,* the noted English Whig paper, prefaced with a letter lauding Hamilton. At about the same time, both Bradfords reprinted an article from the *Barbados Gazette,* published by Keimer, showing that Hamilton's defense was bad law. Franklin, Hamilton, and Zenger are thus ranged against the rival printers Keimer and the two Bradfords.

16. Franklin, *Autobiography,* 1364–65.
17. Ibid., 1398.
18. Stephen Botein, " 'Meer Mechanics' and an Open Press: The Business and Political Strategies of Colonial American Printers," *Perspectives in American History* 9 (1975): 177–91; and see Chapter 10.
19. Miller, *Franklin's Philadelphia Printing,* Appendix A.
20. Franklin, *Autobiography,* 1368.
21. Miller, *Franklin's Philadelphia Printing.*
22. Wroth, *Col. Printer,* 181.
23. Franklin, *Autobiography,* 1397.
24. George Simpson Eddy, *Account Books Kept by Benjamin Franklin: Ledger "D" 1739–1774* (New York: New York Public Library, 1929) shows him sending 1,000 a year or more to Jonas Green in Annapolis, James Parker in New York, his sister in Newport, and Lewis Timothy's widow in Charleston; smaller quantities were sent to two booksellers and a binder in Boston.
25. Franklin, *Autobiography,* 1404.
26. Miller, *Franklin's Philadelphia Printing,* xxxvii.
27. *Pennsylvania Gazette,* June 12, 1740; Franklin, *Autobiography,* 1406.
28. Frank Lambert, *Pedlar in Divinity: George Whitefield and the Transatlantic Revivals, 1737–1770* (Princeton, N.J.: Princeton University Press, 1994).
29. Franklin, *Autobiography,* 1379.
30. Thomas, *Hist. Printing,* 360.
31. *Pennsylvania Gazette,* March 25, 1729.
32. Edwin Wolf, 2nd, et al., *"At the Instance of Benjamin Franklin": A Brief History of the Library Company of Philadelphia,* rev. and enl. ed. (Philadelphia: Library Company, 1995), 5–8.
33. J. Bennett Nolan, *Printer Strahan's Book Account: A Colonial Controversy* (Reading, Pa.: Bar of Berks County, 1939), chap. 2.
34. Giles Barber, "Books from the Old World and for the New: the British International Trade in Books in the Eighteenth Century," *Studies on Voltaire and the Eighteenth Century* 151 (1976): 221–22 (table 3).
35. I am indebted to Leo Lemay for making available to me a very preliminary draft of his forthcoming edition of Franklin's account books. The rather impressionistic conclusions drawn here are my own. The account books are so chaotic that no one has ever attempted to edit them all, but excerpts have been published by George Simpson Eddy.
36. Account books, Ledger B, 345, American Philosophical Society, Philadelphia.
37. See for example in Lemay's edition of Franklin's accounts, October 3, 1746: Franklin bought from William Blair a parcel of Scottish books invoiced in Glasgow at £46 12*s.* 5-½*d* Sterling and "sold at 130 [percent] Ad[vance]" for

£107 4*s.* 11*d.* in Pennsylvania currency. David Hall followed Franklin's practice; for example, he paid Strahan 10*d.* sterling per copy for James Greenwood's *The London Vocabulary* and retailed it at 3*s.*, a 125 percent advance. Cynthia Z. Stiverson and Gregory A. Stiverson, "The Colonial Retail Book Trade: Availability and Affordability of Reading Material in Mid-Eighteenth-century Virginia," in *Printing and Society,* 159–65, found lower markups in Virginia bookstores and do not discuss this booksellers' rule of thumb, but they cite a 1764 reference to "200 p[er] Cent advance" for "Goods in the retail way," and a sale of books to the young Jefferson at 100 percent advance. In 1769 James Rivington quoted the prices of imported books in terms of the advance, the lowest wholesale price being a 100 percent advance (see pp. 282–83).

38. Thus in 1741 Franklin debited the Presbyterian Synod more than £50 for printing the third part of *The Querists,* but on the other side of the ledger (D290), he credited them with more than £10 for 200 copies that he kept to sell. At 18*d.* a copy retail, these would have brought him an extra profit of £5, though he did not sell them all at retail: he sent thirty copies to his sister Ann in Newport and thirty-six copies to a Boston bookseller. For comparable incomes, see Carl Van Doren, *Benjamin Franklin* (New York: Viking, 1938), 188.
39. Thomas, *Hist. Printing,* 213.
40. Beverly McAnear, "William Bradford and the Book of Common Prayer," *PBSA* 43 (1949): 101–10.
41. Evans 2815, 2800, 2950.
42. The following discussion summarizes my article "Benjamin Franklin as Publisher and Bookseller," in *Reappraising Benjamin Franklin,* ed. J. A. Leo Lemay (Newark: University of Delaware Press, 1993), 98–114.
43. *Pennsylvania Gazette,* June 10, 1731.
44. The evidence for a Philadelphia Testament is summarized in Miller, *Franklin's Philadelphia Printing,* 368.
45. Thomas, *Hist. Printing,* 103–04, 120–21; Harry Miller Lydenberg, "The Problem of the Pre-1776 Bible," *PBSA* 48 (1954): 183–94.
46. Ralph Frasca, "Benjamin Franklin's Printing Network," *American Journalism* 5 (1988): 145–58.
47. Ralph Frasca, "From Apprentice to Journeyman to Partner: Benjamin Franklin's Workers and the Growth of the Early American Printing Trade," *PMHB* 114 (1990): 235–37.
48. The contract is reprinted in the *Franklin Papers,* 2:341.
49. Ibid.
50. John William Wallace, *An Old Philadelphian, Colonel William Bradford, The Patriot Printer of 1776* (Philadelphia, 1884), still the only book-length biography, is devoted mainly to his distinguished public and military career.
51. In an adroit political maneuver, Andrew Hamilton managed to have the new county seat located on land he owned. Perhaps Franklin's attempts to endow the town with a press were favors to his great patron and his heirs, since a town with a newspaper was more likely to attract commerce.
52. Like all piracies, Steuart's edition was cheaper: His duodecimo edition cost 3*d.*, compared to the authorized quarto edition at 1*s.* 6*d.*

53. Thomas, *Hist. Printing*, 378–89.
54. Franklin to Hall, April 18, 1759, *Franklin Papers*, 8:319.
55. Dunlap to Franklin, October 1764, *Franklin Papers*, 11:418.
56. Thomas, *Hist. Printing*, 405–26.
57. James Parker, *An Appeal to the Publick of New-York* (New York, 1759), Evans 41071.
58. Beverly McAnear, "James Parker versus William Weyman," *Proceedings of the New Jersey Historical Society* 59 (1941): 1–13.
59. *The Journals of Hugh Gaine, Printer*, ed. Paul Leicester Ford, 2 vols. (New York: Dodd, Mead, 1902), 1:9–19.
60. William H. Benedict, "James Parker, the Printer, of Woodbridge," *Proceedings of the New Jersey Historical Society*, n.s., 8 (1923): 194–99. For the printing history of Smith's *History* see Joseph J. Felcone, *New Jersey Books, 1698–1800* (Princeton, N.J., 1992), 243. 600 copies were printed at a cost of £164 (about 5*s*. 6*d*. per copy not including binding), which was paid in cash by Smith. It was sold by Parker and Hall for 12*s*. bound in sheep.
61. McAnear, "William Weyman," 13–23.
62. Beverly McAnear, "James Parker versus John Holt," *Proceedings of the New Jersey Historical Society* 59 (1941): 77–95, 198–213.
63. John Holt, *An Humble Address to the Publick* (New York, 1766), Evans 41655.
64. Thomas, *Hist. Printing*, 467–70; Leonard W. Levy, *Freedom of Speech and Press in Early American History* (New York: Harper & Row, 1963), 79–85.
65. John Feather, *The Provincial Book Trade in Eighteenth-Century England* (Cambridge: Cambridge University Press, 1985).
66. Warren McDougall, "Copyright Litigation in the Court of Session, 1738–1749, and the Rise of the Scottish Book Trade," *Edinburgh Bibliographical Society Transactions* 5:5 (1988): 2–31; Warren McDougall, "Scottish Books for America in the Mid-18th Century," in *Spreading the Word: The Distribution Networks of Print, 1550–1850*, Robin Myers and Michael Harris, eds. (Winchester: St. Paul's Bibliographies, 1990) 21–24; Mary Pollard, *Dublin's Trade in Books, 1550–1800* (Oxford: Clarendon Press, 1989).
67. Jack P. Greene, *Pursuits of Happiness: The Social Development of Early Modern British Colonies and the Formation of American Culture* (Chapel Hill: University of North Carolina Press, 1988), chap. 8.
68. Franklin to Strahan, July 4, 1744, *Franklin Papers*, 2:409.
69. The contract is printed in the *Franklin Papers*, 3:263–67.
70. Hall papers, American Philosophical Society; J. A. Cochrane, *Dr. Johnson's Printer: The Life of William Strahan* (London: Routledge & Kegan Paul, 1964), chap. 6; Robert D. Harlan, "David Hall's Bookshop and its British Sources of Supply," in *Books in America's Past*, ed. David Kaser (Charlottesville: University of Virginia Press, 1966), 1–24.
71. Harlan, "David Hall's Bookshop," 6.
72. Robert D. Harlan, "A Colonial Printer as Bookseller in Eighteenth-Century Philadelphia: the Case of David Hall," *Studies in Eighteenth-Century Culture* 5 (1976): 355–70.
73. Harlan, "Colonial Printer as Bookseller," 12.
74. Franklin-Hall account, *Franklin Papers*, 13:97.
75. James Green, "Franklin as Publisher," 106–07, 110.

76. Barber, "Books from the Old World," 221–22.
77. Leroy Hewlett, "James Rivington, Tory Printer," in *Books in America's Past,* 165–93; Stephen Botein, "The Anglo-American Book Trade before 1776: Personnel and Strategies," in *Printing and Society,* 73–81.
78. William Strahan to David Hall, March 3, 1755, quoted in Cochrane, *Dr. Johnson's Printer,* 81. See also Cynthia Z. and Gregory A. Stiverson, "The Colonial Retail Book Trade," in *Printing and Society,* 155.
79. Strahan to Hall, March 3, 1755, July 11, 1758, in Cochrane, *Dr. Johnson's Printer,* 81, 84. Stephen Botein, "The Anglo-American Book Trade," 74–75, calls these remainders and other unsalable books "rum books," but Strahan's "waste-paper books" seems a more precise and authentic term. Botein sees "rum books" as emblematic of the peripheral nature of colonial book culture even though Rivington's trade in them was experimental and unsuccessful.
80. Cochrane, *Dr. Johnson's Printer,* 80–87.
81. Strahan to Hall, July 11, 1758, in Cochrane, *Dr. Johnson's Printer,* 84.
82. Strahan to Hall, December 17, 1759, ibid., 86.
83. Richard G. Landon, "'Small Profits Do Great Things': James Lackington and Eighteenth-Century Bookselling," *Studies in Eighteenth-Century Culture* 5 (1976): 387–99.
84. John Feather, "The Publishers and the Pirates: British Copyright Law in Theory and Practice, 1710–1775," *Publishing History* 22 (1987): 5–32.
85. Strahan to Hall, March 24, 1759, in Cochrane, *Dr. Johnson's Printer,* 85.
86. James Raven, *British Fiction, 1750-1770* (Newark: University of Delaware Press, 1987), no. 728.
87. *South Carolina Gazette,* September 29, 1766.
88. This was the so-called third edition, 1766, but it was actually the first collected edition of his poems. Each of his poems had first appeared separately unbound in quarto. The first volume of his *Poems* had been collected and issued in quarto during his lifetime and then reissued posthumously in 1765, but the second volume had previously appeared only in the form of the several separate printings bound together and reissued with a new title, *Poems, Volume II,* 1765.
89. Rivington announced the publication and apologized for the delay in the *New York Journal,* December 15, 1768.
90. This was technically a remainder, but by no means a "rum book." The third edition of 1766 had obviously been a very large one, and sales must have been slow for there to have been 2,200 copies in sheets available two years later. But Rivington's purchase of those copies exhausted the supply, and the book was immediately reprinted in a fourth edition, 1769. In the meantime there had been an unauthorized London duodecimo edition in 1767, which would explain the slow sale of the third edition.
91. "William McCulloch's Additions to Thomas's *History of Printing,*" *Procs. AAS,* n.s., 31:1 (1921): 228, 247.
92. Richard B. Sher, "*Charles V* and the Book Trade: an Episode in Enlightenment Print Culture," in *William Robertson and the Expansion of Empire,* ed. Stewart J. Brown (Cambridge: Cambridge University Press, 1997), 164–95.
93. William Robertson, *The History of the Reign of Charles the Fifth,* 3 vols. (Philadelphia: Bell, 1770–1771), 3:5.

94. Robert Bell, *To the Honorable the Representatives of the Freemen, of the Commonwealth of Pennsylvania, in General Assembly met* (Philadelphia, 1783), Evans 17836.
95. Robert Bell, *Bell's Address to every Free-Man* (Philadelphia, 1784), Evans 18345.
96. Robert Bell, *Memorandum* (Philadelphia, January 17, 1774), Evans 13141.
97. Merchants and traders of the city of Philadelphia, March 10, 1769, Du Simitière papers, no. 89, Library Company of Philadelphia.
98. Leroy Hewlett, "James Rivington," 171; *New York Journal,* October 6, November 10, and November 24, 1768.
99. *Pennsylvania Journal,* June 16, 1768.
100. David Hall to Benjamin Franklin, October 14, 1765.
101. Robert D. Harlan, "David Hall and the Stamp Act," *PBSA* 61 (1967): 13–37.
102. Robert D. Harlan, "David Hall and the Townshend Acts," *PBSA* 68 (1974): 19–38.
103. Ford, *Hugh Gaine,* 1:57.
104. Rollo G. Silver, "Aprons Instead of Uniforms: The Practice of Printing, 1776–1787," *Procs. AAS* 87 (1977): 111–94.
105. Robert Aitken, Waste Book, ms., Library Company of Philadelphia, 356 (May 12, 1777).
106. Michael Zinman, *The Journals of the Continental Congress* (Ardsley, N.Y.: M. Zinman, 1995).
107. Richard Gimbel, *Thomas Paine: A Bibliographical Check List of Common Sense with an Account of Its Publication* (New Haven: Yale University Press, 1956), 15–57.
108. William and Thomas Bradford invoice book, 25, Bradford papers, Historical Society of Pennsylvania.
109. William H. Gaines, Jr., "The Continental Congress Considers the Publication of a Bible, 1777," *SB* 3 (1950): 274–80.
110. Robert Aitken, circular letter, August 11, 1782. The copy at the Massachusetts Historical Society shows the price in manuscript of $2.00 a copy by the dozen bound. I am grateful to Willman Spawn for supplying a photocopy of it.
111. Robert Aitken, waste book, Library Company of Philadelphia.
112. Aitken to John Nicholson, January 20, 1791, Pennsylvania State Archives, Nicholson Papers.
113. McCulloch, "Additions," 235.
114. For an overview of migration, settlement, literacy, and demographic patterns suggesting the relationship of Dutch and German adjustments to the New World, see A. G. Roeber, " 'The Origin of Whatever Is Not English among Us:' The Dutch-speaking and the German-speaking Peoples of Colonial British America," in *Strangers within the Realm: Cultural Margins of the First British Empire,* ed. Bernard Bailyn and Philip D. Morgan (Chapel Hill: University of North Carolina Press, 1991), 220–83.
115. *Die wunderbare neue Welt: German Books about the Americas in the John Carter Brown Library,* comp. Ilse E. Kramer (Providence, R.I.: John Carter Brown Library, 1988); *Handbuch historischer Buchbestände in Deutschland,* ed. Bernhard Fabian, 2 vols. (Hildesheim: Olms-Weidmann, 1991–) on the provenance of books in Germany.

116. I make no attempt here to survey or quantify pamphlets or broadsides printed in Europe promoting migration to America – for example, the Amsterdam or Hamburg versions of William Penn's promotion of Pennsylvania in the late 1670s.
117. The standard work on international Pietism has become *Geschichte descaps Pietismus,* ed. Martin Brecht et al., 2 vols. (Göttingen: Vandenhoeck & Ruprecht, 1993–1995).
118. Claudia Schnurmann, "Kommunikation und soziale Netzwerke: Beziehungen zwischen Bewohnern englischer und niederländischer Kolonien in der amerikanisch-atlantischen Welt, 1648–1713" (Habilitationsschrift, University of Göttingen, 1995), 513–14.
119. Roeber, "Dutch-speaking and German-speaking Peoples," 220–37; Hendrik Edelman, *The Dutch Language Press in America* (Nieuwkoop: De Graaf, 1986), 20–21.
120. I owe much of my information to Ruth Piwonka and her examination of inventories in the New York State Archives. See also *New York Historical Manuscripts: Dutch Kingston Papers,* ed. Peter R. Christoph, Kenneth Scott, and Kenn Stryker-Rodda, trans. Dingman Versteeg (Baltimore, Md.: Genealogical Publishing Co., 1976) 2:568–69; 574. On literacy rates, see David E. Narrett, *Inheritance and Family Life in Colonial New York City* (Ithaca, N.Y.: Cornell University Press, 1992), 222–27.
121. Eric Nooter, "Between Heaven and Earth: Church and Society in Pre-Revolutionary Flatbush, Long Island" (Ph.D. dissertation, Vrije Universiteit, Amsterdam, 1994), discusses both the catechisms and psalmbooks as well as theological treatises found in Flatbush households (131–34).
122. Although scholars have not documented the existence of a Dutch-language printer and press in New Netherland, a clear reference occurs in the correspondence of Jeremias van Rensselaer to his mother, Anna. Writing in 1663, he pointed out news she could glean "from the *neu nederlanse Marcurius." The Correspondence of Jeremias van Rensselaer, 1651–1674,* ed. and trans. A. J. F. van Laer (Albany: University of the State of New York, 1932), 328–39; see also E. B. O'Callaghan, *History of New Netherland, or New York Under the Dutch,* 2 vols. (New York, 1846–1848), 2:552.
123. Harold Jantz, "German-American Literature: Some Further Perspectives," in *America and the Germans: An Assessment of a Three-Hundred-Year History,* eds. Frank Trommler and Joseph McVeigh, 2 vols. (Philadelphia: University of Pennsylvania Press, 1985), 1:283–93. Manuscript compilations of hymnody antedate even these efforts. On the work of Johann Kelpius and his manual of prayer, which received a translation into English in 1761, see Willard Martin, "Johann Kelpius and Johann Gottfried Seelig: Mystics and Hymnists on the Wissahickon" (Ph.D. dissertation, Pennsylvania State University, 1973).
124. A. G. Roeber, *Palatines, Liberty, and Property: German Lutherans in Colonial British America* (Baltimore, Md.: The Johns Hopkins University Press, 1993), 95–132, 177; the relevant studies on literacy are cited in Chapter 11, below.
125. Robert E. Cazden, *A Social History of the German Book Trade in America to the Civil War* (Columbia, S.C.: Camden House, 1984), 4–5, 11.
126. Robert Diehl, *Frankfurt am Main im Spiegel alter Reisebeschreibungen vom 15. bis zum 19. Jahrhundert* (Frankfurt: M. Diesterweg, 1939), 54–106; Johann

Georg Keyßler, *Fortsetzung neuester Reisen durch Teutschland, Böhmen, Hungarn, etc.* (Hanover, 1741); Fried Lübbecke, *Fünfhundert Jahre Buch und Druck in Frankfurt am Main* (Frankfurt: H. Cobet, 1948), 213–16.

127. E. G. Alderfer, *The Ephrata Commune: An Early American Counterculture* (Pittsburgh, Pa.: University of Pittsburgh Press, 1985), 127–30, 154–55, 164–70.

128. I am indebted to Dexter Hawn of Ottawa for checking on the will of the Reverend Johann Samuel Schwerdtfeger and the inventory of books, contained in Archives of Ontario, Microfilm 862333 Registerbook A, 182–86 (will) and inventory of estate Stormont, Dundas and Glengarry Counties, Ontario, Surrogate Court Records, Wills, 1800–1821, 862340. Anton Henrich, *Der hochdeutsche Neu-Schottländische Calender* . . . (Halifax, N.S., 1788).

129. Roeber, *Palatines,* 113–38; 175–88.

130. Renate Wilson, "Public Works and Piety in Ebenezer: The Missing Salzburger Diaries of 1744–1745," *Georgia Historical Quarterly* 78 (1993): 336–66.

131. This and the following paragraph summarize my research at the Archives of the Francke Foundations, Halle/Saale detailing the financial relationships between the Foundations and the German-speaking churches in Georgia and Pennsylvania served by Halle-trained clerics. For Pennsylvania: Abteilung 4: A6 and 9; C 13, 17, and 20; Abteilung D; 2–6; for Georgia, Abteilung 5, A6–A9. Jablonsky's book was issued at Leipzig in 1721, at Königsberg in 1748, and again at Leipzig in 1767.

132. Archives of the Francke Foundations, 4 F/7 pp. 24–25 "Rechnung. . . ."

133. On Berkenmeyer, see Cazden, *German Book Trade,* 6; on Virginia, Roeber, *Palatines,* 138–40; Roeber, "The German-speaking and Dutch-speaking Peoples," 271–72; Mabel Haller, *Early Moravian Education in Pennsylvania* (Nazareth, Pa.: Moravian Historical Society, 1953).

134. The above summarize the entries in Karl John Richard Arndt and Reimer C. Eck, *The First Century of German Language Printing in the United States of America,* 2 vols. (Göttingen: Niedersächsische Staats- und Universitätsbibliothek, 1989). For Schneider and Steinmeyer, the most exhaustive archival treatment of these controversies, albeit from a pro-Carroll and hierarchical point of view, is V. J. Fecher, S.V.D., *A Study of the Movement for German National Parishes in Philadelphia and Baltimore (1787–1802)* (Roma: Apud Aedes Universitatis Gregorianae, 1955); Fecher also does not acknowledge the role of Mainz and its "enlightenment" in the controversies in Baltimore and Philadelphia. See Martin I. J. Griffin, "The Church of the Holy Trinity, Philadelphia. Its First Pastor, the Rev. John Baptist Charles Helbron," and "The Rev. Peter Helbron, Second Pastor of Holy Trinity Church, Philadelphia," *Records of the American Catholic Historical Society of Philadelphia* 21 (1910): 1–45; 22 (1912): 1–22.

135. Cazden, *German Book Trade,* 8–11, and see James O. Knauss, "Christopher Saur the Third," *Procs. AAS* 41 (1931): 242–43. For further bibliographic information, compare the titles to the entries in Arndt and Eck, *First Century.*

136. Henry Miller, "Der Überrest von einer Sammlung Bücher . . . ," in *Neueste, Verbessert- und Zuverlässige Amerikanische Calender* (Philadelphia, 1775), *ad fin.*

137. Renate Wilson, "Medical Literature in North America, 1740–1820: The High End of the Market," paper presented at the annual meeting of the

American Association for the History of Medicine, 1994; Wilson, "The Traffic in Halle Orphanage Medications: Medicinals, Philanthropy, and Colonial Mission," *Caduceus: A Humanities Journal for Medicine and the Health Sciences* 13:1 (Spring, 1997): 6–22; David L. Cowen and Renate Wilson, "The Traffic in Medical Ideas: Popular Medical Texts as German Imports and American Imprints," ibid., 67–80. Reinhard Wittmann, *Geschichte des deutschen Buchhandels: ein Überblick* (Münich: C. H. Beck, 1991) summarizes the history of the book fairs. I thank Professor Martha Woodmansee of Case Western Reserve, Department of English, who is studying copyright law in the Empire during this time for confirming my own failure to find a legal explanation for this phenomenon.

138. Unfortunately, later collections of German-language books rarely distinguish those acquired prior to the Revolution and possibly in North America from those imported after the Revolution. For one such example, see the Uncatalogued Materials, Kurz Collection, Gettysburg Lutheran Seminary, which contains both secular and religious eighteenth-century titles.

139. This and the following paragraphs summarize A. G. Roeber, "Citizens or Subjects? German Lutherans and the Federal Constitution in Pennsylvania, 1789–1800," *Amerikastudien/American Studies* 34 (1989): 49–68; Roeber, "The von Mosheim Society and the Preservation of German Education and Culture in the New Republic, 1789–1813," in Henry Geitz, Jürgen Heideking and Jürgen Herbst, eds., *German Influences on Education in the United States to 1917* (Cambridge: Cambridge University Press, 1995), 157–76; and Roeber, "J. H. C. Helmuth, Evangelical Charity, and the Public Sphere in Pennsylvania, 1793–1800," *PMHB* 121:1–2 (1997): 77–100.

140. This and the succeeding paragraph summarize Christopher L. Dolmetsch, *The German Press of the Shenandoah Valley* (Columbia, S.C.: Camden House, 1984), 57–60; Klaus Wust, *The Virginia Germans* (Charlottesville: University Press of Virginia, 1969), 150–52.

141. *Ben Franklin's Jugendjahre, von ihm selbst für seinen Sohn beschrieben und übersetzt von Gottfried August Burger* (Berlin, 1792).

142. Roeber, "The von Mosheim Society," 160–69; Roeber, *Palatines*, 325–32; Henry Miller, *Verbessertes Hochdeutsch-Reformiertes Namen-Büchlein* (Philadelphia, 1772). As early as 1755 Saur published for the Moravians *Das Kinder-Büchlein in den Brüder Gemeinden* (Germantown, 1750); and Anton Armbrüster, before his conversion to Lutheranism, provided the Moravians with *Des Kinder-Büchleins Tom. vii* (Philadelphia, 1758?). Also designed for children were *Biblia, das ist Die Heilige Schrift* (Germantown, 1776), published by Christopher Saur, and Eberhard Caspar's *Kurze und einfältige Kinderlehr* (Germantown, 1788) published by Michael Billmeyer. Rarely, however, does one find a broader genre of children's literature.

143. See for the connection between Weisse and Berquin, Florence V. Barry, *A Century of Children's Books* (1922, repr. Detroit, Mich.: Singing Tree Press, 1968), 92.

144. Pending the cataloguing of the Society Library and its reopening in 1998, no systematic study of the holdings was possible prior to writing this essay. Helmuth continued to obtain books, as did other American clients, from

the Hermannische Buchladen in Frankfurt, maintaining a tie he established in 1786. See his letter of June 3, 1791 (Lutheran Archives of Philadelphia).

145. I am indebted to Renate Wilson for reminding me of the founding of the Medical College at Cincinnati by German speakers whose antecedents lay in the Jefferson Medical College in Pennsylvania; for further details of this later revival, see Cazden, *German Book Trade,* 121–57.

Chapter 9. The New England Book Trade 1713–1790

1. Bruce C. Daniels, *The Connecticut Town: Growth and Development, 1635–1790* (Middletown, Conn.: Wesleyan University Press, 1979); Richard W. Wilkie and Jack Tager, *Historical Atlas of Massachusetts* (Amherst: University of Massachusetts Press, 1991), pp. 27 ff.
2. Gary B. Nash, "The Social Evolution of Preindustrial American Cities, 1700–1820: Reflections and New Directions," *Journal of Urban History* 13 (1987): 25.
3. David Hancock, "Markets, Merchants, and the Wider World of Boston Wine, 1700–1775," in *Entrepreneurs: The Boston Business Community, 1700–1850,* ed. Conrad E. Wright and K. P. Viens (Boston: Massachusetts Historical Society, 1997), 82–84.
4. See generally Carol Sue Humphrey, *"This Popular Engine": New England Newspapers during the American Revolution, 1775–1789* (Newark: University of Delaware Press, 1992), chaps. 1–4; the best documented account of New England printing to date, though she touches only incidentally, of course, on the importation and distribution of books and pamphlets.
5. On the identification of his youngest son's printing in Boston, see Note 25.
6. Alfred L. Lorenz, *Hugh Gaine: A Colonial Printer-Editor's Odyssey to Loyalism* (Carbondale: Southern Illinois Press, 1972), 26.
7. The circulation figure of 8,000 in 1778 (Humphrey, "*This Popular Engine,*" 73), though generally accepted, is probably too large. As of 1774, the *Courant* had only 700 subscribers, and the printer, Ebenezer Watson, who died on Sept. 16, 1777, had only one press, worth £20. During 1777, he or his widow printed eight sermons, an almanac, one dying words, a reprinting of the *Rules* for the Revolutionary forces, and nine broadsides – to say nothing of job-printing that is either unrecorded or lost; together with a weekly production of 8,000 sheets of the *Courant,* this would almost certainly have exceeded the capacity of a one-press shop during the weeks when the other items, and particularly the almanac, were being printed. See Susan Henry, "Work, Widowhood, and War: Hannah Bunce Watson, Connecticut Printer," *Connecticut Historical Society Bulletin* 48 (1983): 25–31; William DeLoss Love, *The Colonial History of Hartford* (Hartford, Conn.: The author, 1914), 311 n.; and Michael Pollak, "The Performance of the Wooden Printing Press," *Library Quarterly* 42 (1972): 218–64.
8. Milton W. Hamilton, *The Country Printer: New York State, 1785–1830* (New York: Columbia University Press, 1936); the distribution of imprint bibliographies by states tends to obscure such commercial connections. As Harriet S. Tapley's study of Salem shows, cities are more appropriate units.
9. *Diary of Joshua Hempstead of New London, Connecticut, 1711–1758* (New London, Conn.: New London County Historical Society, 1902), 611 & passim.

10. Joseph T. Buckingham, *Personal Memoirs and Recollections of Editorial Life,* 2 vols. (Boston, 1852), 1:20–21.
11. Printed prospectus, 1762 (John E. Alden, *Rhode Island Imprints, 1727–1800* [New York: R.R. Bowker, 1949], no. 246).
12. Hamilton, *Country Printer,* 244.
13. Humphrey, "This Popular Engine," [48–50].
14. James A. Henretta, "Economic Development and Social Structure in Colonial Boston," *WMQ,* 3rd ser., 22 (1965): 75–92. Cf. also Charles Wetherell, "Brokers of the Word: An Essay in the Social History of the Early American Press, 1689–1788" (Ph.D. dissertation, University of New Hampshire, 1980). Wetherell extends the demographic methods used by Lawrence Stone in his *Crisis of the Aristocracy* to argue for the continuing hegemony of the Green family during the eighteenth century; entry to the trade, however, was far less restricted than entry to the British aristocracy, and the thesis is not persuasive.
15. Henry Coulton: *Report of the Record Commissioners of the City of Boston* 29 (1900): 236, granted permission to settle, June 25, 1716; James Cummins: Duniway, *Freedom of the Press,* 80; Irish book-printer: *Boston News-Letter,* June 18/25, 1716.
16. Martin Unwin: Boston Record Commrs., *Rept.* 15 (1886): 53, from London, granted permission to settle June 22, 1737. The others appear in Evans, but on Skinner see also Willman & Carol Spawn, "Francis Skinner, Bookbinder of Newport: An Eighteenth-Century Craftsman Identified by his Tools," *Winterthur Portfolio* 2 (1965): 47–61.
17. William McDuell: Boston Record Commrs., *Rept.* 29 (1900): 293, from Glasgow, granted permission to settle, Jan. 11, 1767; the others appear in Evans.
18. Elizabeth C. Reilly, "The Wages of Piety: The Boston Book Trade of Jeremy Condy," *Printing and Society,* 83–131.
19. Samuel Bass: Daniel Henchman papers (microfilm, American Antiquarian Society, Worcester, Mass.), reel 3; Jared Sparks (ed.), "Bennett's History of New England," *Procs. MHS* 5 (1860–1862): 112, who adds, "the leather is not pretended to be near so good as that which is sent from England."
20. Thomas, *Hist. Printing,* 195–86.
21. This paragraph is based on Daybook no. 1, in the Henchman papers (microfilm, American Antiquarian Society); and cf. Reilly, "Wages of Piety," 108.
22. Bennett, "History," 112; Sparks's transcription has been corrected against the original, Sparks MS 2, Houghton Library, Harvard University.
23. The identity of the two firms appears from Henchman's accounts, which do not distinguish them; for the rental of Number 2 Dock Square, see Boston Record Commrs., *Rept.* 15 (1886): 356.
24. Thomas, *Hist. Printing,* 124 says Bushell "as I have been informed" printed the *Boston Post-Boy* for Huske, and this is confirmed by the ornaments in the banner signed IB; the similarly signed ornaments in the *Boston Gazette* have been wrongly ascribed to Huske's predecessor as postmaster, John Boydell (Sinclair Hamilton, *Early American Book Illustrators and Wood Engravers,* vol. 2 [Princeton, N.J.: Princeton University Press, 1968], no. 1308).

25. Benjamin Franklin V, *Boston Printers, Publishers, and Booksellers: 1640–1800* (Boston, Mass.: G. K. Hall, 1980), following the American Antiquarian Society printers' file, rightly rejects Bristol's identification of this Green with Bartholomew, Jr.'s son, the partner of Green & Russell (1731–1787). His identity with the son of Timothy Green of New London is confirmed by the transfer of ornaments from his Boston edition of the *History of the Holy Jesus* (1748) to his New London edition (1754); cf. Elizabeth C. Reilly, *A Dictionary of Colonial American Printers' Ornaments and Illustrations* (Worcester, Mass.: American Antiquarian Society, 1975), nos. 1253, 1247, 1250, 1256, 1262–63, 1266–67, 1272–73. Reilly no. 1256 first appeared as an illustration in *Blazing Stars, Messengers of Gods Wrath* (Boston: Printed for and are to be sold by Benj. [Gray], 1744), about the time when John Green moved to Boston (cf. a mutilated entry in Hempstead's *Diary,* 433).

26. The best account of Bushell is in the *Dictionary of Canadian Biography,* vol. 3: *1741–1770*; on the earlier tradespeople, see H. Pearson Gundy, *The Spread of Printing: Canada* (Amsterdam: Van Gendt & Co., 1972), 13.

27. Negus appears in only two imprints, 1719, but he was still purchasing books from Henchman in 1738, and he held town office from 1729 until 1742, when he may have died (Robert F. Seybolt, *Town Officials of Colonial Boston, 1634–1775* [Cambridge, Mass.: Harvard University Press, 1939]). Thomas (*Hist. Printing,* 197–98) identifies Starkey as "from London," apparently by confusion with his father, a mariner and member of Second Church. Robert Jr. was baptized on April 25, 1697 and died in 1722 (Suffolk Co. Probate Records, vols. 22: 416; 23: 209). On Checkley, see Edmund F. Slafter, *John Checkley* (Boston, Mass.: Prince Society, 1897).

28. See Chapter 5, Part 2.

29. Rollo G. Silver, "Publishing in Boston, 1726–1757: The Accounts of Daniel Henchman," *Procs. AAS* 66 (1956): 17–36.

30. See generally Michael Winship, "Publishing in America: Needs and Opportunities for Research," in *Needs and Opportunities in the History of the Book: America, 1639–1876,* ed. David D. Hall & John B. Hench (Worcester, Mass.: American Antiquarian Society, 1987), 61–102; and for the transition to modern publishing, Rosalind Remer, *Printers and Men of Capital: Philadelphia Book Publishers in the New Republic* (Philadelphia: University of Pennsylvania Press, 1996), chap. 1. For a definition of publishing, I have paraphrased *Book and Print in New Zealand: A Guide to Print Culture in Aotearoa,* ed. Penny Griffith et al. (Wellington, NZ: Victoria University Press, 1997), 86.

31. Thomas, *Hist. Printing,* 103–104 (where the first edition read "not long after the time when this impression of the Bible came from the press"), and 120–21; the discrepancy was noted by William McCulloch, "Additions to Thomas's *History of Printing,*" *Procs. AAS* 31 (1921): 89–247.

32. The entire bill is transcribed by Silver, "Publishing in Boston," 31–32.

33. Thomas Prince's *Vade Mecum for America* (Evans 3470), which Silver identifies as "The &c.," contained only 14-¼ sheets, nearly all of them printed in England; and if "The &c." in fact cost £3 a sheet, Henchman's £8 5*s.* would have purchased only twenty-two copies of this 127-½-sheet book.

34. Frank Lambert, *"Pedlar in Divinity": George Whitefield and the Transatlantic Revivals, 1737–1770* (Princeton, N.J.: Princeton University Press, 1994), citing Whitefield on "enthusiasm," p. 190.
35. Rosalind Remer, "Old Lights and New Money: A Note on Religion, Economics and the Social Order in 1740 Boston," *WMQ*, 3rd ser., 47 (1990): 571–73.
36. The Strahan Ledgers (microfilm), British Library, Add. Mss. 48,800, fols. 22v and 37v; a second London edition, also of 1,000 copies, followed in 1743.
37. The size of the first Henchman edition is implied by Draper's charges (reprinted in Silver, "Publishing in Boston," 33) at a rate of 75*s*. a thousand for the first edition (2 ½ sheets); a copy of the second edition (not recorded in NAIP, Evans, or Bristol), wanting the title page, is in the Houghton Library, Harvard University. No more American editions appeared after 1741 during the eighteenth century.
38. George S. Eddy, ed., *Account Books Kept by Benjamin Franklin: Ledger "D," 1739–1747* (New York: Columbia University Press, 1929), 53, 70; I have counted only the number of volumes needed to make up sets as the booksellers' actual subscription, assuming that the surplus consisted of subscriptions for individual customers.
39. *Franklin Papers,* 2:242–44.
40. Henchman papers (American Antiquarian Society), DH10.
41. Boston Record Commrs., *Rept.* 29 (1900): 269, permitting Alexander Ferbes [sic] and James Archibald, both from Leith, to settle, Aug. 22, 1765; Thomas, *Hist. Printing*: 149. "Ferbes" is presumably the Alexander Forbes recorded in Edinburgh, 1731 by Robert H. Carnie & R. P. Doig, "Scottish Printers and Booksellers 1668–1775: A Supplement [to Plomer et al., *Dictionary*]," *SB* 12 (1959): [131]–57.
42. My account here is indebted to the illuminating study by John W. Tyler, *Smugglers and Patriots: Boston Merchants and the Advent of the American Revolution* (Boston, Mass.: Northeastern University Press, 1986).
43. Timothy M. Barnes, "The Loyalist Press, 1756–1781" (Ph.D. dissertation, University of New Mexico, 1970), 119–20.
44. Mary Ann Yodelis, "Who Paid the Piper?," *Journalism Monographs* 38 (1975) begs a number of questions: that religion was nearly as central to colonial life as a distrust of taxation without representation hardly implies that religion "paid" for the Revolution; see Appendix 1, for a discussion of her statistics.
45. "The Cornfields" was the sign of the merchant Hopestill Capen (*Boston Gazette,* June 22, 1767); and see Walter Muir Whitehill, *Boston: A Topographical History* (Cambridge, Mass.: Belknap Press, 1959), 30, for the identification of this building.
46. Geyer: *Boston Post-Boy/Massachusetts Gazette,* January 30/February 6, 1775; this seems to be the earliest recorded instance of the manufacture of printing ink in New England. Mitchelson: see Rollo G. Silver, *Typefounding in America, 1787–1825* (Charlottesville: University Press of Virginia, 1965), 6–7, and references there.
47. The classifications are not water-tight: some bookbinders imported stock (e.g., A. Barclay), importers occasionally sold domestic imprints (e.g., P. Freeman, & W. Phillips), and printer–booksellers might also do importing (e.g., J. Boyle). In the print trade, the engravers' main market was mark-

ing silver, not engraving copperplate. *Bookbinders:* A. Barclay, A. Butler Jr., J. Perkins, S. Robinson (d. Feb. 25, 1771), J. Snelling, A. Steele, S. Webb, T. White; *Importers:* T. Bromfield, J. F. Condy, Cox & Berry, P. Freeman, H. Knox, J. Langdon, W. Phillips; *Stationers:* N. Bowes, T. Leverett; *Printer–booksellers:* J. Boyle, N. Coverly, Edes & Gill, J. Edwards, T. & J. Fleet, J. Fleeming, Z. Fowle, W. McAlpine, G. Rogers, E. Russell, I. Thomas; *Printers:* R. Draper, Green & Russell, D. Kneeland, Kneeland & Adams; *Prints, etc.*: N. Hurd, W. Price (d. May 11, 1771), D. Rea Jr., P. Revere, S. Whiting, S. Whiting Jr., W. Williams.

48. *Boston Post-Boy/Massachusetts Gazette,* Feb. 4, 1771; *Boston Evening Post,* May 20, 1771 & August 2, 1773.
49. Bettye Hobbs Pruitt, ed., *The Massachusetts Tax Valuation List of 1771* (Boston: G. K. Hall, 1978); mysteriously, neither Richard Draper, Green & Russell, nor W. McAlpine were rated. The index of wealth used here may not be entirely reliable: see John J. McCusker and Russell R. Menard, *The Economy of British America, 1607–1789* (Chapel Hill: University of North Carolina Press, 1991), 273–74.
50. John E. Alden, "John Mein: Scourge of Patriots," *Pubs. CSM* 34 (1937–42): 571–99. The letterbook of Kincaid & Bell, 1764–1773, is in the Bodleian Library, Oxford, call no. Mss. Eng. lett. c. 20–1.
51. Rollo G. Silver, "Benjamin Edes, Trumpeter of Sedition," *PBSA* 47 (1953): 248–68.
52. Rollo G. Silver, "Aprons instead of Uniforms: The Practice of Printing, 1776–1787," *Procs. AAS* 87 (1987): 111–94.
53. Rollo G. Silver, "Government Printing in Massachusetts, 1751–1801," *SB* 16 (1963): 161–200.
54. Alan Kulikoff, "The Progress of Inequality in Revolutionary Boston," *WMQ*, 3rd ser., 28 (1971): 385.
55. Lawrence W. Towner, "The Indentures of Boston's Poor Apprentices: 1734–1805," *Pubs. CSM* 43 (1956): 417–68. The original indentures are now deposited in the Boston Public Library, Ms. fBos. W1 (5). Interestingly, one of the four children, Anthony Haswell, was apprenticed to Thomas, who also later projected "printers' academies" in Boston and Worcester, where the children of "poor Printers, Booksellers and Bookbinders" might learn English and Latin (Clifford K. Shipton, *Isaiah Thomas: Printer, Patriot and Philanthropist, 1749–1831* [Rochester, N.Y.: Leo Hart, 1948], 77).
56. Gary B. Nash, *The Urban Crucible: The Northern Seaports and the Origins of the American Revolution,* abridged ed. (Cambridge, Mass.: Harvard University Press, 1986), 185–88.
57. Cit. Shipton, *Isaiah Thomas,* 21.
58. Hollis Roger Yarrington, "Isaiah Thomas, Printer" (Ph.D. dissertation, University of Maryland, 1970), 69.
59. Ibid., 157; Shipton, *Isaiah Thomas,* 44, styles it "the most widely circulated almanac of that generation," which can hardly be true.
60. Ibid., 51; my account is much indebted to "The Rise and Fall of Isaiah Thomas's Bookselling Network," an AAS seminar paper presented October 24, 1996 by James N. Green.
61. William Charvat, *Literary Publishing in America, 1790–1850,* [repr.] with a new afterword by Michael Winship (Amherst: University of Massachu-

setts Press, 1993), chap. 1. Charvat's statistics have been silently corrected by reference to the later authority of Shipton & Mooney, *National Index*, and Shaw and Shoemaker, *American Bibliography*, to eliminate ghosts, and erroneous dates and attributions.

62. See *A Catalogue of Books for Sale by Thomas and Thomas* (Walpole, 1803) (copy at the AAS). For a somewhat later period, cf. Jack Larkin, "The Merriams of Brookfield: Printing in the Economy and Culture of Rural Massachusetts in the Early Nineteenth Century," *Procs. AAS* 96 (1986): 39–73, stressing the importance of staple books in the sales of the Merriams' bookstore.
63. Dennie's light-hearted quip threatens to become a canonical proof-text for Charvat's assertions: cf. Lawrence Buell, *New England Literary Culture: From Revolution through Renaissance* (New York: Cambridge University Press, 1986), 27–28; Cathy N. Davidson, *Revolution and the Word: The Rise of the Novel in America* (New York: Oxford University Press, 1986), 21. But see under the title of the *Algerine Captive* in the *Catalogue of Books, for Sale or Circulation, by W. P. & L. Blake* (Boston, 1798); *Catalogue of Books, for Sale by E. Larkin* (Boston, 1798); and [Edward Cotton, comp.], *A Catalogue of All the Books Printed in the United States* (Boston, 1804).
64. William J. Gilmore, *Reading Becomes a Necessity of Life: Material and Cultural Life in Rural New England, 1780–1835* (Knoxville: University of Tennessee Press, 1989), 173. See also his "Peddlers and the Dissemination of Printed Material in Northern New England, 1780–1840," *Annual Proceedings of the Dublin Seminar for New England Folklife* 9 (1984): 76–89, though his account of the "extensive" stock of peddlers may be misleading. They may have had more titles than the "intensive reading" stocked by country stores, but they still sold "small books." The copies of *Charlotte Temple* (1802) and *Pamela* (1800) in a Connecticut peddler's stock of 1802, cited by Gilmore-Lehne, contained only 142 pages and 138 pages, respectively.
65. Cf. "Printers, Editors, and Publishers of Country Newspapers, New York, 1785–1830," in Hamilton, *Country Printer*, [253]–309; and, for the economic reorientation of Connecticut and Long Island, McCusker and Menard, *Economy*, 190.
66. This count is based on the "Miscellaneous" section in Cotton's 1804 *Catalogue*, where most of the literature is classed. For an analysis of the distribution of imprints in other sections, see Adolf Growoll, *Book-Trade Bibliography in the United States in the XIXth Century* (New York: Dibdin Club, 1898), xv–xvi.
67. Samuel G. Goodrich, *Recollections of a Lifetime, or Men and Things I have Seen*, 2 vols. (New York, 1856), 1:412. Cf. Charvat's provocative dictum, that Hartford's "literary publishing up to 1830 was as important as Boston's" (p. 19).

Chapter 10. Periodicals and Politics

1. *OED*, s.v. "journalism."
2. David Paul Nord, "Teleology and News: The Religious Roots of American Journalism, 1630–1730," *Journal of American History* 77 (1990): 9–38.

3. Karl Bücher, *Industrial Evolution,* tr. S. Morely Wickett (1901; repr. New York: A. M. N. Kelly, 1968), 221–33; J. B. Williams, "The Newsbooks and Letters of News of the Restoration," *English Historical Review,* 23 (1905): 252; G. A. Cranfield, *The Development of the Provincial Newspaper, 1700–1760* (Oxford: Oxford University Press, 1962), 31–32; Charles E. Clark, *The Public Prints: The Newspaper in Anglo-American Culture, 1665–1740* (New York: Oxford University Press, 1994), 16–23, 65.
4. See, e.g., Joad Raymond, ed., *Making the News: An Anthology of the Newsbooks of Revolutionary England, 1641–1660* (New York: St. Martin's Press, 1993).
5. David L. Jacobson, ed., *The English Libertarian Heritage* (Indianapolis: Bobbs-Merrill, 1965), xvii–lx.
6. See Chapter 12.
7. Michael Warner, *The Letters of the Republic: Publication and the Public Sphere in Eighteenth-Century America* (Cambridge, Mass.: Harvard University Press, 1990), 38–39. For one critique, see Grantland S. Rice, *The Transformation of Authorship in America* (Chicago, Ill.: University of Chicago Press, 1997), 23–24.
8. Charles E. Clark, "The Newspapers of Provincial America," *Procs. AAS* 100 (1990): 367–89.
9. The only known surviving copy of *Publick Occurrences* is in the Public Record Office, London. A facsimile edition was produced by Calvin P. Otto for the American Antiquarian Society in 1990. Secondary treatments of *Publick Occurrences* and its publisher include Duniway, *Freedom of the Press*; Frank Luther Mott, *American Journalism: A History of Newspapers in the United States Through 250 Years, 1690 to 1940* (New York: Macmillan, 1949), 9–10; Victor Hugo Paltsits, "New Light on 'Publick Occurrences': America's First Newspaper," *Procs. AAS* 59 (1949): 75–88; John Tebbel, "Benjamin Harris" in *Boston Printers, Publishers, and Booksellers, 1640–1800,* ed. Benjamin Franklin V (Boston: G. K. Hall, 1980), 277–80; Judith Serrin, "U.S. Newspapers' 300th Year," *Editor and Publisher,* April 21, 1990, 66–69; and Clark, "The Newspapers of Provincial America." But Ian K. Steele, citing the content and uncertain periodicity of Harris's newssheet, doubts that it qualifies as "America's First Newspaper" at all, *The English Atlantic, 1675–1740: An Exploration of Communication and Community* (New York: Oxford University Press, 1986), 146–47. On the *London Gazette,* see P. M. Handover, *A History of the London Gazette* (London: H. M. Stationery Office, 1965).
10. Cranfield, *Development of the Provincial Newspaper,* 12–16.
11. Not counting either the special case of the *News-Letter* of Dublin begun in 1685, which with its successors served only the small Protestant community in occupied Ireland, or the *Edinburgh Gazette,* which in 1699 revived the title of a short-lived Scottish newspaper of 1680. Robert Munter, *The History of the Irish Newspaper, 1685–1760* (Cambridge: Cambridge University Press, 1967), 5–15; W. J. Couper, *The Edinburgh Periodical Press,* 2 vols. (Stirling, Scotland: Eneas Mackay, 1908), 1:202–54.
12. Those preceding the *News-Letter* were the *Norwich Post* (1701), *Bristol Post-Boy* (1702), and *Sam Farley's Exeter Post-Man* (probably 1704). See list of English provincial newspapers in R. M. Wiles, *Freshest Advices: Early Provincial Newspapers in England* (Columbus: Ohio State University Press, 1965), Appendix B, 373.

13. Letters from Duncan and John Campbell to Gov. Fitz John Winthrop of Connecticut are printed in *Procs. MHS* 9 (1866–1867): 485–501, and 12 (1871–1875): 419–27. In his letter of July 12, 1703 (9: 496–97), John Campbell quotes at length from a letter he had received from New York, parts of which themselves appear to have been copied from London newspapers. Discussions of the Campbells' newsletters include those in Duniway, *Freedom of the Press,* 76–77; *DAB,* s.v. "Campbell, John"; Douglas C. McMurtrie, *The Beginnings of the American Newspaper* (Chicago: Black Cat Press, 1935); Arthur M. Schlesinger, *Prelude to Independence: The Newspaper War on Britain, 1764–1776* (New York: Alfred A. Knopf, 1958), 5–52; and Steele, *The English Atlantic, 1675–1740,* 360 n.
14. Clark, *The Public Prints,* 78–79, 85–86.
15. Ibid., 92–95.
16. Ibid., 105–06, 119–22.
17. *American Weekly Mercury,* Oct. 14, 1721; see discussion in Clark, *The Public Prints,* 118–19.
18. Ibid., 70–72. This argument is developed there at some length.
19. See, e.g., *Boston News-Letter,* June 10, 1706.
20. Clark, *The Public Prints,* 200–07.
21. See Appendix 1, Graph 3.
22. Based mainly on the insights of Michael Warner, who discusses legitimization by the "impersonality" of print in *Letters of the Republic,* 34–43. In the same work, Warner offers a specific interpretation of the *Courant* (82–86) with a different emphasis. For another provocative treatment of the *Courant,* see Thomas C. Leonard, *The Power of the Press: The Birth of American Political Reporting* (New York: Oxford University Press, 1986), 18–32.
23. See Stephen Botein's discussion of the *Weekly Journal*'s use of, and his comparison of that paper with, the anti-Walpole London newspaper, *The Craftsman,* in *'Mr. Zenger's Malice and Falshood': Six Issues of the New-York Weekly Journal, 1733–34* (Worcester, Mass.: American Antiquarian Society, 1985), 5–11; and see the discussion of Zenger in Chapter 8.
24. Botein, "Printers and the American Revolution," *Press & Am. Rev.*, 19. See also Botein, "'Meer Mechanics' and an Open Press: The Business and Political Strategies of Colonial American Printers," *Perspectives in American History* 9 (1975): 127–55. Jeffrey A. Smith's *Printers and Press Freedom: The Ideology of Early American Journalism* (New York: Oxford University Press, 1988) is concerned mainly with the evolution of "press freedom" to criticize government, but in the process explores some related ideas about the ethics and responsibilities of printers. Smith's treatment of Benjamin Franklin and his associates in this regard, 108–67, is especially rich.
25. See again Botein, " 'Meer Mechanics' and an Open Press."
26. Franklin, *Autobiography,* 1398. See Clark, *The Public Prints,* 207–10, for more on printers' policies. The argument that most printer–publishers of the era held a more positive view of their mission than is implied by the phrase "meer mechanics" is developed more fully in Clark, "The Evolution of Newspaper Ethics in Eighteenth Century America," an unpublished pa-

per presented to the Society for the History of Authorship, Reading and Publishing, Worcester, Mass., July 21, 1996.

27. Frank Lambert, *"Pedlar in Divinity": George Whitefield and the Transatlantic Revivals, 1737–1770* (Princeton, N.J.: Princeton University Press, 1994), esp. 95–133.

28. *Boston Evening-Post,* September 29 and October 6, 1740; *Boston Weekly News-Letter,* October 2, 1740.

29. On "Country Party" or "Real Whig" rhetoric in the Boston press, see Richard L. Bushman, *King and People in Provincial Massachusetts* (Chapel Hill: University of North Carolina Press, 1985), 253–67, with specific attention to the transforming role of Edes and Gill, 261. Some sense of the change in emphasis between the older and younger owners can be gained by scanning the *Boston Gazette* for 1754 and early 1755, the last months of Kneeland's ownership (though the final two months of his *Gazette,* February 18–March 31 are missing from the extant file at the AAS), and the first few months of the same paper under the new ownership beginning April 7, 1755. Edes & Gill even gave a partisan cast to the paper's title by changing the name from the *Boston Gazette, or Weekly Advertiser* to *Boston Gazette, or Country Journal.* The quotation from Goddard is from the first number of the *Providence Gazette,* October 30, 1762.

30. David W. Conroy, *In Public Houses: Drink and the Revolution of Authority in Colonial Massachusetts* (Chapel Hill: University of North Carolina Press, 1995), 175–81, 231–36.

31. Charles E. Clark and Charles Wetherell, "The Measure of Maturity: The *Pennsylvania Gazette,* 1728–1765," *WMQ,* 3rd ser., 46 (1989): 279–303.

32. Frank Luther Mott, *A History of American Magazines, 1741–1850,* 5 vols. (Cambridge, Mass.: Harvard University Press, 1957–1968), 1:24–31, 71–79, 787–89.

33. Thomas, *Hist. Printing* is the most accessible edition. For more on Thomas, see Marcus McCorison's Foreword to *Press & Am Rev.,* 1–10.

34. Botein, "Printers and the American Revolution"; Leonard, *The Power of the Press*; and Carol Sue Humphrey, *"This Popular Engine": New England Newspapers during the American Revolution, 1775–1789* (Newark: University of Delaware Press, 1992).

35. Russell Martin has found that of the 483 individual printers between 1701 and 1790 listed by the North American Imprints Project, only 136 had no connection with a newspaper, and of those, 110 were at best marginal participants in the trade.

36. Humphrey, *"This Popular Engine,"* 72–73; see Chapter 9, n. 7.

37. This point is made by Stephen Botein in "Printers and the American Revolution," *Press & Am. Rev.,* 11 and n.

38. Botein, "Printers and the American Revolution," 25–26.

39. Leonard, *The Power of the Press,* 33–58.

40. Botein, "Printers and the American Revolution," 32.

41. See Bernard Bailyn, *Pamphlets of the American Revolution, 1750–1776* (Cambridge, Mass.: Harvard University Press, 1965), 1:3–5, including a quotation of George Orwell.

42. Rice, *Transformation of Authorship,* 40–44.

43. Thomas R. Adams, *American Independence: The Growth of an Idea* (Providence, R.I.: Brown University Press, 1965), xi, 164–71; Thomas R. Adams, *The American Controversy: A Bibliographical Study of the British Pamphlets About the American Dispute, 1764–1783*, 2 vols. (Providence, R.I.: Brown University Press, 1980), 1:422–26.
44. Adams, *American Independence*, 110–13.
45. Ibid., 47–40.
46. Bailyn, *Pamphlets*, reproduction of title page in preface, Pamphlet 7:409–17.
47. John K. Alexander, *The Selling of the Constitutional Convention: A History of News Coverage* (Madison, Wisc.: Madison House, 1990).
48. Elaine F. Crane, "Publius in the Provinces: Where Was *The Federalist* Reprinted Outside New York City?," *WMQ*, 3rd ser., 21 (1964): 589–92.
49. Robert Allen Rutland, "The First Great Newspaper Debate: The Constitutional Crisis of 1787–88," *Procs. AAS* 97 (1987): 43–58. For a closer, semi-popularized look at the role of the newspaper press in one state's ratification process, see Charles E. Clark, *Printers, the People, and Politics: The New Hampshire Press and Ratification* (Concord: New Hampshire Humanities Council, 1989).
50. N. H. Keeble, *The Literary Culture of Nonconformity in Later Seventeenth-Century England* (Leicester: Leicester University Press, 1987), 95–126; Richard D. Brown, *The Strength of a People: The Idea of an Informed Citizenry in America, 1650–1870* (Chapel Hill: University of North Carolina Press, 1996), chap. 1; J. R. Jones, ed., *Liberty Secured? Britain Before and After 1688* (Stanford, Calif.: Stanford University Press, 1992). For a revisionist view of the seventeenth-century colonial experience with freedom of the spoken word, see Larry Eldridge, *A Distant Heritage: The Growth of Free Speech in Early America* (New York: New York University Press, 1994). His analysis of 1,244 seditious speech prosecutions from all the mainland colonies reveals that "colonial authorities came to punish seditious speech much more mildly" and that defendants increasingly called on "juries to decide their cases," thus prefiguring the eighteenth-century experience with printed speech in significant ways (pp. 3, 132).
51. Jeffrey A. Smith, "A Reappraisal of Legislative Privileges and American Colonial Journalism," *Journalism Quarterly* 61 (1984): 97–104; and, in general, Mary P. Clarke, *Parliamentary Privilege in the American Colonies* (New Haven, Conn.: Yale University Press, 1943).
52. Duniway, *Freedom of the Press*, 99; *Royal Instructions to British Colonial Governors, 1670–1776*, ed. Leonard W. Labaree (New York: American Historical Association, 1935), 495–96.
53. Thomas, *Hist. Printing*, 497. The proceedings of Parliament in the early seventeenth century were publicized unofficially, in handwritten "separates" (newsletters) and similar scribally produced documents. At a time of fierce differences between Parliament and James II, it arranged for the publication of its journals. Harold Love, *Scribal Publication in Seventeenth-Century England* (Oxford: Clarendon Press, 1993), 15–22.
54. See Chapters 2, 3, 4, 9, and 12, and the preceding section of this chapter.
55. Duniway, *Freedom of the Press*, 79–96.
56. Such suits could also be directed against authors, with printers involved only secondarily; see, e.g., Thomas, *Hist. Printing*, 443, 466–70.

57. Duniway, *Freedom of the Press,* 108–09.
58. Leonard W. Levy, *Emergence of a Free Press* (New York: Oxford University Press, 1985), chap. 5; James Alexander, *A Brief Narrative of the Case and Trial of John Peter Zenger, Printer of the New York Weekly Journal,* ed. Stanley N. Katz, 2d edition, (Cambridge, Mass.: Harvard University Press, 1972). The original publication of Alexander's text was in 1736; Jeffrey A. Smith, *Printers and Press Freedom: The Ideology of Early American Journalism* (New York: Oxford University Press, 1988). For another appraisal of the Zenger case that attempts to erase the dichotomy between censorship and a free press, see Rice, *Transformation of Authorship,* chap. 2.
59. *A Treatise of the Pleas of the Crown* (London, 1716), quoted in Levy, *Emergence of a Free Press,* 8.
60. Katz, Introduction to *A Brief Narrative,* 13.
61. Ibid.
62. Ibid., 15; Jacobson, ed., *English Libertarian Heritage,* 73–80.
63. Katz, Introduction to *A Brief Narrative,* 24–26.
64. Ibid., 29; Levy, *Emergence of a Free Press,* 8.
65. Smith, *Printers and Press Freedom,* 119–20 (on Franklin).
66. For examples of this latter point, see Chapters 8 and 9.
67. Katz, introduction to *A Brief Narrative,* 36–37.
68. J. A. Leo LeMay, *Men of Letters in Colonial Maryland* (Knoxville: University of Tennessee Press, 1972), 124–25.
69. William Livingston. *The Independent Reflector, or Weekly Essays on Sundry Important Subjects More particularly Adapted to the Province of New-York,* ed. Milton M. Klein (Cambridge, Mass.: Harvard University Press, 1963), 340–41.
70. Ibid., 341–42. Authorship of this piece has not been established with certainty; the evidence is reviewed by Klein, *Independent Reflector,* 343 n. 3, 344 n. 5, and Klein's letter to author, Knoxville, Jan. 31, 1995. Leonard Levy attributes this essay to Livingston in *Emergence of a Free Press* and in his edited *Freedom of the Press from Zenger to Jefferson* (Indianapolis: Bobbs Merrill, 1966).
71. Levy, *Emergence of a Free Press,* 135. *Common Sense* is quoted in ibid., 134.
72. Ibid., 135.
73. Richard Buel, Jr., "Freedom of the Press in Revolutionary America: The Evolution of Libertarianism, 1760–1820," in *Press & Am. Rev.,* 59–97.
74. Stephen Botein, "Printers and the American Revolution," *Press & Am. Rev.,* 11–57; Arthur Meier Schlesinger, *Prelude to Independence: The Newspaper War on Britain, 1764–1776* (New York: Knopf, 1958).
75. Buel, "Freedom of the Press," 77–80; Levy, *Emergence of a Free Press,* 67–68; Mary Ann Yodelis, "Courts, Counting House and Streets: Attempts at Press Control, 1763–1775," *Journalism History* 1 (1974): 11–15.
76. Quoted by Klein, *The Independent Reflector,* 342.
77. Botein, "Printers and the American Revolution," *Press & Am. Rev.,* 38–39; Buel, "Freedom of the Press," ibid., 60; Dwight Teeters, "'King' Sears, the Mob, and Freedom of the Press in New York, 1765–1776," *Journalism Quarterly* 41 (1964): 539–44.
78. Levy, *Emergence of a Free Press,* 188.
79. Ibid., 206–11.

80. In Henry Steele Commager and Milton Cantor, eds., *Documents of American History,* 10th edition, 2 vols. (Englewood Cliffs, N.J.: Prentice-Hall, 1988), 1: 104; Levy, *Emergence of Free Press,* 196.
81. Ibid., 211–13.

Chapter 11. Practices of Reading

1. Franklin, *Autobiography,* 1317, 1311, 1317–19.
2. The rate of increase stabilized in the 1760s before resuming in the early 1770s; see Chapter 5.
3. Devereux Jarratt, *The Life of the Reverend Devereux Jarratt . . . Written by Himself* (Baltimore, 1806), 24–26; Joseph T. Buckingham, *Personal Memoirs and Recollections of Editorial Life,* 2 vols., (Boston, 1852), 1:15–16, 21, 8.
4. Susan O'Brien, "Eighteenth-Century Publishing Networks in the First Years of Transatlantic Evangelicalism," in *Evangelicalism: Comparative Studies of Popular Protestantism in North America, the British Isles, and Beyond 1700–1900,* ed. Mark A. Noll, David W. Babbington, and George A. Rawlyk (New York: Oxford University Press, 1994), 38–57; on Quakers, see Chapter 6.
5. See Note 19.
6. Franklin, *Autobiography,* 1317–23; *Franklin Papers,* 1:6–7.
7. Kenneth A. Lockridge, *Literacy in Colonial New England: An Inquiry into the Social Context of Literacy in the Early Modern West* (New York: W. W. Norton, 1974), 13, 28; Gloria L. Main, "An Inquiry into When and Why Women Learned to Write in Colonial New England," *Journal of Social History* 24 (1991): 580.
8. Main, "Inquiry," 585–86.
9. Linda Auwers, "Reading the Marks of the Past: Exploring Female Literacy in Colonial Windsor, Connecticut," *Historical Methods* 13 (1980): 204–14. For literacy rates in Grafton, Massachusetts, see Ross W. Beales, Jr., "Studying Literacy at the Community Level: A Research Note," *Journal of Interdisciplinary History* 9 (1982): 93–102.
10. William J. Gilmore, "Elementary Literacy on the Eve of the Industrial Revolution: Trends in Rural New England, 1760–1830," *Procs. AAS* 92 (1982): 172.
11. Joel Perlmann and Dennis Shirley, "When Did New England Women Acquire Literacy?", *WMQ,* 3rd ser., 478 (1991): 54.
12. Lockridge, *Literacy,* 72–101; Alan Tully, "Literacy Levels and Educational Development in Rural Pennsylvania, 1729–1775," *Pennsylvania History* 39 (1972): 301–12.
13. Robert E. Gallman, "Changes in the Level of Literacy in a New Community of Early America," *Journal of Economic History* 48 (1988): 574, 568, 582.
14. David Galenson, "British Servants and the Colonial Indenture System in the Eighteenth Century," *Journal of Southern History* 44 (1978): 48–51; Farley Grubb, "Colonial Immigrant Literacy: An Economic Analysis of Pennsylvania-German Evidence, 1727–1775," *Economic History* 21 (1987): 63–76.
15. As is suggested by the runaway notices analyzed in Robert L. Hall, "Slave Resistance in Baltimore City and County, 1747–1790," *MdHM* 84 (1989): 310.

16. *Religious Philanthropy and Colonial Slavery: The American Correspondence of the Associates of Dr. Bray,* ed. John C. Van Horne (Urbana: University of Illinois Press, 1985), 31. Some of the language in this paragraph is taken from chapter 7, "Literacy and the Enslaved," of a work-in-progress on literacy in early America by E. Jennifer Monaghan.
17. Van Horne, *Religious Philanthropy,* passim; Edgar Legare Pennington, "The Reverend Francis Le Jau's Work Among Indian and Native Slaves," *Journal of Southern History* 1 (1935): 442–58.
18. Harvey H. Jackson, "Hugh Bryan and the Evangelical Movement in Colonial South Carolina," *WMQ,* 3rd ser. 43 (1986): 594–614; Jon Butler, "Enlarging the Body of Christ: Slavery, Evangelism, and the Christianization of the South," in *The Evangelical Tradition in America,* ed. Leonard I. Sweet (Macon: University of Georgia Press, 1984), 87–112; Cotton Mather, *Rules for a Society of Negroes* (Boston, 1713). The influence of evangelicalism on black writing is registered in the autobiographies reprinted in *Black Atlantic Writers of the Eighteenth Century: Living the New Exodus in England and the Americas,* ed. Adam Potkay and Sandra Burr (New York: St. Martin's, 1995). Mather, *Diary,* 2:379, 442, 478, 500, 663.
19. Jon Teaford, "The Transformation of Massachusetts Education, 1670–1780," *History of Education Quarterly* 10 (1970): 287–307; E. Jennifer Monaghan, "Readers Writing: The Curriculum of the Writing Schools of Eighteenth-Century Boston," *Visible Language* 21 (1987): 167–213; Tamara Plakins Thornton, *Handwriting in America: A Cultural History* (New Haven, Conn.: Yale University Press, 1996), 6–12. Much light is thrown on the rise and importance of practical instruction by the material gathered in Louis C. Karpinski, *Bibliography of Mathematical Works Printed in America through 1850* (Ann Arbor: University of Michigan Press, 1940), and Florian Cajori, *The Teaching and History of Mathematics in the United States* (Washington, D.C., 1890).
20. This story is told in Thomas Woody, *Early Quaker Education in Pennsylvania* (New York: Teachers College, 1920).
21. See in general Lawrence A. Cremin, *American Education: The Colonial Experience 1607–1783* (New York: Harper & Row, 1970), chaps. 16–18.
22. The traditional curriculum is described in E. Jennifer Monaghan, "Literacy Instruction and Gender in Colonial New England," in *Reading in America: Literature and Social History,* ed. Cathy N. Davidson (Baltimore, Md.: Johns Hopkins University Press, 1989), 54–58.
23. Paul Leicester Ford, *The New-England Primer: A History of its Origins and Development* (New York, 1897); Charles F. Heartman, *American Primers, Indian Primers, Royal Primers, and Thirty-Seven Other Types of Non-New England Primers Issued Prior to 1830* (Highland Park, N.J.: Harry B. Weiss, 1935); the same, *The New-England Primer Issued Prior to 1830* (New York: R. R. Bowker, 1934).
24. Isaac Watts, *The Art of Reading and Writing English: or, the Chief Principles and Rules of Pronouncing Our Mother-Tongue,* 4th ed. (London, 1734), 45.
25. Thomas, *Hist. Printing,* 133.
26. Jeremy Condy Account Book, ms., American Antiquarian Society.
27. Dilworth, *New Guide* (1747), vii; *The Educational Writings of John Locke,* ed. James L. Axtell (Cambridge: Cambridge University Press, 1968), 240–41.

On the importance of Locke's ideas, see Samuel F. Pickering, Jr., *John Locke and Children's Books in Eighteenth-Century England* (Knoxville: University of Tennessee Press, 1981), 9, 11.

28. David H. Watters, "'I Spake as a Child': Authority, Metaphor and *The New-England Primer*," *EAL* 20 (1985–1986): 193–213; *Child's New Play-Thing* (1750), [i], 17–18. For the motif of consumption in alphabets, see Patricia Crain, "The Republic of ABC," paper delivered at the annual meeting of the Society for the History of Authorship, Reading and Publishing, Worcester, Mass., July 1996.
29. J. H. Plumb, "The New World of Children in Eighteenth-Century England," *Past and Present* 67 (1975): 64–95.
30. E. Jennifer Monaghan, *A Common Heritage: Noah Webster's Blue-Back Speller* (Hamden, Conn.: Archon Books, 1983), 31–43; Webster, *A Grammatical Institute of the English Language . . . Part I* (Hartford, 1783), 14, 103; Webster, *American Spelling Book* (Boston, 1817), 43.
31. Royall Tyler, *The Algerine Captive*, ed. Jack B. Moore (Gainesville: University Press of Florida, 1967), vi–ix.
32. See Chapter 6, for book-holdings in early Pennsylvania. Whether probate inventories are representative of the general population is addressed in each of the studies cited in the notes that follow.
33. Joseph T. Wheeler, "Books Owned by Marylanders, 1700–1776," *MdHM* 35 (1940): 337–53.
34. Lois Green Carr and Lorena S. Walsh, "Changing Lifestyles and Consumer Behavior in the Colonial Chesapeake," in *Of Consuming Interest: The Style of Life in the Eighteenth Century*, ed. Cary Carson et al. (Charlottesville: University Press of Virginia, 1994), 59–166.
35. Joseph F. Kett and Patricia A. McClung, "Book Culture in Post-Revolutionary Virginia," *Procs. AAS* 94 (1984): 97–147.
36. Joseph T. Wheeler, "Reading Interests of Maryland Planters and Merchants, 1700–1776," *MdHM* 37 (1942): 26–41; the same, "Books Owned by Marylanders," 338, 342.
37. Minor Myers, Jr., "Letters, Learning, and Politics in Lyme, 1760–1800," in *A Lyme Miscellany, 1776–1976*, ed. George Willauer, Jr. (Middletown, Conn.: Wesleyan University Press, 1977), 50. For a finding of almost universal book ownership among men classified as town leaders (most, however, owned only a few books): Jackson Turner Main, *Society and Economy in Colonial Connecticut* (Princeton, N.J.: Princeton University Press, 1985), 337–38.
38. Gregory A. and Cynthia Z. Stiverson, "Books Useful and Entertaining: A Study of Book Purchases and Reading Habits of Virginians in the Mid-Eighteenth-Century" (research report, Colonial Williamsburg Foundation, 1977), 181–86; these figures would be slightly higher were almanacs included in the count. See also Stiverson and Stiverson, "The Colonial Retail Book Trade: Availability and Affordability of Reading Material in Mid-Eighteenth-Century Virginia," in *Printing and Society*, 132–73; cash sales, though unrecorded, were no more than 20 percent of those on credit.
39. Condy Account Book; Elizabeth C. Reilly, "The Wages of Piety: The Boston Book Trade of Jeremy Condy," in *Printing and Society*, 83–131.

40. Elizabeth C. Reilly, "Common and Learned Readers: Shared and Separate Spheres in Mid-Eighteenth-Century New England" (Ph.D. dissertation, Boston University, 1994), chap. 3, esp. 168 ff.
41. Another measure of customer demand is the number of subscribers listed in books published (in part) by subscription; see, for example, the figures given in William S. Powell, "Patrons of the Press: Subscription Book Purchases in North Carolina, 1733–1850," *North Carolina Historical Review* 39 (1962): 423–99.
42. Reilly, "Common and Learned Readers," chaps. 2 and 3; *The Papers of Thomas Jefferson*, ed. Julian P. Boyd et al., 23 vols. (Princeton, N.J.: Princeton University Press, 1950–), 1:76–81.
43. Stiverson and Stiverson, "Books Useful and Entertaining," 101–04, 106.
44. Robert D. Harlan, "A Colonial Printer as Bookseller in Eighteenth-Century Philadelphia: The Case of David Hall," *Studies in Eighteenth-Century Culture* 5 (1975): 360–61, 364–71.
45. "A paper-covered book or pamphlet, usually measuring some three and a half by six inches, containing 4, 8, 12, 16 or 24 pages." Victor Neuberg, *Popular Literature: A History and Guide* (New York: Penguin Books, 1977), 103.
46. Thomas, *Hist. Printing*, 133; Reilly, "Common and Learned Readers," chap. 4.
47. Henry Knox Papers, vol. 47, nos. 4, 28, 56, 63, and passim, Massachusetts Historical Society.
48. William J. Gilmore, "Peddlers and the Dissemination of Print Culture in Rural New England, 1780–1840," *Annual Proceedings of the Dublin Seminar for New England Folklife* 9 (1989): 76–89; Gregory Nobles, "The Rise of Merchants in Rural Market Towns: A Case Study of Northampton, Massachusetts," *Journal of Social History* 24 (1990): 5–23.
49. Elizabeth Cometti, "Some Early Best Sellers in Piedmont North Carolina," *Journal of Social History* 16 (1950): 324–37; Joseph Towne Wheeler, "Booksellers and Circulating Libraries in Colonial Maryland," *MdHM* 34 (1939): 130–31.
50. James Rivington to Henry Knox, February 6, 1774 (Knox Papers, MHS); and see Appendix 3, "A Note on Book Prices."
51. Reilly, "Common and Learned Readers," chap. 3; Condy Account Book, 17.
52. Thomas Legate, General Store Invoice Book, 1758–1775, Ms., American Antiquarian Society; Thomas, *Hist. Printing*, 124; see also 147, 149; Stiverson and Stiverson, "Colonial Retail Trade," 158 n. 60; C. William Miller, "Franklin's *Poor Richard* Almanacs: Their Printing and Publication," *SB* 14 (1961): 111, 98; *Franklin Papers*, 13:95.
53. Marion Barber Stowell, *Early American Almanacs: The Colonial Weekday Bible* (New York: Burt Franklin, 1977), 236–69; Reilly, "Common and Learned Readers," chaps. 5 and 6; and see Chapter 13.
54. Hall, *Worlds*, 132–33; Hannah Heaton, a Connecticut farm woman, was reading *The Second Spira* in the late eighteenth century (see Note 80).
55. Stiverson and Stiverson, "Books Useful and Entertaining," 108–09.
56. O'Brien, "Eighteenth-Century Publishing Networks," 44; Charles E. Hambrick-Stowe, "The Spirit of the Old Writers: Print Media, the Great Awakening, and Continuity in New England," in *Communication and*

Change in American Religious History, ed. Leonard I. Sweet (Grand Rapids, Mich.: Eerdmans, 1993), 126–40.

57. See Appendix 2, "A Note on Popular Authors and Durable Authors and Titles." The number of printings does not automatically translate into the number of copies, however.
58. O'Brien, "Publishing Networks," 38–39.
59. See Chapters 12 and 13; Reilly, "Common and Learned Readers," chap. 2; James McLachlan, "Classical Names, American Identities: Some Notes on College Students and Classical Tradition in the 1770s," in *Classical Traditions in Early America*, ed. John W. Eadie (Ann Arbor: University of Michigan Press, 1976), 81–98; Richard L. Bushman, *The Refinement of America: Persons, Houses, Cities* (New York: Knopf, 1992).
60. Kathryn Shevelow, *Women and Print Culture: The Construction of Femininity in the Early Periodical* (London: Routledge, 1989), chap. 5 and passim; Mary Beth Norton, *Liberty's Daughters: The Revolutionary Experience of American Women, 1750–1800* (Boston: Little, Brown, 1980), chap. 9; Kevin J. Hayes, *A Colonial Woman's Bookshelf* (Knoxville: University of Tennessee Press, 1997).
61. As is apparent from D'Alté A. Welch, *A Bibliography of American Children's Books Printed Prior to 1821* (Worcester, Mass.: American Antiquarian Society, 1972); see also Elizabeth C. Reilly, *A Dictionary of Colonial American Printers' Ornaments and Illustrations* (Worcester, Mass.: AAS, 1975).
62. As is suggested indirectly by Billy G. Smith, "The Material Lives of Laboring Philadelphians, 1750–1800," *WMQ*, 3rd ser., 38 (1988): 163–208.
63. Powell, "Patrons of the Press," 426. The most careful study demonstrating the limited place of reading in everyday life is David Vincent, *Literacy and Popular Culture: England, 1750–1914* (Cambridge: Cambridge University Press, 1989).
64. Hayes, *Woman's Bookshelf*, chap. 5.
65. Mark Olson and Louis-George Harvey, "Reading in Revolutionary Times: Book Borrowing from the Harvard College Library," *HLB*, n.s., 4 (1993): 57–72; Edmund S. Morgan, *The Gentle Puritan: A Life of Ezra Stiles 1727–1795* (New Haven, Conn.: Yale University Press, 1962), 320, 365–66, 393; Robert B. Winans, "The Growth of a Novel-Reading Public in Late-Eighteenth-Century America," *EAL* 9 (1975): 270.
66. Jackson T. and Gloria Main, "Economic Growth and the Standard of Living in Southern New England, 1640–1774," *Journal of Economic History* 48 (1988): 44; Wheeler, "Books Owned by Marylanders," 341, noting some increase in "literature" vis-à-vis religion.
67. John Edgar Molnar, "Publication and Retail Book Advertisements in the Virginia Gazette, 1736–1780" (Ph.D. dissertation, University of Michigan, 1978).
68. Cometti, "Some Early Best Sellers."
69. Ruth H. Bloch, "The Social and Political Base of Millennial Literature in Late Eighteenth-Century America," *American Quarterly* 40 (1988): 378–96.
70. David W. Conroy, *In Public Houses: Drink and the Revolution of Authority in Colonial Massachusetts* (Chapel Hill: University of North Carolina Press, 1995), 234–39.

71. [Thomas Bray], *Proposals for the Encouragement and Promoting of Religion and Learning in the Foreign Plantations* (London, 1695); Joseph Towne Wheeler, "Thomas Bray and the Maryland Parochial Libraries," *MdHM* 34 (1939): 246–65; the same, "The Laymen's Libraries and the Provincial Library," *MdHM* 35 (1940): 60–73; Edgar L. Pennington, "The Beginnings of the Library in Charles Town, South Carolina, *Procs. AAS* 44 (1934): 159–87; Richard Beale Davis, *A Colonial Southern Bookshelf: Reading in the Eighteenth Century* (Athens: University of Georgia Press, 1979), 5, 73–75.
72. Franklin, *Autobiography*, 1372; Jesse H. Shera, *Foundations of the Public Library: The Origins of the Public Library Movement in New England, 1629–1855* (Chicago, Ill.: University of Chicago Library, 1947), 54–57.
73. E. V. Lamberton, "Colonial Libraries of Pennsylvania," *PMHB* 42 (1918): 196.
74. Harriet Silvester Tapley, *Salem Imprints, 1768–1825: A History of the First Fifty Years of Printing in Salem, Massachusetts* (Salem, Mass.: Essex Institute, 1927), 220, 229; Ruth Willard Robinson, "Four Community Subscription Libraries in Colonial Pennsylvania: Darby, Hatboro, Lancaster and Newtown, 1743–1790" (Ph.D. dissertation, University of Pennsylvania, 1952), 191.
75. Lamberton, "Colonial Libraries," 193–94; Shera, *Origins*, 55, table 3.
76. John Mein, *A Catalogue of Mein's Circulating Library* (Boston, 1765); David Kaser, *A Book for a Sixpence: The Circulating Library in America* (Pittsburgh, Pa.: Phi Beta Mu, 1980), 13–17.
77. Thomas Bradford Library Register, Bradford Papers, Historical Society of Pennsylvania (calculations by James Green).
78. Sewall, *Diary*, 2:970, 973, 982.
79. Welch, *Bibliography of Children's Books*, entry for "The Prodigal Daughter."
80. Barbara E. Lacey, "The World of Hannah Heaton: The Autobiography of an Eighteenth-Century Connecticut Farm Woman," *WMQ*, 3rd ser., 45 (1988): 288–89; Michael Crawford, "The Spiritual Travels of Nathan Cole," *WMQ*, 3rd ser., 33 (1976): 96.
81. Douglas Sloan, ed., *The Great Awakening and American Education: A Documentary History* (New York: Teachers College Press, 1973), 224; see also Cremin, *American Education*, 312–13.
82. Charles Chauncy, *Seasonable Thoughts on the State of Religion in New England* (Boston, 1743), 221–23n; Hermon Husbands, *Some Remarks on Religion, With the Author's Experience in Pursuit thereof* (Philadelphia, 1790), 10, 12, 22; *The Works of Jonathan Edwards* 4: *The Great Awakening*, ed. C. C. Goen (New Haven, Conn.: Yale University Press, 1972), 178.
83. Worthington C. Ford, "Henry Knox and the London Book-Store," *Procs. MHS* 1 (1928): 253.
84. Benjamin Franklin, *Proposals Relating to the Education of Youth in Pensilvania* (1749), in *Franklin Papers*, 3:397–421; Norman Fiering, "The First American Enlightenment: Tillotson, Leverett, and Philosophical Anglicanism," *NEQ* 54 (1981): 307–44; Thomas Jefferson, *Notes on the State of Virginia*, ed. Thomas P. Abernethy (New York: Harper Torchbooks, 1964), 141; Daniel Walker Howe, *Making the American Self: Jonathan Edwards to Abraham Lincoln* (Cambridge, Mass.: Harvard University Press, 1997), chaps. 1–3.

85. *Franklin Papers,* 3:13–14; Hayes, *Colonial Woman's Bookshelf,* 53–54; *Works of Jonathan Edwards,* 5: *Apocalyptic Writings,* ed. Stephen J. Stein (New Haven, Conn.: Yale University Press, 1977), 292.
86. Thomas Walter Herbert, *John Wesley as Editor and Author* (Princeton, N.J.: Princeton University Press, 1940), 37; R. S. Crane, "Suggestions toward a Genealogy of the 'Man of Feeling'," *ELH* 1 (1934): 205–30; Robert Darnton, "Readers Respond to Rousseau: The Fabrication of Romantic Sensitivity," *The Great Cat Massacre and Other Episodes in French Cultural History* (New York: Basic Books, 1984), chap. 6.
87. *Papers of Thomas Jefferson,* 1:74–75, 76–81.
88. G. J. Barker-Benfield, *The Culture of Sensibility: Sex and Society in Eighteenth-Century Britain* (Chicago, Ill.: University of Chicago Press, 1992), chap. 1.
89. Naomi Tadmor, " 'In the even my wife read to me': Women, Reading and Household Life in the Eighteenth Century," in *The Practice and Representation of Reading in England,* ed. James Raven, Helen Small, and Naomi Tadmor (Cambridge: Cambridge University Press, 1996), 162–74; James D. Hart, *The Popular Book* (New York: Oxford University Press, 1950), 25.
90. *The Journal of Esther Edwards Burr 1754–1757,* eds. Carol F. Karlsen and Laurie Crumpacker (New Haven, Conn.: Yale University Press, 1984), 98, 99, 102, 107–08; see also Lucia Bergamasco,"Amitié, amour et spiritualité dans la Nouvelle Angleterre du XVIIIe siècle: l'expérience d'Esther Burr et de Sarah Prince," *Annales* 41 (1986): 295–232; Ned Landsman, "Esther Edwards Burr and the Nature of True Virtue: Books and Conversation, Piety and Virtue in the Presbyterian Enlightenment" (unpublished essay). See also Hayes, *Colonial Woman's Bookshelf,* chaps. 2 and 3.

Chapter 12. Learned Culture in the Eighteenth Century

1. See Chapter 13 for a description of *femmes savantes* and other women writers and literary patrons; see also David S. Shields, *Civil Tongues and Polite Letters in British America* (Chapel Hill: University of North Carolina Press, 1997); Kevin J. Hayes, *A Colonial Woman's Bookshelf* (Knoxville: University of Tennessee Press, 1996), 21–22, 123–27.
2. James McLachlan, "Introduction," *Princetonians: A Biographical Dictionary,* 5 vols. (Princeton, N.J.: Princeton University Press, 1976–91), 1:xvii–xxiv. For matriculants, the actual figures are 537 (a total that would be larger if the data for nongraduates who attended Yale and William and Mary were available) in the 1740s, and 1622 in the 1770s. For graduates with degrees the totals are 479 and 1157, respectively. During the same period, another 400 Americans were educated at British and European colleges and universities. These figures, provided by James McLachlan, are derived from archival and published sources on college matriculation and graduation.
3. Brooke Hindle, *The Pursuit of Science in Revolutionary America* (Chapel Hill: University of North Carolina Press, 1956), 146–65.
4. Subscription lists for certain publications, together with the membership of libraries and learned societies, are a guide to participants in and patrons of learned culture. See, e.g., the identifications of subscribers to Thomas Prince,

A Chronological History of New England (1728), in Samuel G. Drake, *Some Memoirs of the Life and Writings of the Rev. Thomas Prince* (Boston, 1851).

5. A quantitative measure of this dependence is provided in Beverly McAnear, "The Raising of Funds by the Colonial Colleges," *Mississippi Valley Historical Review* 38 (1952): 591–612.
6. Kevin J. Hayes, *The Library of William Byrd of Westover* (Madison, Wisc.: Madison House, 1997), 15 n. 41; Raymond Phineas Stearns, *Science in the British Colonies of America* (Urbana: University of Illinois Press, 1970), 487; Edwin Wolf, 2nd, *The Library of James Logan of Philadelphia, 1674–1751* (Philadelphia, Pa.: Library Company of Philadelphia, 1974), xviii; Hindle, *Pursuit of Science,* 43.
7. Anne S. Pratt, "The Books Sent from England by Jeremiah Dummer to Yale College," in *Papers in Honor of Andrew Keogh* (New Haven, Conn.: privately printed, 1938), 7–44; 423–92; *Samuel Johnson, President of King's College: His Career and Writings,* ed. Herbert and Carol Schneider, 4 vols. (New York: Columbia University Press, 1929), 1:7, 25, etc.; Andrew Keogh, "Bishop Berkeley's Gift of Books in 1733," *Yale Library Gazette* 8 (1934): 1–27.
8. E.g., Robert Boyle, whose role as correspondent is briefly noted in Raymond P. Stearns, "Colonial Fellows of the Royal Society of London, 1661–1788," *WMQ,* 3rd ser., 3(1946): 222–32. See also Bruce T. McCully, "Governor Francis Nicholson, Patron *par excellence* of Religion and Learning in Colonial America," *WMQ,* 3rd ser., 39 (1982): 310–33; Theodore Hornberger, "Samuel Lee (1625–1691), A Clerical Channel for the Flow of Ideas to Seventeenth-Century New England," *Osiris* 1 (1936): 341–55.
9. Hindle, *Pursuit of Science,* chap. 2; Frederick R. Tolles, *James Logan and the Culture of Provincial America* (Boston: Little, Brown, 1957), chap. 12. The correspondence between Colden and Collinson is included in *The Letters and Papers of Cadwallader Colden, Collections of the New York Historical Society,* 51–56 (1918–1923); see also *The Correspondence of John Bartram, 1734–1777,* ed. Edmund and Dorothy Smith Berkeley (Gainesville: University Press of Florida, 1992). Subsequently, Logan's treatise was translated into English by Dr. John Fothergill, another Quaker patron of the colonists and donor of books to Harvard College. In "James Petiver Promoter of Natural Science, c. 1663–1718," *Procs. AAS* 62 (1952): 243–365, Raymond Phineas Stearns describes an English intermediary whose connections were mainly with southern men of learning.
10. Harvard College Records, pt. 5," *Pubs. CSM* 50 (1975): 538–39; Ebenezer Turell, *The Life and Character of the Reverend Benjamin Colman, D.D.* (Boston, 1749), 117; the intellectual context in Boston is sketched in Norman Fiering, " The First American Enlightenment: Tillotson and Philosophical Anglicanism," *NEQ* 54 (1981): 307–44.
11. Caroline Robbins, *The Eighteenth-Century Commonwealth Man* (Cambridge, Mass.: Harvard University Press, 1959), 260–68; W. H. Bond, *Thomas Hollis of Lincoln's Inn: A Whig and His Books* (Cambridge: Cambridge University Press, 1990); Caroline Robbins, "Library of Liberty – Assembled for Harvard College by Thomas Hollis of Lincoln's Inn," *HLB* 5 (1951): 5–23, 181–96, lists some of the books he gave.

12. See Francis J. Bremer, *Congregational Communion: Clerical Friendship in the Anglo-American Puritan Community, 1610–1692* (Boston, Mass.: Northeastern University Press, 1994).
13. Turell, *Life of Colman*, 116, 146–57 (including letters written in Latin to scholars in Germany); Susan O'Brien, "A Transatlantic Community of Saints: The Great Awakening and the First Evangelical Network, 1735–1775," *American Historical Review* 91 (1986): 811–32.
14. Thomas H. Johnson, *The Printed Writings of Jonathan Edwards 1703–1758: A Bibliography* (Princeton, N.J.: Princeton University Press, 1940); *Works of Jonathan Edwards*, 4, *The Great Awakening*, ed. C. C. Goen (New Haven, Conn.: Yale University Press, 1972), 32–46.
15. *Works of Jonathan Edwards*, 16, *Letters and Personal Writings*, ed. George S. Claghorne (New Haven, Conn.: Yale University Press, 1998), 248–49; *Works of Jonathan Edwards*, 9, *A History of the Work of Redemption*, ed. John F. Wilson (New Haven, Conn.: Yale University Press, 1989), 20–23. Some of Erskine's donations of books are noted in Louis Shores, *Origins of the American College Library* (Nashville, Tenn.: George Peabody College, 1934), 66–68, 99. Other exchanges are noted in Henry Moncrieff Wellwood, *Account of the Life and Writings of John Erskine, D.D.* (Edinburgh, 1878), 143, 159–96.
16. As an orthodox Presbyterian, Davies was not always welcomed by more liberal-minded Nonconformists. This troublesome dimension of transatlantic connections is exposed in *The Reverend Samuel Davies Abroad: The Diary of a Journey to England and Scotland, 1753–1755*, ed. George W. Pilcher (Urbana: University of Illinois Press, 1967).
17. See e.g., H. L. Ganter, "William Small, Jefferson's Beloved Teacher," *WMQ*, 3rd ser., 4 (1947): 505–11.
18. William R. and C. Helen Brock, *Scotus Americanus: A Survey of the Sources for Links between Scotland and America in the Eighteenth Century* (Edinburgh: University Press, 1982), chap. 6; John Morgan, *A Discourse upon the Institution of Medical Schools in America . . . With a Preface Containing, amongst other Things, the Author's Apology for Attempting to Introduce the Regular Mode of Practising Physic in Philadelphia* (Philadelphia, 1765). On the title page Morgan was identified as FRS, "correspondent of the Royal Academy of Surgery at Paris; member of the Arcadian Belles Lettres Society at Rome; licentiate of the Royal College of Physicians in London and Edinburgh."
19. Edwin Wolf, 2nd, *The Book Culture of a Colonial American City* (Oxford: Clarendon Press, 1988), 137–63; E. Alfred Jones, *American Members of the Inns of Court* (London: Saint Catherine Press, 1924); Charles Warren, *A History of the American Bar* (Boston: Little, Brown, 1911), 178–79; Herbert A. Johnson, *Imported Eighteenth-Century Law Treatises in American Libraries, 1700–1799* (Knoxville: University of Tennessee Press, 1978); William H. Bryson, *Census of Law Books in Colonial Virginia* (Charlottesville: University Press of Virginia, 1978); the prospectus is illustrated in Chapter 8.
20. Anne Goldgar, *Impolite Learning: Conduct and Community in the Republic of Letters, 1680–1750* (New Haven, Conn.: Yale University Press, 1995), chap. 1; Dena Goodman, *The Republic of Letters: A Cultural History of the French Enlightenment* (Ithaca, N.Y.: Cornell University Press, 1994); John Tren-

chard and Thomas Gordon, *Cato's Letters* (1720–23), repr. in *The English Libertarian Heritage,* ed. David Jacobson (Indianapolis: Bobbs-Merrill, 1965), 190; Stearns, *Science in the British Colonies,* 87, 91, 150n. Goldgar argues that the "Enlightenment" republic of letters, as described by Goodman, must be differentiated from the earlier version, whose participants were not concerned with "public utility" or with politics (p. 6). I have ignored this distinction in describing learned culture in eighteenth-century America.

21. In *The Enlightenment in America* (New York: Oxford University Press, 1976), Henry F. May stresses the influence of the "moderate" wing of the Enlightenment, an argument based in part on his survey of books in college and private libraries, for which see Henry F. May and David Lundberg, "The Enlightened Reader in America," *American Quarterly* 28 (1976): 262–93.
22. Norman Fiering, "The Transatlantic Republic of Letters: A Note on the Circulation of Learned Periodicals to Early Eighteenth-Century America," *WMQ,* 3rd ser., 33 (1976): 642–60; Shores, *Origins College Library,* 80; "Harvard College Records, pt. 1," *Pubs. CSM* 15 (1925): 358.
23. Copies of Bayle: John M. Jennings, *The Library of The College of William and Mary in Virginia, 1693–1793* (Charlottesville: University Press of Virginia, 1968), 57; *A Catalogue of Books Belonging to the Library Company of Philadelphia,* ed. Edwin Wolf, 2nd (1741; repr., Philadelphia: Library Company, 1984), 5; the Harvard College catalogue of 1773, reprinted in Bond and Amory, *Harvard Catalogues;* list prepared by James Madison in 1783, *The Papers of James Madison,* ed. William T. Hutchinson et al., 17 vols. (Chicago, Ill.: University of Chicago Press, 1962–1991), 6:62–115.
24. Fiering, "Transatlantic Republic of Letters"; Thomas H. Johnson, "Jonathan Edwards' Background of Reading," *Pubs. CSM* 28 (1931): 193–222. I have benefitted from an annotated transcription of the "Catalogue" prepared by L. Brian Sullivan; this transcription and the original ms. are in the Edwards Papers, Beinecke Library, Yale University. Not only does Edwards frequently cite a specific periodical (e.g., the "Monthly Catalogue of Books" in the *London Magazine*), he also refers to advertisements at the back of printed books, to the list of recommended reading appended to Cotton Mather, *Manuductio ad Ministerium* (Boston, 1726), and to loans of books and exchange of information among his fellow clergy, both local and international (e.g., "which mr Bull said that mr Chauncy of Boston mentiond"). See also a list drawn up by Samuel Johnson, "A Catalogue Of Books read by me from year to year since I left Yale College," *Samuel Johnson,* eds. Schneider and Schneider, 1:497–526.
25. To cite but a single example: the letterbooks of Charles Carroll (1723–1783) show him ordering a set of the *Gentleman's Magazine.* Richard Beale Davis, *Intellectual Life in the Colonial South,* 3 vols. (Knoxville: University of Tennessee Press, 1978), 2:535; Frank Luther Mott, *A History of American Magazines,* 5 vols. (Cambridge, Mass.: Harvard University Press, 1930–68), 1:71–86; and see Chapter 10.
26. See, e.g., "Of Uniformity in Religion, and the Right of private Judgment defended," *American Magazine and Historical Chronicle* 2 (1745): 102–6; *The Independent Reflector,* ed. Milton Klein (Cambridge, Mass.: Harvard University Press, 1963), 336–42.

27. William E. Lingelbach, "The Library of the American Philosophical Society," *WMQ*, 3rd ser., 3 (1946): 52; *The Papers of John Adams*, ed. Robert J. Taylor et al., 8 vols. (Cambridge, Mass.: Harvard University Press, 1977–), 1:120–22; *Diary and Autobiography of John Adams*, ed. L. H. Butterfield et al., 4 vols. (Cambridge, Mass.: Harvard University Press, 1962), 1:219, 257; Thomas Jefferson, *Notes on the State of Virginia*, ed. Thomas Perkins Abernethy (New York: Harper Torchbooks, 1964), 139–43.
28. See Chapter 13.
29. William Douglass to Cadwallader Colden, February 17, 1735/6, *Coll. MHS*, 4th ser., 2 (1854): 188–89 (describing a medical society and a proposed collection of papers); Hindle, *Pursuit of Science*, 65–66.
30. Ibid., chap. 4; I Bernard Cohen, *Benjamin Franklin's Experiments* (Cambridge, Mass.: Harvard University Press, 1941), 17. *A Catalogue of Choice and Valuable Books to be Sold by B. Franklin, April 11, 1744* (Philadelphia, 1744) "records one of the more elaborate" of Franklin's "ventures as a bookseller," for the catalogue consists almost entirely of imported, learned books. Miller, *Franklin's Philadelphia Printing*, 180.
31. Hindle, *Pursuit of Science*, chap. 7; Lingelbach, "Library of the American Philosophical Society," 50 (Franklin, elected president in absentia, was among the donors of books to the library). For another man's vision of an intercolonial society, see Edmund S. Morgan, *The Gentle Puritan: A Life of Ezra Stiles 1727–1795* (New Haven, Conn.: Yale University Press, 1962), 159–63.
32. *Proposals Relating to the Education of Youth in Pensilvania* (1749), in *Franklin Papers*, 3:397–421.
33. Peter J. Diamond, "Witherspoon, William Smith and the Scottish Philosophy in Revolutionary America," in *Scotland and America in the Age of the Enlightenment*, ed. Richard B. Sher and Jeffrey Smitten (Princeton, N.J.: Princeton University Press, 1990), 115–32; Louis Leonard Tucker, *Puritan Protagonist: President Thomas Clap of Yale College* (Chapel Hill: University of North Carolina Press, 1962), 80–93; Francis L. Broderick, "Pulpit, Physics, and Politics: The Curriculum of the College of New Jersey, 1746–1794," *WMQ*, 3rd ser., 6 (1949): 42–68; Thomas J. Siegel, "Professor Stephen Sewall and the Transformation of Hebrew at Harvard," *Hebrew and the Bible in America: The First Two Centuries*, ed. Shalom Goldman (Dartmouth, N.H.: University Press of New England, 1993), 228–45. Proposals to offer instruction in French proved troubling to the trustees of Yale; *The Literary Diary of Ezra Stiles*, ed. Franklin Bowditch Dexter, 3 vols. (New York: Charles Scribner's Sons, 1901), 2:296–98, 304. See also Morgan, *Gentle Puritan*, 324, 386–88.
34. *Jefferson Papers*, 2:540; Douglas Sloan, *The Scottish Enlightenment and the American College Ideal* (New York: Teachers College Press, 1971), chaps. 3 and 4, 6.
35. Anne S. Pratt, *Isaac Watts and his Gifts of Books to Yale College* (New Haven, Conn.: Yale University Library, 1938).
36. Shores, *Origins College Library*, 56, 85, 98.
37. Preface to *A Catalogue of Books in the Library of the College of New Jersey* (Woodbridge, 1760), quoted in Shores, *Origins College Library*, 114, 85;

Stiles to Bishop James Madison, quoted in Jennings, *Library of William and Mary*, 78.

38. Bond and Amory, *Harvard Catalogues*, xxxvi, 137–59; Shores, *Origins College Library*, 173–74, 188; Ebenezer Thayer, Ms., American Antiquarian Society. See Note 46.

39. Austin Baxter Keep, *History of the New York Society Library* (New York: New York Society Library, 1908), 154, 80; for subsequent orders, see pp. 171–75 (there was no light reading in the earliest order); *Catalogue of Books*, vi–vii; James Logan to Abraham Redwood (August 25, 1749), quoted in Edwin Wolf, 2nd, review of *The 1764 Catalogue of the Redwood Library Company at Newport, Rhode Island*, ed. Marcus A. McCorison (New Haven, Conn.: Yale University Press, 1965), in *WMQ*, 3rd ser., 23 (1966): 27; the same, "Franklin and His Friends Choose Their Books," *PMHB* 80 (1956): 11–36. An undergraduate society's orders of 1770 are indicated in Jennings, *Library of William and Mary*, 60–61; in the same period, Harvard undergraduates and tutors were purchasing books that were not being bought by the library (e.g., those recommended in the *Gentleman's Magazine*): Bond and Amory, *Harvard Catalogues*, xxxv. No library was interested in American imprints; Margaret L. Johnson, "American Imprints and their Donors in the Yale College Library of 1742," in *Papers in Honor of Andrew Keogh*, 355–71.

40. American Philosophical Society, *Library Bulletin* (1943), 80; Robert Darnton describes three systems of classification – Bacon's and two that descend from his, the scheme Ephraim Chambers employed in his *Cyclopaedia* and the one Diderot and d'Alembert used for the *Encyclopédie* – in "Philosophers Trim the Tree of Knowledge: The Epistemological Strategy of the *Encyclopédie*," *The Great Cat Massacre and Other Episodes in French Cultural History* (New York: Basic Books, 1984), chap. 5.

41. Leo E. LaMontagne, *American Library Classification With Special Reference to the Library of Congress* (Hamden, Conn.: Shoe String Press, 1961), chaps. 2, 5, and 6; Tucker, *Puritan Protagonist*, 70–71. See also Anna Monrad, "Historical Notes on the Catalogues and Classifications of the Yale University Library," *Papers in Honor of Andrew Keogh*, 251–56; Norman Fiering, "President Samuel Johnson and the Circle of Knowledge," *WMQ*, 3rd ser., 28 (1971): 199–236.

42. LaMontagne, *American Library Classification*, chap. 2; E. Millicent Sowerby, *Catalogue of the Library of Thomas Jefferson*, 5 vols. (Washington, D.C.: Library of Congress, 1952–59); Douglas L. Wilson, "Sowerby Revisited: The Unfinished Catalogue of Thomas Jefferson's Library," *WMQ*, 3rd ser., 41 (1984): 615–28.

43. Mather, *Manuductio*, 36, 72; Morgan, *Gentle Puritan*, chap. 3, detailing the slowness of the transition.

44. Barbara Shapiro, *Probability and Certainty in Seventeenth-Century England* (Princeton, N.J.: Princeton University Press, 1983); *Samuel Johnson*, ed. Schneider and Schneider, 2:186; 1:6. The full text is printed in 2:56–186.

45. *Literary Diary of Ezra Stiles*, 2:277, 284, 325; Morgan, *Gentle Puritan*, 394–95; *Jefferson's Literary Commonplace Book* (Papers of Thomas Jefferson, Second Series), ed. Douglas L. Wilson (Princeton, N.J.: Princeton University

Press, 1989); John Locke, "A New Method of a Common-Place-Book," *Works of John Locke,* 10 vols. (London, 1823), 3:331–49; Minor Myers, Jr., "A Source for Eighteenth-Century Harvard Master's Questions," *WMQ,* 3rd ser., 38 (1981): 261–67.

46. The best brief survey is Edwin Wolf, 2nd, "Great American Book Collectors to 1800," *Gazette of the Grolier Club,* n.s., 16 (1971): 3–70. References to twenty-two libraries may be found in Johnson, *Imported Eighteenth-Century Law Treatises;* see also Winans, *Book Catalogues.* Wolf's catalogue of James Logan's library is rich in details on how Logan acquired his books, many of which he also annotated. "A Catalogue of Books belonging to Ebenezer Thayer" (ms., AAS) lists 220 sermons and but 14 folios and 16 quartos. References to borrowing abound; see, e.g., Hayes, *Byrd Library,* 42 n. 119.
47. Charles Dexter Allen, *American Book-Plates: A Guide to their Study* (London, 1895); Hannah D. French, *Bookbinding in Early America* (Worcester, Mass.: American Antiquarian Society, 1986); Hayes, *Library of William Byrd,* 91–92.
48. Bond and Amory, *Harvard Catalogues,* xxxv–xxxvi; the consequences of doing so are traced in George Simpson Eddy, "Franklin's Library," *Procs. AAS* 34 (1925): 216–62.
49. The importance of the classics, which my narrative scants, may be discerned from *The Classick Pages: Classical Reading of Eighteenth-Century Americans,* ed. Meyer Reinhold (University Park: Pennsylvania State University Press, 1975); see esp. the bibliography (pp. 223–31).
50. Janice G. Schimmelman, "Architectural Treatises and Building Handbooks Available in American Libraries and Bookstores through 1800," *Procs. AAS* 95 (1985): 317–500.
51. Edwin Wolf, 2nd, "The Dispersal of the Library of William Byrd of Westover," *Procs. AAS* 68 (1958): 19–45; Hayes, *Library of William Byrd,* 95–100. In part because it received little use, the Loganian Library was incorporated into the Library Company of Philadelphia in 1792.
52. Sibley, 5:342; *The Prince Library. A Catalogue of the Collection of Books and Manuscripts . . . Bequeathed to the Old South Church . . . Deposited in the Public Library . . . of Boston* (Boston, 1870), a catalogue that mingles Prince's books with those of other ministers of Old South.
53. Thomas Hutchinson, *The History of the Colony and Province of Massachusetts-Bay,* ed. Lawrence Shaw Mayo, 3 vols. (Cambridge, Mass.: Harvard University Press, 1936), 1:xxvii–xxviii. Though his papers were scattered by the mob that sacked his house in 1765, enough remained for him to publish *A Collection of Original Papers Relative to the History of the Colony of Massachusetts-Bay* (1769); others were printed as appendices in the *History,* notably the "examination" of his ancestress Anne Hutchinson.
54. Richard Beale Davis, "Jefferson as Collector of Virginiana," *SB* 14 (1961): 117–44; Sowerby, *Library of Thomas Jefferson,* 2:242.
55. Morgan Edwards, *Materials towards a History of the Baptists in Pennsylvania* (Philadelphia, 1770), the first of an intended ten-volume series of which but two were published; Isaac Backus, *A History of New England . . . with Particular Reference to the Denomination called Baptists* (Boston, 1777).

56. Jesse H. Shera, "The Beginnings of Systematic Bibliography in America," in *Essays Honoring Lawrence C. Wroth* (Portland, Me.: privately printed, 1951), 263–78; Thomas Bacon, *Laws of Maryland at Large* (Annapolis, 1765–1766), sig. b1 recto.
57. Rollo G. Silver, "Financing the Publication of Early New England Sermons," *SB* 11 (1958): 163–78; Christopher Gould and Richard Parker Morgan, *South Carolina Imprints 1731–1800* (Santa Barbara, Calif.: ABC–CLIO, 1985), 25.
58. Samuel A. Green, "Books Published by Subscription," *American Historical Record* 1 (1872): 19–22; Donald Farren, "Subscription: A Study of the Eighteenth-Century American Book Trade" (D.L.S. thesis, Columbia University, 1982), 53 and passim. Most of the books financed in this manner were not especially "learned."
59. *Franklin Papers,* 5:260–61. Franklin had previously written Johnson in 1750 (4:108) that "I think it scarce necessary to ask for Subscriptions for so small a Work."
60. Wolf, *Library of James Logan,* xxi; Cohen, *Franklin's Experiments,* 148–56; Butterfield et al., *Papers of John Adams,* 1:105; Thomas R. Adams, "The British Pamphlet Press and the American Controversy," *Procs. AAS* 89 (1979): 33–88; C. C. Bonwick, "An English Audience for American Revolutionary Pamphlets," *Historical Journal* 19 (1976): 355–74.
61. Adams, "British Pamphlet Press."
62. *Franklin Papers,* 1:57; Conrad Wright, *The Beginnings of Unitarianism in America* (Boston, Mass.: Skinner House, 1955), 187–91; and see Morgan, *Gentle Puritan,* 167–68. Race was another issue about which writers may have hesitated to express themselves, as Jefferson did in speculating about African-Americans in *Notes on the State of Virginia.*
63. *The Works of Jonathan Edwards,* 7: *Life of David Brainerd,* ed. Norman Pettit (New Haven, Conn.: Yale University Press, 1985), 79–84; Julie Ellison, "The Sociology of Holy Indifference: Sarah Edwards' Narrative," *American Literature* 56 (1984): 479–95.
64. *Gentleman's Progress: The Itinerarium of Alexander Hamilton, 1744,* ed. Carl Bridenbaugh (Chapel Hill: University of North Carolina Press, 1948), 91, 129, 79; Daniel R. Coquillette, "Justinian in Braintree: John Adams, Civilian Learning, and Legal Elitism, 1758–1775," in *Law in Colonial Massachusetts 1630–1800, Pubs. CSM* 62 (1984): 359–418.
65. A good brief summary of these conflicts is provided by May, *Enlightenment in America.*
66. Josiah Quincy, *The History of Harvard University,* 2 vols. (Boston, 1840), 1:559; *A Narrative of the Proceedings of those Ministers in the County of Hampshire* (Boston, 1736), 6, 10, 24.
67. Tucker, *Puritan Protagonist,* 71; *The Works of the Rev. Joseph Bellamy D.D.,* 3 vols. (New York, 1811), 1:35. Bellamy also insisted that the practice of asking ministerial candidates to profess allegiance to an orthodox creed did not amount to "persecution"; Tryon Edwards, "Memoir," *The Works of Joseph Bellamy,* 2 vols. (Boston, 1853), 1:xxxi–xxxii.
68. Tucker, *Puritan Protagonist,* 66, 195; Thomas Clap, *The Religious Constitution of Colleges, Especially of Yale-College in New Haven* (New London, 1754),

12; almost simultaneously, the governing board affirmed the authority of the Westminster Confession.

69. Isaac Backus, *All True Ministers of the Gospel, Are Called into That Work* (1754), repr. in *Isaac Backus on Church, State, and Calvinism*, ed. William G. McLoughlin (Cambridge, Mass.: Harvard University Press, 1968), 75; Samuel Davies, *Sermons on Important Subjects*, 3 vols. (New York, 1841), 3:135; *Life of David Brainerd*, 343–44; Morgan, *Gentle Puritan*, 317, 394; Tucker, *Puritan Protagonist*, 156–57. My interpretation of evangelicalism owes much to Sandra Gustafson.
70. Hall, "The Politics of Writing and Reading in Eighteenth-Century America," in *Publishing and Readership in Revolutionary France and America*, ed. Carol Armbruster (Westport, Conn.: Greenwood Press, 1994), 154–55 and passim; Wolf, *Library of James Logan*, lx; Jefferson, *Notes*, 27–29. Space is lacking to trace the influence of John Locke's advice on how to read the Bible – essentially, to treat it as a historical document and discard all elements of figural interpretation.
71. Figures provided by James McLachlan.
72. The trope of the clergy's scheming, power-hungry "priestcraft," though without foundation in the social history of the colonial churches, was reiterated by William Livingston in *The Independent Reflector;* see also Query XVII, Religion, in Jefferson, *Notes.*
73. I owe this argument to Charles E. Clark, *The Public Prints: The Newspaper in Anglo-American Culture, 1665–1740* (New York: Oxford University Press, 1994), 249 (a reference provided by Michael Schudson).
74. Bernard Bailyn, *The Ideological Origins of the American Revolution* (Cambridge, Mass.: Harvard University Press, 1967), 15–18.
75. Sloan, *Scottish Enlightenment*, 195. That these hopes were not realized is properly the subject of the next volume in this series.
76. *Literary Diary of Ezra Stiles*, 1:131–32.

Chapter 13. Eighteenth-Century Literary Culture

1. David A. Brewer, "Please, Sir, I Want Some More': Prefaces, Sequels and Styles of Reading in the Eighteenth Century," and Jeanne Griggs, "The Preface as Secret Handshake," Session 71, Eighteenth-Century Prefaces: Constructing Readers and Writers, American Society for Eighteenth Century Studies, Tucson, April 8, 1995.
2. See Brigham; Lyon N. Richardson, *A History of Early American Magazines, 1741–1789* (New York: Thomas Nelson, 1931).
3. Ibid., 38–58.
4. Miller, *Franklin's Philadelphia Printing*, 83–84.
5. Harold Love, *Scribal Publication in Seventeenth-Century England* (Oxford: Clarendon Press, 1993).
6. For my attribution, see Shields, "The Wits and Poets of Pennsylvania: New Light on the Rise of Belles Lettres in Provincial Pennsylvania, 1720–1740," *PMHB* 109 (April 1985): 105, n. 9.
7. M. Katherine Jackson, *Outlines of the Literary History of Colonial Pennsylvania* (Lancaster, Pa.: New Era Printing Co., 1906), 34–37.

8. Mary Lou Lustig, *Robert Hunter 1666–1734: New York's Augustan Statesman* (Syracuse, N.Y.: Syracuse University Press, 1983), 50–59. Hunter's appointment as governor of New York is celebrated in the *Tatler* (September 17, 1709).
9. Thomas Wendell, "The Life and Writings of Sir William Keith, Lieutenant-Governor of Pennsylvania and the Three Lower Counties, 1717–1726," (Ph.D. dissertation, University of Washington, 1964).
10. Elizabeth C. Goldsmith, *Exclusive Conversations: the Art of Interaction in Seventeenth-Century France* (Philadelphia: University of Pennsylvania Press, 1988).
11. For an account of Keith's embassy, see Charles P. Keith, *Chronicles of Pennsylvania from the English Revolution to the Peace of Aix-la-Chapelle*, 2 vols. (Philadelphia, 1917), 2:608–14.
12. David S. Shields, *Oracles of Empire* (Chicago: University of Chicago Press, 1990), 141–42, 154–59.
13. John Parke, "Preface," *The Lyric Works of Horace, translated into English Verse; to which are added a number of original poems* (Philadelphia, 1786), Evans 19717.
14. William Becket, Notices and Letters Concerning Incidents at Lewes Town 1724–1744, Ms Am. 0165, Historical Society of Pennsylvania; David S. Shields, "Henry Brooke and the Situation of the First Belletrists in British America," *EAL* 23 (1988): 4–8.
15. "On the lately discover'd Wild Raspberries," ms, Library Company of Philadelphia, printed in Kenneth Silverman, *Colonial American Poetry* (New York: Hafner, 1968); and "The Orchard in Winter" (private collection, Philadelphia).
16. [Francis Harrison], "Cosby the Mild, the happy, good and Great," *New York Gazette*, 428 (Jan. 7, 1733/1734), Lemay 284. "Concerning the Purveyors of Scandal in New York, *New York Gazette*, 442 (April 15, 1734), Lemay 302.
17. See James N. Green, *Library Company Annual Report* (Philadelphia: Library Company, 1989), 8–11.
18. Evans 2846 and 3004; another version of Evans 2846, "A Poem on the Death of King George I, and Accession of King George II," appeared in the *New England Weekly Journal* (September 4, 1727), Lemay 69. See also *On the Death of the Queen. A Poem. Inscribed to His Excellency Governor Belcher* (Boston, 1738), Evans 4229.
19. *New York Gazette*, 206 (October 13, 1729), Lemay 127.
20. Michael Warner, *The Letters of the Republic: Publication and the Public Sphere in Eighteenth-Century America* (Cambridge, Mass.: Harvard University Press, 1990), 29–30.
21. J. A. Leo Lemay, *Men of Letters in Colonial Maryland* (Knoxville: University of Tennessee Press, 1972), 81, 93–94.
22. Cf. also E. Cooke. Laureat, "An Elegy on the Death of the Honourable Nicholas Lowe," *Maryland Gazette*, 67 (December 14, 1728), Lemay 99; "An Elegy on the death of the Honourable William Lock, Esq. . . . 1732. By Ebenezer Cook, Poet Laureate," Bozman-Kerr Papers, MS Division, Library of Congress; Edward H. Cohen, "The Elegies of Ebenezer Cooke," *EAL* 4 (1969): 49–72.

23. Edmund K. Broadus, *The Laureateship: A Study of the Office of Poet Laureate in England, With Some Account of the Poets* (Freeport, N.Y.: Books for Libraries Press, 1966).
24. For Lewis's career, see Lemay, *Men of Letters in Colonial Maryland*, 126–84, and Shields, *Oracles of Empire*, 58–64.
25. Neil T. Eckstein, "The Pastoral and the Primitive in Benjamin Tompson's 'Address to Lord Bellamont,'" *EAL* 8 (1973): 111–16. Benjamin Tompson, "To Lord Bellamont when entering Governour of the Massachusetts," *Benjamin Tompson, Colonial Bard: A Critical Edition*, ed. Peter White (University Park: Pennsylvania State University Press, 1980), 157–60. Ebenezer Parkman sent Byles a copy of the ms. to remind the new volunteer laureate that he had predecessors.
26. For English precedents, see Richard Helgerson, *Self-Crowned Laureates: Spenser, Jonson, Milton, and the Literary System* (Berkeley: University of California Press, 1983); Dustin Griffin, *Literary Patronage in England 1650–1800* (New York: Cambridge University Press, 1996).
27. Jack P. Greene, *The Quest for Power: The Lower Houses of Assembly in the Southern Royal Colonies, 1689–1776* (Chapel Hill: University of North Carolina Press, 1963).
28. Shields, *Oracles of Empire*, 95–172.
29. Franklin, *Autobiography*, 1367–68.
30. See Gerald S. Brown's discussion of the method of administration in *The American Secretary; The Colonial Policy of Lord George Germain, 1775–1778* (Ann Arbor: University of Michigan Press, 1963).
31. Frederick B. Tolles, *James Logan and the Culture of Provincial America* (Boston, Mass.: Little, Brown, 1957).
32. Warner, *Letters of the Republic*, 36–56.
33. Archibald Home, "Memoirs of a Handspike," in his *Poems on Several Occasions*, Laing Manuscripts III, 452, University of Edinburgh Library.
34. Gary B. Nash, *The Urban Crucible: The Northern Seaports and the Origins of the American Revolution*, abridged ed.(Cambridge, Mass.: Harvard University Press, 1986), 45–64.
35. French's translations appear in Parke, *Lyric Works of Horace*, 231–33.
36. Anne Goldgar, *Impolite Learning: Conduct and Community in the Republic of Letters, 1680–1750* (New Haven, Conn.: Yale University Press, 1995).
37. Obituary of Thomas Dale, *South Carolina Gazette* (September 17, 1750).
38. Henry Brooke, "Modern Politeness," Henry Brooke Poetry Collection, Peters Commonplace Book, Peters Family Papers, Historical Society of Pennsylvania.
39. *Pitchero-Threnodia* (Boston, 1724); Evans 2579.
40. Evans 1460 and 2558; see William C. Lane, "A Religious Society at Harvard College, 1719," *Pubs. CSM* 24 (1921): 309–12.
41. William C. Lane, Report on "The Telltale, 1721" and "A Harvard College Society, 1722–23," *Pubs. CSM* 12 (January 1909): 220–31.
42. Members included Robert Treat Paine, Edward Wigglesworth, and later Cotton Tufts. Stephen T. Riley and Edward W. Hanson, eds., *The Papers of Robert Treat Paine, 1746–1756, Coll. MHS* 67 (1992): 22.
43. Jane Carson, *James Innes and his Brothers of the F. H. C.* (Williamsburg, Va.: Colonial Williamsburg Foundation, 1965); George P. Coleman, *The*

Flat Hat Club and the Phi Beta Kappa Society: Some New Light on their History (Richmond, Va.: Dietz Press, 1916).

44. Julius Tuttle, "The Philomusarian Club," *Pubs. CSM* 18 (April 1915): 80.
45. Leon Jackson, "The Rights of Man and the Rites of Youth: Fraternity and Riot at Eighteenth-Century Harvard," *History of Higher Education Annual*, 15 (1995): 5–49.
46. David C. Humphrey, "Anglican 'Infiltration' of Eighteenth-Century Harvard and Yale," *Historical Magazine of the Protestant Episcopal Church* 43 (1974): 247–51.
47. Seymour Martin Lipset, "Political Controversies at Harvard, 1736–1974," *Education and Politics at Harvard* (New York: McGraw-Hill, 1975), 22–23.
48. Ibid.
49. J. E. Morpurgo, *Their Majesties' Royal Colledge; William and Mary in the Seventeenth and Eighteenth Centuries* (Williamsburg, Va.: Endowment Association of The College of William and Mary, 1976), 133.
50. Robert Francis Seybolt, *The Public Schools of Colonial Boston, 1635–1775* (New York: Arno Press, 1969), 14–18, provides the list of tutors and their terms of service.
51. David S. Shields, "Nathaniel Gardner, Jr. and the Literary Culture of Boston in the 1750s," *EAL* 24 (1989): 196–216.
52. Loosely translated, this may be rendered: "I shall briefly remind you how our school trains boys. It can be so wearisome to rehearse the turns, of speech, gender, and noun, and all that stuff in Lily! Let me at times propose a greater task and toil on greater matters! Let me at times show what is fitting and what is dishonorable, how we should return a parent's love, how God's favor, and indeed how harmful it is for boys as well as men to neglect either. So weighty a responsibility is it to form the youthful mind!" Nathaniel Gardner, [Jr.], "The Teacher," *Early American Latin Verse*, ed. Leo M. Kaiser (Chicago: Bochazy-Carducci, 1984), 68.
53. Pamela Regis, *Describing Early America: Bartram, Jefferson, Crèvecoeur, and the Rhetoric of Natural History* (DeKalb: Northern Illinois University Press, 1992), 40–78.
54. Earl G. Swemm, *Brothers of the Spade* (Barre, Mass.: Barre Press, 1957).
55. Jane Colden, *Botanic Manuscript*, ed. H. W. Rickett (New York: Chanticleer Press, 1963). Susanna Wright's ms. correspondence from Pennsylvania awaits publication. See also the activity of Elizabeth Lamboll in Elise Pinckney, *Thomas and Elizabeth Lamboll, Early Charleston Gardeners* (Charleston, S.C.: Charleston Museum, 1969).
56. Richard Lewis, *The Mouse Trap or the Battle of the Cambrians and Mice. A Poem. Translated into English* (Annapolis, 1728), Evans 3038; Lemay, "Richard Lewis, Poet," *Men of Letters in Colonial Maryland*, 126–32.
57. J. A. Leo Lemay, "Richard Lewis and Augustan American Poetry," *PMLA* 83 (1968): 80.
58. Roger E. Stoddard, "Poet and Printer in Colonial and Federal America: Some Bibliographical Perspectives," *Procs. AAS* 93 (1983): 265–361.
59. Aubrey C. Land, "The Planters of Colonial Maryland," *MdHM* 68 (1972): 109–28.
60. R. P. Bond, *English Burlesque Poetry, 1700–1750* (Cambridge, Mass.: Harvard University Press, 1932), 219–22.

61. In Maryland, Sterling used "Musaeus" as his pen-name when publishing his own compositions; J. A. Leo Lemay, *Men of Letters in Colonial Maryland*, 257–312.
62. The manuscript of the translation is in the collection of the Maryland Historical Society. For Chase, see Rosamund R. Beirne, "The Reverend Thomas Chase: Pugnacious Parson," *MdHM* 59 (1964): 1–14.
63. David Curtis Skaggs, *The Poetic Writings of Thomas Cradock 1718–1770* (Newark: University of Delaware Press, 1983).
64. Henry Brooke, "On Reading Mr Pope's Homer 1725.26," Henry Brooke Poetry Collection, Peters Commonplace Book, Peters Collection, Historical Society of Pennsylvania.
65. See, for instance, Grantland S. Rice, *The Transformation of Authorship in America* (Chicago: University of Chicago Press, 1997).
66. [Abigail Coxe], "To the Memory of Archibald Home, Esq. late Secretary of the Jerseys," *Pennsylvania Gazette* 818 (August 16, 1744), Lemay 739. Wife of Daniel Coxe, Abigail was, according to Benjamin Rush, the most intellectually accomplished woman in British America.
67. Samuel Johnson, *Lives of the English Poets*, ed. George Birkbeck Hill, 3 vols. (1905; repr. New York: Octagon Books, 1967), 2:310.
68. C. Lennart Carlson, "Richard Lewis and the Reception of His Work in England," *American Literature* 9 (1937): 301–16; David Shields, "Mental Nocturnes: Night Thoughts on Man and Nature in the Poetry of Eighteenth-Century America," *PMHB* 110 (1986): 245–58.
69. Elizabeth R. McKinsey, "James Ralph," *Procs. Am. Phil. Soc.*, 117 (1973): 59–78.
70. David S. Shields, "The Manuscript in the British American World of Print," *Procs. AAS* 102 (1992):412–16.
71. Alexander Hamilton, "The Itinerarium of Dr. Alexander Hamilton," *Colonial American Travel Narratives*, ed. Wendy Martin (New York: Penguin, 1994), 207.
72. "Song: on Captain Long of the Seaforth Man of Wars being a general Lover when stationed at New-York," "To Miss Katy Hall: A Song," "Black Joke. A Song," "On a Dispute, between two Scotchmen at a St. Andrew's Feast in New-York Anno 1733."
73. Evans 39818; see Shields, *Oracles of Empire*, 206–09 for attribution.
74. *The Letters and Papers of Cadwallader Colden . . . 1711[–1775]*, 9 vols. (New York: The New-York Historical Society, 1918–1937), 8:251–52.
75. John Barry Talley, *Secular Music in Colonial Annapolis: The Tuesday Club 1745–56* (Urbana: University of Illinois Press, 1988), 9–14.
76. David S. Shields, "Henry Brooke and the Situation of the First Belletrists in British America," *EAL* 23 (1988): 4–27.
77. Lawrence E. Klein, "Gender, Conversation, and the Public Sphere in Early Eighteenth-Century England," *Textuality and Sexuality*, ed. Judith Still and Michael Worton (Manchester: Manchester University Press, 1993), 100–15.
78. *The Challenge, sent by a young Lady to Sir Thomas ———, &c, or, The Female War* (London, 1697).
79. Beth Kowalski-Wallace, "Tea, Gender and Domesticity in Eighteenth-Century England," *Studies in Eighteenth-Century Culture*, 23 (1994): 131–45;

David S. Shields, *Civil Tongues and Polite Letters in British America* (Chapel Hill: University of North Carolina Press, 1997).

80. Shields, *Civil Tongues and Polite Letters*, chap. 4.
81. Sarah Kemble Knight, "The Journal of Madam Knight," in *Colonial American Travel Narratives,* ed. Wendy Martin.
82. *New England Courant* (April 2, 1722; August 19, September 16, September 23, November 25, 1723).
83. *South Carolina Gazette* 1039 (May 14, 1754).
84. [Ebenezer Turell], *Memoirs of the Life and Death of the Pious and Ingenious Mrs. Jane Turell* (Boston, 1735); Evans 3969.
85. Simon Gratz, "Some Material for a Biography of Mrs. Elizabeth Fergusson née Graeme," *PMHB* 39 (1915): 257–321, 385–409; 41 (1917): 385–98; Chester T. Hallenbeck, "The Life and Collected Poems of Elizabeth Graeme Ferguson" (M.A. thesis, Columbia University, 1929); Martha C. Slotten, "Elizabeth Graeme Ferguson: A Poet in 'The Athens of North America,'" *PMHB* 108 (1984): 259–88. H. S., "To the Memory of a much lov'd Friend Mrs. Hannah Dale (Relict of Doctor Dale) who died the 9th of April, 1751, aged 29 years," *South Carolina Gazette* 887 (May 13, 1751; corrected version).
86. Carla Mulford, ed., *Only for the Eye of a Friend: The Poems of Annis Boudinot Stockton* (Charlottesville: University Press of Virginia, 1995).
87. Samuel Stanhope Smith, *A Funeral Sermon on Richard Stockton* (Trenton, 1781), Evans 17371.
88. Only recently has the cultural practice of the republican court again attracted the notice of the historians. Prior to the rise of the progressive historians, it was widely discussed: Rufus Wilmot Griswold, *The Republican Court, or American Society in the Days of Washington* (New York, 1855), 256, 260, 342–44; Elizabeth F. L. Ellet, *The Court Circles of the Republic, or the Beauties and Celebrities of the Nation* (Hartford, Conn., 1869); and Anne Hollingsworth Wharton, *Salons Colonial and Republican* (New York, 1900).
89. Fredrika J. Teute and David S. Shields, "The Republican Court and the Historiography of a Woman's Domain in the Public Sphere" (paper presented at the annual meeting of the Society of Historians of the Early American Republic, Boston, July 1994).
90. Published in the *Gazette of the United States* (March 13, 1793); Mulford, *Only for the Eye of a Friend*, 174–75.
91. *National Gazette* (December 19, 22, 29, 1791; January 5, 1792); "mackled" means "blurred or spoiled" (*OED*).
92. Hall, *Worlds.*
93. Victor Hugo Paltsits, *A Bibliography of the Separate and Collected Works of Philip Freneau, together with an Account of his Newspapers* (New York: Dodd, Mead and Company, 1903); Philip M. Marsh, *Philip Freneau, Poet and Journalist* (Minneapolis, Minn.: Dillon Press, 1967); Mary Weatherspoon Bowden, *Philip Freneau* (Boston, Mass.: Twayne, 1976); Jacob Axelrod, *Philip Freneau, Champion of Democracy* (Austin: University of Texas Press, 1967).
94. Marion Barber Stowell, *Early American Almanacs* (New York: Burt Franklin, 1977), 13–36, is the standard introduction.

95. Jacob Taylor, 46 issues, from *An Almanack for the Year 1700* (Philadelphia, 1700) through *Pennsylvania, 1746. An Almanack* (Philadelphia, 1746). Shields, "Wits and Poets of Pennsylvania," 110–21.
96. [*Titan Leeds Almanack for 1733*]. The New-York Historical Society copy is missing the title page and is misfiled under the year 1736. J. A. Leo Lemay discovered this item. A manuscript version lacking a title contains identifications of the persons being satirized: Norris Commonplace Book, Henry E. Huntington Library, HM 164.
97. Matthew A. Stickney, "Almanacs and Their Authors," *EIHC* 8 (1866): 29–31, 101–04, 158–64, 193–205; 14 (1877): 81–93, 212–32, 242–48.
98. See Stowell, *Early American Almanacs*, 315–20, for a listing of the major series.
99. *The Lady's Almanack* (Portsmouth, 1786–1792), Evans 19748 and 23484; *The Lady's Astronomical Diary, Or Almanack, for 1792* (Exeter, 1792), Evans 23485.
100. Mary Kelley, "Designing a Past for the Present: Women Writing Women's History in Nineteenth-Century America," *Procs. AAS* 105(1995): 315–46.
101. See Chapters 3 and 4; examples may be found in Evans 7991, 8289, 12069, 11681, and 6743.
102. Jason Haven, *A Sermon Delivered at a Private Meeting in Framingham* (Boston, 1761).
103. Charles E. Hambrick-Stowe, *The Practice of Piety: Puritan Devotional Disciplines in Seventeenth-Century New England* (Chapel Hill: University of North Carolina Press, 1982), 137–43.
104. Mather, *Diary*, 1:579.
105. Cotton Mather, *The Young Man's Preservative* (Boston, 1701), *Youth Under a Good Conduct* (Boston, 1704), *Youth in its Brightest Glory* (Boston 1709), *Things that Young People Should Think Upon* (Boston, 1700), *Ornaments for the Daughters of Zion* (Cambridge, 1691), *Eureka: The Vertuous Woman Found* (Boston, 1704), and *Tabitha Rediviva* (Boston, 1713), Evans 997, 1181, 1410, 934, 39291, 1121, and 1627, respectively; Benjamin Colman, *Practical Discourses on the Parable of the Ten Virgins* (London, 1713), and *The Honor and Happiness of the Vertuous Woman* (Boston, 1716), Evans 1803.
106. Thomas Walter, *The Grounds and Rules of Musick* (Boston, 1721), Evans 2302. There were six editions during the colonial period. Thomas Walter, *The Sweet Psalmist of Israel* (Boston, 1722), Evans 2404.
107. Isaac Backus, *An Address to the Inhabitants of New-England* (Boston, 1787), *An Appeal to the Public for Religious Liberty* (Boston, 1773), and *A Door Opened for Equal Christian Liberty* (Boston, [1783]), Evans 20212, 13654, and 17824, respectively; Samuel Hopkins, *The System of Doctrines* (Boston, 1793), and *An Inquiry into the Nature of True Holiness* (Newport, 1773), Evans 25634 and 12811, respectively.
108. Samuel Johnson, *A Letter from a Minister* (New York, 1733), *A Second Letter from a Minister of the Church of England* (Boston, 1734), *A Third Letter from a Minister* (Boston, 1737), and *A Letter from Aristocles* (Boston, 1745), Evans 3672, 3784, 4148, and 5614, respectively.
109. *The Journal of Esther Edwards Burr*, eds. Carol F. Karlsen and Laurie Crumpacker (New Haven, Conn.: Yale University Press, 1984).

110. *Milcah Martha Moore's Book: The Commonplace Book of an Eighteenth-Century American,* ed. Catherine La Courreye Blecki and Karin A. Wulf, (University Park: The Pennsylvania State University Press, forthcoming); the editors, however, place this work in a Quaker epistolary tradition, rather than in salon culture.
111. See Chapter 10.
112. William T. Laprade, *Public Opinion and Politics in Eighteenth-Century England to the Fall of Walpole* (London: Macmillan, 1963); Steven Pincus, " 'Coffee Politicians Does Great': Coffee-Houses and Restoration Political Culture," *Journal of Modern History* 67 (1995): 807–34.
113. Anthony Ashley Cooper, Earl of Shaftesbury, *Sensus Communis: an Essay on the Freedom of Wit and Humour* (London, 1709).
114. Alexander Hamilton, *The History of the Ancient and Honorable Tuesday Club*, ed. Robert Micklus, 3 vols. (Chapel Hill: University of North Carolina Press, 1990); Archives of the Schuylkill Fishing Company, 1732–present, ms. collection, Historical Society of Pennsylvania; Records, &c of the Homony Club Instituted the 22nd of December, 1770, Dreer Collection, vol. 15, Historical Society of Pennsylvania.
115. *Transactions of the Society, Instituted in the State of New-York, for the Promotion of Agriculture, Arts, and Manufactures* (New York, 1792–1799); *Constitution of the Ladies Society, Established in New York for the Relief of Poor Widows with Small Children* (New York, 1799), Evans 38101; *Rules and Regulations of the Society for Political Enquiries* (Philadelphia, 1787), Evans 20645.

Afterword

1. Rollo G. Silver, "Aprons instead of Uniforms: The Practice of Printing, 1776–1787," *Procs. AAS* 87 (1978): 111–94.
2. Rollo G. Silver, "Prologue to Copyright in America: 1772," *SB* 11 (1958): 259–62; Irving Lowens, "Copyright and Andrew Law," *PBSA* 53 (1959): 150–53; Bruce W. Bugbee, *Genesis of American Patent and Copyright Law* (Washington, D. C.: Public Affairs Press, 1967), chap. 5; James Gilreath, introduction to *Federal Copyright Records, 1790–1800*, ed. Elizabeth Carter Wills (Washington, D.C.: Library of Congress, 1987). Like most of his fellow psalmodists, William Billings was his own publisher and distributor; unlike literary authors who might try to do the same, Billings found a market for his songsters among the many singing societies in New England.
3. Stuart C. Sherman, ed., "Leman Thomas Rede's 'Bibliotheca Americana,' " *WMQ*, 3rd ser., 4 (1947): 346.
4. Samuel Briggs, *The Essays, Humor, and Poems of Nathaniel Ames, Father and Son . . . 1726–1775* (Cleveland, Ohio, 1891), 33: Nathaniel Jr. proposed a "patent of the Minister of State" for his almanac.
5. Richard J. Moss, *The Life of Jedidiah Morse* (Knoxville: University of Tennessee Press, 1995), 59; Rollo G. Silver, *The American Printer, 1787–1825* (Charlottesville: University Press of Virginia, [1967]), 104.
6. Robert Darnton and Daniel Roche, eds., *Revolution in Print: The Press in France, 1775–1800* (Berkeley and Los Angeles: University of California Press, 1989).

7. Volume 2 in this series takes as its starting point these consequences.
8. D'Alté Welch, *A Bibliography of American Children's Books Printed Prior to 1821* (Worcester, Mass.: American Antiquarian Society, 1972), no. 1242.3: Song V, verse 2; Louis F. Benson, "The American Revisions of Watts's Psalms," *Journal of the Presbyterian Historical Society* 3 (1903): 18–34, 75–89.
9. [Edward Cotton], comp., *A Catalogue of All the Books Printed in the United States* (Boston, 1804), t.p.; for the attribution, see Rollo G. Silver, *The Boston Book Trade, 1800–1825* (New York: New York Public Library, 1949), 11.
10. Charles L. Nichols, "The Literary Fair in the United States," in *Bibliographical Essays: A Tribute to Wilberforce Eames*, ed. G. P. Winship ([Cambridge, Mass.: Harvard University Press], 1924), 83–92.
11. The comparison makes sense because so many of Bell's subscribers were booksellers who planned to retail the multiple copies of their subscription: James Rivington in New York, for example, took 200 copies, and there were many multiple subscribers who styled themselves merchants, booksellers, binders, or printers. Similarly, one may suppose, the country printers who appeared in Cotton's catalogue exchanged a few of the books they printed with Thomas and other masters of bookselling networks.
12. Sherman, "Leman Thomas Rede's 'Bibliotheca Americana,'" 349.
13. Samuel J. Rogal, "A Checklist of Eighteenth-Century British Literature Published in Eighteenth-Century America," *Colby Library Quarterly* 10 (1973): 231–57. Michael T. Gilmore estimates that "About three-quarters of the [literary] books published in the United States before 1820 were of English origin." Gilmore, "Literature of the Revolutionary and Early Modern Periods," in *The Cambridge History of American Literature*, vol. 1: *1590–1820*, ed. Sacvan Bercovitch and C. R. K. Patell (Cambridge: Cambridge University Press, 1994), 547.
14. Gilmore, "Literature of the Revolutionary and Early Modern Periods," 550–54.
15. William Charvat, *Literary Publishing in America, 1790–1850*, with a new afterword by Michael Winship (Amherst: University of Massachusetts Press, 1993).
16. Bugbee, *Genesis*, chap. 5.
17. Freneau, "Literary Importation," quoted in Richard Ruland, *The Native Muse: Theories of American Literature* (New York: E. P. Dutton, 1972), 48, 50.
18. See Chapter 12; here, too, however, regional differences may have been acute, for southern society was not yet significantly penetrated by evangelical Protestantism.
19. Richard Henderson to Cunningham Corbett, July 30, 1774, in *American Archives: Fourth series,* ed. Peter Force, 6 vols. (Washington, D.C., 1837–1846), 3:54.
20. Edmund S. and Helen M. Morgan, *The Stamp Act Crisis: Prologue to Revolution* (1953; repr., New York: Collier Books, 1963), 120–34.
21. *Md. Arch.* 2:54–55.
22. Patricia Cline Cohen, *A Calculating People: The Spread of Numeracy in Early America* (Chicago, Ill.: University of Chicago Press, 1982); Lawrence A. Cremin, *American Education: The Colonial Experience, 1607–1783* (New York: Harper & Row, 1970), Pt. 4.

23. Harry S. Stout, "Religion, Communications, and the Ideological Origins of the American Revolution," *WMQ*, 3rd ser., 34 (1977): 519–44; Gordon S. Wood, "The Democratization of Mind in the American Revolution," in *Leadership in the American Revolution* (Washington, D.C.: Library of Congress, 1974), 68–71.
24. Caroline Robbins, "Library of Liberty – Assembled for Harvard College by Thomas Hollis of Lincoln's Inn," *HLB* 5 (1951): 5–23, 181–96.

Index

This is an index of the names and topics in the text, illustrations, appendixes, and selected notes. Books mentioned in the text that were written, read, or owned by residents in the colonies are fully indexed, but passing references to other names, titles and topics are generally ignored. The heading "booksellers and bookselling" covers printers as well as booksellers and printer-booksellers in the larger cities, unless the reference is exclusively to the production of print.